BRIEF CONTENTS

A WRITER'S GUIDE

A WRITER'S READER

A WRITER'S RESEARCH MANUAL

A WRITER'S HANDBOOK

APPENDICES AND OTHER RESOURCES

The Bedford Guide for College Writers

with Reader, Research Manual, and Handbook

TWELFTH EDITION

X. J. Kennedy · Dorothy M. Kennedy · Marcia F. Muth

bedford/st.martin's
Macmillan Learning

Boston | New York

For Bedford/St. Martin's

Vice President, Editorial, Macmillan Learning Humanities: Leasa Burton
Program Director, English: Stacey Purviance
Senior Program Manager: Laura Arcari
Marketing Manager: Vivian Garcia
Director of Content Development, Humanities: Jane Knetzger
Senior Developmental Editor: Rachel Goldberg
Associate Editor: Suzanne H Chouljian
Assistant Editor: Paola Garcia-Muñiz
Senior Content Project Manager: Kerri A. Cardone
Associate Project Media Editor: Emily Brower
Senior Workflow Manager: Paul W. Rohloff
Text Permissions Manager: Kalina K. Ingham
Photo Researcher: Krystyna Borgen/Lumina Datamatics
Text Permissions Editor: Mark Schaefer, Lumina Datamatics
Photo Permissions Editor: Angela Boehler
Director of Design, Content Management: Diana Blume
Text Design: Lisa Buckley
Cover Design: William Boardman
Cover and Title Page Photo: Hero Images/Getty Images
Composition: Lumina Datamatics, Inc.
Printing and Binding: King Printing Co., Inc.

Manufactured in the United States of America.

1 2 3 4 5 6   24 23 22 21 20

For information, write: Bedford/St. Martin's, 75 Arlington Street, Boston, MA 02116
   (617-399-4000)

ISBN 978-1-319-36153-2 (paperback)

Acknowledgments

Text acknowledgments and copyrights appear at the back of the book on pages A-1–A-2, which constitute an extension of the copyright page. Art acknowledgments and copyrights appear on the same page as the art selections they cover.

Preface

To The Instructor

The twelfth edition of *The Bedford Guide for College Writers* gives students everything they need to succeed as writers. With clear and concise instruction, a flexible organization, and frequent opportunities for active learning, *The Bedford Guide* focuses on the needs of students and instructors, whether meeting face to face or online. It has found enduring success because of its uniquely comprehensive scope. Written and developed as four books in one, *The Bedford Guide* combines a step-by-step rhetoric, a fresh thematic reader, a practical research manual, and a thorough handbook. Hallmark features, such as the handy checklists and Learning by Doing activities, prepare students for future writing and research projects in college and in life.

Recognizing that the college composition course may be one of a student's last classes with in-depth writing instruction, this new edition responds to the excellent suggestions of our reviewers and Advisory Board to the changing needs and habits of students. The twelfth edition sharpens its focus on source-based academic writing, the kinds of writing students actually do in college. It gathers diverse, thought-provoking model essays on topics that speak to students' lives, from how Millennials compare to their grandparents' generation to the way hip-hop has influenced the music industry. The new edition also continues to break down the writing process for each type of assignment, helping students manage their writing projects, aided by a practical new time management planner designed to help students meet their deadlines. Finally, an updated Research Manual addresses the ever-growing need to evaluate online sources critically and consider biases of all kinds. All aspects of this new edition of *The Bedford Guide* are designed with one overarching goal: to help students to become the confident, resourceful, and *independent* writers they will need to be.

BOOK 1 — *A Writer's Guide*

This process-oriented rhetoric helps students of all skill levels become better, more effective writers. In the twelfth edition, *A Writer's Guide* has been streamlined carefully. Now divided into three parts, the *Guide* focuses on the essential processes and assignments in college writing.

Part One, A College Writer's Processes, establishes the interconnected processes at the core of college composition: writing (Chapter 1), reading (Chapter 2), and critical thinking, (Chapter 3). New attention to the genre in Chapter 1 introduces students to the important element of the rhetorical situation.

Part Two, A Writer's Situations, now encapsulates ten core chapters, corresponding to the full range of common first-year writing assignments. Each chapter features two sample readings, one professional selection and one student essay, to give students helpful models and inspiration. The rhetorical situations in Part Two include recalling an experience and observing a scene (Chapter 4), interviewing for information (Chapter 5), comparing and contrasting (Chapter 6), explaining causes and effects (Chapter 7), taking a stand (Chapter 8), proposing a solution (Chapter 9), evaluating and reviewing (Chapter 10), supporting a position with sources (Chapter 11), responding to literature (Chapter 12), and responding to visual representations (Chapter 13). Part Two showcases the range of rigorous academic writing that lies at the heart of the composition course, with flexibility for instructors to rearrange chapters to emphasize argument, source-based writing, or other rhetorical or thematic approaches.

Part Three, A Writer's Strategies, guides students as they delve into composing. The first chapter, Strategies: A Case Study (Chapter 14), features a new source-based student essay and follows a real student as he develops and revises his rhetorical analysis of two relevant and timely sources on teens and smartphone use. It also includes his self-reflective portfolio letter. The next five chapters explain and further illustrate common approaches to generating ideas (Chapter 15), stating a thesis and planning (Chapter 16), drafting (Chapter 17), developing (Chapter 18), revising and editing (Chapter 19), and creating presentations and portfolios (Chapter 20). Marginal annotations in the earlier parts of the book link to these chapters, offering students a toolbox of writing strategies.

BOOK 2   A Writer's Reader

Freshly overhauled for the twelfth edition, A Writer's Reader is a five-chapter thematic reader showcasing excellent source-based selections to get students thinking and writing. The reader offers engaging 25 readings in all — three-quarters of them new — arranged around five provocative themes: America (Chapter 21), Language (Chapter 22), Popular Culture (Chapter 23), Inequality (Chapter 24), and Gender (Chapter 25). From immigration, transgender identity, sexual double-standards, and income inequality, the readings collected here raise issues students care about. Headnotes and analytical questions accompany each reading, along with suggested writing assignments for students to apply what they have learned. A rhetorical table of contents (p. xxi) shows how selections correlate with A Writer's Guide and the writing situations assigned there.

BOOK 3 *A Writer's Research Manual*

Detailed yet practical, *A Writer's Research Manual* covers how to use print, electronic, and field research sources in academic work. This portion of *The Bedford Guide* begins with a unique chapter on defining the research project (Chapter 26), finding sources (Chapter 27), evaluating sources (Chapter 28), working with sources (Chapter 29), and writing the research paper (Chapter 30). A new section addresses critical thinking as part of source evaluation, as well as the importance of authenticating Web sources. *A Writer's Research Manual* ends with extensive coverage of documentation in both MLA (Chapter 31) and APA (Chapter 32) style, including dozens of models in a variety of source types. Updated Source Navigators provide a visual map of how to cite sources correctly for MLA and APA style. In the appendices, the Quick Research Guide offers a brief, convenient review of how to find, evaluate, integrate, cite, and document sources while the Quick Format Guide illustrates academic document design.

BOOK 4 *A Writer's Handbook*

The handbook clearly explains grammar, style, punctuation, and mechanics topics, with examples and explanations that are easy to follow. From parts of speech to additional help for multilingual writers, and almost fifty exercises for additional practice, the handbook gives students a handy reference guide to strengthening their writing. In addition, the Quick Editing Guide in the appendices highlights the most troublesome grammar and editing problems.

New to the Twelfth Edition

Based on the valuable feedback from our editorial board and instructors around the country, the twelfth edition of *The Bedford Guide* strengthens its focus on academic writing from sources. The activities, examples, visuals, and readings all work together to sharpen students' academic writing skills.

A Practical New Time Management Planner in the *Guide*

Especially when they are writing from sources, students often need help planning the steps of their project. This clear timetable lays out manageable goals for each assignment type, ensuring that students organize their essays effectively and meet their deadlines.

More Source-Based Readings

The sample essays in the *Guide* and the *Reader*, both professional and student, provide relevant models of writing from sources — the kinds of assignments students will face throughout their years in college. More argument and analysis pieces illustrate how real writers integrate, synthesize, and cite sources in their essays. In Chapter 14, a new source-based case study follows a real student writer as he responds to and analyzes two magazine articles.

Nineteen Fresh and Diverse New Readings in *A Writer's Reader*

Two entirely new chapters on "America" and "Inequality" highlight current issues, and selections in the "Language," "Popular Culture," and "Gender" amplify important new voices on topics students care about:

- NPR reporter Shankar Vedantam on the myth of American immigration
- An exploration of how the term "Latinx" came to be and what it means
- An academic journal article analyzing the rise of "cute" superheroes
- Psychologist Keith Payne on overcoming the barriers of income inequality
- Acclaimed writer Chimamanda Ngozi Adichie on what "feminism" is — and what it isn't

Crucial Attention to Authenticating Online Sources

The *Research Manual* offers new sections on authenticating sources and steering clear of "fake news." These timely additions respond to crucial gaps in students' media literacy to help them evaluate online sources with a critical eye, move outside their own information bubbles, and recognize bias. The practical Source Navigators — detailed visual models that instruct students on how to cite common source types — now appear in the MLA and APA chapters, right where students need them.

A New *Student's Companion for The Bedford Guide* for Corequisite or ALP Support

Authored by Elizabeth Catanese (Community College of Philadelphia), this supplement offers thorough support for students using *The Bedford Guide* in ALP/co-requisite courses. The text includes coverage of college success strategies; activities to help students develop thoughtful, college-level essays; and additional practice in correcting writing problems, from revising topic sentences and developing paragraphs to correcting fragments.

Bedford/St. Martin's puts you first

From day one, our goal has been simple: to provide inspiring resources that are grounded in best practices for teaching reading and writing. For more than 35 years, Bedford/St. Martin's has partnered with the field, listening to teachers, scholars, and students about the support writers need. We are committed to helping every writing instructor make the most of our resources.

How can we help *you*?

- Our editors can align our resources to your outcomes through correlation and transition guides for your syllabus. Just ask us.
- Our sales representatives specialize in helping you find the right materials to support your course goals.
- Our *Bits* blog on the Bedford/St. Martin's English Community (**community.macmillan.com**) publishes fresh teaching ideas weekly. You'll also find easily downloadable professional resources and links to author webinars on our community site.

Contact your Bedford/St. Martin's sales representative or visit **macmillanlearning.com** to learn more.

Print and Digital Options for *The Bedford Guide for College Writers*

Choose the format that works best for your course, and ask about our packaging options that offer savings for students.

Print

- *Paperback 4-in-1.* To order the paperback edition of the guide, reader, research manual, and handbook, use ISBN 978-1-319-36153-2.
- *Paperback 2-in-1.* To order the paperback edition of the guide and reader, use ISBN 978-1-319-36819-7.
- *A Student's Companion for* The Bedford Guide for College Writers. To package our new ALP supplement with the 4-in-1 or the 2-in-1 versions, contact your sales representative.
- *Loose-leaf edition.* This format does not have a traditional binding; its pages are loose and hole punched to provide flexibility and a lower price to students. It can be packaged with our digital space for additional savings. To order the loose-leaf for the 4-in-1, use ISBN 978-1-319-36815-9. To order the loose-leaf for the 2-in-1, use ISBN 978-1-319-36818-0.

Digital

- *Innovative digital learning space.* Bedford/St. Martin's suite of digital tools makes it easy to get everyone on the same page by putting student writers at the center. For details, visit **macmillanlearning.com/college/us/englishdigital**.

- *Popular e-book formats.* For details about our e-book partners, visit **macmillanlearning.com/ebooks**.

- *Inclusive Access.* Enable every student to receive their course materials through your LMS on the first day of class. Macmillan Learning's Inclusive Access program is the easiest, most affordable way to ensure all students have access to quality educational resources. Find out more at **macmillanlearning.com/inclusiveaccess**.

Your Course, Your Way

No two writing programs or classrooms are exactly alike. Our Curriculum Solutions team works with you to design custom options that provide the resources your students need. (Options below require enrollment minimums.)

- *ForeWords for English.* Customize any print resource to fit the focus of your course or program by choosing from a range of prepared topics, such as Sentence Guides for Academic Writers.

- *Macmillan Author Program (MAP).* Add excerpts or package acclaimed works from Macmillan's trade imprints to connect students with prominent authors and public conversations. A list of popular examples or academic themes is available upon request.

- *Bedford Select.* Build your own print handbook or anthology from a database of more than 800 selections, and add your own materials to create your ideal text. Package with any Bedford/St. Martin's text for additional savings. Visit **macmillanlearning.com/bedfordselect**.

Instructor Resources

You have a lot to do in your course. We want to make it easy for you to find the support you need — and to get it quickly.

Practical Suggestions for Teaching with The Bedford Guide for College Writers is available as a PDF that can be downloaded from **macmillanlearning.com**. In addition to chapter overviews and teaching tips, the instructor's manual includes sample syllabi, correlations to the Council of Writing Program Administrators' Outcomes Statement, classroom activities, and answers to the handbook exercises.

Thanks and Appreciation

Many individuals contributed significantly to the twelfth edition of *The Bedford Guide for College Writers*, and we extend our sincerest thanks to all of them.

Editorial Advisory Board

As we began to prepare this edition, we turned to our trusted editorial advisory board for its opinion on the many significant changes we planned. These dedicated instructors were eager to share ideas about how to make the book more useful to both students and teachers. They responded thoroughly and insightfully to new features of the book and its media, answered innumerable questions, and suggested many ideas, activities, and assignments. They also submitted student papers and in ways large and small helped to shape the twelfth edition. We are extremely grateful to each one of them:

- Marsha Anderson, Wharton Junior College
- Patricia Boyd, Arizona State University
- Jill Dahlman, University of North Alabama
- Kimberly George, Temple College
- Sandra Grady, Community College of Baltimore County Catonsville
- Jennifer Gray, College of Coastal Georgia
- Stephanie Hyman, Gaston College
- Irma Luna, San Antonio College
- Anna McKennon, Fullerton College
- Terry Novak, Johnson & Wales University

Other Colleagues

We also extend our gratitude to the following instructors across the country who took time and care to review this edition, participate in focus groups, respond to surveys, send us their students' work, and share excellent suggestions gleaned from their experience: Susan Achziger, Community College of Aurora; Evan Balkan, Community College of Baltimore County; Kathleen Beauchene, Community College of Rhode Island; Jenny Billings, Rowan-Cabarrus Community College; Martha Brown, Clinton Community College; Kathryn Crowther, Georgia State University-Perimeter College; Melanie DeKerlegand, Gaston College; Meredith Dodson, Olivet College; Michele Domenech, Gaston College; Genevieve Freese, University of Wisconsin-Waukesha; Jennifer Gray, College of Coastal Georgia; Rebecca Kouider, Gaston College; Robbyn Lamb, Colby Community College; Lucinda Ligget, Ivy Tech Community College; Irma Luna, San Antonio College; Kelly Giles McFarland, Community College of Baltimore County; Anna McKennon, Fullerton College; Cindy Ross, Lone Star College, Kingwood; Michelle Stevier-Johanson, Dickinson State University; Elizabeth Stoneberger, Labette Community College; Gina Teel, Southeast Arkansas College; Christopher Thurley, Gaston College; Andrea Trapp, Cincinnati State Technical and Community College; Mary Treglown, Southeast Arkansas College; Donna Wilson, Community College of Baltimore County; Gaye Winter, Mississippi Gulf Coast Community College-Perkinston; Nadia Woods, Jefferson College; Charlotte Wulf,

Community College of Baltimore County; Stephanie Zerkel-Humbert, Maple Woods Community College.

Contributors

The twelfth edition could not have been completed without the help of numerous individuals. Special thanks go to Ellen Thibault, whose thoughtful recommendations and diligence helped shape this edition of the text and the *Practical Suggestions* that accompany it. Valerie Duff-Strautmann (Newbury College) ably developed apparatus and reading comprehension quizzes for the new selections in this edition. We thank both of them for contributing their time and expertise to this edition.

Editorial

We wish to thank Vice President Editorial for the Humanities Leasa Burton; Program Director for English Stacey Purviance; and Senior Program Manager Laura Arcari for their continuing support of this title. Senior Development Editor Rachel Goldberg brought fresh eyes to this edition, encouraging lively innovation. Associate Editor Suzy Chouljian skillfully developed *A Writer's Reader* and lent her insight to many other parts of the book. Assistant Editor Paola Garcia-Muñiz ably and efficiently helped with the many aspects, large and small, of the development of this complex book. Many thanks and heartfelt appreciation also go to unflappable Senior Production Editor Kerri Cardone, who, with an exacting eye, great patience, and good humor, shepherded the book through production. Bridget Leahy deftly copyedited the text. Finally, we once again thank our friends and families for their unwavering patience, understanding, and encouragement.

Contents

BOOK 1

A WRITER'S GUIDE

**BOOK
2**

A WRITER'S READER

Introduction: Reading to Write   330

BOOK 3

A WRITER'S RESEARCH MANUAL

BOOK 4

A WRITER'S HANDBOOK

RHETORICAL CONTENTS

*(Essays listed in order of appearance; * indicates student essays.)*

FEATURES OF *THE BEDFORD GUIDE,* TWELFTH EDITION, AND ANCILLARIES

Correlated to the Writing Program Administrators (WPA) Outcomes Statement

WPA Outcomes	Relevant Features of *The Bedford Guide*
Rhetorical Knowledge	
Learn and use key rhetorical concepts through analyzing and composing a variety of texts	▪ Ch. 1, Writing Processes, including audience and purpose (pp. 4–15) ▪ Ch. 2, Reading Processes, including annotation, literal vs. analytical reading, online and multimodal reading (pp. 16–35) ▪ Ch. 8, Taking a Stand, including finding, testing, and applying evidence; avoiding faulty thinking (pp. 123–147) ▪ Chs. 2, 4–13, 20: Throughout these chapters, Learning from Other Writers activities guide students through rhetorical analysis of texts in a variety of situations/genres (e.g., p. 167). ▪ Chs. 1–19, 26, 33, 35–37: Learning by Doing activities give students opportunities to apply rhetorical concepts to a variety of situations/genres (e.g., p. 116, p. 498). ▪ Chs. 4–13: Learning by Writing assignments and additional writing assignments require students to use key rhetorical concepts to compose texts in a variety of genres (e.g., p. 155, p. 234). ▪ Chs. 21–25 (*A Writer's Reader*) offer additional texts, arranged thematically. Each selection is paired with critical thinking questions and suggestions for student response (e.g., pp. 404–424).
Gain experience reading and composing in several genres to understand how genre conventions shape and are shaped by readers' and writers' practices and purposes	▪ Chs. 4–20 (Part Two, A Writer's Situations, and Part Three, A Writer's Strategies) introduce students to a variety of writing situations and genres, exploring the conventions and purposes of those genres via guided analysis of professional and student texts (Learning from Other Writers) and active practice (Learning by Doing activities, Learning by Writing assignments, Additional Writing Assignments) (pp. 48–328). ▪ Chs. 21–25 (*A Writer's Reader*) are heavily integrated with Part Two of *A Writer's Guide*. Many of the Suggestions for Writing assignments following the texts ask students to respond to the piece in terms of its genre conventions (pp. 331–445). ▪ A rhetorically organized table of contents is available on pages xxi–xxiv.
Develop facility in responding to a variety of situations and contexts, calling for purposeful shifts in voice, tone, level of formality, design, medium, and/or structure	▪ Understanding Your Writing Situation (pp. 8–15) in Ch. 1, Writing Processes ▪ The Learning by Writing sections of each Part Two chapter (e.g., pp. 130–147) ▪ Considering Purpose and Audience (pp. 265–280) in Ch. 16, Strategies for Stating a Thesis and Planning ▪ Ch. 19, Strategies for Revision, including Revising for Audience (pp. 306–307), Working with a Peer Editor (pp. 308–309), Revising for Emphasis, Conciseness, and Clarity (pp. 311–316) ▪ Ch. 36, Word Choice (pp. 641–651)

WPA Outcomes	Relevant Features of *The Bedford Guide*
Rhetorical Knowledge	
Understand and use a variety of technologies to address a range of audiences	■ Visual Activities in Part One, including Reading Online and Multimodal Texts in Ch. 2, Reading Processes (pp. 33–35) ■ Ch. 13, Responding to Visual Representations (pp. 230–242) ■ Ch. 20, Strategies for Creating Presentations and Portfolios, including Using Visuals (pp. 320–322), Visuals for Oral Presentations (pp. 322–324), and Portfolios (pp. 324–328) ■ *A Writer's Research Manual* with online strategies throughout (Chs. 26–32) ■ Quick Format Guide, including a section on integrating and crediting visuals (pp. Q-1–Q-19) ■ Quick Research Guide, including Searching for Recommended Sources (pp. Q-20–Q-36)
Match the capacities of different environments (e.g., print and electronic) to varying rhetorical situations	■ Ch. 20, Strategies for Creating Presentations and Portfolios, including Using Visuals (pp. 320–322), Visuals for Oral Presentations (pp. 322–324), and Portfolios (pp. 324–328) ■ *A Writer's Research Manual* with online strategies throughout (Chs. 26–32) ■ Quick Research Guide, including Searching for Recommended Sources (pp. Q-20–Q-36).
Critical Thinking, Reading, and Composing	
Use composing and reading for inquiry, learning, thinking, and communicating in various rhetorical contexts	■ Chs. 1–3 (Part One, A College Writer's Processes) includes writing, reading, and critical thinking processes. ■ Parts Two and Three emphasize the connection between reading and writing. ■ *A Writer's Reader*, with twenty-five readings grouped thematically (pp. 331–445) ■ Critical reading apparatus in Part Two, A Writer's Situations (e.g., pp. 50–57) and in *A Writer's Reader* (e.g., pp. 331–356) *For instructors* ■ *Practical Suggestions for Teaching with The Bedford Guide for College Writers*, Ch. 3: Teaching Critical Thinking
Read a diverse range of texts, attending especially to relationships between assertion and evidence, to patterns of organization, to interplay between verbal and nonverbal elements, and to how these features function for different audiences and situations	■ Each chapter in Part Two presents multiple text and multimodal selections produced by professional writers and students, organized by situation/genre. Texts are followed by questions that ask students to consider meaning, the effectiveness of the writer's strategies, and other rhetorical matters. ■ *A Writer's Reader* offers twenty-five new text and multimodal selections organized around five timely themes. Diverse readings are followed by questions on critical reading, meaning, writing strategies, and, in the case of multimodal texts, questions on verbal/nonverbal interplay.

WPA Outcomes	Relevant Features of *The Bedford Guide*
Critical Thinking, Reading, and Composing	
Locate and evaluate primary and secondary research materials, including journal articles, essays, books, databases, and informal Internet sources	■ Ch. 11, Supporting a Position with Sources (pp. 182–204) ■ Ch. 26, Defining Your Research Project (pp. 447–456) ■ Ch. 28, Evaluating Sources, including detailed guidance on how to authenticate information and recognize bias in sources (pp. 473–481) ■ Ch. 29, Working with Sources, including capturing information and developing an annotated bibliography (pp. 482–494) ■ Chs. 27–29 on finding, evaluating, integrating, and synthesizing sources from the Internet, the library, and the field (pp. 457–494) ■ Quick Research Guide (pp. Q-20–Q-36) ■ Visual and Source Activity and Source Assignment options in Part Two of *A Writer's Guide* (e.g., p. 34; pp. 180–181)
Use strategies — such as interpretation, synthesis, response, critique, and design/redesign — to compose texts that integrate the writer's ideas with those from appropriate sources	■ *A Writer's Reader* with critical thinking questions, writing suggestions, and paired essays (pp. 331–445) ■ Ch. 11, Supporting a Position with Sources (pp. 181–204) ■ Chs. 27–29 on finding, evaluating, integrating, and synthesizing sources (pp. 457–494) ■ Quick Research Guide (pp. Q-20–Q-36)
Processes	
Develop a writing project through multiple drafts	■ Ch. 1, Writing Processes (pp. 4–15) with process overview ■ Chs. 4–13 with situation-specific process guidance ■ In Part Two, Chs. 4–13, the Managing Your Time planner helps students allocate their time effectively during their writing process. ■ Part Three, A Writer's Strategies, shows writing processes in detail, including Ch. 19, Strategies for Revising and Editing with example of students' revision stages (pp. 245–253; pp. 314–316).
Develop flexible strategies for reading, drafting, reviewing, collaborating, revising, rewriting, rereading, and editing	■ Ch. 1, Writing Processes with an overview of generating ideas, planning, drafting, developing, revising, editing, and proofreading (pp. 4–15) ■ In Part Two, Chs. 4–13, the Managing Your Time planner helps students read, research, draft, review, revise, and edit during their writing process. ■ Part Three, A Writer's Strategies, with detailed coverage of each stage of drafting, revising, and editing (pp. 244–328)
Use composing processes and tools as a means to discover and reconsider ideas	■ Ch. 15, Strategies for Generating Ideas (pp. 255–264) ■ Ch. 19, Strategies for Revising and Editing (pp. 305–318) ■ Learning by Doing activities involve students in applying relevant composing processes to discover and reconsider ideas. ■ Checklists help students consider purpose and audience, discover something to write about, get feedback from a peer, revise their draft, and edit for grammatical correctness (e.g., p. 11).

WPA Outcomes	Relevant Features of *The Bedford Guide*
Processes	
Experience the collaborative and social aspects of writing processes	■ Learning by Doing features including collaborative activities (e.g., p. 82; p. 248) and Peer Response guidelines (Part Three and p. 309) ■ In Part Two, A Writer's Situations, Additional Writing Assignments offer collaborative options (e.g., p. 103) ■ Ch. 14, Strategies: A Case Study, including Rough Draft with Peer and Instructor Responses (pp. 246–253) and Reflective Portfolio Letter (p. 254) ■ Ch. 26, Defining Your Research Project, including advice on planning collaborative research (p. 447–456) ■ Ch. 27, Finding Sources, including Interviewing (p. 469) and Attending Public and Online Events (p. 472) *For instructors* ■ *Practical Suggestions for Teaching with The Bedford Guide for College Writers,* Ch. 2: Creating a Writing Community
Learn to give and act on productive feedback to works in progress	■ Ch. 19, Strategies for Revising and Editing with peer-editing advice (pp. 305–318) ■ Peer Response sections for each chapter in Part Two, A Writer's Situations ■ Ch. 14, Strategies: A Case Study, including Rough Draft with Peer and Instructor Responses (pp. 246–253) and Reflective Portfolio Letter (p. 254) *For instructors* ■ *Practical Suggestions for Teaching with The Bedford Guide for College Writers,* Ch. 2: Creating a Writing Community
Adapt composing processes for a variety of technologies and modalities	■ Visual Activities in Part One and Visual Assignment options in Parts Two and Three ■ Ch. 13, Responding to Visual Representations (pp. 230–242) ■ Reading Online and Multimodal Texts (pp. 33–35) in Ch. 2, Reading Processes ■ Ch. 20, Strategies for Creating Presentations and Portfolios, covers how to utilize digital portfolios to compile written projects over time (pp. 324–328). ■ Quick Format Guide, including a section on integrating and crediting visuals (pp. Q-1–Q-19)
Reflect on the development of composing practices and how those practices influence their work	■ Writing Strategies questions following each text in Parts Two and Three and in *A Writer's Reader* ask students to reflect upon the author's composing practices. ■ Ch. 3, Critical Thinking Processes, including Thinking Critically about Your Own Writing (pp. 38–42) and Self-Reflection (pp. 42–43) ■ Ch. 14, Strategies: A Case Study, with Reflective Portfolio Letter (p. 254) ■ Learning by Doing activities in Part Three ask students to reflect on their practice with the writing strategy covered in the chapter. ■ Checklists help students consider purpose and audience, discover something to write about, get feedback from a peer, revise their drafts, and edit for grammatical correctness (e.g., p. 12). ■ Chs. 4–13 (Parts Two of *A Writer's Guide*): Reviewing and Reflecting activities help students reconsider ideas learned in each chapter (e.g., p. 86)

WPA Outcomes	Relevant Features of *The Bedford Guide*
Knowledge of Conventions	
Develop knowledge of linguistic structures, including grammar, punctuation, and spelling, through practice in composing and revising	■ *A Writer's Handbook* (pp. 558–691) with exercises, including a chapter on basic grammar (Ch. 38) ■ Quick Editing Guide with Editing Checklist (pp. Q-37–Q-64) ■ Part Two, A Writer's Situations, revising and editing advice, including cross-references to relevant topics in the Quick Editing Guide ■ Ch. 19, Strategies for Revising and Editing (pp. 305–318) *For instructors* ■ *Practical Suggestions for Teaching with The Bedford Guide for College Writers*, Ch. 4: Providing Support for Underprepared Students
Understand why genre conventions for structure, paragraphing, tone, and mechanics vary	■ Part Two, A Writer's Situations, and Part Three, A Writer's Strategies ■ Ch. 36, Word Choice, Ch. 37: Punctuation, and Ch. 38: Mechanics ■ Ch. 16, Strategies for Stating a Thesis and Planning, especially Shaping Your Topic for Your Purpose and Your Audience (pp. 265–280) ■ Ch. 19, Strategies for Revising and Editing, especially Revising for Audience (pp. 305–318)
Gain experience negotiating variations in genre conventions	■ Ch. 1, Writing Processes, specifically Writing in Different Genres (pp. 11–13) ■ Part Two, A Writer's Situations, and Part Three, A Writer's Strategies, feature a wide variety of genres
Learn common formats and/ or design features for different kinds of texts	■ Advice on various types of assignments in Parts Two and Three ■ Quick Format Guide with MLA and APA papers, tables, resumes, and letters
Explore the concepts of intellectual property (such as fair use and copyright) that motivate documentation conventions	■ Chs. 27–29 on finding, evaluating, integrating, and synthesizing sources from the Internet, the library, and the field (pp. 457–494) ■ Ch. 28, Evaluating Sources, on assessing reliability in sources (pp. 473–481)
Practice applying citation conventions systematically in their own work	■ Options for source-based activities (Chs. 1–3) and assignments (Chs. 4–17) concluding each chapter ■ Ch. 11, Supporting a Position with Sources (pp. 182–205), ■ Ch. 30, Citing and Integrating Your Sources as You Draft (pp. 496–499) ■ Quick Research Guide (pp. Q-20–Q-36)

How to Use *The Bedford Guide for College Writers*

You may be wondering how any textbook can improve your writing. In fact, a book alone can't make you a better writer, but practice can, and *The Bedford Guide for College Writers* is designed to make your writing practice effective and productive. This text offers help—easy to find and easy to use—for writing the essays most commonly assigned in college.

Underlying *The Bedford Guide* is the idea that writing is a necessary and useful skill beyond the writing course. The skills you learn throughout this book are transferable to other areas of your life—future courses, jobs, and community activities—making *The Bedford Guide* both a time-saver and a money-saver. Read on to discover how you can get the most out of this text.

Finding Information in *The Bedford Guide*

Each of the tools described here directs you to useful information—fast.

Brief Contents. In the Brief Contents (see the first book page), you have at a glance the list of topics covered in *The Bedford Guide*. The quickest way to find a specific chapter is by using the Brief Contents.

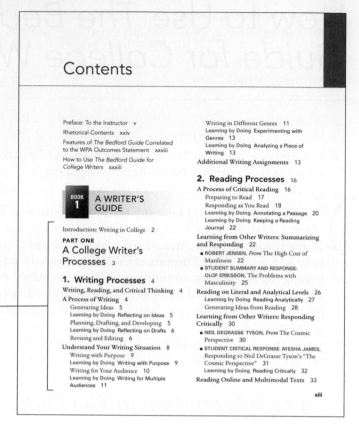

Contents

Contents. Beginning on p. xi, the more detailed list of contents breaks down the topics covered within each chapter. Use this list to find a specific part of a chapter. For example, if you've been asked to read Olof Eriksson's paper "The Problems with Masculinity," a quick scan will show you that it begins on page 25.

Rhetorical Contents. This list, beginning on page xxii, includes all readings in *The Bedford Guide,* organized by writing strategy or situation, such as Explaining Causes and Effects, or Evaluating and Reviewing. Use this list to locate examples of the kind of writing you're doing and to see how other writers approached their material.

Index. The index is an in-depth list of the book's contents. Turn to page I-1 to find the information available for a particular topic. This example shows you where to look for help with analyzing material, a common assignment in college.

Guide to the Handbook. After the index is a guide listing the contents of *A Writer's Handbook.* Turn to this guide for help editing your essays. It gives page numbers for each topic, such as "sentence fragments." If English is not your native language, this guide notes all the Guidelines for Multilingual Writers boxes included in the Handbook, such as What Is the Order for Cumulative Adjectives?

Marginal Cross-References. You can find additional information quickly by using the references in the margins — notes on the sides of each page that tell you where to turn in the book.

Color-Coded Pages. Several sections of *The Bedford Guide* are color-coded to make them easy to find.

- MLA Style (pp. 500–28). For help using MLA guidelines to document the sources in your paper, turn to the green-edged pages.

- APA Style (pp. 529–56). For help using APA guidelines to document the sources in your paper, turn to the blue-edged pages.

- Quick Format Guide (pp. Q-1–Q-19). For help formatting your paper, turn to this section at the back of the book, designated with gold-edged pages.

- Quick Research Guide (pp. Q-20–Q-36). For fast help with research processes, sources, or the basics of MLA or APA style, turn to this section at the back of the book, designated with orange-edged pages.

- Quick Editing Guide (pp. Q-37–Q-64). For help as you edit your writing, turn to this section at the back of the book, designated with blue-edged pages.

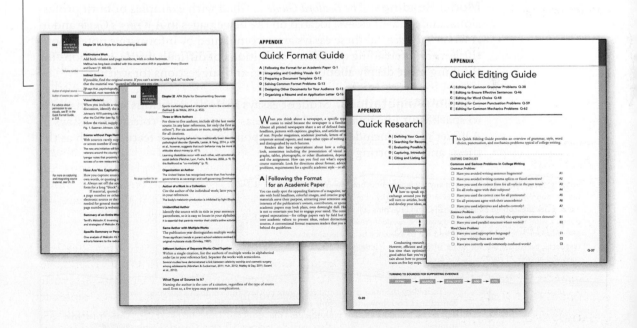

Navigation Tabs. A colored tab in the top left margin of each spread reminds users which book they are in, the Guide, Reader, Research Manual, or Handbook. In addition, tabs at the top of each page in *A Writer's Handbook* link the explanations, examples, and exercises to the particular editing problem. Your instructor may use correction symbols, such as *agr* for subject-verb agreement, to indicate areas in your draft that need editing.

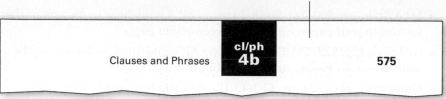

Clauses and Phrases   **cl/ph 4b**   575

Answers to Exercises. As you complete the Handbook exercises, you'll want to know if you're learning what is expected. Turn to the last section of the Handbook to find the correct answers to the lettered exercises.

Becoming a Better Writer by Using *The Bedford Guide*

The Bedford Guide includes readings, checklists, activities, and other features to help you improve your writing and do well in college and on the job.

Model Readings. *The Bedford Guide* is filled with examples of both professional and student essays, located on the beige pages in *A Writer's Guide* and in *A Writer's Reader*. All these essays are accompanied by informative notes about the author, prereading questions, definitions of difficult words, questions for thinking more deeply about the reading, and suggestions for writing.

Reading Annotations. Student essays include questions in the margins to spark your imagination and your ideas as you read. Professional essays in *A Writer's Guide* include annotations to point out notable features, such as the thesis and supporting points.

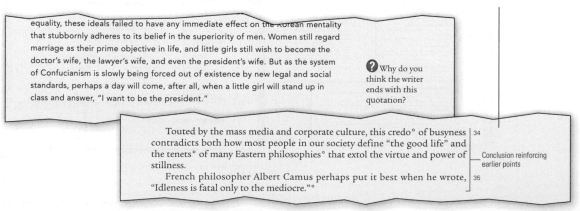

equality, these ideals failed to have any immediate effect on the Korean mentality that stubbornly adheres to its belief in the superiority of men. Women still regard marriage as their prime objective in life, and little girls still wish to become the doctor's wife, the lawyer's wife, and even the president's wife. But as the system of Confucianism is slowly being forced out of existence by new legal and social standards, perhaps a day will come, after all, when a little girl will stand up in class and answer, "I want to be the president."

❓ Why do you think the writer ends with this quotation?

Touted by the mass media and corporate culture, this credo° of busyness contradicts both how most people in our society define "the good life" and the tenets° of many Eastern philosophies° that extol the virtue and power of stillness.

French philosopher Albert Camus perhaps put it best when he wrote, "Idleness is fatal only to the mediocre."°

34

Conclusion reinforcing earlier points

35

Clear Assignments. In Chapters 4–13, the Learning by Writing section presents the assignment for the chapter and guides you through the process of writing that type of essay.

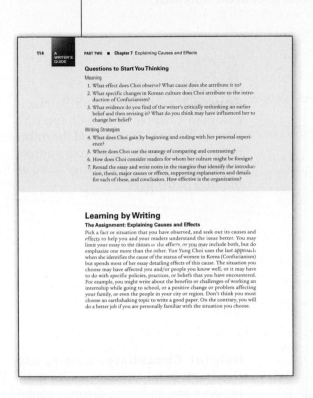

Time Management Planner. A new Managing Your Time box in Chapters 4–13 of *A Writer's Guide* helps you break down each assignment into manageable tasks and plan your time to meet your deadlines. Look for the clock icon to find this helpful planner.

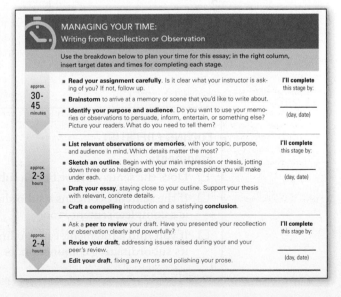

Learning by Doing 🖋 Reflecting on Ideas

Think over past writing experiences at school or work. How do you get ideas? Where do they come from? Where do you turn to gather material to flesh out your ideas? What are your most reliable sources of inspiration and information? Share your experiences with others in class or online, noting any new approaches you would like to try.

Learning by Doing. These activities are designed to let you practice and apply what you are learning to your own writing, whether in other contexts in college or in the workplace.

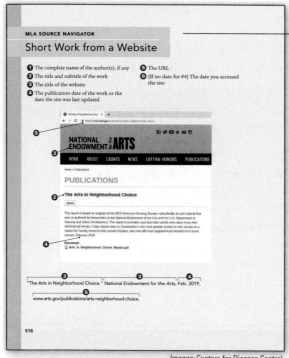

Source Navigators. Source Navigators in Chapter 31 and Chapter 32 show you how to quickly find the information you need to credit your sources correctly. Look for the orange band at the edge of the page.

Images: Centers for Disease Control.

Helpful Checklists. Easy-to-use checklists help you to consider your purpose and audience, discover something to write about, get feedback from a peer, revise your draft, and edit for grammatical correctness, using references to the Quick Editing Guide (pp. Q-37–Q-64).

EDITING CHECKLIST

Fragments

☐ Does the sentence have both a subject and a verb?

☐ If the sentence contains a subordinate clause, does it contain a clause that is a complete sentence too?

☐ If you find a fragment, can you link it to an adjoining sentence, eliminate its subordinating conjunction, or add any missing element?

A WRITER'S GUIDE

Introduction: Writing in College

As a college writer, you may wonder how people who write for a living are able to do so, seemingly without effort. The truth is, they have no magic. What they have is experience and confidence, the products of lots of practice writing, as well as input from others. The purpose of this book is to help you to become a better writer by actually writing. In *A Writer's Guide* we'll give you a lot of practice — and plenty of advice to help you build your skills and confidence.

Part One, "A College Writer's Processes," will help you to write, read, and think critically — essential skills for writing in college.

Part Two, "A Writer's Situations," is the heart of this book. Each chapter presents a writing situation and then guides you as you write a paper in response. You will learn to expertly recall and observe events (Chapter 4), interview to gather information (Chapter 5), compare and contrast ideas (Chapter 6), explain causes and effects (Chapter 7), take a stand (Chapter 8), propose a solution to a problem (Chapter 9), evaluate and review the work of others (Chapter 10), support a position with sources (Chapter 11), write about literature (Chapter 12), and analyze visual works (Chapter 13).

Part Three, "A Writer's Strategies," walks you through another student's strategies, showing how a paper evolves from idea to final form. Other chapters help you generate ideas, plan, draft, develop, revise, edit, create presentations, and keep a portfolio of your writing.

PART ONE

A College Writer's Processes

1 Writing Processes

You are already a writer with long experience. In school you have taken notes, written book reports and term papers, answered exam questions, perhaps kept a journal. In the community or on the job you've composed emails and perhaps letters. You've sent text messages or tweets to friends, made lists, maybe even written songs or poetry. All this experience is about to pay off as you tackle college writing, learning by doing.

Writing, Reading, and Critical Thinking

For more on reading critically, see Ch. 2. For more on thinking critically, see Ch. 3.

In college you will expand what you already know about writing. You may be asked not only to recall an experience but also to reflect upon its significance. Or you may go beyond summarizing positions about an issue to present your own position or propose a solution. Above all, you'll read and think critically — not just stacking up facts, but analyzing what you discover, deciding what it means, and weighing its value. As you read — and write — actively, you will engage with the ideas of others, analyzing and judging those ideas. You will use criteria — models, conventions, principles, standards — to evaluate what you're doing.

In large measure, learning to write well is learning what questions to ask as you write. For that reason, we include questions, suggestions, and activities to help you accomplish your writing tasks and reflect on your own processes as you write, read, and think critically.

A Process of Writing

For full chapters on stages of the writing process, see Chs. 14–20.

Writing can seem at times to be an overwhelming drudgery, worse than scrubbing floors; at other moments, it's a sport full of thrills — like whizzing downhill on skis, not knowing what you'll meet around a bend. Unpredictable as the process may seem, nearly all writers do similar things:

- They generate ideas.
- They plan, draft, and develop their papers.
- They revise and edit.

These three activities form the basis of most effective writing processes, and they lie at the heart of each chapter in Part Two of this book.

Generating Ideas

The first activity in writing — finding a topic and something to say about it — is often the most challenging and least predictable. In Part 2 (Chapters 4–13), each chapter includes a section titled "Generating Ideas" that provides examples, questions, checklists, and visuals designed to spark ideas that will help you begin the writing assignment.

Discovering What to Write About. You may get an idea while texting friends, riding your bike, or staring out the window. Sometimes a topic is from close to home, bubbling up from a conversation or everyday event. Often, your reading will raise questions that call for investigation. Even if an assignment doesn't appeal to you, your challenge is to find an aspect of it that does. Find it, and words will flow — words to draw in your readers and accomplish your purpose.

Finding Sources. To shape and support your ideas, you'll need facts and figures, reports and opinions, examples and illustrations. How do you find supporting material that makes your slant on a topic clear and convincing? Luckily you have many sources at your fingertips. You can recall your experience and knowledge, observe things around you, talk with others who are knowledgeable, read enlightening materials that draw you to new approaches, and think critically about all these sources.

Learning by Doing 🎯 Reflecting on Ideas

Think over past writing experiences at school or work. How do you get ideas? Where do they come from? Where do you turn to gather material to flesh out your ideas? What are your most reliable sources of inspiration and information? Share your experiences with others in class or online, noting any new approaches you would like to try.

Planning, Drafting, and Developing

Next you will plan your paper, write a draft, and develop your ideas further. In each chapter of Part 2 (Chs. 4–13), a section titled "Planning, Drafting, and Developing" will help you through these stages for the assignment in that chapter.

Planning. Having discovered a burning idea to write about (or at least a smoldering one) and some supporting material (but maybe not enough yet), you'll sort out what matters most. Test various ways of stating your main point, or thesis, keeping in mind your purpose and audience:

MAYBE   We need more options for buying food on campus.

OR   We should have a greater variety of food on campus, and introducing food trucks is one way to do that.

Next, add reasoning to support your main point and arrange your ideas and material in a sensible order that will clarify it. For example, you might group and label your ideas, make an outline, or analyze the main point, breaking it down into parts:

> Introducing a variety of food trucks to our campus will offer students 1) interesting choices for meals, 2) the opportunity to try new things, and 3) convenience.

But if no clear thesis emerges quickly, don't worry. You may find one while you draft — that is, while you write an early version of your paper.

Drafting. As your ideas begin to appear, write them down before they can go back into hiding. When you let yourself take risks at this stage, you'll probably be surprised and pleased at what happens, even though your first version will be rough. Writing takes time; a paper usually needs several drafts and maybe a clearer introduction, a stronger conclusion, more convincing evidence, or even a fresh start.

Keep in mind, too, that your writing process may take you in unexpected directions, not necessarily in a straight line. You can skip around, work on several parts at a time, test a fresh approach, circle back over what's already done, or stop to play with a sentence until it clicks.

For advice on using sources, see the Quick Research Guide, pp. Q-20–Q-36.

Developing. Weave in explanations, definitions, examples, and other evidence to make your ideas clear and persuasive. To that end, you may explain the challenges faced by single parents, define an at-risk student, or provide an example of a policy that needs improvement. Concrete evidence helps your readers understand and accept your ideas. If you need specific support for your point, use strategies for developing ideas — or return to those for generating ideas.

As the graphic on p. 7 shows, your writing process may not be a linear one. What is important is that you 1) plan, keeping your writing situation in mind, 2) draft your ideas, allowing early drafts ones to be rough, and 3) develop your ideas, supporting them with concrete evidence that will persuade your readers.

Learning by Doing 🔲 Reflecting on Drafts

Reflect on your past writing experiences. How do you usually plan, draft, and develop your writing? How well do your methods work? How do you adjust them to your writing situation — that is, your purpose, your audience, and the genre in which you're composing? Which part of producing a draft do you most dread, enjoy, or wish to change? Why? Write down your reflections, and then share your experiences with others.

Revising and Editing

You might be tempted to relax once you have a draft, but for most writers, revising begins the work in earnest. Each "Revising and Editing" section provides checklists as well as suggestions for working with a peer.

PLAN

- Identify your purpose and audience
- Decide on one main point
- State a thesis
- Organize ideas by grouping or outlining

DRAFT

- Start and restart
- Build paragraphs
- Open and conclude
- Create coherence

DEVELOP

- Explain and support
- Add definitions, examples, and details
- Supply evidence such as facts, statistics, expert testimony, and observations

Revising. Revising means both reseeing and rewriting, making major changes so your paper does what you want it to. You might reevaluate your purpose, audience, or genre, rework your thesis, decide what details or evidence to include or leave out, move paragraphs around, and connect ideas better. Perhaps you'll add costs to a paper suggesting a solution to a problem or switch attention from mothers to fathers as you consider single parents.

If you put aside your draft for a few hours or a day, you can reread it with fresh eyes and a clear mind. Other students can also help you by responding to your drafts as engaged readers. This is called **peer-reviewing** (see the chart on p. 8 that shows the stages of revising, editing, and proofreading).

For editing advice, see the Quick Editing Guide, pp. Q-37–Q-64. For format advice, see the Quick Format Guide, pp. Q-1–Q-19.

Editing. Editing means refining details, improving wording, and correcting flaws that may stand in the way of your readers' understanding and enjoyment. Don't edit too early, though, because you may waste time on parts that you later revise out. In editing, you usually make these repairs:

- Drop unnecessary words; choose lively and precise words.
- Replace incorrect or inappropriate wording.

- Rearrange words into a clearer, more emphatic order.
- Combine short, choppy sentences, or break up long, confusing ones.
- Refine transitions for continuity of thought.
- Check grammar, usage, punctuation, and mechanics.

Proofreading. Finally you'll proofread, checking correctness and catching any spelling errors you may have missed during your editing stage.

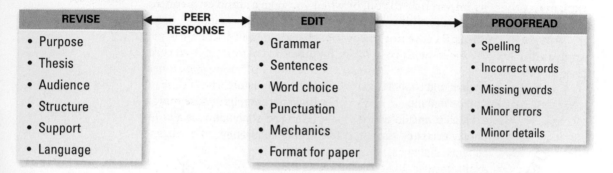

Understand Your Writing Situation

Three considerations — what you want to accomplish as a writer, how you want to appeal to your audience, and what type of document you are writing — will shape the direction of your writing. These considerations of purpose, audience, and genre are essential elements of your writing situation (sometimes referred to as a rhetorical situation). Clarifying your purpose,

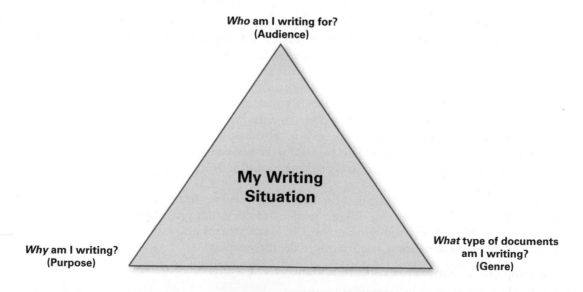

identifying your audience, and determining your genre will increase your confidence as a writer. At any moment in the process, remind yourself of your writing situation. The three questions in the diagram on p. 8 are worth asking.

Writing with Purpose

Like most college writing assignments — and most writing in general — every assignment in this book asks you to write for a definite reason. You write with a purpose in mind, for example, when you recall a memorable experience to explain to others its importance to you, or when you take a stand on a controversy to convey your position and persuade your readers to respect it.

For more on using your purpose for planning, see pp. 265–66, and for revising, see pp. 305–08.

A note of caution: Be sure not to confuse the sources and strategies you apply in these assignments with your ultimate purpose for writing. "To compare and contrast two things" is a strategy, but not a very interesting purpose; "to compare and contrast two websites *to explain which is more reliable*" communicates a real reason for writing. In most college writing, your purpose maybe to explain or analyze something, to inform your readers, to propose a solution to a problem, to evaluate or review an object, or to convince your readers of something.

To sharpen your concentration on your purpose, ask yourself from the start: What do I want to say? And, in revising, Did I say what I meant to say? These practical questions will help you slice out irrelevant information and remove other barriers to getting your paper where you want it to go.

KNOW YOUR WRITING SITUATION

- ☐ Have you identified your purpose?
- ☐ Have you considered your audience?
- ☐ Have you considered the genre (type of writing) in which you are composing in relation to your purpose and audience?
- ☐ Have you clearly stated your point as a thesis or unmistakably implied it?
- ☐ Have you supported your point with enough concrete evidence to persuade your audience?

Learning by Doing 📷 Writing with Purpose

Imagine that you are in the following writing situations. For each, write a sentence that sums up your purpose as a writer.

1. The instructor in your psychology course has assigned a paragraph about the meanings of three essential terms in your readings.

2. You're upset about a change in financial aid procedures and plan to write a letter asking the financial aid director to remedy the problem.

3. You're starting a blog about your first year at college so your extended family can envision the environment and share your experiences.

4. Your Facebook profile seemed appropriate last year, but you want to revise it now that you're attending college and have a job with future prospects.

Writing for Your Audience

For more on planning for your readers, see pp. 265–71. For more on revising for them, see pp. 305–08.

Your audience may or may not be defined in your assignment, but you need to have an audience in mind to write. Consider the following sample assignments.

ASSIGNMENT 1   Discuss the advantages and disadvantages of homeschooling.

ASSIGNMENT 2   In a letter to parents of school-aged children, discuss the advantages and disadvantages of homeschooling.

If your assignment defines an audience, as the second example does, you need to think about how to approach those readers and what information they would want. For example, what points would you include in a discussion aimed at parents? How would you organize your ideas? Would you discuss advantages or disadvantages first?

Now consider how your approach might differ if the assignment read this way:

ASSIGNMENT 3   In a newsletter article for elementary school teachers, discuss the advantages and disadvantages of homeschooling.

Audiences may be identified by characteristics, such as role (parents) or occupation (teachers), that suggest values to which a writer might appeal. As the chart "Assessing Your Audience" suggests, you can analyze the concerns of readers to persuade them more successfully.

For many college assignments, the audience for your writing is your instructor and your classmates. Depending on the assignment and genre, however, your audience may include general readers such as the students on your campus, or even the public. In any case, your readers will expect you to know your subject and support your ideas with concrete, detailed evidence.

WRITING FOR YOUR AUDIENCE

☐ Do you know who your readers are? Do you understand their relationship to you?

☐ Do you have a sense of what your readers know about your topic? Do you know what you want them to learn?

☐ Do you know how much detail your readers will want and need regarding your topic?

☐ Do you know what objections they are likely to raise as they read? Do you have ideas for how to overcome your readers' anticipated objections?

☐ Do you know what is likely to convince your readers? Do you know what is likely to offend them?

Assessing Your Audience

	Instructor	Peers/ Classmates	Work Supervisor	General Audience
Relationship to You	Known briefly in a class context	Known on campus and in social contexts	Known for some time in a job context	Imagined but not known personally
Purpose for Reading Your Writing	To teach knowledge and skills; to evaluate your writing so that you can succeed	To learn about your topic; to provide feedback on your writing; possibly to model their writing on yours	To train and mentor you; to evaluate your writing as it relates to your job performance	To enjoy and learn more about what you have written (with varied levels of curiosity and interest)
Knowledge about Your Topic	Well-informed about college topics; wants to see what you know	Friendly but may or may not be informed about your topic	Well-informed about work-related topics; expects reliable information from you	Level of awareness assumed and gaps addressed with logical presentation
Genres Expected	Essays, reports, research papers, or other academic genres; possibly assigns multimodal genres, such as video or podcasts	Notes, blog entries, social media, or other informal messages; will expect what the instructor assigns	Memos, reports, web pages, emails, letters, recommendations, project plans, and other workplace genres	Essays, articles, letters, reports, videos, websites, podcasts
Amount and Type of Evidence Expected	Enough sound research-based evidence to support your thesis	Will expect what the instructor expects	Enough to inform or persuade colleagues, outside vendors, and more; general or technical information as needed	Enough to inform or persuade

Learning by Doing 🖉 Writing for Multiple Audiences

Imagine that you've been in a minor car accident. Write out the descriptions of the incident you'd give to the following audiences: a close friend, your friends and followers on social media, your parents, a police officer, and your insurance company. What information do you want to convey to each, and for what purposes? How does your language change, if at all? To whom are certain details accentuated or downplayed? Write a paragraph or more to reflect about the differences between the stories.

Writing in Different Genres

A genre is a type of writing or composition. You may know that science fiction and poetry are genres of literature, and that hip hop and reggae are genres of music. Typical genres of college writing include essays and research papers in your composition course.

Academic Genres across Disciplines. Different purposes and audiences may call for other genres. Other genres of academic writing include lab reports (in the fields of science and health), presentations, podcasts, and videos (in communications courses), close readings and analyses of stories, poems, and plays (in literature courses), proposals, reports, and business plans (in business and management courses), news stories and editorials (in journalism courses), and so on.

Each genre has its own characteristics and rules about format, the use of citations (or not), and the type of evidence and detail readers expect. For example, your biology instructor would expect to see the findings from your experiment, while your history and literature instructors might look for relevant quotations from the document or novel you're analyzing.

For a model essay in MLA style, see p. 521.

To write in particular genres, it is helpful to look at models of those genres. For example, if your instructor asks you to write a research paper using the MLA (Modern Language Association) style of documentation, you would need to look at an example of a successful MLA-style paper, learn what qualities make it successful, and follow MLA's rules for integrating sources into your paper.

Composition and Multimodal Genres. In some composition courses, you may be asked to create in multiple modes. For example, you might be assigned to write a paper that integrates visuals, create a video presentation or website based on research, make a poster that informs or persuades an audience, or write a song or poem about an issue you care about.

WRITING IN GENRES

☐ Look at your course syllabus. Do you understand the writing assignments that you are being asked to complete? Do you recognize the genres you are being asked to use?

☐ Has your instructor recommended sample readings or models of completed assignments—including in the genres in which you will compose?

☐ Do you have a sense of your purpose for writing in a given genre? Do you know how your audience approaches the genre?

☐ Do you know if research is required for writing in the genre, and if so, how much and what type? Do you know the kinds of details your readers expect? Do you know the best ways to persuade your readers through this genre?

☐ If you are asked to choose your own genre, do you know which genres will best meet the needs of your purpose and audience?

Learning by Doing ⌧ Experimenting with Genres

The passage below, from the United States Department of Agriculture, explains what a vegetarian diet is. Use this text as the basis for composing something new in a totally different genre, such as an editorial about why more people should adopt a vegetarian diet, an advertisement for a vegetarian cookbook, a review of a vegetarian restaurant, a social media post encouraging vegetarianism, or another genre of your choice. What key changes are needed to transform your writing into a new genre? How do these changes impact your purpose? Who is the audience for your new creation? What do you want them to "get" from your composition?

A vegetarian diet focuses on plants for food. These include fruits, vegetables, dried beans and peas, grains, seeds and nuts. There is no single type of vegetarian diet. Instead, vegetarian eating patterns usually fall into the following groups:

- The vegan diet, which excludes all meat and animal products
- The lacto vegetarian diet, which includes plant foods plus dairy products
- The lacto-ovo vegetarian diet, which includes both dairy products and eggs

People who follow vegetarian diets can get all the nutrients they need. However, they must be careful to eat a wide variety of foods to meet their nutritional needs. Nutrients vegetarians may need to focus on include protein, iron, calcium, zinc and vitamin B12.

Learning by Doing ⌧ Analyzing a Piece of Writing

The letter on p. 14 is directed to subscribers of the magazine, *Zapped!* Examine the letter and determine how well its writer seems to understand his or her writing situation. As you analyze, circle words and make notes in the margins of the page that 1) indicate letter's purpose, 2) describe its target audience, and 3) evaluate how well the choice of genre (a letter, as opposed to a postcard or email) reflects the writer's sense of purpose and audience. To what extent is the letter persuasive? Why?

Additional Writing Assignments

1. Write a few paragraphs or an online post reflecting on your personal goals as a writer. What do you already do well as a writer? What do you need to improve? What do you hope to accomplish? How might you benefit, in college or elsewhere, from improving your writing?

Zapped! misses you.

Dear Dan Morrison,

All last year, *Zapped!* magazine made the trek to
5 Snowden Lane and it was always a great experience.
You took great care of *Zapped!,* and *Zapped!* gave you
hours of entertainment, with news and interviews from
the latest indie bands, honest-as-your-momma reviews
of musical equipment, and your first glimpse of some
of the finest graphic serials being published today.

But, Dan, we haven't heard from you and are starting
to wonder what's up. Don't you miss *Zapped!*? One
thing's for sure: *Zapped!* misses you.

We'd like to re-establish the relationship: if you renew
your subscription by March 1, you'll get 20% off last
year's subscription price. That's only $24 for another
year of great entertainment. Just fill out the other side
of this card and send it back to us; we'll bill you later.

Come on, Dan. Why wait?

Thanks,

Carly Bevins

Carly Bevins
Director of Sales

2. **Source Activity.** Find an article, pamphlet, or web page that interests you.
   Try your hand at rewriting a passage for a new audience, such as a very
   young or very old person. Then write an informal paragraph explaining
   whether this task was easy, challenging, or impossible.

3. **Visual Activity.** Working with a classmate, examine the two texts on p. 15.
   One is from a "tool kit" created by the National Women's Law Center; the
   other is from a scholarly article from the journal *Critical Sociology*. The texts
   address the same topic — the obstacles and unfair treatment that girls of
   color can experience in educational settings — but are composed in different genres, for different purposes, and for different audiences. Begin
   your analysis by identifying the purpose and audience for each text. How
   can you tell what the purpose of the text is? How do you know who the
   audience for the text is? Then, compare and contrast the genres (the tool
   kit/brochure versus the scholarly article), as well as the physical features
   such as page layout, images, color, type size and font, section divisions,
   and source credits. Write a paragraph about each piece, explaining how it
   fulfills a purpose, appeals to its audience, and supports both purpose and
   audience through genre.

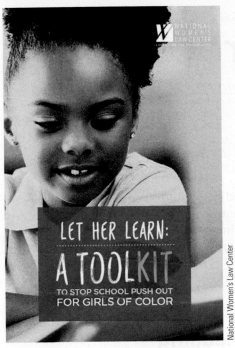

MANY GIRLS OF COLOR ARE **UNFAIRLY DISCIPLINED**

National stats from the 2013-14 school year show that:

- **Black girls are 5.5 times more likely** to be suspended from school as white girls.
- **Black girls are more likely** than any other race or gender to be suspended more than once.
- **Schools are 3.5 times more likely** to suspend Black girls with disabilities than white girls with disabilities.
- **In preschools, Black girls are 20%** of the girls enrolled but 54% of the girls receiving out-of-school suspensions; in K-12, Black girls are 16% of the girls enrolled but 45% of the girls receiving out-of-school suspensions.
- **Schools suspend** American Indian/Alaskan Native girls at more than three times the rate of white girls and at a higher rate than white boys.
- **Latina girls are 1.6 times more likely** to be suspended than white girls are.

These uneven rates of discipline are not because of more frequent or serious misbehavior.

Instead, race and gender bias informs unfair discipline. For instance, schools often punish Black girls who act out because of stereotypes that Black girls are "angry." Or target Latina girls for not following dress codes because of sexualized images of Latinas in the media.

National Women's Law Center

National Women's Law Center

Tool Kit/Brochure. The National Women's Law Center, "Let Her Learn: A Tool Kit to Stop School Push Out for Girls of Color."

Article

Unaccounted Foundations: Black Girls, Anti-Black Racism, and Punishment in Schools

Critical Sociology
2016, Vol. 42(4-5) 737–750
© The Author(s) 2014
Reprints and permissions:
sagepub.co.uk/journalsPermissions.nav
DOI: 10.1177/0896920551456444
crs.sagepub.com
SAGE

Connie Wun
Mills College, USA

Abstract
For nearly three decades, racial formations theory has influenced ideas, discourses and political projects surrounding race and racism in the United States. The theory holds that although race is a permanent feature in the US, the formation, order, and set of meanings inscribed onto racialized subjects are contingent upon historical and political contexts. This framework conceals anti-black racism as an enduring social order that affects policies, policy outcomes and organizes the relationship between non-black and black bodies. One exemplary social institution through which this can be seen is the public education system and its culture of discipline and punishment in the US. Current interrogations of school disciplinary landscapes have focused in on disparities in discipline policies as they affect working-class/working-poor boys of color. While it is useful to examine the uneven rates of suspensions, expulsions, and arrests, focusing on these disciplinary discrepancies misses everyday occurrences of punishment that young black girls experience. This qualitative paper examines school discipline policies and informal punitive practices including the implications that these mechanisms have on the physical and emotional worlds of black girls. The study finds that black girls are rendered structurally vulnerable to discipline and punishment at the hands of adults and peers in ways that exceed or contend with the logics espoused through racial formations theory. Placing black girls at the center of analysis compels us to examine the anti-black logic of discipline and punishment in schools and at large.

Keywords
anti-black racism, anti-blackness, black girls, education, girls of color, intersectionality, race and gender in education, racial formation, school discipline and punishment

Funding
This research received no specific grant from any funding agency in the public, commercial, or not-for-profit sectors.

Note
1. Although this study centers on girls of color in general, most of the girls who met the criteria for the study were black girls. As a result, this study focuses primarily on the experiences that black girls have with discipline at FHS.

References
Advancement Project (2011) *No Child Left Behind Catalyzes 'School-to-Prison Pipeline'*. Washington, DC. Available at: http://www.advancementproject.org/news/entry/press-release-no-child-left-behind-catalyzes-school-to-prison-pipeline.
American Bar Association (2001) *School Discipline: 'Zero tolerance' Policies*. Washington, DC. Available at: http://www.americanbar.org/about_the_aba/contact.html.

Scholarly Journal Article. Connie Wun, "Unaccounted Foundations: Black Girls, Anti-Black Racism, and Punishment in Schools," from the scholarly journal, *Critical Sociology*.

2 Reading Processes

What's so special about the reading you do in college? Don't you just pick up a book, start on the first page, and keep going as you have ever since you met *The Cat in the Hat*? Reading from beginning to end works especially well when you are eager to find out what *happens* next, as in a thriller, or what to *do* next, as in a cookbook. On the other hand, the dense, challenging texts typical of college will require closer reading and deeper thinking—in short, a process for reading critically.

A Process of Critical Reading

For more on critical thinking, see Ch. 3.

Reading critically means approaching whatever you read in an active, questioning manner. This essential college-level skill changes reading from a spectator sport to a contact sport. You no longer sit in the stands, watching graceful skaters glide by. Instead, you charge right into a rough-and-tumble hockey game, gripping your stick and watching out for your teeth.

Critical reading, like critical thinking, is not an activity reserved for college courses. It is a continuum of strategies that thoughtful people use every day to grapple with new information, to integrate it with existing knowledge, and to apply it to problems in daily life:

- They prepare to read actively.
- They respond as they read.
- They read on literal and analytical levels.

Building your critical reading skills will open the door to information you've never encountered and to ideas unlikely to come up with friends. For this course alone, you will be prepared to evaluate strengths and weaknesses of essays by professionals, students, and classmates. If you research a topic, you will be ready to figure out what your sources say, what they assume and imply, whether they are sound, and how you might use them to help make your point. In addition, you can apply your expanded skills in other courses, at your job, and in your community.

Your instructors expect you to do far more than recognize the words on the page. They want you to read their assignments and assigned readings critically and then to think and write critically about what you have read. Your instructors will want you to learn the effective reading strategies that they and other experienced readers apply to complex texts. Some may have you preview a reading so you learn its background or its structure. Others supply reading questions so you know what to look for. Still others may share their own reading processes with you, revealing what they read first (maybe the opening and conclusion) or how they might decide to skip a section (such as the methods section of a report, if they want to read the conclusions first). These strategies appear in the following chart, and in the advice that follows it.

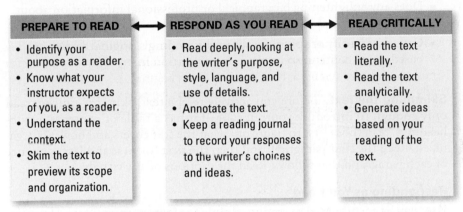

PREPARE TO READ	RESPOND AS YOU READ	READ CRITICALLY
• Identify your purpose as a reader. • Know what your instructor expects of you, as a reader. • Understand the context. • Skim the text to preview its scope and organization.	• Read deeply, looking at the writer's purpose, style, language, and use of details. • Annotate the text. • Keep a reading journal to record your responses to the writer's choices and ideas.	• Read the text literally. • Read the text analytically. • Generate ideas based on your reading of the text.

Strategies for Critical Reading

Preparing to Read

Before you read, think ahead about how to make the most of the experience.

Identifying Your Purpose. When you begin to read, ask questions like these about your immediate purpose:

- What are you reading?
- Why are you reading? What do you want to do with the reading?
- Do you need to memorize details, find main points, or connect ideas?
- How does this reading build on, add to, contrast with, or otherwise relate to other reading assignments in the course?

Knowing What Your Instructor Expects of You. When you are assigned a text to read, ask yourself what your instructor expects you to do once you have done your reading. For example:

- Will you need to be ready to discuss the text during class?
- Will you need to write about it? Write about it during an exam?
- Will you need to identify its purpose, audience, and genre? Find its main points? Sum it up? Compare it? Question it? Spot its strengths and weaknesses? Draw useful details from it?

Understanding the Context. Knowing a reading's context, approach, or frame of reference can help you predict where the reading is likely to go and how it relates to other readings. Begin with your available resources:

- Does the syllabus reveal why your instructor assigned the text?
- What can you learn from reading questions, tips about what to watch for, or connections with other texts?
- Does the text have a book jacket or preface, an introduction or abstract that sums it up, or reading pointers or questions?
- Does any enlightening biographical or professional information about the author accompany the text?
- Can you identify or speculate about the reading's original audience based on its content, style, tone, or publication history?

Skimming the Text. Before you actively read a text, skim it — quickly read only enough to introduce yourself to it. If it has a table of contents or sub-headings, read those first to figure out what the text covers and how it is organized. Read the first paragraph and then the first (or first and last) sentence of each paragraph that follows. Read the captions of any visuals.

Responding as You Read

You may be accustomed to reading simply for facts or main ideas. However, critical reading is far more active than fact hunting. It requires responding, questioning, and challenging as you read. Critical reading requires writing, too, in the form of notes, annotations, highlights, or other marks on the text.

Reading Deeply. Texts assigned in college often require more concentration than other readings do. Use these questions to dive below the surface and to get a sense of the writer's purpose, style, language, and use of details:

- How does the writer begin? What does the opening paragraph or section reveal about the writer's purpose? How does the writer prepare readers for what follows?
- How might you trace the progression of ideas in the reading? How do headings, previews of what's coming up, summaries of what's gone before, and transitions signal the organization?
- Are difficult or technical terms defined in specific ways? How might you highlight, list, or record such terms so that you master them?
- How might you record or recall the details in the reading? How could you track or diagram interrelated ideas to grasp their connections?
- How do word choice, tone, and style alert you to the complex purpose of a reading that is layered or indirect rather than straightforward?
- Does the reading include figurative or descriptive language, references to other works, or recurring themes? How do these enrich the reading?

For more on figurative language, see p. 641.

■ Can you answer any reading questions in your textbook, assignment, or syllabus? Can you restate headings in question form to create your own questions and then supply the answers? For example, change "Major Types of X" to "What are the major types of X?"

For more on evaluating what you read, see Section C in the Quick Research Guide, pp. Q-25–Q-27.

Annotating the Text. Writing notes on the page (or on a copy if the material is not your own) is a useful way to trace the author's points, question them, and add your own comments as they pop up. When you annotate, you make note of the writer's purpose, style, language, and use of details. The following passage is the introduction of Peter Toohey's article "Sibling Rivalry, a History," first published by the *Atlantic*. Notice how one writer annotated the passage.

For a Critical Reading Checklist, see p. 29.

At its most benign, family jealousy between siblings reflects a competition for resources—coupled with the bonds of kinship, which are equally strong. St. Augustine, in his *Confessions*, described having "personally watched and studied a jealous baby. He could not yet speak and, pale with jealousy and bitterness, glared at his brother sharing his mother's milk. Who is unaware of this fact of experience?"

Key point — balance between competition and kinship

True! I've seen this look in my own children's faces.

This heady mix can lead to all sorts of jealous rivalry and internecine warfare. It's evident in the animal kingdom, where actual family cannibalism also takes place. The animal behaviorist Scott Forbes makes some fascinating links between sibling rivalry in animals and humans. This is not sexual jealousy, but involves real birds and bees. Forbes describes how herpetologists, ornithologists, and mammalogists found that "infanticide—including siblicide—was a routine feature of family life in many species," most commonly seen in birds. Some birds lay two eggs "to insure against failure of the first egg to hatch. If both hatch, the second chick is redundant to the parents, and a potentially lethal competitor to the first-hatched progeny." The healthy older chick often kills the younger to eliminate the competition, and some parents actually encourage siblicide when the death of the nest-mate doesn't naturally occur.

Sounds almost like the description of a TV drama

Scary stuff. I wonder how extreme things can get with humans.

Never heard the term "siblicide" before!

Good quote from an authoritative source

Maybe sibling cooperation is also beneficial for survival?

After all, if resources are scarce, it's better that the strongest offspring survive and that their potential efforts go to ensuring that happens. (It's the old story of genetic replication again: Surviving offspring are more likely to have the strongest genes, and they are the ones that have the best chance of reproducing later and passing those genes on.) Forbes thinks that such extreme jealous reactions are not common in the human species, but "the more modest forms of sibling rivalry that are ubiquitous in species with extensive parental care—the scrambles for food and begging competitions—resemble more closely the dynamics that occur in human families."

Will the author explore that angle?

Biology helps drive behavior — in multiple species

When you annotate a reading, don't passively highlight big chunks of text. Instead, respond actively, using pen or pencil on a page or adding a comment to a file. Next, read slowly and carefully so you can absorb what the writer says — and how the writer supports his or her point. Record your reactions to what you read by doing the following:

- Jot down things you already know or have experienced to build your own connection to the reading.
- Circle key words, star or check ideas when you agree or disagree, add arrows to mark connections, or underline key points, ideas, or definitions to learn the reading's vocabulary.
- Add question marks or questions about meaning or implications.
- Separate main points from supporting evidence and detail. Then you can question a conclusion, or challenge the evidence that supports it. (Main points often open a section or paragraph, followed by supporting detail, but sometimes this pattern is reversed.)
- React to quotable sentences or key passages. If they are hard to understand, try restating them in your own words.
- Talk to the writer — maybe even talk back. Challenge weak points, respond with your own thoughts, draw in other views, or boost the writer's persuasive ideas.
- Sum up the writer's main point, supporting ideas, and notable evidence or examples.
- Consider how the reading appeals to your head, heart, or conscience.

Learning by Doing Annotating a Passage

Annotate the following passage from an article published by the National Institutes of Health (NIH) on a study that demonstrated how nonverbal cues from others can affect our stress levels. In the study, a group of men, stressed out about having to give speeches, responded to different kinds of smiles and facial expressions of audience members. "Smiles Affect Response to Stress" by Harrison Wein was posted at the NIH website.

Many people find it stressful to be in situations where other people are judging them, such as public speaking. During such situations, we produce steroid hormones called glucocorticoids that affect many systems throughout the body. The hypothalamic-pituitary-adrenal (HPA) axis — a network involving the hypothalamus and pituitary gland in the brain and the adrenal glands near the kidneys — plays a central role in these effects.   1

A team led by Jared Martin and Dr. Paula Niedenthal at the University of Wisconsin–Madison investigated whether the HPA axis responds to nonverbal feedback, such as facial expressions. Past work from the team identified the characteristics of at least three distinct types of genuine, spontaneous smiles. Each one serves a different social function. "Reward" smiles show happiness and reinforce behavior, "affiliation" smiles strengthen social bonds between people, and "dominance" smiles are derisive and signal   2 feelings of superior social status. The researchers tested how these different smiles affect HPA axis activity.

The team recruited 90 male college students. The men were asked to   3
give three short speeches about themselves in front of a male evaluator who was watching over a web camera. In fact, the evaluator only briefly appeared live, then turned off his camera. After each of the three speeches, the participants were shown videos of their evaluator's facial expressions. They were told these represented spontaneous reactions, but the videos were actually pre-recorded. The men were shown one reward, affiliation, or dominance smile after each of their responses. Each time, they were also shown a control video with a neutral response, such as face-scratching or eye blinks.

The scientists measured levels of the glucocorticoid cortisol in the men's   4
saliva. They also used an electrocardiograph before, during, and after the speech to measure heart activity. . . . The team found that dominance smiles increased levels of cortisol and heart rates. Reward and affiliation smiles, in contrast, tended to buffer the effects of stress. Participants receiving reward or affiliation smiles returned to their base cortisol levels within 30 minutes after their speech, while those who received dominance smile continued to have significantly higher cortisol levels 30 minutes later. . . .

"Our results show that subtle differences in the way you make facial   5
expressions while someone is talking to you can fundamentally change their experience, their body, and the way they feel like you're evaluating them," Martin says.

Keeping a Reading Journal. A reading journal is an excellent place to record not just what you read but how you respond to a given text, and to the writer's choices and ideas. As you read actively, you will build a reservoir of ideas for follow-up writing. Address questions like these in a special notebook or digital file:

For advice on keeping a writer's journal, see Ch. 15.

- What is the subject of the reading? What is the writer's stand or main argument?
- What does the writer take for granted? What assumptions does he or she begin with? Where are these stated or suggested?
- What are the writer's main points? What evidence supports them?
- Do you agree with what the writer has said? Do his or her ideas clash with or question your assumptions?
- Has the writer told you more than you wanted to know or failed to tell you something you wish you knew?
- What conclusions can you draw from the reading?
- How has the reading helped you see the subject in new ways?

Learning by Doing Keeping a Reading Journal

Your instructor may ask you to keep a reading journal in which you record your notes and commentary about each text you've been assigned. Ask questions in your journal. Make observations. What are the advantages of a reading journal? How might keeping a reading journal be effective for your writing process?

Learning from Other Writers: Summarizing and Responding

For another reading response on both literal and analytical levels, see pp. 31–32.

Following are excerpts of an essay by Robert Jensen titled "The High Cost of Masculinity," a text to which student Olof Eriksson responds on page 25. As you read Jensen's article, evaluate it and annotate it with your responses to his argument. What do you think about the text? Why do you think that? Overall, what are the strengths and weaknesses of Jensen's arguments? To what extent do you find them persuasive?

Robert Jensen

Robert Jensen

From The High Cost of Manliness

Robert Jensen (b. 1958) is an author and professor of journalism at the University of Texas at Austin. In the following essay, first published in full on *Alternet* in 2006, Jensen calls for abandoning the prevailing definition of masculinity, arguing that it is "toxic" to both men and women. Note that the following is an excerpt from Jensen's essay.

Author addresses "guys" informally, with humor ("this masculinity thing"); states argument.

Defines "masculinity"; states argument more forcefully.

Discusses concept of masculinity in U.S. culture (competitive, aggressive, sexist, homophobic); gives examples.

So, guys, I have an idea—maybe it's time we stop trying. Maybe this masculinity thing is a bad deal, not just for women but for us. 1

We need to get rid of the whole idea of masculinity. It's time to abandon the claim that there are certain psychological or social traits that inherently come with being biologically male. If we can get past that, we have a chance to create a better world for men and women. 2

The dominant conception of masculinity in U.S. culture is easily summarized: men are assumed to be naturally competitive and aggressive, and being a real man is therefore marked by the struggle for control, conquest, and domination. A man looks at the world, sees what he wants, and takes it. Men who don't measure up are wimps, sissies, fags, girls. The worst insult one man can hurl at another—whether it's boys on the playground or CEOs in the boardroom—is the accusation that a man is like a woman. Although the culture acknowledges that men can in some situations have traits traditionally associated with women (caring, compassion, tenderness), in the end it is men's strength-expressed-as-toughness that defines us and must trump any female-like softness. Those aspects of masculinity must prevail° for a man to be a "real man." 3

prevail: Dominate.

That's not to suggest, of course, that every man adopts that view of masculinity. But it is endorsed in key institutions and activities—most notably in business, the military, and athletics—and is reinforced through the mass media. It is particularly expressed in the way men—straight and gay alike—talk about sexuality and act sexually. And our culture's male heroes reflect those characteristics: they most often are men who take charge rather than seek consensus,° seize power rather than look for ways to share it, and are willing to be violent to achieve their goals.

> **4**
> Further supports argument. Addresses possible objections (not every man is aggressive); gives examples (business, military).

That view of masculinity is dangerous for women. It leads men to seek to control "their" women and define their own pleasure in that control, which leads to epidemic levels of rape and battery. But this view of masculinity is toxic for men as well.

> **5**
> Discusses "toxic" impact on women.

If masculinity is defined as conquest, it means that men will always struggle with each other for dominance. In a system premised on hierarchy° and power, there can be only one king of the hill. Every other man must in some way be subordinated° to the king, and the king has to always be nervous about who is coming up that hill to get him. A friend who once worked on Wall Street—one of the preeminent° sites of masculine competition—described coming to work as like walking into a knife fight when all the good spots along the wall were taken. Masculinity like this is life lived as endless competition and threat.

> **6**
> Discusses negative impact of toxic masculinity on men's lives.

No one man created this system, and perhaps none of us, if given a choice, would choose it. But we live our lives in that system, and it deforms men, narrowing our emotional range and depth. It keeps us from the rich connections with others—not just with women and children, but other men—that make life meaningful but require vulnerability.

> **7**
> More on how toxic masculinity hurts men.

This doesn't mean that the negative consequences of this toxic masculinity are equally dangerous for men and women. As feminists have long pointed out, there's a big difference between women dealing with the possibility of being raped, beaten, and killed by the men in their lives and men not being able to cry. But we can see that the short-term material gains that men get are not adequate compensation for what we men give up in the long haul—which is to surrender part of our humanity to the project of dominance.

> **8**
> Addresses toxic masculinity from feminist perspective.

Of course there are obvious physical differences between men and women—average body size, hormones, reproductive organs. There may be other differences rooted in our biology that we don't yet understand. Yet it's also true that men and women are more similar than we are different, and that given the pernicious° effects of centuries of patriarchy° and its relentless devaluing of things female, we should be skeptical of the perceived differences.

> **9**
> Argues that men and women are in this together, not so different; gives examples.

consensus: Agreement.   **hierarchy:** A grouping based on relative rank.   **subordinated:** Lowered in rank.   **preeminent:** Most important.   **pernicious:** Destructive.   **patriarchy:** Social organization in which the father is supreme; male control of most of the power in a society.

Argues that we don't know enough about the relationship between genetics and human behavior; gives examples.

What we know is simple: in any human population, there is wide individual variation. While there's no doubt that a large part of our behavior is rooted in our DNA, there's also no doubt that our genetic endowment is highly influenced by culture. Beyond that, it's difficult to say much with any certainty. It's true that only women can bear children and breastfeed. That fact likely has some bearing on aspects of men's and women's personalities. But we don't know much about what the effect is, and given the limits of our tools to understand human behavior, it's possible we may never know much.   10

Argues that even if we find that genetics affect male and female behavior, institutional sexism blurs what we can understand.

At the moment, the culture seems obsessed with gender differences, in the context of a recurring intellectual fad (called "evolutionary psychology" this time around, and "sociobiology" in a previous incarnation) that wants to explain all complex behaviors as simple evolutionary adaptations—if a pattern of human behavior exists, it must be because it's adaptive in some ways. In the long run, that's true by definition. But in the short term it's hardly a convincing argument to say, "Look at how men and women behave so differently; it must be because men and women are fundamentally different," when a political system has been creating differences between men and women.   11

. . .

Concludes with restatement of thesis/ argument; gives example of what is at stake.

I don't think the planet can long survive if the current conception of masculinity endures. We face political and ecological challenges that can't be met with this old model of what it means to be a man. At the more intimate level, the stakes are just as high. For those of us who are biologically male, we have a simple choice: we men can settle for being men, or we can strive to be human beings.   12

Olof Eriksson's instructor asked his class to write a one-page reading response to Robert Jensen's essay "The High Cost of Manliness" and include a summary and a personal response. Your instructor will likely ask you to respond to the articles and other texts that you read for your composition course. Whether you're asked to keep a reading journal or to submit or post online your responses to those texts, you might be required to provide the following:

- Summary: a short statement in your own words of the reading's main points (without your opinion, evaluation, or judgment)
- Paraphrase: a restatement of a passage using your own words and sentences
- Quotation: a noteworthy expression or statement in the author's exact words, presented in quotation marks and correctly cited
- Personal response: a statement and explanation of your reaction to the reading
- Critique: your evaluation of the strengths or weaknesses of the reading
- Analysis: a close study and interpretation
- Personal connection/application: a statement about the relationship between a text and your experience
- Question: a point that you wish the writer had covered

As you read Olof Eriksson's paper, pay attention to how he recaps Jensen's argument and supports his own responses.

Olof Eriksson   Student Summary and Response

The Problems with Masculinity

Robert Jensen writes in his essay "The High Cost of Manliness" about masculinity and how our culture creates expectations of certain traits from the males in our society. He strongly opposes this view of masculinity and would prefer that sociological constructs such as masculinity and femininity were abolished. As examples of expected traits, he mentions strength and competition. Males are supposed to take what they want and avoid showing weaknesses. Then Jensen points out negative consequences of enforcing masculinity, such as men having trouble showing vulnerability and, worse, men committing rape. He counters the argument that there are differences in biology between men and women by pointing out that we do not know which or how much behavior comes from biology and how much comes from culture, but that both certainly matter and we should do what we can. He is also concerned about identifying positive attributes as features of masculinity, because doing so would imply that they only belong with men. Jensen ends by observing that we now face challenges that require us to change our current view of masculinity.

1

Summarizes the argument that author presents.

Paraphrases author's ideas.

I agree with what Jensen says, and I find it a problem today that the definition of masculinity is so closely connected to competition and aggression. Even so, I find that my own definition of masculinity is not so different. I would say that to be masculine is to be strong and determined, to be always winning. Many people may share this view, even as they disagree with it, logically. That is why we need to make an effort to change our culture, just as Jensen argues. If we can either abolish our ideas about masculinity and femininity or simply change them so that they are more neutral and closely related terms, then we will be a lot closer to real equality between the genders. This change will not only help remove most of the negative impacts Jensen brought up, but will also help pave a better way for future generations, reducing their problems.

States personal response to author's argument.

2

Gives analysis of essay.

Connects the essay with personal experience.

Concludes by restating author's argument; seeks to persuade readers; supports response to his own argument with examples.

Work Cited

Jensen, Robert. "The High Cost of Manliness." *The Bedford Guide for College Writers with Reader, Research Manual, and Handbook*, edited by X. J. Kennedy, Dorothy M. Kennedy, and Marcia F. Muth, 12th ed., Bedford/St. Martin's, 2020, pp. 22–24.

——*Cites source.*

Questions to Start You Thinking

Meaning

1. According to Eriksson, what is Jensen's topic and Jensen's position on this topic? Where in his essay does Eriksson present this information?
2. Identify the places in his essay where Eriksson summarizes parts of Jensen's argument. How effective or ineffective are his summaries? What makes them so?
3. What is Eriksson's personal response to the essay? Where does he present his views?

Writing Strategies

4. How does Eriksson consider his audience as he organizes and develops his summary and response?

5. What kinds of material from the essay does Eriksson use to develop his summary?

Reading on Literal and Analytical Levels

Educational expert Benjamin S. Bloom identified six levels of cognitive activity: knowledge, comprehension, application, analysis, synthesis, and evaluation.[1] (A recent update recasts *synthesis* as *creating* and moves it above evaluation to the highest level.) Each level acts as a foundation for the next. Each also demands higher thinking skills than the previous one. Experienced readers, however, jump among these levels, gathering information and insight as they occur.

The first three levels are literal skills, building blocks of thought. The last three levels — analysis, synthesis, and evaluation — are analytical skills that your instructors especially want you to develop. To read critically, you must engage with a reading on both literal and analytical levels. Suppose you read in your history book a passage about Franklin Delano Roosevelt (FDR), the only American president elected to four consecutive terms.

Knowing. Once you read the passage, even if you have little background in American history, you can decode and recall the information it presents about FDR and his four terms in office.

Comprehending. To understand the passage, you need to know that a term for a U.S. president is four years and that *consecutive* means "continuous." Thus FDR was elected to serve for sixteen years.

Connecting Personally/Applying. To connect this knowledge to what you already know (or have experienced), you think of other presidents — George Washington, who served two terms; Grover Cleveland, who served two terms but not consecutively; Jimmy Carter, who served one term; the second George Bush, who served two terms. You realize that four terms are quite unusual. In fact, the Twenty-Second Amendment to the Constitution, ratified in 1951, now limits a president to two terms.

Analyzing. You can scrutinize FDR's election to four terms from various angles, selecting a principle for analysis that suits your purpose. Then you can use this principle to break the information into its components or parts.

---

[1] Information from Benjamin S. Bloom et al., *Taxonomy of Educational Objectives, Handbook 1: Cognitive Domain*. Longman, 1956. See also the update in David R. Krathwohl, "A Revision of Bloom's Taxonomy: An Overview." *Theory into Practice*, vol. 41, no. 4, Fall 2002, pp. 212–218.

For example, you might analyze FDR's tenure in relation to that of other presidents. Why has FDR been the only president elected to serve four terms? What circumstances contributed to three reelections?

Synthesizing. To answer your questions, you may read more or review past readings. Then you begin synthesizing—creating a new approach or combination by pulling together facts and opinions, identifying evidence accepted by all or most sources, examining any controversial evidence, and drawing conclusions that reliable evidence seems to support. For example, you might logically conclude that the special circumstances of the Great Depression and World War II contributed to FDR's election to four terms, not that Americans reelected him out of pity because he had polio.

Evaluating. Finally, you evaluate the significance of your new knowledge for understanding Depression-era politics and assessing your history book's approach. You might ask yourself, Why has the book's author chosen to make this point? How does it affect the rest of the discussion? You may also have concluded that FDR's four-term presidency is understandable in light of the events of the 1930s and 1940s, that the author has mentioned this fact to highlight the era's unique political atmosphere, and that it is evidence neither for nor against FDR's excellence as a president.

Learning by Doing 🔲 Reading Analytically

Think back to something you've read recently — a book, an article, a social media post — that helped you make a decision. How did you analyze what you read, breaking the information into parts? How did you synthesize it, combining it with what you already knew? How did you evaluate it, judging its significance for your decision?

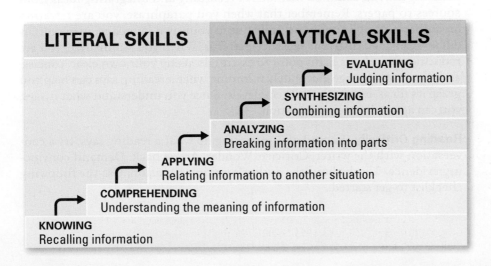

LITERAL SKILLS   **ANALYTICAL SKILLS**

EVALUATING
Judging information

SYNTHESIZING
Combining information

ANALYZING
Breaking information into parts

APPLYING
Relating information to another situation

COMPREHENDING
Understanding the meaning of information

KNOWING
Recalling information

Generating Ideas from Reading

For more on generating ideas, see Ch. 15.

Like flint that strikes steel and causes sparks, readers and writers provoke one another. For example, when your class discusses an essay, you may be surprised by the range of insights your classmates report. Of course, they may be equally surprised by what you see. Above all, reading is a dynamic process. It may change your ideas instead of support them. Here are suggestions for unlocking the potential of a good text.

Looking for Meaty Pieces.   Spur your thinking about current topics by browsing through essay collections or magazines in the library or online. Try the *Atlantic, Harper's, New Republic, Commentary,* or special-interest magazines such as *Architectural Digest* or *Scientific American.* Check editorials and op-ed columns in your local newspaper, the *New York Times,* or the *Wall Street Journal.* Search the Internet on intriguing topics (such as silent-film technology) or issues (such as homeless children). Look for meaty, not superficial, articles written to inform and convince, not entertain or amuse. Consider also browsing your library's databases for scholarly journal articles on topics that interest you. Such articles contribute to your knowledge and can also be drawn on in a research paper.

Logging Your Reading.   For several days keep a log of the articles that you find. Record the author, title, and source for each promising piece so that you can easily find it again. Briefly note the subject and point of view as well, so you can identify a range of possibilities.

Recalling Something You Have Already Read.   What have you read lately that started you thinking? Return to a reading—a chapter in a history book, an article for sociology, a research report for biology.

For more on paraphrase and summary, see Ch. 11 and D4–D5 in the Quick Research Guide, pp. Q-29–Q-30.

Paraphrasing and Summarizing Complex Ideas.   Do you feel overwhelmed by challenging reading? If so, read slowly and carefully. Paraphrasing and summarizing are two common methods of recording and integrating ideas from sources to papers. Remember that when you paraphrase, you are restating an author's complicated ideas fully but in your own language, using different wording and different sentence patterns. When you summarize, you are reducing an author's main point to essentials, using your own clear, concise, and accurate language. Accurately recording what a reading says can help you grasp its ideas, especially on literal levels. Once you understand what it says, you can agree, disagree, or question.

Reading Critically.   Instead of just soaking up what a reading says, try a conversation with the writer. Criticize. Wonder. Argue back. Demand convincing evidence. Think about the author's writing situation. Use the following checklist to get started.

READING CRITICALLY

- ☐ What problems and issues does the author raise?

- ☐ What is the author's purpose? Is it to explain or inform? To persuade? To amuse? In addition to this overall purpose, is the author trying to accomplish some other agenda?

- ☐ How does the author appeal to you as a reader? Where do you agree and disagree? Where do you want to say "Yeah, right!" or "I don't think so!"? Does the topic or approach engage you?

- ☐ How does this piece relate to your own experiences or thoughts? Have you encountered anything similar?

- ☐ Are there important words or ideas that you don't understand? If so, do you need to reread or turn to a dictionary or reference book?

- ☐ What is the author's point of view? What does the author assume or take for granted? Where does the author reveal these assumptions? Do they make the selection seem weak or biased?

- ☐ Which statements are facts, verifiable by observation, firsthand testimony, or research? Which are opinions? Does one or the other dominate?

- ☐ Is the writer's evidence accurate, relevant, and sufficient? Is it persuasive?

For more on facts and opinions, see Ch. 8.

For more on evaluating evidence, see C1–C3 in the Quick Research Guide, pp. Q-25–Q-27.

Analyzing Writing Strategies. Reading widely and deeply can reveal what others say and how they shape it. For some readings in this book, notes in the margin identify key features such as the introduction, thesis statement or main idea, major points, and supporting evidence. To identify an author's writing strategies, ask the questions presented in the following checklist.

ANALYZING WRITING STRATEGIES

- ☐ Does the author introduce the text and try to engage the audience?

- ☐ Do you see where the author either states or implies the thesis?

- ☐ Is the text clearly organized, and what main points develop the thesis?

- ☐ Does the author support his or her thesis (or argument) with facts, data, expert opinions, explanations, examples, or other information?

- ☐ Does the author connect or emphasize ideas for readers?

- ☐ Does the author conclude the text in a satisfying way?

- ☐ Do you recognize the author's tone — and how the choice of words and examples reveals the author's attitude, biases, or assumptions?

Learning from Other Writers: Responding Critically

Following is an excerpt from an essay by Neil deGrasse Tyson titled "The Cosmic Perspective." Student Ayesha James was asked to read the essay and respond to it on both the literal and analytical levels. As you read Tyson's essay, evaluate the text and Ayesha's annotations to the points he makes. Then read her essay on pp. 31–32.

Sthanlee B. Mirador/ Sipa USA/AP Images

Neil deGrasse Tyson

From The Cosmic Perspective

Neil deGrasse Tyson is an astrophysicist and author. His essay "The Cosmic Perspective" first appeared in the magazine *Natural History* in 2007; the full text is available at his website (haydenplanetarium.org/tyson/).

> Of all the sciences cultivated by mankind, Astronomy is acknowledged to be, and undoubtedly is, the most sublime, the most interesting, and the most useful. For, by knowledge derived from this science, not only the bulk of the Earth is discovered . . . ; but our very faculties are enlarged with the grandeur of the ideas it conveys, our minds exalted above [their] low contracted prejudices.
>
> —James Ferguson, *Astronomy Explained upon Sir Isaac Newton's Principles, and Made Easy to Those Who Have Not Studied Mathematics* (1757)

Argument: humans are part of nature.

W e are one with . . . nature, fitting neither above nor below, but within. 1
        Need [some] ego softeners? Simple comparisons of quantity, size, and scale do the job well. 2

Socrates? Cool. Also gross!

Take water. It's simple, common, and vital. There are more molecules of water 3 in an eight-ounce cup of the stuff than there are cups of water in all the world's oceans. Every cup that passes through a single person and eventually rejoins the world's water supply holds enough molecules to mix 1,500 of them into every other cup of water in the world. No way around it: Some of the water you just drank passed through the kidneys of Socrates, Genghis Khan, and Joan of Arc.

More evidence supports argument.

How about air? Also vital. A single breathful draws in more air molecules 4 than there are breathfuls of air in Earth's entire atmosphere. That means some of the air you just breathed passed through the lungs of Napoleon, Beethoven, Lincoln, and Billy the Kid.

Okay, starting to feel insignificant.

Time to get cosmic. There are more stars in the universe than grains of sand 5 on any beach, more stars than seconds have passed since Earth formed, more stars than words and sounds ever uttered by all the humans who ever lived.

Cosmic evolution, constant change.

Want a sweeping view of the past? Our unfolding cosmic perspective takes 6 you there. Light takes time to reach Earth's observatories from the depths of space, and so you see objects and phenomena not as they are but as they once were. That means the universe acts like a giant time machine: The farther away you look, the further back in time you see — back almost to the beginning of time itself. Within that horizon of reckoning, cosmic evolution unfolds continuously, in full view.

Want to know what we're made of? Again, the cosmic perspective offers a bigger answer than you might expect. The chemical elements of the universe are forged in the fires of high-mass stars that end their lives in stupendous explosions, enriching their host galaxies with the chemical arsenal of life as we know it. The result? The four most common chemically active elements in the universe — hydrogen, oxygen, carbon, and nitrogen — are the four most common elements of life on Earth. We are not simply in the universe. The universe is in us.

> 7
>
> We are made of what Earth is made of.

Ayesha James   Student Critical Response

Responding to Neil deGrasse Tyson's "The Cosmic Perspective"

In his essay "The Cosmic Perspective," Neil deGrasse Tyson, reminds us that, as human beings, it's too easy for us to separate ourselves from the natural world around us, and think that we are somehow above it. For example, he begins by stating that "We are one . . . with nature, fitting neither above nor below, but within."

> 1
>
> Identifies the issue that the author presents, on a literal level; includes example.

We are all connected, past and present, on a molecular level, the author explains. He supports that claim by stating that the water we drink and the air we breathe has also passed through the bodies of Socrates and Beethoven. As Tyson informs readers that we are part of nature and the cosmos, he also argues and seeks to persuade us that nature and the cosmos are much bigger than us. He wants us to put human life in perspective, and he uses facts (the water and air examples) and humor ("Need [some] ego softeners?").

> 2
>
> States the author's purposes and provides critique on an analytical level; includes examples.

I can relate to the point that the author makes, that humans need to understand our place in the universe. It is humbling to think about, but humans need to feel more humility, in general, especially when it comes to how we treat the environment, for example.

> 3
>
> Makes personal and critical connection with author's purpose; explains his appeal to her as a reader.

In the essay, there were many ideas that I hadn't thought of before, for example, that, like our planet, we are also made of "hydrogen, oxygen, carbon, and nitrogen." That fact is very persuasive for me, in terms of connecting humans to nature. Mainly, the vocabulary used in the essay is straightforward and aimed at a general audience. It seems to me that the author assumes that his readers are intelligent and articulate, but not experts in astrophysics, which is why he explains things so clearly and does not use specialized or scientific language.

> 4
>
> Provides critical reading of ideas, language, and assumptions of author; includes examples.

Notes author's expertise; gives an example of something she did not totally understand (space and time).

Because of his expertise as an astrophysicist, the author can make major claims 5 about the cosmos that are credible to me. I have to admit, though, that I got a little lost when he talks about space and time. He writes that "the universe acts like a giant time machine: The farther away you look, the further back in time you see." I need to think some more about that, and maybe do some further reading.

Concludes with a personal and critical evaluation; includes example.

Overall, I found this essay to be informative, entertaining and funny, and 6 persuasive. I have new knowledge and appreciation of my relationship to the earth, the stars, and to other people. As Tyson proves in this piece, "We are not simply in the universe. The universe is in us."

Work Cited

Cites source. —— DeGrasse Tyson, Neil. "The Cosmic Perspective." *The Bedford Guide for College Writers with Reader, Research Manual, and Handbook*, edited by X. J. Kennedy, Dorothy M. Kennedy, and Marcia F. Muth, 12th ed., Bedford/St. Martin's, 2020, pp. 30–31.

Questions to Start You Thinking

Meaning

1. According to James, what is the issue that Tyson raises, and what is his position on this topic? Where does James present this information?
2. What are main points in her analysis?
3. How does James apply this reading to her own life?

Writing Strategies

4. How has James demonstrated both literal and critical reading responses?
5. How does James develop her analysis? What kinds of material does she draw from the essay?

Learning by Doing 🔟 Reading Critically

For a sample annotated passage, see p. 19.

Using the advice in this chapter, choose a selection from *A Writer's Reader* (p. 329) and read it critically. First, add notes and comments in the margin, responding on both literal and analytical levels. Second, add notes about writing strategies. (Ayesha James's annotations on Tyson's essay are a good model.) Finally, use those notes to write a brief critical response to the reading.

Reading Online and Multimodal Texts

Traditionally, a literate person is someone who can read and write. This definition remains current, but technologies have vastly increased the complexity of reading and writing. Many online texts are multimodal, combining written materials with images, sounds, and video. Such texts can't be confined to the fixed form of a printed page and may be routinely updated. They also may be accessed flexibly as a reader wanders through sites by following links rather than paging through the defined sequence of a bound book.

For more on responding to images, see Ch. 13.

Learning to read and write effectively has likewise increased in complexity. Eye-movement studies show that, rather than moving from one word to the next, readers actually jump back and forth, skip letters and words, and guess at words the eye skips. Online readers also may jump from line to line or from chunk to chunk, scanning the page. In addition, multimodal texts may draw the eye to, or from, the typical left-to-right, top-to-bottom path with an image. Analyzing the meaning or impact of an image may require "reading" its placement and arrangement.

What might these changes mean for you as a reader and writer? Your critical reading skills are likely to be increasingly useful, as the essential challenge of deep, thoughtful reading applies to graphic novels, blogs, photo essays, and YouTube videos just as it does to printed books, articles, and essays. In fact, some argue that texts with multiple components that appeal to multiple senses, require even more thorough scrutiny on the part of readers in order to grasp what writers are saying and how they are saying it. Here are some suggestions about how you might apply your critical skills in these often media-rich contexts:

- Concentrate on your purpose when you read online or multimodal texts, especially if those texts tug you further and further away from your original search or material.

- Create a reading journal or blog so that you have a handy location for responding to new materials.

- Bookmark (or subscribe to) meaty online readings, sites, or multimodal texts so you can easily return to examine their details. Consider what you see or hear, what the material suggests, and how it appeals to you.

- Read the features and effects of visual or multimodal texts as carefully as you read words in print texts. Observe composition, symmetry, sequence, shape, color, texture, brightness, and other visual components.

- Listen for the impact of audio characteristics such as sound effects (accuracy, clarity, volume, timing, emotional power), speech (pitch, tone, dialect, accent, pace), and music (instrumentation, vocals, melody, rhythm, harmony, musical roots, cuts, and any parts that may have been remixed).

- Examine visual or multimodal materials critically — analyzing components, synthesizing varied information, and evaluating effects.

- Evaluate research material that supports your points or that challenges other views so you can draw on trustworthy sources.
- Secure any necessary permission to add someone else's visual or other material to your text and credit your source appropriately.
- Generate even more ideas by rereading this chapter and thinking about how you could apply the skills presented here in new situations.

Learning by Doing Reading a Website

Examine this nonprofit organization's website: idahorivers.org. Using this chapter as a guide, consider the following questions as you evaluate or "read" the site: Based on the URL, what kind of information do you expect to find on this site? Looking at the pictures on the home page, what do you think this organization does? How is information presented? How easy is it to navigate the page? Is everything understandable? Do the creators of the site use special language or jargon? What might that language tell you about the organization? Does the information seem credible? Why, or why not? Identify specific features on the site that support your position. Write a short reflection to capture your observations. What will you remember the next time you "read" a website?

Additional Writing Assignments

1. **Source Activity.** Select an essay from *A Writer's Reader* (see the table of contents on p. 329.) Annotate the reading, marking both its key ideas and your own reactions to it. Review the text and your annotations, and then write two paragraphs, one summarizing the reading and the other explaining your personal response to it.

2. **Source Activity.** Follow up on Activity 1, working with others who have responded to the same essay. Share your summaries, noting the strengths of each. Then develop a collaborative summary that briefly and fairly presents the main points of the reading. (You can merge your existing summaries or make a fresh start.) When you finish the group summary, decide which methods of summarizing work best.

3. **Source Activity.** Follow up on Activity 1 by adding a critical reading analysis and response.

4. **Source Activity.** Select a passage from the readings for one of your other courses. Annotate the passage, and make some notes using the Reading Critically and the Analyzing Writing Strategies checklists in this chapter (p. 29) as guides. Pay special attention to the reading's purpose and its

assumptions about its audience. Write a paragraph or two about your critical examination of the passage.

5. **Visual Activity.** Take a close look at this visual text—a vintage travel guide for California. Read it critically, adapting the reading processes and skills from this chapter. Annotate the image, then write a short critical response.

Library of Congress, Prints & Photographs Division [LC-USZC2-964]

3 Critical Thinking Processes

*C*ritic, from the Greek word *kritikos*, means "one who can judge and discern" — in short, someone who thinks critically. College will have been worth your time and effort if it leaves you better able to determine what is more and less important, to make distinctions and recognize differences, to generalize from specifics, to draw conclusions from evidence, to grasp complex concepts, to choose wisely. The effective thinking that you'll need in college, on the job, and in daily life is active and purposeful, not passive and ambling. It is critical thinking.

A Process of Critical Thinking

For more on critical reading, see Ch. 2.

When you approach college reading and writing tasks, instructors will expect you (and you should expect yourself) to read, think, write, and think some more. This process often involves returning to prior steps; after you draft something, for instance, you may need to go back and read more sources, think some more about them, and write some more about what you have learned.

A Process for Critical Thinking: Read, Think, Write, Think

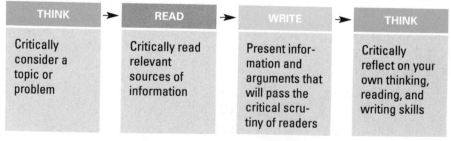

THINK	READ	WRITE	THINK
Critically consider a topic or problem	Critically read relevant sources of information	Present information and arguments that will pass the critical scrutiny of readers	Critically reflect on your own thinking, reading, and writing skills

Critical thinking, like critical reading, draws on a cluster of intellectual strategies and skills.

Strategies for Critical Thinking: Analysis, Synthesis, Evaluation

Critical Thinking Skill	Definition	Readers	Writers
Analysis	Breaking down information into its parts and elements	Readers analyze a text to grasp the facts and concepts it contains.	Writers analyze events, ideas, processes, and structures to understand them and explain them to readers.
Synthesis	Putting together elements and parts to form new wholes	Readers synthesize a text (or texts) to examine implications and draw conclusions supported by evidence.	Writers synthesize texts with their own thoughts (and with other texts) to share with readers the resulting unique combination of ideas.
Evaluation	Judging according to standards	Readers evaluate a text by determining and applying standards for judging to arrive at a conclusion about the text's value, significance, or credibility.	Writers evaluate something to convince readers that their standards for judging are reasonable and that the subject of their evaluation either does or does not meet those standards.

These three activities — **analysis**, **synthesis**, and **evaluation** — are the core of critical thinking. They are not new to you, but applying them rigorously to college-level reading and writing may be.

Applying Critical Thinking in Daily Life

You use critical thinking every day to explore problems step by step and reach solutions. Suppose you don't have enough money both to pay your tuition and to buy the car you need. First, you might pin down the causes of your financial problem. Next, you might examine your options to find the best solution, as shown in the chart that follows.

You can follow the same steps to examine many types of issues, helping you analyze a situation or dilemma, creatively synthesize to develop alternatives, and evaluate a possible course of action.

Learning by Doing 🎯 Thinking Critically When Facing a Problem

You've worked hard on a group presentation that will be a major part of your grade — and each member of the group will get the same grade. Two days before the project is due, you discover that one group member has plagiarized heavily from sources well known to your instructor. Working together with classmates, use critical thinking to explore your problem and determine what you might do.

Critical Thinking in Action

IDENTIFY PROBLEM	ANALYZE	SYNTHESIZE	EVALUATE	FINALIZE SOLUTIONS
	Break problem into parts and elements based on a principle.	Combine parts and elements to form new wholes.	Judge according to standards or criteria.	
You can't afford your college tuition.	*Causes of the problem:*	*Possible actions:*	*Value judgement:*	
	Job loss	Get a new job. Take out a loan. Borrow money.	A paid internship or work study job could help long term. An additional loan would still need to be paid back.	Look for a paid internship or work study job. Investigate loan options (ask family/friends, work out payback timetable).
	Credit card debt	Consolidate debt to lower payments.	Consolidating debt means paying less in interest.	Take steps to consolidate debt.
	Tuition increase	Take fewer courses to lower tuition.	Bad idea to drop courses. Fewer credits would affect eligibility for current loan.	Keep full course load to stay eligible for current student loan.

Applying Critical Thinking to Academic Problems

For advice on supporting critical thinking with evidence, see pp. 135–40.

As you grapple with academic problems and papers, you'll be expected to use your critical thinking skills — analyzing, synthesizing, and evaluating — in your reading and writing. You may simply dive in, using each skill as needed. However, the very wording of an assignment may alert you to a skill that your instructor expects you to use, as the first sample assignment in each set illustrates in the chart on page 39.

Thinking Critically about Your Own Writing: Self-Reflection

The word *reflection* may bring to mind the quiet contemplation of a poet or philosopher, and it may seem to have little to do with the process of learning new academic skills or applying them successfully. However, reflecting on

Applying Strategies for Critical Thinking to Academic Problems

Critical Thinking Skill	College Writing Assignments
Analyze Break problem into parts and elements based on a principle.	■ Trace the stages through which a bill becomes a law. ■ Define *romanticism*, identifying and illustrating its major characteristics.
Synthesize Combine parts and elements to form new wholes.	■ Discuss the following statement: Opposition to slavery was only one cause of the animosity between the North and South that in 1861 escalated into civil war. (Synthesize by combining the causes or elements of the North-South animosity, going beyond the opposition to slavery, to form a new whole: your conclusion, in which you argue three major causes of the escalation into civil war.) ■ Imagine that you are a trial lawyer in 1921 charged with defending Nicola Sacco and Bartolomeo Vanzetti, two anarchists accused of murder. Argue for their acquittal on whatever grounds you can justify.
Evaluate Judge according to standards or criteria.	■ Present and evaluate the most widely accepted theories that explain the disappearance of the dinosaurs. (Evaluate—based on standards such as scientific merit—the credibility of each theory.) ■ Defend or challenge the idea that houses and public buildings should be constructed to last no longer than twenty years.

your writing and writing processes — that is, thinking through the difficulties, questions, and successes that arise as you draft and revise papers — can help you become a more active learner. In short, self-reflection and active learning can help you make lasting improvements in your writing skills. With time and practice, you'll become more comfortable applying those skills in any writing situation, both in college and beyond.

How to Reflect on Your Own Writing

Self-reflection involves metacognition, with *meta* meaning "beyond" and *cognition* referring to the process of thinking, learning, or understanding. In the context of writing, *metacognition* means thinking about your own thinking — and about your writing process. Throughout the process of writing, you ask yourself questions like these:

REFLECTING ON YOUR OWN WRITING

Before Writing

☐ Do I understand the purpose or reason for the writing assignment I've been asked to complete? Would this type of writing be relevant beyond this particular assignment or class?

☐ Am I clear on the requirements of this assignment? If not, what questions should I ask my instructor?

☐ Am I having a hard time starting the assignment? Do I know what is getting in my way?

During Writing

☐ Are some aspects of the writing assignment fairly easy for me to complete? Are some more challenging, and do I know why?

☐ Do I enjoy some parts of the writing process more than others? Do I know why?

After Writing

☐ Did I use the most successful strategies that I could to write this paper? Could I have done anything differently or better?

☐ Did I learn something valuable from completing this writing assignment?

☐ Is there anything that what would have been helpful for me to know, early in the process of writing?

☐ Does the feedback that I received from my instructor (or peers) make sense to me? Do I have any remaining questions for my instructor or peers?

☐ Would I give myself an "A" on this piece of writing? Why or why not?

☐ Do I know how to best work on the next draft of this paper, or on my next writing assignment?

The syllabus for this and other courses might specify desired learning outcomes. If your instructor has provided learning outcomes or rubrics (criteria for successful papers), use them for self-reflection, too. For example, let's say that in an economics course, the rubric for research papers makes this statement:

> Successful papers will give a new insight into the topic—an insight not provided in lectures, class discussions, or readings.

As the writer generates ideas, he or she might repeatedly ask, "Can I draw fresh conclusions from the evidence I've gathered? Would additional research be helpful?" And when it's time to draft a thesis stating the paper's main point, the writer might ask, "Is this truly an original insight? Do I need to spend more time thinking about what I've read?" The central aim of self-reflection should be to learn more about what is working well and what needs more effort and attention—both in your writing process in general and in your specific writing assignments.

You might record your self-reflections in a designated notebook or journal, or in a digital file. Or you might post your reflections to a blog. Unless your instructor specifies a format for this type of writing, choose the one that is most comfortable and convenient for you.

Learning by Doing 🔟 Reflecting on Your College Career

Consider what Keith Hjortshoj says in his book *The Transition to College Writing*: "Students who get the most out of college usually take the most active responsibility for determining what, how, and why they should learn."[1] Reflect on your own motivation for going to college. Why are you here? How should you adapt your own study habits (or lack thereof) to adjust to college life? How will the work in this course benefit you in later courses and beyond college? How can your classmates help you succeed? What do you think you need to do to become invested in your classwork and your learning?

For details on keeping a journal for self-reflection, see pp. 262–63.

Contexts for Self-Reflection

You can record your reflections in your reading journal. Additionally, your instructor might assign self-reflective writing at various points in the course. For example, you might be asked to respond to a "midterm reflection" prompt like the one Khalia Nadam received (see p. 42). If you are required to keep a writing portfolio for your course, you might be asked to complete a series of self-reflections as part of that process. Any ongoing evaluation of your thinking and writing processes will certainly help you write the introduction or cover letter that usually accompanies the portfolio. These documents are a form of self-assessment in which you discuss your best or most challenging papers, detail your writing and revision process, and so on. The more you practice self-reflection, the more helpful the process will be.

For details on self-reflection and self-assessment in portfolio keeping, see pp. 325–27.

Self-Reflection in Peer Review. In addition to building your thinking and writing skills, self-reflection can help you get more out of peer review. In particular, it will allow you to ask peers more specific questions about your writing, encouraging more helpful responses. Consider the differences between the following sets of questions, and the likely benefits of the more specific ones.

VAGUE QUESTIONS	Did you like my paper or not? What did you think of my paper?
SPECIFIC QUESTIONS	I struggled with how to organize the paragraphs supporting my argument. Does the order of them make sense to you? If not, why not?
	I'm not sure that my argument responds adequately to opposing views. Can you think of any counter arguments that I haven't addressed?

[1] Keith Hjortshoj, *The Transition to College Writing*, (Boston/New York: Bedford/St. Martin's, 2009).

Learning by Doing Reflecting on Your Course Syllabus

Working with a classmate or a small group, look over the syllabus for this course, paying special attention to the stated goals, which may be called "outcomes" or "objectives." Write a short reflection about the syllabus. How does it differ from others you may have received in college or high school? Do the goals raise any questions for you? Which ones do you think might be the most challenging and why? Examine your syllabus further. If assignments are listed, do any look particularly difficult? What skills do you currently have that would help you tackle them?

Learning from Another Writer: Self-Reflection

In the following piece of writing, student Khalia Nadam responded to this "midterm reflection" prompt for a course on writing in the biological sciences:

> "Which writing assignment in this course has been the most valuable so far, and why? How might you use what you've learned from this assignment in other contexts?"

As you read Nadam's writing, notice how she applied critical thinking skills by *analyzing* the challenges of her policy-recommendation assignment and *evaluating* her response to it.

Khalia Nadam   **Student Self-Reflection**
What I Learned from My Research Project

Reflects on and states the value of her writing assignment.

The most valuable piece of writing I have done so far in this course is the policy-recommendation paper. It is one of the most challenging assignments that I have ever worked on. But in spite of that difficulty, or maybe because of it, it has also been the most rewarding.   1

Identifies aspects of writing that were easiest.

As you know from my first draft, I recommended that Kenworth County's land management agencies use social media to keep the public and other stakeholders informed about land management policies, controversies, and other issues. The idea came to me rather easily, because I interned at one of such agency last summer and witnessed the old-school communication strategies. (For one thing, the Communications Department was still snail-mailing press releases to local media and had a weak Internet presence.)   2

Identifies aspects of writing that were most difficult.

The hard part was researching the full scope of the problem and determining possible solutions. I interviewed key personnel and asked questions like these: Why does your agency have no social media presence? Why is there no news feed   3 on the website? Other than the press releases being sent to local newspapers and radio stations, what else is being done to get agency news out?

I would say that the most valuable lessons I've learned from this assignment are that (1) when researching a current and local issue, interviews can be one of the most valuable ways to gather evidence, (2) the research process took a lot longer than I thought it would, so I'll try to get an earlier start on future research projects, and (3) I should have created an outline before diving in on my first draft. I ended up doing a ton of reorganizing after that draft, andeven a rough outline would have helped me think through the structure of my writing in advance.

> 4 Reflects on process and states what she learned.

In terms of what I need to work on more, again, I need to get an earlier start on research for future writing projects and do a better job of planning. It is also clear from the feedback I received on my first draft that I need to spend more time on editing and proofreading. Because the final draft is due next Monday, I'm going to devote at least a couple of evenings to both tasks.

> 5 Reflects on process and feedback; observes what she can improve upon in the future.

I'm confident that I can apply what I've learned in other contexts. In fact, I've already started doing that. Because of what the policy-rec paper taught me about the value of outlining, I prepared a pretty detailed outline for a history paper I'm working on, and that really helped. The insights I got from this project should be helpful to me in future courses and in the workplace as well.

> 6 States how she can apply her process in other writing situations.

Questions to Start You Thinking

Meaning

1. According to Nadam, what made the policy-recommendation assignment so challenging?

2. How would you summarize the main lessons that she learned from the assignment?

Writing Strategies

3. Nadam could have responded to the reflection prompt in a single paragraph. What might have been the benefits of going into greater detail about the challenges of her policy-recommendation project?

4. If Nadam had written this reflection just for herself instead of in response to an assignment, might she have used a different approach? For example, can you imagine her using a less formal structure? What might be the benefits of that?

Additional Writing Assignments

1. With classmates, identify a common problem for students at your college—juggling a busy schedule, parking on campus, or some other issue. Working together, use critical thinking to explore the problem and identify possible solutions. Make notes as you explore the problem and solutions, and put your findings into writing.

2. Working with a classmate or small group, select a sample assignment (not already explained) from the chart on page 39 or from one of your classes. Demonstrate your critical thinking by explaining, in writing, how you would approach the assignment. Also, share your strategies for tackling college assignments.

3. Think back over the past month at college, at work (if you hold a job), and in your day-to-day life. Then respond to these two self-reflection prompts: (a) Which experiences have been the most important, because they taught you something valuable, gave you confidence in your abilities, or supported your personal growth in some other way? (b) Which experiences have been the most challenging, and why?

4. **Source Activity**. Using your college's library, or using research tools available on the library's website, identify two or three sources that cover (a) a topic you are investigating for a college course or (b) a topic you find personally interesting. Keeping in mind at least three key questions that you have about your topic, read over the sources and try to answer these questions, making notes. (In case you want to revisit these sources later, make sure to record their titles and authors, the publications they came from, and any page numbers.) Afterward, respond to these self-reflection questions: Was it easy to find relevant and helpful sources, or was it more difficult than you expected? Why? To what degree did the sources answer your questions? Do you still feel the need to track down additional information? If so, will you adjust your search strategy in any way? How?

5. **Visual Activity**. Working with a classmate or small group, study the images on the next page or gather your own set of images to examine—for example, from your student newspaper or a magazine or from a favorite social media site. Then, using the critical thinking skills discussed in this chapter, share your impressions of the images. For example, you might analyze the images by considering their various parts and discussing how they work together or set one another apart. Or you might evaluate the images by considering their lighting, their composition, the distance or perspective from which the subjects were photographed, the mood created, and so on.

miljko/E+/Getty Images

Godong/UIG/Getty Images

A Writer's Situations

4 Recalling and Observing

fstop123/Getty Images

Responding to an Image

Look carefully at the photograph above. In your view, when was this photograph taken? Who might the people be? Where are they, and why are they there? What are they doing? What relationships and emotions does the picture suggest with its focal point and arrangement? Which details do you notice? Write about an event you experienced or observed that the image helps you recall or about a possible explanation of events in this picture. Use vivid detail to convey what happened to you or what might have happened to the people in the picture.

Why Recalling and Observing Matter

Writing from recall is writing from memory, a writer's richest — and handiest — resource. Recall is clearly necessary when you write of a personal experience, a favorite place, a memorable person, or an interesting scene. Recall also helps you probe your memories of specific events. For example, in a literacy narrative you might examine the significance of your experiences learning to read or write. On the other hand, in a reflection you might begin with an incident or scene that you recall and then explore the ideas that evolve from it.

Most writers begin to write by recalling what they know. Then they look around and add what they observe. Some writing consists almost entirely of observation — a reporter's eyewitness account of a fire, a clinical report by a nurse detailing a patient's condition, a traveler's blog or photo essay. In fact, observation plays a large role for writers whenever they describe a person, place, or thing. Through observation, writers provide details to make a point clear or convincing. For example, writers can make the dry statistics of a case study more vivid by including compelling observations.

Even when an instructor hands you a subject that seems to have nothing to do with you — say, the history of carnival or fair food in the United States — your memory is the first place to look. Jot down what you remember of specific visits to fairs of your childhood. If you need more to write about, open your eyes — and your other senses. Take in what you can see, hear, smell, touch, and taste. As you write, report your observations and memories in concrete detail. Of course, you can't record everything you observe or recall. You must be selective based on what's important and relevant for your purpose and audience.

The abilities to observe the world around you and recall your memories benefit you in various contexts, including the following:

In a College Course

- You recall and record both routine and unusual events in a journal that you are asked to keep throughout a course, internship, or clinical experience.
- You write essays in which you discuss memories about a specific event or experience that shaped your life.
- You observe and report compelling information from field trips in sociology, criminal justice, or anthropology as well as impressions of a play, an exhibit, or a historical site for a humanities class.
- You observe clinical practices in health or education, habitats for plants and animals, the changing night sky, or lab experiments to report accurate information and to improve your own future practice.

In the Workplace

- At your job, you might recall past successes, failures, customer comments, or other feedback to persuade colleagues to adopt your proposals for changing a product or service.
- You observe and analyze to lend credibility to your case study as a nurse, teacher, or social worker or to your site report as an engineer or architect.

In Your Community

- You recall your own experiences taking standardized tests as part of an appeal to the local school board to change the testing program at your child's school.

- You observe, photograph, and report on hazards (a dangerous intersection, a poorly lit park, a run-down building) or needs (a soccer arena, a performing arts center) to motivate action by authorities or fellow citizens.

  ❓ When have you presented observed scenes or recalled memories in your writing? What did these observations or recollections add to your writing? In what future writing situations might you rely on observation or recollection?

Learning from Other Writers

Here are two samples of good writing from observation and recollection—one by a professional writer, one by a college student. To help you analyze the first reading, look at the notes in the margin. They identify features such as the main idea, or thesis, and the supporting details that describe a recalled event or observation. As you read these observations and recollections, ask yourself the following questions:

1. What does the writer recall or observe? Experiences? Places? People? Behavior? Things?

2. What senses does the writer draw upon? What sensory images does the writer develop? Find some striking passages in which the writer reports observations. What makes these passages memorable to you?

3. Why does the writer incorporate observation into the text? What realization or conclusion does the writer draw from reflecting on the observations?

4. How does the realization or conclusion change the writer?

Rachael Warecki

Margaret Rhee

Returning to My Father's Koreatown

In this essay from the travel site *On She Goes* (2017), writer and poet Margaret Rhee, in her own words, "look[s] back at family, food, and memories in [a] Los Angeles neighborhood."

Introduction with thesis. Writer observes a place and people; recalls family's background.

F or many, Koreatown's bright signage, plethora° of restaurants, and popular bars make it an exotic and trendy section of Los Angeles to visit. But for me, within its large communities of ethnic diversity—Salvadorian,   1

plethora: Abundance or large amount.

Mexican, and Korean immigrants — is where I feel at home. My parents immigrated to the US from Korea in the 1970s, and I was born in Los Angeles. They first settled in Koreatown, then soon moved to the northern part of Orange County, where I grew up.

It wasn't *The O.C.* you remember from the popular TV show; it was less dense and more sprawling, with modest cream-colored homes in our suburban neighborhood. It had quiet residential streets, not like the bustling streets of Koreatown lit up with signs in Korean. After my parents divorced in my early teens, my father moved to a small apartment in Koreatown. Whenever I went to visit, we would frequent restaurants in the city together for lunch or dinner.

When I was younger, my experience of travel was mainly with my father. I would visit him in Koreatown, and we took road trips to the nearby bordering states of Nevada and Utah. We'd visit national parks and spend time in the outdoors, and my father loved to document the nature we saw. Although he immigrated as an auto mechanic, my father dreamed of traveling the US and taking video of national parks. At one point, in his characteristically eccentric way, he thought he would sell the video footage to other Koreans thinking of immigrating to the US. Usually it would be me and him, but when my sister was home from college, she would join us too. Once we even attended an air show in the desert, and in Vegas we visited the bustling and busy casinos where my father would gamble. Like the games in the casinos we frequented, my father's immigration was a gamble, one he often did not win because he was unable to pursue much outside of his daily work because of his limited English language skills.

The travel wasn't to Italy, Switzerland, or even Korea, but when I visited my father in Los Angeles, it felt like another world. Although the community where I grew up in Orange County had a sizable Korean population, it lacked a variety of Korean restaurants that my father and I could frequent together. After the divorce, the hour-long lunches and dinners we planned, mostly every two weeks, would be the only time I would see my father. He would always let me choose the place, but if he could choose, he would take us to a "Omma Jip" restaurant. Often my choice would be to let him choose, so Omma would be where we'd go.

Omma Jip means "Mother's House" in Korean, and it was appropriately named for the comfort it offered. These storefront restaurants are small, comfortable, and no-nonsense. Prices were cheap, with the caveat that you would only get one small dish of banchan° along with your bowl of soup and stew. But that was okay. For the steaming seolleongtang° stew, with its green onions and thick white soup, one would only need a side of kimchi° anyway. There are a couple of Omma Jip restaurants that still exist, with names such as Halmae Restaurant ("Grandmother's Restaurant"), and they still serve people who would like a simple and cheap Korean meal, and a comforting space in the busy city.

banchan: In Korean cuisine, small side dishes of food served with rice. **seolleongtang:** In Korean cuisine, ox bone soup. **kimchi:** In Korean cuisine, a side dish of salted and fermented vegetables.

These Korean restaurants would never make a "best-of" list — they were   6
not hot spots. These restaurants, I soon realized, were also a place where bach-
elors could go eat alone. The atmosphere was antithetical° to trendy. There
were no tourists here, just simple wood tables and chairs, and an ah juh ma°
who would serve you swiftly and without frills. During the times I went to
Omma Jip with my father, I noticed that there were not many families there.
Instead, there were single, older Korean men who could eat Korean food at
low prices, without the self-consciousness of not belonging. My father, who
had no family to eat dinner with, would often come here to have a Korean
meal. I was happy to visit the restaurant with him.

When I reflect on it now, I feel sad that my father would have to go to these   7
restaurants for a home-cooked meal, but I am comforted that they existed. I
wish we could have cooked for him more, even if his apartment didn't have a
large kitchen, or even if there was not much I could make at that young age.
However, when we went to the restaurant together, I felt it was a time to connect. At Omma Jip, we could enjoy a Korean meal and talk about school or
how my father was doing with his work. If we had time afterward, we would
stop by the nearby cafe for dessert. It was just a block away and a "trendier"
place — Korean pop music, large white sofas, and young Korean waitresses
and waiters dressed in black. While it was more expensive than Omma Jip,
my father never complained when we ordered bing soo, the popular Korean
ice cream, or his overpriced Korean tea. We sat outside and watched as people
went about their day in K-Town.

> Writer reflects further on her father; gives details about restaurants visited; supports her thesis that she feels most at home in Koreatown.

Koreatown is densely packed with terra-cotta apartment buildings, tower-   8
ing palm trees planted on sidewalks, and folks walking in the neighborhood.
Bright signs with Korean lettering are juxtaposed with high-rise buildings.
Along with newer blue glass buildings, there are Korean BBQ restaurants
and countless karaoke bars. Rental signs are in Korean, Spanish, and English.
My father's apartment was near a laundry/fast-food restaurant where you
could eat french fries while waiting for your clothes to dry. If we didn't meet
at Omma Jip, we often met him there because it was convenient. Going to
K-Town was also a way to connect to Korean culture and language. Since we
didn't visit Korea when I was a child, Koreatown was a stand-in for my understanding of diaspora° and the first country my father called home.

My father passed away now almost fifteen years ago, and I've almost forgot-   9
ten those times we spent at the restaurants. My nostalgia and grief changed into
trying to remember, but I do not attempt to place the memories in language. My
father, while he could not take me to many places growing up, prompted a love
for travel in me, even if only in words. My father loved to explore the US, and he
loved to see the new country he adopted as his own. Through travel, I believe it
was his way of feeling he belonged. The author Edwidge Danticat° wrote something that I always found resonant, but I am reminded of it even more when I
think of my father and why I write:

> Writer recalls her father's death; observes that he found a home as an immigrant.

antithetical: Being directly opposite or opposed.   **ah juh ma:** Korean for aunt, "ma'am," or
unrelated woman.   **diaspora:** People living far away from their ancestral homelands, or a
reference to the place where they now live.   **Edwidge Danticat:** A Haitian-American writer.

> . . . [T]he immigrant artist must quantify the price of the American dream in flesh and bone. All this while living with the more 'regular' fears of any other artist. Do I know enough about where I've come from? Will I ever know enough about where I am? Even if someone has died for me to stay here, will I ever truly belong?

Writer cites another writer's observations on belonging as an immigrant.

I hold Danticat's words on the fears of the immigrant artist. I realize my   10
father's American dream was quite simple. I think back on one of our trips, when we traveled out to the ports in Southern California. There we stood, looking through the round windows of ships, where he shared he would like to live on a boat and travel. He dreamed of travel and how it offered a sense of autonomy° and belonging, something oftentimes withheld from the grasp of immigrants' hands. I wonder what I inherited, if I will "ever know enough," and even with my father's passing, "will I ever truly belong?"

Writing, like travel, is a means of escape. It is also a way to belong, even   11
if only on the page, or on the airplane. After 15 years of devoting myself to writing and with my first book coming later this year,[1] I was suddenly reminded of my father and why I travel and write. My book isn't about my father, Los Angeles, or immigrants. It is a poetry collection about robots and love. But the experience of taking author photos for the book in Koreatown reminded me of how a place has so much to do with memory and family.

Writer considers the current significance of Koreatown; realizes its impact on her and memories of her father.

I had decided that I would return to K-Town to have my photos taken,   12
for a small portrait on my first book that would forever serve as a reminder of home. The photographer met me off Wilshire Boulevard, not too far from where my father had lived off Bonnie Brae Street. At one point, we walked on Wilshire, past Western Avenue and into an alleyway with two Korean newspaper vending machines. The photographer asked me to lean against the green metal box with black and white Korean lettering, and I was suddenly struck with a memory of my father.

Growing up, my father loved to read the Korean newspaper. When he was   13
ill, before I went to the hospital, I would stop by these vending machines to buy a newspaper for him. I remember holding the newspaper up with both hands so he could read from his hospital bed. I turned the pages as he read the headlines. I remember him telling me, after reading each headline in his usual curmudgeonly° way, that the headlines were no good.

Writer recalls her father's illness; his character.

In his last days when he was ill in the hospital, I remember him telling me in   14
Korean, I can't wait until you, me, and your sister travel and drink soda again.

My father never was able to travel with my sister and me again. Sadly, he   15
passed away soon after. On the day we took the author photos, I had almost forgotten the memory that helped explain why I had returned to Koreatown to take these photos to accompany my own writing. Since I write about science-fiction worlds, the book reminded me of how I too travel, even if only

autonomy: Independence.   **curmudgeonly:** bad-tempered, cantankerous.

---

[1] Rhee refers to her poetry collection, *Love, Robot*, published in 2017 by The Operating System.

through literature. Perhaps I write in order to remind myself that through language we all belong. After I said goodbye to the photographer, I stood for a moment at an intersection on Wilshire. The cars passed me, fast and hurried squares of color. As I stood there, the cool California breeze softly met my face. When the traffic lights turned, I began walking. I was not lost. I knew exactly where to go.

Writer solidifies her father's (and Koreatown's) place in her memory and heart. Her observations and recollections helped her realize that she belongs.

Questions to Start You Thinking

Meaning

1. In your own words, state what Rhee concludes about her father. What incidents or statements help identify this observation for readers?

2. Why do you think Rhee wrote this essay?

Writing Strategies

3. What is the effect, in paragraph 5, of Rhee's use of Korean words for food? What other devices does she use to characterize Koreatown, or specifically Omma Jip, vividly?

4. What does the quotation from Edwidge Danticat add to Rhee's account? Had the quotation been omitted, what would have been lost?

5. How does Rhee organize her essay? Why does she use this order? Is this organization effective? Why, or why not?

Robert G. Schreiner   **Student Essay**
What Is a Hunter?

In this college essay, Robert G. Schreiner uses vivid details to bring to life a significant childhood event.

What is a hunter? This is a simple question with a relatively straightforward answer. A hunter is, according to *Webster's New Collegiate Dictionary*, a person who hunts game (game being various types of animals hunted or pursued for various reasons). However, a second question is just as simple but without such a straightforward answer: What characteristics make up a hunter? As a child, I had always considered the most important aspect of the hunter's person to be his ability to use a rifle, bow, or whatever weapon was appropriate to the type of hunting being done. Having many relatives in rural areas of Virginia and Kansas, I had been exposed to rifles a great deal. I had done extensive target shooting and considered myself to be quite proficient in the use of firearms. I had never been hunting, but I had always thought that since I could fire a rifle accurately I would make a good hunter.

One Christmas holiday, while we were visiting our grandparents in Kansas, my grandfather asked me if I wanted to go jackrabbit hunting with him. I eagerly accepted, anxious to show off my prowess° with a rifle. A younger cousin of mine also wanted to come, so we all went out into the garage, loaded two .22 caliber rifles and a 20-gauge shotgun, hopped into the pickup truck, and drove out of town. It had snowed the night before, and to either side of the narrow road swept six-foot-deep powdery drifts. The wind twirled the fine crystalline snow into whirling vortexes° that bounced along the icy road and sprayed snow into the open windows of the pickup. As we drove, my grandfather gave us some pointers about both spotting and shooting jackrabbits. He told us that when it snows, jackrabbits like to dig out a hollow in the top of a snowdrift, usually near a fencepost, and lie there soaking up the sunshine. He told us that even though jackrabbits are a grayish brown, this coloration is excellent camouflage in the snow, for the curled-up rabbits resemble rocks. He then pointed out a few rabbits in such positions as we drove along, showing us how to distinguish them from exposed rocks and dirt. He then explained that the only way to be sure that we killed the rabbit was to shoot for the head and, in particular, the eye, for this was on a direct line with the rabbit's brain. Since we were using solid point bullets, which deform into a ball upon impact, a hit anywhere but the head would most likely only wound the rabbit.

> **❓** How does the writer convey his grandfather's definition of hunting?

My grandfather then slowed down the pickup and told us to look out for the rabbits hidden in the snowdrifts. We eventually spotted one about thirty feet from the road in a snow-filled gully. My cousin wished to shoot the first one, so he hopped out of the truck, balanced the .22 on the hood, and fired. A spray of snow erupted about a foot to the left of the rabbit's hollow. My cousin fired again, and again, and again, the shots pockmarking the slope of the drift. He fired once more and the rabbit bounced out of its hollow, its head rocking from side to side. He was hit. My cousin eagerly gamboled into the snow to claim his quarry.° He brought it back holding it by the hind legs, proudly displaying it as would a warrior the severed head of his enemy. The bullet had entered the rabbit's right shoulder and exited through the neck. In both places a thin trickle of crimson marred the gray sheen of the rabbit's pelt. It quivered slightly and its rib cage pulsed with its labored breathing. My cousin was about to toss it into the back of the pickup when my grandfather pointed out that it would be cruel to allow the rabbit to bleed slowly to death and instructed my cousin to bang its head against the side of the pickup to kill it. My cousin then proceeded to bang the rabbit's head against the yellow metal. Thump, thump, thump, thump; after a minute or so my cousin loudly proclaimed that it was dead and hopped back into the truck.

> **❓** Why do you think that the writer reacts as he does?

prowess: Superior skill.   **vortex:** Rotation around an axis, as in a whirlwind.   **quarry:** Prey.

The whole episode sickened me to some degree, and at the time I did   4
not know why. We continued to hunt throughout the afternoon, and feigning
boredom, I allowed my cousin and grandfather to shoot all of the rabbits. Often,
the shots didn't kill the rabbits outright so they had to be killed against the
pickup. The thump, thump, thump of the rabbits' skulls against the metal began
to irritate me, and I was strangely glad when we turned around and headed back
toward home. We were a few miles from the city limits when my grandfather
slowed the truck to a stop, then backed up a few yards. My grandfather said
he spotted two huge "jacks" sitting in the sun in a field just off the road. He
pointed them out and handed me the .22, saying that if I didn't shoot something
the whole afternoon would have been a wasted trip for me. I hesitated and then
reluctantly accepted the rifle. I stepped out onto the road, my feet crunching
on the ice. The two rabbits were about seventy feet away, both sitting upright
in the sun. I cocked and leveled the rifle, my elbow held almost horizontal in the
military fashion I had learned to employ. I brought the sights to bear on the right
eye of the first rabbit, compensated° for distance, and fired. There was a harsh
snap like the crack of a whip and a small jolt to my shoulder. The first rabbit was
gone, presumably knocked over the side of the snowdrift. The second rabbit
hadn't moved a muscle; it just sat there staring with that black eye. I cocked
the rifle once more and sighted a second time, the bead of the rifle just barely
above the glassy black orb that regarded me so passively. I squeezed the trigger.
Again the crack, again the jolt, and again the rabbit disappeared over the top of
the drift. I handed the rifle to my cousin and began making my way toward the
rabbits. I sank into powdery snow up to my waist as I clambered to the top of the
drift and looked over.

On the other side of the drift was a sight that I doubt I will ever forget. There   5
was a shallow, snow-covered ditch on the leeward side of the drift and it was
into this ditch that the rabbits had fallen, at least what was left of the rabbits.
The entire ditch, in an area about ten feet wide, was spattered with splashes of
crimson blood, pink gobbets of brain, and splintered fragments of bone. The
twisted corpses of the rabbits lay in the bottom of the ditch in small pools of
streaming blood. Of both the rabbits, only the bodies remained, the heads being
completely gone. Stumps of vertebrae protruded obscenely from the mangled
bodies, and one rabbit's hind legs twitched spasmodically. I realized that my
cousin must have made a mistake and loaded the rifle with hollow point explosive
bullets instead of solid ones.

I shouted back to the pickup, explaining the situation, and asked if I should   6
bring them back anyway. My grandfather shouted back, "No, don't worry about
it, just leave them there. I'm gonna toss these jacks by the side of the road
anyway; jackrabbits aren't any good for eatin'."

compensated: Counterbalanced.

Looking at the dead, twitching bodies I thought only of the incredible waste of life that the afternoon had been, and I realized that there was much more to being a hunter than knowing how to use a rifle. I turned and walked back to the pickup, riding the rest of the way home in silence.

7 ❓ Why do you think the writer returns in silence?

Questions to Start You Thinking

Meaning

1. How would you characterize the writer's grandfather? How would you characterize his cousin?

2. How did the writer's understanding of himself change as a result of this hunting experience?

Writing Strategies

3. What are some of Schreiner's memorable descriptions? What senses does he use most effectively? Point to a few examples to support your choice.

Learning by Writing

The Assignment: Recalling a Personal Experience or Observing a Scene

You have two options for this assignment:

Writing from recollection.

First, you can write about a personal experience that changed how you acted, thought, or felt. Pick an event that is not too personal, too subjective, or too big to convey effectively to others. Use your experience as a springboard for reflection. Your purpose is not merely to tell an interesting story but to show your readers the importance of that experience for you.

Writing from observation.

Alternatively, observe a place near your campus, home, or job and the people who frequent it. Open all your senses so that you see, smell, taste, hear, and feel. Then write a paper that describes the place, the people, and their actions so as to convey the spirit of the place and offer some insight into its impact on the people. Your purpose is not only to describe the scene but also to express thoughts and feelings connected with what you observe. When you select the scene you wish to observe, find out from the person in charge whether you'll need to request permission to observe there, as you might at a school, a business, or another restricted or privately owned site.

MANAGING YOUR TIME:
Writing from Recollection or Observation

Use the breakdown below to plan your time for this essay; in the right column, insert target dates and times for completing each stage.

approx. 30-45 minutes

- **Read your assignment carefully**. Is it clear what your instructor is asking of you? If not, follow up.
- **Brainstorm** to arrive at a memory or scene that you'd like to write about.
- **Identify your purpose and audience**. Do you want to use your memories or observations to persuade, inform, entertain, or something else? Picture your readers. What do you need to tell them?

I'll complete this stage by:

_____
(day, date)

approx. 2-3 hours

- **List relevant observations or memories**, with your topic, purpose, and audience in mind. Which details matter the most?
- **Sketch an outline**. Begin with your main impression or thesis, jotting down three or so headings and the two or three points you will make under each.
- **Draft your essay**, staying close to your outline. Support your thesis with relevant, concrete details.
- **Craft a compelling** introduction and a satisfying **conclusion**.

I'll complete this stage by:

_____
(day, date)

approx. 2-4 hours

- Ask a **peer to review** your draft. Have you presented your recollection or observation clearly and powerfully?
- **Revise your draft**, addressing issues raised during your and your peer's review.
- **Edit your draft**, fixing any errors and polishing your prose.

I'll complete this stage by:

_____
(day, date)

Generating Ideas

If you are **writing from recollection**, give yourself time for your memories to surface. Ask yourself, what experiences — positive, painful, or otherwise — have you learned from? When a promising recollection emerges, write it down.

For more on each strategy for generating ideas in this section or for additional strategies, see Ch. 18.

If you are **writing from observation**, give yourself the opportunity to observe a place, a group of people, or whatever subject you plan to write about.

Although setting down memories or observations might seem cut-and-dried, to many writers it is true discovery. Here are some ways to stir your memories and generate observations.

Brainstorm to find a topic. When you brainstorm, you write down as many ideas as you can.

Writing from recollection.

You can start with a suggestive idea — *disobedience, painful lesson, childhood, celebration* — and list whatever occurs through free association. You can also draw on your memories by asking yourself the following questions.

- Have I ever broken an important rule or rebelled against authority? What did I learn from my actions?

- Have I ever succumbed to peer pressure? What were the results of going along with the crowd? What did I learn?

- Have I ever regarded a person in a certain way and later changed my opinion of him or her? What produced this change?

Writing from observation.

First, list potential scenes to observe. What places interest you? Which are memorable? Start brainstorming, rapidly listing any ideas that come to mind. Here are a few questions to get you started with your list.

- Where do people gather for specific activities (a gym, a classroom), events (a stadium, a place of worship, a wedding), or performances (a theater)?

- Where do people pause on their way to yet another destination (an Amtrak station, a bus or subway station, an airport, a rest stop on a highway)?

If nothing on your list strikes you as compelling, plunge into the world to see what you see. Visit a city street or country hillside, a student event or practice field, a lively scene — a mall, a street fair — or a scene with only a few people sunbathing, walking dogs, or playing basketball. Observe for a while, and then mix and move to gain different views.

Try Doodling or Sketching. If you are writing about a memory such as learning to drive, try sketching whatever helps you recollect the event and its significance. If you are writing based on observation, make a sketch of the person, place, or thing that you are observing. Turn doodles into words by adding comments on main events, dialogue, notable details, and their impact on you.

Record Your Memories and Observations. Try asking "the five **W**'s and an **H**" that journalists find useful:

1. **Who** was involved?
2. **What** happened?
3. **Where** did it take place?
4. **When** did it happen?
5. **Why** did it happen?
6. **How** did the events unfold?

Any question might lead to further questions — and to further discovery.

■ **Who** was involved? ⟶ What did the others look like?
⟶ What did they say or do?
⟶ Would their words supply any lively quotations?

■ **What** happened? ⟶ What did you think as the event unfolded?
⟶ When did you understand its importance?

Writing from recollection.

In her essay, Margaret Rhee incorporated vivid memories of the Koreatown of her youth. She was able to mine those memories for details to bring her subject to life. For your own essay, record all the details you can recall about your subject — the people, statements, events, locations, and related physical details. Your notes on a subject — or tentative subject — can be taken in any order or methodically.

Writing from observation.

It may be helpful to draw up an "observation sheet." First, fold a sheet of paper in half lengthwise. Label the left column "Objective," and impartially list what you see, like a zoologist looking at a new species of moth. Label the right column "Subjective," and list your thoughts and feelings about what you observe. The quality of your paper will depend in large part on the truthfulness and accuracy of your observations. Your objective notes will trigger more subjective ones.

Sample Observation Sheet

Objective	Subjective
The ticket holders form a line on the weathered sidewalk outside the old brick hall, standing two or three deep all the way down the block.	This place has seen concerts of all kinds — you can feel the history as you wait, as if the hall protects the crowds and the music.
Everyone shuffles forward when the doors open, looking around at the crowd and edging toward the entrance.	The excitement and energy grow with the wait, but it's the concert ritual — the prelude to a perfect night.

Consider Sources of Support. Because our minds both retain and drop details, you may want to double-check your recollections of an experience. Did you keep a journal at the time? Do your memories match those of a friend or relative who was there? Was the experience (big game, new home, birth of a child) a turning point that you or your family would have photographed? Was it a public event that was in the news? If so, these resources can remind you of forgotten details. Similarly, depending on how recent your observations are, you may want to check them against other sources, such as people who also observed the person, place, or thing that is your subject.

Include a Range of Images. As we experience the world, we're bombarded by sensory details, but our task as writers is to choose those that bring a subject alive for readers. For example, describing an oak as "a big tree with green leaves" is too vague to help readers envision the tree or grasp its unique qualities. In thinking about the experience you are recalling or the scene you're observing, ask yourself:

- What colors, shapes, and sizes did I see?
- What tones, pitches, and rhythms did I hear?
- What textures, grains, and physical features did I feel?
- What fragrances and odors did I smell?
- What sweet, spicy, or other flavors did I taste?

After recording the details that define the scene, ask two more questions:

- What overall main impression do these details establish?
- Which specific details will best show the spirit of this event to a reader?

Your answers will help you decide which details to include in your paper. Consider, too, how other writers use *images* to evoke sensory experience, to record what they sense. For instance, in the memoir *Northern Farm*, naturalist Henry Beston describes a remarkable sound: "the voice of ice," the midwinter sound of a whole frozen pond settling and expanding in its bed.

> Sometimes there was a sort of hollow oboe sound, and sometimes a groan with a delicate undertone of thunder. . . . Just as I turned to go, there came from below one curious and sinister crack which ran off into a sound like the whine of a giant whip of steel lashed through the moonlit air.

Planning, Drafting, and Developing

Now, how will you tell the stories you recall or present your observations to your readers? Look over your notes, highlighting whatever looks useful. When you start drafting, throw out details that don't matter. Plan how you will organize your essay by creating a simple scratch outline.

For more strategies for planning, drafting, and developing, see Chs. 17, 18, and 19.

Start with a Main Impression, Idea, or Thesis
Writing from recollection.

When writing from recall, a major challenge can be figuring out and focusing on a main idea. It can be tempting to include every detail that comes to mind. It is also easy to overlook details that would make the story clearer and more relevant to readers. When you are certain of your purpose in writing about a personal experience or event — that is, you know whether your goal is to inform, persuade, critique, and so on — you can transform a laundry list of details into a story narrative that connects events clearly around a main idea.

Start by jotting down a few words that identify your experience. Next, begin to shape these words into a sentence that states why the experience

For more on stating a thesis, see Ch. 16.

matters to you. If you're not yet sure about the main idea that you want to convey, just begin writing. You can work on your thesis as you revise.

| TOPIC IDEA + SLANT | Reunion in Georgia + liked meeting family |
| WORKING THESIS | When I went to Georgia for a family reunion, I enjoyed meeting my relatives. |

Writing from observation.

What main insight or impression do you want to convey? Answering this question will help you decide which details to include, which to omit, and how to avoid a dry list of facts.

PLACE OBSERVED	Smalley Green after lunch
MAIN IMPRESSION	Relaxing activity is good after a morning of classes.
WORKING THESIS	After their morning classes, students have fun relaxing on Smalley Green with their dogs and Frisbees.

If the details you've gathered overwhelm your ability to arrive at a main impression, take a break (and maybe a walk) and try to think of a statement that sums things up.

Organize with Your Purpose and Audience in Mind
Writing from recollection.

For more organization strategies, see pp. 271–80.

If you are recalling an experience for your readers, you can either establish the chronology of your story or tell it through flashbacks. Telling your story in the order that the events took place is the simplest way to reach your readers. On the other hand, you may want to start a story in the middle and then, through flashbacks, fill in whatever background a reader needs to know.

Writing from observation.

For transitions that mark place or direction, see p. 291.

If you are sharing your observations, map them out in a way that conveys the main impression you want to create for readers. Whatever your choice, add transitions that mark place or direction — words or phrases to guide the reader from one vantage point, location, or idea to the next. As you create your "picture," use details that bring a place to life and capture its spirit.

Revising and Editing

For more revising and editing strategies, see Ch. 21.

After you have written an early draft, put it aside for a few days. Then reread it carefully. Try to see it through the eyes of your readers, noting both pleasing and confusing spots, then revise it to make your writing clearer and stronger.

Focus on Your Main Idea, Impression, or Thesis. Revising your thesis or main idea helps you emphasize the point of your recollections or observations, to answer the question "So what?"

Writing from recollection.

As you reread your essay, return to your purpose: What was so important about the experience you're writing about? What makes it memorable? Will readers see why it was crucial to your life — and how it has changed you?

WORKING THESIS	When I went to Georgia for a family reunion, I enjoyed meeting my relatives.
REVISED THESIS	Meeting my Georgia relatives showed me how powerfully two values — generosity and resilience — unite my family.

Writing from observation.

As you begin to revise, have a friend read your observation, or read it yourself as if you had never seen the place you observed. Note gaps that would puzzle a reader, restate the spirit of the place, or sharpen the description of the main impression you want to convey in your thesis.

WORKING THESIS	After morning classes, students have fun relaxing on Smalley Green with their dogs and Frisbees.
REVISED THESIS	When students, dogs, and Frisbees accumulate on Smalley Green after lunch, they show how much campus learning takes place outside of class.

Learning by Doing 🔘 Strengthen Your Main Idea, Impression, or Thesis

As you read and revise your paper, strengthen your thesis by completing the following three sentences.

- The most important thing about my experience is _____.
- The main impression that I want to show my audience is _____.
- I want to share this so that my readers _____.

Next, exchange sentences with a classmate. Hone your thesis by asking each other questions to sharpen your statements about the experiences you're both describing.

STRENGTHENING YOUR THESIS

☐ Does the thesis convey your main impression or idea?

☐ Does the thesis clearly state why the experience or scene you are writing about was significant and memorable?

☐ Does the thesis focus on a single main idea, as opposed to various aspects of the experience or scene?

☐ Does the thesis need to be refined in response to any new insights you've gained while reflecting, researching, or writing?

Add Relevant, Powerful, and Concrete Details. Next, check your selection of details. Ask yourself whether you have made events or scenes come alive for your audience by recalling them in sufficient concrete detail. Be specific enough that your readers can see, smell, taste, hear, and feel what you experienced. Make sure that all details support your main idea or thesis. In student Robert Schreiner's essay "What Is a Hunter?," notice the focus in his second paragraph on the world outside his own skin: his close recall of the snow, of his grandfather's pointers about the habits of jackrabbits and the way to shoot them. Consider whether your own descriptions could be more vivid, powerful, or concrete. Could vague words such as *very, really, great,* or *beautiful* be replaced with more specific words? (Use the Find function to locate repetition, so you can reword for variety.)

Revisit the Organization of Your Essay
Writing from recollection.

Be sure you have followed a clear sequence. Reconsider the order of events, looking for changes that will make your essay easier for readers to follow. For example, if a classmate seems puzzled about the sequence of your draft, make a rough outline or list of main events to check the clarity of your arrangement. Or, add more transitions to connect events more clearly.

Writing from observation.

Check that you have presented your observations in an order that shows readers what your main impression is. Remove any extraneous or confusing details.

Peer Response 👥 Recalling and Observing

For general questions for a peer editor, see p. 309.

As you revise your draft, ask for feedback on it from a peer, such as a classmate or friend. Ask your peer editor to review your draft with the following questions in mind:

- What main insight or impression do you carry away from my draft?
- Which senses do I draw on particularly well? Which senses, if any, have I neglected?
- Can you see and feel what I experienced? Would more detail be more compelling? Put check marks wherever you want more details.
- How well have I used evidence from my senses to build a main impression? Which sensory impressions contribute most strongly to the overall picture? Which seem superfluous?
- If this paper were yours, what one thing would you work on?

REVISING YOUR DRAFT

Writing from recollection

☐ Where have you shown why this experience was important and how it changed your life?

☐ How have you engaged readers so they will keep reading? Will they see and feel your experience?

☐ If the events are not in chronological order, how have you made your organization easy for readers to follow?

☐ In what ways does the ending provide a sense of finality?

☐ Do you stick to a point? Is everything in the essay relevant to your main idea or thesis?

☐ If you portray people, how have you made their importance clear? Which details make them seem real, not just shadowy figures?

Writing from observation

☐ Have you accomplished your purpose — to convey to readers your overall impression of the subject and to share insights about it?

☐ What can you assume readers know? What do you need to tell them? Have you gathered enough observations to describe the subject? Have you observed with *all* your senses when possible — even smell and taste?

☐ Is your organizational pattern the best choice for your subject? Is it easy for your readers to follow? Would another pattern work better?

After you revise your essay, edit and proofread it. Carefully check the grammar, word choice, punctuation, and mechanics — and then correct any problems. If you added details, consider whether they're sufficiently blended with the ideas already there. Also check your paper's format using the Quick Format Guide. Follow the style expected by your instructor for features such as the heading, title, running head, page numbers, margins, and paragraph indentation.

For more editing and proofreading strategies, see pp. 316–18.

EDITING FOR DRAFT

☐ Is your sentence structure correct? Have you avoided writing fragments, comma splices, or fused sentences? **A1, A2**

☐ Have you used correct verb tenses and forms? When you present a sequence of past events, is it clear what happened first and what happened next? **A3**

☐ When you use transitions and other introductory elements to connect events, have you placed any needed commas after them? **D1**

☐ In your dialogue, have you placed commas and periods before (inside) the closing quotation mark? **D3**

For more help, find the relevant checklist sections in the Quick Editing Guide on p. Q-37. Turn also to the Quick Format Guide beginning on p. Q-1.

☐ Have you spelled everything correctly, especially the names of people and places? Have you capitalized names correctly?   E1, E2

☐ Have you used parallel structure wherever needed, especially in lists or comparisons?   B2

Reviewing and Reflecting

Writing from recollection

REVIEW Working with classmates or independently, respond to the following questions:

1. What is the major challenge of writing from recall? What is the best way to address this challenge?

2. Asking reporters' questions is one good strategy for recalling an experience. What are those questions? Try asking them about a significant experience you've had at school, in the workplace, or in your everyday life.

REFLECT Reflect in writing about how you might apply the insights gained from this assignment to another situation, in or outside of college, in which you recall an experience. Consider how your purpose might affect decisions about how you will tell your story and about the most relevant and significant details to include.

Writing from observation

REVIEW Working with classmates or independently, respond to the following questions:

1. To write a compelling description of a scene, you need to gather a lot of sensory details. How do you decide which ones to include or leave out?

2. What are the benefits of making both objective and subjective observations about a scene that you want to describe? Before answering the question, think of an interesting scene that you have observed on your campus or elsewhere and then make objective and subjective observations about it. How did this process deepen or enrich your perspective?

REFLECT Reflect in writing about how you might apply the insights that you drew from this assignment to another situation — in or outside of college — in which you have to observe a scene. In your reflection, consider the types of details you might include to get across your main impression.

Additional Writing Assignments

Writing from recollection

1. Choose a person outside your immediate family who has had a marked effect on your life, either good or bad. Jot down ten details that might show what that person was like: physical appearance, way of talking, habits, or memorable incidents. Then look back at "Returning to My Father's Koreatown" to identify the kinds of detail that Margaret Rhee uses to portray her father, noting any that you might add to your list. Write your paper, including details to help readers experience the person's impact on you.

2. Recall a place you were fond of as a child — your grandmother's kitchen, a tree house, a library, a locker room, a vacation spot. What made it different from other places? Why was it important? What do you feel when you remember it? Write a paper in which you use specific, concrete details to explain to readers why this place was memorable. If you have a photograph of the place, look at it to jog your memory, and consider adding it to your paper.

3. Write a paper or a podcast text to recall a familiar ceremony, ritual, or observation, perhaps a rite of passage (confirmation, bar or bat mitzvah, college orientation, graduation, etc.). How did the tradition originate? Who takes part? How has it changed over the years? What does it add to the lives of those who observe it? Share with readers the importance of the tradition to you.

4. **Visual assignment.** Examine the image below. Can you relate to it in any way? Can you recall a similar event in your life? If so, what was its importance to you? How did the experience affect or even change you? Write an essay in which you briefly recall your experience and then reflect on its significance for you.

wundervisuals/E+/Getty Images

Writing from observation

1. To develop your powers of observation, go for a walk through an unfa-miliar scene or one worth a closer look (such as a supermarket or an open field). Avoid a familiar subject. Record your observations in two or three detailed paragraphs. Sum up your impression of the place, including any opinion you form through close observation.

2. Select an observation site that relates to your career plans. You might choose a medical facility (for nursing or medical school), a school or play-ground (for education), or an office complex, financial district, or work site (for business). Observe carefully, noting details that contribute to your main impression of the place and your insight about work done there. Write an essay to convey these points to an audience interested in the same career path.

For advice on analyzing an image, see Ch. 13, Responding to Visual Representations.

3. **Visual Assignment**. Look the following photograph to explore the importance of the observer's point of view. After a preliminary look at the scene, select your vantage point as an observer, and identify the audience your essay will address (for example, readers who would or would not share your perspective). Observe the image carefully, and use its details to support your main impression of the scene from your perspective. Direct your specific insight about it to your audience.

Zoran Milich/Moment Mobile/Getty Images

Interviewing for Information

Maddie Meyer/Getty Images

Responding to an Image

Suppose that you had an opportunity to interview the American gymnast and Olympic Gold medalist, Simone Biles. What questions would you most like to ask her? Based on Biles's public image and personality, as revealed in this photo, what kind of response would you expect to receive? How do you think the photographer has tried to suggest something about Biles?

Why Interviewing for Information Matters

Do you need ideas for what to write about? Or, do you have a topic in mind, and aren't sure what to do first? Go talk with someone. Meet for half an hour with an anthropology professor, and you will likely gather enough material for a paper. Just as likely, you can get a paper's worth of information from a ten-minute exchange with a mechanic who relines brakes. Both the mechanic and the professor are experts. But even people who aren't usually considered experts may provide you with material.

You can direct a conversation by asking questions designed to draw out the information you want. You do so in an *interview* — a conversation with a purpose. Interviews can help you get to know other people, understand their perspectives, and discover what they know. You may use what you learn to profile the individuals interviewed. Other purposes for an interview include: gathering expert information about a topic, collecting information from samples of representative people, and accessing firsthand accounts of an event or an era.

Interviewing skills can help you in various contexts, including the following:

In a College Course

- For your American Studies course, you gather firsthand knowledge about a moment in history by interviewing a veteran, a civil rights activist, a disaster survivor, or a person who experienced a local event.

- You might interview a person who mentors students or who sponsors internships that provide students with career advice (perhaps an internship with an early childhood educator, an artist, or a catering manager).

In the Workplace

- You interview an "informed source" for a news site, a benefits specialist for a profile in your company newsletter, or your customers or clients for feedback on company products and services.

In Your Community

- You contact experts to learn about composting food waste through the new city program or about installing a ramp to make your home wheelchair accessible.

? Whom would you like to interview as an intriguing personality? Whom would you like to interview for answers or advice? In what situations might you conduct interviews in the future?

Learning from Other Writers

The writers of the following two essays drew on interviews with others. In their essays, they report on their conversations, using direct quotations and telling details. To help you analyze the readings, look at the notes in the margin. They identify features such as the main idea, or thesis, and the quotations that provide support. As you read these interview essays, ask yourself the following questions:

1. Did the writer conduct an informal talk or a planned interview? In the essay, does the writer report the conversation directly or indirectly?

2. What does the writer reveal about the character and personality of the speaker (interviewee)? What does the writer (interviewer) reveal about him- or herself? And, what specialized or expert information does the writer draw from the interviewee?

3. For the writer, what value does the interview bring to the essay?

Jon Ronson

How One Stupid Tweet Blew Up Justine Sacco's Life

Jon Ronson is a journalist, a radio personality, the author of several books, and a documentary filmmaker. The following selections from an article published in the *New York Times Magazine* capture his interviews of Justine Sacco, who was widely shamed on social media after posting a tweet that many considered racially offensive. The article was adapted from Ronson's book *So You've Been Publicly Shamed* (2015).

Geraint Lewis/AP Images

1   As she made the long journey from New York to South Africa, to visit family during the holidays in 2013, Justine Sacco, thirty years old and the senior director of corporate communications at IAC [InterActiveCorp], began tweeting acerbic° little jokes about the indignities° of travel. There was one about a fellow passenger on the flight from John F. Kennedy International Airport:

2   " 'Weird German Dude: You're in First Class. It's 2014. Get some deodorant.' — Inner monologue as I inhale BO. Thank God for pharmaceuticals."

3   Then, during her layover at Heathrow:°

4   "Chilly — cucumber sandwiches — bad teeth. Back in London!"

5   And on December 20, before the final leg of her trip to Cape Town:

6   "Going to Africa. Hope I don't get AIDS. Just kidding. I'm white!"

7   She chuckled to herself as she pressed send on this last one, then wandered around Heathrow's international terminal for half an hour, sporadically° checking her phone. No one replied, which didn't surprise her. She had only 170 Twitter followers.

8   Sacco boarded the plane. It was an eleven-hour flight, so she slept. When the plane landed in Cape Town and was taxiing on the runway, she turned on her phone. Right away, she got a text from someone she hadn't spoken to since high school: "I'm so sorry to see what's happening." Sacco looked at it, baffled.

> Vivid story about the interview subject provides context for the interview

9   Then another text: "You need to call me immediately." It was from her best friend, Hannah. Then her phone exploded with more texts and alerts. And then it rang. It was Hannah. "You're the No. 1 worldwide trend on Twitter right now," she said.

10   Sacco's Twitter feed had become a horror show. "In light of @Justine Sacco disgusting racist tweet, I'm donating to @care today" and "How did @Justine-Sacco get a PR job?! Her level of racist ignorance belongs on Fox News. #AIDS can affect anyone!" and "I'm an IAC employee and I don't want @JustineSacco doing any communications on our behalf ever again. Ever." And then one from her employer, IAC, the corporate owner of The Daily Beast, OKCupid, and Vimeo: "This is an outrageous, offensive comment. Employee in question currently unreachable on an intl flight." The anger soon turned to excitement: "All I want for Christmas is to see @JustineSacco's face when her plane lands

---

acerbic: Harsh.   **indignities:** Humiliations.   **Heathrow:** A major airport in west London, England.   **sporadically:** Occasionally.

and she checks her inbox/voicemail" and "Oh man, @JustineSacco is going to have the most painful phone-turning-on moment ever when her plane lands" and "We are about to watch this @JustineSacco bitch get fired. In REAL time. Before she even KNOWS she's getting fired."

By the time Sacco had touched down, tens of thousands of angry tweets had been sent in response to her joke. Hannah, meanwhile, frantically deleted her friend's tweet and her account—Sacco didn't want to look—but it was far too late. "Sorry @JustineSacco," wrote one Twitter user, "your tweet lives on forever."   11

In the early days of Twitter, I was a keen shamer. When newspaper columnists made racist or homophobic statements, I joined the pile-on. Sometimes I led it. . . .   12

[Interviewer explains why he is personally interested in the interviewee's predicament]

[I]n those early days, the collective fury felt righteous, powerful, and effective. It felt as if hierarchies° were being dismantled, as if justice were being democratized. As time passed, though, I watched these shame campaigns multiply, to the point that they targeted not just powerful institutions and public figures but really anyone perceived to have done something offensive. I also began to marvel at the disconnect between the severity of the crime and the gleeful savagery of the punishment. It almost felt as if shamings were now happening for their own sake, as if they were following a script. . . .   13

Late one afternoon last year, I met Justine Sacco in New York, at a restaurant in Chelsea called Cookshop. Dressed in rather chic business attire, Sacco ordered a glass of white wine. Just three weeks had passed since her trip to Africa, and she was still a person of interest to the media. Web sites had already ransacked° her Twitter feed for more horrors. (For example, "I had a sex dream about an autistic kid last night," from 2012, was unearthed by BuzzFeed in the article "16 Tweets Justine Sacco Regrets.") A *New York Post* photographer had been following her to the gym.   14

"Only an insane person would think that white people don't get AIDS," she told me. It was about the first thing she said to me when we sat down.   15

[Quotations show the interviewee's personality and concerns]

Sacco had been three hours or so into her flight when retweets of her joke began to overwhelm my Twitter feed. I could understand why some people found it offensive. Read literally, she said that white people don't get AIDS, but it seems doubtful many interpreted it that way. More likely it was her apparently gleeful flaunting° of her privilege that angered people. But after thinking about her tweet for a few seconds more, I began to suspect that it wasn't racist but a reflexive° critique of white privilege—on our tendency to naively imagine ourselves immune from life's horrors. Sacco . . . had been yanked violently out of the context of her small social circle. Right?   16

"To me it was so insane of a comment for anyone to make," she said. "I thought there was no way that anyone could possibly think it was literal."° (She would later write me an email to elaborate on this point. "Unfortunately, I am not a character on *South Park* or a comedian, so I had no business commenting on the epidemic in such a politically incorrect manner on a   17

hierarchies: Systems in which certain people or offices are placed higher than others. **ransacked:** Raided. **flaunting:** Displaying. **reflexive:** Automatic. **literal:** True; authentic.

public platform," she wrote. "To put it simply, I wasn't trying to raise awareness of AIDS or piss off the world or ruin my life. Living in America puts us in
a bit of a bubble when it comes to what is going on in the third world. I was
making fun of that bubble.")

I would be the only person she spoke to on the record about what   18
happened to her, she said. It was just too harrowing° — and "as a publicist,"
inadvisable — but she felt it was necessary, to show how "crazy" her situation
was, how her punishment simply didn't fit the crime.

"I cried out my body weight in the first twenty-four hours," she told me.   19
"It was incredibly traumatic. You don't sleep. You wake up in the middle of
the night forgetting where you are." She released an apology statement and
cut short her vacation. Workers were threatening to strike at the hotels she
had booked if she showed up. She was told no one could guarantee her safety.

Her extended family in South Africa were African National Congress   20
supporters — the party of Nelson Mandela.° They were longtime activists for
racial equality. When Justine arrived at the family home from the airport,
one of the first things her aunt said to her was: "This is not what our family
stands for. And now, by association, you've almost tarnished the family."

As she told me this, Sacco started to cry. I sat looking at her for a moment.   21
Then I tried to improve the mood. I told her that "sometimes, things need to
reach a brutal nadir° before people see sense."

More quotations from
tho interviewee convey
her emotional state

"Wow," she said. She dried her eyes. "Of all the things I could have been in soci-   22
ety's collective consciousness, it never struck me that I'd end up a brutal nadir."

She glanced at her watch. It was nearly 6 p.m. The reason she wanted to   23
meet me at this restaurant, and that she was wearing her work clothes, was
that it was only a few blocks away from her office. At 6, she was due in there
to clean out her desk.

"All of a sudden you don't know what you're supposed to do," she said. "If   24
I don't start making steps to reclaim my identity and remind myself of who I
am on a daily basis, then I might lose myself."

The restaurant's manager approached our table. She sat down next to   25
Sacco, fixed her with a look and said something in such a low volume I couldn't
hear it, only Sacco's reply: "Oh, you think I'm going to be grateful for this?"

We agreed to meet again, but not for several months. She was determined   26
to prove that she could turn her life around. "I can't just sit at home and
watch movies every day and cry and feel sorry for myself," she said. "I'm going
to come back."

After she left, Sacco later told me, she got only as far as the lobby of her   27
office building before she broke down crying. . . .

It's possible that Sacco's fate would have been different had an anonymous   28
tip not led a writer named Sam Biddle to the offending tweet. Biddle was then
the editor of Valleywag, Gawker Media's tech-industry blog. He retweeted it to
his 15,000 followers and eventually posted it on Valleywag, accompanied by
the headline, "And Now, a Funny Holiday Joke from IAC's P.R. Boss."

harrowing: Agonizing.   **Nelson Mandela:** South Africa's first black president and a central
figure in overturning the country's system of racial segregation and oppression.   **nadir:** The
lowest point.

In January 2014, I received an email from Biddle, explaining his reasoning. 29
"The fact that she was a P.R. chief made it delicious," he wrote. "It's satisfying to be able to say, 'O.K., let's make a racist tweet by a senior IAC employee count this time.' And it did. I'd do it again." Biddle said he was surprised to see how quickly her life was upended, however. "I never wake up and hope I [get someone fired] that day—and certainly never hope to ruin anyone's life." Still, he ended his email by saying that he had a feeling she'd be "fine eventually, if not already."

He added: "Everyone's attention span is so short. They'll be mad about 30 something new today."

Four months after we first met, Justine Sacco made good on her promise. 31
We met for lunch at a French bistro downtown. I told her what Biddle had said—about how she was probably fine now. I was sure he wasn't being deliberately glib,° but like everyone who participates in mass online destruction, uninterested in learning that it comes with a cost.

"Well, I'm not fine yet," Sacco said to me. "I had a great career, and I loved 32 my job, and it was taken away from me, and there was a lot of glory in that. Everybody else was very happy about that."

Sacco pushed her food around on her plate, and let me in on one of the 33 hidden costs of her experience. "I'm single; so it's not like I can date, because we Google everyone we might date," she said. "That's been taken away from me too." She was down, but I did notice one positive change in her. When I first met her, she talked about the shame she had brought on her family. But she no longer felt that way. Instead, she said, she just felt personally humiliated.

Biddle was almost right about one thing: Sacco did get a job offer right 34 away. But it was an odd one, from the owner of a Florida yachting company. "He said: 'I saw what happened to you. I'm fully on your side,' " she told me. Sacco knew nothing about yachts, and she questioned his motives. ("Was he a crazy person who thinks white people can't get AIDS?") Eventually she turned him down.

After that, she left New York, going as far away as she could, to Addis 35 Ababa, Ethiopia. She flew there alone and got a volunteer job doing P.R. for an NGO° working to reduce maternal-mortality rates. "It was fantastic," she said. She was on her own, and she was working. If she was going to be made to suffer for a joke, she figured she should get something out of it. "I never would have lived in Addis Ababa for a month otherwise," she told me. She was struck by how different life was there. Rural areas had only intermittent° power and no running water or Internet. Even the capital, she said, had few street names or house addresses.

Addis Ababa was great for a month, but she knew going in that she would 36 not be there long. She was a New York City person. Sacco is nervy and sassy and sort of debonair.° And so she returned to work at Hot or Not, which had

More background
on the interviewee's
predicament

---

glib: Smooth-talking.   **NGO:** Non-governmental organization.   **intermittent:** Occasional.
debonair: Charming.

been a popular site for rating strangers' looks on the pre-social Internet and was reinventing itself as a dating app.

But despite her near invisibility on social media, she was still ridiculed 37 and demonized across the Internet. Biddle wrote a Valleywag post after she returned to the workforce: "Sacco, who apparently spent the last month hiding in Ethiopia after infuriating our species with an idiotic AIDS joke, is now a 'marketing and promotion' director at Hot or Not."

"How perfect!" he wrote. "Two lousy has-beens, gunning for a comeback 38 together." . . .

Recently, I wrote to Sacco to tell her I was putting her story in the *Times*, 39 and I asked her to meet me one final time to update me on her life. Her response was speedy. "No way." She explained that she had a new job in communications, though she wouldn't say where. She said, "Anything that puts the spotlight on me is a negative."

It was a profound° reversal for Sacco. When I first met her, she was 40 desperate to tell the tens of thousands of people who tore her apart how they had wronged her and to repair what remained of her public persona.° But perhaps she had now come to understand that her shaming wasn't really about her at all. Social media is so perfectly designed to manipulate our desire for approval, and that is what led to her undoing. Her tormentors were instantly congratulated as they took Sacco down, bit by bit, and so they continued to do so. Their motivation was much the same as Sacco's own — a bid for the attention of strangers — as she milled° about Heathrow, hoping to amuse people she couldn't see.

THESIS gives dominant impression of interviewee and makes a larger point

profound: Deep; significant.   **persona:** Someone's perceived personality.   **milled:** Wandered aimlessly.

Questions to Start You Thinking

Meaning

1. What faults did Twitter users find in Justine Sacco's tweet about AIDS in Africa? What did Sacco actually mean by the tweet, according to her explanation to Ronson?

2. Why was Ronson personally interested in the public shaming of Sacco? In his view, how have "shame campaigns" changed over the years (paragraph 13)?

3. In the final paragraph, Ronson says, "perhaps [Sacco] had now come to understand that her shaming wasn't really about her at all." What, according to Ronson, might have been the actual purpose of the public ridicule she faced?

Writing Strategies

4. Ronson provides a good deal of background about Sacco's tweeting fiasco and its consequences before presenting the content of his interviews with her. Do you think this is an effective strategy? Why, or why not?

5. As Ronson indicates, he conducted two separate interviews with Sacco. How, if at all, did the passage of time affect the nature of her responses? What might be the advantages or disadvantages of conducting separate interviews over time?

6. Ronson waits until the end of his essay to make a larger point about Sacco and the motivations behind public shaming. Do you think this is the best place to make this point, or should it have been presented earlier? Explain your reasoning.

Lorena A. Ryan-Hines   Student Essay

Looking Backwards, Moving Forward

Lorena Ryan-Hines, a student in a nursing program, wrote this essay after interviewing an experienced professional in her field.

Someone once said, "You cannot truly know where you are going unless you know where you have come from." I don't think I understood this statement until I got the opportunity to sit down with Joan Gilmore, assistant director of nursing at Smithville Health Care Center. With the blur of everyday activities going on during the change of third shift to first shift at the nursing home, I had never recognized what value Joan could bring to the younger nurses. Once we started to talk, I began to realize that, although I am a nurse, I don't know much about how nursing has evolved over the years. During our conversation, I discovered how much history, wisdom, and advice Joan has to share.

❓ Can you identify with Ryan-Hines's work environment and relationship with Joan? In what ways?

Joan tries to stay as active as she can working on the floor so she does not use an office. We decided to sit down in one of the multi-purpose conference rooms. Joan looks very good for a woman of her age. In fact, no one would ever suspect by looking at her that she is sixty-four years old. She is approximately 5'2" tall and dressed in white scrub pants with a flowered scrub top. She is not flashy or outspoken, but she knows what she is doing. However, if she has a question, she does not have a problem asking someone else.

When we first sat down, we started talking about how she grew up. She was the third child of seven children. Her father worked in a factory and also farmed over one hundred acres. Her mom stayed home to take care of the children. As I watched her talk about her upbringing, I could see a slight twinkle in her eyes. She almost appeared to have traveled back in time to her childhood. She went on to explain to me that she decided to go to nursing school because it was one of the few jobs, forty-five years ago, that could be productive for a woman.

❓ Why do you think that the "dignity cap" was so important for Joan?

She decided to enter the three-year program at St. Elizabeth Hospital's School for Nursing in Dayton, Ohio. Students were not allowed to be married and had to live in the nursing school's brick dormitory. Whenever they were in class and on the floors of the hospital, they were required to wear their uniforms, light blue dresses with white pinstripes. The student nursing cap, the "dignity cap" as Joan called it, was all white. When students graduated, they earned their black stripe which distinguished them as registered nurses. Joan said that she did not think that the all-white uniforms or nursing caps were practical. However, she conveyed a sense of sadness when she said, "I think we have gone too far because now everyone dresses and looks the same. I think as a nurse you have worked hard and earned the right to stand out somehow."

I asked Joan about the pros and cons of being a registered nurse and whether she ever regretted her decision. Her philosophy is that being a nurse is a calling. Although nursing pay is generally considered a decent living wage, sometimes dealing with management, long hours, and the grief of tough cases is hard. Through experience and commitment, a nurse learns to take each day as it comes and to grow with it. Even though life-and-death situations can be very stressful and the fast-paced world of nursing can be draining, nurses can never forget that patients are people who need our care. For Joan, when patients are demanding and short-fused, they are not really angry at the nurses but at the situation they are in. She believes that a nurse is always able to help her patients in some way, be it physical or emotional.

The advice Joan gave me about becoming a new registered nurse may be some of the best advice of my life. Each registered nursing specialty has its demands. She recommended working for a while in a medical surgery area. This area is a great place to gain knowledge and experience about multiple acute illnesses and disease processes. From there, nurses can move forward and find the specialty areas that best suit them. This fit is important because nurses need to be knowledgeable and confident, leaders who are not afraid to ask questions when they do not know the answers. To gain the respect of others, nurses also must be willing to help and to let others help them because no one can be a nurse all alone, in a vacuum. Joan recommends being courteous, saying "please" and "thank you" when asking someone to do something, and encouraging others with different talents. Lastly, she urged me to always do my best and be proud of my accomplishments.

Afterwards, I thanked her for the advice and her time. She got up smiling and simply walked out of the room and back to the job she has loved for so many years. I found myself sitting back down for a few minutes to reflect on everything she had just told me. Nursing from yesterday to today has changed not only with the technological advances but even the simplest things. Uniforms are nothing like they were forty years ago. The rules back then could never be enforced today. Some things will never change though, like the simple respect a nurse gives another human being. The profound advice Joan gave me is something I will carry with me for the rest of my personal and professional career.

5

6

7

❓ Have you ever received valuable advice from someone like Joan? How has that advice affected you and your decisions?

Work Cited

Gilmore, Joan. Personal interview, 4 June 2018.

Questions to Start You Thinking

Meaning

1. What is the main point of Ryan-Hines's essay?

2. What kind of person is Joan Gilmore? How does Ryan-Hines feel about her?

3. How is Gilmore's history the history of nursing during the last few decades? Is an interview an effective method of relating the history of a profession? Why, or why not?

Writing Strategies

4. Why does Ryan-Hines begin her essay with a quotation and an impression of the nursing home? How does this opening serve as a frame for her conversation with Joan?

5. How much of the interview does Ryan-Hines quote directly? Why does she choose to quote directly rather than paraphrase in these places? Would her essay be stronger if she used more of Joan's own words?

6. Using highlighters or marginal notes, identify the essay's introduction, thesis, major emphases, supporting details for each emphasis, and conclusion. How effective is the organization of this essay?

Learning by Writing

The Assignment: Writing an Essay Based on an Interview

Interview someone who is knowledgeable in an area you would like to learn about, then write an informative essay about it. Base your paper primarily on your interview with that person. Select any acquaintance, relative, or person you have heard about whose traits, interests, and knowledge will intrigue your readers. Your purpose is to 1) show this person's character and personality — to bring your interviewee to life for your readers — and 2) share with readers the specific knowledge that your interviewee possesses.

Generating Ideas

For more on each strategy for generating ideas in this section, or for additional strategies, see Ch. 15.

If an image of the perfect subject has flashed into your mind, consider yourself lucky, and set up an appointment with that person at once. If you have drawn a blank, you'll need to cast about for a likely interview subject.

Brainstorm for Possible People to Interview. Try brainstorming for a few minutes to see what pops into your mind. Your subject need not be spectacular or unusual; ordinary lives can make fascinating reading.

MANAGING YOUR TIME
Writing an Essay Based on an Interview

Use the breakdown below to plan your time for this essay; in the right column, insert target dates and times for completing each stage.

approx. 30-45 minutes

- **Read your assignment carefully.** Is it clear what your instructor is asking of you? If not, follow up.
- **Brainstorm** to arrive at a topic or area of interest that you'd like to write about, and identify a person who can provide insights and knowledge on that topic.
- **Identify your purpose and audience.** What do you want to learn from your interviewee? What will your readers be most interested in?

I'll complete this stage by:

———————
(day, date)

approx. 1 hour

- **Draft interview questions.** What questions will help you to learn about your topic? What questions can your interviewee shed light on and the topic he or she is going to discuss with you?
- **Ask peers to review your interview questions.** Revise as needed.

I'll complete this stage by:

———————
(day, date)

approx. 2-3 hours

- **Contact your interviewee,** set up your interview, and send your questions so that he or she can prepare.
- **Conduct your interview.** Record your interview (in audio or video), if your interviewee agrees to that. Take notes of major points.
- **Evaluate your material.** Identify the most significant information or insights that your interviewee shared.

I'll complete this stage by:

———————
(day, date)

approx. 2-3 hours

- **Sketch an outline.** Begin with your thesis, jotting down the two or three main points you will make under each.
- **Draft your essay,** staying close to your outline. Support your thesis with relevant details and quotations from the interview.
- Craft an engaging **introduction** and a satisfying **conclusion.**

I'll complete this stage by:

———————
(day, date)

approx. 2-4 hours

- Ask a **peer to review** your draft. Have you described your interviewee in a memorable way? Have you conveyed the most significant knowledge that your interviewee shared?
- **Revise your draft,** addressing issues raised during your and your peer's review.
- **Edit your draft,** fixing any errors and polishing your prose.

I'll complete this stage by:

———————
(day, date)

IDENTIFYING A PERSON TO INTERVIEW

☐ Is there an expert or a leader whom you admire or are puzzled by?

☐ Do you know someone whose job or hobby interests you?

☐ Are you acquainted with anyone who has specialized knowledge on a topic?

☐ What older person could tell you about life thirty or even fifty years ago?

☐ Who has passionate convictions about society, politics, sex, community, or family?

☐ Whose background and life history would you like to know more about?

☐ Whose lifestyle, values, or attitudes are utterly different from your own and from those of most people you know?

Tap Local Interview Resources. Investigate campus resources such as departmental or faculty Web pages, student activity officers and sponsors, recent yearbook photographs, stories from the newspaper archives, or facilities such as the theater, media, or sports centers. Look on campus, at work, or in your community for people with intriguing backgrounds or experiences. Identify several prospects in case your first choice isn't available.

Set Up the Interview. Find out whether your prospect will grant an interview, talk at length—an hour, say—and agree to appear in your paper. If you sense reluctance, reach out to someone else. Don't be timid about asking for an interview. After all, your request is flattering, acknowledging that person as someone with valuable things to say. Try to schedule the interview on your subject's own ground—his or her home or workplace. The details you observe in those surroundings can make your essay more vivid. A phone or an email interview sounds easy but lacks the interplay you can achieve face-to-face. You'll miss observing or seeing smiles, frowns, or other body language that reveals personality. Meet in person if possible, or set up an online video chat.

Prepare Questions. The interview will go better if you are an informed interviewer with prepared questions. To develop thoughtful questions, consider what you want to learn about your topic. Questions that ask "how?" or "why?" will lead to better discussion than simple "yes/no" questions. Find out a bit about your subject's life history, experience, affiliations, and interests, too. It's also a good idea to send your questions to your interviewee well before the interview so that he or she can prepare thoughtful responses. Ask about the person's background, everyday tasks, or favorite parts of his or her job. Focus on whatever aspects best reveal what you want to convey. Good questions will help you lead the conversation where you want it to go, get it back on track when it strays, and avoid awkward silences. To interview someone with an unusual job or hobby, try questions like these:

- How long have you been a _____ ?
- How did you get involved in this work?

- What is the most surprising thing about your field?
- What happens in a typical day? What do you like most or least?
- How has this job changed your life or your concerns?
- What are your plans and hopes for the future?

One good question can get some people talking for hours, and four or five may be enough for any interview, but it's better to prepare too many than too few.

Learning by Doing 🎙 Analyzing Interview Questions

Listen to several radio interviews on a local station or National Public Radio (which archives many types of interviews, including programs such as *Fresh Air*). As you listen, jot down the names of the interviewer and interviewee, the topic, and any particularly fruitful or useless questions. Working with others in person or online, discuss your conclusions about the success of the interviews you heard. Collaborate on a set of guidelines for preparing good questions and dodging bad ones.

Be Flexible and Observant. Sometimes a question won't interest your subject. Or the person may seem reluctant to answer, especially if you're unwittingly trespassing into private territory, such as someone's love life. Don't badger. If you wait silently for a bit, you might be rewarded. If not, just go on to the next question. Should the conversation drift, steer it back: "But to get back to what you were saying about. . . ." Sometimes the most rewarding question simply grows out of what the subject says or an item you note in the environment. Observing your subject's clothing, expressions, mannerisms, or equipment may also suggest unexpected facets of personality. For example, Ryan-Hines describes Joan Gilmore's appearance as she introduces her character.

For more on using observation, see Ch. 4.

Peer Response 👥 Get Feedback on Your Interview Questions

Ask a classmate to read the questions you plan to use in your interview. Then interview your classmate, asking the following:

- Are the questions appropriate for the person who will be interviewed?
- Will the questions help gather the information I am seeking?
- Are any of the questions unclear? How could I rephrase them?
- Do any of the questions seem redundant? Irrelevant?
- What additional questions would you suggest that I ask?

Record the Interview. Many interviewers use only paper and pen to take notes unobtrusively. Even though they can't write down everything the person says, they want to look the subject in the eye and keep the conversation lively. As you take notes, be sure to include details on the scene—names and dates, numbers, addresses, surroundings, physical appearance. Also jot down memorable words exactly as the speaker says them, and put quotation marks around them. When you transcribe your notes, you will know that they are quoted directly.

Many professionals advise against using a recorder because it may inhibit the subject and make the interviewer lazy about concentrating on the subject's responses. Too often, the objections go, it tempts the interviewer simply to quote rambling conversation without shaping it into good writing. If you do bring a recorder to your interview, be sure that the person you're talking with has no objections. Even if you record, write down the interviewee's main points; later, use your recording to check quotations for accuracy or add more words from the interview. As soon you complete your interview, write down everything you recall but couldn't record. The questions you prepared for the interview will guide your memory, as will notes you took while talking.

Learning by Doing Practicing by Interviewing a Classmate

Interview a classmate to learn more about him or her. Record specific details about that person's life, identifying commonalities between the two of you. Perhaps you both attended the same school or share a birthday month. Look for differences, too. For example, your interview partner might have unique skills or talents, knowledge about a subject that is unfamiliar to you, or memories that he or she considers especially significant. Use your notes to write a one-paragraph "spotlight" feature on your classmate.

Planning, Drafting, and Developing

For more strategies for planning, drafting, and developing, see Chs. 16, 17, and 18.

After your interview, you may have a good idea of what to include in your first draft, what to emphasize, what to quote directly, and what to summarize. But if your notes seem to be a confused jumble, what should you do?

Evaluate Your Material. As you review the material you gathered during your interview, remember your purpose: to present information that your interviewee supplied on his or her area of interest or expertise. Start by listing details you're likely to include in your essay. Photographs, sketches, or your doodles also may help you find a focus. As you sift your material, consider the following:

- Overall, what did you learn from your interviewee? What aspects of his or her expertise and knowledge are most valuable to you?

- What specific parts of your interviewee's responses will be most informative and interesting to your audience?
- Which direct quotations reveal the most about your topic? Which are the most informative, surprising, or insightful?

Focus Your Thesis. Once you have the reviewed your material, identify the most interesting pieces of information you learned from your interview. What questions did the interview answer, and what conclusions can you draw about the topic? Pick details from the interview that best illustrate the points you want to make. Develop your thesis based on both your dominant impression of the interviewee and the statements and details that will interest your readers.

For more on stating a thesis, see pp. 266–71.

| DOMINANT IMPRESSION | Del talked a lot about freedom of the press. |
| WORKING THESIS | According to Del Sampat, freedom of the press is a huge concern for journalists today. |

Once you have a working thesis, list the evidence from the interview you can use to support each point. If you are writing your interview essay in the first person, as Ryan-Hines did, you may personalize the thesis statement by including yourself as the observer:

| RYAN-HINES'S THESIS | During our conversation, I discovered how much history, wisdom, and advice Joan has to share. |

Bring Your Subject to Life. To bring a little color to your informative essay, think how you can convey your interviewee's personality. A quotation, a physical description, a detail about your subject at home or at work can bring the person instantly to life in your reader's mind. A carefully placed image can supplement but not overshadow your essay.

For more on selecting and presenting quotations, see D3 (pp. Q-28–Q-29) and D6 (pp. Q-30–Q-31) in the Quick Research Guide. For more on using visuals, see pp. 320–23.

When you quote directly, be as accurate as possible, and don't put into quotation marks anything your interviewee didn't say. Sometimes you may quote a whole sentence or more, sometimes just a phrase. Be selective and strategic. Use quotations to reveal the information that you wish to emphasize — along with your own perspective and observations of what the interviewee said.

Double-Check Important Information. Maybe you can't read your hasty handwriting or some crucial information escaped your notes. In such a case, call or email the person you interviewed to ask specific questions. You might also read back any direct quotations you plan to use so your subject can confirm their accuracy.

Revising and Editing

As you read over your first draft, keep in mind that your purpose was to convey information and make your interviewee come alive for your reader.

For more revising and editing strategies, see Ch. 19.

Peer Response 👥 Get Feedback on Your Essay

For general questions for a peer editor, see p. 309.

Have a classmate or friend read your draft and answer these questions to make the portrait more vivid, complete, and clear:

- Does the opening make you want to know more about the topic? If so, how has the writer interested you? If not, what gets in your way?
- What makes the interviewee interesting to the writer?
- What is the writer's dominant impression of the person interviewed?
- What knowledge does the interviewee share with the writer? Is it engaging and well-supported? Is it presented in a way that makes you want to continue reading?
- Do the quoted words or reported speech "sound" real to you? What words or phrases did the interviewee use that were particularly memorable or insightful?
- Do you have questions about the interviewee or the subject(s) discussed in the essay?
- If this paper were yours, what is the one thing you would be sure to work on before handing it in?

Support Your Thesis. Once you have finished a draft, you may still feel swamped by too much information. Will readers find your essay overloaded? Will they understand the main idea you want to convey? To be certain that they will, polish and refine your thesis, giving readers a preview of the points you will make in your essay.

WORKING THESIS	According to Del Sampat, freedom of the press is a huge concern for journalists today.
REVISED THESIS	According to Del Sampat, news editor for the *Campus Times*, freedom of the press is at risk of being eroded both in the United States and worldwide.

In this example, the revised thesis identifies the interviewee and lets readers know that the essay will focus on both domestic and international attacks on the press.

STRENGTHENING YOUR THESIS

- ☐ Does the thesis get across them main points you want to make?
- ☐ Does it convey these points as clearly as possible?
- ☐ Could you make the thesis more specific or vivid based on insights you gathered from your interview?
- ☐ Is there sufficient evidence to support each point?

Learning by Doing 🔲 Supporting a Thesis

Examine an essay you wrote for this class or another, underlining your thesis. Using highlighters or the highlighting tool on your word-processing program, highlight the main points the essay makes, assigning each one a distinct color. Go through the essay and highlight the evidence that supports each point, using its assigned color. Afterward, examine your essay. Do the colors appear out of order, suggesting a disorganized essay? Check for balance. Are any colors over- or underrepresented? Consider using this color coding strategy to help with longer essays.

Spend time rereading the body of your essay, making sure each paragraph is focused and specific.

REVISING YOUR DRAFT

☐ Does your paper need a stronger beginning to interest your readers? Does your ending give readers a satisfactory takeaway from your interview?

☐ Are readers given sufficient background information to understand the interviewee's points? Does any jargon or technical terms need to be explained?

☐ Should some quotations be summarized or indirectly quoted? Should some explanations be enlivened by adding specific quotations?

☐ When your direct quotations are read out loud, do they sound as if they come from the mouth of the person you're portraying?

☐ Have you included your own pertinent observations and insights?

☐ Does any of your material strike you now as irrelevant or dull?

After you have revised your essay, edit and proofread it. Carefully check the grammar, word choice, punctuation, and mechanics — and then correct any problems you find.

EDITING FOR CLARITY

☐ Is it clear what each *he, she, they,* or other pronoun refers to? Does each pronoun agree with (match) its antecedent?   **A6**

☐ Have you used the correct case (*he* or *him*) for all your pronouns?   **A5**

☐ Is your sentence structure correct? Have you avoided writing fragments, comma splices, or fused sentences?   **A1, A2**

☐ Have you used quotation marks, ellipses (to show the omission of words), and other punctuation correctly in all quotations?   **D3**

For more editing and proofreading strategies, see pp. 316–18.

For more help, find the relevant checklist sections in the Quick Editing Guide on p. Q-37. Turn also to the Quick Format Guide beginning on p. Q-1.

Reviewing and Reflecting

REVIEW Working with classmates or independently, respond to the following questions:

1. What are some strategies for finding an interesting person to interview? Using one or more of these strategies, identify two or three possible interview candidates.

2. Once you have conducted an interview, what strategies can you use to evaluate the information that you've gathered and to identify the most useful material?

3. In interview-based essays, what should the thesis do? Examine the thesis in an informative essay that draws on an interview as its main source. It can be written by you or a peer, or by a journalist. Does the thesis accomplish this goal? Why, or why not?

REFLECT Reflect in writing about how you might apply the insights that you drew from this assignment to another situation—in or outside of college—in which you have to conduct an interview. In your reflection, consider the types of questions that you might ask and how you might bring your interview subject to life.

Additional Writing Assignments

1. Interview someone whose profession interests you or whose advice can help you solve a problem or make a decision. Your purpose will be to communicate what you have learned, not to characterize the person you interview.

2. Write a paper based on an interview with at least two members of your extended family about some incident that in your family lore. Direct your paper to younger relatives. If accounts of the event don't always agree, combine them into one vivid account, noting that some details may be more trustworthy than others. Give credit to your sources.

3. Briefly talk with ten students on your campus to find out their career goals and their reasons for their choices. Are they feeling uncertain about a career, pursuing the one they've always wanted, or changing careers for better employment options? Are most looking for security, income, or personal satisfaction? Write a short essay summing up what you find out. Provide some quotations to flesh out your survey and perhaps characterize your classmates. Are they materialists? Idealists? Practical people? (Ask your instructor if any campus permission is needed before you begin these interviews.)

4. **Source Assignment.** In a small group, collaborate to interview someone from campus or the local community with special knowledge about a matter that concerns the group. Prepare by turning to background sources: your interviewee's Web page, social media presence, or publications; or any campus or local news coverage. Plan the interview by working together on these questions:

   - What do you want to find out?
   - What lines of questioning will you pursue?
   - What topic will each student ask about?
   - How much time will each have to ask a series of questions?
   - Who will record the interview (if your subject agrees)?
   - Who will take notes (as your record or backup)?

   Preview each other's questions to avoid duplication. Ask open-ended questions—not "yes or no" questions—to encourage discussion. Be sure to credit all of your sources.

5. **Visual Assignment.** Working with the image below, explore the experience of an interview from the standpoint of what is communicated through expression, body language, clothing, environment, and other nonverbal cues. Use your analysis of the image to support your thesis about the interview relationship it portrays.

   For advice on analyzing an image, see Ch. 13, Responding to Visual Representations.

FEMA/Getty Images

6 Comparing and Contrasting

Bettmann/Getty Images

U.S. Customs and Border Protection's Rio Grande Valley Sector/AP Photo

Responding to an Image

Both of these pictures show images of children who left their home countries to immigrate to the United States. The left photo shows immigrant children from Europe being examined by a doctor upon arrival at Ellis Island in 1911. At that time, immigration was at its peak (1900–1914) and between 5,000 and 10,000 people were processed at the New York immigration center each day; though most carried no identification papers, 80 percent were processed within a few hours. The right photograph, taken in September 2018, shows children from Guatemala, Honduras, and El Salvador being held in a Texas facility near the Mexican border. Following the so-called "Zero-Tolerance Policy" of former Attorney General Jeff Sessions, put in place in April 2018, children—including infants—were routinely separated from the adults they arrived with. By the end of 2018, more than 14,000 unaccompanied children were held as the Department of Health and Human Services attempted to place the children with their closest relatives in the United States, or in foster care. Examine the two photographs carefully, noting similarities and differences. What do these and other similarities or differences say about the years the photos were taken or the policies that affected immigration of the past and present?

Why Comparing and Contrasting Matter

Which city—Dallas or Atlanta—has more advantages or drawbacks for a young single person thinking of settling down to a career? Which of two ads for the same toy appeals more effectively to parents who want educational value for their money? As singers and songwriters, how are Cardi B and Taylor Swift similar and dissimilar? Such questions invite answers that set two subjects side by side.

When you compare, you point out similarities; when you contrast, you discuss differences. When you write about two complicated subjects, usually you need to do both. Considering Mozart and Bach, you might find that each has traits the other has — or lacks. Instead of concluding that one is great and the other inferior, you might conclude that they're two distinct composers, each with an individual style. On the other hand, if your main purpose is to judge between two subjects (such as moving either to Dallas or to Atlanta), you would look especially for positive and negative features, weigh the attractions and faults of each city, and then stick your neck out and make your choice.

Drawing comparisons and identifying contrasts in the world around you is important in many contexts, including the following:

In a College Course

- You compare and contrast to evaluate the relative merits of Norman Rockwell and N. C. Wyeth in an art history course or the relative accuracy of two Civil War websites for a history course.

- You compare and contrast to describe a little-known subject, such as medieval funeral customs, by setting it next to a similar yet familiar subject, such as modern funeral traditions.

In the Workplace

- You compare and contrast your company's products or services with those of competitors.

In Your Community

- You compare and contrast your options in choosing a financial aid package, cell phone contract, childcare provider, bike helmet, or new mayor.

  ❓ What are some instances when you compare or contrast products, services, opportunities, options, solutions, or other things? When might you use comparison, contrast, or both in your writing? What would you expect them to contribute?

Learning from Other Writers

In this chapter you will be asked to write a paper in which you set two subjects side by side and compare and contrast them. Let's see how two other writers have used these familiar habits of thought in their writing. To help you analyze the first reading, look at the notes in the margin. They identify features such as the thesis, or main idea, the sequence of the broad subjects considered, and the specific points of comparison and contrast. As you read these essays, ask yourself the following questions:

1. What two (or more) items are compared and contrasted? Do the writers use comparison or contrast only? Do they combine the two? Why?
2. What is the purpose of comparing and contrasting in the essay? What idea does the information support or refute?
3. How do the writers organize their essays? Why?

Richard Fry, Ruth Igielnik, and Eileen Patten

How Millennials Today Compare with Their Grandparents of 50 Years Ago

Richard Fry and Ruth Igielnik are senior researchers, and Eileen Patten is a former research analyst, for the Pew Research Center, a nonpartisan fact tank that informs the public on social issues and attitudes and demographic trends in the United States. The following excerpt comes from an article originally published in 2015 and updated in 2018 at PewResearch.org.

Thesis — The past five decades — spanning from the time when the Silent   1
Generation° (today, in their 70s and 80s) was entering adulthood to the adulthood of today's Millennials° — have seen large shifts in U.S. society and culture. It has been a period during which Americans, especially Millennials, have become more detached from major institutions such as political parties, religion, the military and marriage. At the same time, the racial and ethnic makeup of the country has changed, college attainment has spiked and women have greatly increased their participation in the nation's workforce.

Our analysis finds several distinctive ways that Millennials stand out when compared with the Silent Generation, a group of Americans old enough to be grandparents to many Millennials:

Point 1 — **1. Today's young adults (Millennials ages 21 to 36 in 2017) are much   2
better educated than the Silent Generation.** The educational trajectory° of young women across the generations has been especially steep. Among Silent

Subject A (Silent Generation) — Generation women, only 9% had completed at least four years of college when they were young. By comparison, Millennial women are four times (36%) as likely as their Silent predecessors were to have at least a bachelor's degree at the same age. Educational gains are not limited to women, as Millennial men

Subject B (Millennials) — are also better educated than earlier generations of young men. Three-in-ten Millennial men (29%) have at least a bachelor's degree, compared with 15% of their young Silent counterparts. These higher levels of educational

---

Silent Generation (aka "Greatest Generation"): People born before 1946, currently ages 73 and older.   **Millennials:** People born between 1981 and 1996, currently ages 21–26. **trajectory:** Course or path.

attainment at ages 21 to 36 suggest that Millennials — especially Millennial women — are on track to be our most educated generation by the time they complete their educational journeys.

2. Young women today are much more likely to be working, compared with Silent Generation women during their young adult years. In 1965, when Silent women were young, a majority (58%) were not participating in the labor force and 40% were employed. Among Millennials, that pattern has flipped. Today, 71% of young Millennial women are employed, while 26% are not in the labor force. This shift to more women in the workplace occurred as early as 1985, when Boomers° were young. Then, nearly seven-in-ten young Boomer women (66%) were employed and 29% were not in the labor force.

3 — Point 2

Subject A (Silent Generation)

Subject B (Millennials)

3. Millennials today are more than three times as likely to have never married as Silents were when they were young. About six-in-ten Millennials (57%) have never been married, reflecting broader societal shifts toward marriage later in life. In 1965, the typical American woman first married at age 21 and the typical man wed at 23. By 2017, those figures climbed to 27 for women and 29.5 for men. When members of the Silent Generation were the same age as Millennials are now, just 17% had never been married. Still, about two-thirds of never-married Millennials (65%) say they would like to get married someday. When asked the reasons they have not gotten married, 29% say they are not financially prepared, while 26% say they have not found someone who has the qualities they are looking for; an additional 26% say they are too young and not ready to settle down.

4 — Point 3

Subject B (Millennials)

Subject A (Silent Generation)

Subject B (Millennials)

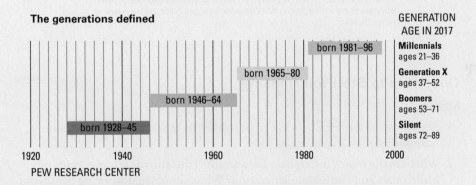

The generations defined

GENERATION
AGE IN 2017

born 1981–96   **Millennials**
ages 21–36

born 1965–80   **Generation X**
ages 37–52

born 1946–64   **Boomers**
ages 53–71

born 1928–45   **Silent**
ages 72–89

1920   1940   1960   1980   2000

PEW RESEARCH CENTER

4. Millennials are much more likely to be racial or ethnic minorities than were members of the Silent Generation. Fifty years ago, America was less racially and ethnically diverse than it is today. Large-scale immigration from Asia and Latin America, the rise of racial intermarriage and differences in fertility patterns across racial and ethnic groups have contributed to Millennials being more racially and ethnically diverse than prior generations.

5 — Point 4

Subject B (Millennials)

Boomers: The Baby Boom generation, or people born between 1946 and 1964, currently ages 53–27.

Subject A (Silent Generation)

Subject B (Millennials)

In 2017, fewer than six-in-ten Millennials (56%) were non-Hispanic whites, compared with more than eight-in-ten (84%) Silents. The share who are Hispanic is five times as large among Millennials as among Silents (21% v. 4%), and the share who are Asian has also increased. However, the share who are black has remained roughly the same.

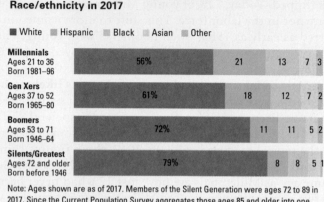

Race/ethnicity in 2017

■ White   ■ Hispanic   ■ Black   ■ Asian   ■ Other

Millennials Ages 21 to 36 Born 1981–96	56% 21 13 7 3	
Gen Xers Ages 37 to 52 Born 1965–80	61% 18 12 7 2	
Boomers Ages 53 to 71 Born 1946–64	72% 11 11 5 2	
Silents/Greatest Ages 72 and older Born before 1946	79% 8 8 5 1	

Note: Ages shown are as of 2017. Members of the Silent Generation were ages 72 to 89 in 2017. Since the Current Population Survey aggregates those ages 85 and older into one category, outcomes for members of the Silent and Greatest generations cannot be separately shown. Whites, blacks and Asians include only single-race non-Hispanics. Hispanics art of any race. Asians include Pacific Islanders. "other races" includes non-Hispanics of other races and non-Hispanics who identify with multiple races. Figures may not add to 100% due to rounding.

Source: Pew Research Center tabulations of the 2017 Current Population Survey Annual Social and Economic Supplement (ASEC) from the Integrated Public Use Microdata Series (IPUMS).

Questions to Start You Thinking

Meaning

1. According to the article, what major shifts in U.S. society and culture have Millennials experienced?

2. What are the major differences between the educational achievements of Millennials and the Silent Generation? What about their working lives? And how do their attitudes toward marriage and other institutions compare?

3. What is the authors' purpose in contrasting these two groups? Is their goal to explain or convince? Or is it something else?

Writing Strategies

4. The writers chose to include with their essay graphs that offer statistics. How do the text and graphs work together (or against each other)? How effective would the text be without the graphs, and why?

5. Which method of organization do the writers use to arrange the essay? How effectively do they switch between the two subjects?

6. How would you describe the writers' attitude toward their subjects, especially toward the end of the essay? Support your response by referring to specific parts of the text.

Isaac Sinclair   Student Essay

E-Cigarettes Pose a Hidden Danger

For his campus newspaper, Iowa State University student Isaac Sinclair examined the risks of vaping, or e-cigarettes, comparing and contrasting them with the traditional tobacco alternative.

Are e-cigarettes popular on your campus too?

By this point in time, everyone has heard of or knows someone who smokes e-cigarettes, or "vapes." This may seem like a healthy alternative to cigarettes, and it sure is advertised as just that.   1

Despite what it may seem, this is far from the truth. E-cigarettes and vaping have similar dangers to cigarettes, are falsely advertised as beneficial products and should have more regulations put upon them.   2

E-cigarettes, according to the FDA, "are devices that allow users to inhale an aerosol containing nicotine or other substances." They are powered by batteries and have refillable tanks.   3

The tank is filled with a liquid that provides the flavoring and nicotine found in e-cigarettes. This liquid is heated and turns into the vapor that you inhale when you smoke an e-cigarette.   4

When e-cigarettes first came out on the market, they were advertised as a healthy alternative to cigarettes. They were presented as a tool to help people quit smoking cigarettes by providing a healthy substitute that would slowly wean people off cigarettes.   5

The problem with these claims is that e-cigarettes are still addictive and dangerous in hauntingly similar ways to cigarettes. One risk of ecigarettes is that in the flavoring, there are many toxins and chemicals that are safe to ingest, but not to inhale. There is very little regulation on the FDA's part in this area, leaving the safety of these flavoring liquids as a large unknown. There needs to be stronger regulations on the flavoring liquids and more research needs to be put into the effects of inhaling these chemicals.   6

The largest and most dangerous risk of e-cigarettes is that they contain nicotine, which is one of the primary ingredients found in cigarettes. Nicotine is an addictive substance that is an easy addiction to pick up, but almost impossible to break. Nicotine is especially dangerous to teens and young adults.   7

If adolescents inhale nicotine, it can cause behavioral and cognitive problems. Adolescent brains are not fully developed, and the nicotine can disturb its development, especially in the areas that affect attention and memory.   8

Considering how addictive and dangerous nicotine is to young adults, it is especially concerning to learn that "more than 18 million U.S. middle and high   9

? Do you agree with the author that e-cigarette advertisements are aimed at teens and young adults?

school youth were exposed to e-cigarette ads in 2014." These advertisements are aimed directly at young adults. They frame ecigarettes in a manner that makes them seem like a cool, hip activity that all teenagers are currently a part of.

Advertisements also hit home the flavoring of e-cigarettes, one of the biggest selling points for teens. What is even more ridiculous is that spending on e-cigarette advertisements has increased from $6.4 million in 2011 to $115 million in 2014. Not only is the most vulnerable group being aggressively targeted, but more money than ever is being funneled into this effort. 10

And it's working. The surgeon general found that between 2011 and 2015, "e-cigarette use among high school students increased by 900 percent." That is an incredible increase in such a short span of time. 11

Now, even with all this clear evidence of e-cigarette risks, I must admit that e-cigarettes are slightly better than smoking cigarettes. But this does not mean e-cigarettes are the way to go. 12

In 2016, a study found that teens "that never smoked but used e-cigs were six times more likely to try cigarettes compared to kids who don't vape." Even if e-cigarettes are barely better than cigarettes, they can have almost the opposite effect than intended or advertised. 13

Teens who smoke e-cigarettes will seek a bigger dose of nicotine after a certain point, and cigarettes provide that bigger dose that they are looking for. E-cigarettes don't slowly wean people off cigarettes; they actually slowly lead them to cigarettes. 14

The change that needs to happen is in how these products are presented and regulated. I believe there needs to be more honest advertising about these products. Companies shouldn't be able to convince young adults to smoke their life away because e-cigarettes are cherry flavored. 15

And, yes, you can say smoking is a choice, but corporations must be held accountable for what they say about their products and make sure their messages are presented in an honest way. In terms of regulation, the FDA needs to have stricter regulations on e-cigarettes. More oversight will lead to more research and information on the safety of these products — something consumers should have available to them. 16

? How else might the author have concluded his essay?

E-cigarettes being regulated by the FDA as a tobacco product is a great start, but there is much more that can be done. There needs to be more responsibility taken by the FDA and corporations that produce ecigarettes in order to protect the health of Americans. 17

Sources:
https://www.lung.org/stop-smoking/smoking-facts/e-cigarettes-and-lung-health.html
https://www.lung.org/stop-smoking/smoking-facts/e-cigarettes-and-lung-health.html
https://www.drugabuse.gov/publications/research-reports/
    tobacco-nicotine-e-cigarettes/nicotine-addictive
https://www.cdc.gov/vitalsigns/ecigarette-ads/

https://www.cdc.gov/vitalsigns/ecigarette-ads/

https://www.lung.org/stop-smoking/smoking-facts/e-cigarettes-and-lung-health.html

https://www.webmd.com/smoking-cessation/features/vape-debate-electronic
  -cigarettes

https://drugfree.org/learn/drug-and-alcohol-news/fda-plans-to-regulate
  -e-cigarettes-as-tobacco-products-not-drug-delivery-devices/

Questions to Start You Thinking

Meaning

1. How does Sinclair define e-cigarettes? In what ways are they similar to regular cigarettes? In what ways are these two different? Do the similarities outweigh the differences, or vice versa?

2. Can you think of other types of similarities and differences that Sinclair might have included?

Writing Strategies

3. Is Sinclair's comparison and contrast sufficient and balanced? Explain.

4. What is Sinclair's thesis? Why does Sinclair state it where he does?

5. What kinds of evidence does Sinclair use to support his claims?

6. Using highlighters or marginal notes, identify the essay's introduction, thesis, contrasting subjects, points of comparison and contrast, and conclusion. How effective is the organization of this essay?

Learning by Writing

The Assignment: Comparing and Contrasting

Write a paper in which you compare and contrast two items to enlighten readers about both subjects. The specific points of similarity and difference will be important, but you will go beyond them to draw a conclusion from your analysis. This conclusion, your thesis, needs to be more than "point A is different from point B" or "I prefer subject B to subject A." You will need to explain why you have drawn your conclusion. You'll also need to provide specific evidence supporting your position and to convince your readers of its soundness. You may choose two people, two events, two places, two objects, two activities, or two ideas, but be sure to choose two you care about. You might write an impartial paper that distinctly portrays both subjects, or you might show why you favor one over the other.

MANAGING YOUR TIME
Writing a Comparison/Contrast Essay

Use the breakdown below to plan your time for this essay; in the right column, insert target dates and times for completing each stage.

approx. 30-45 minutes

- **Read your assignment carefully.** Is it clear what your instructor is asking of you? If not, follow up.
- **Brainstorm** to identify two related subjects that you'd like to learn and write about.
- **Identify your purpose and audience.** Do you want to inform, persuade, or entertain your readers? Which topics will your readers be most interested in?
- **Ask peers to give you feedback on your choice of subjects.** Is there enough material to compare and contrast?

I'll complete this stage by:

_____
(day, date)

approx. 2-3 hours

- **Sketch an outline of your essay.** Begin with your thesis. What would you like to say, ultimately, about the two subjects you are writing about?
- Consider how you would like to **organize your essay.** Will you use an opposing pattern or an alternating pattern?
- **Draft your essay,** staying close to your outline. Support your thesis with relevant details.
- Craft a compelling **introduction** and a satisfying **conclusion.**

I'll complete this stage by:

_____
(day, date)

approx. 2-4 hours

- Ask a **peer to review** your draft. Have you presented both subjects clearly? Have you presented your points and evidence in a way that makes sense?
- **Revise your draft,** addressing issues raised during your and your peer's review.
- **Edit your draft,** fixing any errors, and polishing your prose.

I'll complete this stage by:

_____
(day, date)

Generating Ideas

For strategies for generating ideas, see Ch. 15.

Find Two Subjects. Pick subjects you can compare and contrast purposefully. An examination question may give them to you, ready-made: "Compare and contrast ancient Roman sculpture with that of the ancient Egyptians." But suppose you have to find your subjects for yourself. You'll need to choose things that have a sensible basis for comparison, a common element.

coral reefs + stars = no common element

Jimmy Fallon + Trevor Noah = television talk-show personalities

Besides having a common element, the subjects should share enough to compare but differ enough to throw each other into sharp relief.

sports cars + racing cars = common element + telling differences

sports cars + oil tankers = limited common element + unpromising differences

Try generating a list or brainstorming. Recall what you've recently read, discussed, or spotted on the Web. Let your mind skitter around in search of pairs that go together, or play the game of *free association*, jotting down a word and whatever it brings to mind: Democrats? Republicans. Urban? Rural. Facebook? LinkedIn. Or try the following questions:

- Do you know two people who are strikingly different in attitude or behavior (perhaps your parents or two brothers, two friends, two teachers)?
- Can you think of two groups that are both alike and different (perhaps two sports teams, two clubs, two sets of relatives)?
- Have you taken two courses that were quite different but both valuable?
- Can you recall two events in your life that shared similar aspects but turned out to be quite different (perhaps two performances, two jobs, two romances, two vacations, the births of two children, an event then and now)?
- Can you compare and contrast two holidays or two family customs? Or two recipes that are special to you and your family or friends?
- Are you familiar with two writers, two artists, or two musicians who seem to have similar goals but quite different accomplishments?

Once you have a list of pairs, put a star by those that seem promising. Ask yourself what similarities immediately come to mind. What differences? Can you jot down several of each? Are these striking, significant similarities and differences? If not, move on until you discover a workable pair.

Limit Your Scope. If you want to compare and contrast Japanese literature and American literature in 750 words, your task is probably impossible. But to cut down the size of your subject, you might compare and contrast, say, a haiku of Bashō about a snake with a short poem by Emily Dickinson about a snake. This topic you could cover in 750 words.

Develop Your Pair to Build Support. As you examine your subjects, your goal is twofold. First, analyze each using a similar approach so you have a reasonable basis for comparison and contrast. Then find details and examples that will support your points. Here are some tips for developing your subjects.

For more on interviewing, see Ch. 5.

For advice on finding a few useful sources, turn to B1–B2 in the Quick Research Guide, pp. Q-24–Q-25. For more on using sources for support, see Ch. 11.

- Ask a reporter's questions — the 5 *W*'s (who, what, where, when, why) and an *H* (how).
- Interview someone at each event you're contrasting, or read news or other accounts.
- Read or listen to contrasting views.
- Browse online for websites that supply different examples.
- Look for articles reporting studies or government statistics.

Learning by Doing 👁 Making a Comparison-and-Contrast Table

For more on planning, drafting, and developing, see Chs. 19, 20, and 21. For more about informal outlines, see pp. 275–77.

After deciding which items to compare, take notes on what you know about subject A and then subject B. First identify what the two have in common (similarities); then, in a 3-column table, list their differences. Use the first column to characterize those differences. Here's one example:

Similarities: house pets, have fur, good sense of smell, playful		
Differences	**Subject A: Cats**	**Subject B: Dogs**
personality	fairly self-sufficient	dependent; require a lot of attention

Planning, Drafting, and Developing

Plan to cover both subjects in a similar fashion. Return to your table or make a scratch outline so that you can refine your points of comparison or contrast, consolidate supporting details, and spot gaps in your information. Remind yourself of your goal. What is it you want to show, argue, or find out?

State Your Purpose in a Thesis. You need a reason to place two subjects side by side — a reason that you and your audience will find compelling and worthwhile. If you prefer one subject over the other, what reasons can you give for your preference? If you don't have a preference, try instead to understand them more clearly, making a point about each or both. Comparing and contrasting need not be a meaningless exercise. Instead, think clearly and pointedly in order to explain an idea you care about.

For more on stating a thesis, see pp. 266–71.

TWO SUBJECTS	Two teaching styles in required biology courses.
REASON	To show why one style is better.
WORKING THESIS	Although students learn a lot in both of the required introductory biology courses, one class teaches information and the other teaches how to be a good learner.

Sometimes comparison and contrast is used to make an argument — an argument beyond why, say, subject 1 is better than subject 2. Notice the argument that Isaac Sinclair makes in his thesis statement about e-cigarettes:

ISAAC'S THESIS   E-cigarettes and vaping have similar dangers to cigarettes, are falsely advertised as beneficial products, and should have more regulations put upon them.

Select a Pattern of Organization. Besides understanding your purpose and thesis, readers also need to follow your supporting evidence — the clusters of details that reveal the nature of each subject you consider. They're likely to expect you to follow one of two ways to organize a comparison-and-contrast essay. Both patterns present the same information, but each has its own advantages and disadvantages.

OPPOSING PATTERN, SUBJECT BY SUBJECT	ALTERNATING PATTERN, POINT BY POINT
Subject A	**Point 1**
Point 1	Subject A
Point 2	Subject B
Point 3	
	Point 2
Subject B	Subject A
Point 1	Subject B
Point 2	
Point 3	**Point 3**
	Subject A
	Subject B

When you use the opposing pattern of subject by subject, you state all your observations about subject A and then do the same for subject B. In the following paragraph from *Whole-Brain Thinking*, Jacquelyn Wonder and Priscilla Donovan use the opposing pattern of organization to explain the differences in the brains of females and males.

For more on outlines, see pp. 273–80.

At birth there are basic differences between male and female brains. The female cortex is more fully developed. The sound of the human voice elicits more left-brain activity in infant girls than in infant boys, accounting in part for the earlier development in females of language. Baby girls have larger connectors between the brain's hemispheres and thus integrate information more skillfully. This flexibility bestows greater verbal and intuitive skills. Male infants lack this ready communication between the brain's lobes; therefore, messages are routed and rerouted to the right brain, producing larger right hemispheres. The size advantage accounts for males having greater spatial and physical abilities and explains why they may become more highly lateralized and skilled in specific areas.

Subject A: Female brain

Point 1: Development

Point 2: Consequences

Shift to subject B: Male brain
Point 1: Development
Point 2: Consequences

Using the opposing pattern in a single paragraph or a short essay can effectively unify all the details about each subject. For a long essay or a complicated subject, it has a drawback: readers might find it difficult to remember all the separate information about subject A while reading about subject B.

Using the alternating pattern, you take up one point at a time, applying it first to one subject and then to the other. In their report on the differences between Millennials and their grandparents of the Silent Generation (now in their 70s and 80s), researchers Richard Fry, Ruth Igielnik, and Eileen Patten use this pattern to lead the reader along clearly and carefully through four factors — overall level of education; participation of women in the workforce; marriage; and racial and ethnic diversity — comparing the two generations for each factor.

For more on transitions, refer students to pp. 290–92.

Add Transitions.   Once your essay is organized, you can bring cohesion to it through effective transitional words and phrases — *on the other hand, in contrast, also, both, yet, although, finally, unlike.* Your choice of wording will depend on the content, but keep it varied and smooth. Jarring, choppy transitions distract readers instead of contributing to a unified essay, each part working to support a meaningful thesis.

Learning by Doing Building Cohesion with Transitions

Working on paper or in a file, highlight each transitional word or phrase. For passages without much highlighting, decide whether your audience will need more cues to see how your ideas connect. Next, check each spot where you switch from one subject or point to another to be sure that readers can easily make the shift. Finally, smooth out the wording of your transitions so that they are clear and helpful, not repetitious or mechanical. Test your changes on a reader by exchanging drafts with a classmate.

Revising and Editing

For more on revising and editing strategies, see Ch. 19.

Focus on Your Thesis.   Reflect on your purpose when you review your draft. If your purpose is to illuminate two subjects impartially, ask whether you have given readers a balanced view. Obviously it would be unfair to set forth all the advantages of Oklahoma City and all the disadvantages of Honolulu and then conclude that Oklahoma City is superior on every count.

It's fine to take a stand and favor one option, but you will want to include the same points about each option. One useful way to check for balance or thoroughness is to outline your draft and give the outline a critical look.

Peer Response 🔲 Get Feedback on Your Compare-and-Contrast Essay

Ask a classmate or friend respond to your draft and answer these questions, suggesting how to present your two subjects more clearly:

For general questions for a peer editor, see p. 309.

- How does the introduction motivate you to read the entire essay?
- What is the point of the comparison and contrast of the two subjects? Is the thesis stated in the essay, or is it implied?
- Is the essay clearly organized? Is the pattern appropriate, or would the other one work better?
- Are the same categories discussed for each item? If not, should they be?
- Are there enough details for you to understand the comparison and contrast? Put a check where more details or examples would be useful.
- If this paper were yours, what is the one thing you would be sure to work on before handing it in?

Use your classmates' suggestions as you rework your thesis.

STRENGTHENING YOUR THESIS

☐ Does the thesis make clear the purpose of your comparison and contrast?

☐ Can you sharpen the distinctions between the subjects that you are comparing or contrasting?

☐ Could you make the thesis more compelling based on details that you gathered while planning, drafting, or developing your essay?

Vary Your Wording. Make sure, as you go over your draft, that you have escaped a monotonous drone: A does this, B does that; A has these advantages, B has those. Comparison and contrast needn't result in a paper as symmetrical as a pair of sneakers. Revising and editing give you a chance to add lively details, transitions, dashes of color, and especially variety:

The menu is another major difference between the Cozy Cafe and the Wilton Inn. For lunch, the Cozy Cafe offers sandwiches, hamburgers, and chili. ~~For~~ *L* ~~lunch~~ *at*, the Wilton Inn ~~offers~~ *features* dishes such as fajitas, shrimp salads, and onion soup topped with Swiss cheese. ~~For dinner, the Cozy Cafe continues to serve the lunch menu and adds~~ *adding* home-style comfort foods such as meatloaf, stew, macaroni and cheese, and barbecued ribs. ~~By dinner~~ *after five o'clock*, the Wilton's specialties for the day are posted—perhaps marinated buffalo steak or orange-pecan salmon.

REVISING YOUR DRAFT

☐ Does your introduction present your topic and main point clearly? Is it interesting enough to make a reader want to read the whole essay?

☐ Is your purpose for comparing and contrasting unmistakably clear? What do you want to demonstrate, argue for, or find out?

☐ Have you used the same categories for each item so that you treat them fairly?

☐ Have you selected points of comparison and supporting details that will intrigue, enlighten, and persuade your audience?

☐ What have you concluded about the two? Do you prefer one to the other? If so, is this preference (and your rationale for it) clear?

☐ Does your draft look thin at any point for lack of evidence? If so, how might you develop your ideas?

☐ Have you used the best arrangement, given your subjects and your point?

For more editing and proofreading strategies, see pp. 316–18.

☐ Are there any spots where you need to revise a boringly mechanical, monotonous style ("On one hand, . . . now on the other hand")?

After you have revised your comparison-and-contrast essay, edit and proofread it. Carefully check the grammar, word choice, punctuation, and mechanics—and then correct any problems you may find.

EDITING FOR CLARITY

For more help, find the relevant checklist sections in the Quick Editing Guide on p. Q-37. Turn also to the Quick Format Guide beginning on p. Q-1.

☐ Have you used the correct comparative forms (for two things) and superlative forms (for three or more) for adjectives and adverbs?   A7

☐ Is your sentence structure correct? Have you avoided writing fragments, comma splices, or fused sentences?   A2

☐ Have you used parallel structure in your comparisons
and contrasts? Are your sentences as balanced as your ideas?   B2

☐ Have you used commas correctly after introductory
phrases and other transitions?   D1

Reviewing and Reflecting

REVIEW Working with classmates or independently, respond to the following questions:

1. What are some characteristics of good subjects for comparison-and-contrast papers? Based on these characteristics, identify some promising subjects.

2. Name a key strategy for developing a strong thesis for a comparison-and-contrast paper. Examine the thesis of a comparison-and-contrast essay — one written by you or a peer, or by a journalist. Did the writer seem to employ this strategy? Why, or why not?

3. Describe the opposing and alternating patterns for organizing a comparison-and-contrast essay. If you have written or are writing a comparison-and-contrast paper, which pattern did you decide to use, and why?

REFLECT Reflect in writing about topics that lend themselves to being compared and contrasted. How can the technique be best used to persuade your readers? What have text(s) have you encountered in which the writer uses this organizational strategy? How effectively did the writer compare and contrast the subjects?

Additional Writing Assignments

1. Listen to two different recordings of the same piece of music as performed by two different groups, orchestras, or singers. What elements of the music does each stress? What contrasting attitudes toward the music do you detect? In an essay, compare and contrast these versions.

2. With a classmate or small group, choose a topic, problem, or campus issue about which your views differ to some extent. Agree on several main points of contrast that you want each writer to consider. Then have each person write a paragraph summing up his or her point of view, concentrating on those main points. Collaborate on an introduction that outlines the issue, identifies the main points, and previews the contrasting views. Arrange the paragraphs effectively, add transitions, and write a collaborative conclusion. Revise and edit as needed to produce an orderly, coherent essay.

For more on using sources to support a position, see Ch. 11 and the Quick Research Guide beginning on p. Q-20.

3. Compare and contrast yourself with a classmate in a collaborative essay. Decide together what your focus will be: Your backgrounds? Your paths to college? Your career goals? Your taste in music or clothes? Have each writer use this focus to work on a detailed analysis of himself or herself. Draft a clear thesis comparing your analyses, and decide how to shape the essay. If your instructor approves, you might prepare a mixed-media presentation or post your essay to introduce yourselves to the class.

4. **Source Assignment.** Write an essay in which you compare and contrast one of the following pairs to shed light on both subjects. Turn to readings or essay pairs from this book, a source from the library, news coverage, a website or image, or another relevant source for details and support. Be sure to credit your sources. Possible pairs:

   ■ The coverage of a world event on television and on online news sites
   ■ The experience of watching a film at home and in a theater
   ■ The styles of two athletes playing in the same position (two pitchers, two point guards, two goalies)
   ■ Northern and Southern California (or two other regions)
   ■ Two similar works of architecture (two churches, two skyscrapers, two city halls, two museums, two campus buildings)
   ■ Two articles, essays, or websites about the same topic
   ■ Two articles or other types of sources for an upcoming research paper

5. **Visual Assignment.** The following images show a classroom in Bosso, Nigeria, and a classroom in Wellsville, New York. Compare and contrast the images in an essay, following the advice in this chapter. Be sure that you identify the purpose of your comparison, organize your subjects and points effectively, and support your points with details that you observe in the images.

Pupils attend class at a Koranic school in Bosso, Nigeria. ISSOUF SANOGO/AFP/Getty Images

A student poses a question during a math class in Wellsville, New York. Education Images/Getty Images

7 Explaining Causes and Effects

Larry Washburn/Getty Images

Responding to an Image

That first domino is standing, but for how long? The slightest tap will set the line of dominoes in motion, tipping them into an unstoppable, satisfying ripple of movement. You can almost hear the sound, the soft clickity-click of each tile collapsing onto the next, a wave of cause and effect. What other images and situations can you think of that suggest both cause and effect?

Why Explaining Causes and Effects Matters

In a *New York Times* article titled "How to Be Happy," Tara Parker-Pope writes: "Behavioral scientists have spent a lot of time studying what makes us happy (and what doesn't). We know happiness can predict health and longevity, and happiness scales can be used to measure social progress and the success of public policies." Parker-Pope writes that to obtain these benefits, we can make ourselves happier by making small changes to how we behave, where we live, and who we invite into our lives. So, our happiness (cause) can improve our health and success (effects). But there are things that "cause" happiness. Among the variables that that influence or "cause" happiness is simply being generous toward others. According to the World Happiness Report, generous people are happier than selfish people. And according to a recent study published in the journal *Nature*, being generous with your time and resources — even just *thinking* about being generous — activates the part of the brain that processes happiness.

Often in college you are asked to investigate and think like a behavioral scientist, tracing causes, identifying effects, and suggesting ways to address or solve a problem. To do so, you have to gather information to marshal evidence.

In a College Course

- You explore causes or effects to add depth to your paper, whether you are investigating teen parenthood in sociology, romanticism in American fiction, or head traumas in speech pathology.

- You identify causes (such as those for the decline or the revival of the U.S. auto industry) or effects (such as those of widespread unemployment in Detroit) in essay exams.

In the Workplace

- You consider causes and effects when you recommend changing from one advertising campaign to another to improve sales or from an old procedure to a new one to improve quality, efficiency, or safety.

In Your Community

- You use causal analysis to help you advocate for more rigorous standards for the fuel efficiency of new vehicles or for stronger school board support for early childhood programs.

❓ When have you explained causes, effects, or both in your writing? What situations are likely to require this kind of analysis?

Learning from Other Writers

The following essays explore causes and effects, each examining a different situation. To help you begin to analyze the first reading, look at the notes in the margin. They identify features such as the writer's thesis, or main idea, and the first of the causes or effects that the paper analyzes. As you read these case-and-effect essays, ask yourself the following questions:

1. Do the writers explain causes? Or effects? Or both? Why?

2. Do the writers perceive and explain a chain or series of causal relationships? That is, do they make clear that one event is the result of the occurrence of the other event? If so, how are the various causes and effects connected?

3. What evidence do the writers supply? To what extent does the evidence clarify the causal relationships and to provide credibility to the essay?

Simon Gottschalk

Simon Gottschalk

In Praise of Doing Nothing: Why Leisure Time Is Good for Productivity

Simon Gottschalk, a professor of sociology at the University of Nevada, Las Vegas, argues that "modern life seems to encourage acceleration for the sake of acceleration." But, he asks, "to what end?" The following essay was published in 2018 by the nonprofit evidence-based journal *The Conversation* (theconversation.com).

Introduction to situation

In the 1950s, scholars worried that, thanks to technological innovations, Americans wouldn't know what to do with all of their leisure time. 1

Yet today, as sociologist Juliet Schor notes, Americans are overworked, putting in more hours than at any time since the Depression° and more than in any other in Western society.° 2

It's probably not unrelated to the fact that instant and constant access has become de rigueur,° and our devices constantly expose us to a barrage of colliding and clamoring messages: "Urgent," "Breaking News," "For immediate release," "Answer needed ASAP." 3

It disturbs our leisure time, our family time — even our consciousness. 4

Over the past decade, I've tried to understand the social and psychological effects of our growing interactions with new information and communication technologies. . . . In this 24/7, "always on" age, the prospect of doing nothing might sound unrealistic and unreasonable. 5

Thesis

But it's never been more important. 6

Acceleration for the Sake of Acceleration

In an age of incredible advancements that can enhance our human potential and planetary health, why does daily life seem so overwhelming and anxiety-inducing? 7

Why aren't things easier? 8

It's a complex question, but one way to explain this irrational state of affairs is something called the force of acceleration. 9

Expert sources and examples cited to back thesis

According to German critical theorist Hartmut Rosa, accelerated technological developments have driven the acceleration in the pace of change in social institutions. 10

We see this on factory floors, where "just-in-time" manufacturing demands maximum efficiency and the ability to nimbly respond to market forces, and in university classrooms, where computer software instructs teachers how to "move students quickly" through the material. Whether it's in the grocery store or in the airport, procedures are implemented,° for better or for worse, with one goal in mind: speed. 11

Depression (aka "Great Depression"): In the U.S., from 1929 to 1939, the worst economic downturn in the history of industrialized world.   **Western society:** A broad term used to describe beliefs, traditions, and systems associated with Europe.   *de rigueur:* "Of strictness" (French); describes something that is customarily required or expected. **implemented:** Applied; put into effect.

Noticeable acceleration began more than two centuries ago, during the | 12
Industrial Revolution.° But this acceleration has itself . . . accelerated. Guided
by neither logical objectives nor agreed-upon rationale,° propelled by its own
momentum, and encountering little resistance, acceleration seems to have
begotten more acceleration, for the sake of acceleration.

To Rosa, this acceleration eerily mimics the criteria of a totalitarian° | 13
power: 1) it exerts pressure on the wills and actions of subjects; 2) it is ines-
capable; 3) it is all-pervasive; and 4) it is hard or almost impossible to criticize
and fight.

The Oppression of Speed

Unchecked acceleration has consequences.   14

At the environmental level, it extracts resources from nature faster than   15
they can replenish themselves and produces waste faster than it can be
processed.

At the personal level, it distorts how we experience time and space. It   16
deteriorates how we approach our everyday activities, deforms how we relate
to each other, and erodes a stable sense of self. It leads to burnout at one
end of the continuum and to depression at the other. Cognitively, it inhibits
sustained focus and critical evaluation. Physiologically, it can stress our bodies and disrupt vital functions.

For example, research finds two to three times more self-reported health ⌉ 17
problems, from anxiety to sleeping issues, among workers who frequently
work in high-speed environments compared with those who do not.

When our environment accelerates, we must pedal faster in order to keep | 18
up with the pace. Workers receive more emails than ever before—a number
that's only expected to grow. The more emails you receive, the more time you
need to process them. It requires that you either accomplish this or another   Evidence supporting
task in less time, that you perform several tasks at once, or that you take less   thesis that acceleration
time in between reading and responding to emails.   (cause) is harmful
                                                                                   (effects)
American workers' productivity has increased dramatically since 1973.   19
What has also increased sharply during that same period is the pay gap
between productivity and pay. While productivity between 1973 and 2016
has increased by 73.7 percent, hourly pay has increased by only 12.5 percent.
In other words, productivity has increased at about six times the rate of
hourly pay.   ⌋

Clearly, acceleration demands more work—and to what end? There   20
are only so many hours in a day, and this additional expenditure of energy
reduces individuals' ability to engage in life's essential activities: family,
leisure, community, citizenship, spiritual yearnings and self-development.

It's a vicious loop: Acceleration imposes more stress on individuals and 21
curtails° their ability to manage its effects, thereby worsening it.

Industrial Revolution: The period from 1760 to 1840, marked by the transition from old
manufacturing processes to new ones; a time when rural, farm-based societies became more
industrialized and urban.   **rationale:** Underlying reason.   **totalitarian:** Relating to a system
of governance that is centralized, undemocratic, dictatorial, tyrannical.   **curtails:** Reduces,
lessens.

Doing Nothing and "Being"

In a hypermodern society propelled by the twin engines of acceleration   22
and excess, doing nothing is equated with waste, laziness, lack of ambition,
boredom or "down" time.

But this betrays a rather instrumental grasp of human existence.   23

Much research — and many spiritual and philosophical systems — suggest   24
that detaching from daily concerns and spending time in simple reflection
and contemplation are essential to health, sanity, and personal growth.

Similarly, to equate "doing nothing" with nonproductivity betrays a   25
short-sighted understanding of productivity. In fact, psychological research
suggests that doing nothing is essential for creativity and innovation, and a
person's seeming inactivity might actually cultivate new insights, inventions,
or melodies.

Evidence supporting idea that acceleration (cause) lowers productivity and creativity (effect)

As legends go, Isaac Newton grasped the law of gravity sitting under an   26
apple tree. Archimedes discovered the law of buoyancy relaxing in his bathtub,
while Albert Einstein was well-known for staring for hours into space in his
office.

The academic sabbatical° is centered on the understanding that the mind   27
needs to rest and be allowed to explore in order to germinate° new ideas.

Doing nothing — or just being — is as important to human well-being as   28
doing something.

The key is to balance the two.   29

Taking Your Foot Off the Pedal

Since it will probably be difficult to go cold turkey° from an accelerated   30
pace of existence to doing nothing, one first step consists in decelerating. One
relatively easy way to do so is to simply turn off all the technological devices
that connect us to the internet — at least for a while — and assess what happens to us when we do.

Ideas for countering acceleration

Danish researchers found that students who disconnected from Facebook   31
for just one week reported notable increases in life satisfaction and positive
emotions. In another experiment, neuroscientists who went on a nature trip
reported enhanced cognitive° performance.

Different social movements are addressing the problem of acceleration.   32
The Slow Food movement, for example, is a grassroots campaign° that advocates a form of deceleration by rejecting fast food and factory farming.

As we race along, it seems as though we're not taking the time to seriously   33
examine the rationale behind our frenetic° lives — and mistakenly assume
that those who are very busy must be involved in important projects.

---

academic sabbatical: A paid period of leave from teaching at a university.   **germinate:**
To sprout, develop, come into existence.   **to go cold turkey:** To suddenly quit something to
which you are addicted.   **cognitive:** Of or related to conscious intellectual activity, such as
thinking.   **grassroots campaign:** A type of campaign aimed at getting individuals (rather
than authorities, such as politicians) to persuade others and/or take action.   **frenetic:**
Frenzied, frantic.

Touted by the mass media and corporate culture, this credo° of busyness contradicts both how most people in our society define "the good life" and the tenets° of many Eastern philosophies° that extol the virtue and power of stillness.

French philosopher Albert Camus perhaps put it best when he wrote, "Idleness is fatal only to the mediocre."°

34

Conclusion reinforcing earlier points

35

credo: A guiding set of beliefs.   **tenets:** Principles on which beliefs are based.   **Eastern philosophies:** A broad term used to describe beliefs associated with East and South Asia. **mediocre:** Ordinary, average, uninspired, not very good.

Questions to Start You Thinking

Meaning

1. What are Gottschalk's criticisms of the emphasis on acceleration and productivity? What evidence does he use to support his critique?

2. According to Gottschalk, what are the effects of "acceleration for the sake of acceleration" on human beings?

3. In Gottschalk's view, what might be the results of "doing nothing," of just "being"?

Writing Strategies

4. In paragraph 3, Gottschalk presents a barrage of messages ("Urgent," "Breaking News") that urge us to be tuned in 24/7. What is the effect of his choice to include these specific terms rather than to describe the situation?

5. Gottschalk backs his thesis with various types of evidence, such as input from sociologists and theorists. In your opinion, does he provide the right mix of evidence? Why, or why not? Can you think of any other types of sources he might have consulted?

6. Does Gottschalk deal predominantly with causes or effects? Where and to what degree does he examine each of these? How would the essay change if he altered his focus?

Yun Yung Choi   **Student Essay**

Invisible Women

Yun Yung Choi examines the adoption of a new state religion in her native Korea and the effects of that adoption on Korean women. South Korea elected its first woman president, Park Geun-hye in August 2013, and she served through March 2017. The election of Park, who is the daughter of a previous president of Korea, Park Chung-hee, was considered a major milestone in gender equality for South Korea. Unfortunately, Park Geun-hye was found guilty of the abuse of power and, in 2018, was sentenced to 25 years in jail. Choi wrote this essay prior to Park Geun-hye's election.

For me, growing up in a small suburb on the outskirts of Seoul, the adults' preference for boys seemed quite natural. All the important people that I knew —doctors, lawyers, policemen, and soldiers—were men. On the other hand, most of the women that I knew were either housekeepers or housewives whose duty seemed to be to obey and please the men of the family. When my teachers at school asked me what I wanted to be when I grew up, I would answer, "I want to be the wife of the president." Because all women must become wives and mothers, I thought, becoming the wife of the president would be the highest achievement for a woman. I knew that the birth of a boy was a greatly desired and celebrated event, whereas the birth of a girl was a disappointing one, accompanied by the frequent words of consolation for the sad parents: "A daughter is her mother's chief help in keeping house." 1

These attitudes toward women, widely considered the continuation of an unbroken chain of tradition, are, in fact, only a few hundred years old, a relatively short period considering Korea's long history. During the first half of the Yi dynasty, which lasted from 1392 to 1910, and during the Koryo period, which preceded the Yi dynasty, women were treated almost as equals with many privileges that were denied them during the latter half of the Yi dynasty. This turnabout in women's place in Korean society was brought about by one of the greatest influences that shaped the government, literature, and thoughts of the Korean people—Confucianism.° 2

Throughout the Koryo period, which lasted from 918 to 1392, and throughout the first half of the Yi dynasty, according to Laurel Kendall in her book *View from the Inner Room*, women were important and contributing members of the society and not marginal and dependent as they later became. Women were, to a large extent, in command of their own lives. They were permitted to own property and receive inheritances from their fathers. Wedding ceremonies were held in the bride's house, where the couple lived, and the wife retained her surname. Women were also allowed freedom of movement—that is, they were able to go outside the house without any feelings of shame or embarrassment. 3

With the introduction of Confucianism, however, the rights and privileges that women enjoyed were confiscated. The government of the Yi dynasty made great efforts to incorporate into society the Confucian ideologies, including the principle of *agnation*. This principle, according to Kendall, made men the important members of society and relegated° women to a dependent position. The government succeeded in Confucianizing the country and encouraging the acceptance of Confucian proverbs such as the following: "Men are honored, but women are abased." "A daughter is a 'robber woman' who carries household wealth away when she marries." 4

? How would you have answered this question?

? How do you respond to this historical background?

Confucianism: System of philosophy and ethics based on the teachings of Chinese philosopher Confucius (551–479 BCE).   **relegated:** Reduced to a less important position.

The unfortunate effects of this Confucianization in the lives of women were numerous. The most noticeable was the virtual confinement of women. They were forced to remain unseen in the *anbang*, the inner room of the house. This room was the women's domain, or, rather, the women's prison. Outside, a woman was carried through the streets in a closed sedan chair. Walking outside, she had to wear a veil that covered her face and could travel abroad only after nightfall. Thus, it is no wonder that Westerners traveling through Korea in the late nineteenth century expressed surprise at the apparent absence of women in the country.   5

Women received no formal education. Their only schooling came from government textbooks. By giving instruction on the virtuous° conduct of women, these books attempted to fit women into the Confucian stereotype — meek, quiet, and obedient. Thus, this Confucian society acclaimed particular women not for their talent or achievement but for the degree of perfection with which they were able to mimic the stereotype.   6

A woman even lost her identity in such a society. Once married, she became a stranger to her natal° family, becoming a member of her husband's family. Her name was omitted from the family *chokpo*, or genealogy book, and was entered in the *chokpo* of her in-laws as a mere "wife" next to her husband's name.   7

Even a desirable marriage, the ultimate hope for a woman, failed to provide financial and emotional security for her. Failure to produce a son was legal grounds for sending the wife back to her natal home, thereby subjecting the woman to the greatest humiliation and to a life of continued shame. And because the Confucian ideology stressed a wife's devotion to her husband as the greatest of womanly virtues, widows were forced to avoid social disgrace by remaining faithfully unmarried, no matter how young they were. As women lost their rights to own or inherit property, these widows, with no means to support themselves, suffered great hardships. As Sandra Martielle says in *Virtues in Conflict*, what the government considered "the ugly custom of remarriage" was slowly eliminated at the expense of women's happiness.   8

This male-dominated system of Confucianism is one of the surviving traditions from the Yi dynasty. Although the Constitution of the Republic of Korea, proclaimed on July 17, 1948, guarantees individual freedom and sexual equality, these ideals failed to have any immediate effect on the Korean mentality that stubbornly adheres to its belief in the superiority of men. Women still regard marriage as their prime objective in life, and little girls still wish to become the doctor's wife, the lawyer's wife, and even the president's wife. But as the system of Confucianism is slowly being forced out of existence by new legal and social standards, perhaps a day will come, after all, when a little girl will stand up in class and answer, "I want to be the president."   9

❓Why do you think the writer ends with this quotation?

---

virtuous: Moral, honorable, pure.   **natal:** Relating to one's birth.

Questions to Start You Thinking

Meaning

1. What effect does Choi observe? What cause does she attribute it to?

2. What specific changes in Korean culture does Choi attribute to the introduction of Confucianism?

3. What evidence do you find of the writer's critically rethinking an earlier belief and then revising it? What do you think may have influenced her to change her belief?

Writing Strategies

4. What does Choi gain by beginning and ending with her personal experience?

5. Where does Choi use the strategy of comparing and contrasting?

6. How does Choi consider readers for whom her culture might be foreign?

7. Reread the essay and write notes in the margins that identify the introduction, thesis, major causes or effects, supporting explanations and details for each of these, and conclusion. How effective is the organization?

Learning by Writing

The Assignment: Explaining Causes and Effects

Pick a fact or situation that you have observed, and seek out its causes and effects to help you and your readers understand the issue better. You may limit your essay to the causes *or* the effects, or you may include both, but do emphasize one more than the other. Yun Yung Choi uses the last approach when she identifies the cause of the status of women in Korea (Confucianism) but spends most of her essay detailing effects of this cause. The situation you choose may have affected you and/or people you know well, or it may have to do with specific policies, practices, or beliefs that you have encountered. For example, you might write about the benefits or challenges of working an internship while going to school, or a positive change or problem affecting your family, or even the people in your city or region. Don't think you must choose an earthshaking topic to write a good paper. On the contrary, you will do a better job if you are personally familiar with the situation you choose.

MANAGING YOUR TIME
Writing a Cause-and-Effect Essay

Use the breakdown below to plan your time for this essay; in the right column, insert target dates and times for completing each stage.

approx. **30–45** minutes	■ **Read your assignment carefully.** Is it clear what your instructor is asking of you? If not, follow up. ■ **Brainstorm** to find a topic. Choose a familiar situation, issue, or problem. What are its causes? Its effects? How can looking at both help you better understand the issue?	**I'll complete** this stage by: _____ (day, date)
approx. **2–3** hours	■ **Read** about your topic; list the causes and/or effects that you will discuss. Gather sources of support. What **evidence** will help you explain the situation or issue — how the situation came about (causes) and what followed as a result (effects)? ■ **Sketch an outline of your essay.** Begin with your thesis. What would you like to say, ultimately, about your topic? ■ Consider how you would like to **organize your essay.** Will you discuss the situation and its causes? The situation and its effects? Or all three? In what sequence?	**I'll complete** this stage by: _____ (day, date)
approx. **2–3** hours	■ **Draft your essay,** staying close to your outline. Support your thesis with evidence. ■ Craft a compelling **introduction** and a satisfying **conclusion.**	**I'll complete** this stage by: _____ (day, date)
approx. **2–4** hours	■ Ask a **peer to review** your draft. Have you explained the causes (and not just listed them)? Are they plausible? Are the effects the result of the situation described? ■ **Revise your draft,** addressing issues raised during your and your peer's review. ■ **Edit your draft,** fixing any errors and polishing your prose.	**I'll complete** this stage by: _____ (day, date)

Generating Ideas

Find a Topic. What familiar situation would be informative or instructive to explore? This assignment leaves you the option of writing from what you know, what you can find out, or a combination of the two. Begin by letting your thoughts wander over a particular situation you're familiar with — on campus, in your workplace, in your state, or globally. Has the situation always been this way? Or has it changed in the last few years? Have things gotten better or worse?

For more strategies for generating ideas, see Ch. 15.

When your thoughts begin to percolate, jot down likely topics. Then choose the idea that you care most about and that promises to be neither too large nor too small. A paper confined to the causes of a family's move from New Jersey to Montana might be a single sentence: "My father's company transferred him." But the subsequent effects of the move on the family might become an interesting essay. On the other hand, a topic like the effects of technology in schools could yield hundreds of pages of analysis. You would probably want to narrow your focus and look at, for example, the effects of using tablets to teach literacy.

The following questions can help you brainstorm topics for a cause-and-effect essay:

- Have you experienced a major change in your life (a lost job or a new one; a fluctuation in income; new family dynamics due to marriage, death, or divorce; a new school)?
- Has the environment changed (due to a drought, a flood or a storm, a fire, a new industry, new policies)?
- Has a new invention (the tablet, GPS, social-media platforms, the smartphone) changed your habits or preferences?
- Are employment trends changing (more women in management, fewer young people in rural areas, more men in nursing)?

Learning by Doing Determining Causes and Effects

Determine the cause and effect of each of these situations:

- Because Taylor studied, she earned an A on her test.
- Due to the lack of rainfall in Texas, water restrictions are in effect.
- Janine was injured in a roller derby match because she was not wearing all her safety equipment.
- Although Austin had parked for only five minutes in a handicapped parking spot, he received a ticket because he didn't have the required placard.
- Because Denmark's homes and businesses are powered solely by wind, its residents enjoy a lower cost of energy.

List Causes and Effects. Once you figure out the basic causal relationships, probe for contributing factors. As you draft, these ideas will be a rich resource, but remember to focus on only the most important causes or effects. When you explore a given phenomenon — such as local employment opportunities or the success of your favorite musical artist — don't overwhelm your readers with all possible causes and effects. Instead, decide what you want to emphasize.

Gather Sources of Support. After identifying the topic you would like to cover, it's time find examples. Let's say you've identified a topic to write about, for example: What causes the natural phenomenon of known as the Northern Lights (the Aurora Borealis)? As you gather texts that explain the "cause" of the effect (Northern Lights) you will write about, star, highlight, or underline passages that stand out as major causes. Ask yourself about each: How significant is this cause? Would the situation exist without it? And what about the effect? Has the appearance of the Northern Lights had an impact on the environment or on the people who view it? How much detail do you need to give about the results?

Next, consider what evidence you have and what you still need to gather. As you set priorities — identifying major causes or effects and noting missing information — plan to talk with others, search online, or browse the your library's subject guides and databases for sources of supporting ideas, details, and statistics. You might look for images or illustrations of the phenomenon or problem you're addressing, or charts showing current data and projections.

For advice on finding a few pertinent sources, turn to the Quick Research Guide, beginning on p. Q-20.

Planning, Drafting, and Developing

Start with a Scratch Outline and Thesis. Yun Yung Choi's "Invisible Women" (on pages 111–14) follows a clear plan based on a brief scratch outline that simply lists the effects of the change:

For Choi's complete essay, see pp. 111–14. For more about informal outlines, see pp. 275–77.

Intro — Personal anecdote
   - Tie with Korean history
   - Then add working thesis: The turnabout for women resulted from the influence of Confucianism in all aspects of society.
Comparison and contrast of status of women before and after Confucianism
Effects of Confucianism on women
       1. Confinement
       2. Little education
       3. Loss of identity in marriage
       4. No property rights
Conclusion: Impact still evident in Korea today but some hints of change

In her paper, Choi makes this point: Confucianism is the reason for the status of Korean women. She then details four specific effects of Confucianism on women in Korean society. She shows that cause and effect are closely related: Confucianism is the cause of the change in the status of Korean women; and Confucianism has had specific effects on Korean women.

For more about stating your main point in a thesis, see pp. 266–69.

Organize to Show Causes and Effects to Your Audience. Your paper's core — showing how the situation came about (the causes), what followed as a result (the effects), or both — likely will follow one of these patterns:

I. The situation	I. The situation	I. The situation
II. Its causes	II. Its effects	II. Its causes
		III. Its effects

Try planning by grouping causes and effects. If you are writing about how spending time in nature improves your health, after doing some reading, you might list the following:

Cause	Effects
spending time in nature	improves physical health
	reduces anxiety and depression
	improves sense of wellbeing and satisfaction

Although the benefits to physical health are interesting, you might decide that you are more interested in the specific ways that a walk in the park can improve your mental state. You could then organize the effects from least to most important, giving the major effect more space and placing it last. When your plan seems logical, discuss it or share a draft with a classmate, a friend, or your instructor. Ask whether your organization will make sense to someone else.

Introduce the Situation. Begin your draft by describing the situation you want to explain in no more than two or three paragraphs. Tell readers your task — explaining causes, effects, or both. Instead of doing this in a flat, mechanical fashion ("Now I am going to explain the causes"), announce your task casually, as if you were talking to someone: "At first, Sarah Delgado didn't realize that keeping beehives in her backyard would bother the neighbors." Or tantalize your readers as one writer did in a paper about her father's sudden move to a Trappist monastery: "The real reason for Father's decision didn't become clear to me for a long while."

Learning by Doing 🎯 Focusing Your Introduction

Read aloud the draft of your introduction for a classmate or small group, or post it for online discussion. Ask your readers first to identify where you state the main point of your essay — why you are explaining causes or effects. Then ask them if that statement is clear or if your introduction gets bogged down in detail or skips over essentials.

Integrate Your Evidence. Some writers want to rough out a cause-and-effect draft, positioning all the major points first and then circling back to pull in supporting explanations and details. Others want to plunge deeply into each section—stating the main point, elaborating, and working in the evidence all at once. Tables, charts, and graphs can often consolidate information that illustrates causes or effects. Place any graphics near the related text discussion, supporting but not duplicating it. Be sure to cite your sources according to the documentation style your instructor has assigned.

For more on using sources for support, see Ch. 11 or the Quick Research Guide beginning on p. Q-20.

Revising and Editing

Because explaining causes and effects takes concentration, set aside plenty of time for rewriting. As Yun Yung Choi approached the final version of her paper, she wanted to rework her thesis for greater precision with more detail.

For more revising and editing strategies, see Ch. 19.

> WORKING THESIS   The turnabout for women resulted from the influence of Confucianism in all aspects of society.

> REVISED THESIS   This turnabout in women's place in Korean society was brought about by one of the greatest influences that shaped the government, literature, and thoughts of the Korean people—Confucianism.

Taking a cue from Choi, ask yourself the following questions about your thesis when you revise any cause-and-effect paper.

STRENGTHENING YOUR THESIS

- ☐ Is the purpose of your cause-and-effect analysis clear from your thesis? Is the rest of the paper focused on this purpose?

- ☐ Could the thesis be more specific about the causes or effect you will be discussing?

- ☐ Could you make the thesis more compelling based on details that you gathered while planning, drafting, or developing your essay?

Choi also faced a problem pointed out by classmates: how to make a smooth transition from recalling her own experience to probing causes.

(emphasize that underline{everyone} thinks that) ——→ *widely*
These attitudes toward women, ~~which I once~~ believed to be the

continuation of an unbroken chain of tradition, are, in fact, only a few hun-   *, a relatively short time, considering Korea's long history*

dred years old. During the first half of the Yi dynasty, which lasted from
[tell when]
1392 to 1910, and during *[the Koryo period,]* women were treated almost

as equals, with many privileges that were denied them during the latter

half of the Yi dynasty. This upheaval in women's place in Korean society

was brought about by one of the greatest influences that shaped the

government, literature, and thoughts of the Korean people: Confucianism.

Because of Confucianism, my birth was not greeted with joy and

celebration but rather with these words of consolation: "A daughter is

her mother's chief help in keeping house."

(belongs in opening paragraph)

Peer Response 👥 Get Feedback on Your Cause-and-Effect Essay

For general questions for a peer editor, see p. 309.

Ask a classmate or friend to read your draft and answer these questions, considering how you've analyzed causes or effects:

- Does the writer explain, rather than merely list, causes?
- Do the causes seem logical and possible? Are there other causes that the writer might consider?
- Do all the effects seem to be results of the situation the writer describes? Are there other effects that the writer might consider?
- What is the writer's thesis? Does the explanation of causes or effects help the writer accomplish the purpose of the essay?
- Is the order of supporting ideas clear? Can you suggest a better organization?
- Are you convinced by the writer's logic? Do you see any logical fallacies?
- Do the writer's evidence and detail convince you? Put stars where more or better evidence is needed.
- If this paper were yours, what is the one thing you would be sure to work on before handing it in?

REVISING YOUR ESSAY

For more on evidence, see pp. 136–39.

☐ Have you shown your readers your purpose in presenting causes or effects?

☐ Is your explanation thoughtful, searching, and reasonable?

☐ Where might you need to reorganize or add transitions so your paper is easy for readers to follow?

☐ Do you need to add any significant causes or effects or drop any remote ones?

☐ Might you need more evidence to convince readers that the causal relationships are valid, not just guesses?

☐ Could any effect have resulted not from the cause you describe but from some other cause?

After you have revised your cause-and-effect essay, edit and proofread it. Carefully check the grammar, word choice, punctuation, and mechanics — and then correct any problems you find.

For more editing and proofreading strategies, see pp. 316–18.

EDITING FOR CLARITY

☐ Have you used correct verb tenses and forms throughout? When you describe events in the past, is it clear what happened first and what happened next?   A3

☐ Have you avoided creating fragments when adding causes or effects? (Check revisions carefully, especially those beginning "Because . . ." or "Causing . . .") Have you avoided comma splices or fused sentences when integrating ideas?   A1, A2

☐ Do your transitions and other introductory elements have commas after them, if these are needed?   D1

For more help, find the relevant checklist sections in the Quick Editing Guide on p. Q-37. Turn also to the Quick Format Guide beginning on p. Q-1.

Reviewing and Reflecting

REVIEW Working with classmates or independently, respond to the following questions:

1. What are some strategies for keeping a cause-and-effect paper focused and not overwhelming for readers?

2. What questions might you ask yourself to identify a topic for a cause-and-effect paper?

3. What are some strategies for organizing a cause-and-effect paper? If you have written or are writing a cause-and-effect paper, which organizational strategies did you find most helpful? Why?

REFLECT Reflect in writing about how you might apply the insights that you drew from this assignment to another situation — in or outside of college — in which you have to explain causes or effects. In your reflection, consider how you might keep your examination of causes and effects focused on your purpose.

Additional Writing Assignments

1. Write an essay about a noticeable, lasting change that has taken place in your lifetime, exploring its causes, effects, or both to help you and your audience understand that change better. The change might have affected only you (such as a move), or it might have affected your community, region, or society at large (such as a medical breakthrough).

2. Identify a major event, individual, circumstance, habit, or other factor that shaped you as a person. In your journal, write informally about this cause and its effects on you. Use this entry to develop a cause-and-effect essay that will enlighten readers about how you came to be the person that you are now.

3. Write a formal letter addressed to someone who could make a change that you advocate. Support this change by explaining causes, effects, or both. For example, address a college official to support a change in a campus policy, the principal to advocate for a change at your child's school, or your work supervisor to encourage a change in office procedures.

4. **Source Assignment.** Find a news or magazine article that probes the causes of a current problem: the shortage of certain types of jobs, for instance, or tuition increases in your state. Write an essay in which you argue that the author has or has not done a good job of explaining the causes of this problem. Be sure to credit the article correctly.

5. **Visual Assignment.** Write an essay explaining the causes, effects, or both captured or implied in the graph below. Establish the purpose of your explanation, effectively identify and organize the causes or effects, and support your points with details that you observe in the graph. It shows a decrease in the percentage of households with landline phones and an increase in the number of households that own only cell phones over a ten-year period.

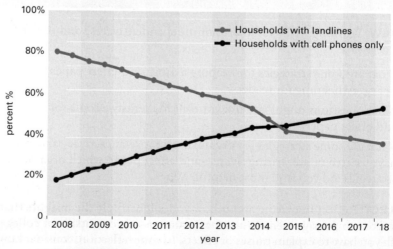

Growth in Cell Phone–Only Households, 2008–2017

Data from the National Center for Health Statistics and the Centers for Disease Control and Prevention.

Taking a Stand

Luiz Rampelotto/Pacific Press/LightRocket/Getty Images

Responding to an Image

Malala Yousafzai (b. 1997) is an activist for girls' education. As a child in Pakistan, she was shot in the head by the Taliban for attending school and speaking out about the importance of education. After her recovery, she founded a nonprofit organization dedicated to providing girls around the world with access to education, and she was awarded the Nobel Peace Prize for her activism. What motivates Malala to continue to take a stand as an advocate for human rights for girls and women? How is she a role model for speaking out?

Why Taking a Stand Matters

Both in and outside of class, you hear controversial issues discussed — health care costs, immigration policy, policing practices, use of alternative energy sources, and the global outsourcing of jobs. Such controversies can be international, national, regional, or local. Educating ourselves and participating in these discussions, whatever our viewpoints may be, is part of what makes a democracy function. Taking a stand in response to such issues will help you understand the controversy and clarify what you believe. Such writing is common in genres such as editorials, letters to the editor, or opinion columns in print and digital news outlets. It is also the foundation of persuasive brochures, partisan blogs, and websites that take a position on an issue.

Writing of this kind has a twofold purpose — to express and to win your readers' respect for your opinion. What you say might or might not change a reader's opinion. But if you fulfill your purpose, a reader at least will see good reasons for your views. In taking a stand, you do the following:

- You state your opinion or stand.
- You give reasons with evidence to support your position.
- You enlist your readers' trust.
- You consider and respect what your readers may think and feel.

Taking a stand is common in situations like the following:

In a College Course

- You take a stand in an essay or exam when you respond, pro or con, to a statement such as "The Internet is an invention that has transformed human communication for the better."
- You take a stand when you write a research paper that supports your position on juvenile sentencing, state funding for higher education, or greater access to affordable housing.

In the Workplace

- You take a stand when you persuade others that your financial strategy will increase revenue or that your customer service initiative will attract new business.

In Your Community

- You take a stand when you write a letter to the editor appealing to voters to support new legalizing medical marijuana.

❓ When have you taken a stand in your writing?

Learning from Other Writers

In the following two essays, the writers take a stand on issues of importance to them. To help you analyze the first reading, look at the notes in the margin. They identify the thesis, or main idea, and the first supporting point in a paper that takes a stand. As you read these essays that take a stand, ask yourself the following questions:

1. What stand does the writer take? Is it a popular opinion, or does it break from commonly accepted beliefs?
2. How does the writer appeal to readers?
3. How does the writer support his or her position? Is the evidence sufficient to gain your respect? Why, or why not?

Suzan Shown Harjo

Last Rites for Indian Dead

Suzan Shown Harjo is a writer and political activist, advocating for Native American legal rights and cultural protections. As a result of the efforts of Harjo and others like her, the Native American Graves Protection and Repatriation Act was passed in 1990.

MANUEL BALCE CENETA/
AP Images

What if museums, universities, and government agencies could put your dead relatives on display or keep them in boxes to be cut up and otherwise studied? What if you believed that the spirits of the dead could not rest until their human remains were placed in a sacred area?

Introduction appeals to readers

The ordinary American would say there ought to be a law — and there is, for ordinary Americans. The problem for American Indians is that there are too many laws of the kind that make us the archaeological property of the United States and too few of the kind that protect us from such insults.

THESIS taking a stand

Some of my own Cheyenne relatives' skulls are in the Smithsonian Institution today, along with those of at least 4,500 other Indian people who were violated in the 1800s by the U.S. Army for an "Indian Crania Study." It wasn't enough that these unarmed Cheyenne people were mowed down by the cavalry at the infamous Sand Creek massacre; many were decapitated and their heads shipped to Washington as freight. (The Army Medical Museum's collection is now in the Smithsonian.) Some had been exhumed° only hours after being buried. Imagine their grieving families' reaction on finding their loved ones disinterred° and headless.

Point 1

Supporting evidence

Native Americans march with a truck returning 2,000 skeletal remains of Jemez Pueblo Indian ancestors for reburial in New Mexico. The remains had been in the collections Harvard University. AP Images/Eddie Moore

exhumed: Dug up out of the earth.   **disinterred:** Taken out of a place of burial.

Some targets of the army's study were killed in noncombat situations 4 and beheaded immediately. The officer's account of the decapitation of the Apache chief Mangas Coloradas in 1863 shows the pseudoscientific nature of the exercise. "I weighed the brain and measured the skull," the good doctor wrote, "and found that while the skull was smaller, the brain was larger than that of Daniel Webster."

These journal accounts exist in excruciating detail, yet missing are any 5 records of overall comparisons, conclusions, or final reports of the army study. Since it is unlike the army not to leave a paper trail, one must wonder about the motive for its collection.

The total Indian body count in the Smithsonian collection is more than 6 19,000, and it is not the largest in the country. It is not inconceivable that the 1.5 million of us living today are outnumbered by our dead stored in museums, educational institutions, federal agencies, state historical societies, and private collections. The Indian people are further dehumanized by being exhibited alongside the mastodons and dinosaurs and other extinct creatures.

Where we have buried our dead in peace, more often than not the sites 7 have been desecrated. For more than two hundred years, relic-hunting has been a popular pursuit. Lately, the market in Indian artifacts has brought this abhorrent activity to a fever pitch in some areas. And when scavengers come upon Indian burial sites, everything found becomes fair game, including sacred burial offerings, teeth, and skeletal remains.

One unusually well-publicized example of Indian grave desecration 8 occurred in a western Kentucky field known as Slack Farm, the site of an Indian village five centuries ago. Ten men — one with a business card stating "Have Shovel, Will Travel" — paid the landowner $10,000 to lease digging rights between planting seasons. They dug extensively on the forty-acre farm, rummaging through an estimated 650 graves, collecting burial goods, tools, and ceremonial items. Skeletons were strewn about like litter.

What motivates people to do something like this? Financial gain is the 9 first answer. Indian relic-collecting has become a multimillion-dollar industry. The price tag on a bead necklace can easily top $1,000; rare pieces fetch tens of thousands.

And it is not just collectors of the macabre° who pay for skeletal remains. 10 Scientists say that these deceased Indians are needed for research that someday could benefit the health and welfare of living Indians. But just how many dead Indians must they examine? Nineteen thousand?

There is doubt as to whether permanent curation of our dead really 11 benefits Indians. Dr. Emery A. Johnson, [a] former assistant Surgeon General, observed, "I am not aware of any current medical diagnostic or treatment procedure that has been derived from research on such skeletal remains. Nor am I aware of any during the thirty-four years that I have been involved in American Indian . . . health care."

macabre: Gruesome, ghastly.

Indian remains are still being collected for racial biological studies. While 12
the intentions may be honorable, the ethics of using human remains this way
without the full consent of relatives must be questioned.

Some relief for Indian people has come on the state level. Almost half of 13
the states, including California, have passed laws protecting Indian burial
sites and restricting the sale of Indian bones, burial offerings, and other
sacred items. . . . However, no legislation has attacked the problem head-on
by imposing stiff penalties at the marketplace, or by changing laws that make
dead Indians the nation's property.

Some universities — notably Stanford, Nebraska, Minnesota, and Seattle 14
— have returned, or agreed to return, Indian human remains; it is fitting that
institutions of higher education should lead the way. . . .

The country must recognize that the bodies of dead American Indian 15
people are not artifacts to be bought and sold as collector's items. It is not
appropriate to store tens of thousands of our ancestors for possible future
research. They are our family. They deserve to be returned to their sacred
burial grounds and given a chance to rest.

Conclusion proposes action

The plunder of our people's graves has gone on too long. Let us rebury 16
our dead and remove this shameful past from America's future.

Questions to Start You Thinking

Meaning

1. What is the issue that Harjo identifies? How extensive does she show
   it to be?

2. What is Harjo's position on this issue? Where does she first state it?

3. What evidence does Harjo present to refute the claim that housing
   skeletal remains of Native Americans in museums is necessary for medical research and may benefit living Indians?

Writing Strategies

4. What assumptions do you think Harjo makes about her audience?

5. How does Harjo use her status as a Native American to enhance her
   position? Would her argument be as credible if it were written by
   someone of another background?

6. How does she appeal to the emotions of the readers in the essay? In what
   ways do these strategies strengthen or detract from her logical reasons?

Marjorie Lee Garretson   **Student Essay**

More Pros Than Cons in a Meat-Free Life

Marjorie Lee Garretson's opinion piece originally appeared in the *Daily Mississippian*, the student newspaper of the University of Mississippi.

What would you say if I told you there was a way to improve your overall health, decrease environmental waste, and save animals from inhumane treatment at the same time? You would probably ask how this is possible. The answer is quite simple: go vegetarian. Vegetarians are often labeled as different or odd, but if you take a closer look at their actions, vegetarians reap multiple benefits meat eaters often overlook or choose to ignore for convenience.

1

The health benefits vegetarians acquire lead us to wonder why more people are not jumping on the meat-free bandwagon. On average, vegetarians have a lower body mass index,° significantly decreased cancer rates, and longer life expectancies. In addition, Alzheimer's disease° and osteoporosis° were linked to diets containing dairy, eggs, and meat.

2

The environment also encounters benefits from vegetarians. It takes less energy and waste to produce vegetables and grains than the energy required to produce meat. Producing one pound of meat is estimated to require 16 pounds of grain and up to 5,000 gallons of water, which comes from adding the water used to grow the grain crop as well as the animal's personal water consumption. Also, according to the Environmental Protection Agency, the runoff of fecal matter from meat factories is the single most detrimental° pollutant to our water supply. In fact, it is said to be the most significant pollutant in comparison to sources of all other industries combined.

3

The inhumane treatment of animals is common at most animal factories. The living conditions chickens, cows, pigs, and other livestock are forced into are far removed from their natural habitats. The goal of animal agriculture nowadays seems to be minimizing costs without attention to the sacrifices being made to do so. Animals are crammed into small cages where they often cannot even turn around. Exercise is denied to the animals to increase energy toward the production of meat. Female cows are pumped with hormones to allow their bodies to produce triple the amount of milk they are naturally capable of. Chickens are stuffed tightly into wire cages, and conditions are manipulated to increase egg production cycles. When chickens no longer lay eggs and cows cannot produce milk, they are transported to slaughterhouses where their lives are taken from them—often piece by piece.

4

Animal factory farms do a great job convincing Americans that their industry is vital to our health because of the protein, calcium, and other nutrients available

5

Do you find Garretson's discussion of the health benefits of vegetarianism convincing? Why, or why not?

Is it possible to decrease damage to the environment from factory farms without becoming a vegetarian? What other options might there be?

---

body mass index: A measurement of body fat, based on height and weight.   **Alzheimer's disease:** An incurable brain disorder causing memory loss and dementia.   **osteoporosis:** A disease that increases risk of bone fractures.   **detrimental:** Harmful.

in chicken, beef, and milk. We are bombarded with "Got Milk?" ads featuring various celebrities with white milk mustaches. We are told the egg is a healthy breakfast choice and lean protein is the basis of many good weight loss diets. What all of the ads and campaigns for animal products leave out are all the hormones injected into the animals to maximize production. Also, the tight living conditions allow for feces to contaminate the animals, their environment, and the potential meat they are growing. It is ironic how irate° Americans react to puppy mills and the inhumane treatment of household pets, but for our meat and dairy products we look the other way. We pretend it is fine to confine cows, pigs, and chickens to tiny spaces and give them hormones and treat them inhumanely in their life and often in the way they are killed. We then cook and consume them at our dinner tables with our families and friends.

> ❓ Do you agree that Americans are hypocritical about the different treatment of household pets and farm animals? Why, or why not?

Therefore, I encourage you to consider a meat-free lifestyle not only for the sake of the animals and the environment, but most importantly your personal health. All of your daily nutrients can be found in plant-based sources, and oftentimes when you make the switch to being a vegetarian, your food choices expand because you are willing to use vegetables and grains in innovative ways at the dinner table. Going vegetarian is a life-changing decision and one you can be proud of because you know it is for your own health as well as the greater good.   6

Questions to Start You Thinking

Meaning

1. What points does Garretson make to support her position that vegetarianism has multiple benefits?

2. In the author's view, why is it especially troubling that we are willing to "look the other way" (paragraph 5) on the inhumane treatment of farm animals?

Writing Strategies

3. What kind of support does Garretson use to back up her claims about the benefits of vegetarianism? Do you find her argument effective? Why, or why not?

4. To what extent does Garretson account for other points of view? How does the inclusion (or absence) of opposing views affect your opinion on the issue?

5. This article was written as an editorial for a student newspaper. How might Garretson change the article if she were submitting it as an essay or a research paper?

6. Using highlighters or marginal notes, identify the essay's introduction, thesis, major points or reasons, supporting evidence for each point, and conclusion. How effective is the organization of this essay?

irate: Angry.

Learning by Writing

The Assignment: Taking a Stand

Find a controversy that rouses your interest. It might be a current issue, a long-standing one, or a matter of personal concern: the pros and cons of trigger warnings on college syllabi, the contribution of sports to a school's educational mission, or the need for menu changes at the cafeteria to accommodate ethnic, religious, and personal preferences. Your purpose isn't to solve a social or moral problem but to make clear exactly where you stand on an issue and to persuade your readers to respect your position, perhaps even to accept it. As you reflect on your topic, you may change your position, but don't shift positions in the middle of your essay.

Assume that your readers may not be familiar with the controversy, so provide relevant background or an overview to help them understand the situation. They also may not have taken sides yet or may hold a position different from yours. You'll need to consider their views and choose strategies to enlist their support.

Emma Gonzalez, survivor of the school shooting in Parkland, Florida, took a stand in favor of gun control. Abaca Press/AP Images

MANAGING YOUR TIME
Taking a Stand: Writing an Argument Essay

Use the breakdown below to plan your time for this essay; in the right column, insert target dates and times for completing each stage.

approx. **30- 45** minutes	■ **Read your assignment carefully.** Is it clear what your instructor is asking of you? If not, follow up. ■ **Brainstorm** to identify a controversial issue that interests you and that will interest your readers. Ask yourself which topic you're most concerned about and why. What is your position on the issue? How can you best defend that position?	**I'll complete** this stage by: _____ (day, date)
approx. **2-3** hours	■ **Read** about your topic, identifying the arguments and counterarguments of other writers. ■ Begin with a debatable question that you will revise into a **thesis** with a clearly stated position. ■ Identify **evidence** that you can use to support your position, such as facts, statistics, photos and illustrations, expert testimony, and first-hand observations.	**I'll complete** this stage by: _____ (day, date)
approx. **2-3** hours	■ **Sketch an outline of your essay,** beginning with your thesis. Apply reasoning (formal or informal) to refine your position. Support your thesis with relevant evidence. Consider organizing your argument around each claim. ■ **Draft your essay,** staying close to your outline. Think of your readers as you draft, and appeal to them using logic, emotion, and ethics. Back yourself up with facts, and be sure to credit your sources as you write. ■ Craft a compelling **introduction** and a satisfying **conclusion** by appealing to your readers to accept your position and/or to take a specific action.	**I'll complete** this stage by: _____ (day, date)
approx. **2-4** hours	■ Ask a **peer to review** your draft. Is your position tenable? Have you supported it with persuasive enough evidence? Have you acknowledge and rebutted counterarguments? ■ **Revise your draft,** addressing issues raised during your and your peer's review. ■ **Edit your draft,** fixing any errors and polishing your prose.	**I'll complete** this stage by: _____ (day, date)

For more strategies for generating ideas, see Ch. 15.

Generating Ideas

For this assignment, you will need to select an issue, take a stand, develop a clear position, and assemble evidence that supports your view.

Find an Issue. Choose an issue or a controversy that interests both you and your audience. Try brainstorming a list of these issues. Start with the headlines of a newspaper or news magazine, review the letters to the editor, check the political cartoons on the opinion page, or watch for stories on demonstrations or protests. You might also consult the library index to *CQ Researcher* (a respected source for reporting), browse news or opinion websites, talk with friends, or consider topics raised in class. If you keep a journal, look over your entries to see what has perplexed or angered you. If you are considering an issue but aren't sure you want to take a stand on it, investigate by freewriting, reading, or turning to other sources.

Learning by Doing 🎯 Testing Potential Topics

Take your list of possible issues or controversies and eliminate topics that are too broad, too narrow, or not focused. For example, if you are limited to one thousand words, do you have enough space to write about the hunger in the United States? Weed out anything that might not hold your — or your readers' — interest. You might exchange topic lists with other students and discuss which topics are most or least promising.

As you refine your list, ask yourself:

- Among the issues or controversies you've listed, which one most concerns you, and why?
- What position or "stand" do you want to take on the issue? What evidence might you need to support it?
- How can you translate your position on the issue into a working thesis?

Start with a Question and a Thesis. Try to pose the issue you've chosen as a question — one that you will answer through the position you take. Convert vague questions into questions that allow different stands.

VAGUE QUESTION	Is stereotyping bad?
CLEARLY DEBATABLE	Should we fight gender stereotypes in advertising?

For more on stating a thesis, see pp. 266–70.

Next, focus your position by stating it in a thesis — one sentence that answers the question you've posed.

WORKING THESIS	We should expect advertisers to fight rather than reinforce gender stereotypes.

Your thesis should invite continued debate by taking a strong position that can be argued rather than stating a fact.

FACT	Women in TV commercials are far more likely than men to be depicted in the kitchen.
WORKING THESIS	Advertisers need to catch up to the changes in gender roles and depict both men and women in the workplace and at home.

Notice that both Suzan Shown Harjo and Marjorie Lee Garretson pose questions in their introductory paragraphs that are then addressed in their thesis statements. If you came up with a debatable question, you might revisit and revise this question later, to develop a strong introduction.

Use Formal Reasoning to Refine Your Position. As you take a stand on an issue, you are likely to use reasoning and specific evidence to support your position. A *syllogism* is a series of statements used in traditional formal logic to lead deductively to a logical conclusion.

MAJOR STATEMENT	All students must pay tuition.
MINOR STATEMENT	You are a student.
CONCLUSION	Therefore, you must pay tuition.

But the truth of a syllogism depends on whether you accept the statements. In the example above, what about students whose families pay for their tuition or who get loans or scholarships? What about veterans or others who receive tuition waivers under special programs? In real-life arguments, the tidiness of a syllogism may be hard to achieve.

Use Informal Toulmin Reasoning to Refine Your Position. A contemporary approach to logic was presented by the philosopher Stephen Toulmin (1922–2009) in *The Uses of Argument*. He described an informal way of arguing that acknowledges the kinds of assumptions we make in our day-to-day reasoning. This approach starts with a concise statement that makes a *claim* and supplies a *reason* to support it.

CLAIM   REASON

Students should boycott the café <u>because</u> the food costs too much.

You develop a claim by supporting your reasons with *evidence*, also known as grounds. In this example, your evidence might include facts about the cost of lunches on campus or statistics about the limited budgets of most students at your campus.

Toulmin recognized that most practical arguments rely on a *warrant*, which is the often unspoken thinking or assumption that connects the claim, reason, and evidence. State your warrant directly to ensure that readers will see the connection that you do.

WARRANT

The campus cafe should set prices that are reasonable for student budgets.

Back up your warrant, if necessary, in various ways:

- Use facts, perhaps based on quality and cost comparisons with food service operations on other campuses.
- Use logic, perhaps based on research about the importance of good nutrition for brain function and learning.
- Draw on the college mission statement or other expressions of the school's commitment to students.

As you develop your reasoning, you might adjust your claim or the evidence you present to suit your audience, your issue, or your refined thinking. For instance, you might *qualify* your claim by limiting it in some way; for example, perhaps you will object only to the prices of entrees. You might also add a *rebuttal* by identifying an *exception* to the argument; perhaps you would exclude the fortunate, but few, students without financial worries. You might even reconsider your claim, concluding that the campus café is, after all, convenient for students and that the manager might be willing to offer more inexpensive options without a student boycott.

REVISED CLAIM   REVISED REASON

The café should offer less expensive options **because** most students can't afford a balanced meal at current prices.

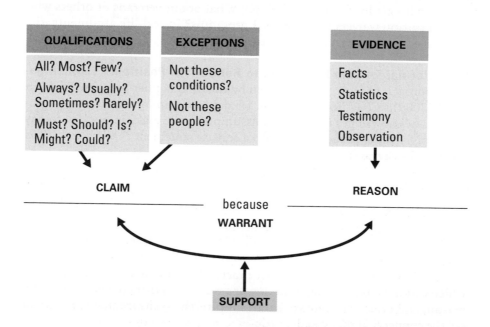

Understand Types of Claims — and How to Support Each. As you begin to look for supporting evidence, consider the issue in terms of the three general types of claims — claims that require substantiation, claims that provide evaluation, and claims that endorse policy. Understanding the type of claim will help you select appropriate evidence.

1. **Claims of Substantiation: What Happened?**

   These claims require examining and interpreting information in order to resolve disputes about facts, circumstances, causes or effects, definitions, or the extent of a problem.

   Sample Claims:
   - The development of e-cigarettes and vapes has significantly increased smoking among teenagers.
   - Although body cameras worn by police will not always prevent unnecessary use of force, they are showing promise in reducing police brutality.
   - On the whole, bilingual education programs actually help students learn English more quickly than total immersion programs do.

   Possible Supporting Evidence:
   - Facts and information: statistics, numbers, examples of teens who vape vs. teens who smoke cigarettes; use-of-force incidents with and without body cameras; or English proficiency test scores for students in bilingual programs vs. total immersion programs.
   - Clear definitions of terms: *police brutality* or *total immersion*.

2. **Claims of Evaluation: What Is Right?**

   These claims consider right or wrong, appropriateness or inappropriateness, and worth or lack of worth involved in an issue.

   Sample Claims:
   - Research using fetal tissue is unethical in a civilized society.
   - English-only legislation promotes cultural intolerance in our society.
   - Keeping children in foster care for years, instead of releasing them for adoption, is wrong.

   Possible Supporting Evidence:
   - Explanations or definitions of appropriate criteria for judging: deciding what's "unethical in a civilized society" or what constitutes "cultural intolerance."

3. **Claims of Policy: What Should Be Done?**

   These claims challenge or defend approaches for achieving generally accepted goals.

   Sample Claims:
   - The federal government should support the distribution of medications that block opioid overdoses to reduce fatalities.
   - Denying children of undocumented workers enrollment in public schools will reduce the problem of illegal immigration.
   - All teenagers accused of murder should be tried as adults.

Possible Supporting Evidence:

- Definition of the policy goal: reducing fatal opioid overdoses, lowering the number of immigrants entering the U. S. illegally, or trying murderers in the same way regardless of age.
- Detailed explanations showing how your policy recommendation would meet the goal or what its limitations are: results of trials using opioid blockers or examples of cases involving teen murderers.

Consider Your Audience as You Develop Your Claim. The nature of your audience might influence the type of claim you choose to make. For example, suppose that the nurse at the local high school has proposed distributing free condoms to students. Consider how different audiences might respond to the idea depending on how the claim was formulated. For example, if you are the parent of a teenager, what type of claim would best address both your general views and your specific concerns about your own child? If you are a school administrator, what type of claim would most effectively persuade you? Ask the following questions to analyze your audience:

- What are their attitudes? Interests? Priorities?
- What do they already know about the issue?
- What do they expect you to say?

As you develop your claims, try to put yourself in the place of your audience. Remember, if you consider the views of your readers, they are more likely to respect your opinion, even if they don't agree with it.

Select Evidence to Support Your Claim. Now that you've stated your claim, you'll need evidence to support it. That evidence can be anything that demonstrates the soundness of your position and the points you make — facts, statistics, observations, expert testimony, illustrations, examples, and case studies. To decide how to support a claim, try to reduce it to its core question. Then figure out what reliable and persuasive evidence might answer the question.

For more about using sources, see Ch. 11 and the Quick Research Guide beginning on p. Q-20.

Facts. Facts are statements that can be verified objectively, by observation or by reading a reliable account. They are usually stated straightforwardly: "If you leave the milk out on the counter, eventually it will spoil." Of course, we accept many of our facts based on the testimony of others. For example, we believe that the Great Wall of China exists, although we may never have seen it with our own eyes.

Sometimes people say facts are true statements, but truth and sound evidence may be confused. Consider the truth of these statements:

The tree in my yard is oak.	(verifiable fact)
A kilometer is 1,000 meters.	(verifiable fact)
My favorite food is pizza.	(opinion)
Murder is wrong.	(value judgment)

When you think critically, you should avoid treating opinions, beliefs, value judgments, or personal experience as true in the same sense that verifiable facts are true.

Statistics. Statistics are facts expressed in numbers. What portion of American children are poor? According to statistics from the National Center for Children in Poverty, 41 percent of children in the U.S. lived in low-income families in 2016, down from the 45-percent rate in 2010. Clear as such figures seem, they may raise complex questions. For example, how significant is this decrease in the rate of low-income families? Is it an aberration or part of a longer trend?

Most writers, without trying to be dishonest, interpret statistics to help their causes. The statement "Fifty percent of the populace have incomes above the poverty level" might substantiate the fine job done by the government of a developing nation. Putting the statement another way — "Fifty percent of the populace have incomes below the poverty level" — might use the same statistic to show the inadequacy of the government's efforts.

Even though a writer is free to interpret a statistic, statistics should not be used to mislead. On the wrapper of a candy bar, we read that a one-ounce serving contains only 150 calories. The claim is true, but the bar weighs 1.6 ounces. Gobble it all — more likely than eating 62 percent of it — and you'll ingest 240 calories, a heftier snack than the innocent statistic on the wrapper suggests. Because abuses make some readers automatically distrustful, use figures fairly when you write, and make sure they are accurate. If you doubt a statistic, check several other sources. Distrust a statistical report that differs from every other report unless it is backed by further evidence.

Few people save some of a candy bar to eat later.
iStockphoto.com/pidjoe/Getty Images

Expert Testimony. By "experts," we mean people with knowledge gained from study and experience in a particular field. The test of an expert is whether his or her expertise stands up to the scrutiny of others who are knowledgeable in that field. The views of Tom Brady on how to play offense in football carry authority. So do the views of historian and essayist Jill Lepore on the origins of America. However, Brady's take on American history or Lepore's thoughts on football might not be authoritative. Also consider whether the expert has any bias or special interest that would affect reliability. Statistics on cases of lung cancer attributed to smoking might be better taken from government sources than from the tobacco industry.

Should you want to contact a campus expert, turn to Ch. 5 for advice about interviews.

Firsthand Observation. Firsthand observation is persuasive. It can add concrete reality to abstract or complex points. You might support the claim "The Meadowfield waste recycling plant fails to meet state guidelines" by recalling your own observations: "When I visited the plant last January, I was struck by the number of open waste canisters and by the lack of protective gear for the workers who handle these toxic materials daily."

For more on observation, see Ch. 4.

For more on logical fallacies, see p. 145.

As readers, most of us tend to trust the writer who declares, "I was there. This is what I saw." Sometimes that trust is misplaced, however, so always be wary of a writer's claim to have seen something that no other evidence supports. Ask yourself, Is this writer biased? Might the writer have (intentionally or unintentionally) misinterpreted what he or she saw? Of course, your readers will scrutinize your firsthand observations, too; take care to reassure them that your observations are unbiased and accurate. Evidence must be used carefully to avoid logical fallacies — common mistakes in thinking — or statements that lead to wrong conclusions. Examples are easy to misuse; for instance, just because two professors you know are dissatisfied with state-mandated testing programs, you can't claim that all — or even most — professors are. For that, you would need to conduct scientific surveys, access reliable statistics from the library or Internet, or solicit the views of a respected expert.

Learning by Doing 🎬 Supporting a Claim

Write out, in one complete sentence, the claim you plan to support. Working in a small group, drop everyone's position statements into a hat, with no names attached. Then read each aloud in turn, inviting the group to suggest useful supporting evidence and possible sources for it. Ask someone in the group to record the suggestions. Finally, match up writers with claims, and share reactions. If this activity causes you to alter your position, be thankful: it will be easier to revise now rather than later.

For more on testing evidence, see B in the Quick Research Guide, pp. Q-24–Q-25.

Check Your Evidence. Record your evidence in a notebook or digital file, noting the complete source information. Then get ready to sift through it and decide which information to use. Always critically test and question evidence to see whether it is strong enough to carry the weight of your claims.

For advice on evaluating sources of evidence, see C in the Quick Research Guide, pp. Q-25–Q-27.

CHECKING YOUR EVIDENCE

☐ Is it accurate?

- Do the facts seem accurate based on other published sources?
- Are figures or quoted facts copied correctly?

☐ Is it reliable?

- Is the source trustworthy and well regarded?
- Does the source acknowledge any bias that might affect the quality of its information?
- Is the writer respected as an expert or someone with appropriate credentials or experience?

- [ ] Is it up-to-date?
  - Are facts and statistics current?
  - Is the information from the latest sources?
- [ ] Is it to the point?
  - Does the evidence back the exact claim made?
  - Is the evidence all pertinent?
- [ ] Is it representative?
  - Are examples typical rather than outliers?
  - Are examples balanced? Do they present the topic or issue fairly?
  - Are contrary examples acknowledged?
- [ ] Is it appropriately complex?
  - Is the evidence sufficient to account for the claim made?
  - Does it avoid treating complex things superficially?
  - Does it avoid needlessly complicating simple things?
- [ ] Is it sufficient and strong enough to back the claim and persuade readers?
  - Are the amount and quality of the evidence appropriate for the claim?
  - Is the evidence aligned with the existing knowledge of readers?
  - Does the evidence answer the questions readers are likely to ask?
  - Is the evidence vivid and significant?

For information on mistakes in thinking, see p. 145.

You may find that your evidence supports a different stand than you intended to take. Do you need facts, testimony, and observations to support your original position after all? Or should you rethink your position? If so, revise your working thesis. Does your evidence cluster around several points or reasons? If so, use your evidence to plan the sequence of your essay.

In addition, consider whether information presented visually would strengthen your case or make your evidence easier for readers to grasp.

For more on the use of visuals and their placement, see section B in the Quick Format Guide, pp. Q-7–Q-12.

- Graphs can effectively show facts or figures.
- Tables can convey terms or comparisons.
- Photos or other illustrations can help support your claims.

Test each visual as you would test other evidence for accuracy, reliability, and relevance. Mention each visual in your text, and place the visual close to that reference. Cite the source of any visual you use and of any data you consolidate in your own graph or table.

Address Counterarguments. Most effective argument writers take opposing viewpoints into consideration whenever possible. Doing so demonstrates that the writer respects those viewpoints. Providing evidence that refutes opposing viewpoints can strengthen an argument. Use these questions to help you assess your evidence from this standpoint.

Focus on opposing viewpoints

- What are the opposition's claims?
- What is their evidence?
- Who supports their positions?

Acknowledge and rebut the counterarguments

- What are the strengths of other positions? What might you want to concede or grant to be accurate or relevant?
- What are the limitations of other positions? What might you want to question or challenge?
- What facts, statistics, testimony, observations, or other evidence can you use to show why their claims are weak, only partially true, misguided, or just plain wrong?

Learning by Doing Addressing Counterarguments

State your thesis on a debatable issue and list two or three main reasons why you support this position. Think about what a reader would need to understand or consider in order to be persuaded that your position is correct. This will be the nucleus of your argument. Next, consider arguments that might be made in opposition to your views and questions that might be raised. Write some notes on how you would answer or refute these questions and counterarguments. Exchange papers with a partner to see if he or she has anything to contribute.

Planning, Drafting, and Developing

Reassess Your Position and Your Thesis. Now that you have looked further into the issue you chose, what is your current position? If necessary, revise the thesis that you formulated earlier. Then summarize your reasons for holding this view, and list your supporting evidence.

WORKING THESIS	We should expect advertisers to fight rather than reinforce gender stereotypes.
REFINED THESIS	Consumers should spend their shopping dollars thoughtfully in order to hold advertisers accountable for reinforcing rather than resisting gender stereotypes.

STRENGTHENING YOUR THESIS

☐ Is it clearly debatable — something that you can take a position on? Is it more than just a factual statement?

☐ Does it take a strong position?

☐ Does it need to be refined or qualified in response to evidence that you've gathered?

Organize Your Material Persuasively. Arrange your notes into the order you think you'll follow, perhaps making an outline. One useful pattern is the classical form of argument:

For more on outlines, see pp. 273–80.

1. Introduce the subject to gain your readers' interest.
2. State your thesis.
3. If useful, supply historical background or an overview of the situation.
4. Present your claims, and provide evidence to support them.
5. Refute the opposing arguments.
6. Reaffirm your thesis.

Most academic essays are organized *deductively* — that is, they begin with a general statement (often a thesis) and then present particular claims to support or apply it. However, when you expect readers to be hostile to your position, stating your position too early might alienate resistant readers or make them defensive. Instead, you may want to refute the opposition first, then replace those views by building a logical chain of evidence that leads to your main point, and finally state your position. Papers that begin with particular details and evidence and then lead up to a larger claim are organized *inductively*. Of course, you can always try both approaches to see which one works better. Note also that some papers will be mostly based on refutation (countering opposing

DEDUCTIVE PATTERN

FIRST: Broad generalization or conclusion. **THEN:** Details, examples, facts, and supporting particulars.

FIRST: Particulars, details, examples, facts. **THEN:** Concluding generalization.

INDUCTIVE PATTERN

views) and some mostly on confirmation (directly supporting your position). Others might even alternate between refuting and confirming a position.

Attend to Logical, Emotional, and Ethical Appeals. Logical appeals engage readers' intellect; emotional appeals touch their hearts; ethical appeals draw on their sense of fairness and reasonableness. A persuasive argument usually operates on all three levels. The following table illustrates how appeals support a thesis about the need to curb accidental gunshot deaths.

Type of Appeal	Ways of Making the Appeal	Possible Supporting Evidence
Logical (logos)	■ Rely on clear reasoning and sound evidence to influence a reader's thinking. ■ Demonstrate what you claim, and don't claim what you can't demonstrate. ■ Test and select your evidence.	■ Supply current and reliable statistics about gun ownership and accidental shootings. ■ Prepare a bar graph showing the number of incidents each year during the past ten years, using data from county records. ■ Describe the immediate and long-term consequences of a typical shooting accident.
Emotional (pathos)	■ Choose examples and language that will influence a reader's feelings. ■ Include effective images, but don't overdo them. ■ Complement logical appeals, but don't replace them.	■ Describe a wrenching scenario of accidental gun violence, such as a college student who unexpectedly returns home at 3 A.M. and the parent who mistakes him for an intruder and shoots him. ■ Use quotations and descriptions from newspaper accounts to show reactions of family and friends.
Ethical (ethos)	■ Use a tone and approach that appeal to your reader's sense of fairness and reasonableness. ■ Spell out your values and beliefs, and acknowledge the values and beliefs of others with different opinions. ■ Establish your credentials or the credentials of experts you cite. ■ Instill confidence in your readers so that they see you as caring and trustworthy.	■ Establish your reasonable approach by acknowledging the views of law-abiding gun owners who follow recommended safety procedures. ■ Supply the credentials or affiliation of experts ("Ray Fontaine, public safety director for the county").

Learning by Doing Identifying Types of Appeals

Bring to class or post links for the editorial or opinion page from a newspaper, newsmagazine, or blog with a strong point of view. Read some of the pieces, and identify the types of appeals used by each author to support his or her point. With classmates, evaluate the effectiveness of these appeals.

Credit Your Sources. As you write, make your sources of evidence clear. One simple way to do so is to incorporate your source into the text: "As analyzed in an article in the May 25, 2015, issue of *Time*" or "According to historian Harry Cleghorn. . . ."

For pointers on integrating and documenting sources, see Ch. 30 and D6 (pp. Q-30–Q-31) and E1–E2 (pp. Q-31–Q-36) in the Quick Research Guide.

Revising and Editing

When you're writing a paper that takes a stand, you may fall in love with the evidence you've gone to such trouble to collect. Taking out information is hard to do, but if it is irrelevant, redundant, or weak, the evidence won't help your case. Play the crusty critic as you reread your paper. Consider outlining it so that you can check for missing or unnecessary points or evidence. Pay special attention to the suggestions of friends or classmates who read your draft for you. Apply their advice by ruthlessly cutting unneeded material, as in the following passage:

For more revising and editing strategies, see Ch. 19.

> The school boundary system requires children who are homeless or whose families move frequently to change schools repeatedly. ~~They often lack clean clothes, winter coats, and required school supplies.~~ As a result, these children struggle to establish strong relationships with teachers, to find caring advocates at school, and even to make friends to join for recess or lunch.

Peer Response 🖐 Get Feedback on Your Argument Essay

Enlist several other students to read your draft critically and answer these questions:

For general questions for a peer editor, see p. 309.

- Can you state the writer's claim?
- Do you have any problems following or accepting the reasons for the writer's position? Would you make any changes in the reasoning?
- How persuasive is the writer's evidence? What questions do you have about it? Can you suggest good evidence the writer has overlooked?
- Has the writer provided transitions to guide you through the argument?
- Has the writer made a strong case? Are you persuaded by his or her point of view? If not, is there any objection that the writer could address to make the argument more compelling?
- If this paper were yours, what is the one thing you would be sure to work on before handing it in?

REVISING YOUR DRAFT

- ☐ Have you developed your reasoning on a solid foundation? Are your initial assumptions sound? Do you need to identify, explain, or justify them?
- ☐ Is your main point, or thesis, clear? Do you stick to it?

☐ Have you defined all necessary terms and explained your points clearly?

☐ Have you arranged your reasons in a sequence that will make sense to your audience? Have you used transitions to introduce and connect them?

☐ Have you used evidence that your audience will respect to support each reason you present? Have you favored objective, research-based evidence (facts, statistics, and expert testimony that others can substantiate) rather than personal experiences or beliefs that others may not share?

☐ Have you explained your evidence so that your audience can see how it supports your points?

☐ Have you enhanced your own credibility by acknowledging, rather than ignoring, other points of view or possible objections? Have you integrated or countered these views?

☐ Have you adjusted your tone and style so you come across as reasonable and fair-minded? Have you avoided arrogant claims about proving (rather than showing) points?

☐ In rereading your paper, do you have any excellent, fresh thoughts? If so, where might you make room for them?

☐ Have you credited any sources as expected by academic readers?

Learning by Doing 🎬 Reflecting on Your Draft

Reflect on a draft of a current essay that makes an argument. What have you found most challenging about the process of drafting an argument essay? What have you found most rewarding? How, if at all, has the work of producing multiple drafts caused you to rethink the argument or how you have constructed and supported it?

For more editing and proofreading strategies, see pp. 316–18.

After you have revised your argument, edit and proofread it. Carefully check the grammar, word choice, punctuation, and mechanics — and then correct any problems you find. Wherever you have given facts and figures as evidence, check for errors in names and numbers.

EDITING FOR CLARITY

For more help, find the relevant checklist sections in the Quick Editing Guide on p. Q-37. Turn also to the Quick Format Guide beginning on p. Q-1.

☐ Is it clear what each pronoun refers to? Does each pronoun agree with (match) its antecedent? Do pronouns used as subjects agree with their verbs?   A6

☐ Have you used adjectives and adverbs correctly? Have you used the correct form when comparing two or more things?   A7

☐ Have you set off your transitions, other introductory elements, and interrupters with commas, if these are needed?   D1

☐ Have you correctly punctuated quotations?   D3

☐ Have you spelled and capitalized everything correctly,   E1, E2
especially names of people and organizations?

Recognize Logical Fallacies. Logical fallacies are common mistakes in thinking that may lead to wrong conclusions or distort evidence. Here are a few familiar logical fallacies.

Term	Explanation	Example
Ad Hominem	Attacking an individual's opinion by attacking his or her character, thus deflecting attention from the merit of a proposal; Latin for "against the man"	Diaz may argue that we need to save the polar bears, but he's the type who gets emotional over nothing.
Allness	Stating or implying that something is true of an entire class of things, often using *all, everyone, no one, always,* or *never*	Students enjoy studying. (All students? All subjects? All the time?)
Bandwagon Argument	Suggesting that everyone is joining the group and that readers who don't may miss out on happiness, success, or a reward	Purchasing the new Global Glimmer admits you to the nation's most elite group of smartphone users.
Begging the Question	Proving a statement already taken for granted, often by repeating it in different words or by defining a word in terms of itself	Rapists are dangerous because they are menaces. Happiness is the state of being happy.
Circular Reasoning	Supporting a statement with itself; a form of begging the question	He is a liar because he simply isn't telling the truth.
Either/Or Reasoning	Oversimplifying by assuming that an issue has only two sides, a statement must be true or false, a question demands a yes or no answer, or a problem has only two possible solutions	What are we going to do about global warming? Either we stop using all of the energy-consuming products that cause it, or we just learn to live with it.
Non Sequitur	Stating a claim that doesn't follow from your first premise or statement; Latin for "it does not follow"	Jenn should marry Mateo. In college he got all A's.
Oversimplification	Offering easy solutions for complicated problems	If we want to end substance abuse, let's send every drug user to prison for life. (Even aspirin users?)
Post Hoc, Ergo Propter Hoc	Assuming that because one event preceded another, there must be a cause-and-effect relationship; Latin for "after this, therefore because of this"	After Jenny's black cat crossed my path, everything went wrong, and I failed my midterm.
Proof by Too Few Examples	Presenting an example as proof rather than as illustration or clarification; overgeneralizing	Armenians are great chefs. My neighbor is Armenian, and can he cook!

Reviewing and Reflecting

REVIEW Working with classmates or independently, respond to the following questions:

1. What characteristics make an issue or a question a good subject for a paper that takes a stand? What characteristics make an issue or a question a weaker subject? With these criteria in mind, think of an issue on campus or in the news that would be a good topic for a taking-a-stand paper.

2. Why is evidence so important in writing that takes a stand?

3. Why is it important to address opposing views in an argument? If you identified a good topic in your answer to question 1, try to state a position on it and list two or three opposing views.

REFLECT Reflect in writing about how you might apply the insights that you drew from this assignment to an argument assignment for another course or to a writing situation outside of college. In your reflection, consider such factors as your audience's interests, level of knowledge, or possible objections; the types of evidence that you might supply to support your position; the type of reasoning that might be most effective; and so on.

Additional Writing Assignments

1. Write a letter to the editor of your newspaper or a newsmagazine in which you agree or disagree with the publication's editorial stand on a current question. Make clear your reasons for holding your view.

2. Write one claim each of substantiation, evaluation, and policy for or against a specific policy or proposal. Indicate an audience each claim might address effectively. Then list reasons and types of evidence you might need to support one of these claims and indicate what opposing viewpoints you would need to consider and how you could best do so.

3. Write a short paper, blog entry, or class posting expressing your view on one of these topics or another that comes to mind. Make clear your reasons for thinking as you do.

Raising the minimum wage
Bilingual education
Twitter activism
Sexual harassment in the
    workplace
Controlling terrorism

Requiring public school
    students to be vaccinated
Crimes committed by
    professional athletes
Protecting the gray wolf

4. Working with a classmate or a small group online, develop a blog to inform your audience about multiple points of view on an issue, with each member representing a different view. Present the most compelling reasons and

evidence to support each view. Counter other views as appropriate with reasons and evidence, but avoid emotional outbursts attacking them. Considering your purpose and audience, also decide whether the blog should cover certain points or be organized in a particular way. Draft it in a location or file where you can save and return to it, taking time to revise and edit before you post your contribution.

5. **Source Assignment.** Find a letter to the editor, opinion piece, or blog post that takes a stand that you disagree with. Write a response to that piece, countering its points, presenting your points, and supporting them with evidence. Be sure to cite the other piece, and identify any quotations or summaries from it. Decide which audience to address: The writer? Readers likely to support the other selection? Readers with interest in the issue but without loyalty to the original publication? Some other group?

For more on supporting a position with sources, see Ch. 11.

6. **Visual Assignment.** Study the following image and note its persuasive visual elements. Write an essay that first explains what argument the image might be making, including its topic and its visual appeals to viewers, and then agrees with, disagrees with, or qualifies that argument.

Children playing on their smartphones in Soweto, South Africa. Per-Anders Pettersson/Corbis News/Getty Images

9 Proposing a Solution

Student Government Resource Center, a project of Student Organizing Inc

Responding to an Image

The National Student Campaign Against Hunger and Homelessness is a student-led effort to combat the problem of hunger and homelessness at their colleges and universities. Among the solutions they offer on their website is a toolkit to help make a case for and run a campus food pantry. How would you characterize the group's attitude toward solving the problems of hunger and homelessness?

Why Proposing a Solution Matters

Sometimes when you learn of a problem such as the destruction caused by a natural disaster, homelessness, or climate change, you say to yourself, "Something should be done about that." You can do something constructive yourself—through powerful and persuasive writing.

Your purpose in such writing, as political leaders and advertisers well know, is to rouse your audience to action. At college, you might write a letter to your college newspaper or to someone in authority and try to stir your readers to do something. Does some college policy irk you? Would you urge students to attend a rally for a cause or a charity? Do you want to address the problem of student hunger and homelessness, perhaps following the lead of the National Student Campaign Against Hunger and Homelessness, mentioned above?

You can use the power of your writing to solve a problem, to make something better, to implement change. In Chapter 8, you took a stand and backed it up with evidence. Now go a step further, writing a *proposal*—a recommendation for taking action. If, for instance, you have made the claim "Our national parks are in sorry condition," you might urge readers to write to their representatives in Congress or to visit a national park and pick up trash. This paper would be a call to immediate action on the part of your readers. On the other hand, you might suggest that the Department of the Interior be given a budget increase to hire more park rangers, purchase additional park land to accommodate more visitors, and buy more cleanup equipment. This second paper would attempt to forge a consensus about what needs to be done.

We propose solutions to problems all the time, including situations like the following:

In a College Course

- You identify a societal problem and propose a solution, tackling issues such as sealed adoption records, rising costs of prescriptions, and violence in prisons.

- You propose a field research study, explaining and justifying your purposes and methods, in order to gain faculty and institutional approval for your capstone project.

In the Workplace

- You propose expanding into a new market to increase your company's profits.

In Your Community

- You plan a tutoring program at the library for the many adults in your region with limited literacy skills.

❓ What situations have encouraged you to write proposals?

Learning from Other Writers

The writers of the following two essays propose sensible solutions for pressing problems. To help you analyze the first reading, look at the notes in the margin, which point out the problem, the thesis or main idea, and the proposed solution. As you read these proposals, ask yourself the following questions:

1. What problem does the writer identify? Does the writer rouse you to want to do something about the problem?
2. What solution does the writer propose? What evidence supports the solution? Does the writer convince you to agree with this solution?
3. How is the writer qualified to write on this subject?

Wilbert Rideau

Wilbert Rideau

Why Prisons Don't Work

Wilbert Rideau (b. 1942) was editor of the *Angolite*, the Louisiana State Penitentiary newsmagazine, during his incarceration there. His memoir, *In the Place of Justice* (2010), offers a voice seldom heard in the debate over crime control—that of the criminal.

Introduction of the problem

I was among thirty-one murderers sent to the Louisiana State Penitentiary in 1962 to be executed or imprisoned for life. We weren't much different from those we found here, or those who had preceded us. We were unskilled, impulsive, and uneducated misfits, mostly black, who had done dumb, impulsive things—failures, rejects from the larger society. Now a generation has come of age and gone since I've been here, and everything is much the same as I found it. The faces of the prisoners are different, but behind them are the same impulsive, uneducated, unskilled minds that made dumb, impulsive *THESIS stating the problem* choices that got them into more trouble than they ever thought existed. The vast majority of us are consigned to suffer and die here so politicians can sell the illusion that permanently exiling people to prison will make society safe.

Getting tough has always been a "silver bullet," a quick fix for the crime and violence that society fears. Each year in Louisiana—where excess is a way of life—lawmakers have tried to outdo each other in legislating harsher mandatory penalties and in reducing avenues of release. The only thing to do with criminals, they say, is get tougher. They have. In the process, the purpose of prison began to change. The state boasts one of the highest lockup rates in the country, imposes the most severe penalties in the nation, and vies to execute more criminals per capita than anywhere else. This state is so tough that last year, when prison authorities here wanted to punish an inmate in solitary confinement for an infraction,° the most they could inflict on him was to deprive him of his underwear. It was all he had left.

1

2

infraction: Violation.

If getting tough resulted in public safety, Louisiana citizens would be   3
the safest in the nation. They're not. Louisiana has the highest murder rate
among states. Prison, like the police and the courts, has a minimal impact on
crime because it is a response after the fact, a mop-up operation. It doesn't
work. The idea of punishing the few to deter the many is counterfeit because
potential criminals either think they're not going to get caught or they're so
emotionally desperate or psychologically distressed that they don't care about
the consequences of their actions. The threatened punishment, regardless of
its severity, is never a factor in the equation. But society, like the incorrigible°
criminal it abhors, is unable to learn from its mistakes.

Prison has a role in public safety, but it is not a cure-all. Its value is lim-   4
ited, and its use should also be limited to what it does best: isolating young
criminals long enough to give them a chance to grow up and get a grip on
their impulses. It is a traumatic experience, certainly, but it should be only
a temporary one, not a way of life. Prisoners kept too long tend to embrace
the criminal culture, its distorted values and beliefs; they have little choice —
prison is their life. There are some prisoners who cannot be returned to
society — serial killers, serial rapists, professional hit men, and the like — but
the monsters who need to die in prison are rare exceptions in the criminal
landscape.

Introduction of the proposed solution

Crime is a young man's game. Most of the nation's random violence is   5
committed by young urban terrorists. But because of long, mandatory sentences, most prisoners here are much older, having spent fifteen, twenty,
thirty, or more years behind bars, long past necessity. Rather than pay for new
prisons, society would be well served by releasing some of its older prisoners
who pose no threat and using the money to catch young street thugs. Warden
John Whitley agrees that many older prisoners here could be freed tomorrow
with little or no danger to society. Release, however, is governed by law or by
politicians, not by penal professionals. Even murderers, those most feared by
society, pose little risk. Historically, for example, the domestic staff at Louisiana's Governor's mansion has been made up of murderers, hand-picked to
work among the chief-of-state and his family. Penologists° have long known
that murder is almost always a once-in-a-lifetime act. The most dangerous
criminal is the one who has not yet killed but has a history of escalating
offenses. He's the one to watch.

Transitions (underlined) for coherence

Rehabilitation can work. Everyone changes in time. The trick is to influ-   6
ence the direction that change takes. The problem with prisons is that they
don't do more to rehabilitate those confined in them. The convict who enters
prison illiterate will probably leave the same way. Most convicts want to be
better than they are, but education is not a priority. This prison houses 4,600
men and offers academic training to 240, vocational training to a like number. Perhaps it doesn't matter. About 90 percent of the men here may never
leave this prison alive.

---

incorrigible: Incapable of reform.   **penologists:** Those who study prison management and
criminal justice.

Conclusion summing up solution

The only effective way to curb crime is for society to work to prevent the   7
criminal act in the first place, to come between the perpetrator° and crime.
Our youngsters must be taught to respect the humanity of others and to handle disputes without violence. It is essential to educate and equip them with
the skills to pursue their life ambitions in a meaningful way. As a community,
we must address the adverse life circumstances that spawn criminality. These
things are not quick, and they're not easy, but they're effective. Politicians
think that's too hard a sell. They want to be on record for doing something
now, something they can point to at reelection time. So the drumbeat goes on
for more police, more prisons, more of the same failed policies.

Ever see a dog chase its tail?   8

perpetrator: One who is responsible for an action or a crime.

Questions to Start You Thinking

Meaning

1. Does Rideau convince you that the belief that "permanently exiling
people to prison will make society safe" is an "illusion" (paragraph 1)?

2. According to Rideau, why don't prisons work?

3. What does he propose as solutions to the problem of escalating crime?
What other solutions can you think of?

Writing Strategies

4. What evidence does the author provide to support his assertion that
Louisiana's "getting tough" policy has not worked? Does he provide
sufficient evidence to convince you? Does he persuade you that action is
necessary?

5. Other than himself, what authorities does Rideau cite? Why do you think
he does this? Also, why do you think he mentions that he is a convicted
criminal?

6. How do you interpret the last line, "Ever see a dog chase its tail?" Is this
line an effective way for Rideau to end his essay? Explain.

Lacey Taylor   **Student Essay**

It's Not Just a Bike

Lacey Taylor drew on personal experience in her essay to identify a problem on
her campus and to propose solutions for it.

❓ What compara-
ble local problems
have you experi-
enced or observed?

Imagine one day waking up to find that your car had been stolen. To many students,   1
a bicycle is just like a car. They depend on their bicycles for all their transportation
needs, getting to and from classes and work. Too many bicycles are being stolen on

campus, and this situation has become a major problem for students who depend on them. In the past year, one friend has had two new bicycles stolen. Just three months ago, I went home for the weekend, and when I got back, my bicycle was gone. I could not believe that anyone would do such a horrible thing, but I was wrong, and someone did do it. This theft was a major blow to me because my bicycle was my only transportation to work. I am not the only person and will not be the last to have my bicycle taken, so something should be done and should be done soon. The campus community should use methods such as posting warning signs, starting an awareness program, and investing in new technology like cameras, chain alarms, and tracking devices to help solve this problem.

Although many solutions are available to help alleviate this problem, some may be as simple as posting signs. Signs are a cheap and easy way to alleviate bike theft. The signs should read that bicycle theft is a crime, punishable by law, and they should explain the consequences that go along with stealing bicycles. The signs would need to be posted at all the bicycle racks just like the signs posted at every parking spot warning about being a tow-away zone. These signs would not completely solve the problem, but they would discourage some potential bicycle thieves.

2

The school also needs to begin a bicycle-theft awareness program. The program should inform students about bicycle theft, warning that it happens all the time and that it could happen to them. The program also would need to tell students about certain steps that they could take to avoid becoming victims of bike theft. For example, it could provide information about different methods of bicycle security such as keeping the serial number in case the bike is stolen and engraving a name on the bike so that it can be easily identified. The program also should tell students what to do if a bicycle is actually stolen such as calling the police and filing a report. This awareness program would prevent many students from ending up with stolen bicycles.

3 ❓ What simple informative and preventive methods have been used in your community or on your campus to solve problems?

A more advanced method for solving this problem would be to install security cameras all around campus. The cameras would keep track of all the activity going on at the bicycle racks and let the person watching the camera know if someone is stealing a bicycle. If no one sees the illegal act take place, then the camera tape could be pulled, watched, and used as evidence against the bike thief. For this solution to succeed, the cameras should be placed a certain way, all facing the bike racks and close enough for a viewer to tell what is going on at the racks. The cameras also need to be in plain sight for everyone to see so that anyone considering stealing a bicycle would think twice before acting. After all, no one wants to be caught doing something illegal on camera. Finally, these cameras should be linked to a TV in the lobby of each dorm. Keeping an eye on the TV, watching for any strange activity, should be part of the job of the resident assistant on duty. The resident assistant then could report a bicycle being stolen to the campus police. These cameras would not only ward off some potential criminals but also help to catch the ones who were not scared off.

4

A creative solution would be to invest in chain alarms. These chains contain   5
small wires; if the chains are cut, an alarm in the lock goes off just like a car alarm.
This alarm would alert people nearby that someone was stealing a bicycle. The
sound also might scare the thief into dropping the bike and running off. These
chains could be rented out to students by the transportation department. If the
rental cost around ten dollars a semester, the chains would pay for themselves
over a short period of time and eventually make a profit for the transportation
department. If someone never returned the chain at the end of the semester,
the student should be fined, and a hold should be placed on his or her account
just as the library does with book fines that must be paid before graduation.
These chains would help to catch the bike thieves and also, just like the signs and
cameras, help to scare off potential thieves.

Finally tracking devices could be placed on all campus bicycles. This would   6
be the most effective solution to the bicycle theft problem because these tracking
devices would come into play if all the other solutions failed to do the job. These
devices should be small and placed in a hard-to-find spot on the bicycle. If a bike
is stolen, then the bike could be traced on a campus police computer and its
location identified. Then the police could go through the proper procedure to
catch the thief. These tracking devices could be rented out just like the bicycle
chains. Even though this method would not stop bicycles from being stolen, it
would make it easy to find the bikes and catch the thieves.

Bicycle theft is a major problem that deserves attention. Too many bicycles   7
are being stolen, and bikes are too important to everyday campus life to let this
problem go unnoticed. The campus should use simple methods such as posting
warning signs or sponsoring an awareness program and also invest in new
technology like cameras, chain alarms, and tracking devices to help solve this
problem. Bicycle riders should be aware that theft is a problem that could happen
to them at any time, but bicycle thieves should not be able to take whatever they
like with no action being taken against them. Bicycles, like cars, provide essential
transportation, and no one wants to have that necessity stolen.

? Would students
on your campus wel-
come technological
solutions to prob-
lems like bike theft,
or would they worry
about privacy, costs,
or other issues?

Questions to Start You Thinking

Meaning

1. What problem does Taylor identify? Does she convince you that this is an
   important problem? Why, or why not?

2. What solutions does she propose? Why does she arrange them as she
   does? Which is her strongest solution? Her least convincing? Can you
   think of other ideas that she might have included?

3. How effectively would Taylor's proposal persuade various members of a
   campus audience? Which people would she easily persuade? Which might
   need more convincing? Can you think of other arguments that would
   appeal to specific readers?

Writing Strategies

4. Is Taylor's argument easy to follow? Why, or why not? What kinds of transitions does she use to lead readers through her points? How effective do you find them?

5. Is Taylor's evidence specific and sufficient? Explain.

6. What qualifies Taylor to write about this topic? How do these qualifications contribute to her ability to persuade?

Learning by Writing

The Assignment: Proposing a Solution

In this essay you'll first carefully analyze and explain a specific social, economic, political, civic, or environmental problem — a problem you care about and strongly wish to see resolved. The problem may be large or small, but it shouldn't be trivial. It may affect the whole country or mainly people from your city, campus, or classroom. Show your readers that this problem really exists, that it matters to you and to them, and perhaps even why it exists. Write for an audience who, once aware of the problem, may be expected to help do something about it.

The second thing you are to accomplish is to propose one or more ways to solve or at least alleviate the problem. In making a proposal, you urge action by using words like *should*, *ought*, and *must*: "This city ought to have a Bureau of Missing Persons"; "Small private aircraft should be banned from flying close to a major commercial airport." Lay out the reasons why your proposal deserves to be implemented; supply evidence that your solution is reasonable and can work.

A "living wall," a wall that is completely or partially covered with plants, addresses the problem of energy consumption and air pollution. Nano Calvo/VW Pics/ZUMAPRESS.com

MANAGING YOUR TIME
Writing a Proposal

Use the breakdown below to plan your time for this essay; in the right column, insert target dates and times for completing each stage.

approx. 30-45 minutes	■ **Read your assignment carefully.** Is it clear what your instructor is asking of you? If not, follow up. ■ **Brainstorm** to identify a **problem** that you would like to solve—and **possible solutions** to that problem. How will you draw in your readers?	**I'll complete** this stage by: _____ (day, date)
approx. 2-3 hours	■ **Read** about the problem you've chosen—its scope, causes, effects, or components—and what solutions have already been tried or discussed. ■ Formulate your **thesis** by clearly stating the problem and proposing your solution. How will your solution improve the situation? ■ Identify **evidence** that you can use to demonstrate the value of your solution, such as facts, statistics, and examples.	**I'll complete** this stage by: _____ (day, date)
approx. 2-3 hours	■ **Sketch an outline of your essay.** Begin by stating the problem you will solve, then discuss the solutions that have been tried before. Present your solution persuasively. ■ **Draft your essay,** staying close to your outline. Back yourself up with facts, and be sure to credit your sources as you write. ■ Craft a compelling **introduction** and a satisfying **conclusion** by appealing to your readers to accept your solution and/or to take a specific action.	**I'll complete** this stage by: _____ (day, date)
approx. 2-4 hours	■ Ask a **peer to review** your draft. Have you identified a compelling problem? Have you offered valuable, concrete solutions to it? Have you supported it with persuasive evidence? ■ **Revise your draft,** addressing issues raised during your and your peer's review. ■ **Edit your draft,** fixing any errors and polishing your prose.	**I'll complete** this stage by: _____ (day, date)

Generating Ideas

Identify a Problem. Brainstorm by writing down all the problems that come to mind. Observe events around you to identify irritating campus or community problems you would like to solve. Watch for ideas in the news. Browse through issue-oriented websites or blogs. Listen to radio programs or podcasts to learn about current issues. Be sure to stick to problems that you want to solve, and star the ideas that seem to have the most potential.

■ What problems do you meet every day or occasionally? What problems concern people near you?

- What conditions in need of improvement have you observed on television, on the radio, or on the Web? What action is called for?
- What problems have been discussed recently on campus or in class?
- What problems are discussed in blogs, newspapers, or magazines such as *Time, The Week,* or *U.S. News & World Report*?

Use the critical thinking skills you learned in Chapter 3 (p. 36) to analyze the problem you have identified. Can you break it down into distinct parts? Can you identify its causes or effects?

Consider Your Audience. Readers need to believe that your problem is real and your solution is feasible. If you are addressing classmates, maybe they haven't thought about the problem before. Look for ways to make it personal, to show that it affects them and deserves their attention.

Learning by Doing 🖭 Describing Your Audience

Write a paragraph describing the audience you intend to address. Who are they, and why should they care about this problem? Which of their circumstances, interests, traits, social circles, attitudes, and values best prepare them to face the problem? Which make them most (or least) receptive to your solution? Consider how to present your ideas most persuasively to this audience. If you want a second opinion, share your analysis with a classmate.

Think about Solutions. Once you've chosen a problem, brainstorm — alone or with classmates — possible solutions, or use your imagination. Critically evaluate (see p. 37) each potential solution to see which ones have merit. Some problems, such as reducing international tensions, present no easy solutions. Still, give some strategic thought to any problem that seriously concerns you, even if it has stumped experts. Sometimes a solution reveals itself to a novice thinker, and even a partial solution is worth offering.

Finding solutions is much harder than finding problems. Convincing readers that you have found a reasonable, workable solution is harder still. Try to anticipate the concerns and experiences of your audience, so you can develop a realistic solution that fully addresses a problem and satisfies the people the problem affects.

Consider Sources of Support. To show that the problem really exists, you'll need evidence and examples. If further library research will help you justify the problem, now is the time to do it. Consider whether local history archives, newspaper stories, accounts of public meetings, interviews, or relevant websites might help you develop your solution.

For more on using evidence to support an argument, see pp. 136–39.

For advice on finding sources, see sections A and B in the Quick Research Guide, pp. Q-20–Q-25.

For more on stating a thesis, see pp. 266–71.

Planning, Drafting, and Developing

Start with Your Thesis. A basic approach is to state your proposal in a sentence that can act as your thesis.

PROPOSAL	Let people get divorced without having to go to court.
WORKING THESIS	The legislature should pass a law allowing couples to divorce without the problem of going to court.

From such a statement, the rest of the argument may start to unfold, often falling naturally into a simple two-part shape:

1. *The problem statement*, which explains the problem and supplies evidence of its significance — for example, the costs and stress of divorce court for a couple and their family.

2. *The suggested solution*, which proposes what should be done about the problem — for example, new laws to authorize other options such as mediation.

For more on outlines, see pp. 273–80.

These two parts can grow naturally into an informal outline.

1. Introduction
   Overview of the situation
   Working thesis stating your proposal
2. Problem
   Explanation of its nature
   Evidence of its significance
3. Solution
   Explanation of its nature
   Evidence of its effectiveness and practicality
4. Conclusion

You can then expand your outline and make your proposal more persuasive by including some or all of the following elements:

- Knowledge or experience that qualifies you to propose a solution (your experience as a player or a coach, for example, that establishes your credibility as an authority on Little League or soccer clubs)
- Values, beliefs, or assumptions that have caused you to feel strongly about the need for action
- An estimate of the resources — money, people, skills, material — and the time required to implement the solution (perhaps including what is available now and what needs to be obtained)
- Step-by-step actions needed to achieve your solution
- Controls or quality checks to monitor implementation
- Possible obstacles or difficulties that may need to be overcome

- Reasons your solution is better than others proposed or tried already
- Any other evidence that shows that your suggestion is practical, reasonable in cost, and likely to be effective

A sign from part of a popular and successful antilittering campaign emphasizes its simplicity. AP Images/Donna McWilliam

Learning by Doing 🔯 Proposing a Solution

Academic or workplace stress is a problem for most people, but there are ways to manage it. In what aspect of your life do you experience stress or observe it in others? How might you or others manage that stress? Consider various solutions to the problem of stress, such as improving communication with supervisors or instructors, setting reasonable goals and expectations, taking time to exercise and meditate, and accessing any available mental health care and benefits. Conduct research as needed and make a brief outline of an essay proposing your solution. Be sure to provide step-by-step actions, identify obstacles, and state reasons that your solution is a good one, backing your statements with evidence. Cite any sources you draw on.

Imagine Possible Objections. Once you have drawn readers into the problem and the solution, think of objections they might raise — reservations about the cost, complexity, or workability of your plan, or new problems that your solution might cause. Persuade readers by anticipating and laying to rest their likely objections.

For pointers on integrating and documenting sources, see Ch. 11 and D6 and E1–E2 (pp. Q-30–Q-36) in the Quick Research Guide.

Cite Sources Carefully. When you collect evidence from outside sources, you need to document where you found everything. Follow the documentation style, such as MLA or APA, that your instructor wants you to use. Generally, it is good practice to identify sources as you introduce them to assure a reader that they are authoritative.

> According to *Newsweek* correspondent Josie Fair, . . .

> In his biography *FDR: The New Deal Years*, Davis reports . . .

> While working as a Senate page in the summer of 2019, I observed . . .

Introduce visual evidence (tables, graphs, drawings, maps, photos), too.

> As the 2018 unemployment figures in Table 1 indicate, . . .

> The photograph showing the run-down condition of the dog park (see Fig. 2) . . .

For more about integrating visuals, see section B (pp. Q-7–Q-12) in the Quick Format Guide.

Revising and Editing

For more revising and editing strategies, see Ch. 19.

As you revise, concentrate on a clear explanation of the problem and solid supporting evidence for the solution. Make your essay coherent and its parts clear to help convince your readers.

Clarify Your Thesis. Your thesis should identify the problem and possibly preview your solution. Look again at your thesis from a reader's point of view.

WORKING THESIS	The legislature should pass a law allowing couples to divorce without the problem of going to court.
REVISED THESIS	Because divorce court can be expensive, adversarial, and stressful, passing a law that allows couples to divorce without a trip to court would encourage simpler, more harmonious ways to end a marriage.

STRENGTHENING YOUR THESIS

☐ Does your thesis clearly identify the problem?

☐ Does it suggest a solution?

☐ Could the thesis be refined or made more specific based on evidence or insights that you gathered while developing your essay?

Reorganize for Unity and Coherence. When one student revised her first draft, she focused on clarifying the presentation of her problem: the decline of college agriculture programs.

Why would high schools in farming communities drop agriculture

The main reason that

classes and the FFA program? ₅ Small schools are cutting ag programs

is that

~~because~~ the state has not provided significant funding for the schools to

operate. The small schools have to make cuts, and some small schools

are deciding that the agriculture classes are not as important as other

courses. Some small schools are consolidating to receive more aid. Many

of these schools have been able to save their ag programs.

Move main reason last for emphasis

Why did I put a solution here? Move to end!

One reason is that m

Many colleges are demanding that students have two years of foreign

language. In small schools, like my own, the students could take either

foreign language or ag classes. Therefore, students choose language

classes to fill the college requirement. When the students leave the ag

classes to take foreign language, the number of students declines, which

makes it easier for school administrators to cut ag classes.

Rewrite this! Not really college requirements but college-prep courses vs. others when budget is tight

The revised paper was more forcefully organized and more coherent, making it easier for readers to follow. The bridges between ideas were now on paper, not just in the writer's mind.

For strategies for achieving coherence, see pp. 292–94.

Learning by Doing 🔄 Revising for Clear Organization

Check the organization of your draft against your plans and the two-part structure commonly used in proposals (see p. 158). Outline what you've actually written, not what you intended, to see your organization as readers will. Does your draft open with a sufficient overview for your audience? Do you state your actual proposal clearly? Does your draft progress from problem to solution without mixing ideas? Have you addressed the needs and concerns of your audience? Reorganize and revise as needed. Exchange drafts with a classmate if you want a second opinion on organization.

Be Reasonable. Exaggerated claims for a solution will not persuade readers. Neither will oversimplifying the problem so the solution seems more workable. Don't be afraid to express reasonable doubts about the completeness of your solution. If necessary, rethink both problem and solution.

Peer Response ⟨⟩ Proposing a Solution

Ask several classmates or friends to review your proposal and solution, answering questions such as these:

For general questions for a peer editor, see p. 309.

- What is your overall reaction to this proposal? Does it make you want to go out and do something about the problem?
- Are you convinced that the problem is of concern to you? If not, why not?
- Are you persuaded that the writer's solution is workable? Why, or why not?
- Has the writer paid enough attention to readers and their concerns?
- Restate what you understand to be the proposal's major points:

  Problem

  Explanation of problem and why it matters

  Proposed solution

  Explanation of proposal and its practicality

  Reasons and procedure to implement proposal

  Proposal's advantages, disadvantages, and responses to other solutions

  Final recommendation
- If this paper were yours, what one thing would you work on?

REVISING YOUR DRAFT

☐ Does your introduction invite the reader into the discussion?

☐ Is your problem clear and relevant to readers?

☐ Have you clearly outlined the steps necessary to solve the problem?

☐ Where have you demonstrated the benefits of your solution?

☐ Have you considered other solutions before rejecting them or anticipated the doubts readers may have about your solution?

☐ Have you avoided promising that your solution will do more than it can possibly do?

☐ Do you sound reasonable, willing to admit that you don't know everything? If you sound preachy, have you overused *should* and *must*?

For more editing and proofreading strategies, see pp. 316–18. For more on documenting sources, see E1–E2 in the Quick Research Guide, pp. Q-31–Q-36.

After you have revised your proposal, edit and proofread it. Carefully check the grammar, word choice, punctuation, and mechanics — and then correct any problems you find. If you have used sources, be sure that you have cited them correctly in your text and added a list of works cited.

Your sentence structure should help you make your points clearly and directly. Using the active voice allows you to emphasize the actor (subject) performing the sentence's action (verb). For example, the sentence "The dean should remedy the problem by spending money on prevention" explicitly identifies and emphasizes the actor (the dean) and does so succinctly. Using the passive voice, by contrast, results in a sentence that doesn't specify the actor: "The problem should be remedied by spending money on prevention." Readers may struggle to determine your intended focus — is it on the dean, or on the problem?

EDITING FOR CLARITY

☐ Is it clear what each pronoun refers to? Is any *this* or *that* ambiguous? Does each pronoun agree with its antecedent?   A6

☐ Is your sentence structure correct? Have you avoided writing fragments, comma splices, or fused sentences?   A1, A2

☐ Do your transitions and other introductory elements have commas after them, if these are needed?   D1

☐ Have you spelled and capitalized everything correctly, especially names of people and organizations?   E1, E2

For more help, find the relevant checklist sections in the Quick Editing Guide on p. Q-37. Turn also to the Quick Format Guide beginning on p. Q-1.

Reviewing and Reflecting

REVIEW Working with classmates or independently, respond to the following questions:

1. What strategies can you use to identify a problem that interests you — a problem with potential solutions?

2. What questions can you ask to learn more about the audience of a paper that proposes a solution to a problem? Think of a topic for such a paper, and ask these questions about the potential audience. Did going through this process make you think differently about how you might approach the topic? If so, how?

3. What types of information might flesh out an outline for a paper that proposes a solution to a problem, making the proposal more persuasive? If you have written or are writing a proposal paper, ask yourself if you could add any of this type of information to make your paper more effective.

REFLECT Reflect in writing about how you might apply the insights that you drew from this assignment to another situation — in or outside of college — in which you have to propose a solution to a problem. In your reflection, consider the types of solutions that might be most appealing to your potential audience.

Additional Writing Assignments

1. If you followed the assignment in Chapter 8 and took a stand, now write a few paragraphs extending that paper to propose a solution that argues for action.

2. Brainstorm with classmates to develop a list of campus problems that irritate students or complicate their lives. Write an essay that tackles one of these problems by explaining it and proposing a practical, workable solution. (If you can't identify a workable solution, select a different problem.) Address an audience on your campus or in your college system that could implement a solution. Present your ideas tactfully. After all, they may also be the ones responsible for creating or at least not solving the problem earlier.

3. Write a memo to your supervisor at work in which you propose an innovation (related to procedures, schedules, policies, or similar matters) that could benefit your department or company.

4. **Source Assignment.** The following are practice that attempt to solve a problem. Choose one that you find inefficient, unethical, or unfair. In a few paragraphs, give reasons for your objections. Then narrow the issue as needed to propose a better solution in a persuasive essay. Locate, use, and cite some statistics or other data to help raise readers' awareness.

   Companies censoring bad online reviews   Genetic engineering of foods

   Using child labor to produce consumer goods   Outsourcing jobs

   Conducting laboratory experiments on animals   Dumping waste in the ocean

5. **Visual Assignment.** Select one of the following images on page 165. Write an essay that analyzes the problem that it identifies, noting how elements of the image draw the viewer into the problem. Include any solution suggested or implied by the image or your own solution to the problem.

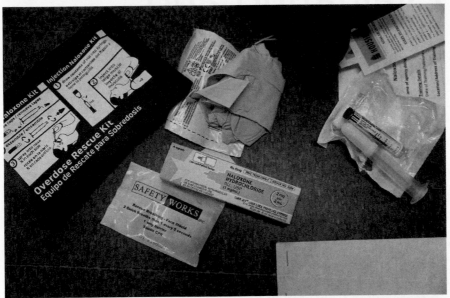

Spencer Platt/Getty Images

AP Images/The Brownsville Herald/Brad Doherty

10 Evaluating and Reviewing

Justin Sullivan/Getty Images

Responding to an Image

In what respects does this photograph of a giant-pumpkin weigh-in capture the essence of such competitions? What overall impression does the image convey? What details contribute to this impression? How does the photograph direct the viewer's eye? In what ways does this image suggest, represent, or comment on a particular set of criteria and process of evaluation?

Why Evaluating and Reviewing Matter

Evaluating means judging. You do it when you decide what candidate to vote for, pick which smartphone to buy, or recommend a new restaurant to your friends. All of us pass judgments — often snap judgments — as we move through a day's routine. A friend asks, "How was that movie you saw last night?" and you reply, "Terrific — don't miss it" or maybe "Pretty good, but it had too much blood and gore for me."

But to *write* an evaluation calls for you to think more critically. As a writer you first decide on *criteria*, or standards for judging, and then come up with evidence to back up your judgment. You zero in on a subject that you inspect carefully in order to reach a considered opinion. The subject might be a film, a book, or a performance that you review. Or it might be a sports team, a product, or a body of research that you evaluate. The possibilities are endless. Here are just some of the ways we evaluate every day:

In a College Course

- You evaluate theories and methods in the fields you study, including long-standing controversies and new approaches.
- You evaluate instructors, courses, and sometimes campus facilities and services to help improve your college.

In the Workplace

- You evaluate people, projects, goals, and results, just as your performance is evaluated as an employee.

In Your Community

- You evaluate video games for yourself or your children and review films, music, shows, and restaurants as you decide how to spend your money and time.

❓ What have you evaluated within the last few weeks? How have you incorporated evaluations and reviews into your writing?

Learning from Other Writers

Here are evaluations by a professional and a student. To help you analyze the first reading, look at the notes in the margin, which identify features such as the thesis, or main idea, and the criteria for evaluation. As you read these evaluations, ask yourself the following questions:

1. Do you consider the writer qualified to evaluate the subject he or she chose? What biases and prejudices might the writer bring to the task?

2. What criteria for evaluation does the writer establish? Are these reasonable standards for evaluating the subject?

3. What is the writer's assessment of the subject? Does the writer provide sufficient evidence to convince you of his or her evaluation?

James Bennett II

If You're Mad about *DAMN.*, You Probably Need to Listen to More Hip-Hop

New York Public Radio

James Bennet II is a digital writer and editor at WQXR-FM, a New York Public Radio station. Originally from the Chesapeake Bay area, Bennett moved to New York City, where he graduated from Columbia University. He contributed the following essay to NYPR's "New Sounds" program. It is both a review of the album *DAMN.* and an evaluation of the criticism faced by the first hip-hop artist to win the Pulitzer Prize for Music.

I don't think anyone really expected the announcement that Kendrick Lamar won the Pulitzer Prize° for Music, for his album *DAMN.*, would prompt musicians and composers and critics of all colors and creeds to join hands and sing *Kumbaya*.° But I was still surprised at how many of us considered Lamar's win a musical apocalypse, signaling the end of any meaning the Pulitzer Prize for Music once held. (A quick peek at the comments of your favorite blog/media outlet's post on the news will tell you everything you need to know about this). With that in mind, there's really only two things to say:

THESIS

1. For many a hip-hop listener, this is what the Grammys feel like every *DAMN.* year and

2. Once again, the classical community — contemporary or otherwise — needs to look inwards and determine the causes of this particular reaction's violent apoplexy.° (Hint: it's probably about race. Actually, it's always about race.)

Evaluation criterion 1: Attitudes toward hip-hop

Many of the criticisms aimed at Kendrick (and hip-hop music in general) are truly baffling.° Some complain that since rappers often work with songwriters and producers, rappers shouldn't be eligible for these awards (as if your favorite composer always wrote their own librettos, or it's routine for orchestras to engineer and produce their own recordings). Others argue that it can't truly be "music" because all those loops and repetitive phrases can't amount of art worthy of critical merit (in which case I have some terrible news about this acclaimed composer named Steve Reich).° And all of this is couched in language that discredits hip-hop as an art form.

Evaluation criterion 2: Analysis of the response to hip-hop's Pulitzer win

It's disheartening to read these opinions from self-professed "non-listeners" of hip-hop music, and it also assumes the Pulitzer for Music is reserved for compositions born of the Western European classical tradition, despite the Pulitzer's 2004 declaration to expand the works up for consideration in order to "honor the full range of distinguished American musical compositions"

Pulitzer Prize: A prize for founded in 1917 by Joseph Pulitzer for achievements in journalism and the arts.   ***Kumbaya:*** An American spiritual folk song meant to signify unity and harmony, sometimes invoked sarcastically.   **apoplexy:** Brain hemorrhage; intense, uncontrollable anger.   **baffling:** Extremely confusing.   **Steve Reich:** American composer of minimalist music.

(Paul Moravec's *Tempest Fantasy*° was that year's winner). But while it's tempting to roast these opinions, this isn't the place for that. Twitter is the place for that. Instead, we're going to appreciate what this win means for hip-hop and for music rooted in the Black American tradition.

Hip-hop, since it was born in the Bronx almost four decades ago, has long been America's cultural bastard. Early beats were cobbled together with new technologies — "something from nothing," as the saying goes. But even though it eventually surpassed the limits of novelty, the rest of the musical establishment was reluctant to give it a seat at the table. So it fixed itself a plate and kept itself fueled.

4 Evaluation criterion 3: Definition of/context for hip-hop

Metaphor: hip-hop as a guest at a dinner party

Fueled despite poor television coverage at the Grammys, political pundits' and terrified suburban parents' efforts to censor or ban the music, and whatever the hell Dee Dee Ramone° was up to in the late 80's. But even in recent years, the questions of ownership in hip-hop and the lack of mainstream recognition for some of its most talented artists seem to be sticking around. Kendrick is a fine artist to consider in this respect. If you use the Grammys as a metric for how well a certain sound is "accepted" by old judges, Kendrick Lamar is a terrible rapper. His albums *Good Kid, M.A.A.D. City* (2012), *To Pimp a Butterfly* (2014) and *DAMN.* (2017) were all nominated for album of the year — but lost to efforts by Daft Punk, Taylor Swift and Bruno Mars, respectively. That *Good Kid* loss was extra puzzling, not because it lost to Daft Punk (who produced a solid cut with Random Access Memories), but because it lost Rap Album of the Year to Macklemore and Ryan Lewis' *The Heist* — a move that any hip-hop listener would be quick to contest.

5

Evaluation criterion 4: Analysis of mainstream/Grammy award recognition of hip-hop

And maybe that's part of the problem. I'm willing to bet that a great deal of people arguing that *DAMN.* is undeserving of such accolades° haven't listened to the album, or listened to much hip-hop at all. And that's OK! What *is* a bad thing, is if I go to some kind of international potluck, take one look at food I have never tasted, pass on it, and then proceed with the rest of dinner bad mouthing what very well may be delicious cuisine.

6 Evaluation criterion 5: Analysis of critics of hip-hop

Continued metaphor: hip-hop as a guest at a dinner party

In the conversations *DAMN.* has encouraged, people have been pointing out that since the Prize was first awarded in 1943, this is the first time it has gone to a non-classical or jazz piece. The problem with that statement is that it implies jazz has always been treated by the Pulitzer jury with dignity. It has not. In 1965 Duke Ellington° was denied a Pulitzer citation — and there was no Prize given at all.

7

Evaluation criterion 6: Comparison/contrast of Pulitzer jury attitudes toward jazz and hip-hop; bias against non-European music

Sometimes we like to tell ourselves awards like these don't matter — game will always recognize game, trophy or not — but even someone like Ellington understood the function of such an honor. As he told critic Nat Hentoff after the denial, he couldn't be surprised that his contributions to black music would remain unrecognized. "Most Americans still take it for granted that

8

Tempest Fantasy: A work of chamber music by American composer Paul Moravec (b. 1957). **Dee Dee Ramone:** (1951–2002) Born Douglas Glen Colvin; the original bass player for the American punk rock band The Ramones.   **accolade:** Praise and honor, usually to acknowledge a person or his or her accomplishments.   **Duke Ellington:** (1899–1974) Edward Kennedy "Duke" Ellington; an American composer, pianist, and jazz bandleader.

European-based-classical music, if you will, is the only really respectable kind. By and large, in this country, jazz has always been the kind of man you wouldn't want your daughter to associate with." It's not difficult to see hip-hop in the same situation.

After the Pulitzers were announced, Pulitzer Prize Administrator Dana Canedy spoke with *Billboard* about the decision to recognize Kendrick. "[The jury was] considering a piece of music they felt had hip-hop influences and said, 'Well if we're considering a piece of music that has hip-hop influences, why aren't we considering hip-hop?'," Canedy explained. "And someone said, 'That's exactly what we should do.'" So next time you have the urge to dismiss this album or think a piece that falls into whatever your working recognition of music is, I encourage you to breathe, sit down and be humble.

Evaluation criterion 7: Analysis of how Pulitzer jury decides

Continued metaphor: hip-hop as a guest at a dinner party, with quote from Lamar's song "Humble"

9

Questions to Start You Thinking

Meaning

1. How does Bennett describe the negative criticism aimed at Kendrick Lamar's music — and at hip-hop in general? Why are some people upset that Lamar won the Pulitzer for Music? And what does Bennett think about that?

2. According to Bennett, what does Lamar's win mean for hip-hop and "other music rooted in the African American tradition" (paragraph 3)?

3. What does Bennett mean when he writes that "the musical establishment was reluctant to give it [hip-hop] a seat at the table" (paragraph 4)?

Writing Strategies

4. What is Bennett's assessment of the Grammy awards, in relation to hip-hop? What evidence does he use to support this judgment? How effective is his evidence?

5. How does quoting Duke Ellington contribute to Bennett's argument about the lack of recognition for Black music in America (paragraphs 7 and 8)?

6. Reread the last sentence of Bennett's essay (paragraph 9). How does the metaphor he uses here connect with those he includes earlier in the piece? How do these metaphors contribute to Bennett's tone and attitude toward his topic and his readers?

Elizabeth Erion   Student Essay

Internship Program Falls Short

Elizabeth Erion drew on two valuable resources for her evaluation: her investigation of the campus internship program and her own experience as an intern. An earlier version of her essay appeared as an editorial in the campus student newspaper.

Since its creation in 1978, the Coram Internship Program has been a mainstay of the Career Development Center. The program matches interested students – usually those entering their junior year – with companies offering paid summer employment. Participating companies vary by year but range from the Guggenheim Museum in New York to the Keck School of Medicine in Los Angeles. In 2011, the program placed thirteen students from the class of 2012 at eleven companies or organizations. While this statistic may at first sound impressive, it accounts for only 2.8% of the class of 2012. Given the popularity of summer internships to lead into one's junior year, it is surprising that a higher percentage of the student body didn't make use of such a seemingly excellent, paid opportunity. But the program's low participation rate may be explained by one of its biggest flaws: its inherently restrictive nature.

1

? What would you want to gain from an internship program?

By offering funded opportunities at only a certain set of companies, the Coram program limits its utility to a certain set of students – those whose career interests match the industries and whose geographical options match the locations of companies participating during a particular summer. What's more, certain locations and industries are heavily privileged over others. In 2012, nine of the fourteen companies were located in the Boston area. This regionalism is understandable given the college's location in Maine and the high percentage of students and alumni from the Boston area, but it still represents a concerning lack of geographic diversity.

2

Massachusetts natives probably would find this location far more doable than would students who hail from elsewhere. Local students might have the opportunity to live at home and save significant money (the program stipend does not cover living or travel expenses) or might have an easier time finding roommates or an apartment to sublet due to a strong network of friends and family in the area. They would incur no significant travel costs for a flight, a long train ride, or long-distance gas mileage to arrive and depart from their summer destination. A student from elsewhere who could not afford such expenses or who could not relocate for a personal reason – perhaps a family member who is ill – is at a disadvantage. If students were able to select the locations of their internships, they would be much more likely to participate in the program.

3

? What advice would you give a nonlocal student?

Similarly, students are restricted to opportunities in a certain set of industries. Four of the participating programs in 2012 were in the financial services sector. Five were in science and medicine. Only one opportunity was available for students interested in museum work. The aspiring journalist is out of luck, as the program offers no journalism internships. So too is the student wishing to gain exposure to law firm work. These students are forced to look elsewhere, at both paid and unpaid opportunities. In many sectors – especially the arts – unpaid internships abound, usually located in prohibitively expensive metropolitan areas. Students who cannot afford to take unpaid internships are then left with no options, which jeopardizes their entry into the job market after graduating. Had the Coram program offered internships in the desired fields

4

of such students, those students could have spent the summer attaining the experience they needed.

The Coram Internship Program offers an excellent opportunity for the   5
fortunate student who finds a good employment fit with a geographically convenient company. Unfortunately, the percentage of students who are able to find such a fit is prohibitively small, as illustrated by the program's low participation rate. The program's structure denies the chance of obtaining rewarding, paid opportunities to the majority of the college's students, which is problematic given the importance of internships in gaining entry-level employment. Ultimately, the Coram Internship Program proves itself an ineffective career resource for a geographically and professionally diverse student community.

? What kinds of internship opportunities would students on your campus want?

Questions to Start You Thinking

Meaning

1. Why does Erion feel that evaluating the internship program is important? Who might belong to the audience that she would like to influence?

2. Based on her evaluation, what changes do you think Erion would want the Career Development Center or the internship program to make?

Writing Strategies

3. What criteria does Erion use to judge the internship program? To what extent has the program met these criteria, according to Erion?

4. Do you find Erion's use of statistics effective? Why, or why not?

5. Using highlighters or marginal notes, identify the essay's introduction, thesis, criteria for evaluation, supporting evidence, and conclusion. How effective is the organization of the essay?

Learning by Writing

The Assignment: Writing an Evaluation

Pick a subject to evaluate — one you have personal experience with and feel competent to evaluate. This subject might be a movie, a TV program, a piece of music, a work of art, a new product or service, a campus facility or policy, a novel or poem, or anything else you can think of. Then, in a thoughtful essay, analyze your subject and evaluate it. You will need to determine specific criteria for evaluation and make them clear to your readers. Your purpose is twofold: (1) to set forth your assessment of the quality of your subject and (2) to convince your readers that your judgment is reasonable.

MANAGING YOUR TIME
Writing an Evaluation

Use the breakdown below to plan your time for this essay; in the right column, insert target dates and times for completing each stage.

approx. **30-45** minutes	■ **Read your assignment carefully.** Is it clear what kinds of subjects you can choose to evaluate (movies, books, art, video games, products, food, etc.)? If not, follow up. ■ **Brainstorm** to identify something to evaluate. Ask yourself which topic interests you most—and which will be the most interesting to evaluate.	**I'll complete** this stage by: _____ (day, date)
approx. **2-3** hours	■ **Read** about your topic to better understand it and develop your judgment. Look for examples of reviews that others have written about your subject. ■ Identify **criteria** for evaluating your topic. What specific aspects of your topic will you consider in your evaluation? How will you convey those criteria to your readers? ■ Formulate your clearly stated judgment into a **thesis** that you will later refine. ■ Identify **evidence** that you can use to support your judgment, such as facts, statistics, photos and illustrations, or firsthand observations.	**I'll complete** this stage by: _____ (day, date)
approx. **2-3** hours	■ **Sketch an outline of your essay.** Will it be more effective to begin with your thesis and support it with evidence, or present your evidence first and end with your overall judgment? Be sure to list the criteria by which you are evaluating your subject. ■ **Draft your essay,** staying close to your outline. Think of your readers as you draft. Back yourself up with facts and specific detail. ■ Craft a compelling **introduction** and a satisfying **conclusion** by appealing to your readers to accept your evaluation.	**I'll complete** this stage by: _____ (day, date)
approx. **2-4** hours	■ Ask a **peer to review** your draft. Have you clearly stated your overall judgement and supported it with evidence? Have you been fair? ■ **Revise your draft,** addressing issues raised during your and your peer's review. ■ **Edit your draft,** fixing any errors and polishing your prose.	**I'll complete** this stage by: _____ (day, date)

Generating Ideas

Find Something to Evaluate. Try *brainstorming* or *mapping* to identify as many possible topics as you can. Test your understanding of each possible topic by concisely describing or summarizing it.

For more strategies for generating ideas, see Ch. 15.

Consider Sources of Support. You'll want to spend time finding material to help you develop a judgment. Watch a television program on your subject, or read an article about it. Review several examples of your subject: watch several films or campus plays, listen to several albums, examine several works of art, or test several products.

Establish Your Criteria. Criteria are standards to apply to your subject based on its particular features, not just whether you like the subject or not. How well, for example, does a popular entertainer score on musical skill, rapport with the audience, selection of material, originality? In evaluating Portland as a home for a young professional, you might ask: Does it offer ample entry-level positions in growth firms? Any criterion for evaluation has to fit your subject, audience, and purpose. After all, entry-level job opportunities might not matter to an audience of retirees.

Once you've chosen a topic, identify your standards for evaluating it:

- What features or aspects will you use as criteria for evaluating?
- How could you briefly explain each of the criteria to your readers?
- What judgment or evaluation about your topic do the criteria support?

In the body of your essay, examine each of the criteria in turn. Explaining your criteria will ensure that you move beyond a summary to an opinion or judgment that you can justify to your readers.

For more on comparing and contrasting, see Ch. 6.

Try Comparing and Contrasting. Often you can readily size up the worth of a thing by setting it next to another of its kind. You can compare, pointing to similarities, or you can contrast, noting differences. To be comparable, of course, your two subjects need to have plenty in common. The quality of a Harley-Davidson motorcycle might be judged by contrasting it with a Honda but not with a school bus.

For example, if you are writing a paper for a film history course, you might compare and contrast the classic 1931 horror movie *Dracula* with the 1992 version of that film, concluding that the original film was more artistic. Try listing characteristics of each film, point by point.

By jotting down each point and each bit of evidence side by side, you can outline your comparison and contrast with great efficiency. Once you have listed them, decide on a possible order for the points.

Bela Lugosi as Count Dracula and Dwight Frye as Renfield (Jonathan Harker) in the 1931 film, *Dracula*. Universal/Kobal/Shutterstock

	Dracula (1931)	*Bram Stoker's Dracula* (1992)
Sets	Elaborate but stark and cold, with sharp angles, metal objects	Elaborate but warm and inviting, with wood and fabrics
Color and Lighting	Black and white; strong contrast between bright light and dark shadows	Color, hues of red, brown, gold; soft golden light; subtler, softer shadows
Costumes	Formal dress. Dracula is sharp and polished in a tuxedo. Harker's hair is severely parted, combed back. Rigid.	Loose, casual clothing, rich fabrics. Dracula is in a flowing dressing gown. Harker has his sleeves rolled up, vest unbuttoned. Sensual.

Try Defining Your Subject. Another technique for evaluating is to define your subject so clearly that your readers understand it — its structure, habitat, functions. In evaluating a classic television show such as *Friends*, you might want to include an extended definition of sitcoms over the years, their techniques, views of women, effects on the audience. Unlike a dictionary definition, an extended definition is intended not simply to explain but to judge: What is the nature of my subject? What qualities make it unique, unlike others of its sort?

Gary Oldman as Count Dracula and Keanu Reeves as Jonathan Harker in the 1992 film, *Bram Stoker's Dracula*. Moviestore Collection/Shutterstock

For more on defining, see pp. 297–99.

Learning by Doing 🔘 Developing Criteria

With a small group of classmates, discuss the subjects each of you plan to evaluate. If possible, share a product, show a photograph of artwork, play a song, or read aloud a short literary work. Ask your classmates to explain the reasons for their own evaluations. Maybe they'll suggest criteria or evidence that hadn't occurred to you.

Planning, Drafting, and Developing

Start with a Thesis. Reflect a moment: What is your purpose? What is the main point you are making about your subject: Is it good, worthwhile, significant, exemplary, preferable — or not? Try writing a thesis that summarizes your main point and conveys the judgment you are making.

For more on stating a thesis, see pp. 266–71.

TOPIC + JUDGMENT	Campus revival of *South Pacific*—liked the performers featured in it plus the problems the revival raised
WORKING THESIS	Chosen to showcase the achievements of graduating seniors, the campus revival of *South Pacific* also brings up societal problems.

In reviews of books, movies, and other forms of entertainment, the thesis may consider how the subject conforms — or doesn't conform — to certain standards. This is the approach that James Bennett II used in his evaluation of the response to Kendrick Lamar's Pulitzer for Music (see p. 168).

> Once again, the classical community—contemporary or otherwise— needs to look inwards and determine the causes of this particular reaction's violent apoplexy.° (Hint: it's probably about race. Actually, it's always about race.)

Consider Your Criteria. Many writers find that a list of specific criteria gives them confidence and generates ideas. Consider filling in a chart with three columns — criteria, evidence, judgment — to focus your thinking.

Learning by Doing 🖐 Stating Your Overall Judgment

Build your criteria into your working thesis statement by filling in this

sentence: _____ is _____ because it _____.
       (your subject)   (your judgment)   (your criteria)

With a classmate, compare sentences and share ideas about improving your statement of your judgment and criteria. Use this advice to rework and sharpen your working thesis.

Develop an Organization. You may want to begin with a direct statement of your judgment:

THESIS OR MAIN POINT → SUPPORTING EVIDENCE → RETURN TO THESIS

> Based on durability, cost, and comfort, the Classic 7 is an ideal campus backpack.

On the other hand, you may want to reserve judgment by opening with a question about your subject:

OPENING QUESTION → SUPPORTING EVIDENCE → OVERALL JUDGMENT

> How good a film is *Mad Max: Fury Road*?

Each approach suggests a different organization. Either way, you'll supply lots of evidence — details, examples, maybe comparisons or contrasts — to make your case compelling. You'll also cluster evidence around your points or criteria for judgment so that readers know how and why you reach your judgment. You might try both patterns of organization to see which works better for your subject and purpose.

Most writers find that an outline — even a rough list — helps them keep track of points to make. If approved by your instructor, you also might include a sketch, photograph, or other illustration of your subject or develop a comparative table summarizing the features of similar items you have compared.

Learning by Doing 📷 Reflecting on Product Reviews

Locate and examine three reviews of a specific car model in consumer information sources such as Kelley Blue Book, *Consumer Reports*, or edmunds.com. Which review appears most reliable and why? Least reliable and why? What evidence did the reviewers use to persuade or dissuade potential car buyers? Reflect on language, pictures, or data that influenced your opinion about whether your chosen car model is worth purchasing.

Revising and Editing

Focus Your Thesis. Make your thesis as precise and clear as possible, eliminating wordy or vague phrases.

For more revising and editing strategies, see Ch. 19.

WORKING THESIS	Chosen to showcase the achievements of graduating seniors, the campus revival of *South Pacific* also brings up societal problems.
REVISED THESIS	The senior showcase, the musical *South Pacific*, spotlights outstanding performers and raises timely societal issues such as prejudice.

STRENGTHENING YOUR THESIS

- ☐ Does the thesis clearly convey your judgment of the topic?
- ☐ Can you see ways to make your thesis more precise or detailed?
- ☐ Can you make the thesis more persuasive or specific based on information that you gathered while developing your essay?

Be Fair. Make your judgments reasonable, not extreme. A reviewer can find fault with a film and still conclude that it is worth seeing. There's nothing wrong, of course, with a fervent judgment ("This play is the trashiest excuse for a drama I have ever suffered through"), but consider your readers and their likely reactions. Read some reviews in your local newspaper or online, or watch some movie critics on television to see how they balance their judgments. Because readers will have more confidence in your opinions if you seem fair and reasonable, revise your tone where needed. For example, one writer revised his opening after he realized that he was criticizing the audience rather than evaluating the performance.

The most recent performance by a favorite campus group—Rock

Mountain—was an ~~incredibly revolting~~ *disappointing concert* experience. ~~The~~ *Although t*he ~~outlandish~~ crowd

ignored the DJ who introduced the group, and a few ~~nameless members~~ *people*

~~of one social group spent their time~~ toss~~ing~~ *ed* around trash cans in front of

the stage, *, the opening number still announced the group's powerful musical presence.*

Peer Response 👥 Evaluating and Reviewing

For general questions for a peer editor, see p. 309.

Ask a classmate or friend to review your evaluation, answering questions like these:

- What is your overall reaction to this essay? Does the writer persuade you to agree with his or her evaluation?
- Can you tell exactly what the writer thinks of the subject? Where does the writer express this opinion?
- How do you know what criteria the writer is using for evaluation?
- Does the writer give you sufficient evidence for his or her judgment? Put stars wherever more or better evidence is needed.
- What audience does the writer seem to have in mind?
- Would you recommend any changes in the essay's organization?

For more on comparison and contrast, see Ch. 6.

- If this paper were yours, what is the one thing you would be sure to work on before handing it in?

REVISING YOUR DRAFT

- ☐ Is the judgment you pass on your subject unmistakably clear?
- ☐ Have you given your readers evidence to support each point you make?
- ☐ Have you been fair, acknowledging the subject's admirable traits as well as its disadvantages or faults?

For more editing and proofreading strategies, see pp. 316–18.

- ☐ Have you anticipated and answered readers' possible objections?
- ☐ If you compare two things, do you look at the same points in both?

After you have revised your evaluation, edit and proofread it. Carefully check the grammar, word choice, punctuation, and mechanics — and then correct any problems you find. Make sentences in which you describe the subject of your evaluation as precise and useful as possible. If you have used comparisons or contrasts, make sure these are clear: don't lose your readers in a fog of vague pronouns or confusing references.

For more help, find the relevant checklist sections in the Quick Editing Guide on p. Q-37. Turn also to the Quick Format Guide beginning on p. Q-1.

EDITING FOR CLARITY

☐ Is it clear what each pronoun refers to? Does each pronoun agree with (match) its antecedent? A6

☐ Is it clear what each modifier in a sentence modifies? Have you created any dangling or misplaced modifiers, especially in descriptions of your subject? B1

☐ Have you used parallel structure wherever needed, especially in lists or comparisons? B2

Reviewing and Reflecting

REVIEW Working with classmates or independently, respond to the following questions:

1. How can you establish criteria for evaluating a subject? If you have written or are writing an evaluation or a review, what criteria did you decide upon? Why did you make these particular choices?

2. Why are comparing and contrasting, as well as defining, potentially useful strategies for evaluating and reviewing? If you have used one or both of these strategies, what benefits or challenges did they bring?

3. In writing an evaluation or a review, why is it important to make judgments reasonable, not extreme?

REFLECT Reflect in writing about how you might apply the insights that you drew from this evaluation assignment to another situation — in or outside of college — in which you have to or review something.

Additional Writing Assignments

1. Evaluate an unfamiliar magazine, a proposal being considered at work, a source you've read for a college class, or an academic website about an area that interests you. Specify your criteria for evaluation, and identify the evidence that supports your judgments.

2. Evaluate a product that you might want to purchase. Establish criteria that matter to you and to other prospective purchasers. Consider, for example,

the product's features, construction, utility, beauty, color, and cost. Make a clear recommendation to your audience: buy or not.

3. Go to a restaurant, museum, or tourist attraction, and evaluate it for others who might consider a visit. Present your evaluation as an essay, an article for a travel or lifestyle magazine, or a travel blog. Specify your criteria, and include plenty of detail to create the local color your audience will expect.

For more on responding to literature, see Ch. 12.

4. **Source Assignment.** Read these two poems focused on a single animal, and decide which seems to you the better poem. In a brief essay, set forth your evaluation. Consider which criteria to apply, such as the choice of concrete words that appeal to the senses and the poet's awareness of his or his audience. Quote, paraphrase, summarize, and accurately credit supporting evidence from the poems.

The Cow in Apple Time
ROBERT FROST (1874–1963)

Something inspires the only cow of late
To make no more of a wall than an open gate,
And think no more of wall-builders than fools.
Her face is flecked with pomace and she drools
A cider syrup. Having tasted fruit,
She scorns a pasture withering to the root.
She runs from tree to tree where lie and sweeten
The windfalls spiked with stubble and worm-eaten.
She leaves them bitten when she has to fly.
She bellows on a knoll against the sky.
Her udder shrivels and the milk goes dry.

A Jelly-Fish
MARIANNE MOORE (1887–1972)

Visible, invisible,
A fluctuating charm,
An amber-colored amethyst
Inhabits it; your arm
Approaches, and
It opens and
It closes;
You have meant
To catch it,
And it shrivels;
You abandon
Your intent —
It opens, and it
Closes and you
Reach for it —
The blue
Surrounding it
Grows cloudy, and
It floats away
From you.

5. **Visual Assignment.** Examine the following pair of images carefully. Write an essay that evaluates the images themselves, specifying for your audience your criteria for judging.

Church at Auvers-sur-Oise, France (2002). PIERRE-FRANCK COLOMBIER/AFP/Getty Images

The Church in Auvers-sur-Oise (1890), painted by Vincent van Gogh (1853–1890). Buyenlarge/Hulton Fine Art Collection/Getty Images

11 Supporting a Position with Sources

Caiaimage/Sam Edwards/Getty Images

Journal-Courier/Steve Warmowski/The Image Works

Greg Hinsdale/Corbis/Glow Images

Responding to an Image

These images show activities that might help a student gather evidence from sources to support a position in a college paper. What does each image suggest about possible sources? What do the images suggest about the process of inquiry? Which activities look most intriguing? What other activities might have appeared in images on this page?

Why Supporting with Sources Matters

The typical college writing assignment might boil down to reading a few texts and writing a paper about them. Simple as this description sounds, it suggests what you probably expect from a college education: an opportunity to absorb and think seriously about provocative ideas. It also suggests the values that lie behind college expectations — a deep respect for the process of inquiry (the academic method of asking and investigating intriguing questions) and for the products of inquiry (the analyses, interpretations, and studies in each academic field).

When you first tackle such assignments, you may wonder "How do I figure out what my instructor really wants?" or "How could I possibly do that?" In response, you may turn to questions such as "How long does my paper have to be?" or "How many sources do I have to use?" Instead, try to face the central question: "How can I learn the skills I need to use a few sources to develop and support a position in a college paper?"

Unlike a debate or a Super Bowl game, a paper that takes a position generally doesn't have two sides or a single winner. Instead, the writer typically joins the ongoing exchange of ideas about an intriguing topic in the field. Each paper builds on the exchanges of the past — the articles, essays, reports, and books that convey the perspectives, research findings, and conclusions of others. Although reading such sources may seem daunting, you are not expected to know everything yourself but simply to work hard at learning what others know. Your paper, in turn, advances the exchange to convey your well-grounded point of view or to defend your well-reasoned interpretation.

In a College Course

- You write a history paper about an event, synthesizing a first-person account, a contemporary newspaper story, and a scholarly article.
- You analyze a short story after reading several critical essays about it.

In the Workplace

- You write a report pulling together multiple accounts and records to support your recommendation.

In Your Community

- You write a well-substantiated letter to the editor about a recent article.

❓ When have you used sources to support a position in your writing? What source-based writing might you do at work or in your community?

Learning from Other Writers

The writers of the following two essays draw on evidence from sources to support their points. To help you analyze the first reading, look at the notes in the margin, which point out the thesis and some methods for integrating information from sources. As you read these essays, ask yourself the following questions:

1. What thesis, or main idea, expresses the position supported by the essay? How does the writer try to help readers appreciate the importance of this position?

2. How does the writer use information from sources to support a thesis? Do you find this information relevant and persuasive?

3. How does the writer vary the way each source is introduced and the way information is drawn from it?

Charles M. Blow

Black Dads Are Doing Best of All

Charles M. Blow (b. 1970) is a columnist for the *New York Times*, where the following piece appeared. He has served at the *Times* as graphics editor, graphics director, and design director for news, and he is the author of the memoir *Fire Shut Up in My Bones*. The sources that Blow refers to have been adapted to illustrate the MLA (Modern Language Association) documentation style.

Damon Winter/
The New York Times/Redux

One of the most persistent statistical bludgeons° of people who want to blame Black people for any injustice or inequity they encounter is this: According to data from the Centers for Disease Control and Prevention (C.D.C.), nearly 72 percent of births to non-Hispanic Black women, the mothers were unmarried[1].

Background information including statistics

It has always seemed to me that embedded in the "If only Black men would marry the women they have babies with . . ." rhetoric was a more insidious° suggestion: that there is something fundamental, and intrinsic° about black men that is flawed, that black fathers are pathologically° prone to desertion of their offspring and therefore largely responsible for Black community "dysfunction."°

THESIS presenting position

There is an astounding amount of mythology loaded into this stereotype, one that echoes a history of efforts to rob black masculinity of honor and fidelity.

Josh Levs points this out in his book, *All In*, in a chapter titled "How Black Dads Are Doing Best of All (But There's Still a Crisis)." One fact that Levs quickly establishes is that most Black fathers in America live with their children: "There are about 2.5 million Black fathers living with their children and about 1.7 million living apart from them" (149).

Direct quotation

1

2

3

4

bludgeons: Heavy clubs; tools for bullying or coercion.   **insidious:** Dangerous or deceitful.
intrinsic: belonging to a thing by its very nature.   **pathologically:** In a disease-like fashion.
dysfunction: A serious breakdown or malfunction.

[1] The statistic provided by the author is from 2014. The latest information from the CDC (2017) indicates that the percentage of such births has decreased from 72 percent to 69.4 percent. —Ed.

"So then," you may ask, "how is it that 72 percent of black children are born to single mothers? How can both be true?" Good question. | 5 | Central question, referring back to introductory statistics

Here are two things to consider: | 6 |

First, there are a growing number of people who live together but don't marry. Those mothers are still single, even though the child's father may be in the home. And, as the *Washington Post* reported last year: | 7 |

"The share of unmarried couples who opted to have 'shotgun cohabitations' — moving in together after a pregnancy — surpassed 'shotgun marriages' for the first time during the last decade, according to a forthcoming paper from the National Center for Health Statistics, part of the Centers for Disease Control and Prevention" (Yen). | 8 | One response to the central question, supported by evidence

Furthermore, a C.D.C. report found that black and Hispanic women are far more likely to experience a pregnancy during the first year of cohabitation than white and Asian women (Copen et al.). | 9 |

Second, some of these men have children by more than one woman, but they can only live in one home at a time. This phenomenon° means that a father can live with some but not all of his children. Levs calls these men "serial impregnators," but I think something more than promiscuity° and irresponsibility are at play here. | 10 | Paraphrase, and another response to the central question

As *Forbes* reported on Ferguson, Missouri:° | 11 |

"An important but unreported indicator of Ferguson's dilemma is that half of young African American men are missing from the community. According to the U.S. Census Bureau, while there are 1,182 African American women between the ages of 25 and 34 living in Ferguson, there are only 577 African American men in this age group. In other words there are more than two young Black women for each young black man in Ferguson" (Ozimek). | 12 | Supporting evidence

In April, the *New York Times* extended this line of reporting, pointing out that nationally, there are 1.5 million missing Black men. As the paper put it: "Incarceration and early deaths are the overwhelming drivers of the gap. Of the 1.5 million missing Black men from 25 to 54 — which demographers° call the prime-age years — higher imprisonment rates account for almost 600,000. Almost one in 12 Black men in this age group are behind bars, compared with one in 60 non-Black men in the age group, one in 200 Black women and one in 500 non-Black women" (Wolfers et al.). For context, there are about 8 million African American men in that age group overall. | 13 | Additional statistical support

Mass incarceration has disproportionately ensnared° young Black men, sucking hundreds of thousands of marriage-age men out of the community. | 14 |

Another thing to consider is something that the *Atlantic*'s Ta-Nehisi Coates has pointed out: "The drop in the birthrate for unmarried Black women is mirrored by an even steeper drop among married Black women. Indeed, whereas at one point married Black women were having more kids than married white women, they are now having less." This means that births to unmarried black women are disproportionately represented in the statistics. | 15 |

phenomenon: Fact or situation.   **promiscuity:** Having sex with multiple partners. **Ferguson, Missouri:** Scene of the August 2014 police shooting of an unarmed black teenager; the investigation of the shooting exposed, among other things, deep racial divisions in the city. **demographers:** Researchers who produce and study population statistics.   **ensnared:** Captured; entrapped.

Additional responses to the central question, followed by evidence

Now to the mythology of the black male dereliction° as dads: While it is true that Black parents are less likely to marry before a child is born, it is not true that Black fathers suffer a pathology of neglect. In fact, a C.D.C. report found that Black fathers were the most involved with their children daily, on a number of measures, of any other group of fathers—and in many cases, that was among fathers who didn't live with their children, as well as those who did (Jones and Mosher). 16

Conclusion reinforcing the author's position

There is no doubt that the 72 percent statistic is real and may even be worrisome, but it represents more than choice. It exists in a social context, one at odds with the corrosive° mythology about Black fathers. 17

Works Cited

Each source cited in Blow's essay listed alphabetically by author, with full publication information

First line of entry placed at left margin, with subsequent lines indented ½ inch

Coates, Ta-Nehisi. "Understanding Out-of-Wedlock Births in Black America." *The Atlantic*, 21 June 2013, theatlantic.com/sexes/archive/2013/06/understanding-out-of-wedlock-births-in-black-america/277084/.

Copen, Casey E., et al. "First Premarital Cohabitation in the United States: 2006–2010 National Survey of Family Growth." National Health Statistics Reports, no. 64, National Center for Health Statistics, 4 Apr. 2013, cdc.gov/nchs/data/nhsr/nhsr064.pdf.

Jones, Jo, and William D. Mosher. "Fathers' Involvement with Their Children: United States, 2006–2010." *National Health Statistics Reports*, no. 71, National Center for Health Statistics, 20 Dec. 2013, cdc.gov/nchs/data/nhsr/nhsr071.pdf.

Levs, Josh. *All In: How Our Work-First Culture Fails Dads, Families, and Businesses—And How We Can Fix It Together*. HarperCollins, 2015.

Ozimek, Adam. "Half of Ferguson's Young African American Men Are Missing." *Forbes*, 18 Mar. 2015, forbes.com/sites/modeledbehavior/2015/03/18/half-of-fergusons-young-african-american-men-are-missing/#273f5c58119b.

United States, Centers for Disease Control and Prevention. "About Natality, 2007–2014." *CDC Wonder*, 9 Feb. 2016, wonder.cdc.gov/natality-current.html.

Wolfers, Justin, et al. "1.5 Million Missing Black Men." *The New York Times*, 20 Apr. 2015, nyti.ms/1P5Gpa7.

Yen, Hope. "More Couples Who Become Parents Are Living Together But Not Marrying, Data Show." *The Washington Post*, 7 Jan. 2014, washingtonpost.com/politics/more-couples-who-become-parents-are-living-together-but-not-marrying-data-show/2014/01/07/2b639a86-77d5-11e3-b1c5-739e63e9c9a7_story.html.

dereliction: Negligence.   **corrosive:** Destructive.

Questions to Start You Thinking

Meaning

1. According to Blow, what are the prevailing stereotypes about black fathers? What position does he take about these stereotypes?

2. What major points does Blow make to counter prevailing views about black fathers?

3. How are demographic changes that pertain to women — in particular, birthrates among married black women — contributing to the "statistical bludgeons" Blow describes in his first paragraph?

Writing Strategies

4. What types of evidence does Blow use to support his position? How convincing is this evidence to you?

5. Blow alternates between stating some source information in his own words and quoting some directly. What are the advantages and disadvantages of these two approaches?

6. How would you describe Blow's tone, the quality of his writing that reveals his attitude toward his topic and his readers? What specific words, phrases, or sentences contribute to his tone? Does the tone seem appropriate for his purpose and audience? Why, or why not?

Abigail Marchand   Student Essay

The Family Dynamic

Abigail Marchand wrote this essay in response to a reading assigned in her composition class. She used MLA style to cite and list sources.

Children are resilient creatures, and often adults underestimate their vast emotional capabilities, their compassion, and their ability to find the good in everything. When babies are brought home from the hospital, they don't care if their parents are same sex or not. They only ant to feel safe, to be held, and most of all to be loved. It is unfortunate that we as a human race allow our own petty ideals to interfere with these simple needs.

1

The notion that a child can thrive only in a "nuclear" family has long been dispelled. With the increase in the divorce rate and the number of children born to single mothers, many children are not raised in that traditional family. Thus, the idea of a child being raised by a same-sex couple really shouldn't seem that foreign. According to 2017 data from the U.S. Census Bureau, there are more than 935,000 same-sex couples in the country, and 16.4% — roughly 150,000 of them — include children. As pediatrician and researcher Jacky Hewitt points out, "experts repeatedly come to the same conclusion: children raised by same-sex parents are no different from those raised by heterosexual parents."

2

? What does a "nuclear" family mean to you?

For a variety of reasons, many children today are growing up in a completely different environment than that of their grandparents of the 1950s and 1960s. However, as Hewitt says, those differences do not mean poorer outcomes for the children: "Young people from same-sex parented families have without fail been among the most wanted, loved, and well raised and cared for children I have seen." Regardless of whether a family has two mothers, two fathers, one single

3

parent, or even a grandparent, what should matter is not the quantity of love a child receives but the quality of that love.

A child's development will neither be hurt nor helped by a same-sex family. 4 Frankly, the makeup of the family and specifically the absence of an opposite-sex partner have little impact on the day-to-day lives of most children. As two sociologists who reviewed past research studies on parenting concluded, "The gender of parents correlates in novel ways with parent-child relationships but has minor significance for children's psychological adjustment and social success" (Biblarz and Stacey 3). Many same-sex households involve members of the opposite sex in some capacity, whether as friend, aunt, uncle, or cousin. In addition, as children from same-sex families attend schools, they encounter any number of people, both male and female. The argument that the child would interact only with one gender is ludicrous.

The advantages of a same-sex household are similar to those of a standard 5 father-and-mother household: Two people are there to help raise the children. Compared to a single parent raising a child alone, the same-sex household would benefit from having another person to shoulder some of the responsibilities. As a parent of four sons, I know the benefits of having a second person to help with transportation to various events, dinner preparation, or homework. Navigating the treacherous landscape of child rearing is far easier with an ally.

On a developmental level, a same-sex household would not affect the child's 6 ability to grow and become a productive member of society. Certainly most children can adapt to any situation, and in the case of same-sex relationships, a child usually is brought into the home as a baby, so that environment is all he or she would know. The absence of an opposite-sex parent would never come into question since most children don't concern themselves with the gender of their family members. Instead, they view their caregivers as any other child would—as mommy or daddy.

The only disadvantage children in same-sex households experience stems from 7 those who are bent on "explaining" to them how their parental unit is somehow doing something wrong. These naysayers pose the greatest risk because children are vulnerable to the criticism of others, despite the fact that most same-sex households function better than many "traditional" ones. Photographer Gabriela Herman interviewed children of same-sex parents from 2010 to 2017 and captured the impact of societal disapproval. One of her subjects, Jaz, who was raised by two moms, shares an example of this negative response: "One of my best friends growing up who I'm still very close with—she wasn't allowed to sleep over for a while, and then when her parents finally said that she could sleep over, her mother took my mom aside and was like, 'You can't kiss in front of my daughter'" (Herman 138). In his memoir about growing up in a same-sex household, Iowa state senator Zach Wahls echoes this sentiment: "Though society regularly informs me that my family structure is different, I feel as though I'm being told that I am wearing different colored socks. Yes, you might not like how they look, but beyond inciting the occasional bout of aesthetic displeasure, how does it affect your life?" (xvi).

In fact, most people are unlikely to recognize a child being raised in a same- 8 sex household unless they specifically know the child's parents. My son attends

How do you view the role of family structure in a child's development?

daycare with two brothers who have two mothers. I never would have known this if I hadn't personally met both mothers. Their children are well-adjusted little boys who are fortunate to have two caring women in their lives.

The real focus should be on whether all of the child's needs are met. It shouldn't matter if those needs are met by a mother and father, two mothers, or two fathers. Children should feel loved and cared for above all else. Unfortunately, in the case of same-sex households, external pressures can potentially shatter a child's well-being when "well-meaning" people attempt to interfere with something they know nothing about. It is amazing that people are more focused on the bedroom activities, activities that never enter a child's consciousness anyway, than on the run-of-the-mill activities that most same-sex couples encounter in the rearing of a child. The only real disadvantage to these households lies solely with the closed minds of intolerance.

9

❓ What do you think that children need from parents and from society?

Works Cited

Biblarz, Timothy J., and Judith Stacey. "How Does the Gender of Parents Matter?" *Journal of Marriage and Family*, vol. 72, no. 1, Feb. 2010, pp. 3–22.

Hermin, Gabriela. *The Kids: The Children of LGBTQ Parents in the USA*. The New Press, 2017.

Hewitt, Jacky. "There is no harm caused by same-sex parenting. Studies suggesting otherwise are skewed." *The Guardian View*, 12 Sep. 2017, https://www.theguardian .com/commentisfree/2017/sep/13/there-is-no-harm-caused-by-same-sex-parenting -studies-suggesting-otherwise-are-skewed.

United States Census Bureau. *Characteristics of Same-Sex Couple Households, 2005 to Present*, 2017, www.census.gov/data/tables/time-series/demo /same-sex-couples/ssc-house-characteristics.html.

Wahls, Zach. *My Two Moms: Lessons of Love, Strength, and What Makes a Family*. Avery, 2013.

For more on MLA citation style, see E1–E2 in the Quick Research Guide, pp. Q-20–Q-36.

Questions to Start You Thinking

Meaning

1. What position does Marchand support in her essay?
2. What reasons for her view does Marchand supply?

Writing Strategies

3. What types of evidence does Marchand use to support her position? How convincing is this evidence to you?
4. Has Marchand considered alternative views? How does the inclusion (or lack) of these views contribute to or detract from the essay?
5. Marchand uses specific examples in several places. Which of these seem most effective to you? Why?
6. Using highlighters or marginal notes, identify the essay's introduction, thesis, major points, supporting evidence for each point, and conclusion. How effective is the organization of this essay?

Learning by Writing

The Assignment: Supporting a Position with Sources

See the contents of *A Writer's Reader* on p. 329.

Identify a cluster of readings about a topic that interests you. For example, choose related readings from this book or from other readings assigned in your class. If your topic is assigned and you don't begin with much interest in it, develop your curiosity. Look for an angle that will engage you. Relate the topic in some way to your experience. Read (or reread) the selections, considering how each supports, challenges, or deepens your understanding of the topic.

Based on the information you've gathered from your reading, develop a position about the topic that you'd like to share with an audience of college readers. Support your position—your working thesis—using quotations, paraphrases, summaries, and syntheses of the information in the readings as evidence. Present your information from sources clearly, and credit your sources appropriately.

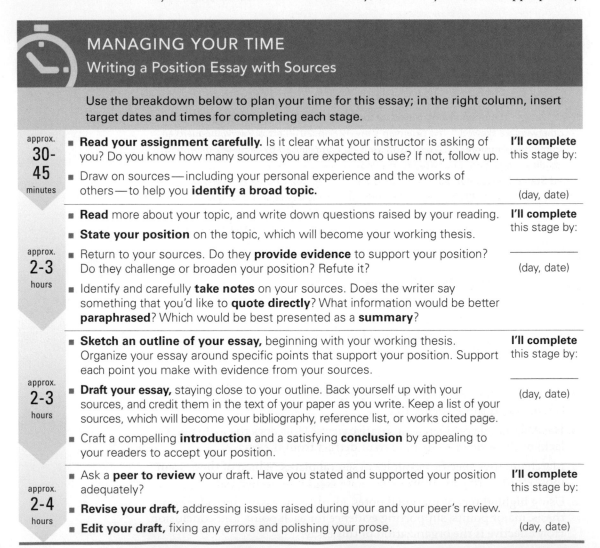

MANAGING YOUR TIME
Writing a Position Essay with Sources

Use the breakdown below to plan your time for this essay; in the right column, insert target dates and times for completing each stage.

approx. 30-45 minutes

- **Read your assignment carefully.** Is it clear what your instructor is asking of you? Do you know how many sources you are expected to use? If not, follow up.
- Draw on sources—including your personal experience and the works of others—to help you **identify a broad topic.**

I'll complete this stage by:
_____
(day, date)

approx. 2-3 hours

- **Read** more about your topic, and write down questions raised by your reading.
- **State your position** on the topic, which will become your working thesis.
- Return to your sources. Do they **provide evidence** to support your position? Do they challenge or broaden your position? Refute it?
- Identify and carefully **take notes** on your sources. Does the writer say something that you'd like to **quote directly**? What information would be better **paraphrased**? Which would be best presented as a **summary**?

I'll complete this stage by:
_____
(day, date)

approx. 2-3 hours

- **Sketch an outline of your essay,** beginning with your working thesis. Organize your essay around specific points that support your position. Support each point you make with evidence from your sources.
- **Draft your essay,** staying close to your outline. Back yourself up with your sources, and credit them in the text of your paper as you write. Keep a list of your sources, which will become your bibliography, reference list, or works cited page.
- Craft a compelling **introduction** and a satisfying **conclusion** by appealing to your readers to accept your position.

I'll complete this stage by:
_____
(day, date)

approx. 2-4 hours

- Ask a **peer to review** your draft. Have you stated and supported your position adequately?
- **Revise your draft,** addressing issues raised during your and your peer's review.
- **Edit your draft,** fixing any errors and polishing your prose.

I'll complete this stage by:
_____
(day, date)

Generating Ideas

Pin Down Your Topic and Sources. It may be that your instructor has assigned the topic and required readings to use as sources. If not, figure out what limits your instructor has set and which decisions are yours. Draw on your experiences, interests, conversations, and imagination as you decide on your topic and sources. Instead of hunting only for sources that support your initial views on the topic, look for a variety of sources that will broaden and challenge your perspective. Ask yourself:

For more strategies for generating ideas, see Ch. 19.

- What topic have I chosen (or been assigned)? What position do I hold and how might that change?

- What readings will I use as sources? Some from this book? Others? What do I want to learn from skimming them?

- What is my purpose in writing this paper? Who is my primary audience? What will my instructor expect me to accomplish?

Skim Your Sources. When you work with a cluster of readings, you'll probably need to read them repeatedly. Start out, however, by skimming — quickly reading only enough to find out what direction a selection takes.

For advice about finding and evaluating academic sources, turn to sections B and C in the Quick Research Guide, pp. Q-24–Q-27.

- Leaf through the reading; glance at any headings or figure labels.

- Return to the first paragraph; read it in full. Then read only the first sentence of each paragraph. At the end, read the final paragraph in full.

- Stop to consider what you've already learned.

Do the same with your other sources, classifying or comparing them as you begin to think about what they might contribute to your paper.

Planning, Drafting, and Developing

Start with a Working Thesis. Sometimes you start reading for a source-based position paper with a clear position in mind; other times, you begin simply with your initial response to your sources. Either way, try to state your main idea as a working thesis even if you expect to rewrite it — or replace it — later on. Once your thesis takes shape in words, you can assess the richness and relevance of your reading based on a clear main idea.

Here is how one student responded to the sources she read.

For more on reading critically, see Ch. 2.

For more on stating a thesis, see pp. 266–71.

FIRST RESPONSE TO SOURCES	Joe Robinson, author of "Four Weeks Vacation," and others say that workers need more vacation time, but I can't see my boss agreeing to this.
WORKING THESIS	Although most workers would like longer vacations, many employers do not believe that they would benefit from this, too.

Sometimes a thesis statement for a position paper will push back against common perceptions or stereotypes. This is the approach that Abigail Marchand and Charles M. Blow use for their thesis statements.

MARCHAND'S THESIS   It is unfortunate that we as a human race allow our own petty ideals to interfere with these simple needs [of children].

BLOW'S THESIS   There is an astounding amount of mythology loaded into this stereotype [about African American fathers], one that echoes a history of efforts to rob Black masculinity of honor and fidelity.

Learning by Doing 🎯 Strengthening Your Position as You Gather Evidence

Evaluating your position is a good first step in planning your search for supporting evidence — or for additional evidence if your thesis is based on some initial reading. For example, the student described on page 191 planned searches based on her working thesis: "Employers need to consider the advantages to them and to their workers in allowing employees to take longer vacations." She made a list of the following key terms to search her library's databases:

■ benefits of vacation time for employers / employees

■ workplace morale; productivity; profit

■ preventing employee burnout

■ census statistics on vacation time, employers, employees

■ potential downside / negative effects / unintended consequences of time off

To plan your search, jot down key terms that could help you refine your position or more effectively address challenges to it.

Read Each Source Thoughtfully. Before you begin quoting, taking notes, or highlighting a source, simply read, slowly and carefully. Once you have figured out what the writer is saying, you are ready to decide how you might use that source to support your ideas. Read again, this time sifting and selecting what's relevant to your thesis. Consider the following:

■ How does the writer of this piece use sources to support her position?

■ How does the writer integrate her sources? Chronologically (by date), thematically (by topic), or by some other method?

■ Does the writer use sources to supply background on her position? Does she compare her position or research findings with those of other studies?

■ Who is her main audience? What is her purpose in writing?

■ How might you draw on this source in your own work?

Record Source Details. A well-researched article that follows academic conventions identifies its sources for several reasons. It gives honest credit to the work on which it relies — work done by other researchers and writers. The article also informs you about its sources so you, or any other reader, could find them yourself.

Carefully citing your sources enhances your credibility as a careful writer. As you take notes, identify the source (author, title, etc.) and the exact location of the material you are using (page number, URL, etc.). Doing so will help you avoid accidental plagiarism (using someone else's words or ideas without giving the credit due) and correctly integrate your sources into your draft. Add this information when you first use the source, even if you are just dropping it in so you don't forget it. Later, you won't have to hunt for the details.

Join the Academic Exchange. When you read and respond to the work of others, you join the academic exchange, raising questions, seeking answers, evaluating information, and advancing knowledge. In your writing, you will investigate your topic using reliable sources that include articles, essays, reports, books, Web pages, and other reliable materials. You'll be expected to quote, paraphrase, and summarize information from these sources and to introduce and credit them properly. Follow your instructor's preferred style of documentation; MLA style (Modern Language Association) is widely used in composition and English courses, and APA style (American Psychological Association) is often used in psychology and other social science courses.

For more on plagiarism, see D1 in the Quick Research Guide, p. Q-28. For more on documenting sources, see E1 and E2 in the Quick Research Guide, pp. Q-31–Q-36.

You can see how the academic exchange works in the following example. A student interested in the health benefits of exercise found an article by journalist Janet Lee in the popular magazine *Consumer Reports*. In the article, Lee quotes Alpa Patel, a lead researcher at the American Cancer Society. The student followed up on this quotation and found the research findings of Patel's study published in the scholarly journal *Cancer Causes & Control*.

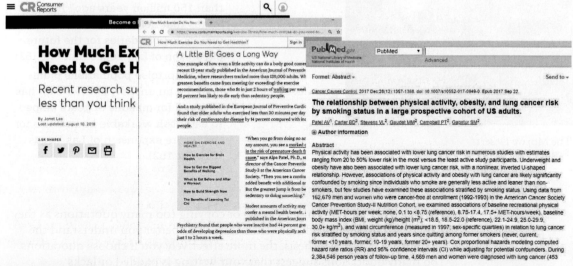

These articles from *Consumer Reports* and a scholarly journal are part of the academic exchange about the health benefits of exercise.

To use these sources in her essay, the student can summarize the key results of Patel's study, paraphrase in her own words Lee's article about the research findings, or quote an exact passage from either source as evidence to support her own working thesis.

Identify Material to Quote. When a writer communicates an idea so memorably that you want to include their exact words in your paper, quote them word for word. Direct quotations can add life, color, and authority; too many can drown your voice and overshadow your point. Consider this example for a paper that connects land use and threats to wildlife.

ORIGINAL

The tortoise is a creature that has survived virtually unchanged since it first appeared in the geologic record more than 150 million years ago. The species became threatened, however, when ranchers began driving their herds onto Mojave Desert lands for spring grazing, at the very time that the tortoise awakens from hibernation and emerges from its burrows to graze on the greening desert shrubs and grasses. As livestock trampled the burrows and monopolized the scarce desert vegetation, tortoise populations plummeted. (page 152)

Babbitt, Bruce. *Cities in the Wilderness: A New Vision of Land Use in America*. Island Press-Shearwater, 2005.

The Mojave Desert.
iStockphoto.com/KateLeigh/Getty Images

TOO MUCH QUOTATION

When "tortoise populations plummeted," a species "that has survived virtually unchanged since it first appeared in the geologic record more than 150 million years ago" had losses that helped to justify setting workable boundaries for the future expansion of Las Vegas (Babbitt 152).

MEMORABLE QUOTATION

When "tortoise populations plummeted," an unlikely species that has endured for millions of years helped to establish workable boundaries for the future expansion of Las Vegas (Babbitt 152).

Writers often begin by highlighting or copying too many quotations as they struggle to master the ideas in the source. The better you understand the reading and your own thesis, the more effectively you'll choose quotations. Too many quotations suggest that your writing is padded or lacks originality.

HOW TO QUOTE

- Select a quotation from your source that is relevant to your thesis — and memorable.
- Record it accurately, including exact punctuation and capitalization.
- Surround it with quotation marks. If the quotation is longer than four lines, place it in a block of text indented by one half inch and omit quotation marks.
- Note the page or other location where the quotation appears. If the quotation begins on one page but ends on another, mark where the switch occurs so you can credit it properly later.
- Double-check the accuracy of each quotation as you record it.
- Place in brackets any words that you have added to the quotation.

    EXAMPLE   She assured her that "[although] she was a seamstress and a governess, she was comfortable in the homes of the rich" (Carroll 15).

- Use ellipses marks to indicate that you have deleted words from a quotation.

    EXAMPLE   She assured her that "[although] she was . . . a governess, she was comfortable in the homes of the rich" (Carroll 15).

For more on quotations, see D3 in the Quick Research Guide, pp. Q-28–Q-29.

Paraphrase Specific Passages in Your Own Words. Paraphrasing involves restating an author's ideas in your own language. A paraphrase is generally about the same length as the original. It conveys the ideas and emphasis of the original in your words and sentences, which brings your voice to the fore. A fresh and creative paraphrase expresses your style without awkwardly jumping between it and your source's style. Be sure to name your source in the text of your paper so that readers know exactly where you move from one to the other.

Look back at the original passage by Bruce Babbitt on page 194, then at the following sloppy paraphrase. Note how it uses too many words from the original. (The borrowed words are underlined in the paraphrase.) Those words need to be expressed in the writer's own language or identified as direct quotations with quotation marks.

For more on punctuating quotations and using ellipsis marks, see D3 in the Quick Editing Guide, pp. Q-61–Q-62.

SLOPPY PARAPHRASE   Babbitt says that the tortoise is a creature in the Mojave that is virtually unchanged over 150 million years. Over the millennia, the tortoise would awaken from hibernation just in time for spring grazing on the new growth of the region's shrubs and grasses. In recent years the species became threatened. When cattle started to compete for the same food, the livestock trampled the tortoise burrows and monopolized the desert vegetation while the tortoise populations plummeted (152).

To avoid picking up language from the original as you paraphrase, state each sentence afresh instead of just changing a few words in the original. If possible, take a short break, and then check each sentence against the original. Highlight any identical words or sentence patterns, and rework your paraphrase again. Proper nouns or exact terms for the topic (such as *tortoise*) do not need to be rephrased.

The next example avoids parroting the original by making different word choices while reversing or varying sentence patterns.

PARAPHRASE
> As Babbitt explains, a tenacious survivor in the Mojave is the 150-million-year-old desert tortoise. Over the millennia, the hibernating tortoise would rouse itself each spring just in time to enjoy the new growth of the limited regional plants. In recent years, as cattle became rivals for this desert territory, the larger animals destroyed tortoise homes, ate tortoise food, and thus eliminated many of the tortoises themselves (152).

A common option is to blend paraphrase with brief quotation, carefully using quotation marks to identify any exact words drawn from the source. Even in a brief paraphrase, be careful to avoid slipping in the author's words or closely shadowing the original sentence structure.

HOW TO PARAPHRASE

For more on paraphrases, see D4 in the Quick Research Guide, p. Q-29.

- Select a passage that is relevant to your thesis.
- Reword that passage: represent it accurately, but use your own language.
- Change the sentence patterns of the passage, simplify long sentences, and reorder information.
- Note the page or other location of the passage, as it appears in your source.
- After a break, recheck your paraphrase against the original to be certain that it does not repeat the same words or merely replace a few with synonyms. Revise as needed.

Summarize an Overall Point. Summarizing is a useful way of incorporating the general point of a whole paragraph, section, or work. You briefly state the main sense of the original in your own words and also identify the source. Like a paraphrase, a summary uses your own language. However, a summary is shorter than the original; it expresses only the most important ideas — the essence — of the original. This example summarizes the section of Babbitt's book containing the passage quoted on page 194.

SUMMARY
> According to Bruce Babbitt, desert tortoises have been around for millions of years, but they only became endangered when ranchers allowed their livestock to graze on public lands.

HOW TO SUMMARIZE

- Select a passage whose main idea bears on your thesis.
- Read the selection carefully until you have mastered its overall point.
- Write a sentence or a series of sentences that states its essence in your own words.
- Revise your summary until it is as concise, clear, and accurate as possible. Replace any vague generalizations with precise words.
- Name your source as you begin your summary, or identify it in parentheses.

For more on summaries, see D5 in the Quick Research Guide, pp. Q-28–Q-29.

The following table can help you choose the best method for capturing information from your sources.

Capturing Information from Sources

	Quote	**Paraphrase**	**Summarize**
Advantages	Authoritative	In your voice	Brief
Format	Use exact words of the original passage; use brackets to show additions and ellipses to show deletions.	Use your own words. Use your own sentence structure. Make briefer than, or same length as, original passage.	Use your own words. Use your own sentence structure. Reduce the original passage to its essence.
What to avoid	Quoting too much or doing so inaccurately	Accidentally using author's words and sentence patterns	Giving too much detail

Learning by Doing 🔲 Avoiding Accidental Plagiarism

When writing a position paper supported by sources, make sure that you have identified and cited all information or evidence drawn from the works of others. Read your draft line by line, and compare each direct quotation, paraphrase, and summary with the original passage from the relevant source. Check that you have mentioned the author and page number in the text of your paper and that each in-text citation has a corresponding entry in your references or works cited list.

For more on quotations, paraphrases, and summaries, see D3, D4, and D5 in the Quick Research Guide, pp. Q-28–Q-30.

Interpret Supporting Evidence. No matter how many quotations, paraphrases, and summaries you assemble, chunks of evidence captured from sources do not — on their own — make a solid paper. You need to interpret and

For advice on MLA and APA styles, see Chs. 31 and 32.

explain that evidence for your readers, helping them to see exactly why, how, and to what extent it supports your position.

To organize a solid draft, many writers rely on one of two methods, beginning either with the evidence or with the position they wish to support:

Method 1. Start with your evidence. Arrange quotations, paraphrases, and summaries in a logical, compelling order. Next, add commentary to connect the chunks for your readers: introduce, conclude, and link pieces of evidence with your explanations and interpretations. (Ignore any leftovers from sources unless they cover key points that you still need to integrate.) Let your draft expand as you alternate evidence and interpretation.

Method 2. Start with your position. State your case boldly and directly, explaining your thesis and supporting points in your own words. Use this structure to identify where to embed evidence from your sources. Let your draft grow as you pull in your sources and expand your comments.

INTEGRATING SOURCES CHECKLIST

For more on quotations, paraphrases, and summaries, see D3, D4, and D5 in the Quick Research Guide, pp. Q-28–Q-30.

☐ Do the passages that you've quoted add support and authority to your paper?

☐ Are the quotations accurate? Have you used quotation marks correctly?

☐ Have you paraphrased accurately — and in your own words and sentence structure?

☐ Have you summarized effectively and omitted unnecessary details?

☐ Have you identified the source of every quotation, paraphrase, or summary?

☐ Have you cited your sources correctly, according to your instructor's required documentation style?

☐ Have you stated your position clearly and interpreted the evidence that you've drawn from sources? Have you done so in your own voice?

Revising and Editing

For more on revising and editing strategies, see Ch. 19.

As you read over the draft of your paper, remember what you wanted to accomplish: to develop a clear position about your topic and to share this position with a college audience, using sources to support your ideas.

Strengthen Your Thesis. As you begin to revise, you may decide that your thesis is ambiguous, poorly worded, hard to support, or simply off the mark. Revise it so that it clearly alerts readers to your position. In this example, the student revised her thesis to take a clear position on the issue.

WORKING THESIS   Although most workers would like longer vacations, many employers do not believe that they would benefit, too.

REVISED THESIS   Despite assumptions to the contrary, employers who increase vacation time for workers also are likely to increase creativity, productivity, and the bottom line.

STRENGTHENING YOUR THESIS

☐ Is your thesis, or main idea, clear?

☐ Is it as specific as possible?

☐ Does it stand out from the points made by your sources?

☐ Have you taken a strong (enough) position?

☐ Should you refine your position based on what you've learned from other sources? Have you changed your thinking about the subject?

Introduce and Cite Each Source. Whenever you quote, paraphrase, summarize, or refer to a source, give it a suitable introduction. An effective introduction or signal phrase sets the scene for your source material, prepares your reader to accept it, and marks the transition from your words and ideas to those of the source. In your introductory sentence, identify the source by the author's last name or, if the author isn't named, by a short version of the title. When you quote or paraphrase from a specific page, include that exact location. The following examples introduce the source about endangered tortoises mentioned earlier (see page 194) and cite them in MLA style:

For more about introducing sources (and using signal phrases), see D6 in the Quick Research Guide, pp. Q-30–Q-31.

> <u>According to Babbitt,</u> while tortoises have been around for millions of years, they became endangered when ranchers allowed their livestock to graze in the dessert <u>(152)</u>.

Here the writer introduces the source by naming the author directly in the sentence and provides the relevant page number in parentheses.

If you do not include a signal phrase, identify both the author's name and the location of the source material in parentheses at the end of the sentence:

> While tortoises have been around for millions of years, they became endangered when ranchers allowed their livestock to graze in the dessert <u>(Babbitt 152).</u>

Then try to suggest why you've mentioned this source at this point, perhaps noting its vantage point, or relationship to other sources.

Vary your signal phrases to avoid tedium and to add emphasis. Here are some typical patterns to introduce sources:

> As Yung demonstrates, . . .

> The classic definition of . . . (Bagette 18).

> Although Zeffir maintains . . . , Matson suggests . . .

For sample source citations and lists, see the MLA and APA examples in E in the Quick Research Guide, pp. Q-31–Q-36, and in A in the Quick Format Guide, pp. Q-1–Q-6.

Many schools educated the young but also unified the community (Hill 22). . . .

In *Forward March*, Smith's study of the children of military personnel, . . .

Another common recommendation is . . . ("Safety Manual").

Tapping into her experience as a travel consultant, Lee explains . . .

Benton distinguishes four typical steps in this process (248–51).

Synthesize Several Sources. Often you will compare, contrast, or relate two or three sources to deepen your discussion or to illustrate a range of views. When you synthesize, you pull together several sources in the same passage to build a new interpretation or reach a new conclusion. You go beyond the separate contributions of the individual sources to relate the sources to each other and to connect them to your thesis. A synthesis should be easy to follow and should use your own wording.

HOW TO SYNTHESIZE

- Summarize (see pages 196–97) each of the sources you want to synthesize. Boil down each summary to its essence.
- State in a few sentences — in your own words — how the sources are linked. For example, are they similar, different, or related? Do they share assumptions and conclusions, or do they represent alternatives?
- Explain what the relationships among the sources mean for the position you develop in your paper.
- Refine your synthesis statements until they are clear. Embed them as you reach new interpretations or conclusions that go beyond the separate sources.

SYNTHESIS
Using different methods, three separate studies reached a similar conclusion: Tortoises are in serious trouble (Barber et al.; Carroll; Jones and Henderson).

Use Your Own Voice. Writers create voices through their choices of language and angle of vision. Finding your own voice may be difficult in a source-based paper. By the time you have supported your position by quoting, paraphrasing, or summarizing relevant readings, you may worry that your sources have taken over your paper.

As you develop your voice, you'll learn to restrict sources to their proper role as supporting evidence. Don't let them dominate your writing. Use these questions to help you strengthen your voice:

- What do you want readers to hear in your voice? Have you balanced passion and personality with logic and reason? Can you revise your draft with that in mind?

- Have you used your own voice — and not quotations or paraphrases from sources — to introduce your topic, state your thesis, and draw conclusions? To state your position and to support it with evidence?

- Have you used your own voice to introduce source material — and to explain or interpret it in the context of your position/thesis?

To make sure your voice dominates your paper, reread your drafts and identify where the voices of others have become louder than yours.

DRAFT

Writers Lisa Jo Rudy and Giulia Rhodes <u>say</u> that screen-based activities can benefit children on the autism spectrum. Simon Baron Cohen, a professor of developmental psychopathology at the University of Cambridge, <u>says</u>: "We can use computers to teach emotion recognition and to simplify communication by stripping out facial and vocal emotional expressions and slowing it down using e-mail instead of face-to-face real-time modes" (Rhodes). Christopher R. Engelhardt, a researcher at the University of Missouri-Columbia, <u>says</u>, "In-room media access was associated with about 1.5 fewer hours of sleep per night in the group with autism" (Doyle).

Whole passage repeats "say"/ "says"

Jumps from one source to the next; no explanations or transitions

When your sources overshadow your voice and thesis, revise to restore balance. Try strategies such as these to regain control of your draft:

- Interpret your source information clearly so that your readers can distinguish your voice from the others.

- Explain the value of drawing on a specific source. State why you're including a quote, paraphrase, or summary. Recognize alternative views to strengthen your credibility.

- Use transitions and arrange information logically, not in the order in which you read it.

- Revise to vary your sentence openings and avoid repetition.

Thoughtful revision can help readers grasp what you want to say, why you have included each source, and how you think that it supports your thesis.

REVISION

As the parent of a child on the autism spectrum, I have long questioned whether I should limit my son's screen time in some way. Based on my recent research, I have concluded that it is probably beneficial to allow him to play video games, one of his favorite activities, but that I should place some restrictions on his access to them.

Clearly, participating in screen-based activities can provide certain benefits for children on the autism spectrum. <u>For example</u>, these activities can aid these children's learning, help them connect with peers, and give them a greater sense of control over their environment (Rudy, Rhodes). Simon Baron Cohen, a professor of developmental psychopathology at the University of Cambridge, has noted the

Identifies author's experience to add to credibility; draws conclusions based on her research

Adds a transition and introduces a summary

Introduces a quotation

benefits of computers to people with autism: "We can use computers to teach emotion recognition and to simplify communication by stripping out facial and vocal emotional expressions and slowing it down using e-mail instead of face-to-face real-time modes" (Rhodes).

Adds more transitions and introduces additional source material

However, unrestricted screen access is not without drawbacks. Recently, for example, a group of researchers at the University of Missouri-Columbia found that boys on the autism spectrum who had bedtime access to television, computers, and video games slept less each night (Engelhardt, Mazurek, and Sohl).

According to Christopher R. Engelhardt, the researcher who led the study, "In-room media access was associated with about 1.5 fewer hours of sleep per night in the group with autism" (Doyle).

Cite Your Sources as College Readers Expect. You'll be expected to identify your sources twice: briefly when you draw information from them and fully when you list them at the end of your paper, following a conventional system such as MLA or APA style. For example, the writer of the draft in the previous section listed her sources in MLA style:

Doyle, Kathryn. "Bedroom Computers, TV May Add to Autism Sleep Issues." *Reuters*, 18 Nov. 2013, www.reuters.com/article/us-bedroom-sleep -idUSBRE9AH11V20131118.

Mazurek, Micah O., et al. "Bedtime Electronic Media Use and Sleep in Children with Autism Spectrum Disorder." *Journal of Developmental and Behavioral Pediatrics*, vol. 37, no. 7, Sep. 2016, pp. 525–31, doi: 10.1097/DBP.0000000000000314.

Menhall, Jamie. "Emerging Technologies and the Frontiers of Autism Research." *The Clay Center for Young Healthy Minds,* 26 Mar. 2018, www.mghclaycenter.org/parenting-concerns/families/emerging -technologies-and-the-frontiers-of-autism-research/.

Rudy, Lisa Jo. "Top 10 Good Reasons for Allowing Autistic Children to Watch TV and Videos." *About.com*, 13 May 2015, autism.about.com/od /inspirationideas/tp/TVOK.htm.

Peer Response: 🕮 Get Feedback on Your Position Paper

For more about using either MLA or APA style, see D6 and E in the Quick Research Guide, pp. Q-30–Q-36.

For general questions for a peer editor, see p. 309.

Ask peers to consider the following questions.

■ What is the writer's position on the topic?

■ Do the writer's points connect clearly with the supporting evidence from sources?

■ How effectively does the writer capture the information from sources? Should any of the quotations, paraphrases, or summaries be presented differently?

- Are any of the source citations unclear?
- Is the writer's voice clear? Do the sources drown it out in any spots?
- If this paper were yours, what is the one thing you would be sure to work on before handing it in?

REVISING YOUR DRAFT

☐ Have you used your voice effectively? Have you interpreted your sources instead of letting them dominate the paper?

☐ Have you moved smoothly back and forth between your explanations and source material?

☐ Have you quoted, paraphrased, summarized, and credited each source accurately and ethically?

After you have revised your paper, edit and proofread it. Carefully check the grammar, word choice, punctuation, and mechanics — and then correct any problems you find. Be certain to check the punctuation with your quotations, making sure that each quotation mark is correctly placed and that you have used other punctuation, such as commas, correctly.

As you edit your draft, ask yourself the following.

EDITING FOR CLARITY

☐ Do all the verbs agree with their subjects, especially when you switch from your words to those of a source?   A4

☐ Do all pronouns agree with their antecedents, especially when you use your own words with a quotation from a source?   A6

☐ Have you used commas correctly, especially where you integrate material from sources?   D1

☐ Have you punctuated all quotations correctly?   D3

For more help, find the relevant checklist sections in the Quick Editing Guide on p. Q-37. Turn also to the Quick Format Guide beginning on p. Q-1.

Reviewing and Reflecting

REVIEW Working with classmates or independently, respond to the following questions:

1. What are some strategies for making sure that your voice shines through in a source-based position paper?

2. Briefly define each of the following methods for capturing information from sources: quoting, paraphrasing, and summarizing.

3. What does it mean to introduce a source in your paper? What do you do to prepare an effective signal phrase?

REFLECT Reflect in writing about how you might apply the insights that you drew from this assignment to another situation — in or outside of college — in which you have to support a position with sources. In your reflection, consider how you would draw on various evidence to support your position.

Additional Writing Assignments

For more on interviewing, see Ch. 5. For more on reviewing and evaluating, see Ch. 10.

1. **Source Assignment.** Read three sources that address the same topic, such as three essays from the thematic chapters in the Reader. Instead of using these texts as evidence to support a position, analyze how well they function as sources. State your thesis about them, and evaluate their strengths and weaknesses, using clear criteria. (See, for example, the criteria in C3 in the Quick Research Guide, pp. Q-26–Q-27.)

2. **Source Assignment.** Locate two different accounts of a notable event. Draw on newspapers, magazines, published letters or journals, books, blogs, social media, or other sources, depending on the time when the event occurred. State and support a thesis that explains the differences among the accounts. Use the accounts as evidence to support your position.

3. **Source Assignment.** Browse in your library's new book area (on site or online) or in specialty search engines to identify a current topic of interest to you. Gather and evaluate three sources on your topic. Write an essay using those sources to support your position about the new development.

4. **Source Assignment.** Following the directions of your instructor, use sources to support your position in an essay. One option might be to select paired readings (from this book), and to interview someone with the background or experience to act as another valuable source of information. A second option might be to view and evaluate a film, television program, radio show, podcast, blog, website, art exhibit, or performance or other event. Then supplement your review by reading several articles that review the same topic, evaluate a different or related production, or discuss criteria for similar types of items or events.

5. **Visual Assignment.** Examine the following images, and analyze one of them. Use the image to support your position in an essay, perhaps a conclusion about the image or about what it portrays. Point out relevant details to persuade your audience of your view. Cite the images correctly, using the style your instructor specifies.

Sharp Increase in Opioid Prescriptions ⟶ Increase in Deaths

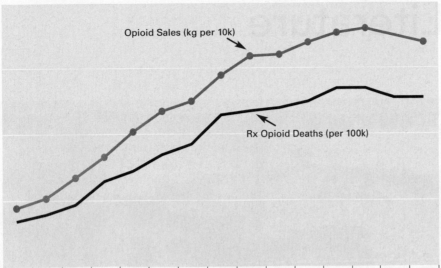

Opioid Sales (kg per 10k)

Rx Opioid Deaths (per 100k)

1999 2000 2001 2002 2003 2004 2005 2006 2007 2008 2009 2010 2011 2012 2013

Sharp Increase in Opioid Prescriptions. National Vital Statistics System, DEA Automation of Reports and Consolidated Orders System

Dragon dancers at a Chinese New Year celebration. Greg Baker/AFP/Getty Images

12 Responding to Literature

Responding to an image

The Tale of Genji, written in eleventh-century Japan by Lady Murasaki Shikibu, is the world's first novel. As it chronicles the life and many loves of Prince Genji, the novel deals with the universal themes of coming of age, desire, and the passage of time, making it relevant even to today's readers. The decorative screen shown here is illustrated with scenes from the novel. What stories do you see? What aspects about those stories might you relate to?

Why Responding to Literature Matters

As countless readers know, reading fiction gives pleasure and delight. Whether you read Stephen King or Stephen Crane, you can be swept up into an imaginative world where you journey to distant lands and meet exotic people. You may also meet characters like yourself with familiar or new ways of viewing life. On a deeper level, by sharing the experiences of literary characters, you gain insights into your own life and the lives of others. You gain perspective on the human experience and develop more empathy toward humankind.

Typically, a writing assignment in a literature or humanities course requires you to read closely a literary work (short story, novel, play, or poem) and then to divide it into elements, explain its meaning, and support your interpretation with evidence from the work. You might also be asked to evaluate a selection or to compare and contrast several readings. Such analysis is not an end; its purpose is to illuminate the meaning of the work, to help you and others understand it better.

In a College Course

- You apply methods of literary analysis to identify themes, images, symbols, and figures of speech in history speeches, political essays, or business case studies.
- You respond to plays in your theater class, novels in cultural studies, essays in philosophy, or poetry in upper-level literature courses.

In the Workplace

- You use literary analysis as you critique the setting, point of view, and theme for your company's advertising campaign.

In Your Community

- You support the library's story hour for your children, the community theater's plays, and the hospital's journal project for wounded veterans.

❓ When have you responded to a short story, novel, poem, or play? In what situations might you respond to literature in future writing?

Learning from Other Writers

Student Amina Khan was assigned to write a literary analysis of "Clothes," a provocative short story by Chitra Banerjee Divakaruni published in her 1995 collection *Arranged Marriage*. Read this story yourself to understand its meaning. Then read on to see how Khan responded to it.

Chitra Banerjee Divakaruni

Clothes

The water of the women's lake laps against my breasts, cool, calming. I can feel it beginning to wash the hot nervousness away from my body. The little waves tickle my armpits, make my sari° float up around me, wet and yellow, like a sunflower after rain. I close my eyes and smell the sweet brown odor

1

Krishna Giri © 1995 by Chitra Divakaruni. First appeared in ARRANGED MARRIAGE

sari: A draped garment worn by women of south Asia, made of a piece of fabric that wraps around the waist and over one shoulder.

of the *ritha*° pulp my friends Deepali and Radha are working into my hair so it will glisten with little lights this evening. They scrub with more vigor than usual and wash it out more carefully, because today is a special day. It is the day of my bride-viewing.

"Ei, Sumita! Mita! Are you deaf?" Radha says. "This is the third time I've asked you the same question."

"Look at her, already dreaming about her husband, and she hasn't even seen him yet!" Deepali jokes. Then she adds, the envy in her voice only half hidden, "Who cares about friends from a little Indian village when you're about to go live in America?"

I want to deny it, to say that I will always love them and all the things we did together through my growing-up years—visiting the charak fair where we always ate too many sweets, raiding the neighbor's guava tree summer afternoons while the grown-ups slept, telling fairy tales while we braided each other's hair in elaborate patterns we'd invented. *And she married the handsome prince who took her to his kingdom beyond the seven seas.* But already the activities of our girlhood seem to be far in my past, the colors leached out of them, like old sepia° photographs.

His name is Somesh Sen, the man who is coming to our house with his parents today and who will be my husband "if I'm lucky enough to be chosen," as my aunt says. He is coming all the way from California. Father showed it to me yesterday, on the metal globe that sits on his desk, a chunky pink wedge on the side of a multicolored slab marked *Untd. Sts. of America*. I touched it and felt the excitement leap all the way up my arm like an electric shock. Then it died away, leaving only a beaten-metal coldness against my fingertips.

For the first time it occurred to me that if things worked out the way everyone was hoping, I'd be going halfway around the world to live with a man I hadn't even met. Would I ever see my parents again? Don't send me so far away, I wanted to cry, but of course I didn't. It would be ungrateful. Father had worked so hard to find this match for me. Besides, wasn't it every woman's destiny, as Mother was always telling me, to leave the known for the unknown? She had done it, and her mother before her. *A married woman belongs to her husband, her in-laws.* Hot seeds of tears pricked my eyelids at the unfairness of it.

"Mita Moni, little jewel," Father said, calling me by my childhood name. He put out his hand as though he wanted to touch my face, then let it fall to his side. "He's a good man. Comes from a fine family. He will be kind to you." He was silent for a while. Finally he said, "Come, let me show you the special sari I bought in Calcutta for you to wear at the bride-viewing."

"Are you nervous?" Radha asks as she wraps my hair in a soft cotton towel. Her parents are also trying to arrange a marriage for her. So far three families have come to see her, but no one has chosen her because her skin-color is considered too dark. "Isn't it terrible, not knowing what's going to happen?"

---

ritha: Also called soapnut; a medicinal herb used to beautify the skin and hair.   **sepia:** A reddish-brown pigment sometimes used to tint black-and-white photographs in the nineteenth century.

I nod because I don't want to disagree, don't want to make her feel bad 9 by saying that sometimes it's worse when you know what's coming, like I do. I knew it as soon as Father unlocked his mahogany *almirah*° and took out the sari.

It was the most expensive sari I had ever seen, and surely the most beau- 10 tiful. Its body was a pale pink, like the dawn sky over the women's lake. The color of transition. Embroidered all over it were tiny stars made out of real gold *zari*° thread.

"Here, hold it," said Father. 11

The sari was unexpectedly heavy in my hands, silk-slippery, a sari to walk 12 carefully in. A sari that could change one's life. I stood there holding it, wanting to weep. I knew that when I wore it, it would hang in perfect pleats to my feet and shimmer in the light of the evening lamps. It would dazzle Somesh and his parents and they would choose me to be his bride.

When the plane takes off, I try to stay calm, to take deep, slow breaths like 13 Father does when he practices yoga. But my hands clench themselves on to the folds of my sari and when I force them open, after the *fasten seat belt* and *no smoking* signs have blinked off, I see they have left damp blotches on the delicate crushed fabric.

We had some arguments about this sari. I wanted a blue one for the jour- 14 ney, because blue is the color of possibility, the color of the sky through which I would be traveling. But Mother said there must be red in it because red is the color of luck for married women. Finally, Father found one to satisfy us both: midnight-blue with a thin red border the same color as the marriage mark I'm wearing on my forehead.

It is hard for me to think of myself as a married woman. I whisper my 15 new name to myself, Mrs. Sumita Sen, but the syllables rustle uneasily in my mouth like a stiff satin that's never been worn.

Somesh had to leave for America just a week after the wedding. He had to get 16 back to the store, he explained to me. He had promised his partner. The store. It seems more real to me than Somesh — perhaps because I know more about it. It was what we had mostly talked about the night after the wedding, the first night we were together alone. It stayed open twenty-four hours, yes, all night, every night, not like the Indian stores which closed at dinnertime and sometimes in the hottest part of the afternoon. That's why his partner needed him back.

The store was called 7-Eleven. I thought it a strange name, exotic, risky. All 17 the stores I knew were piously° named after gods and goddesses — Ganesh° Sweet House, Lakshmi Vastralaya for Fine Saris — to bring the owners luck.

The store sold all kinds of amazing things — apple juice in cardboard 18 cartons that never leaked; American bread that came in cellophane packages, already cut up; canisters of potato chips, each large grainy flake curved

---

almirah: Wardrobe, cabinet where clothing is stored.   *zari*: Gold thread used to enhance Indian clothing.   **piously**: Reverentially; with awe or respect.   **Ganesh**: A god in Hindu mythology who has the head of an elephant; Ganesh is also worshipped by Jainists and Buddhists.

exactly like the next. The large refrigerator with see-through glass doors held beer and wine, which Somesh said were the most popular items.

"That's where the money comes from, especially in the neighborhood where our store is," said Somesh, smiling at the shocked look on my face. (The only places I knew of that sold alcohol were the village toddy shops, "dark, stinking dens of vice," Father called them.) "A lot of Americans drink, you know. It's a part of their culture, not considered immoral, like it is here. And really, there's nothing wrong with it." He touched my lips lightly with his finger. "When you come to California, I'll get you some sweet white wine and you'll see how good it makes you feel. . . ." Now his fingers were stroking my cheeks, my throat, moving downward. I closed my eyes and tried not to jerk away because after all it was my wifely duty.

"It helps if you can think about something else," my friend Madhavi said when she warned me about what most husbands demanded on the very first night. Two years married, she already had one child and was pregnant with a second one.

I tried to think of the women's lake, the dark cloudy green of the *shapla*° leaves that float on the water, but his lips were hot against my skin, his fingers fumbling with buttons, pulling at the cotton night-sari I wore. I couldn't breathe.

"Bite hard on your tongue," Madhavi had advised. "The pain will keep your mind off what's going on down there."

But when I bit down, it hurt so much that I cried out. I couldn't help it although I was ashamed. Somesh lifted his head. I don't know what he saw on my face, but he stopped right away.

"Shhh," he said, although I had made myself silent already. "It's OK, we'll wait until you feel like it." I tried to apologize but he smiled it away and started telling me some more about the store.

And that's how it was the rest of the week until he left. We would lie side by side on the big white bridal pillow I had embroidered with a pair of doves for married harmony, and Somesh would describe how the store's front windows were decorated with a flashing neon Dewar's sign and a lighted Budweiser waterfall this big. I would watch his hands moving excitedly through the dim air of the bedroom and think that Father had been right, he was a good man, my husband, a kind, patient man. And so handsome, too, I would add, stealing a quick look at the strong curve of his jaw, feeling luckier than I had any right to be.

The night before he left, Somesh confessed that the store wasn't making much money yet. "I'm not worried, I'm sure it soon will," he added, his fingers pleating the edge of my sari. "But I just don't want to give you the wrong impression, don't want you to be disappointed."

In the half dark I could see he had turned toward me. His face, with two vertical lines between the brows, looked young, apprehensive, in need of protection. I'd never seen that on a man's face before. Something rose in me like a wave.

19

20

21

22

23

24

25

26

27

---

shapla: Bengali for *water lily*.

"It's all right," I said, as though to a child, and pulled his head down to my 28
breast. His hair smelled faintly of the American cigarettes he smoked. "I won't
be disappointed. I'll help you." And a sudden happiness filled me.

That night I dreamed I was at the store. Soft American music floated in 29
the background as I moved between shelves stocked high with brightly colored cans and elegant-necked bottles, turning their labels carefully to the
front, polishing them until they shone.

Now, sitting inside this metal shell that is hurtling through emptiness, I 30
try to remember other things about my husband: how gentle his hands had
been, and his lips, surprisingly soft, like a woman's. How I've longed for them
through those drawn-out nights while I waited for my visa to arrive. He will
be standing at the customs gate, and when I reach him, he will lower his face
to mine. We will kiss in front of everyone, not caring, like Americans, then
pull back, look each other in the eye, and smile.

But suddenly, as I am thinking this, I realize I cannot recall Somesh's face. 31
I try and try until my head hurts, but I can only visualize the black air swirling
outside the plane, too thin for breathing. My own breath grows ragged with
panic as I think of it and my mouth fills with sour fluid the way it does just
before I throw up.

I grope for something to hold on to, something beautiful and talismanic° 32
from my old life. And then I remember. Somewhere down under me, low
in the belly of the plane, inside my new brown case which is stacked in the
dark with a hundred others, are my saris. Thick Kanjeepuram° silks in solid
purples and golden yellows, the thin hand-woven cottons of the Bengal
countryside, green as a young banana plant, gray as the women's lake on a
monsoon morning. Already I can feel my shoulders loosening up, my breath
steadying. My wedding Benarasi,° flame-orange, with a wide *palloo*° of gold-
embroidered dancing peacocks. Fold upon fold of Dhakais° so fine they can
be pulled through a ring. Into each fold my mother has tucked a small sachet°
of sandalwood powder to protect the saris from the unknown insects of
America. Little silk sachets, made from her old saris—I can smell their calm
fragrance as I watch the American air hostess wheeling the dinner cart toward
my seat. It is the smell of my mother's hands.

I know then that everything will be all right. And when the air hostess 33
bends her curly golden head to ask me what I would like to eat, I understand
every word in spite of her strange accent and answer her without stumbling
even once over the unfamiliar English phrases.

Late at night I stand in front of our bedroom mirror trying on the 34
clothes Somesh has bought for me and smuggled in past his parents. I model
each one for him, walking back and forth, clasping my hands behind my head,
lips pouted, left hip thrust out just like the models on TV, while he whispers

---

talismanic: Possessing magical or protective powers.   **Kanjeepuram:** An ancient city in the
southern Indian state of Tamil Nadu.   **Benarasi:** A fine sari made in the city of Varanasi
(also known as Benares or Banaras).   *palloo:* The end of a sari that hangs loose.   **Dhakais:**
Saris made in the city of Dhaka in Bangladesh.   **sachet:** A small bag or packet containing
perfumed powder, used to scent clothes and sheets.

applause. I'm breathless with suppressed laughter (Father and Mother Sen must not hear us) and my cheeks are hot with the delicious excitement of conspiracy. We've stuffed a towel at the bottom of the door so no light will shine through.

I'm wearing a pair of jeans now, marveling at the curves of my hips and   35
thighs, which have always been hidden under the flowing lines of my saris. I love the color, the same pale blue as the *nayantara*° flowers that grow in my parents' garden. The solid comforting weight. The jeans come with a closefitting T-shirt which outlines my breasts.

I scold Somesh to hide my embarrassed pleasure. He shouldn't have been   36
so extravagant. We can't afford it. He just smiles.

The T-shirt is sunrise-orange — the color, I decide, of joy, of my new Ameri-   37
can life. Across its middle, in large black letters, is written *Great America*. I was sure the letters referred to the country, but Somesh told me it is the name of an amusement park, a place where people go to have fun. I think it a wonderful concept, novel. Above the letters is the picture of a train. Only it's not a train, Somesh tells me, it's a roller coaster. He tries to explain how it moves, the insane speed, the dizzy ground falling away, then gives up. "I'll take you there, Mita sweetheart," he says, "as soon as we move into our own place."

That's our dream (mine more than his, I suspect) — moving out of this   38
two-room apartment where it seems to me if we all breathed in at once, there would be no air left. Where I must cover my head with the edge of my Japan nylon sari (my expensive Indian ones are to be saved for special occasions — trips to the temple, Bengali New Year) and serve tea to the old women that come to visit Mother Sen, where like a good Indian wife I must never address my husband by his name. Where even in our bed we kiss guiltily, uneasily, listening for the giveaway creak of springs. Sometimes I laugh to myself, thinking how ironic it is that after all my fears about America, my life has turned out to be no different from Deepali's or Radha's. But at other times I feel caught in a world where everything is frozen in place, like a scene inside a glass paperweight. It is a world so small that if I were to stretch out my arms, I would touch its cold unyielding edges. I stand inside this glass world, watching helplessly as America rushes by, wanting to scream. Then I'm ashamed. Mita, I tell myself, you're growing westernized. Back home you'd never have felt this way.

We must be patient. I know that. Tactful, loving children. That is the   39
Indian way. "I'm their life," Somesh tells me as we lie beside each other, lazy from lovemaking. He's not boasting, merely stating a fact. "They've always been there when I needed them. I could never abandon them at some old people's home." For a moment I feel rage. You're constantly thinking of them, I want to scream. But what about me? Then I remember my own parents, Mother's hands cool on my sweat-drenched body through nights of fever, Father teaching me to read, his finger moving along the crisp black angles of the alphabet, transforming them magically into things I knew, water, dog, mango tree. I beat back my unreasonable desire and nod agreement.

nayantara: A flowering plant also known as the periwinkle.

Somesh has bought me a cream blouse with a long brown skirt. They 40
match beautifully, like the inside and outside of an almond. "For when you
begin working," he says. But first he wants me to start college. Get a degree,
perhaps in teaching. I picture myself in front of a classroom of girls with
blond pigtails and blue uniforms, like a scene out of an English movie I saw
long ago in Calcutta. They raise their hands respectfully when I ask a question. "Do you really think I can?" I ask. "Of course," he replies.

I am gratified he has such confidence in me. But I have another plan, a 41
secret that I will divulge to him once we move. What I really want is to work
in the store. I want to stand behind the counter in the cream-and-brown skirt
set (color of earth, color of seeds) and ring up purchases. The register drawer
will glide open. Confident, I will count out green dollars and silver quarters.
Gleaming copper pennies. I will dust the jars of gilt-wrapped chocolates on
the counter. Will straighten, on the far wall, posters of smiling young men
raising their beer mugs to toast scantily clad redheads with huge spiky eye-
lashes. (I have never visited the store — my in-laws don't consider it proper
for a wife — but of course I know exactly what it looks like.) I will charm the
customers with my smile, so that they will return again and again just to hear
me telling them to have a nice day.

Meanwhile, I will the store to make money for us. Quickly. Because when 42
we move, we'll be paying for two households. But so far it hasn't worked.
They're running at a loss, Somesh tells me. They had to let the hired help go.
This means most nights Somesh has to take the graveyard shift (that horrible
word, like a cold hand up my spine) because his partner refuses to.

"The bastard!" Somesh spat out once. "Just because he put in more money 43
he thinks he can order me around. I'll show him!" I was frightened by the
vicious twist of his mouth. Somehow I'd never imagined that he could be
angry.

Often Somesh leaves as soon as he has dinner and doesn't get back till 44
after I've made morning tea for Father and Mother Sen. I lie mostly awake
those nights, picturing masked intruders crouching in the shadowed back
of the store, like I've seen on the police shows that Father Sen sometimes
watches. But Somesh insists there's nothing to worry about, they have bars
on the windows and a burglar alarm. "And remember," he says, "the extra cash
will help us move out that much quicker."

I'm wearing a nightie now, my very first one. It's black and lacy, with a 45
bit of a shine to it, and it glides over my hips to stop outrageously at mid-
thigh. My mouth is an O of surprise in the mirror, my legs long and pale and
sleek from the hair remover I asked Somesh to buy me last week. The legs of
a movie star. Somesh laughs at the look on my face, then says, "You're beautiful." His voice starts a flutter low in my belly.

"Do you really think so," I ask, mostly because I want to hear him say it 46
again. No one has called me beautiful before. My father would have thought
it inappropriate, my mother that it would make me vain.

Somesh draws me close. "Very beautiful," he whispers. "The most beau- 47
tiful woman in the whole world." His eyes are not joking as they usually are.
I want to turn off the light, but "Please," he says, "I want to keep seeing your

face." His fingers are taking the pins from my hair, undoing my braids. The escaped strands fall on his face like dark rain. We have already decided where we will hide my new American clothes — the jeans and T-shirt camouflaged on a hanger among Somesh's pants, the skirt set and nightie at the bottom of my suitcase, a sandalwood sachet tucked between them, waiting.

I stand in the middle of our empty bedroom, my hair still wet from the purification bath, my back to the stripped bed I can't bear to look at. I hold in my hands the plain white sari I'm supposed to wear. I must hurry. Any minute now there'll be a knock at the door. They are afraid to leave me alone too long, afraid I might do something to myself.   48

The sari, a thick voile° that will bunch around the waist when worn, is borrowed. White. Widow's color, color of endings. I try to tuck it into the top of the petticoat,° but my fingers are numb, disobedient. It spills through them and there are waves and waves of white around my feet. I kick out in sudden rage, but the sari is too soft, it gives too easily. I grab up an edge, clamp down with my teeth and pull, feeling a fierce, bitter satisfaction when I hear it rip.   49

There's a cut, still stinging, on the side of my right arm, halfway to the elbow. It is from the bangle-breaking ceremony. Old Mrs. Ghosh performed the ritual, since she's a widow, too. She took my hands in hers and brought them down hard on the bedpost, so that the glass bangles I was wearing shattered and multicolored shards flew out in every direction. Some landed on the body that was on the bed, covered with a sheet. I can't call it Somesh. He was gone already. She took an edge of the sheet and rubbed the red marriage mark off my forehead. She was crying. All the women in the room were crying except me. I watched them as though from the far end of a tunnel. Their flared nostrils, their red-veined eyes, the runnels of tears, salt-corrosive, down their cheeks.   50

It happened last night. He was at the store. "It isn't too bad," he would tell me on the days when he was in a good mood. "Not too many customers. I can put up my feet and watch MTV all night. I can sing along with Michael Jackson as loud as I want." He had a good voice, Somesh. Sometimes he would sing softly at night, lying in bed, holding me. Hindi° songs of love, *Mee Sapnon K Rani*, queen of my dreams. (He would not sing American songs at home out of respect for his parents, who thought they were decadent.) I would feel his warm breath on my hair as I fell asleep.   51

Someone came into the store last night. He took all the money, even the little rolls of pennies I had helped Somesh make up. Before he left he emptied the bullets from his gun into my husband's chest.   52

"Only thing is," Somesh would say about the night shifts, "I really miss you. I sit there and think of you asleep in bed. Do you know that when you sleep you make your hands into fists, like a baby? When we move out, will you come along some nights to keep me company?"   53

voile: A lightweight, somewhat sheer fabric used for women's summer clothes.   **petticoat:** A woman's light undergarment; a slip.   **Hindi:** A language of northern India.

My in-laws are good people, kind. They made sure the body was covered ⁵⁴ before they let me into the room. When someone asked if my hair should be cut off, as they sometimes do with widows back home, they said no. They said I could stay at the apartment with Mrs. Ghosh if I didn't want to go to the crematorium. They asked Dr. Das to give me something to calm me down when I couldn't stop shivering. They didn't say, even once, as people would surely have in the village, that it was my bad luck that brought death to their son so soon after his marriage.

They will probably go back to India now. There's nothing here for them ⁵⁵ anymore. They will want me to go with them. You're like our daughter, they will say. Your home is with us, for as long as you want. For the rest of your life. *The rest of my life.* I can't think about that yet. It makes me dizzy. Fragments are flying about my head, multicolored and piercing sharp like bits of bangle glass.

I want you to go to college. Choose a career. I stand in front of a classroom ⁵⁶ of smiling children who love me in my cream-and-brown American dress. A faceless parade straggles across my eyelids: all those customers at the store that I will never meet. The lace nightie, fragrant with sandalwood, waiting in its blackness inside my suitcase. The savings book where we have $3605.33. *Four thousand and we can move out, maybe next month.* The name of the panty hose I'd asked him to buy me for my birthday: sheer golden-beige. His lips, unexpectedly soft, woman-smooth. Elegant-necked wine bottles swept off shelves, shattering on the floor.

I know Somesh would not have tried to stop the gunman. I can picture ⁵⁷ his silhouette° against the lighted Dewar's sign, hands raised. He is trying to find the right expression to put on his face, calm, reassuring, reasonable. *OK, take the money. No, I won't call the police.* His hands tremble just a little. His eyes darken with disbelief as his fingers touch his chest and come away wet.

I yanked away the cover. I had to see. *Great America, a place where people go to* ⁵⁸ *have fun.* My breath roller-coasting through my body, my unlived life gathering itself into a scream. I'd expected blood, a lot of blood, the deep red-black of it crusting his chest. But they must have cleaned him up at the hospital. He was dressed in his silk wedding *kurta.°* Against its warm ivory his face appeared remote, stem. The musky aroma of his aftershave lotion that someone must have sprinkled on the body. It didn't quite hide that other smell, thin, sour, metallic. The smell of death. The floor shifted under me, tilting like a wave.

I'm lying on the floor now, on the spilled white sari. I feel sleepy. Or per- ⁵⁹ haps it is some other feeling I don't have a word for. The sari is seductive-soft, drawing me into its folds.

Sometimes, bathing at the lake, I would move away from my friends, their ⁶⁰ endless chatter. I'd swim toward the middle of the water with a lazy back-stroke, gazing at the sky, its enormous blueness drawing me up until I felt weightless and dizzy. Once in a while there would be a plane, a small silver

---

silhouette: An outline; a dark shape and outline against a light background.   **kurta:** A long, loose, collarless shirt worn in India.

needle drawn through the clouds, in and out, until it disappeared. Sometimes the thought came to me, as I floated in the middle of the lake with the sun beating down on my closed eyelids, that it would be so easy to let go, to drop into the dim brown world of mud, of water weeds fine as hair.

Once I almost did it. I curled my body inward, tight as a fist, and felt it start to sink. The sun grew pale and shapeless; the water, suddenly cold, licked at the insides of my ears in welcome. But in the end I couldn't. 61

They are knocking on the door now, calling my name. I push myself off the floor, my body almost too heavy to lift up, as when one climbs out after a long swim. I'm surprised at how vividly it comes to me, this memory I haven't called up in years: the desperate flailing of arms and legs as I fought my way upward; the press of the water on me, heavy as terror; the wild animal trapped inside my chest, clawing at my lungs. The day returning to me as searing air, the way I drew it in, in, in, as though I would never have enough of it. 62

That's when I know I cannot go back. I don't know yet how I'll manage, here in this new, dangerous land. I only know I must. Because all over India, at this very moment, widows in white saris are bowing their veiled heads, serving tea to in-laws. Doves with cut-off wings. 63

I am standing in front of the mirror now, gathering up the sari. I tuck in the ripped end so it lies next to my skin, my secret. I make myself think of the store, although it hurts. Inside the refrigerated unit, blue milk cartons neatly lined up by Somesh's hands. The exotic smell of Hills Brothers coffee brewed black and strong, the glisten of sugar-glazed donuts nestled in tissue. The neon Budweiser emblem winking on and off like a risky invitation. 64

I straighten my shoulders and stand taller, take a deep breath. Air fills me —the same air that traveled through Somesh's lungs a little while ago. The thought is like an unexpected, intimate gift. I tilt my chin, readying myself for the arguments of the coming weeks, the remonstrations. In the mirror a woman holds my gaze, her eyes apprehensive yet steady. She wears a blouse and skirt the color of almonds. 65

Questions to Start You Thinking

Meaning

1. Where does this story take place? When? How do the story's multiple settings contribute to its meaning and to your experience as a reader?

2. What is Sumita's attitude toward getting married? Once wedded, how does she feel about her marriage? About her new husband?

3. What does Sumita think about Somesh's store? What does the store symbolize for her? How does that symbolism compare with the reality of what the store is and what happens there?

Writing Strategies

4. Describe Sumita's voice, as the speaker in the story. Choose a passage that was particularly memorable to you and reread it. How do her words and use of sensory imagery contribute to the overall tone and feel of the story?

5. Why is this story titled "Clothes"? What is the significance of Sumita's clothes in the story? With what does she associate the cream-colored blouse and brown skirt?

6. Are the events in the story believable? Why or why not? For Sumita, by the story's end, how has her outlook shifted? How do you know?

7. In addition to clothes and change, some of the story's themes include family, traditional gender roles, marriage, falling in love, the American Dream, loss and grief, hope and transformation, and the natural world. Which of these themes interests you most as a reader and writer? Are there others not mentioned here that you see in the story?

Preparing to Write a Literary Analysis

As Amina Khan first read "Clothes," she was carried along by Sumita's story of identity, family, marriage, hope, loss, and change. When she reached the ending, Khan understood the events of the story on a literal level. She then reread the story slowly in order to connect with it on a deeper level. She analyzed some of the literary elements at work in the story (see glossary on p. 222), including setting, character, imagery, and symbolism. She started to think about what she might have to say about "Clothes."

Then she considered the characters in the story, especially Sumita, the protagonist who narrates the story through the lens of her clothing. Rather than discussing character traits, Khan decided to focus on the different kinds of "journeys" Sumita takes, both literal (moving to the United States) and metaphorical (growing and changing). The metaphorical growth of Sumita, in the context of a traditional upbringing and her new life, interested Khan. She asked herself: "How did the author, Chitra Banerjee Divakaruni, develop and demonstrate how Sumita has evolved?" Khan thought it had to do with Sumita's clothes, which after all, is the title of the story.

To focus her thinking, Khan brainstormed for possible titles for her essay. "Control, Color, and Change," "A Subtle Change," "From Tradition to Independence", and her final choice, "Saris, Jeans, and Independence: The Symbolism of 'Clothes' by Chitra Banerjee Divakaruni." After reviewing her notes, Khan realized that Divakaruni uses symbolism and metaphor to tell Sumita's story through the various garments and situations. Khan jotted down some headings that occurred to her, thinking they might later help her to organize her paper.

Title: Saris, Jeans, and Independence: The Symbolism of Chitra Banerjee Divakaruni's "Clothes"

For more on stating a thesis, organizing ideas, and outlining, see Ch. 16.

Working Thesis: In "Clothes" by Chitra Banerjee Divakaruni, one of the major themes is that choice is essential to female evolution and independence. That choice is expressed in this story through clothing.

1. The colors of change: examples of clothing expressing independence
   - The pale pink viewing-day sari
   - The blue (possibility) sari and red (good luck) travel-day sari

2. The move from control to aspirations of her own
   - The traditional family members who "decide" on her clothes
   - Somesh buying her clothes for study and work, showing confidence in her
   - The beginning of Sumita's shift
3. Saris, panty hose, and thoughts of independence
   - The ornamentation of her pink sari
   - Sumita's love for her husband
4. Tragedy, independence, a choice to live
   - Death of Somesh and widowhood garments
   - White grieving sari, bitten and torn
   - "Blouse and skirt the color of almonds"

Then she drafted the following introduction:

For more on introductions, see pp. 286–88.

"Clothes" is a story of Indian womanhood experienced through the arranged marriage tradition. Clothes are often seen as objects of feminine vanity, or as a luxury for privileged fashionistas. But in Divakaruni's story, Sumita's saris and her new "American" clothes connect her to family, tradition, new experience, and culture, but they also signify changes that she experiences as eventually she is able to act for herself.

With her working thesis and her informal outline, Khan revised the introduction and wrote her essay.

Amina Khan   Student Essay

Saris, Jeans, and Independence: The Symbolism of Chitra Banerjee Divakaruni's "Clothes"

"Clothes" is a story about female identity and Hindu identity. Sumita, the main   1
character and narrator of the story, is a woman who hopes, loves, and grieves—
and who also aspires to a better, freer life. As the story's title suggests, Sumita's
strong attachment to her clothes is the main focus of the story. Her personal
growth is represented by the color of her clothes and by who chooses them for
her. It is through her clothes—her saris *and* her t-shirt and jeans—that Sumita
reveals the layers of her life and inner thoughts. In "Clothes," Chitra Banerjee
Divakaruni shows that when women have choice, they can grow and change and
evolve into independent beings, into who they want to be.

While some might dismiss clothes as objects of vanity, or as a luxury for those   2
who are privileged and shallow, Divakaruni's way of weaving them in her narrative
reinforces their significance as something more. The story begins with the pink
sari that Sumita's father brings for her bride-viewing day:

The numbers in parentheses are page-number citations following MLA style. For more on citing and listing sources, see D6 and E (pp. Q-30–Q-36) in the Quick Research Guide.

It was the most expensive sari I had ever seen, and surely the most beautiful.
Its body was a pale pink, like the dawn sky over the women's lake. The color
of transition. Embroidered all over it were tiny stars made out of real gold
zari thread. (209)

Like the dawn, this sari is a symbol of Sumita's transition from young girl to adult, from single to married, and ultimately, from India to America. She does not choose the sari for herself but is pleased by her father's choice. This is a direct metaphor for how an arranged marriage is set up in India. The pale pink sari is "beautiful" and "unexpectedly heavy," similar to Sumita's new phase of life (209).

While *what* Sumita wears is important, the bigger issue is *who* gets to decide on the clothes in the first place; for most of the story the "deciders" are her parents and in-laws. For instance, the sari Sumita will wear to travel to the U.S causes "some arguments"; she had wanted it to be blue, "the color of possibility" and modernity, but her mother wanted red, "the color of luck for married women" and tradition (209). The argument over the sari is a metaphor for her breaking away from her mother's home to define her independence and individuality.

Once she has moved to the U.S. it is Sumita's husband, Somesh, who adds a new style to her wardrobe. Somesh loves his wife, and he respects her. He has faith in Sumita. He wants her to go to college and then to have a career. The American-style clothes he buys her give her confidence to dream of her future: "I picture myself in front of a classroom of girls with blond pigtails and blue uniforms, like a scene out of an English movie I saw a long time ago in Calcutta" (213). The smuggling of Western attire and lingerie, and even their conspiratorial laughter, become secrets that bring them closer as a married couple.

As Sumita describes her clothes poetically, noting their touch and feel and their varied shades and hues, she reveals changes in herself. The item Sumita desires is panty hose, "sheer golden-beige" (215). Of all the things she could have asked for, Sumita chooses something subtle, almost unnoticeable garment, but it is an assertion of who she sees herself becoming. She emerges slowly and carefully, a butterfly who wants to break out from her cocoon without getting in trouble with her in-laws.

Eventually, and only after great loss, Sumita will pick out her own clothes. When her kind and supportive husband is tragically murdered, Sumita is immediately embraced by the protective women of the family. They dress her in widow's clothes — "White. Widow's color, color of endings" — smash the glass bangles she wears, as is the tradition, and rub out the red mark of marriage from her forehead (214). While this is done with kindness, Sumita feels lost, breathless, suffocating as she imagines her future as a widow. In pain and fury she bites and tears into the fabric of the white grieving sari, tucking the damaged end so that no one will see this small thing she's done for herself (217). Sumita makes a choice, and that is to live. As the story ends, Sumita is no longer wearing the white mourning sari but is dressed instead in "a blouse and skirt the color of almonds" (216). In choosing these clothes — the ones Somesh had bought for her — Sumita chooses her future.

Works Cited

Divakaruni, Chitra Banerjee. "Clothes." 1995, *The Bedford Guide for College Writers,*
edited by Kennedy, X.J,. et al., Macmillan Learning, 2020, pp. 207–16.

Questions to Start You Thinking

Meaning

1. What is Khan's thesis? What specific passages from the story does she include as evidence to support that thesis?

2. What does Khan mean by "personal growth" in her first paragraph? How does the story show Sumita's personal growth?

Writing Strategies

3. What literary terms does Khan analyze in this essay? What is their significance?

4. Overall, is Khan's analysis of "Clothes" persuasive? Why or why not? If you were peer-reviewing her paper, what advice, if any, would you give her?

5. Is Khan's introduction effective? Compare and contrast it with her first draft (p. 218). What did she change? Which version do you prefer?

6. How do Khan's use of language and choice of organization contribute to your experience of her essay? Would discussing Sumita's evolution in a different way or in a different order be more effective? Why or why not?

Learning by Writing

The Assignment: Analyzing a Literary Work

For this assignment, you are to be a literary critic — analyzing, interpreting, and evaluating a work of literature for your peers. Your purpose is to deepen their understanding based on the time and effort you have spent digging out the work's meaning.

Choose a literary work that intrigues you. Your selection might be a short story, a poem, a play, a novel, or a graphic novel. After analyzing it carefully, write an essay as an expert critic: explain the meaning you've uncovered, support your interpretation with evidence from that work, and evaluate the author's use of literary elements (see the Glossary of Terms for Literary Analysis on page 222).

You cannot include everything about the work in your paper, so focus on one element (such as character, setting, or theme) or the interrelationship of two or three elements (such as characterization and symbolism). Although a summary, or *synopsis*, of the plot can help check your understanding of the work, retelling the story is not a satisfactory literary analysis. Your readers will expect a clear thesis that presents your specific interpretation. They want to see how you analyze the work and which features of the work you use to support your position about it.

MANAGING YOUR TIME
Writing a Literary Analysis

Use the breakdown below to plan your time for this essay; in the right column, insert target dates and times for completing each stage.

approx. **45-60** minutes	■ **Read your assignment carefully.** Can you choose the literary work you will focus on, or is it assigned to you? Is it clear what your instructor is asking of you? If not, follow up. ■ **Perform a close reading of the literary work.** First make sure you understand the literal meaning thoroughly, then consider its figurative meaning. ■ **Brainstorm to identify element(s)** in the literary work that interest you. Consult a glossary of literary terms for ideas.	**I'll complete** this stage by: _____ (day, date)
approx. **2-3** hours	■ **Draft a thesis statement** that roughly conveys your interpretation of the literary work. ■ **Annotate the literary work to identify evidence to use in your analysis.** Look for powerful passages you can use as quotations to support your claims. Consider which aspects of the work could be paraphrased or summarized for your readers.	**I'll complete** this stage by: _____ (day, date)
approx. **2-3** hours	■ **Sketch an outline of your essay,** beginning with your working thesis. Organize your essay around specific points that support your interpretation. Support each point you make with evidence from the text. ■ **Draft your essay,** staying close to your outline. Back yourself up with specific references to the text. ■ **Cite your sources accurately,** both in the text of the essay and in the reference list, or works cited page. ■ Craft a compelling **introduction** and a satisfying **conclusion** by appealing to your readers to accept your interpretation.	**I'll complete** this stage by: _____ (day, date)
approx. **2-4** hours	■ Ask a **peer to review** your draft. Have you stated and supported your interpretation adequately? ■ **Revise your draft,** addressing issues raised during your and your peer's review. ■ **Edit your draft,** fixing any errors and polishing your prose.	**I'll complete** this stage by: _____ (day, date)

A Glossary of Terms for Literary Analysis

Characters are imagined people. The author shows what they are like through their actions, speech, thoughts, attitudes, background, and even physical characteristics or names.

Figures of Speech are lively or fresh expressions that vary the expected phrasing or sense of words. Some common types of figurative language are *simile*, a comparison using *like* or *as*; *metaphor*, an implied comparison; and *personification*, the attribution of human qualities to nonhuman creatures or things.

Imagery is a group of words that convey sensory experience: seeing, hearing, smelling, tasting, touching, or feeling.

Irony results from readers' sense of discrepancy. A simple kind of irony, *sarcasm*, occurs when you say one thing but mean the opposite: "I just love scrubbing the floor." In literature, an *ironic situation* sets up a contrast or incongruity. *Ironic dialogue* occurs when a character says one thing, but the audience or reader is aware of another meaning. A story has an *ironic point of view* when readers sense a difference between the author and the narrator or the character who perceives the story.

Plot is the arrangement of the events of the story — what happens to whom, where, when, and why. Most plots place the *protagonist*, or main character, in a *conflict* with the *antagonist*, some other person or group, so that the two forces trying to conquer each other or resist being conquered. *External conflicts* occur outside an individual — between two people or groups, or even between a character and the environment. *Internal conflicts* between two opposing forces or desires occur within an individual. The conflict propels the action of the story and leads to the *climax*, the moment when the outcome or *resolution* is inevitable. Some stories let events unfold without any apparent plot — action and change occur inside the characters.

Point of View is the angle from which a story is told. The *narrator*, the one who tells the story and perceives the events, might be the author or a character. Two common points of view are those of a *first-person narrator* (*I*), the *speaker* who tells the story from personal perspective, and a *third-person narrator* (*he, she*), who tells the story from an outside perspective. The point of view may be *omniscient* (the speaker knows all and has access to every character's thoughts and feelings); *limited omniscient* (the speaker knows the thoughts and feelings of one or more characters, but not all); or *objective* (the speaker observes the characters but cannot share their thoughts or feelings).

Setting refers to the time and place of events and may include the season, the weather, and the people in the background. The setting often helps establish a literary work's *mood* or *atmosphere*, the emotional climate that a reader senses.

Symbols are tangible objects, visible actions, or characters that hint at meanings beyond themselves. (For example, a book might be a symbol of knowledge.)

Theme is a work's main idea or insight — the author's observation about life, society, or human nature. Sometimes you can sum up a theme in a sentence ("Human beings cannot live without illusion"); other times, a theme may be implied.

Generating Ideas

Read several literary works from the course options to find two or three you like. Next, reread those that interest you. Select one that strikes you as especially significant—realistic or universal, moving or disturbing, believable or shocking—with a meaning you wish to share with classmates.

Reading Closely and Critically. In order to perform *literary analysis*, you must read the work closely and critically. Close, critical reading requires you to slow down, absorbing each line and every word so that you can analyze, interpret, and evaluate the work. First, check your comprehension of the work. Do you understand its literal meaning? Write a few sentences explaining what happens to whom, where, when, why, and how. Look up any unfamiliar words as well as words whose familiar meanings don't fit the context. Reread the work *at least* twice more, each time checking your interpretations and identifying possible evidence to back up your claims as you analyze and evaluate. Because literary analysis has its own vocabulary, consult the glossary of terms used to discuss the elements of fiction, poetry, and drama (see p. 222). Use these questions to guide you in your analysis of any literary work:

ANALYZING A LITERARY WORK

- ☐ What is your reaction to the story, poem, or play? Jot it down.
- ☐ Who is the *narrator* or *speaker*—not the author, but the one who tells the story?
- ☐ What is the *point of view*?
- ☐ What is the *setting* (time and place)? What is the *atmosphere* or *mood*?
- ☐ How does the *plot* unfold? Write a synopsis, or summary, of the events in sequence.
- ☐ What are the *characters* like? Describe their personalities and motivations based on their actions or speech. What strategies does the author use to develop the characters? Who is the *protagonist*? Is there an *antagonist*? Do any characters change? Are the changes believable?
- ☐ How would you describe the text's *style*, or use of language? Is it informal, conversational, or formal? Does the story use dialect or foreign words? Does it use irony or figurative language: *imagery, metaphor, personification*?
- ☐ What is the *central conflict* of the work? Express the conflicts using the word *versus*, for example, "dreams versus reality" or "the individual versus society."
- ☐ What is the *climax* of the story? Is there any *resolution*?
- ☐ What does the *title* of the work mean?
- ☐ What are the *themes* of the work? Are they universal (applicable to all people everywhere at all times)? Write down your interpretation of the main theme. How is this theme related to your own life?

The questions above apply to all types of literary works. In addition, here are some specific issues to consider when analyzing poems, which often incorporate rhythm and rhyme, and plays, which are written to be seen and heard, not read:

ANALYZING A POEM

☐ Is the poem *lyric* (expressing emotion) or *narrative* (telling a story)?

☐ What is striking about the poem's *language*? Is it informal or formal? Consider *connotations*, the suggestions conjured by the words: *house* versus *home,* though both refer to the same place.

☐ Is there repetition in words or sounds? What meaning does that repetition add?

☐ How is the poem structured or divided? Does it use *couplets* (two consecutive rhyming lines), *quatrains* (units of four lines), or other units? How do the beginning and end relate to each other and to the poem as a whole?

☐ Does the poem use *rhyme* (words that sound alike)? If so, how does the rhyme contribute to the meaning?

☐ Does the poem have *rhythm* (regular meter or beat, patterns of accented and unaccented syllables)? How does the rhythm contribute to the meaning?

ANALYZING A PLAY

☐ Is the play a serious *tragedy* (arousing pity and fear in the audience and usually ending with the downfall of the *tragic hero*)? Or is it a *comedy* (aiming to amuse and usually ending happily)? What is its *mood*?

☐ What are the characters like? Are there *foil characters* who contrast with the protagonist and reveal his or her traits? Which characters are in conflict? Which change?

☐ Which speeches seem especially significant?

☐ What is the *climax* of the play? Is there a *resolution* to the action?

☐ Can you identify any *dramatic irony*, words or actions of a character that carry meaning unperceived by the character but evident to the audience?

Learning by Doing 🔂 Writing a Paraphrase of a Poem

Paraphrasing a poem — expressing its content in your own words, without adding any interpretations or opinions — is a good way to make sure you understand what the poem is saying. A paraphrase forces you to divide the poem into logical sections, then to figure out what the poet says in each section and how the parts relate. It also prepares you to state the theme in a sentence or two. Choose a poem that interests you, either from a course reading or by browsing the Poetry Foundation website <https://www.poetryfoundation.org/poems>. Draft a paraphrase that conveys the meaning of the poem and its main theme or insight.

Planning, Drafting, and Developing

When you write your analysis, your purpose is to explain the work's deeper meaning. Don't try to impress readers with your brilliance. Instead, regard them as friends who are familiar with the work, though they may not have studied it as carefully as you have. This assumption will help you decide how much evidence from the work to include and will reduce summarizing.

For more on planning, drafting, and developing, see Chs. 16, 17, and 18.

Learning by Doing 🖉 Examining Fiction Genres

Compare two stories that you have both read and watched on film or TV (for example, stories from the *Harry Potter* or *Game of Thrones* series). Choose a single scene that appears in both the book and the adaptation and reflect on the two versions. How do the book and film or TV version differ? What might account for those differences? In responding to these questions, consider how the genre (book or film) affects the presentation. You may also wish to consider a book that has been converted to a graphic novel. How do those genres differ?

For more on stating a thesis, see pp. 266–71.

Identify Your Support. After you have determined the major element(s) that you intend to focus on, go through the work again to find all the passages that relate to your main point. Mark them as you find them, or put them on note cards or in a computer file, along with the page references. If you use any quotations, quote exactly.

Develop Your Main Idea or Thesis. Begin by trying to express your point in a thesis statement that identifies the literary work and the author.

WORKING THESIS   In "Clothes," Chitra Banerjee Divakaruni reveals a theme.

But this statement is too vague, so you rewrite it to be more precise:

IMPROVED THESIS   In "Clothes" by Chitra Banerjee Divakaruni, tradition and change are themes.

This thesis is better but still doesn't state the theme clearly or precisely.

IMPROVED THESIS   In "Clothes" by Chitra Banerjee Divakaruni, one of the major themes is female independence.

Adding *one of* shows that this is not the story's only theme, but the rest is vague. What does the story say about female independence?

> MORE PRECISE
>
> In "Clothes" by Chitra Banerjee Divakaruni, one of the major themes is that choice is essential to female independence.

This thesis is better but may change as you write. For instance, you might go beyond interpretation of Divakaruni's ideas by adding your evaluation of her point about women's freedom. Convey what is significant about the theme.

> EVALUATION ADDED
>
> In "Clothes," Chitra Banerjee Divakaruni shows that when women have choice, they can grow and change and evolve into independent beings, into who they want to be.

Focus on analyzing ideas, not retelling events. Maintain that focus by analyzing your thesis: divide it into parts, and then develop each part in turn. The thesis just presented could be divided into (1) use of symbolism to reveal theme and (2) use of irony to reveal theme. Similarly, you might divide a thesis about character change into the character's original traits, the events that cause change, and the character's new traits.

Learning by Doing 🔲 Developing Your Thesis

Follow the preceding pattern for developing a thesis statement. Start with your working thesis. Then improve it, make it more precise, and consider adding an evaluation of why the thesis matters or why it is significant. Present your thesis drafts to a classmate or small group, perhaps asking questions like these: What wording needs to be clearer? What idea could I narrow down? What point sounds intriguing? What might a reader want me to emphasize? Continue to refine your thesis as you work on your essay.

For more on introductions, see pp. 288–90.

Introduce Your Essay. Tie your beginning to your main idea, or thesis. If you are uncertain how to begin, try one of these openings:

- Focus on a character's universality.
- Focus on a theme's universality.
- Quote a striking line from the work.
- Make a statement about the work's point, your reaction when you read it, a parallel personal experience, or the writer's technique.
- Ask a "Have you ever?" question to draw readers into your interpretation.

Peer Response 🔖 Getting Feedback on Your Literary Analysis

For general questions for a peer editor, see p. 309.

Ask your peer editor to answer questions such as these:

- What is your first reaction to the literary analysis?
- In what ways does the analysis add to your understanding of the literary work? To your insights about life?
- Does the introduction make you want to read on? What changes would you suggest to strengthen the opening?
- Is the main idea clear? Is there sufficient relevant evidence from the work to support that point? Put stars wherever additional evidence is needed. Put a check mark by any irrelevant information.
- Does the essay go beyond plot summary to analyze elements, interpret meaning, and evaluate literary merit? If not, how might the writer revise?
- If this paper were yours, what is the one thing you would be sure to work on before handing it in?

Support Your Interpretation. As you develop your analysis, include supporting evidence — descriptions of setting and character, summaries of events, quotations of dialogue, and other specifics. Cite page numbers (for prose) or line numbers (for poetry) where the details can be found in the work. Integrate evidence from the story with your comments and ideas.

For more on citing and listing literary works, see MLA style in E (pp. Q-31–Q-36) in the Quick Research Guide.

Conclude Your Essay. When you reach the end, don't just stop. Close as you might open — with a personal experience, a comment on technique, a quotation — to provide a sense of finality. Refer to or reaffirm your thesis. Often an effective conclusion ties in directly with the introduction.

For more on conclusions, see pp. 288–90.

Revising and Editing

As you read over your draft, keep in mind your thesis and the evidence that supports it.

For more revising and editing strategies, see Ch. 19.

REVISING YOUR DRAFT

- ☐ Have you clearly identified the literary work and the author near the beginning of the analysis?
- ☐ Is your thesis clear? Does everything else relate to it?
- ☐ Have you focused on one element in your analysis? On more than one? Have you organized around ideas rather than events?
- ☐ Are your interpretations supported by evidence from the literary work? Do you need to add examples of dialogue, action, or description?
- ☐ Have you woven the details from the work smoothly into your text? Have you cited their correct page or line numbers? Have you quoted and cited carefully?
- ☐ Do you understand all the words and literary terms you use?

After you have revised your literary analysis, check the grammar, word choice, punctuation, and mechanics — and then correct any problems you find. Make sure that you smoothly introduce all of your quotations and references to the work and weave them into your own discussion.

For more editing and proofreading strategies, see pp. 316–18.

For more help, find the relevant checklist sections in the Quick Editing Guide on p. Q-37. Turn also to the Quick Format Guide beginning on p. Q-1.

EDITING FOR CLARITY

☐ Have you used the present tense for events in the literary work and for comments about the author's presentation? **A3**

☐ Have you used quotation marks correctly whenever you give the exact words of the literary work? **D3**

☐ Have you used correct manuscript format for your paper?

Reviewing and Reflecting

REVIEW Working with classmates or independently, respond to the following questions:

1. Describe the major tasks involved in a literary analysis. What is the major challenge of this type of writing?

2. What problems should you look for in a draft of a literary analysis — problems that you can take action on to strengthen the analysis? If you have prepared a draft of a literary analysis, can you identify any of these issues in your work? If so, what revisions might help? Make notes about these.

3. How does a synopsis differ from a literary analysis? In what contexts are synopses used?

REFLECT After completing a literary analysis, reflect in writing about how you might apply the insights that you drew from the literary analysis to another situation — in or outside of college — in which you have to analyze something. In your reflection, consider the advantages and challenges of going beyond a straight summary of material.

Additional Writing Assignments

For more on writing a comparison-and-contrast essay, see Ch. 6.

1. **Source Assignment**. Write an essay comparing and contrasting a literary element in two or three assigned or optional short stories or poems.

2. **Source Assignment**. Write an essay comparing and contrasting a literary element in a short story and another type of narrative such as a novel or film that tells a story. Use specific evidence from each narrative to support your conclusions.

3. **Source Assignment.** Read the poem below by Robert Frost (1874–1963). Write an essay using a paraphrase of the poem as a springboard for your thoughts on a fork in the road of your life—a decision that made a difference for you.

The Road Not Taken

Two roads diverged in a yellow wood,
And sorry I could not travel both
And be one traveler, long I stood
And looked down one as far as I could
To where it bent in the undergrowth;

Then took the other, as just as fair,
And having perhaps the better claim,
Because it was grassy and wanted wear;
Though as for that the passing there
Had worn them really about the same,

And both that morning equally lay
In leaves no step had trodden black.
Oh, I kept the first for another day!
Yet knowing how way leads on to way,
I doubted if I should ever come back.

I shall be telling this with a sigh
Somewhere ages and ages hence:
Two roads diverged in a wood, and I—
I took the one less traveled by,
And that has made all the difference.

For another poem by Robert Frost, see p. 180.

4. **Source Assignment.** Write a critical analysis of a song, a movie, or a television show. Play or view it several times to pull out specific evidence to support your interpretation. If your instructor approves, present your analysis in a podcast, a multimedia format, or a series of Web pages.

5. **Visual Assignment.** Go back to the images of *The Tale of Genji* included in the ornamental screen on page 206 of this chapter. Choose two or three of the scenes illustrated there. What stories do they suggest? Write a thesis for each image. Alternatively, use the glossary of literary terms on page 222, and apply a few of these elements in your analysis of the ornamental screen, such as setting, character, tone, plot, and more.

For more about analyzing visuals, see Ch. 13. For more on analysis in general, see Ch. 18.

13 Responding to Visual Representations

National Weather Service

Responding to an Image

According to recent estimates, of all the information transmitted to our brains each day, 90 percent is visual. We process visuals incredibly fast and learn and retain 400 times better when information is conveyed visually. And, as the saying goes, "You can't un-see something." Even if we remember only a portion of what we read, we do not forget what we've seen. What do you notice first about the infographic shown here? Where do your eyes rest? Why? How effective is the graphic in conveying information? What will you remember about this infographic tomorrow?

Why Responding to Visual Representations Matters

Images are a constant and persistent presence in our lives. A billboard invites us to visit a local museum. The lettering on a pickup truck urges us to call for a free landscaping estimate. Advertising images surround us, trying to shape our opinions about everything from personal hygiene products to snack foods to political issues.

Besides ads, all sorts of cartoons, photos, drawings, paintings, logos, graphics, and other media work to evoke responses. The critical skills you develop for analyzing these still images also apply to other visual representations, including commercials, films, and stage productions. Whether visual images provoke a smile or a scream, one thing is certain: visuals help to structure our views of reality.

In a College Course

- You perform visual analysis in your composition, art history, and marketing classes.
- You consider visual representations of data in your health-sciences lab or clinical experience.

In the Workplace

- You evaluate the values conveyed by proposed images for a new Web page.

In Your Community

- You gather recent newspaper images of local teens to document the need for a community sports program.

? When have you responded to visuals in your writing? In what situations might you analyze images in future writing?

Learning from Another Writer

Following is an analysis of an advertisement in which student writer Logan Sikora analyzes a commercial to investigate how advertisers influence our perceptions.

Logan Sikora   **Student Essay**

The Attention Test

The commercial for Škoda Fabia has gotten a lot of media attention, including   1
headlines like this one: "You Won't Be Able to Take Your Eyes Off This Cheap
Škoda Hatchback" (Sorokanich). Although this claim certainly is warranted, the
attention viewers pay to the Škoda Fabia has little to do with the car and almost
everything to do with the design and content of the commercial, an instructive
example of how advertisers shape our perceptions to their advantage.

At the start of the commercial, the following words appear on the screen: 2
"The Attention Test" (Škoda). We are then taken to a street scene that features
an unimpressive blue hatchback parked between a scooter and a black van, with
shops in the background. (The car is the Škoda Fabia, an economy car built by

the Czech subsidiary of Volkswagen.) At this point the voiceover begins, and throughout it the camera never veers from the parked Fabia:

> To test just how much attention the attention-stealing design of the new Škoda Fabia actually steals, we left one parked on this ordinary road in West London. We wanted to see if its sharp, crystalline shapes, bold lines, and lower, wider profile would attract the desired level of attention. Will the seventeen-inch black alloy wheels stop passers-by in their tracks? Will the angular headlights attract the attention of other road users? Will a crowd gather to check out its fresh, sporty look? Well, not quite. But did the attention-stealing design distract *you* from noticing that the entire street has been changing right before your very eyes? Don't believe us? Have another look. Did you spot the van changing to a taxi? How about the scooter changing to a pair of bicycles? Or the lady holding a pig? Let alone the fact that the entire street is now completely different. Didn't think so. So there we have it. Proof that the new Škoda Fabia is truly attention-stealing. (Škoda)

The narrator is right: it is likely that most viewers' eyes will stay trained on the blue car, not noticing all the changes that take place in the background until the narrator points them out. The car remains the center of attention because it is the focal point not only of the camera but also of much of the narrator's commentary, which refers to the Fabia's "attention-stealing design," "sharp, crystalline shapes," and so on. The lesson here is that an automobile company doesn't need a sports car to attract this kind of attention; it just needs the right kind of advertising.   3

Viewers' focus on the car in the Škoda commercial is an example of selective attention, a result of the fact that we can pay attention to only so many things at the same time. As writer and psychology expert Kendra Cherry has noted, "Attention acts somewhat like a spotlight, highlighting the details that we need   4

Fig. 1. "The Škoda Fabia Attention Test." Škoda Australia. *YouTube,* 26 Feb. 2015, www.youtube.com/watch?v=qpPYdMs97eE.

to focus on and casting irrelevant information to the sidelines of our perception."
Effective advertising trains that spotlight carefully, setting our visual priorities to
advertisers' advantage.

Another appealing aspect of the Škoda commercial is its tongue-in-cheek   5
humor, from references to the "fresh, sporty look" of the plain-looking car to the
mention of the "lady holding a pig." The advertiser wants us to feel as if we are
in on the joke, while also making a pitch for the Fabia. As noted in a blog post
from Lumen, an "attention technology" company, humor is an especially effective
approach for reaching Millennials, an important audience for advertisers.

Given its design, content, and humor, the Škoda commercial certainly   6
is appealing; more than that, it sheds an interesting light on strategies that
advertisers use to attract, and hold, our attention.

Works Cited

Cherry, Kendra. "What Is Selective Attention?" *About Education*, psychologyabout
    .com/od/cognitivepsychology/fl/What-Is-Selective-Attention.htm. Accessed
    5 Sept. 2019.

"Marketing to Millennials: Is It a Tougher Task?" *Lumen Research*, 8 Apr. 2015,
    lumenresearch.com/new-blog/marketing-to-millennials. Accessed 10 Sept. 2019.

Škoda. "The Škoda Fabia Attention Test." *YouTube*, 26 Feb. 2015, www.youtube
    .com/watch?v=qpPYdMs97eE. Advertisement.

Sorokanich, Bob. "Video: You Won't Be Able to Take Your Eyes Off This Cheap Škoda
    Hatchback." *Car and Driver*, 4 Mar. 2015, blog.caranddriver.com/video-you-wont-be
    -able-to-take-your-eyes-off-this-cheap-skoda-hatchback/. Accessed 8 Sept. 2019.

Questions to Start You Thinking

Meaning

1. How does the commercial keep viewers focused on the blue car?

2. In what way is this focus an example of selective attention?

3. What other strategies does the commercial use to appeal to viewers?

Writing Strategies

4. Where does Sikora introduce her thesis and her major supporting points?

5. How does Sikora ensure that readers know enough about the commercial
   to follow her discussion?

6. What different kinds of support does Sikora draw from her sources?

Learning by Writing

The Assignment: Writing a Visual Analysis

Find an ad that presents a visual image to promote a product, service, or non-profit group. Study the ad carefully, observe the characteristics of the image, and interpret its meaning. Write an essay analyzing how the ad's visual elements persuade viewers to accept its message. Include a copy of the ad with your essay (citing the source just as you would if it were a print text) or link to it. You can also choose to analyze a different visual work such as a brochure, billboard, graphic, photo essay, artwork, or landmark.

MANAGING YOUR TIME
Writing a Visual Analysis

Use the breakdown below to plan your time for this essay; in the right column, insert target dates and times for completing each stage.

approx. **30-45** minutes	■ **Read your assignment carefully.** Do you understand what your instructor expects from you? If not, follow up. ■ **Brainstorm** to find a photograph, ad, or other visual to analyze.	**I'll complete** this stage by: _____ (day, date)
approx. **2-3** hours	■ **Begin your close reading** of the image by seeing the "big picture." Identify its source, context, and author, as well as its purpose and audience. ■ **Examine the characteristics of the image, including** objects, characters, story, design, composition, and typeface. ■ **Interpret the meaning** of the image by considering mood, attitudes, language, symbols, and themes. ■ **Formulate a thesis** that states your interpretation of the image, and **identify details** to support your thesis.	**I'll complete** this stage by: _____ (day, date)
approx. **2-3** hours	■ **Sketch an outline of your essay.** ■ **Draft your essay,** staying close to your outline. ■ Craft a compelling **introduction** and satisfying **conclusion,** appealing to your readers to accept your analysis and interpretation.	**I'll complete** this stage by: _____ (day, date)
approx. **2-4** hours	■ Ask a **peer to review** your draft. Have you clearly stated your interpretation of the image? Is it well-supported with evidence? ■ **Revise your draft,** addressing issues raised during your and your peer's review. ■ **Edit your draft,** fixing any errors and polishing your prose.	**I'll complete** this stage by: _____ (day, date)

Generating Ideas

Browse through print or online publications to gather several possible images or ads that make clear appeals to viewers. Look for visuals that catch your eye and promise rich detail for analysis. Just as you annotate a written text, do the same to record your observations of an image.

For more strategies for generating ideas, see Ch. 15.

Consider the Writing Situation.   Once you have chosen an image, begin your close reading by discovering all that you can about its origins. Find out who created it and when and where it was first published or exhibited. What is its purpose? What audience does it aim to attract, and how does it appeal to that audience?

See the "Big Picture."   Looking at the image as a whole can help you examine its composition and determine its focal point. First, see if there is a single prominent element that immediately attracts attention. For example, in the public service announcement shown here, the child is the obvious prominent element. Her dark eyes, framed by her dark hair, draw the viewer to her alert, intent expression. That expression suggests her capacity to learn from all she observes. The text above and below her image reinforces this message, cautioning adults to be careful what they teach children through their own conduct.

On the other hand, a more complex image of a whole scene invites many interpretations. What draws your eye in the photograph on the next page? The neon sign, framed in the left window panel, is a bright spot in an otherwise black-and-white toned image. People who read from left to right and top to bottom, including most Americans and Europeans, tend to read photos in the same way. For this reason, artists and photographers often position key elements — those they want viewers to see right away — somewhere in the upper left quadrant to draw the eye.

The neon sign also says a lot about the café: It tells the audience that this is an inexpensive, down-to-earth place, offering simple fare. It probably opens early and closes late, serving average people of modest means. As a focal point, the neon sign sets up a point of contrast with the unusual customer seated at the right.

A public service announcement with one prominent element.

Ian Pool

For more on literal and critical reading of texts, see Ch. 2.

Learning by Doing 🔘 Seeing the Big Picture

Working with a classmate or a small group, select another image in this book, such as one that opens or closes a chapter. Consider the image's purpose and audience (in its original context or in this book), but concentrate on its prominent element, which draws the viewer's eye, and its focal point, which suggests the center of its action or moment. Share analyses in a class discussion, or report or post yours for another group.

Observe the "Literal" Aspects of the Image. Before you begin to look in depth for meaning, determine exactly what the image depicts. First, ask what the story or "plot" of the image is. What moment does it capture? What action is taking place, and where and when? Identify the people or animals that appear in the image, paying attention to characters' facial expressions, poses, hairstyles, ages, sexes, ethnicity, apparent relationships, and so on. For instance, the photograph above shows Batman eating a quick dinner or late-night snack on a winter night. It hints at the earlier part of the story: driving to the place, parking outside, ordering his food, and taking a seat at a small corner table.

Notice how the objects in the image are arranged. What colors and shapes are depicted? How much empty white space is there? Are light and dark areas symmetrical? How much is visible in the image? A photographer, for example, might use a close-up, medium, or wide-angle shot, and also decide on the angle and lighting. The wide angle of the Batman photo allows us to see both the inside and outside of the café. The interior of the café is bright as day — safe, warm, and cozy; this accentuates the cold dark, dangerous night outside. Batman is positioned on the edge, between bright and dark. The four large window panels stretching across the front of the café suggest the grid layout of a comic book with its neat frames. But here there is no "thought balloon" to let viewers know what Batman is thinking. Viewers must imagine and interpret for themselves.

Look closely at how the form of the image relates to its function. Consider, for instance, the Sherwin Williams paint ad below. This image asserts that there are many ways to design — and many colors to paint — an object. The composition of the image makes it easy for us to take in all 24 options by placing them in a white-framed grid. The orderly repetition of the multicolored objects, along with the logo and minimal text in apple green, demonstrates that "Color changes everything."

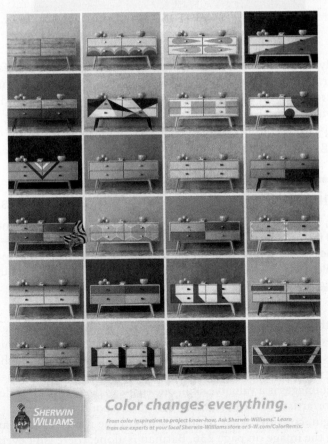

An advertisement for the paint company Sherwin Williams.
The Sherwin-Williams Company

A typeface that contributes to meaning. Andrew Dillon Bustin.

For sample presentation visuals, see pp. 321–23. For sample tables and figures, see B (pp. Q-7–Q-12) in the Quick Format Guide. For sample photographs, turn to the images opening Chs. 4–12 and 21–25.

Finally, notice how text is used in the image. Does the typeface convey a mood or impression? For example, Times New Roman is a common typeface, easy to read and somewhat conservative, whereas the rounded font of the Sherwin Williams' ad is less formal and suggests handwriting. The plain slanted type in the photograph above suggests movement toward the future, reinforcing the message of the words.

Learning by Doing 📷 Observing Characteristics

Working with a classmate or a small group, continue analyzing the image you selected for the activity on page 236. Examine a major characteristic — such as characters, story, design, or artistic choices — to determine exactly what it shows. Report or post your conclusions for your class or another group.

Interpret the Meaning of the Image. When you read a written text analytically, you examine its parts, synthesize the material with other information, and evaluate its significance. When you interpret an image, you do much the same, examining what the image suggests and interpreting what it means. Learning to interpret images is a valuable skill, one that can deepen your understanding of an author/artist's motives — and of why you respond as you do.

To begin, consider what feeling or mood the image creates and how it does so. In the image on page 236, Batman is alone; there isn't even a cashier behind the counter. The mood is one of loneliness and isolation. In contrast, the image at right evokes very different moods. The warm sunset colors evoke a feeling of nostalgia, while in the foreground, the tilt of the amusement ride suggests a slight risk or menace.

Photograph conveying a mood. Thomas Janisch/Getty Images

An image can also convey a variety of social, political, or cultural attitudes. On the surface, the Sherwin Williams ad (p. 237) is simply an attempt to sell paint. But it does more than that: it conveys a subtle "DIY/do-it-yourself" message, that with the right paint and ideas, you can transform a plain, cast-off piece of furniture into something fabulous. A different attitude is communicated in the public service message on the bottom right on this page. This ad deliberately contrasts presence and absence: the missing spoon represents a missing meal for those suffering from hunger.

Examine the words, phrases, and sentences in an image to interpret their meaning. Does the language inform? Appeal to emotions? Does it carry overtones, issue a challenge, or offer a philosophy of life? Many images also carry signs and symbols, such as product logos. Ask yourself what messages they convey. Sometimes a product logo alone is enough, as in the holiday ads featuring little more than a single Hershey's Kiss.

A public service advertisement using a missing element to convey its message. Feeding America, 360i and the Ad Council

Finally, ask what the theme of the image is. The plot of an image tells us what happens in the image; the theme tells us what the image is about. An ad for a diamond ring may tell the story of a man surprising his wife on their anniversary, but the theme may be sex, romance, commitment, or some other concept. The poster on the next page

Poster conveying a theme.

appears to provide a recipe for a tasty margarita, but the list of ingredients reveals the theme: excess alcohol and risky behavior carry severe consequences.

Learning by Doing 🔄 Interpreting Meaning

Return to the image you selected for the activity on page 236 and consider how the following are expressed: feeling or mood, attitude, language, signs or symbols, and overall theme. Write an analysis of how the image conveys meaning through these aspects.

Planning, Drafting, and Developing

Start with a Thesis. Now that you have examined both the visual makeup and the meaning of the image, draft a thesis that states how it tries to attract and influence viewers. Let's imagine that you are working with an ad for dog food. Begin by stating how the ad's creators try to attract and influence viewers. You might identify a consistent persuasive appeal or show how several components work together to persuade viewers.

WORKING THESIS   The dog food ad includes photos of puppies to
                   interest animal lovers.

Organize Support for Your Thesis. As you state your thesis more precisely, break down the position it expresses into main points. Then list the relevant supporting detail from the ad that can clarify and develop each point. Identify details and explain their significance to guide readers through your supporting evidence. Help them see exactly which visual elements create an impression, solidify an appeal, or connect with a viewer as you say that they do. Avoid general description for its own sake, but supply enough relevant description to make your points clear.

REVISED THESIS   The Precious Pooch dog food ad includes photos of cuddly puppies to appeal to dog owners.

MORE PRECISE   The Precious Pooch dog food ad shows carefully designed photos of cuddly puppies to soften the hearts and wallets of devoted dog owners.

Open and Conclude Effectively. Begin by introducing to your audience the image and your thesis about it. Describe the image briefly, providing readers with an understanding of its structure and primary features. Conclude by pulling together your main points and confirming your thesis.

Revising and Editing

Exchange drafts with a peer to learn what is—or isn't—clear to someone who is not immersed in the image you have chosen. Then revise as needed.

REVISING YOUR DRAFT

☐ Have you described the image clearly?

☐ Have you stated your thesis about the author/artist's main point?

☐ Have you analyzed how its creators try to appeal to viewers?

☐ Have you identified features and details that support your thesis?

☐ Have you considered the story, design, artistic choices, and functionality of the image?

☐ Have you interpreted the feeling, attitude, theme, or meaning conveyed by the image?

After you have revised your visual analysis, check the grammar, word choice, punctuation, and mechanics—then correct any problems you find.

For more help, find the relevant checklist sections in the Quick Editing Guide on p. Q-37. Turn also to the Quick Format Guide beginning on p. Q-1.

Reviewing and Reflecting

REVIEW Working with classmates or independently, respond to the following questions:

1. What are some strategies for conducting a close reading of an image? If you haven't done so already, try applying these strategies to an advertisement, to a photo accompanying a news story, or to some other image. Make notes about what you discover.

2. What do you do when you interpret an image, as opposed to making a straightforward observation of it?

3. What is the major challenge of analyzing an image? How do you see your-self addressing this challenge? Jot down some possible answers.

REFLECT Reflect in writing about how you might apply the insights that you drew from this assignment to another situation — in or outside of college — in which you have to respond to visual representations.

Additional Writing Assignments

1. **Visual Activity.** Select an image such as an advertisement, a photograph from a magazine or image database, or album cover. Make notes on its "literal" characteristics (see pp. 236–38). Then bring your image and notes to class. In small groups of three to five students, share your images and discuss your literal readings.

2. **Visual Activity.** In a small group, pick one or two of the images analyzed for activity 1. Ask each group member, in turn, to suggest possible inter-pretations of the images. (For guidance, see pp. 238–40.) What different interpretations do group members suggest? How do you account for the differences? Share your findings with the rest of the class.

3. **Visual Assignment.** Compile a design notebook. Over several weeks, col-lect ten or twelve images that appeal to you. Your teacher may assign a genre, such as snack food ads, portraits, photos of campus landmarks, or landscape paintings. On the other hand, your collection might revolve around a theme, such as friendship, competition, community, or romance. "Read" each image closely, and write short responses explaining your reactions. At the end of the collection period, choose two or three images. Write an essay to compare or contrast them, perhaps analyzing how they illustrate the same genre, convey a theme, or appeal to different audiences.

4. **Visual Assignment.** Prepare your own visual essay on a topic that engages or concerns you. Decide on the purpose and audience for your essay. Take, select, and arrange photographs that will help to achieve this purpose. (Use the guidelines in this chapter to help you evaluate your own photos.) Add concise text to accompany the photos. Ask your classmates to review your essay to help you reach the clearest and most effective final form.

5. **Visual Assignment.** Using the advice in this chapter, analyze an episode in a television series, a film, a blog, a YouTube or other video, a television commercial, or a campus theater, dance, or other production. Analyze the visual elements of your selection, and also evaluate it in terms of criteria that you explain to your audience.

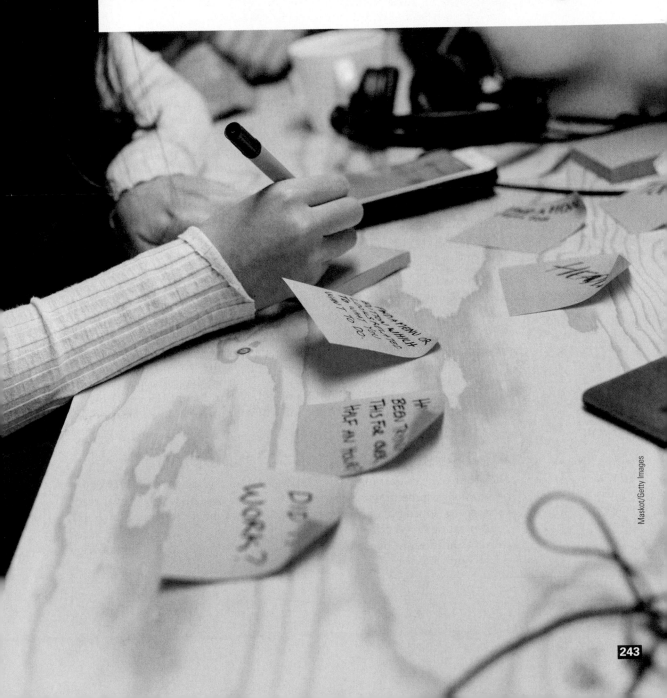

PART THREE

A Writer's Strategies

14 Strategies: A Case Study

Nick Catizone's favorite assignment in Composition I focused on an issue he could relate to — how smartphones affect our lives. Nick and his classmates had to choose two of the course readings on the issue and analyze the articles' content, tone, use of evidence, and conclusions. In this chapter, you can follow Nick's writing processes as he generates ideas, develops a first draft, gathers responses from readers, revises and edits his draft, and writes a reflective letter to accompany the essay in his writing portfolio.

Generating Ideas

? Use the questions in the margin to help you develop your own essay alongside Nick.

Having gotten his first smartphone as a tween, Nick knew firsthand both the benefits and drawbacks of using technology at a young age. He brainstormed ideas about the topic and jotted them down. Next, Nick skimmed the course reading and decided to focus on an article by Jean M. Twenge first published in the *Atlantic* and a response by Alexandra Samuel, published online at *JSTOR Daily*. He reread the sources, highlighting significant quotations as he went, and summarized the main ideas of each one. Using his brainstorming list and the notes he made on his sources, Nick started mapping ideas to make connections (see p. 245). When he finished, Nick felt confident that he had something substantial to say on the topic of young people and smartphones.

Planning, Drafting, and Developing

? What organization would suit your needs?

Nick figured he'd draft his essay as an evaluation, assessing whether Twenge's or Samuel's argument was better. Once he looked over his notes, he was ready to start developing his ideas. He started drafting his first version by hand, concentrating on getting ideas from his cluster down on the page. He inserted words as he thought of them and crossed out false starts, including his original second sentence.

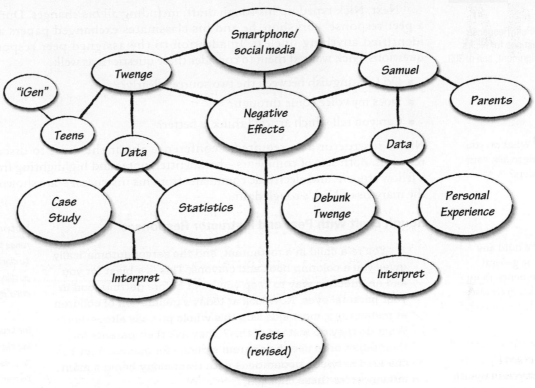

Mapping Ideas

Nick Catizone

First Draft

A lot

~~Lots~~ has changed between generations with technology being a main

influencer for these changes. These changes can be viewed as both positive

in a multitude of ways

and negative, and they affect different generations. Jean M. Twenge

wrote the article "Has the Smartphone Destroyed a Generation?" that

discusses how smartphones and social media use have affected today's

children, while Alexandra Samuel wrote the article "Yes, Smartphones Are

Destroying a Generation, But Not of Kids" as a response to the former

article to say that smartphones are affecting today's parents the most.

~~Samuel's argument is superior to Twenge's because Samuel draws on her~~

~~own experience with children.~~ There are many similarities and differences

between these essays, but Samuel does a superior job at delivering her

argument.

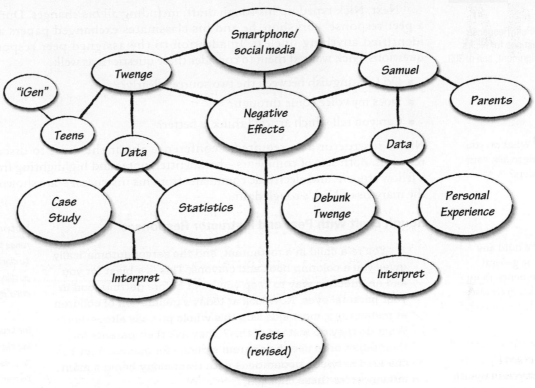
How are you
starting your draft?
What process works
for you?

For Peer Response questions for Nick's assignment, see p. 309.

Next, Nick typed up his rough draft, including all his changes. During a peer response workshop, he and his classmates exchanged papers and identified anything unclear. In addition to the assigned peer response questions, Nick wanted them to consider these questions as well:

- Do I distinguish between the two sources clearly?
- Does my voice come through?
- Can you tell which article I think is better?

? What do you want to ask your readers?

Nick's instructor also required a conference about the draft to discuss revisions. Both sets of comments—handwritten notes and highlighting from a fellow student and electronic comments from his instructor—are shown in the margins of Nick's rough draft.

Rough Draft with Peer and Instructor Responses

? Would any of the general comments about Nick's draft also apply to yours?

You're a child in a restaurant, and the server automatically gives you a coloring book and crayons. This is a blast for you and an effective way to keep you quiet before getting food in your parents' eyes. Now look at today's generation of children at restaurants; most kids skip this whole process altogether. What do they do instead of this? They ask their parents for their tablet or to use their parent's phone for games. A lot has changed between generations with technology being a main influencer for these changes.

Instructor: Rearrange this sentence to clarify meaning. Try putting "in your parents' eyes" first.

Peer: Nice comparison of how kids keep themselves busy with electronics instead of old school activities, but the overall "process" is still the same—distracting hungry kids. Maybe re-word this part for clarity.

These changes can be viewed as both positive and negative, and they affect different generations in a multitude of ways. Jean M. Twenge wrote the article "Has the Smartphone Destroyed a Generation?" that discusses how smartphones and social media use have affected today's children, while Alexandra Samuel wrote the article "Yes, Smartphones Are Destroying a Generation, But Not of Kids" as a response to the former article to say that smartphones are affecting today's parents the most. There are many similarities and differences between these essays, but Samuel does a superior job at delivering her argument.

Instructor: Combining these two sentences to tie in the two articles you're comparing would help you construct a clear thesis statement.

Instructor: Re-work your thesis to analyze the similarities/differences between these two articles instead of evaluating which one is better.

Instructor: Streamline your introductory sentences and make your writing more concise by diving straight into your first main point.

Some exposition must obviously be made before explaining why Samuel did a better job than Twenge in her essay. Let us begin by discussing the major similarities that the essays share. The main topic remains consistent in both of these essays. Both essays talk about the impact smartphones have made on generations with their presence, and they also focus mostly on the negative effects it has engraved on said generations. The essays also share the objective to inform the audience on these events. Smartphones obviously have made negative impacts on generations, but each author chooses to inform the readers on how they specifically have affected generations through the use of statistics and graphs. Personal evidence is also provided throughout each of these essays through each

Peer: Great overview of the sources.

authors' personal experiences. Twenge uses her case study to convey her argument in her own essay, while Samuel uses her own experience with her children to communicate her argument. Lastly, both authors seem to reach a similar consensus on how to deal with the situation at hand. Both authors believe that monitoring your children is a great solution to ending the apparent issues that social media and cell phone usage can impose. It is important to remember the similarities of essays when deciding which one was more effective.

Peer: Do you really need to say this here?

Next we should address the ways in which each essay is different from the other. The major difference in these essays is who each author believes cell phones and social media affects the most. Twenge believes that today's kids, whom she calls "iGen," is the most affected by technological advancement when she says the following, "There is compelling evidence that the devices we've placed in young people's hands are having profound effects on their lives—and making them seriously unhappy" (61). She links many studies on how depressed students are becoming due to it, how they are less sexually active, less inclined to drive, and that they are less functioning members of society in general because of this disastrous development. Samuel on the other hand believes that it's not the children, but that it is the parents who are affected the most by cell phones and social media when she states her thesis, "No, I don't believe that smartphones are 'destroying' a generation, and I'm somewhat insulted at that suggestion on my kids' behalf." She explains that smartphones are disrupting a generation because today's parents are also glued to their phones, and it's affecting how they are parenting their children. This idea very much deviates from Twenge's idea of how technology has been affecting generations, and makes it very easy to see both sides of an argument.

Peer: Great use of a quotation from the source to support your statement.

Peer: I like that you point the main difference out right away, before diving into more detailed differences. It helps me keep a clear picture in my mind of each author and their main points.

Peer: I'm not sure this is the right quote to support your previous statement. Maybe find a quote from Samuel that focuses on parents, not kids.

These articles also differed in how each author structured their essays. A lot of Twenge's article was supported with evidence in the form of statistics with less personal experience. A lot of graphs and numbers can be seen throughout her article, which could appeal to certain audiences more than others. Nearly a quarter of Twenge's article was presented through her case study. The opposite could be said about Samuel's article. A lot of Samuel's essay can be seen using her own experience with a little bit of statistics thrown in at the beginning. Some of her use of personal experience can be seen when she discusses her children and how her technology has affected their life. These are some of the more subtle differences between the articles, but they can make a huge difference in how the audience is reached.

Instructor: Since the similarities and differences aren't your main points, try connecting them back to your thesis.

Instructor: This is a great opportunity to practice writing in active voice. I'd like to see you move away from passive writing.

Peer: Pointing out their different interpretations of the same study helps set these authors apart. You can definitely connect back to your thesis.

Finally, these articles are differentiated by the fact that they use different logic in interpreting their evidence. Both of authors looked at the same study about how unhappy students felt in correlation to their time spent of social media. Twenge decided to focus on the more unhappy eighth graders in the study that provided the data that she wanted to show her audience. Samuel looked at the same study however and found that there was basically no relation between unhappiness and social media use when looking at the behavior of twelfth graders. Samuel states this in her "How unhappy are teens, anyhow?" section of her article when comparing her data and Twenge's data. These different perspectives grant the readers (if they decide to read up on both sides) a bigger picture of how to look at an argument to formulate their own opinion. These differences define each article; if it were not for these differences, we would not even have an argument to discuss.

Learning by Doing 🎯 Responding as a Peer

If Nick were in your class, what questions would you want to ask him? What advice for revision would you offer in your peer response?

Revising and Editing

Nick collected the comments about his draft. To help him focus on the purpose of the essay, he reread the assignment. He decided that he needed to analyze the authors' different approaches to smartphones, rather than just evaluating which argument was better.

Nick concentrated first on revising his thesis statement, as his instructor had suggested. Then he went back to the beginning to make other changes, responding to comments and editing details. The following draft shows Nick's commenting on some of his revision and editing decisions.

Part of Revised and Edited Draft

❓ What is your revision plan for your draft?

❓ What changes do you want to mark in your draft?

Add a title — something informative and creative. How about "Smartphone and Social Media Addiction: Which Generation Is to Blame?"

I need a better opener to set the scene and introduce my topic.

You're a child in a restaurant, and the server automatically gives you a coloring book and crayons. This is a blast for you and ~~an~~ effective way *in your parents' eyes* to keep you quiet before getting food ~~in your parents' eyes~~. Now look at today's generation of children at restaurants. Most kids skip this whole process altogether. What do they do instead of this? They ask their parents for their tablet or to use their parent's phone for games. *Changes in technology have influenced* ~~A lot has changed between generations~~ with technology ~~being a main influencer for these changes. These changes can be viewed as both positive and negative, and they affect~~ different generations in a multitude of positive and negative ways. Jean M. Twenge wrote the article "Has the Smartphone Destroyed a Generation?" that discusses how smartphones and social media use *negatively* have ^affected today's children, while Alexandra Samuel wrote the article "Yes, Smartphones Are Destroying a Generation, But Not of Kids" as a response to Twenge, ~~to say~~ *asserting* that smartphones are affecting today's parents the most. There are many similarities and differences between these essays, but Samuel does a superior job at delivering her argument.

~~Some exposition must obviously be made before explaining why Samuel did a better job than Twenge in her essay. Let us begin by discussing the major similarities that the essays share.~~ The main topic remains consistent in both of these essays. Both essays talk about the impact smartphones have made on generations, and they also focus mostly on the negative effects it has had on said generations. The essays also share the objective to inform the audience on these events. Smartphones obviously have made negative impacts on generations, ~~with their presence~~ but each author chooses to inform the readers on how they specifically have affected generations through the use of statistics and graphs. ~~Personal evidence is also provided~~ Each author also provides their personal experiences throughout the essays ~~through each author's personal experiences~~. Twenge uses her case study to convey her argument in her own essay, while Samuel uses her own experience with her children to communicate her argument. Lastly, both authors seem to reach a similar consensus on how to deal with the situation at hand. Both authors believe that ~~monitoring your children~~ *some form of parental intervention* is a great solution to ending the apparent issues that social media and cell phone usage can impose. ~~It is important to remember the similarities of essays when deciding which one was more effective.~~

~~Next we should address the ways in which each essay is different from the other.~~ The major difference in these essays is ~~who~~ *whom* each author believes cell phones and social media affects the most. Twenge believes that today's kids, whom she calls "iGen," is the most affected by technological advancement when she says the following, ~~her thesis~~ "There is compelling evidence that the devices we've placed in young people's hands are having profound effects on their lives—and making them seriously unhappy" (61). She links many studies on how depressed students are becoming due to it, how they are less sexually active, less inclined to drive, and that they are less functioning members of society in general because of this disastrous development. Samuel on the other hand believes that it's not the children, but that it is the parents who are affected the most by cell phones and social media when she states ~~her thesis~~, "No, I don't believe that smartphones are 'destroying' a generation, and I'm somewhat insulted at that suggestion on my kids' behalf." She explains that smartphones are disrupting a generation because today's parents are also glued to their phones, and it's affecting how they are parenting their children. This idea very much deviates from Twenge's idea of how technology

I need to revise my thesis to focus on the big similarities and differences between these articles. I can pull these points from my body paragraphs below.

I discuss a lot of relevant similarities here. That should be the first part of my revised thesis.

This major difference will be the second item in my revised thesis.

I almost forgot to double check for plagiarism. For my final draft, I should make sure my in-text citations appear correctly.

Must replace this quote with one that focuses on parents.

has been affecting generations, and makes it very easy to see both sides of an argument.

Differences in how the essays are structured can be another point in my revised thesis.

These articles also differed in how each author structured their essays. A lot of Twenge's article was supported with evidence in the form of statistics with less personal experience. A lot of graphs and numbers can be seen throughout her article, which could appeal to certain audiences more than others. Nearly a quarter of Twenge's article was presented through her case study. The opposite ~~could be said about~~ *is true of* Samuel's article. A lot of Samuel's essay ~~can be seen using~~ *describes* her own experience with a little bit of statistics thrown in at the beginning. Some of her use of personal experience ~~can be~~ *is* seen when she discusses her children and how her technology has affected their life. These are some of the more subtle differences between the articles, but they can make a huge difference in how the audience is reached.

Their different interpretations will be the last point in my new thesis.

Finally, these articles are differentiated by the fact that they use different logic in interpreting their evidence. Both of authors looked at the same study about how unhappy students felt in correlation to their time spent of social media. Twenge decided to focus on the more unhappy eighth graders in the study that provided the data that she wanted to show her audience. Samuel looked at the same study however and found that there was basically no relation between unhappiness and social media use when looking at the behavior of twelfth graders. Samuel states this in her "How unhappy are teens, anyhow?" section of her article when comparing her data and Twenge's data. These different perspectives grant the readers (if they decide to read up on both sides) a bigger picture of how to look at an argument to formulate their own opinion. These differences define each article; if it were not for these differences, we would not even have an argument to discuss.

Since I'm revising my thesis, I can salvage parts of the last few paragraphs to support my new main points.

With the similarities and differences established, it is time to discuss why I believe that Samuel delivered a better argument. First, Samuel. . . .

After Nick finished revising and editing, he spell-checked his final version and double-checked his citations. He proofread it one more time, then he submitted his final draft.

Final Draft for Submission

Nick Catizone
Professor Chandler
ENGL 1010.280
24 October 2019

For more on MLA format, see the Quick Format Guide, p. Q-2.

Smartphone Addiction: Which Generation Is to Blame?

Picture yourself in a restaurant when you were a child. The server seats you and your family and automatically gives you a children's menu, a coloring book, and crayons. This is a blast for you and, in your parents' eyes, an effective way to keep you quiet before getting food. Now think of today's generation of children at restaurants. What do they do instead of this? They ask their parents for their tablet or to use their parent's phone for games. Notice that the parents are also probably distracting themselves by tuning into their own devices. Changes in technology have influenced different generations in a multitude of positive and negative ways. Two authors who explore these influences are Jean M. Twenge and Alexandra Samuel. Twenge, who wrote "Has the Smartphone Destroyed a Generation?" discusses how smartphones and social media use have negatively affected today's children, while Samuel, author of "Yes, Smartphones Are Destroying a Generation, But Not of Kids," debunks some of Twenge's claims and asserts that smartphones are affecting today's parents the most. While both articles seek to inform readers of the negative effects of smartphone addiction, they target opposing generations, support their arguments with different types of evidence, and interpret their findings in different ways.

Twenge and Samuel both examine the impact smartphones and social media have made on younger and older generations, focusing on the negative effects they have had on said generations. Twenge connects the increasing amount of time that teens spend in front of screens with rising suicide rates and feeling generally unhappy (63), while Samuel ties together the boom of social media usage by parents and disengagement from their children. The essays also share the objective of informing the audience of these effects through the use of statistics, graphs, and personal experiences. Twenge describes the personal experiences of a teenager she spoke with as a lead-in to discussing data from her case study to convey her argument (59). Samuel uses her own experience with her children, coupled with references to results of numerous studies to communicate her argument. Lastly, both authors seem to reach a similar consensus on how to deal with the situation at hand. Both authors believe that some form of parental intervention is a great solution to ending the apparent issues that social media and cell phone usage can impose.

The first major difference in these essays is whom each author believes cell phones and social media affect the most. Twenge believes that today's teens, whom she calls "iGen," are the most affected by technological advancement: "There is compelling evidence that the devices we've placed in young people's hands are having profound effects on their lives—and making them seriously unhappy" (61). She links many studies on how depressed and isolated teens are becoming due to their screen time, how they are less sexually active, less inclined to drive, and that they are less functioning members of society in general because they are addicted to their screens (Twenge 61).

Samuel, on the other hand, believes that parents, not their teens, are affected the most by cell phones and social media when she states, "Fellow parents, it's time for us to consider another possible explanation for why our kids are increasingly disengaged. It's because we've disengaged ourselves; we're too busy looking down at our screens to look up at our kids." Samuel explains that smartphones are disrupting a generation because today's parents are also glued to their phones, and it's affecting how they are parenting their children. It's clear that the two authors are targeting opposing generations while explaining the negative effects of smartphone and social media addiction.

These articles also differed in how each author supports their arguments. While both authors incorporate statistical data and personal experiences, Twenge's article is supported more heavily with evidence in the form of statistics, with less personal experience:

> Those who spend six to nine hours a week on social media are still 47 percent more likely to say they are unhappy than those who use social media even less. . . . Those who spend an above-average amount of time with their friends in person are 20 percent less likely to say they're unhappy than those who hang out for a below-average amount of time (Twenge 63).

She includes many graphs and numbers throughout her article, which could appeal to certain audiences more than others.

The majority of Twenge's article is presented through her case study. That's not quite true about Samuel's article. About half of Samuel's essay describes her own experience, with statistics thrown in at the beginning. Some of Samuel's use of personal experience is seen when she discusses her children and how her technology has affected their life: "My entire experience of parenthood has been lived in the tug-of-war between child and screen; my kids can't remember a time when they didn't have to compete with my iPhone in order to get my attention. . . ." It's also true that, unlike Twenge, Samuel's presentation of data in the beginning of her essay is structured to address and debunk some of Twenge's claims. These are some of the more subtle differences between the articles, but they can make a huge difference in how the audience is reached.

Finally, these articles are differentiated by the fact that they interpret the available evidence differently. Both authors looked at the same studies about how unhappy students felt in correlation to their time spent on social media. Twenge decided to focus on the more unhappy eighth graders in the study that provided the data that she wanted to show her audience: "Psychologically . . . they [iGen] are more vulnerable than Millennials were: Rates of teen depression and suicide have skyrocketed since 2011. It's not an exaggeration to describe iGen as being on the brink of the worst mental-health crisis in decades" (61).

Samuel looked at the same study, however, and found that there was basically no relation between unhappiness and social media use as reflected in the behavior of twelfth graders: "[These] teens report near identical levels of happiness regardless whether they're on the higher or lower end of social media usage." She also noted that the unhappiest teens are "those poor twelfth graders who don't use social media at all" (Samuel).

In response to Twenge's data-based claim that the release of the iPhone ". . . radically changed every aspect of teenagers' lives, from the nature of their social interactions to their mental health" (61), Samuel also examined a study and showed that the "fastest growth during that time was among young adults (18–29) and 30-to-49-year-olds." Samuel goes on to state that "One year before the iPhone, only 6% of people aged 30-to-49 were on social networks. By 2009, that had leapt up to 44%: that's absolutely explosive growth." Samuel connects the dots between this study and her own experience as a parent to why social media/cell phones are making so much of an impact on children. Her thoughts that parents are the reason for the depression or lack of maturity in children and teens was something that Twenge never touched upon.

Twenge also mentions that teens nowadays are having sex and getting their driver's license later than previous generations (61), yet Samuel questions her intention of bringing this up. Samuel challenges Twenge's interpretation of these findings when she suggests that it's a good thing that teens are waiting until they are more mature before they make decisions such as these. Samuel states that it is better to wait so that way early pregnancies and car accidents do not happen due to the fact that these teens do not feel as if they are ready to take on these responsibilities.

Jean M. Twenge and Alexandra Samuel address the same topic, with similar goals and solutions in mind. They also have many differences, as we can see in the generations they target, the types of evidence they use to support their claims, and their interpretations of similar evidence. These essays are further differentiated by the fact that Twenge constructs her argument based largely upon her own case study and related data, while Samuel's essay is built on isolating Twenge's claims and debunking them. Both authors, however, admit that smartphone and social media addiction presents problems for younger and older generations, and that an effective solution requires some level of parental involvement to bridge the gap between these generations.

Works Cited

Samuel, Alexandra. "Yes, Smartphones Are Destroying a Generation, But Not of Kids." *JSTOR Daily*, 2017, 8 Aug. 2017, https://daily.jstor.org/yes-smartphones-are-destroying-a-generation-but-not-of-kids.

Twenge, Jean. "Has the Smartphone Destroyed a Generation?" *The Atlantic*, Sept. 2017, pp. 58–65.

Reflecting as a Writer

Nick's instructor required a reflective letter to accompany his final draft, following the time-honored advice of writer and teacher Peter Elbow. Here Nick needed to consider his goals, strengths, remaining challenges, and responses to readers during his writing process. The letter and the essay would become part of his writer's portfolio due at the end of the term.

For more about portfolios, see Ch. 20.

Learning by Doing Writing a Reflective Letter

Select one of the following options, and write a reflective letter to your instructor.

1. Reflect on your responses to Nick's writing strategies and processes. For example, you might consider how his processes do and do not relate to yours or what you have learned from him that you might like to apply to your writing.

2. Reflect on a source-based essay, as Nick did. Consider your goals, strengths, remaining challenges, and responses to readers.

Reflective Portfolio Letter

For sample business letter formats, see E in the Quick Format Guide, pp. Q-13–Q-16.

Campus Box A-456
November 9, 2019

Professor Mollie Chandler
English Department
State University
1234 University Road
Campustown, OH 23456

Dear Dr. Chandler:

? What do you want to say in a reflective letter?

The main goal of my essay was to analyze the approaches of two contemporary writers discussing the dangers of smartphone addiction among kids. When writing the essay I was analyzing how the authors presented different ideas on the subject and the kinds of evidence they used to support their ideas.

The strengths I had in writing this essay were in reading both essays critically and analytically. I believe my analysis accurately presented the reader with each writer's points. I began my writing process by mapping my ideas in a diagram, emphasizing the contrast between Twenge's and Samuel's articles. However, if I could revise the essay further, I would focus more on why these differences are significant. I would also revise and strengthen my concluding paragraph.

The feedback I received regarding my essay was mostly positive. However, almost all feedback suggested that I needed to revise thesis to make it more analytical, instead of focusing on which article was better. I believe this strengthened my essay overall. I would like readers to say that my essay gave them new insight into a topic that affects all of us and helped them think critically about their own smartphone use or that of their children.

I may be contacted regarding this essay at ncatizone@campus.edu or 555-555-5555.

Sincerely,

Nick Catizone

Strategies for Generating Ideas

15

For most writers, the hardest part of writing comes first—confronting a blank page. Fortunately, you can prepare for that moment by finding ideas and getting ready to write. All the tested techniques here have worked for writers—professionals and students—and some may work for you.

Finding Ideas

When you begin to write, ideas may appear effortlessly on the paper or screen, perhaps triggered by resources around you—something you read, see, hear, discuss, or think about. (See the top half of the graphic below.) But at other times you need idea generators, strategies to try when your ideas dry up. If one strategy doesn't work for your task, try another. (See the lower half of the graphic.)

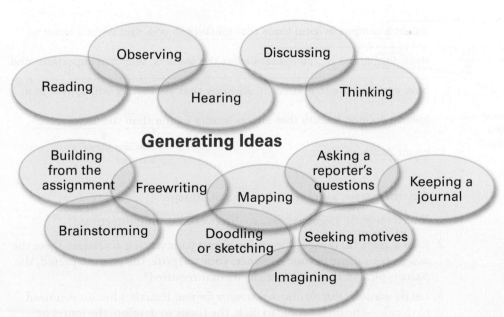

Observing   Discussing

Reading   Hearing   Thinking

Generating Ideas

Building from the assignment   Freewriting   Mapping   Asking a reporter's questions   Keeping a journal

Brainstorming   Doodling or sketching   Seeking motives

Imagining

Building from Your Assignment

For more about writing from personal experience, see Ch. 4.

Learning to write is learning what questions to ask yourself. Your assignment may trigger this process, raising some questions and answering others. For example, Ben Tran jotted the following notes as his instructor and classmates discussed his first assignment — recalling a personal experience.

What event? What consequences?

Tell the story but do more — reflect & show importance.

What readers? Class + prof.

Write about one specific experience that changed how you acted, thought, or felt. Use your experience as a springboard for reflection. Your purpose is not merely to tell an interesting story but to show your readers — your instructor and your classmates — the importance of that experience for you.

2 parts to purpose

The assignment clarified what audience to address and what purpose to set. Ben saw three big questions: Which experience should I pick? How did it change me? Why was it so important for me? Ben still didn't know what he'd write about, but he had figured out the questions to tackle first.

Sometimes assignments assume that you already know something critical — how to address a particular audience or what to include in some type of writing. When Amalia Blackhawk read her argument assignment, she jotted down questions to ask her instructor.

Any issue OK?

My classmates? The publication's readers?

Editor of what?

What's my purpose? Persuading readers to respect my view or to agree?

Select a campus or local issue that matters to you, and write a letter to the editor about it. Tell readers what the issue is, why it is important, and how you propose to address it. Assume that your letter will appear in a special opinion feature that allows letters longer than the usual word-count limits.

How long should that be?

Try these steps as you examine an assignment:

1. *Read through the assignment once* to discover its overall direction.

2. *Read it again,* marking information about your writing situation. Does the assignment identify your audience, your purpose, the genre expected, the parts typical of that genre, or the format required?

3. *List the questions that the assignment raises for you.* Exactly what do you need to decide — the broad topic to pick, the focus to develop, the issues or aspects to consider, the sources to consult? If the assignment doesn't give you answers, ask your instructor.

Brainstorming and Freewriting

A *brainstorm* is a sudden insight or inspiration. As a writing strategy, brainstorming uses free association to stimulate a chain of ideas, often to personalize a topic and break it down into specifics. Start with a word or phrase, and spend a set period of time simply listing ideas as rapidly as possible. Write down whatever comes to mind with no editing or going back.

As a group activity, brainstorming benefits from varied perspectives. At work, it can fill a specific need — finding a name for a product or an advertising slogan. In college, you can brainstorm with a few others or your entire class. Sit facing one another. Designate one person to record the suggestions on paper, screen, or chalkboard. After several minutes of calling out ideas, look over the list for useful results.

On your own, brainstorm to define a topic, generate an example, or find a title for a finished paper. Angie Ortiz brainstormed after her instructor assigned an essay ("Demonstrate from your experience how digital technology affects our lives"). She wrote *digital technology* on the page, set her alarm for fifteen minutes, and began to scribble.

> Digital technology
> Cell phone, laptop, tablet. Alexa, Siri, cable, streaming music and movies. Too much?!
> Always on call — at home, in car, at school. Always something playing.
> Spend so much time in electronic world — phone calls, texting, Skype,
>   social media. Less time really hanging with friends — face-to-face time.
> Less aware of my surroundings outside of the electronic world?

When her alarm went off, Angie took a break. After returning to her list, she crossed out ideas that did not interest her and circled her final promising question. A focus began to emerge: the capacity of the electronic world to expand information but reduce awareness.

To tap your unconscious by *freewriting*, simply write sentences without stopping for about fifteen minutes. The sentences don't have to be grammatical, coherent, or stylish; just keep them flowing to unlock an idea's potential. Angie Ortiz wrote her topic at the top of a page — and then explored her rough ideas.

> Electronic devices — do they isolate us? I chat online and text on my phone all day, but that's quick communication, not in-depth conversation. I don't really spend much time hanging with friends and getting to know what's going on with them. I love listening to music on my phone, but maybe I'm not as aware of my surroundings as I could be. I miss seeing things, like the new art gallery that I walk by every day. I didn't even notice the new sculpture park in front! Then, at night, I do assignments on my computer, browse the Web, and watch some YouTube. I'm in my own little electronic world most of the time. I love technology, but what else am I missing?

Angie's result wasn't polished prose. Still, in a short time she produced a paragraph to serve as a springboard for her essay.

When you want to brainstorm and freewrite, try this advice:

1. *Start with a key word or phrase.* If you need a topic, try a general term (*climate change*); if you need an example for a paragraph in progress, try specifics (*effects of climate change on weather*).

2. *Set a time limit.* Ten minutes (or so) is enough for strenuous thinking.

3. *Don't stop writing.* Express whatever comes to mind, even "My mind is blank," until a new thought floats up. Don't cross out false starts or grammar errors. Don't worry about connecting ideas or finding perfect words. Don't worry about spelling, repetition, or relevance. Don't judge, and don't arrange: just produce.

When you finish, circle anything intriguing. Cross out whatever looks useless or dull. Then try some conscious organizing: Are any thoughts related? Can you group them? Does the group suggest a topic? In freewriting, it's helpful to repeat the process, looping back to expand a good idea, if you wish.

Learning by Doing 🖊 Brainstorming or Freewriting

From the following list, choose a subject that interests you, that you know something about, and that you'd like to learn more about — in other words, something that you might like to write about.

challenges/fears	the environment	health/fitness
dreams	family	pets
education	food	technology/social media
entertainment	friends	work

For ten minutes write as quickly as you can about your subject, listing everything that comes to mind about it, including all pertinent details. You may prefer to brainstorm with short phrases, words, or ideas, or to freewrite in complete sentences. If your writing brings up a debatable issue (such as whether or not workplaces should offer flexible schedules), consider pros, cons, and alternative points of view. If it calls to mind an event (such as a memorable family occasion), list the details of the event in chronological order. Exchange your work with a peer, and see if you can add new ideas or insights to each other's brainstorming.

Doodling or Sketching

If you fill the margins of your notebooks with doodles, harness this artistic energy to generate ideas for writing. Elena Lopez began to sketch her collision with a teammate during a soccer tournament. She added stick figures, notes, symbols, and color as she outlined a series of events.

Try this advice as you develop ideas by doodling or sketching:

1. *Give your ideas room to grow.* Open a new file using a drawing program, doodle in pencil on a blank page, or sketch on a series of pages.

2. *Concentrate on your topic, but welcome new ideas.* Begin with a key visual in the center or at the top of a page. Add sketches or doodles as they occur to you to embellish, expand, define, or redirect your topic.

3. *Add icons, symbols, colors, figures, labels, notes, or questions.* Freely mix visuals and text, recording ideas without stopping to refine them.

4. *Clarify in writing.* After a break, add notes to make connections, identify sequences, or convert visuals into descriptive sentences.

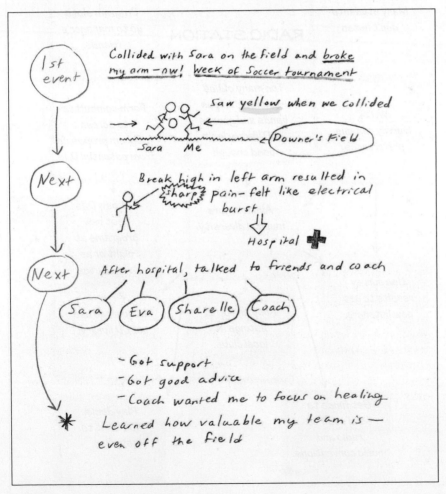

Doodling or sketching to generate ideas.

Mapping

Mapping taps your visual and spatial creativity as you position ideas on the page to show their relationships or relative importance. Ideas might radiate outward from a key term in the center, drop down from a key word at the top, sprout upward from a root idea, branch out from a trunk, flow across page or screen in a chronological or causal sequence, or follow a circular, spiral, or other form.

Andrew Choi used mapping to gather ideas for his proposal for revitalizing the campus radio station. He noted ideas on colored sticky notes—blue for problems, yellow for solutions, and pink for implementation details. Then he moved the sticky notes around on a blank page, arranging them as he connected ideas.

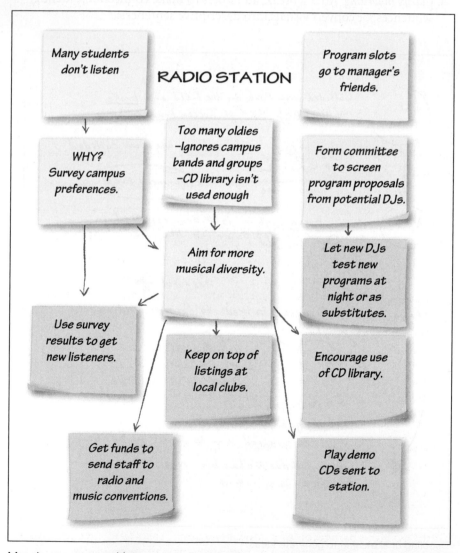

Mapping to generate ideas

Here are some suggestions for mapping:

1. *Give your ideas space.* Open a new file, or try using a poster board for arranging sticky notes or cards.

2. *Begin with a topic or key idea.* Using your imagination, memory, class notes, or reading, place a key word at the center or top of a page.

3. *Add related ideas, examples, issues, or questions.* Quickly and spontaneously place these points above, below, or beside your key word.

4. *Make connections.* As your map evolves, use lines, arrows, or loops to connect ideas; box or circle them to focus attention; add colors to relate points or to distinguish source materials from your own ideas.

After a break, continue mapping to refine the structure, add detail, or build an alternate map from a different viewpoint.

Imagining

Your imagination is a valuable resource for analyzing an option, evaluating an alternative, or solving a problem — and for discovering surprising ideas.

Suppose you asked, "What if the average North American lived more than a century?" No doubt many more people would be old. How would that shift affect doctors, nurses, and medical facilities? How might city planners respond? What would the change mean for shopping centers? For television programming? For leisure activities? For Social Security?

Use some of the following strategies to unleash your imagination:

1. *Speculate about changes, alternatives, and options.* What common assumption might you question or deny? What deplorable condition would you remedy? What changes in policy, practice, or attitude might avoid problems? What different paths in life might you take?

2. *Experiment with a different point of view.* How would someone on the opposing side respond? A plant, an animal, a Martian? Shift the debate (whether retirees, not teens, should be allowed to drink) or the time (present to past or future).

3. *Synthesize.* Synthesis (generating new ideas by combining previously separate ideas) is the opposite of analysis (breaking ideas down into component parts). Synthesize to make fresh connections, fusing materials — perhaps old or familiar — into something new.

For more about analysis and synthesis, see pp. 26–27.

Asking a Reporter's Questions

Journalists, assembling facts to write a news story, ask themselves six simple questions — the five *W*'s and an *H*:

Who?	Where?	Why?
What?	When?	How?

In the opening paragraph of a good news story, the writer tries to condense the whole story into a sentence or two, answering all six questions.

A giant homemade fire balloon [*what*] startled residents of Costa Mesa [*where*] last night [*when*] as Ambrose Barker, 79, [*who*] zigzagged across the sky at nearly 300 miles per hour [*how*] in an attempt to set a new altitude record [*why*].

Later in the news story, the reporter will add details, using the six basic questions to generate more about what happened and why.

A similar set of questions focusing on the act (what happened), actor (who did the action), agency (how the action came about), and the motive (the purpose behind the action) can help you understand human behavior. In a history paper, you might consider how George Washington's conduct shaped the presidency. In a literature essay, you might analyze the motives of Hester Prynne in *The Scarlet Letter*.

For more on writing about literature, see Ch. 12.

For your college writing, use these sets of questions to generate details. They can help you explore the significance of a childhood experience, analyze what happened at a moment in history, or investigate a campus problem. For a topic that is not based on your personal experience, you may need to do reading or interviewing to answer some of the questions. As you learn more, your questions about the topic will naturally lead to further questions. Don't worry if some questions go nowhere or are repetitious. Later you'll weed out irrelevant points and keep those that look promising.

Learning by Doing 🔘 Asking a Reporter's Questions

Choose one of the following topics, or use one of your own:

- A memorable event in history or in your life
- A concert or other performance that you have attended
- An accomplishment on campus or an occurrence in your city
- An important speech or a proposal for change
- A questionable stand someone has taken

Answer the six reporter's questions about the topic. Then write a sentence or two synthesizing the answers to the six questions. Incorporate that sentence into an introductory paragraph for an essay that you might write later.

Keeping a Journal

For ideas about keeping a reading journal, see pp. 21–22.

Journal writing richly rewards anyone who engages in it regularly. You can write anywhere or anytime: all you need is a few minutes to record an entry and the willingness to set down what you think and feel. Your journal will become a mine studded with priceless nuggets—thoughts, observations, reactions, and revelations that are yours for the taking. As you write, you can rifle your well-stocked journal for topics, insights, examples, and other material.

The best type of journal is the one that's useful to *you*. Reflective journals help you think about what you do or see, hear or read, learn or believe. An entry can be a list or an outline, a paragraph or an essay, a poem or a letter you don't intend to send. Describe a person or a place, set down a conversation, or record insights into actions. Consider your pet peeves, fears, dreams, treasures, or moral dilemmas. Use your experience as a writer to nourish and inspire your writing, recording what worked, what didn't, and how you reacted to each. Sometimes you *respond* to something in particular — an assigned reading, a classroom discussion, a movie. Responsive journal entries can give you plenty of material to use in a writing project. Journals can be on paper on in an electronic file, organized by date or subject. Like traditional journals, blogs aim for frank, honest, immediate entries. Unlike journals, they often explore a specific topic and may be available publicly on the Web or privately by invitation. Especially in an online class, you might blog about your writing or research processes.

Learning by Doing 🔊 Keeping a Journal

Keep a journal for at least a week. Each day record your thoughts, feelings, observations, and reactions. Reflect on what happens, and respond to what you read, including selections from this book. Then bring your journal to class, and read aloud to your classmates the entry you like best.

Getting Ready to Write

Once you have generated a suitable topic and some ideas about it, you can get down to the job of actually writing.

Setting Up Circumstances

Some writers find that a ritual relaxes them and helps them get started. If you can write only with your shoes off or with a can of soda nearby, set yourself up that way. Some writers need to hear blaring rap music; others need quiet. Create an environment that puts you in the mood for writing.

Find the Right Spot. Choose a place with good lighting and space to spread out. It may be a desk in your room, the dining room table, or a quiet library cubicle — someplace where no one will bother you, where your mind and body will settle in, and preferably where you can leave projects and keep handy your computer and materials. If you're stuck, try moving from library to home or from kitchen to bedroom. Try an unfamiliar place — a restaurant, an airport, a park.

Reduce Distractions. Most of us can't prevent interruptions, but we can reduce them. If you expect your boyfriend to call, call him before you start writing. If you have small children, write when they are asleep or at school.

Turn off your phone, and concentrate hard. Let others know you are serious about writing; allow yourself to give it full attention.

Write at Your Best Time. Some think best early in the morning; others favor the small hours when their stern self-critic might be asleep, too. Either time can also reduce distractions from others.

Write on a Schedule. Writing at a predictable time of day worked marvels for English novelist Anthony Trollope, who would start at 5:30 A.M., write 2,500 words before 8:30 A.M., and then go to his job at the post office. (He wrote more than sixty books.) Even if you can't set aside the same time every day, it may help to decide, "Today from four to five, I'll write."

Being Open to Ideas

Ideas, images, or powerful urges to write may arrive like sudden miracles. Encourage such moments by opening your mind to inspiration.

Talk about Your Writing. Discuss ideas in person, by phone, or online with a classmate or friend, encouraging questions, comments, and suggestions. Describe what you want to write about and how you'll lay it out. Or talk to yourself, recording your thoughts on your phone while you walk your dog or wait for your laundry to dry.

Keep a Notebook or Journal Handy. Always keep some paper in your backpack or on the night table to write down good ideas that pop into your mind. Imagination may strike in the grocery checkout line, in the doctor's waiting room, or during a lull on the job.

Read. The step from reading to writing is a short one. Even when you're reading for fun, you're involved with words. You might hit on something for your paper. Or read purposefully: set out to read and take notes.

Strategies for Stating a Thesis and Planning

16

Starting to write often seems a chaotic activity, but the strategies in this chapter can help create order. For most papers, you will want to consider your purpose and audience and then focus on a central point by discovering, stating, and improving a thesis. To help you arrange your material, the chapter also includes advice on organizing and outlining.

Considering Purpose and Audience

As you work on your college papers, you may feel as if you're juggling — selecting weighty points and lively details, tossing them into the air, keeping them all moving in sequence. Your performance also draws a crowd — your instructor, classmates, or other readers. They'll expect your attention, too.

Think carefully about your audience and purpose as you plan. If you want to show your classmates and instructor the importance of an event, start by deciding how much detail they need. Give them context to understand the event. Whether your purpose is informing, explaining, or persuading, you'll need to go beyond *what* happened to *why* the event matters. Support your idea with reasons and evidence, such as statistics, expert opinion, or personal testimonies that help convince readers to accept your main point.

Plan for your purpose and audience using questions such as these:

- *What is your general purpose?* What do you want to accomplish? Do you want readers to smile, think, or agree? To learn, accept, respect, care, change, or reply? How might your writing accomplish your aims?

- *Who are your readers?* If they are not clearly identified by your assignment or situation, what do you assume about them? What do they know or want to know? What opinions do they hold? What do they find informative or persuasive?

- *How can you narrow and focus your ideas,* given what you know about your purpose and audience? Which slant would best achieve your purpose? What points would appeal most strongly to your readers? What details would engage or persuade them?

Stating and Using a Thesis

Most pieces of effective writing are unified around one main point. That is, all the subpoints and supporting details are relevant to that point. Generally, after you have read an essay, you can sum up the writer's main point in a sentence. We call this summary statement a *thesis*.

Read more by Judith Ortiz Cofer on p. 338 of A Writer's Reader.

Explicit Thesis. Often a thesis will be explicit, plainly stated, in the selection itself. In "The Myth of the Latin Woman: I Just Met a Girl Named María" from *The Latin Deli* (University of Georgia Press, 1993), Judith Ortiz Cofer states her thesis at the end of the first paragraph: "You can leave the Island, master the English language, and travel as far as you can, but if you are a Latina, especially one like me who so obviously belongs to Rita Moreno's gene pool, the Island travels with you." This clear statement, strategically placed, helps readers see her point.

Implicit Thesis. Sometimes a thesis is implicit, indirectly suggested rather than directly stated. In "The Niceness Solution," a selection from Bruce Bawer's *Beyond Queer* (Free Press, 1996), Paul Varnell describes an ordinance "banning rude behavior, including rude speech," passed in Raritan, New Jersey. He then identifies four objections to such attempts to limit free speech and concludes with this sentence: "Sensibly, Raritan Police Chief Joseph Sferro said he would not enforce the new ordinance." Although Varnell does not state his main point in one concise sentence, readers understand that he opposes the Raritan law and any other attempts to legislate "niceness."

The purpose of most academic and workplace writing is to inform, to explain, or to convince. To achieve any of these purposes, you must make your main point crystal clear. A thesis sentence helps you clarify your idea and stay on track as you write. It also helps your readers see your point and follow your discussion. Sometimes you may want to imply your thesis, but if you state it explicitly, you ensure that readers cannot miss it.

Learning by Doing 📷 Identifying Theses

Working in a small group, select and read five essays from Chapters 4–13. Then, individually, write out the thesis for each essay. Some thesis statements are stated outright (explicit), but others are indirect (implicit). Compare and contrast the thesis statements you identified with those your classmates found. How do you account for differences? Try to agree on a thesis statement for each essay.

In Chs. 4–13, look for specific advice under headings that mention a thesis and for the Strengthening Your Thesis checklists. Also, watch for the pink labels that identify thesis examples in the readings.

How to Discover a Working Thesis

It's rare for a writer to develop a perfect thesis statement early in the writing process and then to write an effective essay that fits it exactly. What you should aim for is a *working thesis* — a statement that can guide you but that you will ultimately refine.

Your topic identifies the area you want to explore. To convert a topic to a thesis, you need to add your own slant, attitude, or point. A useful thesis contains not only the key words that identify your topic but also the *point* you want to make or the *attitude* you intend to express.

Topic   +   Slant or Attitude or Point   =   Working Thesis

Suppose you want to identify and write about a specific societal change.

TOPIC   old-fashioned formal courtesy

Now you experiment, testing ideas to make the topic your own.

TRIAL THESIS   Old-fashioned formal courtesy is a thing of the past.

Although your trial sentence emphasizes change, it's still circular, repeating rather than advancing a workable point. It doesn't say anything new about old-fashioned formal courtesy; it simply defines *old-fashioned.* You still need to state your own slant—maybe why things have changed.

TOPIC IDEA + SLANT   old-fashioned formal courtesy: how have chang-
                         ing gender roles affected it?

WORKING THESIS   As the roles of men and women have changed in our
                         society, old-fashioned formal courtesy has declined.

This working thesis sets you up for a cause-and-effect essay about the impact of changing gender roles upon courtesy. Later, you may refine your thesis further—perhaps focusing on courtesy toward the elderly, toward women, or, despite stereotypes, toward men.

For advice about revising a thesis, see pp. 306–07.

Ask yourself these questions as you draft your working thesis:

- Can you state the specific topic? Can you add your slant or attitude to it?
- Can you spell out your viewpoint or judgment of the topic?
- Can you draft several possible alternative theses to consider?
- Can you think of a catchy title that might be converted into a thesis statement?
- Can you write a summary of your main point? Can you explain it to a friend?

Once you have a working thesis, be sure it makes a substantial point. Suppose your assignment asks you to compare and contrast two local newspapers' coverage of a Senate election. Ask yourself why that comparison and contrast matters. Simply noting a difference won't be enough to satisfy most readers.

NO SPECIFIC POINT   The *Herald*'s coverage of the Senate elections was
                         different from the *Courier*'s.

WORKING THESIS   The *Herald*'s coverage of the Senate elections was
                         more thorough than the *Courier*'s, with detailed
                         analysis of recent demographic changes.

How to State and Improve a Thesis

Once you have a topic and main point, use the advice below to improve your thesis.

■ *State the thesis precisely.* Replace vague or general wording with concise, detailed, and down-to-earth language.

TOO GENERAL	There are a lot of problems with chemical wastes.

Are you going to address all chemical wastes, throughout all of history, all over the world? Will you list all the troubles they can cause?

MORE SPECIFIC	Careless dumping of leftover paint is to blame for a recent outbreak of skin rashes in Atlanta.

Here the thesis statement focuses on one chemical waste in one geographic area. For an argument, you need to take a stand on a debatable issue that would allow others to take different positions. State yours exactly.

SPECIFIC STAND	The recent health consequences of carelessly dumping leftover paint require Atlanta officials both to regulate and to educate.

■ *State just one central idea in the thesis sentence.* If your paper is to focus on one point, your thesis should state only one main idea.

TOO MANY IDEAS	Careless dumping of leftover paint has caused a serious problem in Atlanta, and a new kind of biodegradable paint has been developed, and it offers a promising solution to one chemical waste dilemma.
ONE CENTRAL IDEA	Careless dumping of leftover paint has caused a serious problem in Atlanta.
OR	A new kind of biodegradable paint offers a promising solution to one chemical waste dilemma.

■ *State your thesis positively.* You can usually find evidence to support a positive statement, but you'd have to rule out every possible exception in order to prove a negative one. Negative statements also may sound half-hearted and seem to lead nowhere.

NEGATIVE	Researchers do not know what causes breast cancer.
POSITIVE	The causes of breast cancer still challenge researchers.

Presenting the topic positively as a "challenge" can lead to a paper about the latest research.

■ *Limit your thesis to a debatable statement that you can demonstrate.* A workable thesis can be supported with convincing evidence given the length and the time available to you. The shorter the essay, the less development your thesis should require. Likewise, the longer the essay, the more development and complexity your thesis should suggest.

DIFFICULT TO SHOW	For centuries, popular music has announced vital trends in Western society.
NOT DEBATABLE	My favorite piece of music is Beethoven's Fifth Symphony.

You would need a whole encyclopedia of music to support the first thesis adequately. And the second thesis states your opinion, which is not a fruitful thesis.

Unlike a vague statement or a broad, unrestricted claim, a limited thesis narrows and refines a topic, restricting your essay to a reasonable scope.

TOO VAGUE	Native American blankets are very beautiful.
TOO BROAD	Native Americans have adapted to cultural shifts.
POSSIBLE TO SHOW	For some members of the Apache tribe, working in high-rise construction has allowed both economic stability and cultural integrity.

Whether yours is a first effort or a refined version, your thesis can probably benefit from improvement. Ask yourself the following questions to hone your thesis:

For more on revising a thesis, see pp. 306–08.

■ Could I define or state my **topic** more clearly?

■ Could I define or state my **slant** more clearly?

■ Could I **limit my thesis** to develop it more successfully?

But what if your thesis simply won't take shape? First, relax. Your thesis will slowly develop as your thinking matures and you figure out your paper's true direction, as peer readers spot the idea in your paper you're too close to see, or as you talk with your instructor. In the meantime, keep planning and writing so that you allow your thesis to emerge.

Learning by Doing 🎞 Examining Thesis Statements

You have been assigned an essay of one thousand words (approximately four double-spaced pages). Review the following thesis statements with your classmates and discuss the merits of each. Is the thesis stated clearly? Does it tackle just one idea? Is it debatable? Is it too broad or too narrow? How might each thesis be improved?

1. Violence in television shows or movies can be harmful to children.
2. Students have developed a variety of techniques to disguise cheating.
3. I don't know how to cook.
4. Volunteering at a women's shelter gave me an inside look at the consequences of domestic abuse, and I learned how to incorporate volunteer work into my busy schedule.
5. Trophy hunting of animals should be outlawed.
6. No war is a just war.
7. The government's "war on drugs" is a failure.

How to Use a Thesis to Organize

For more on using a thesis to develop an outline, see pp. 274–75.

Often a good, clear thesis will suggest an organization for your ideas.

WORKING THESIS	Despite the disadvantages of living in a downtown business district, I wouldn't live anywhere else.
FIRST ¶S	Disadvantages of living in the business district
NEXT ¶S	Advantages of living there
LAST ¶	Affirmation of your preference for downtown life

Just putting your working thesis into words can help organize you and keep you on track. A clear thesis can guide you as you select details and connect sections of the essay.

In addition, your thesis can prepare your readers for the pattern of development or sequence of ideas that you plan to present. As a writer, you look for key words (such as *compare, propose,* or *evaluate*) when you size up an assignment. Such words alert you to what's expected. When you write or revise your thesis, you can use such terms or their equivalents (such as *benefit* or *consequence* instead of *effect*) to preview for readers the likely direction of your paper. Then they, too, will know what to expect.

WORKING THESIS	Expanding the campus program for energy conservation would bring welcome financial and environmental benefits.
FIRST ¶S	Explanation of the campus energy situation
NEXT ¶S	Justification of the need for the proposed expansion
NEXT ¶S	Financial benefits for the college and students
NEXT ¶S	Environmental benefits for the region and beyond
LAST ¶	Concluding assertion of the value of the expansion

For an example of changing your thesis during revision, see Nick Catizone's revision on p. 248.

As you write, however, you don't have to cling to a thesis for dear life. If further investigation changes your thinking, you can change your thesis. In the example below, the writer's research and reflection led her to reverse her thesis entirely.

| WORKING THESIS | Because wolves are a menace to people and farm animals, they ought to be exterminated. |
| REVISED THESIS | The wolf, a relatively peaceful animal useful in nature's scheme of things, ought to be protected. |

You can restate a thesis any time: as you write, revise, or revise again.

Learning by Doing 🖉 Using a Thesis to Preview

Each of the following thesis statements is from a student paper in a different field. With your classmates, consider how each one previews the essay to come and jot down how you would expect the essay to be organized into sections.

1. Although the intent of inclusion is to provide the best care for all children by treating both special- and general-education students equally, some people in the field believe that the full inclusion of disabled children in mainstream classrooms may not be in the best interest of either type of student. (From "Is Inclusion the Answer?" by Sarah E. Goers)

2. With ancient Asian roots and contemporary European influences, the Japanese language has continued to change and to reflect cultural change as well. (From "Japanese: Linguistic Diversity" by Stephanie Hawkins)

3. *Manifest destiny* was an expression by leaders and politicians in the 1840s to clarify continental extension and expansion and in a sense revitalize the mission and national destiny for Americans. (From ethnic studies examination answer by Angela Mendy)

4. By comparing the *Aeneid* with *Troilus and Criseyde,* one can easily see the effects of the code of courtly love on literature. (From "The Effect of the Code of Courtly Love: A Comparison of Virgil's *Aeneid* and Chaucer's *Troilus and Criseyde*" by Cindy Keeler)

5. The effects of pollutants on the endangered Least Tern entering the Upper Newport Bay should be quantified so that necessary action can be taken to further protect and encourage the species. (From "Contaminant Residues in Least Tern [*Sterna antillarum*] Eggs Nesting in Upper Newport Bay" by Susanna Olsen)

Organizing Your Ideas

When you organize an essay, you present the parts in an order that makes sense and shows your readers how the ideas are connected. Often your organization will not only help a reader follow your points but also reinforce what you most want to emphasize by moving from beginning to end or from least to most significant, as the following table illustrates.

Organization	Movement	Typical Use	Example
SPATIAL	Left to right, right to left, bottom to top, top to bottom, front to back, outside to inside	■ Describing a place, a scene, or an environment ■ Describing a person's physical appearance	Describe an ocean vista, moving from the tidepools on the rocky shore to the plastic buoys floating offshore to the sparkling water meeting the sunset sky.
CHRONOLOGICAL	What happens first, second, and next, continuing until the end	■ Narrating an event ■ Explaining steps in a procedure ■ Explaining the development of an idea or a trend	Narrate the events that led up to an accident: leaving home late, stopping for an errand, checking messages while rushing along the highway, racing up to the intersection.
LOGICAL	General to specific (or the reverse), least important to most, cause to effect, problem to solution	■ Explaining an idea ■ Persuading readers to accept a stand, a proposal, or an evaluation	Analyze the effects of last year's storms by selecting four major consequences, placing the most important one last for emphasis.

Grouping Your Ideas

While exploring a topic, you will usually find a few ideas that seem to belong together — two facts on New York traffic jams, four actions of New York drivers, three problems with New York streets. But similar ideas seldom appear together in your notes because you did not discover them all at the same time. For this reason, you need to sort your ideas into groups and arrange them in sequences. Here are six ways to work:

1. *Rainbow connections.* List the main points you're going to express. Highlight points that go together with the same color. When you write, follow the color code, and integrate related ideas at the same time.

2. *Emphasizing ideas.* Make a copy of your notes. Use your software tools to highlight, categorize, and shape your thinking by grouping or distinguishing ideas. Mark similar or related ideas in the same way; call out major points. Then move related materials into groups.

Highlighting	• Adding bullets
Boxing	1. Numbering
Showing color	Changing fonts
Using **bold,** *italics,* <u>underlining</u>	Varying print sizes

3. *Linking.* List major points, and then draw lines (in color if you wish) to link related ideas. The following figure illustrates a linked list for an essay on Manhattan driving. The writer has connected related points, numbered their sequence, and jotted down a heading for each group. Each heading will probably inspire a topic sentence to introduce a major division of the essay. Because one point, chauffeured luxury cars, failed to relate to any other, the writer has a choice: drop it or develop it.

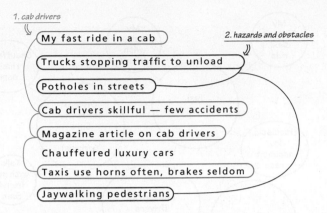

Grouping ideas by linking

4. *Solitaire.* Collect notes and ideas on roomy (5-by-8-inch) file cards, especially to write about literature or research. To organize, spread out the cards; arrange and rearrange them. When each idea seems to lead to the next, gather the cards into a deck in this order. As you write, deal yourself a card at a time, and turn its contents into sentences.

5. *Slide show.* Use presentation software to write your notes and ideas on "slides." When you're done, view your slides one by one or as a collection. Sort your slides into the most promising order.

6. *Clustering.* Clustering is a visual method for generating as well as grouping ideas. In the middle of a page, write your topic in a word or a phrase. Then think of the major divisions into which you might break your topic. For an essay on Manhattan drivers, your major divisions might be *types* of drivers: (1) taxi drivers, (2) bus drivers, (3) truck drivers, (4) New York drivers of private cars, and (5) out-of-town drivers of private cars. Arrange these divisions around your topic, circle them, and draw lines out from the major topic.

Around each division, make another cluster of details you might include — examples, illustrations, facts, statistics, opinions. Circle each specific item, connect it to the appropriate type of driver, and then expand the details into a paragraph. This technique lets you know where you have enough specific information to make your paper clear and interesting — and where you don't. If one subtopic has no branches leading out from it (such as "Bus Drivers"), either add specifics to expand it or drop it. You now have a rough plan for an essay (see p. 274).

Outlining

A familiar way to organize is to outline. A written outline, whether brief or detailed, acts as a map that you make before a journey. It shows where to leave from, where to stop along the way, and where to arrive. If you forget where you are going or what you want to say, you can consult your outline to get back on track. When you turn in your essay, your instructor may request an outline as both a map for readers and a skeletal summary.

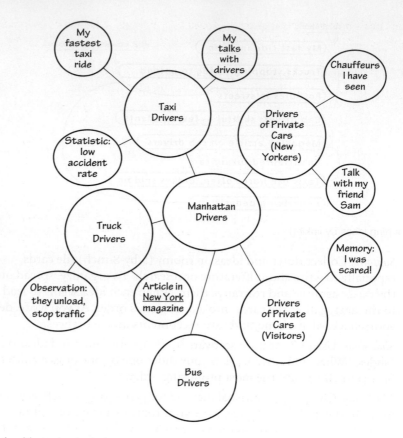

Grouping ideas via clustering

- Some writers like to begin with a working thesis. If it's clear, it may suggest how to develop or expand an outline, allowing the plan for the paper to grow naturally from the idea behind it.

For more on using outlining for revision, see pp. 307–08.

- Others prefer to start with a loose informal outline — perhaps just a list of points to make. If readers find your papers mechanical, such an outline may free up your writing.

- Still others, especially for research papers or complicated arguments, like to lay out a complex job very carefully in a detailed formal outline. If readers find your writing disorganized and hard to follow, this more detailed plan might be especially useful.

Thesis-Guided Outlines. Your working thesis may point to ideas you can use to organize your paper. (If it doesn't, you may want to revise your thesis and then return to your outline or vice versa.) Suppose you are assigned an anthropology paper on the people of Melanesia. You focus on this point:

Working Thesis: Although the Melanesian pattern of family life may look strange to Westerners, it fosters a degree of independence that rivals our own.

This thesis statement suggests an essay that naturally falls into two parts—features that seem strange and admirable results.

1. Features that appear strange to Westerners
   - —A woman supported by her brother, not her husband
   - —Trial marriages common
   - —Divorce from her children possible for any mother
2. Admirable results of system
   - —Wives not dependent on husbands for support
   - —Divorce between mates uncommon
   - —Greater freedom for parents and children

When you create a thesis-guided outline, look for the key element that shapes your working thesis. This key element can suggest both the approach you are taking and an organization. Note how the italicized words in the examples below reflect the approach taken in each thesis statement:

Advantages or benefits:

A varied personal exercise program has four main *advantages.*

This essay would likely present each of the four advantages in order.

Proposals, problem/solution approach, arguments advocating an action or decision (using *should, must, need to, or ought to*):

In spite of these tough economic times, the student senate *should* strongly recommend extended hours for the computer lab.

This essay would likely present the reasons and evidence supporting the argument, then turn to the counterarguments.

Qualifications such as *despite, because, since, or although:*

Although the new wetland preserve will protect only some wildlife, it will bring several long-term benefits to the region.

This essay would likely address the qualification (the *although* portion) first, and then turn to discuss the main statement.

Informal Outlines. For in-class writing, brief essays, and familiar topics, a short or informal outline, also called a *scratch outline,* may serve your needs. Jot down a list of points in the order you plan to make them. Use this outline, for your eyes only, to help you get organized, stick to the point, and remember ideas under pressure. The following is a scratch outline for a short paper explaining how outdoor enthusiasts can avoid illnesses carried by unsafe drinking water. It simply lists the methods for treating potentially unsafe water that the writer plans to explain.

Working Thesis: Campers and hikers need to ensure the safety of the water that they drink from rivers or streams.

Introduction: Treatments for potentially unsafe drinking water

1. Small commercial filter
   –Remove bacteria and protozoa including salmonella and *E. coli*
   –Use brands convenient for campers and hikers
2. Chemicals
   –Use bleach, chlorine, or iodine
   –Follow general rule: 12 drops per gallon of water
3. Boiling
   –Boil for 5 minutes (Red Cross) to 15 minutes (National Safety Council)
   –Store in a clean, covered container

Conclusion: Using one of three methods of treating water, campers and hikers can enjoy safe water from natural sources.

An informal outline can be even briefer than the preceding one. For an exam question or a very short paper, your outline might be no more than three or four phrases jotted in a list, such as this outline for an essay on one state's employment challenges:

Isolation of region

Tradition of family businesses

Growth of tele-commuting

Learning by Doing 🖰 Moving from Outline to Thesis

Based on each of the following informal outlines, write a thesis statement expressing a possible slant, attitude, or point (even if you aren't sure that the position is entirely defensible). Compare thesis statements with classmates. What similarities and differences do you find?

1. Smartphones

   Get the financial and service plans of various smartphone companies.

   Read the phone contracts as well as the promotional offers.

   Look for the time period, flexibility, and cancellation provisions.

   Check the display, keyboard, camera, apps, and other features.

2. Popular Mystery Novels

   Both Tony Hillerman and Margaret Coel have written mysteries with Native American characters and settings.

   Hillerman's novels feature members of the Navajo Tribal Police.

   Coel's novels feature a female attorney who is an Arapaho and a Jesuit priest at the reservation mission who grew up in Boston.

Hillerman's stories take place mostly on the extensive Navajo Reservation in Arizona, New Mexico, and Utah.

Coel's are set mostly on the large Wind River Reservation in Wyoming.

Hillerman and Coel try to convey tribal culture accurately, although their mysteries involve different tribes.

Both also explore similarities, differences, and conflicts between Native American cultures and the dominant culture.

3. Downtown Playspace

Downtown Playspace has financial and volunteer support but needs more.

Statistics show the need for a regional expansion of options for children.

Downtown Playspace will serve visitors at the Children's Museum and local children in Head Start, preschool, and elementary schools.

It will combine an outdoor playground with indoor technology space.

Land and a building are available, but both require renovation.

Formal Outlines. A *formal outline* is an elaborate guide, built with time and care, for a long, complex paper. A formal outline shows how ideas relate one to another — which are equal and important (*coordinate*) and which are less important (*subordinate*). It clearly and logically spells out where you are going. If you outline again after writing a draft, you can use the revised outline to check your logic then as well, perhaps revealing where to revise.

When you make a full formal outline, follow these steps:

- Place your thesis statement at the beginning.

- List the major points that support and develop your thesis, labeling them with roman numerals (I, II, III).

- Break down the major points into subordinate points using capital letters (A, B, C), subdivide those using arabic numerals (1, 2, 3), and subdivide those using small letters (a, b, c). Continue until your outline is fully developed. A very complex project would further subdivide using arabic numerals and small letters in parentheses.

- Indent each level of division in turn: the deeper the indentation, the more specific the ideas. Align like-numbered or -lettered headings under one another.

- Phrase all headings in parallel grammatical form: phrases or sentences, but not both in the same outline.

For more on parallelism, see B2 (pp. Q-47–Q-48) in the Quick Editing Guide.

For more on analysis and division, see pp. 299–302.

Because an outline divides or analyzes ideas, some readers and instructors disapprove of categories with only one subpoint, reasoning that you can't divide anything into one part. Let's imagine you've drafted the following outline on earthquakes:

D. Effects of an earthquake include structural damage.

    1. House foundations crack.

Logically, if you are going to discuss the effects of an earthquake, you should include more than one result:

D. Effects of an earthquake include structural damage.

    1. House foundations crack.

    2. Road surfaces are damaged.

    3. Water mains break.

Not only have you now come up with more points, but you have also emphasized the one placed last.

A *formal topic outline* for a long paper might include several levels of ideas, as this outline for Linn Bourgeau's research paper does. Such an outline can help you work out both a persuasive sequence for the parts of a paper and a logical order for any information from sources.

Crucial Choices: Who Will Save the Wetlands If Everyone Is at the Mall?

Working Thesis: Federal regulations need to foster state laws and educational requirements that will help protect the few wetlands that are left, restore as many as possible of those that have been destroyed, and take measures to improve the damage from overdevelopment.

I.   Nature's ecosystem
    A. Loss of wetlands nationally
    B. Loss of wetlands in Illinois

        1. More flooding and poorer water quality

        2. Lost ability to prevent floods, clean water, and store water
    C. Need to protect humankind

II.   Dramatic floods
    A. Midwestern floods in 1993 and 2011

        1. Lost wetlands in Illinois and other states

        2. Devastation in some states
    B. Cost in dollars and lives

        1. Deaths during recent flooding

        2. Costs in millions of dollars a year
    C. Flood prevention

        1. Plants and soil

        2. Floodplain overflow

III. Wetland laws
   A. Inadequately informed legislators
      1. Watersheds
      2. Interconnections in natural water systems
   B. Water purification
      1. Wetlands and water
      2. Pavement and lawns
IV. Need to save wetlands
   A. New federal laws
   B. Reeducation about interconnectedness
      1. Ecology at every grade level
      2. Education for politicians, developers, and legislators
   C. Choices in schools, legislature, and people's daily lives

A topic outline helps you work out a clear sequence of ideas, but it does not usually elaborate on them. A *formal sentence outline,* on the other hand, clarifies exactly what you want to say. It also moves you a step closer to drafting topic sentences. Notice how this portion of Linn's sentence outline expands her ideas.

Crucial Choices: Who Will Save the Wetlands If Everyone Is at the Mall?

Working Thesis: Federal regulations need to foster state laws and educational requirements that will help protect the few wetlands that are left, restore as many as possible of those that have been destroyed, and take measures to improve the damage from overdevelopment.

I. Each person, as part of nature's ecosystem, chooses how to interact with nature, including wetlands.
   A. The nation has lost over half its wetlands since Columbus arrived.
   B. Illinois has lost even more by legislating and draining them away.
      1. Destroying wetlands creates more flooding and poorer water quality.
      2. The wetlands could prevent floods, clean the water supply, and store water.
   C. The wetlands need to be protected because they protect and serve humankind.
II. Floods are dramatic and visible consequences of not protecting wetlands.
   A. The midwestern floods of 1993 and 2011 were disastrous.
      1. Illinois and other states had lost their wetlands.
      2. Those states also suffered the most devastation.
   B. The cost of flooding can be tallied in dollars spent and in lives lost.
      1. Nearly thirty people died in floods between 1995 and 2011.
      2. Flooding in 2011 cost Illinois about $216 million.

C. Preventing floods is a valuable role of wetlands.

   1. Plants and soil manage excess water.

   2. The Mississippi River floodplain was reduced from 60 days of water overflow to 12.

Learning by Doing 🔟 Outlining

1. Using one of the ideas you came up with in the Learning by Doing activities in Chapter 15, construct a formal topic outline that might serve as a guide for an essay.

2. Now turn that topic outline into a formal sentence outline.

3. Discuss both outlines with your classmates and instructor, bringing up any difficulties you met. If you think of improvements, reorganize the outline.

Strategies for Drafting

17

Learning to write well involves learning what key questions to ask yourself: How can I begin this draft? What should I do if I get stuck? How can I flesh out the bones of my paper? How can I end effectively? How can I keep my readers engaged? This chapter gives you advice on guiding readers through your writing—using opening paragraphs to draw them in, topic sentences to focus and control body paragraphs, and concluding paragraphs to wrap up the discussion.

Making a Start Enjoyable

A playful start may get you hard at work before you know it.

- **Time Yourself.** Set your watch or phone alarm for ten minutes or so, and vow to draft a page before the buzzer sounds. Don't stop for anything. If you're writing nonsense, just push on. You can cross out later.
- **Slow to a Crawl.** If speed quotas don't work, time yourself to write with exaggerated laziness, maybe a sentence every fifteen minutes.
- **Scribble on a Scrap.** If you dread the blank paper or screen, try starting on scrap paper, the back of a list, or a small notebook page.
- **Begin Wherever Is Most Appetizing.** Start in the middle or at the end, wherever thoughts come easily to mind. As novelist Bill Downey observes, "Writers are allowed to have their dessert first."
- **State Your Purpose.** Set forth what you want to achieve: To tell a story? To explain something? To win a reader over to your ideas?
- **Slip into a Reader's Shoes.** Put yourself in your reader's place. Start writing what you'd like to find out from the paper.
- **Nutshell It.** Summarize the paper you want to write. Condense your ideas into one small, tight paragraph. Later you can expand each sentence until the meaning is clear and all points are adequately supported.
- **Start Small.** Break the writing task into small parts, and tackle only the first, perhaps just two paragraphs.
- **Think of a Provocative Title.** Write down a dozen possible titles for your paper. If one sounds strikingly good, don't let it go to waste!

- **Record Yourself.** Talk a first draft into a recorder or your phone. Play it back. Then write. Even if it is hard to transcribe your spoken words, this technique may set your mind in motion.
- **Speak Up.** On your feet, before an imaginary cheering crowd, spontaneously utter a first paragraph. Then — quick! — record it or write it out.
- **Take Short Breaks.** Even if you don't feel tired, take a break every half hour or so. Get up, walk around the room, stretch, or get a drink of water. Two or three minutes should be enough to refresh your mind.

Restarting

When you have to write a long or demanding essay that you can't finish in one sitting, you may return to it only to find yourself stalled. You crank your starter and nothing happens. Your engine seems reluctant to turn over. Try the following suggestions for getting back on the road.

- **Leave Yourself Breadcrumbs.** If you're ready to quit, jot down what might come next or the first sentence of the next section. When you return, you can pick up the trail.
- **Pause Midstream.** Try breaking off in midsentence or mid-paragraph. Just leave a sentence trailing off into space, even if you know its closing words. When you return, you can start writing again immediately.
- **Repeat.** If you can't think of the next sentence, simply recopy the last one until that shy creature emerges on the page.
- **Reread.** When you return to work, spend a few minutes rereading what you have already written.
- **Switch Instruments.** Do you compose on a laptop? Try longhand. Write on note cards or colored paper. Or drop your pen and type instead.
- **Change Activities.** When words won't come, turn to something quite different. Run, cook a meal, or nap. Or reward yourself — after you reach a certain point — with a call to a friend or a game. All the while, your unconscious mind will keep working on your writing task.

Paragraphing

For more on developing ideas within paragraphs, see Ch. 18.

An essay is not a single, indigestible lump; rather, it is written in *paragraphs* — small units, each more or less self-contained, each contributing some new idea in support of the essay's thesis. Writers dwell on one idea at a time, stating it, developing it, illustrating it with examples or a few facts — *showing* readers, with detailed evidence, exactly what they mean.

Paragraphs can be as short as one sentence or as long as a page. Sometimes length is governed by audience, purpose, or medium. Journalists expect newspaper readers to gobble up facts like popcorn, quickly skimming short one- or two-sentence paragraphs. College writers, in contrast, should assume their readers expect well-developed paragraphs.

Using Topic Sentences

A *topic sentence* spells out the main idea of a paragraph in the body of an essay. As the topic sentence establishes the focus of the paragraph, it also relates the paragraph to the topic and thesis of the essay as a whole. (Much of the advice on topic sentences for paragraphs also extends to thesis statements for essays.) To convert an idea to a topic sentence, add your own slant, attitude, or point.

For more on thesis statements, see pp. 266–71.

Main Idea   +   Slant or Attitude or Point   =   Topic Sentence

How do you write a good topic sentence? Make it interesting, accurate, and limited. The more pointed and lively it is, the more it will interest readers. Even a dull, vague start is enlivened once you zero in on a specific point.

MAIN IDEA + SLANT	television + everything that's wrong with it
DULL START	There are many things wrong with television.
POINTED TOPIC SENTENCE	Of all the disappointing television programming, what I dislike most is melodramatic news.

A topic sentence also should be an accurate guide to the rest of the paragraph so that readers expect what's coming. Imagine your paragraph lists the steps for emergency preparedness, then consider these two topic sentences.

| INACCURATE GUIDE | All types of household emergencies can catch people off guard. |

The topic sentence above sets up the reader to expect a paragraph on the range of emergencies.

| ACCURATE TOPIC SENTENCE | Although an emergency may not be a common event, emergency preparedness should be routine at home. |

In contrast, this topic sentence matches the focus of the paragraph: emergency preparedness at home.

Finally, a topic sentence should be limited so you don't mislead or frustrate readers about what the paragraph covers.

| MISLEADING | Seven factors have contributed to the increasing obesity of the average American. |

This topic sentence would be misleading for a paragraph that focuses only on one factor — portion size.

| LIMITED TOPIC SENTENCE | Portion size is a major factor that contributes to the increasing obesity of average Americans. |

The limited topic sentence clearly announces the focus of the paragraph. The rest of the paragraph would go on to define healthy portion sizes and contrast them with the oversized portions at restaurants and in packaged foods.

Open with a Topic Sentence. Usually the topic sentence appears first in the paragraph, followed by sentences that clarify, illustrate, and support what it says. It is typically a statement but can sometimes be a question, alerting the reader to the topic without giving away the punchline. In this paragraph from his book *Excellent Sheep: The Miseducation of the American Elite and the Way to a Meaningful Life* (2014), literary critic William Deresiewicz examines the purpose and benefits of a college education.

> The first thing that college is for is to teach you to think. That's a cliché, but it does actually mean something, and a great deal more than what is usually intended. It doesn't simply mean developing the mental skills particular to individual disciplines—how to solve and equation or construct a study or analyze at text—or even acquiring the ability to work across the disciplines. It means developing the habit of skepticism and the capacity to put it into practice. It means learning not to take things for granted, so you can reach your own conclusions.

This paragraph moves from the general to the specific. The topic sentence clearly states at the outset what the paragraph is about. The rest of the paragraph probes exactly what learning to think involves and provides concise illustrations of the central point.

Place a Topic Sentence near the Beginning. Sometimes the first sentence of a paragraph acts as a transition, linking what is to come with what has gone before. Then the *second* sentence might be the topic sentence, as illustrated in the following paragraph from *Tim Gunn's Fashion Bible: The Fascinating History of Everything in Your Closet* by Tim Gunn with Ada Calhoun (Gallery Books, 2012). The paragraph immediately before this one summarizes how early shoe designers often tried to balance competing desires for modesty, alluring beauty, and practicality. This prior paragraph begins, "Modesty got the better of the shoe industry in the seventeenth century," and concludes, "It wasn't until the late 1930s that sling-backs and open-toed heels gave us another glimpse at the toes and heels."

> Heel height has fluctuated ever since, as have platforms. One goal of a high shoe is to elevate the wearer out of the muck. Before there was pavement (asphalt didn't even appear until 1824, in Paris), streets were very muddy. People often wore one kind of shoe indoors, like a satin slipper, and another outside, perhaps with some kind of overshoe. One type of overshoe was called pattens, which were made of leather, wood, or iron, and lifted the wearer up a couple of inches or more from the sidewalk to protect the sole of the shoe from grime. Men and women wore these from the fourteenth to the mid-nineteenth century, when street conditions started to become slightly less disgusting.

End with a Topic Sentence. Occasionally a writer trying to persuade the reader to agree by first acknowledging counterarguments. Then, with a dramatic flourish, the writer *concludes* with the topic sentence, as author Donna Freitas does in her book *The Happiness Effect: How Social Media Is Driving a Generation to Appear Perfect at Any Cost* (2017).

There are many benefits to social media, primary among them (according to student participants in this research) the ability to connect with friends and loved ones who are far away. It is a basic tool for making real-life plans. Social media can allow us to be playful, expressive, poetic, flirty, and even silly. But it is clear that image-consciousness and professional concerns among young adults are eclipsing these benefits.

This paragraph starts by conceding the positives about social media. The last sentence, however, puts those benefits in perspective by focusing on the risks that come with them.

Imply a Topic Sentence. It is also possible to find a perfectly unified, well-organized paragraph that has no topic sentence at all, like the following from "New York" (*Esquire,* July 1960) by Gay Talese:

Each afternoon in New York a rather seedy saxophone player, his cheeks blown out like a spinnaker, stands on the sidewalk playing "Danny Boy" in such a sad, sensitive way that he soon has half the neighborhood peeking out of windows tossing nickels, dimes, and quarters at his feet. Some of the coins roll under parked cars, but most of them are caught in his outstretched hand. The saxophone player is a street musician named Joe Gabler; for the past thirty years he has serenaded every block in New York and has sometimes been tossed as much as $100 a day in coins. He is also hit with buckets of water, empty beer cans and eggs, and chased by wild dogs. He is believed to be the last of New York's ancient street musicians.

No one sentence neatly sums up the writer's idea. Like most effective paragraphs that do not state a topic sentence, this one contains something just as good—a *topic idea.* The author doesn't wander aimlessly. He knows exactly what he wants to achieve—a description of how the famous Joe Gabler plies his trade. Because Talese keeps this purpose firmly in mind, the main point—that Gabler meets both reward and abuse—is clear to the reader as well.

Learning by Doing 🎯 Shaping Topic Sentences

In a small group, answer these questions about each topic sentence below:

- Will it catch readers' attention? Is it accurate? Is it limited?
- How might you develop the idea in the rest of the paragraph?
- Can you improve it?

1. Television commercials stereotype people.
2. Living away from home for the first time is hard.
3. It's good for a child to have a pet.
4. A flea market is a good place to buy jewelry.
5. Pollution should be controlled.
6. Everybody should use public transportation.

Writing an Opening

Even writers with something to say may find it hard to begin. Often they are so intent on a brilliant opening that they freeze. They forget even the essentials — set up the topic, stick to what's relevant, and establish a thesis. If you feel like a deer paralyzed by headlights, try these ways of opening:

- Start with your thesis statement, with or without a full opening paragraph. Fill in the rest later.
- Write your thesis statement — the one you planned or one you'd now like to develop — in the middle of a page. Above it, concisely add the background a reader needs to see where you're going.
- Write a long beginning for your first draft; then cut it down to the most dramatic, exciting, or interesting essentials.
- Simply set down words — any words — on paper, without trying to write an arresting opening. Rewrite later.
- Write the first paragraph last, after you know where your essay goes.
- Move your conclusion to the beginning, and write a new ending.
- Write a summary for yourself and your readers.

Your opening should intrigue readers — engaging their minds and hearts, exciting their curiosity, drawing them into the world set forth in your writing. A striking example, surprising fact, or lively quotation are all compelling ways to introduce your point. Alternatively, your introduction can set the scene for your essay or prepare the reader for what will come.

Begin with a Story.   Often a simple anecdote can capture your readers' interest and thus serve as a good beginning. Here is how Dan Leeth opens his essay "Trails of Treasure" (*Encompass,* November/December 2013):

> It was my first ever hike. I was 9 years old when my father's friend, Scotty, invited us to join him on a trek into the Superstition Mountains, a rugged jumble of bluffs, buttes, crags, cliffs and canyons rising 35 miles east of Phoenix. Naturally, I wore my Roy Rogers cowboy boots. Six blisters later, I realized why Roy rode and seldom walked. Only Scotty's tales of treasure kept me going.

Most of us, after an anecdote, want to read on. What will the writer say next? How does the anecdote launch the essay? Leeth continues, explaining that the hike introduced him to the territory of the long-lost golden treasure trove known as the Lost Dutchman Mine.

Make an Observation.   Sometimes a writer starts with an observation and expands on it, bringing in vital details, as Greg Lukianoff and Jonathan Haidt do to open their article "The Coddling of the American Mind" (*Atlantic,* September 2015):

> Something strange is happening at America's colleges and universities. A movement is arising, undirected and driven largely by students, to scrub campuses clean of words, ideas, and subjects that might cause discomfort or give offense.

After announcing what they see, Lukianoff and Haidt continue by supplying a series of anecdotes from college campuses to support that viewpoint.

Ask a Question. An essay can begin with a question and answer, as James H. Austin begins "Four Kinds of Chance," in *Chase, Chance, and Creativity: The Lucky Art of Novelty* (Columbia UP, 1978):

> What is chance? Dictionaries define it as something fortuitous that happens unpredictably without discernible human intention. Chance is unintentional and capricious, but we needn't conclude that chance is immune from human intervention. Indeed, chance plays several distinct roles when humans react creatively with one another and with their environment.

Beginning to answer the question in the first paragraph leads readers to expect the rest of the essay to continue the answer.

End with the Thesis Statement. Opening paragraphs often end by stating the essay's main point. Here, after giving example upon example, sports writer Michael Mandelbaum ends with the question that will guide the rest of his book, *The Meaning of Sports* (2005):

For more on thesis statements, see pp. 266–71.

> Baseball, football, and basketball loom large in American life. The annual professional football championship game, the Super Bowl, regularly attracts the largest television audience of the year: As many as half of all Americans tune in to watch it. The attention that team sports command is not only broad, it is also intense. A Web site for loyal supporters of the perennially unsuccessful Chicago Cubs baseball team called CubsAnonymous offers a 12-step program for curing an addiction to the team. Why are these sports so important? Why do people invest so much of their time, money, and emotional energy in following them? Why do team sports mean so much to Americans, and what is it that they mean?

Learning by Doing 🖋 Trying Different Methods of Writing an Opening

Write (or rewrite) an introduction to a paper, using three methods of writing an opening. Select from the following list:

- Begin with a story.
- Make an observation.
- Ask a question.
- Offer a startling statistic or an unusual fact.

- Introduce a quotation or a bit of dialogue.
- Provide historical background.
- Define a key term or concept.
- State a problem, contradiction, or dilemma.
- Use a vivid example or image.
- Develop an analogy.

Which method do you think is most effective and engaging, and why? Swap introductions with a writing partner and ask your partner which introduction he or she thinks is most effective and why.

Writing a Conclusion

The final paragraphs of an essay linger longest for readers, as in E. B. White's "Once More to the Lake" from *One Man's Meat* (Tilbury House, 1941). White describes his return with his young son to a vacation spot he had loved as a child. As the essay ends in an unforgettable image, he realizes the inevitable passing of generations.

> When the others went swimming my son said he was going in, too. He pulled his dripping trunks from the line where they had hung all through the shower and wrung them out. Languidly, and with no thought of going in, I watched him, his hard little body, skinny and bare, saw him wince slightly as he pulled up around his vitals the small, soggy, icy garment. As he buckled the swollen belt, suddenly my groin felt the chill of death.

White's classic ending opens with a sentence that points back to the previous paragraph as it also looks ahead. Then White leads us quickly to his final, chilling insight. And then he stops.

It's easy to say what *not* to do at the end of an essay: don't leave your readers half expecting you to go on. Don't restate all you've just said. Don't introduce a brand-new topic that leads away from your point. And don't signal that the end is near with an obvious phrase like "As I have said." How *do* you write an ending, then? Try answering these questions:

- What restatement of your thesis would give readers satisfying closure?
- What provocative implications of your thesis might answer "What now?" or "What's the significance of what I've said?"
- What closing facts or statistics might confirm the merit of your point?
- What final anecdote, incident, or example might round out your ideas?
- What question has your essay answered?
- What assertion or claim might you want to restate?
- What summary might help a reader pull together what you've said?
- What would make a reader sorry to finish such a satisfying essay?

End with a Quotation. An apt quotation can neatly round out an essay, as literary critic Malcolm Cowley shows in *The View from Eighty* (Viking, 1980), his discussion of the pitfalls and compensations of old age.

> "Eighty years old!" the great Catholic poet Paul Claudel wrote in his journal. "No eyes left, no ears, no teeth, no legs, no wind! And when all is said and done, how astonishingly well one does without them!"

State or Restate Your Thesis. In a sharp criticism of American schools, humorist Russell Baker in "School vs. Education" ends by stating his main point, that schools do not educate.

> Afterward, the former student's destiny fulfilled, his life rich with Oriental carpets, rare porcelain, and full bank accounts, he may one day find himself with the leisure and the inclination to open a book with a curious mind, and start to become educated.

End with a Brief Emphatic Sentence. For an essay that traces causes or effects, evaluates, or argues, a pointed concluding thought can reinforce your main idea. Stick to academic language, but craft a concise, pointed sentence, maybe with a twist. Nathaniel Rich ends his review of Gary Rivlin's *Katrina: After the Flood* (*New York Times*, 5 August 2015) with a short, solemn sentence that invokes the sentiment of the previous sentence for additional impact:

> New Orleans has always been a place where utopian fantasies and dystopian realities mingle harmoniously. May New Orleans always remain so. Or at least may it always remain.

Stop When the Story Is Over. Even a quiet ending can be effective, as long as it signals clearly that the essay is finished. When *Smithsonian* (November 2013) featured articles on "101 Objects That Made America," space-age historian Andrew Chaikin prepared the selection on "Neil Armstrong's Spacesuit." His engaging account of the suit's model number, cost, construction, technical qualities, and wearability describes the essential features that protected Armstrong as he took his famous first step on the moon. Then Chaikin concludes his article with this succinct paragraph:

> "Its true beauty, however," said Armstrong, "was that it worked."

For more on punctuating quotations, see D3 (pp. Q-61–Q-62) in the Quick Editing Guide.

Learning by Doing 🎯 Evaluating Openings and Conclusions

Openings and conclusions frame an essay, contributing to the unity of the whole. The opening sets up the topic and main idea; the conclusion reaffirms the thesis and rounds off the ideas. Discuss the following with your classmates.

1. Here are two possible opening paragraphs from a student essay on the importance of teaching children how to swim.

   A. Humans inhabit a world made up of over 70 percent water. In addition to these great bodies of water, we have built millions of swimming pools for sports and leisure activities. At one time or another most people will be faced with either the danger of drowning or the challenge of aquatic recreation. For these reasons, it is essential that we learn to swim. Being a competitive swimmer and a swimming instructor, I fully realize the importance of knowing how to swim.

   B. Four-year-old Carl, curious like most children, last spring ventured out onto his pool patio. He fell into the pool and, not knowing how to swim, helplessly sank to the bottom. Minutes later his uncle found the child and brought him to the surface. Because Carl had no pulse, his uncle administered CPR until the paramedics arrived. Eventually the child was revived. During his stay in the hospital, his mother signed him up for beginning swimming classes. Carl was a lucky one. Unlike thousands of other children and adults, he got a second chance.

   ■ Which introduction is more effective? Why?

   ■ What would the body of this essay consist of? What kinds of evidence would be included?

   ■ Write a suitable conclusion for this essay.

Adding Cues and Connections

Effective writing proceeds in a sensible order, each sentence following naturally from the one before it. Yet even well-organized prose can be hard to read unless it is *coherent* and smoothly integrates its elements. Readers need cues and connections — devices to tie together words in a sentence, sentences in a paragraph, paragraphs in an essay.

Add Transitional Words and Sentences. Transitions are words and phrases that indicate connections between or within sentences and paragraphs. You use transitions every day as cues or signals to help others follow your train of thought. For example, you might say to a friend, "Well, *on the one hand,* a second job would help me save money for tuition. *On the other hand,* I'd have less time to study." But some writers rush through, omitting links between thoughts or mistakenly assuming that connections they see will automatically be clear to readers. Often just a word, phrase, or sentence of transition inserted in the right place transforms a disconnected passage into a coherent one. In the chart on the next page, *transitional markers* are grouped by purpose or the kind of relation or connection they establish.

Occasionally a whole sentence serves as a transition. The opening of one paragraph may hark back to the last one while revealing a new or narrower direction. The next excerpt is from "Preservation Basics: Why Preserve Film?" a Web page of the National Film Preservation Foundation (NFPF) at film-preservation.org. The first paragraph introduces the organization's mission;

the next opens with a transitional sentence (italics ours) that introduces major challenges to that mission.

> Movies have documented America for more than one hundred years. Since Thomas Edison introduced the movie camera in 1893, amateur and professional filmmakers have used motion pictures to tell stories, record communities, explain the work of business and government, and illustrate current events. They captured, with the immediacy unique to the moving image, how generations of Americans have lived, worked, and dreamed. By preserving these films, we save a century of history.
>
> *Unfortunately, movies are not made to last.* Created on perishable plastic, film decays within years if not properly stored. Already the losses are high. . . .

The first paragraph establishes the value of *preserving* the American film legacy. The next paragraph uses key words related to preservation and its absence (*perishable, decays, losses, lost*) to clarify that what follows builds on what has gone before. The paragraph opens with a short, dramatic transition to one of

Common Transitions	
TO MARK TIME	then, soon, first, second, next, recently, the following day, in a little while, meanwhile, after, later, in the past, finally
TO MARK PLACE OR DIRECTION	in the distance, close by, near, far away, above, below, to the right, on the other side, opposite, to the west, next door
TO SUMMARIZE OR RESTATE	in other words, to put it another way, in brief, in simpler terms, on the whole, in fact, in a word, to sum up, in short, in conclusion, to conclude, therefore
TO RELATE CAUSE AND EFFECT	therefore, accordingly, hence, thus, for, so, consequently, as a result, because of, due to, eventually, inevitably
TO ADD, AMPLIFY, OR LIST	and, also, too, besides, as well, moreover, in addition, furthermore, in effect, second, in the second place, again, next
TO COMPARE	similarly, likewise, in like manner, in the same way
TO CONCEDE	whereas, on the other hand, with that in mind, still, and yet, even so, in spite of, despite, at least, of course, no doubt, even though
TO CONTRAST	on the other hand, but, or, however, unlike, nevertheless, on the contrary, conversely, in contrast, instead, counter to
TO INDICATE PURPOSE	to this end, for this purpose, with this aim
TO EXPRESS CONDITION	although, though
TO GIVE EXAMPLES OR SPECIFY	for example, for instance, in this case, in particular, to illustrate
TO QUALIFY	for the most part, by and large, with few exceptions, mainly, in most cases, generally, some, sometimes, typically, frequently, rarely
TO EMPHASIZE	it is true, truly, indeed, of course, to be sure, obviously, without doubt, evidently, clearly, understandably

the major problems — time and existing loss — and continues by giving specific information about those losses.

Supply Transition Paragraphs. Transitions may be even longer than sentences. In a long and complicated essay, moving clearly from one idea to the next will sometimes require a short paragraph of transition. In the example below, a short transition paragraph connects an earlier section on the effects of extreme long-distance driving and the subsequent section on its causes.

> So far, the physical and psychological effects of driving nonstop for hundreds of miles seem clear. The next consideration is why drivers do this. What causes people to become addicted to their steering wheels?

You can use a transition paragraph when you sense that your readers might get lost if you don't patiently lead them by the hand. A transition paragraph also can help you move between one branch of argument and your main trunk or between a digression and your main direction.

Repeat Selectively. Another way to clarify the relationship between two sentences, paragraphs, or ideas is to repeat a key word or phrase. Such purposeful repetition almost guarantees that readers will understand how all the parts of a passage fit together. Note the word *anger* in the following paragraph (italics ours) from *Of Woman Born* (Norton, 1976), poet Adrienne Rich's exploration of her relationship with her mother.

> And I know there must be deep reservoirs of *anger* in her; every mother has known overwhelming, unacceptable *anger* at her children. When I think of the conditions under which my mother became a mother, the impossible expectations, my father's distaste for pregnant women, his hatred of all that he could not control, my *anger* at her dissolves into grief and *anger* for her, and then dissolves back again into *anger* at her: the ancient, unpurged *anger* of the child.

Strengthen Pronouns. Because they always refer back to nouns or other pronouns, pronouns serve as transitions by making readers refer back as well. Note how certain pronouns (in italics) hold together the following paragraph from "Misunderstood Michelle" by columnist Ellen Goodman in *At Large* (Summit Books, 1981):

> I have two friends who moved in together many years ago. *He* looked upon this step as a trial marriage. *She* looked upon it as, well, moving in together. *He* was sure that in a matter of time, after *they* had built up trust and confidence, *she* would agree that marriage was the next logical step. *She,* on the other hand, was thrilled that here at last was a man *who* would never push *her* back to the altar.

The paragraph uses other transitions, too: time markers (*many years ago, in a matter of time, after*), *on the other hand* to show a contrast, and repetition of words related to marriage (*trial marriage, marriage, the altar*). All serve the main purpose of transitions — keeping readers on track.

Strategies for Developing

18

How can you spice up your general ideas with the stuff of real life? How can you tug your readers deeper and deeper into your essays until they say, "I see just what you mean"? Well-developed essays have such power because they back up general points with evidence that comes alive for readers. This chapter covers eight indispensable methods of development—giving examples, providing details, defining, reasoning inductively and deductively, analyzing a process, dividing and classifying, comparing and contrasting, and identifying causes and effects. A strong essay almost always requires a combination of these strategies.

Whenever you draft or revise a piece of writing, you face a challenge of deciding how to develop your points. The answers to such questions are individual, depending on your writing situation, the clarity of your main idea or thesis, and the state of your draft.

For lists of essays using various methods of development, turn to the Rhetorical Contents on p. xxiv.

DEVELOPING YOUR IDEAS

Purpose

☐ Does your assignment recommend specific methods of development?

☐ Which methods might work best for explaining, informing, or persuading?

☐ What type of development might best achieve your specific purpose?

Audience

☐ Which strategies would best clarify your topic for readers?

☐ Which would best demonstrate your thesis to your readers?

☐ What kinds of evidence will your specific readers prefer? Which strategies might develop this evidence most effectively?

☐ Where might your readers have trouble following or understanding without more or better development?

Thesis

☐ What development does your thesis promise or imply that you will supply?

☐ What sequence of development strategies would best support your thesis?

Paragraph Development

☐ Should any paragraphs with one or two sentences be developed more fully?

☐ Should any long paragraphs with generalizations, repetition, and wordy phrasing be developed differently so that they are richer and deeper?

Giving Examples

An example—the word comes from the Latin *exemplum,* "one thing chosen from among many"—is a typical instance that illustrates a whole type or kind. Giving examples to support a generalization is probably the most often used means of development. This example, from *In Search of Excellence* (Harper and Row, 1982) by Thomas J. Peters and Robert H. Waterman Jr., explains the success of America's top corporations:

> Although he's not a company, our favorite illustration of closeness to the customer is car salesman Joe Girard. He sold more new cars and trucks, each year, for eleven years running, than any other human being. In fact, in a typical year, Joe sold more than twice as many units as who-ever was in second place. In explaining his secret of success, Joe said: "I sent out over thirteen thousand [thank-you] cards every month."
>
> Why start with Joe? Because his magic is the magic of IBM and many of the rest of the excellent companies. It is simply service, overpowering service, especially after-sales service. . . .

Notice how Peters and Waterman focus on a single example, Joe Girard. They don't write *corporation employees* or even *car salespeople.* Instead, they zero in on one particular man to make the point come alive.

Joe Girard	Level 4: Specific Example
car salespeople	Level 3: Even More Specific Group
corporation employees	Level 2: More Specific Group
America's top corporations	Level 1: General Group or Category

A ladder of abstraction moves from general to specific.

This ladder of abstraction moves from the general—America's top corporations—to a specific person—Joe Girard. The specific example of Joe Girard makes good customer service *concrete* to readers: he is someone readers can relate to. To check the level of specificity in a paragraph or even a broad essay topic, draw a ladder of abstraction for it. If you haven't climbed to the fourth or fifth level, you are probably too general and need to add specifics.

An example doesn't have to be a specific individual. Sometimes you can create a picture of something unfamiliar or give an abstraction a personality. In this paragraph from *Beyond Addiction: How Science and Kindness Help People Change* (Scribner, 2014), the authors clarify the effects of drug abuse on the brain, after referring to the fried-egg image from the old "This is your brain on drugs" advertisements:

> Our colleague John Mariani, M.D., an addiction psychiatrist, teacher, clinician, and researcher at Columbia University, suggests we think of a broken leg instead of a fried egg. A bone breaks, and with help—a cast and crutches to prevent reinjury while the person returns to a normal routine, physical therapy to regain strength and flexibility, and family and friends to help and to keep up morale—the bone heals and the person can work, play, run, and jump again. The leg may be more vulnerable to breaking after all that, and the person will need to take care to protect it, but the person can adapt and, for the most part, the body heals. The brain is no exception. Given help and time, therapy and sometimes medication, concerted effort, and measures to safeguard against returning to substance use, brains do heal from the effects of drugs—perhaps not without a trace, but with enough resilience to justify optimism.

An example isn't a trivial doodad you add to a paragraph for decoration; it is what holds your readers' attention and makes an idea concrete and tangible. To give plenty of examples is one of the writer's chief tasks, and you can generate more at any point in the writing process. Begin with your experience, even with an unfamiliar topic, or try conversing with others, reading, digging in the library, or browsing on the Web.

For ways to generate ideas, see Ch. 15.

Learning by Doing 🖉 Giving Examples

To help you get in the habit of thinking specifically, fill in a ladder of abstraction for five of the following general subjects. Then share your ladders with classmates, and compare and contrast your specifics with theirs.

Examples:

animals	foods	sports
art	movies	television
college courses	music	vacations

Providing Details

A *detail* is any specific, concrete piece of information—a fact, a bit of the historical record, your own observation. Details make scenes and images more realistic and vivid for readers. They also back up generalizations, convincing readers that the writer can make broad assertions with authority.

Mary Harris "Mother" Jones told the story of her life as a labor organizer in *The Autobiography of Mother Jones* (1925). She lends conviction to her generalization about a nineteenth-century coal miner's lot with ample evidence from her own experience and observations.

> Mining at its best is wretched work, and the life and surroundings of the miner are hard and ugly. His work is down in the black depths of the earth. He works alone in a drift. There can be little friendly companionship as there is in the factory; as there is among men who build bridges and houses, working together in groups. The work is dirty. Coal dust grinds itself into the skin, never to be removed. The miner must stoop as he works in the drift. He becomes bent like a gnome.
>
> His work is utterly fatiguing. Muscles and bones ache. His lungs breathe coal dust and the strange, damp air of places that are never filled with sunlight. His house is a poor makeshift and there is little to encourage him to make it attractive. The company owns the ground it stands on, and the miner feels the precariousness of his hold. Around his house is mud and slush. Great mounds of culm [the refuse left after coal is screened], black and sullen, surround him. His children are perpetually grimy from playing on the culm mounds. The wife struggles with dirt, with inadequate water supply, with small wages, with overcrowded shacks.

Although Mother Jones, not a learned writer, relies on short, simple sentences, her writing is clear and powerful because of the specific details she uses. Her opening states two generalizations: (1) "Mining . . . is wretched work," and (2) the miner's "life and surroundings" are "hard and ugly." She supports these with a barrage of factual evidence and detail, including well-chosen verbs: "Coal dust *grinds* itself into the skin." The result is a moving, convincingly detailed portrait of the miner and his family.

Quite different from such personal, descriptive details are the comparative statistics in *Families and Faith: How Religion Is Passed Down across Generations* by Vern L. Bengtson, with Norella M. Putney and Susan Harris (Oxford University Press, 2013). Bengtson sums up societal changes during his ongoing research project, begun over thirty-five years ago and surveying grandparents, parents, participants, and now their offspring.

> Since World War II, there has been unprecedented change at the most intimate level of American society: family life. The rate of divorce increased slowly through the first half of the twentieth century and then rose dramatically over the next few decades. By 1990, one out of every two marriages ended in divorce, and by the end of the century, almost as many children lived in single-parent households —most headed by mothers—as in dual-parent households. Of those children in two-parent households, one-quarter lived in "blended" families with stepparents and stepsiblings.

Providing details is a simple yet effective way to develop ideas. All it takes is close attention and precise wording to communicate details to readers. What would they see, hear, smell, or feel on the scene? What fact or statistic would have impact on the reader? Effective details must have a specific purpose: to make your images more evocative or your point more convincing as they support—in some way—your main idea.

Learning by Doing 🎯 Providing Details

With classmates or alone, brainstorm specific details on one of the following topics. Include details that appeal to all five senses and write a paragraph or two using them. Begin by stating a main idea that conveys an engaging impression of your topic (not "My grandmother's house was in Topeka, Kansas" but "My grandmother's house was my childhood haven").

For more on brainstorming, see pp. 257–59.

a childhood memory	a memorable event	a challenging game
the things in my room	a TV or movie star	the cafeteria
my favorite restaurant	a good friend	a favorite song

Defining

Define means "to set bounds to." You define a thing, word, or concept by describing it to distinguish it from all similar things. If people don't agree on the meaning of a word or an idea, they can't share knowledge about it. Scientists take special care to define their terms precisely. "Climate Engineering," a State of the Science Fact Sheet from the National Oceanic and Atmospheric Administration, opens with a definition:

> Climate engineering, also called geoengineering, refers to deliberate, large-scale manipulation of Earth's climate intended to counteract human-caused climate change.

After outlining why this topic needs study, the fact sheet identifies its two main subdivisions:

> Two different climate engineering approaches are commonly considered:
>
> - Removing some CO_2 from the atmosphere to reduce its greenhouse gas effect
> - Increasing the reflection of sunlight away from Earth back to space, thus cooling the planet

If you use a word in a special sense or invent a word, you have to explain it or your readers will be lost. In a 2017 *Fast Company* article about workplace culture, reporter Lydia Dishman explores one common reason workers say they would quit a job immediately: an unsafe, offensive, or intimidating company culture. In describing what contributes to such a problematic work environment, Dishman then introduces and defines a term.

> One of the factors that can breed such negative working conditions is microaggressions. The term "microaggression" has been used in

academic circles since the 1970s to describe small casual verbal and behavioral indignities against people of color, but has entered more popular use in the last few years to encompass intentional and unintentional slights against any socially marginalized group.

You might define an unfamiliar word to save readers a trip to the dictionary or a familiar but often misunderstood concept — such as *guerrilla, liberal,* or *minimum wage* — to clarify the meaning you intend. The more complex or ambiguous the idea, thing, movement, phenomenon, or organization, the longer the definition you will need to clarify the term for your readers.

Learning by Doing 🎯 Developing an Extended Definition

Write an extended definition (a paragraph or so) of a word listed below. Begin with a one-sentence definition of the word. Then, instead of turning to a dictionary, expand and clarify your ideas using strategies in this chapter — examples, details, induction or deduction, analysis, division, classification, comparison, contrast. You may also use *negation* (explaining what something is by stating what it is not). Share your definition with classmates.

dieting	intelligence/ignorance	plagiarism	success
fear	love	privacy	sustainability
gender	peace	racism	war

Reasoning Inductively and Deductively

For more on the statement-support pattern, see A2 (pp. Q-22–Q-24) in the Quick Research Guide.

Most paragraphs rely on both generalizations and particulars. A *generalization* is a broad statement that establishes a point, viewpoint, or conclusion. A *particular* is an instance, a detail, or an example — specific evidence that a general statement is reasonable. Your particulars support your generalizations; compelling instances, details, and examples back up your broader point. Likewise, your generalizations pull together your particulars, identifying patterns or connections that relate individual cases.

For more on induction and deduction, see Ch. 8.

To link particulars and generalizations, you can use an inductive or a deductive process. An *inductive process* begins with the particulars — a convincing number of instances, examples, tests, or experiments that, together, substantiate a larger generalization. Long-term studies of weight loss that point to the benefits of walking, eating vegetables, or some other variable are inductive. Less formally, inductive reasoning is common as people *infer* or draw a conclusion about a particular situation. If your sister ate strawberries three times and got a rash each time, she might infer that she is allergic to them. A *deductive process* begins with a generalization and applies it to another set of particulars. When your sister says no to a piece of strawberry pie, she does so because she has *deduced* that it, too, will trigger a rash.

Once you have reached your conclusions — either by using particulars to support generalizations or by applying reliable generalizations to other particulars — you need to decide how to present your reasoning to readers. Do you want them to follow your process, perhaps examining many cases before reaching a conclusion about them? Or do you want them to learn your conclusion first and then review the evidence? Because academic audiences tend to expect conclusions first, many writers begin essays with thesis statements and paragraphs with topic sentences. On the other hand, if your readers are likely to reject an unexpected thesis initially, you may need to show them the evidence first and then lead them gently to your point.

In "Disaster Planning for Libraries: Lessons from California State University, Northridge," librarian Mary M. Finley opened her presentation at the Eighth Annual Federal Depository Library Conference with a broad generalization and then supported it with specifics from her campus:

> In Northridge we learned that a university with facilities for over 25,000 students can be changed in less than thirty seconds into a university with no usable buildings, no electrical power, no water, and no telephone service. California State University, Northridge (CSUN) is about a mile from the epicenter of the Northridge Earthquake of January 17, 1994, and the damage total for the campus stands at over 400 million dollars. The earthquake happened at 4:31 A.M. on a holiday during semester break, so only a few people were in university buildings during the quake. Fortunately, no one was seriously injured on campus. All of the buildings on campus were damaged, some beyond repair.

Finley's thesis statement presents her conclusion about the effects of the earthquake, and the rest of her paragraph supports that thesis with details and examples.

When using reasoning, make sure your particulars are numerous and substantial enough to support your generalization, and that your generalization follows logically from those particulars. Ask yourself if readers will be able to follow your reasoning clearly.

Analyzing a Process

When you *analyze,* you look closely at your subject's parts and examine them one at a time. If you have taken any chemistry, you probably analyzed water: you separated it into hydrogen and oxygen, its two elements. You've heard many a commentator or blogger analyze the news, telling us what made up an event — who participated, where it occurred, what happened. Analysis helps readers grasp something complex: they can more readily take it in as a series of bites rather than in one gulp.

One type of analysis is analyzing a process — telling step-by-step how something is, was, or could be done. You can analyze an action or a phenomenon — how a skyscraper is built, how a revolution begins, how sunspots form. You can also explain large, long-ago events or complex technical processes.

The *directive,* or "how-to," process analysis tells readers how to do something (how to box, invest for retirement, clean a painting) or how to make something (how to draw a map, blaze a trail, fix chili). Especially on Web sites, directions may consist of simple step-by-step lists with quick advice. In essays and articles, the basics may be supplemented with advice, encouragement, or relevant experience. In "How to Catch More Trout" (*Outdoor Life,* May 2006), Joe Brooks identifies the first stage of trout fishing:

> The first thing you should do is stand by the pool and study it awhile before you fish. Locate the trout that are rising consistently. Choose one (the lowest in the pool, preferably), and work on him. If you rush right in and start casting, you'll probably put down several fish that you haven't seen. And you can scare still more fish by false-casting all over the place. A dozen fish you might have caught with a more careful approach may see the line and go down before you even drop the fly on the surface.

He continues with stages and advice until he reaches the last step, landing the fish. Brooks skillfully addresses his audience; as readers of *Outdoor Life,* they are people who probably already know how to fish and hunt. As his title indicates, Brooks isn't explaining how to catch trout but how to catch *more* trout. For this reason, he skips topics for beginners (such as how to cast) and instead urges readers to try more sophisticated tactics to increase their catch.

Process analysis can also turn to humor, as in this paragraph from "How to Heal a Broken Heart (in One Day)" by student Lindsey Schendel.

> To begin your first day of mourning, you will wake up at 11 A.M., thus banishing any feelings of fatigue. Forget eating a healthy breakfast; toast two waffles, and plaster them with chocolate syrup instead of maple. Then make sure you have a room of serenity so you may cry in peace. It is important that you go through the necessary phases of denial and depression. Call up a friend or family member while you are still in your serious, somber mood. Explain to that person the hardships you are facing and how you don't know if you can go on. Immediately afterwards, turn on any empowering music, get up, and dance.

For more on transitions, see pp. 290–92.

Like more serious process directions, this paragraph includes steps or stages (sleeping late, eating breakfast, crying and calling, getting up and dancing) arranged in chronological order with transitions marking the movement from one to the other (*To begin, then, while, immediately afterwards*).

Process analyses are wonderful ways to show readers the inside workings of events or systems, but they can be difficult to follow. Start by making sure you understand the process thoroughly. Divide it into logical steps or stages, and put the steps in chronological order. Add details or examples wherever your description might be ambiguous; use transitions to mark the end of one step and the beginning of the next.

Learning by Doing 🎯 Analyzing a Process

Analyze one of the following processes or procedures in a paragraph or short essay. Then share your process analysis with classmates. Can they follow your analysis easily? Do they spot anything you left out?

administering CPR   job hunting

bathing a pet   making a smoothie

buying a car   planning a party

Dividing and Classifying

To divide is to break something down, identifying or analyzing its components. The thing divided may be as concrete as a medical center (which you might divide into specialty units) or as abstract as knowledge of art (which you might divide into sculpture, painting, drawing, and other forms). To classify is to make sense of a potentially bewildering array of things — works of literature, this year's movies — by sorting them into categories (*types* or *classes*) that you can deal with one at a time. Literature is customarily arranged by genre — novels, stories, poems, plays. Movies might be sorted by audience (children, teenagers, mature adults). Dividing and classifying are like two sides of the same coin. In theory, any broad subject can be *divided* into components, which can then be *classified* into categories. In practice, it's often difficult to tell where division stops and classification begins.

In the following paragraph from *David and Goliath: Underdogs, Misfits, and the Art of Battling Giants* (Little, Brown, 2013), Malcolm Gladwell uses division to simplify for modern readers what might be an unfamiliar subject: the types of warriors deployed in ancient battles.

> Ancient armies had three kinds of warriors. The first was cavalry — armed men on horseback or in chariots. The second was infantry — foot soldiers wearing armor and carrying swords and shields. The third were projectile warriors, or what today would be called artillery: archers and, most important, slingers. Slingers had a leather pouch attached on two sides by a long strand of rope. They would put a rock or lead ball into the pouch, swing it around in increasingly wider and faster circles, and then release one end of the rope, hurling the rock forward.

Gladwell's intent, however, is less to enlighten readers about historical warfare than, as the book's subtitle suggests, to help them think differently about contemporary contests by considering the advantages of disadvantages. After he classifies Goliath as "heavy infantry" and David as "a slinger, and slingers beat infantry, hands down," readers are equipped to interpret their ancient Biblical contest differently.

Classification also helps to identify patterns and relationships that might otherwise be missed. In "How Wonder Works" (Aeon, 21 June 2013), Jessie

Prinz explores the nature of wonder, "humanity's most important emotion," fed and unified by science, religion, and art. To do so, he classifies various human reactions to novelty, spectacle, and all sorts of natural and creative works — in short, responses that identify and express wonder.

> These bodily symptoms point to three dimensions that might in fact be essential components of wonder. The first is sensory: wondrous things engage our senses — we stare and widen our eyes. The second is cognitive: such things are perplexing because we cannot rely on past experience to comprehend them. This leads to a suspension of breath, akin to the freezing response that kicks in when we are startled: we gasp and say "Wow!" Finally, wonder has a dimension that can be described as spiritual: we look upwards in veneration; hence Smith's invocation of the swelling heart.

When you divide and classify, your goal is to make order out of a complex or overwhelming jumble. Make sure the components and categories you identify are sensible, and follow the same principle of classification or division for all categories. Group apples with apples, not with oranges, so that all the components or categories are roughly equivalent. For example, if you're classifying television shows and you've come up with *reality shows, dramas, talk shows, children's shows, news,* and *cartoons,* then you've got a problem: the last category is probably part of *children's shows.*

Comparing and Contrasting

For sample essays and advice on writing a comparison-and-contrast essay, see Ch. 6.

Set a pair of subjects side by side to compare and contrast them. When you compare, you point out similarities; when you contrast, you discuss differences. You can use two basic methods of organization for comparison and contrast — the opposing pattern, which addresses everything about one subject first, and then turns to the second subject; and the alternating pattern, which looks at a single point within both subjects. The example below illustrates a comparison and contrast of two colleges.

SUBJECT BY SUBJECT

Subject A: Big State University
    Point 1: Academics
    Point 2: Campus Life
    Point 3: Cost
Subject B: Township Community College
    Point 1: Academics
    Point 2: Campus Life
    Point 3: Cost

POINT BY POINT

Point 1: Academics
    Subject A: Big State U.
    Subject B: Township Community College
Point 2: Campus Life
    Subject A: Big State U.
    Subject B: Township CC
Point 3: Cost
    Subject A: Big State U.
    Subject B: Township CC

Generally we compare and contrast for a reason, such as to evaluate two products or to make a decision about which solution is more promising.

The next selection comes from a government Web site on childhood obesity. To answer "How did we get here?" this passage begins with the point-by-point pattern, first contrasting lifestyles (in alternating paragraphs) for children three decades ago and children today.

> Thirty years ago, most people led lives that kept them at a healthy weight. Kids walked to and from school every day, ran around at recess, participated in gym class, and played for hours after school before dinner. Meals were home-cooked with reasonable portion sizes and there was always a vegetable on the plate. Eating fast food was rare and snacking between meals was an occasional treat.
>
> Today, children experience a very different lifestyle. Walks to and from school have been replaced by car and bus rides. Gym class and after-school sports have been cut; afternoons are now spent with TV, video games, and the Internet. Parents are busier than ever and families eat fewer home-cooked meals. Snacking between meals is now commonplace.

The article continues by looking at snacks, portion sizes, and total caloric intake, alternating each point within its own paragraph.

Use comparison and contrast to support your thesis, and be sure to focus on major similarities and differences. As with classification, compare and contrast like items, and treat both subjects fairly.

Learning by Doing 🎯 Comparing and Contrasting

Write a paragraph or two in which you compare and contrast the subjects in one of the following pairs. Exchange drafts with classmates for response, using the following questions as a guide: Does the paragraph address the major similarities and/or differences between the subjects? Are the points of comparison and supporting details informative? Are the two subjects being treated fairly?

> cash versus credit
> childhood versus adulthood
> living in an apartment (or dorm) and living in a house
> big city life versus country life
> *Wonder Woman* versus *Black Panther*
> two classes you are taking

Identifying Causes and Effects

From the time we are children, we ask why. Why can't I go out and play? Why is the sky blue? Why did my goldfish die? Seeking causes and effects continues into adulthood, so it's a common method of development. To explain causal relationships successfully, think about the subject critically, gather evidence, draw judicious conclusions, and clarify relationships.

For sample essays and advice on writing a cause-and-effect essay, see Ch. 7.

In the following passage from "On the Origin of Celebrity" (*Nautilus*, Issue 5), Professor Robert Sapolsky brings his background in biology and neurology to his topic.

> We all feel the magnetic pull of celebrities—we track them, know their net worth, their tastes in furniture, the absurd names of their pets and children. We go under the knives of cosmetic surgeons to look like them. We feel personal connections with them, are let down by their moral failings, care about their tragedies....
>
> Why the obsession? Because we're primates with vested interests in tracking social hierarchies and patterns of social affiliation. And celebrities provide our primate minds with stimulating gyrations of hierarchy and affiliation (who is sleeping with, feuding with, out-earning whom). Celebrities also reflect the peculiar distance we have traveled culturally since our hominid past, and reveal how distorted our minds can become in our virtual world. We obsess over celebrities because, for better or worse, we feel a deep personal sense of connection with people who aren't real.

Instead of focusing on causes *or* effects, often writers trace a *chain* of cause-and-effect relationships. Looking holistically at the ripple effect or subsequent links between causes and effects is particularly useful for analyzing complex or long-term situations, such as climate change or the political instability of a nation.

When you identify cause-and-effect relationships in your writing, be sure to support your assertions with persuasive evidence. Don't rely on conjecture. Draw conclusions judiciously, avoiding faulty thinking and logical fallacies.

Learning by Doing 🖳 Identifying Causes and Effects

For more on faulty thinking and logical fallacies, see p. 145.

Identify some of the causes and effects of one of the following, doing a little research as needed. How might you use the chain of causes and effects in an essay? Discuss your findings with your classmates.

the Supreme Court decision to legalize gay marriage
peer-to-peer businesses in the sharing economy (for example, Uber or Airbnb)
the #metoo movement against sexual harassment and assault
rising sea levels
increasing rates of ADHD diagnoses among children
concussions among football players

Strategies for Revising and Editing

19

ood writing is rewriting. In this chapter we provide strategies for revising and editing—ways to rethink muddy ideas and emphasize important ones, to rephrase obscure passages and restructure garbled sentences. Our advice applies not only to rewriting whole essays but also to rewriting, editing, and proofreading sentences and paragraphs.

Re-viewing and Revising

Revision means "seeing again"—discovering again, conceiving again, shaping again. It may occur at any and all stages of the writing process, as a writer's thinking evolves and develops based on things she reads, hears, sees, or considers. Revision happens on two levels: *macro revising* is making large, global, or fundamental changes that affect the overall direction or impact of writing —its purpose, organization, or audience; *micro revising* involves paying attention to sentences, words, punctuation, and grammar—including ways to create emphasis and eliminate wordiness.

MACRO REVISING	MICRO REVISING
• **PURPOSE:** Have you refined what you want to accomplish?	• **EMPHASIS:** Can you position your ideas more effectively?
• **THESIS:** Could you state your main point more accurately?	• **CONCISENESS:** Can you spot extra words that you might cut?
• **AUDIENCE:** Should you address your readers differently?	• **CLARITY:** Can you make any sentences and words clearer?
• **STRUCTURE:** Should you reorganize any part of your writing?	
• **SUPPORT:** Do you need to add, drop, or rework your support?	

Macro and Micro Revising

Revising for Purpose and Thesis

For more on stating and improving a working thesis, see pp. 268–69.

When you revise for purpose, you make sure that your writing accomplishes what you want it to do — to persuade your readers to take a certain course of action, to inform readers about an issue, to reflect on an experience. As your project develops, your purpose may evolve, too. To revise for purpose, try to step back and see your writing as other readers will. Concentrate on what's actually in your paper, not what you planned to write. Does anything need to be recast to reflect your current thinking? Look closely at how accurately your thesis represents your main idea. If your idea has deepened, your topic become more complex, or your essay developed along new lines, refine or expand your thesis accordingly.

WORKING THESIS	The *Herald*'s coverage of the Senate elections was more thorough than the *Courier*'s.
REVISED THESIS	The *Herald*'s coverage of the Senate elections was less timely but more thorough and more impartial than the *Courier*'s.
WORKING THESIS	As the roles of men and women have changed in our society, old-fashioned formal courtesy has declined.
REVISED THESIS	As the roles of men and women have changed in our society, old-fashioned formal courtesy has declined not only toward women but also toward men.

REVISING FOR YOUR THESIS

☐ Do you know exactly what you want your essay to accomplish? Is your thesis stated in concise yet detailed language?

☐ Is your thesis stated outright in the essay? If not, have you provided clues so that your readers will know precisely what it is?

☐ Is your thesis focused on only one main idea? Is it limited to a demonstrable or arguable statement?

Revising for Audience

What works with one audience can fall flat with another. Your organization, selection of details, word choice, and tone all affect your particular readers. Visualize one of them poring over the essay, reacting to what you have written. What expressions do you see on that reader's face? Where does he or she have trouble understanding? Where have you hit the mark?

REVISING FOR YOUR AUDIENCE

☐ Does the opening of the essay mislead your readers by promising something that the essay never delivers?

☐ Are there places where readers might get bored? Can you shorten, delete, or liven up such passages?

☐ Have you anticipated questions your audience might ask?

☐ Where might readers raise objections? How might you answer them?

☐ Have you used any specialized or technical language that your readers might not understand? If so, have you worked in brief definitions?

☐ What is your attitude toward your audience? Are you chummy, angry, superior, apologetic, preachy? Should you revise to improve your attitude?

Revising for Structure and Support

When you revise for structure and support, you make sure that the order of your ideas, your selection of supporting material, and its arrangement are as effective as possible. You may have all the ingredients of a successful essay — but they may be a confusing mess.

In a well-structured essay, each paragraph, sentence, and phrase serves a clear function. Are your opening and closing paragraphs relevant, concise, and interesting? Is everything in each paragraph on the same topic? Are all ideas adequately developed? Are the paragraphs arranged in the best possible order? Finally, do you lead readers from one idea to the next with clear and painless transitions?

For more on paragraphs, topic sentences, and transitions, see Ch. 17.

An outline can help you discover what you've succeeded in getting on paper. Find the topic sentence of each paragraph in your draft, and list them in order. Label the sentences *I.*, *II.*, *A.*, *B.*, and so on, to show the logical relationships of ideas. Do the same with the supporting details under each topic sentence, labeling them also with letters and numbers and indenting appropriately. Now look at the outline. Does it make sense on its own, without the essay to explain it? Would a different order or arrangement be more effective? Do any sections look thin and need more evidence? Are the connections between parts on paper, not just in your head? Maybe too many ideas are jammed into too few paragraphs. Maybe you need more specific details and examples — or stronger ones. Strengthen the outline and then rewrite to follow it.

For more on using outlining for planning, see pp. 273–80.

REVISING FOR STRUCTURE AND SUPPORT

☐ Does your introduction set up the whole essay? Does it both grab readers' attention and hint at what is to follow?

☐ Is the main idea of each paragraph clear? Is it stated in a topic sentence?

☐ Is the main idea of each paragraph fully developed? Where might you need more or better evidence? Should you omit or move any stray bits?

☐ Is each detail or piece of evidence relevant to the topic sentence of the paragraph and the main point of the essay?

☐ Would any paragraphs make more sense in a different order?

☐ Does everything follow clearly? Does one point smoothly lead to the next? Would transitions help make the connections clearer?

☐ Does the conclusion follow logically or does it seem tacked on?

Learning by Doing Tackling Macro Revision

Select a draft that would benefit from revision. Then, based on your sense of its greatest need, choose one of the revision checklists above to guide a first revision. Let the draft sit for a while. Then work with one of the remaining checklists.

Working with a Peer Editor

There's no substitute for having someone else read your draft. Whether you are writing for your instructor, for the town council, or for readers of *Time,* having a classmate go over your essay is a worthwhile revision strategy. To gain all you can as a writer from a peer review, you need to play an active part:

- Ask your reader questions. (See page 309 for ideas.) Or bring a "Dear Editor" letter or memo, written ahead, to your meeting.
- Be open to new ideas — for focus, organization, or details.
- Use what's helpful, but trust yourself as the writer.

Be a helpful peer editor: offer honest, intelligent feedback, not judgment.

See specific checklists in the Revising and Editing sections in Chs. 4–12.

- Look at the big picture: purpose, focus, thesis, clarity, coherence, organization, support.
- When you spot strengths or weaknesses, be specific yet constructive: note examples, and be kind.
- Answer the writer's questions and others in this book to focus on essentials, not details.

Questions for a Peer Editor

Overall Responses

- What is your first reaction to this paper?
- What is this writer trying to tell you?
- What are this paper's greatest strengths?
- Does it have any major weaknesses?
- What one change would most improve the paper?

Questions on Meaning

- Do you understand everything? Is the draft missing any information that you need to know?
- Does this paper tell you anything you didn't know before?
- Is the writer trying to cover too much territory? Too little?
- Does any point need to be more fully explained or illustrated?
- When you come to the end, has the paper delivered what it promised?

Questions on Organization

- Does the beginning grab your interest and draw you into the main idea? Or can you find a better beginning at a later point?
- Does the paper have a clear main idea? Would the main idea stand out better if anything were removed or added?
- Might the ideas in the paper be more effectively arranged?
- Can you follow the ideas easily? Are transitions needed? If so, where?
- Does the writer keep to one point of view — one angle of seeing?
- Does the ending seem deliberate, as if the writer meant to conclude, not just run out of gas? How might the writer strengthen the conclusion?

Questions on Writing Strategies

- Do you feel that this paper addresses you personally?
- Does the writer's word choice and tone fit the essay well?
- Does the draft contain anything that distracts you or seems unnecessary?
- Do you get bored at any point? How might the writer keep you reading?
- Is the language of this paper too lofty and abstract? If so, where does the writer need to come down to earth and get specific?
- Do you understand all the words used? Do any specialized words need clearer definitions?

Meeting with Your Instructor

Prepare for your conference on a draft as you prepare for a peer review. Reread your paper; then write out your questions, concerns, or current revision plans. Whether you are meeting face-to-face, online, or by phone, arrive on time. Remember that your instructor is an experienced reader who wants to help you improve your writing.

- If you already have received comments from your instructor, ask about anything you can't read, don't understand, or can't figure out how to do.
- If you are unsure about comments from peers, get your instructor's view.
- If you have a revision plan, ask for suggestions or priorities.
- If more questions arise after your conference, especially about comments on a draft returned there, follow up with your instructor.

Instructors often use two kinds of comments. *Summary comments* appear on your first or last page. These general comments may compliment strengths, identify recurring issues, acknowledge changes between drafts, make broad suggestions, or end with a grade. Throughout the essay, *specific comments*—brief notes or questions added in the margins—typically pinpoint issues in the text.

Although brief comments may seem like cryptic code or shorthand, they usually rely on key words to note common, recurring problems. They also may act as reminders, identifying issues that your instructor expects you to look up in your book and solve. Tally up the repeated comments to figure out priorities for revision and editing. Some sample comments and the area they focus on follow with translations, but turn to your instructor if you need a specific explanation.

PURPOSE	Thesis? Vague; Broad; Clarify; What's your point? So? So what?
TRANSLATION	= State your thesis more clearly and directly so that a reader knows what matters. Concentrate on rewording so that your main idea is plain.
ORGANIZATION	Hard to follow; Logic? Sequence? Add transitions? Jumpy
TRANSLATION	= Organize more logically so your paper is easy for a reader to follow without jumping from point to point. Add transitions or other cues to guide a reader.
WORDING	Unclear; Clarify; Awk; Repetition; Too informal
TRANSLATION	= Refine your wording so your sentences are easier to read. Rework awkward passages, reduce repetition, and stick to academic language.

EVIDENCE	Specify; Focus; Narrow down; Develop this more; Seems thin
TRANSLATION	= Provide more concrete evidence or explain how your evidence is relevant. Check that you support each main point with plenty of pertinent and compelling evidence.
SOURCES	Source? Add quotation marks? Too many quotes; Summarize? Synthesize; Cite source?
TRANSLATION	= This wording sound like a source, not like you, so your quotation marks or citation might be missing. Instead of tossing in quotations, use your critical thinking skills to sum up ideas, relate them to each other, and introduce them more effectively.
CITATIONS	Cite? Author? Page? MLA? APA? Comma? Period? Cap? Space? Parens?
TRANSLATION	= Add missing source citations to your text. Use the expected academic format to present them correctly. Check the model citation entries in this book and follow the punctuation and format exactly.

Revising for Emphasis, Conciseness, and Clarity

After you've revised for the large issues in your draft—purpose, thesis, audience, structure, and support—you're ready to turn your attention to micro revising. Paying close attention to the language of your draft can strengthen your distinctive voice and style as a writer.

Stressing What Counts

An effective writer decides what matters most and shines a bright light on it using the most emphatic positions in an essay, a paragraph, or a sentence—the beginning and the end.

Stating It First. In an essay, you might start with the most important point. For an economics paper on import quotas (such as the number of foreign cars allowed into a country), student Donna Waite stated her main point directly.

> Although an import quota has many effects, both for the nation imposing the quota and for the nation whose industries must suffer from it, I believe that the most important effect is generally felt at home. A native industry gains a chance to thrive in a marketplace of lessened competition.

To take a stand or make a proposal, you might open with your position.

> Our state's antiquated system of justices of the peace is inefficient.

In a single sentence, start with what you want to emphasize.

> UNEMPHATIC   When Congress debates the Hall-Hayes Act removing existing protections for endangered species, as now seems likely to occur on May 12, it will be a considerable misfortune if this bill should pass, since the extinction of many rare birds and animals would certainly result.

The beginning of the sentence is wasted on the debate and its probable timing. Here's a better use of this emphatic position:

> REVISED   The extinction of many rare birds and animals would certainly follow passage of the Hall-Hayes Act.

Now the writer stresses what she most fears—the dire consequences of the act.

Stating It Last. To place an idea last can also throw weight on it. This structure dramatically builds up and up to a climax. Giving evidence first and leading up to the thesis at the end is particularly effective in editorials and informal persuasive essays. This sentence by novelist Julian Green suspends its point until the end.

> Amid chaos of illusions into which we are cast headlong, there is one thing that stands out as true, and that is—love.

Cutting and Whittling

Like gardeners who trim dead leaves and twigs, good writers remove needless words that clog their prose. One of the chief joys of revising is to watch 200 meandering words shrink to a direct 150. Here are some strategies for reducing wordiness.

For more on transitions, see pp. 290–92.

Cut the Fanfare. Why bother to announce that you're going to say something? Just say it.

> WORDY   As far as getting ready for winter is concerned, I put antifreeze in my car.
>
> REVISED   To get ready for winter, I put antifreeze in my car.

Cutting empty phrases such as "In this paper I intend to . . ." or "In conclusion I would like to say that . . ." allows the writer to simply state the main point directly.

Use Strong Verbs. *There is* or *There are* and other forms of the verb *be* (*am, is, are, was, were*) can make a statement wordy. Replace such weak verbs with active ones. Replace passive constructions, where it's unclear who is performing the action, with active ones.

WORDY	The Akron game was a disappointment to the fans.
REVISED	The Akron game disappointed the fans.
WORDY	There are many people who dislike flying.
REVISED	Many people dislike flying.

Use Relative Pronouns with Caution. When a clause begins with a relative pronoun (*who, which, that*), you often can whittle it to a phrase.

WORDY	Venus, which is the second planet of the solar system, is called the evening star.
REVISED	Venus, the second planet of the solar system, is called the evening star.

Cut Out Deadwood. Empty phrases such as *on the subject of, in regard to, in terms of,* and *as far as . . . is concerned* often simply fill space. Try reading the sentences below without the words in *italics*.

Howell spoke for the sophomores, and Janet *also spoke* for the seniors.

He is *something of* a clown but *sort of the* lovable *type*.

As a major in *the field of* economics, I plan to concentrate on *the area of* international banking.

The decision as to whether *or not* to go is up to you.

Cut Descriptors. Adjectives and adverbs are often dispensable.

WORDY	Johnson's extremely significant research led to highly important major discoveries.
REVISED	Johnson's research led to major discoveries.

Be Short, Not Long. In general, favor short words over long ones. Instead of *the remainder*, write *the rest*; instead of *activate, start* or *begin*; instead of *adequate* or *sufficient, enough*. Look for the right word — one that wraps an idea in a smaller package.

WORDY	Andy has a left fist that has a lot of power in it.
REVISED	Andy has a potent left.

From reading widely, you absorb words like *potent* and set them to work for you.

Keeping It Clear

Combine these strategies of choosing what to emphasize and trimming away unnecessarily long or wordy phrases to achieve your goal: communicating clearly with your readers.

WORDY	He is more or less a pretty outstanding person in regard to good looks.
REVISED	He is strikingly handsome.

Read your draft with fresh eyes. Return, after a break, to passages that have been a struggle and focus on clarity.

UNCLEAR	Thus, after a lot of thought, it should be approved by the city council to raise property taxes to fund construction of the new high school even though it will be expensive because it has wide support from the community and furthermore the current high school is in terrible condition.
CLEAR	Given the poor condition of the current high school and the wide community support for building a new one, the city council should increase property taxes to fund construction of the new high school.

REVISING FOR EMPHASIS, CONCISENESS, AND CLARITY

- ☐ Have you emphasized your main point by placing it at the beginning or the end?
- ☐ Do you announce an idea before you state it? If so, chop out the announcement.
- ☐ Can you substitute an active verb where you use a form of *be* (*is, was, were*)?
- ☐ Can you recast any passive sentences beginning with *There is* or *There are*?
- ☐ Have you added deadwood or too many adjectives and adverbs?
- ☐ Do you see any long words where short words would do?
- ☐ Have you kept your writing clear, direct, and forceful?

For his composition class, Daniel Matthews wrote a paper about an "urban legend," a widely accepted and emotionally appealing — but untrue — tale about events. The following selection from his first draft, "The Truth about 'Taps,'" introduces his topic, briefly explaining the legend and the true story about it. Macro revisions are noted in the margin, and micro revisions are marked in the text); the clear and concise final version follows.

FIRST DRAFT

Avoid "you" in case readers have not shared this experience.

Anyone who has ever
~~As you know, whenever you have~~ attended the funeral services for a

fallen veteran of the United States of America, ~~you have~~ *has* stood fast as a lone

bugler filled the air with the mournful ~~and sullenly appropriate~~ last tribute to a defender of the ~~United States of America~~ *nation*. ~~As most of us know,~~ *T*he name of

the bugle call is "Taps," and the ~~story~~ *legend* behind its origin ~~is one that is~~ gain~~ing~~ *has* *ed*

a popularity ~~of its own~~ as it ~~is more and more frequently being~~ *has* circulated in

this time of war and terror. Although ~~it is clear that~~ this tale ~~of the origin~~ of a

beautiful ode to a fallen warrior is heartfelt ~~and full of purposeful intent~~, it is

an "urban legend." ~~It~~ *As such, i*t fails to provide due justice to the memories of the men

responsible for the ~~true~~ origin of "Taps."

General Daniel Butterfield is the originator of the bugle call "Taps," *true* ⊙

~~formerly known as "Lights Out."~~ Butterfield served ~~as a general~~ in the Union

army during the Civil War and was awarded the Medal of Honor for actions

during that time. One of his most endearing claims to fame is the bugle call

"Taps," which he composed at Harrison's Landing in 1862 (Warner 167). ~~The~~

~~bugle call~~ "Taps" originates from another call named "Lights Out"*,*~~; this call~~

~~was~~ used by the Army to signal the end of the day. Butterfield, wanting a new

and original call unique to his command, summoned bugler Oliver Willcox

Norton to his tent one night. ~~and~~ *R*ather than compose an altogether new tune,

he instead modified the notes to the call "Lights Out" (US Military District of

Washington). ~~Then~~ *Shortly thereafter* this call could be heard ~~being used~~ up and down the Union

lines as the other commanders ~~who had~~ heard the call ~~liked it~~ and adapted

it for their own use. ~~This call, the modified version of "Lights Out" is also in~~ *and itself*

~~a way~~ a derivative of ~~the~~ British bugle call ~~"Tattoo" which is very~~ *"Tattoo," a* similar in

both sound and purpose ~~to "Lights Out,"~~ (Villanueva). ~~notes this as well in his~~

~~paper "24 Notes That Tap Deep Emotion."~~

Rework paragraph to summarize legend when first mentioned.

INSERT:
According to this story, Union captain Robert Ellicombe discovered that a Confederate casualty was, in fact, his son, a music student in the South. The father found "Taps" in his son's pocket, and the tune was first played at a military burial as his son was laid to rest (Coulter).

Group all the discussion of the versions in one place.

Divide long sentence to keep it clear.

Strengthen paragraph conclusion by sticking to its focus.

REVISED DRAFT

Anyone who has ever attended the funeral services for a fallen veteran of the United States of America has stood fast as a lone bugler filled the air with a mournful last tribute to a defender of the nation. The name of the bugle call is "Taps," and the legend behind its origin has gained popularity as it has circulated in this time of war and terror. According to this story, Union captain Robert Ellicombe discovered that a Confederate casualty was, in fact, his son, a music student in the South. The father found "Taps" in his son's pocket, and the tune was first played at a military burial as his son was laid to rest (Coulter). Although this tale of a beautiful ode to a fallen warrior is heartfelt, it is an "urban legend." As such, it fails to provide due justice to the memories of the men responsible for the true origin of "Taps."

General Daniel Butterfield is the true originator of the bugle call "Taps." Butterfield served in the Union army during the Civil War and was awarded the Medal of Honor for actions during that time. One of his most endearing claims to fame is the bugle call "Taps," which he composed at Harrison's Landing in 1862 (Warner 167). "Taps" originates from another call named "Lights Out," used by the army to signal the end of the day and itself a derivative of "Tattoo," a British bugle call similar in both sound and purpose (Villanueva). Butterfield, wanting a new and original call unique to his command, summoned bugler Oliver Willcox Norton to his tent one night. Rather than compose an altogether new tune, he instead modified the notes to the call "Lights Out" (US Military District of Washington). Shortly thereafter this call could be heard up and down the Union lines as other commanders heard the call and adapted it for their own use.

Editing and Proofreading

Editing means correcting and refining grammar, punctuation, and mechanics. Proofreading means taking a final look to check correctness and to catch spelling or word-processing errors. Don't edit and proofread too soon. Misspellings or grammatical errors may be cut in a later version, so it's best to wait until you have revised to refine and correct. In college, good editing and proofreading can make the difference between a C and an A. On the job, it may help you get promoted. Readers, teachers, and bosses like careful writers who take time to edit and proofread.

Editing

As you edit, whenever you question whether a word or construction is correct, consult a good reference handbook. Learn the grammar conventions you don't understand so you can spot and eliminate problems in your own writing. Practice until you easily recognize major errors such as fragments and comma splices. Ask for assistance from a peer editor or a tutor in the writing center if your campus has one.

Use the Quick Editing Guide (beginning on p. Q-37) to review grammar, style, punctuation, and mechanics problems typically found in college writing. Look for definitions, examples, and a checklist to help you tackle each one.

EDITING FOR CLARITY

The following cross-references refer to the Quick Editing Guide section at the back of this book.

Grammar Problems   *Section Number*

☐ Have you avoided writing sentence fragments?   A1

☐ Have you corrected any comma splices or fused sentences?   A2

☐ Have you used the correct form for all verbs in the past tense?   A3

☐ Do all verbs agree with their subjects?   A4

☐ Have you used the correct case for all pronouns?   A5

☐ Do all pronouns agree with their antecedents?   A6

☐ Have you used adjectives and adverbs correctly?   A7

Sentence Problems

☐ Does each modifier clearly modify the appropriate element?   B1

☐ Have you used parallel structure where necessary?   B2

Word Choice Problems

☐ Have you used appropriate language?   C1

☐ Is your writing clean and concise?   C2

☐ Have you correctly used commonly confused words?   C3

Punctuation Problems

☐ Have you used commas correctly?   D1

☐ Have you used apostrophes correctly?   D2

☐ Have you punctuated quotations correctly?   D3

Mechanics Problems

☐ Have you used capital letters correctly?   E1

☐ Have you spelled all words correctly?   E2

For help documenting any sources in your paper, turn to sections D6 and E1–E2 in the Quick Research Guide (pp. Q-30–Q-36).

Proofreading

All writers make mistakes as they put ideas on paper. Because the mind works faster than the pencil (or the computer), a moment's break in concentration — when someone talks or your phone rings — can lead to errors. Making such mistakes isn't bad—you simply need to take the time to find and correct them.

- Let a paper sit several days, overnight, or at least a few hours before proofreading so that you allow time to gain perspective.
- Budget enough time to proofread thoroughly. For a long essay or complex research paper with a list of sources, schedule several sessions.
- Ask someone else to read your paper and tell you if it is free of errors. But take pride in your own work. *Don't* let someone else do it for you.
- Use a spell-checker cautiously, remembering that it recognizes only correct spelling, not correct choices.
- Keep a list of your habitual errors, especially those your instructor has already pointed out (such as leaving off *-s* or *-ed* endings or putting in unnecessary commas), and double-check for them.

Proofreading does take patience but is a skill you can develop. When you proofread, try to look at all the letters in each word— not just the first and last letters —and the punctuation marks between words. Slow down and concentrate.

PROOFREADING CHECKLIST

☐ Have you read your draft very slowly, looking at every word and letter?

☐ Have you read your paper aloud so you can see and hear mistakes?

☐ Have you read the essay backward so that you look at each word instead of getting caught up in the flow of ideas?

☐ Have you read your essay several times, focusing each time on a specific area of difficulty? (For example, read once for spelling, once for punctuation, and once for any problem that recurs in your writing.)

Learning by Doing Reflecting on Past Grades and Comments

Examine at least two graded pieces of writing from this class or another. What types of comments or suggestions did your instructor(s) make on your work? Did you notice that any particular issues or errors were pointed out on more than one occasion? How might you address those trouble spots as you write or revise future papers? Answer these questions in a brief reflection.

Strategies for Creating Presentations and Portfolios

20

In addition to the writing situations covered in Part Two, presentations and portfolios are other types of assessments commonly used in composition courses. This chapter offers advice on how to present your writing—a useful skill in both academic and workplace settings.

Presentations

Presentations allow a writer to deliver his or her ideas directly to an audience. In college, students might use a presentation to summarize final essays, research reports, or capstone projects. Small groups or teams might prepare pro-and-con debates, roundtable presentations of viewpoints, organized analyses, problem–solution proposals, or field reports. In the workplace, you might present a summary of your current project to colleagues or present a proposal to clients. Some presentations use visual aids such as posters or PowerPoint slides, while others might be done entirely online, as videos or podcasts. All presentations require thoughtful written materials and confident delivery.

Because presentations draw on multiple skills, you may feel anxious or uncertain about how to prepare. You need to write under pressure, preparing a script or notes as well as text for any presentation slides. You need to speak under pressure, making your presentation and possibly fielding questions. You may be assessed on both your prepared content and your actual presentation. Online presentations may add technical challenges of lighting, video, and sound. Nevertheless, each presentation provides valuable experience, preparing you for future classes, job interviews, workplace reports, professional talks, and community involvement.

Preparing Presentations

Whether you are presenting in person to your composition course or online to a wider audience, preparing a presentation involves some basic steps.

Start Early. Get organized, don't procrastinate, and draw on your writing strategies when a presentation looms. Review your assignment and any assessment criteria; be sure you understand what is expected. If you are reporting on a paper or project, finish it well ahead of the deadline. If your presentation requires separate reading or research, get it done early. If you are working with a group, establish a timetable with regular face-to-face meetings or online checkpoints so everyone is prepared. This advance work is necessary to leave time to plan the presentation as a separate activity — and avoid just walking in, looking disorganized or ill-prepared.

Consider Your Format. Your instructor may assign a specific type of presentation — oral, online, multimodal — or you may be able to choose the type of presentation you want to give. As you mull over your options, think about your purpose and audience. Will a face-to-face presentation be more effective at accomplishing your goal than an online presentation? Which format will allow you to incorporate audio or video? Which will meet the needs and limitations of your audience?

Develop Your Presentation. As you work on the presentation itself, keep in mind the time allotted and the formality expected. Think hard about an engaging start — something surprising, intriguing, or notable to help your audience focus. Map out the main points appropriate for your audience and situation. Preview them so your words tell listeners what's major, what's minor, and what's coming up. Instead of writing out a speech like an essay, record your main points on cards or on a page using easy-to-read type. Be selective: listeners can absorb only limited detail.

Using Visuals

As your talk takes shape, work on any slides or images for projection or distribution. Listeners appreciate concise visuals that support — not repeat — your words. Instead, visuals should provide information to support or offer fresh insights into the speaker's points. For example, a speaker discussing rising graduation rates over a five-year period might show a bar chart that makes the trend instantly clear.

Similarly, speakers shouldn't read from their slides, an approach that can bore the audience quickly. Remember that slides should be seen as engaging support for a presentation, not as a teleprompter for the speaker. Try to align the pacing of your slides with your main points so they appear steadily and appropriately. All this preparation will improve your presentation and reduce any fears about public speaking.

Design Your Presentation Visuals. Slides, posters, and photographs give your audience a visual focal point during your presentation. Aim for a simple, professional look without busy designs or dramatic colors. Use design elements such as fonts and type sizes, bulleted lists, white space, headings, repetition, color, and images to direct your audience's attention to key points.

Effective use of space is important in presentation slides. Providing ample space and limiting the text on each slide helps readers absorb your major points. Notice the spacing on the slide below, which is aimed at recruiting participants for a service learning program.

This slide has too much text, making it hard to read and potentially distracting. Almost no margin at the top and bottom of the slide gives it an overcrowded feeling.

Service Learning Participation

- Training workshops — 2 a week for the first 2 weeks of the semester
- After-school tutoring — 3 two-hour sessions per week at designated site
- Journal-keeping — 1 entry per session
- Submission of journal and final report — report should describe 3 most important things learned and should be 5–10 pages

Presentation slide with too much text and too little space

In contrast, this next slide has less text and more open space, making each point easier to read. Its bullets highlight the main points using key words and phrases, rather than including every detail. The type sizes for the slides are large enough for comfortable viewing: 44 points for the heading and 32 points for the body.

Service Learning Participation

- Training workshops
- After-school tutoring
- Journal-keeping
- Submission of journal and final report

Presentation slide with brief text and effective use of space

In the examples above, the "white space" around the text is actually blue. Some public-speaking experts believe that black type on a white background can be too stark; instead, they recommend a dark blue background with yellow or white type. Others believe that black on white is fine and may be what the audience is used to. Presentation software makes it easy to experiment with these options. Ask if your instructor has a preference.

Be Prepared. It is a good idea to save backup copies of your slides in case your original file is lost or corrupted. Email the file to yourself or copy it onto a thumb drive. If it contains animation or videos, consider copying it onto an external hard drive.

Then practice—speaking out loud, timing yourself, revising your notes, testing your talk on a friend, or maybe recording yourself so you can catch rough spots. If you feel nervous, practice taking a deep breath or counting to five before you begin. Also practice looking around the room, making eye contact. Connecting with your audience turns anonymous faces into sympathetic people.

If possible, test out the room where you will be presenting. Run through your presentation and project a few slides. Have a friend sit where your audience will be. Can she hear you? Can she see read the text and/or graphics on your slides?

PRESENTATION CHECKLIST

☐ Do you begin and end with an engaging flair?

☐ Have you stated your points clearly in an order easy to follow?

☐ Are your words, tone, and level of formality well chosen for the situation?

☐ Have you practiced enough to look relaxed and avoid getting lost?

☐ Have you practiced making eye contact as you present?

☐ Have you practiced projecting your voice and speaking slowly so everyone can hear?

☐ Does your appearance—posture, dress—increase your credibility?

☐ Do you stick to the expected time, format, procedure, or other guidelines?

☐ Are your visuals clear, spacious, and easy to read?

☐ Do the design, text, and presentation of your visuals complement your talk?

Learning from Another Writer: Visuals for an Oral Presentation

This slide on urban design was prepared by a student for a face-to-face presentation in his geography class. As this student reported on urbanization, the accompanying presentation slides provided summaries of key points from sources as well as images of the ten most populous cities in the world. Traditional Urban Design, the example shown here, combines text and images.

Andrew Dillon Bustin   **Face-to-Face Class Presentation**

Traditional Urban Design

TRADITIONAL URBAN DESIGN

- ❖ High residential densities
- ❖ Mixed land uses
- ❖ Gridded street patterns
- ❖ Land use plans that maximize social contact, spatial efficiency, and local economy

Arthur Tilley/Getty Images

David C Phillips/Garden Photo World/Corbis

The Granger Collection, NYC

Questions to Start You Thinking

Meaning

1. What information does the slide present?
2. How do the images relate to the words?

Writing Strategies

3. How does the slide try to appeal to an audience of classmates?
4. If the presenter were your classmate, what helpful comments would you make about his slide?

Learning by Doing 🎤 Reflecting on Oral Presentations

Based on what you have read in this chapter, reflect on a previous oral presentation that you made in this or any other class, or for your job. What skills or suggestions from this chapter might have made your presentation better? What new skills might you apply as you prepare your next oral presentation? Write a paragraph reflecting on these strategies and how they might improve your presentation skills.

Portfolios

When your writing course ends, your days using the writing, reading, and thinking skills you've acquired there are not over. The assumption — and the hope — is that your experience in your writing class will equip you to write successfully in your future courses, workplaces, and community. If your writing instructor has asked you to maintain a portfolio or a journal or to complete the reflective activities throughout this book, you'll likely find an encouraging record of the skills you've mastered in the course.

Keeping a Portfolio

Courses that require portfolios typically emphasize revision and reflection — your ability to identify and discuss your decisions, strengths, or learning processes. Portfolios give you a chance to demonstrate how you have developed as a writer. To build your portfolio, save all your drafts and notes, keep track of your choices and changes, and eventually select and submit your best writing.

The portfolio, whether in print or digital, collects pieces of writing that represent the writer's best work. Compiled over time and across projects, it showcases a writer's talent, hard work, and ability to make thoughtful choices. A course portfolio is usually due as the term ends and includes pieces written and revised for that class. Portfolios may also include an introduction or a reflective letter (often a self-assessment or rationale) for readers, who might be teachers, supervisors, evaluators, parents, or classmates.

Understanding Portfolio Assessment

The portfolio method of evaluation and teaching shapes the whole course, beginning to end. Your course will probably emphasize responses to your writing — from your classmates and instructor — but not necessarily grades on separate papers. This method shifts attention to the writing process — to discovery, planning, drafting, peer response, revision, editing — allowing time for your skills to develop before the portfolio is graded. Because this method is flexible, read your assignments carefully, and listen well to determine the kind of portfolio you'll need to keep, such as the following types.

A Writing Folder. Students submit all drafts, notes, outlines, doodles, and messy pages — all writing for the course, finished or unfinished. Students may also revise two or three promising pieces for a "presentation portfolio." This type of portfolio usually does not have a reflective cover letter.

A Learning (or Open) Portfolio. Students submit a variety of materials that have contributed to their learning. They may even determine the contents, organization, and presentation of the portfolio, which might include photos, other images, or nonprint objects that demonstrate learning.

A Closed Portfolio. Students must turn in assignments that are specified by the instructor; often, their options for what to include may be limited.

A Midterm Portfolio. The portfolio is given a trial run at midterm, or the midterm grade is determined by one or two papers that are submitted for evaluation, perhaps with a brief self-assessment.

A Final or Presentation Portfolio. The portfolio is evaluated at the end of the course after being revised, edited, and polished for presentation.

A Modified or Combination Portfolio. The student has some, but not unlimited, choice in what to include. For example, the instructor may ask for three entries that show certain features or parts of the course.

If you have been assigned to compile a portfolio, find out what your instructor has in mind. For example, your combination portfolio might contain three revised papers (out of five or six required). You decide, late in the term, which three to revise and edit. You also may reflect on how those choices define you as a writer, show your learning, or explain your decisions while writing. Here are some questions your instructor, syllabus, or assignment sheets may answer:

- Is the portfolio paper or digital?
- How many assignments should you include in the portfolio?
- Do all the assignments need to be revised? If so, what level of revision is expected? What criteria will be used to assess them?
- How much of the course grade is determined by the portfolio? Are entries graded separately, or does the portfolio receive one grade?
- May you include multimodal entries — such as those incorporating photos, videos, maps, Web pages, or other visuals?
- Do you need an introduction or a cover letter? What approach is expected: Description? Explanation? Exploration? Reflection? Self-assessment?
- Does each entry need its own cover sheet? Should descriptions of your processes or choices appear before or after each entry?

Tips for Keeping a Portfolio

Keep Everything, and Stay Organized. Don't throw anything away! Keep all your notes, lists, drafts, outlines, clusters, responses from readers, copied articles, and source references. *Back up everything*, whether on your own laptop or on a portable drive. For hard copies, organize your files, and invest in a good folder with pockets. Label and store drafts, notes, outlines, and peer-review forms for each assignment.

Manage Your Time. It may be tempting to put off thinking about the portfolio, since it usually isn't due until midterm or the end of the course. However, planning ahead can save you time and frustration. As your instructor returns each assignment with comments, make changes in response while the ideas are fresh. If you don't understand or know how to approach those comments, ask your instructor right away. Make notes about what you want to do. Then, even if you want to let a paper simmer, you will have both a plan and fresh insight ready when you work on it again.

For more help with self-assessment, see the Peer Response questions and Revision Checklists throughout *The Bedford Guide*.

Practice Self-Assessment. For writing, like many complex activities, you can learn a lot by stepping back and evaluating your own performance. Maybe you have great ideas but find it hard to organize them. Maybe you write powerful thesis statements but run out of ideas to support them. Don't wait until the portfolio cover letter is due to begin assessing your strengths, weaknesses, or preferences.

Practice self-assessment from the start. After reviewing the syllabus, write a paragraph or two about how you expect to do in this course. What might you do well? Why? What may be hard? Why? For each paper you share with peers or hand in, write a journal entry about what the paper does well and what it still needs. Keep track of your process as you plan, research, or draft each paper—where you get stuck and where things click.

Choose the Portfolio Entries Carefully. If you can select what to include, consider the course emphasis. Of course, you want to select pieces your evaluator will think are "the best," but also consider which show the most promise or potential. Which drafts show creativity, insight, or an unusual approach? Which show variety—different purposes, audiences, or voices? Which show depth—your ability to do thorough research or stay with a topic for several weeks? Which illustrate how your writing has improved over the duration of the course? Also consider the order of the entries—which piece might work best first or last, and how each placement affects the whole.

For a sample reflective portfolio letter, see p. 254.

Write a Strong Introduction. Your introduction—usually a self-assessment in the form of a reflective cover letter, a statement, or a description for each of your entries—could be the most important text you write all semester. Besides introducing your collection and offering a portrait of you as a writer, it explains your choices in putting the portfolio together. It shows that you can evaluate your work and your writing process. Like a "final exam," your reflective introduction tests what you've learned about good writing, readers' needs, and the details of a careful self-presentation.

Consider the following questions as you draft your reflective letter:

- Who will read this reflection?
- What qualities of writing will your reader value?
- Will the reader suggest changes or evaluate your work?
- What will the outcome of the reading be? How much can you influence it?

- What do you want to emphasize about your writing? What are you proud of? What have you learned? What did you have trouble with?
- How can you present your writing ability in the best light?

If your reader is your instructor, look back over his or her comments on your returned papers. Review the course syllabus and assignment sheets. What patterns do you see in the feedback or directions? What could you tell a friend about this reader's expectations — or pet peeves? Use what you've learned to develop a convincing introduction or cover letter.

If your readers are unknown, ask your instructor for as much information as possible so you can decide which logical, ethical, or emotional appeals might be most effective. Although you won't know your readers personally, it's safe to assume that they will be trained in portfolio assessment and will share many of your instructor's ideas about good writing. If your college writing program has guidelines, consult them, too. For more on appeals, see p. 142.

How long should your introduction or cover letter be? Check with your instructor, but regardless of length, develop your ideas or support your claims as in any effective writing. If you are asked to present your introduction as a letter, follow the format for a business letter: include the date, a salutation, and a closing.

In writing your reflective introduction, you might try some of the following (but don't try to use all of them):

- Discuss your best entry, and explain why it is your best.
- Detail your revisions — the improvements you want readers to notice.
- Review everything included, touching on the strengths of each.
- Outline your writing and revising process for one or more entries.
- State what the portfolio illustrates about you as a writer, student, researcher, or critical thinker.
- Acknowledge your weaknesses, but show how you've worked to overcome them.
- Acknowledge the influence of your readers on your entries.
- Reflect on what you've learned about writing and reading.
- Lay the groundwork for a positive evaluation of your work.

Polish the Final Portfolio. From the first page to the last, print or digital, your portfolio should be ready for public presentation. Review and proofread each item carefully. Take pride in your portfolio. Think about creative ways to give it a final distinctive feature, such as adding a colorful cover, illustrations, a table of contents, or a running head. Although a cheerful cover will not make up for weak writing or careless editing, readers will value your extra effort.

Learning by Doing Reflecting on This Class

Write a reflection about your experiences in this class and how they have affected you. As you write the reflection, think about "the five W's and an H" of journalism: *Who? What? Where? When? Why?* and *How?* Who were you as a writer and academic at the beginning of the semester? How have you progressed as both an academic and a writer? What have you learned? How have you learned it? Where did you find the most success? The greatest struggles? How did you overcome any difficulties this semester? When do you foresee yourself using the skills you learned this semester? Finally, why does this reflection matter?

A WRITER'S READER

Contents

Introduction: Reading to Write

A *Writer's Reader* is a collection of twenty-five professional essays. We hope, first of all, that you will read these pieces simply for the sake of reading—enjoying and responding to their ideas. Second, we hope that you will actively study these essays as solid examples of the situations and strategies explored in *A Writer's Guide*. The authors represented in this reader have faced the same problems and choices you do when you write. You can learn from studying their decisions, structures, and techniques. Finally, we hope that you will find the content of the essays intriguing—and along with the questions posed after each one, a source of ideas to write about.

Each chapter in *A Writer's Reader* concentrates on a broad theme—America, language, popular culture, inequality, and gender. Some essays focus on the inner world of personal experience and opinion. Others turn to the outer world with information and persuasion. In each chapter, the last two selections explore the same subject, illustrating how different writers use different strategies to address similar issues.

Each chapter in the reader begins with an image and a visual activity to stimulate your thinking and writing. Each selection is preceded by biographical information, placing the author—and the piece itself—in a cultural and informational context. Next a reading note, As You Read, suggests a way to consider the selection. Following each reading are five Questions to Start You Thinking that consistently cover meaning, writing strategies, critical thinking, vocabulary, and connections with other selections in *A Writer's Reader*. Paired essays in each chapter are juxtaposed to highlight the links between those two essays. Finally, two possible assignments make specific suggestions for writing. The first is directed toward your inner world, asking you to draw generally on your personal experience and your understanding of the essay. The second is outer directed, asking you to look outside yourself and write an evaluative or argumentative paper that may require further reading or research.

21

America

Lisa Howeler/Alamy

Responding to an Image

Take a look at the photograph above. As a symbol of our nation, the American flag represents many things, including honor, freedom, courage, and respect. Consider your own relationship to the symbols that represent America. When you think of America, what do you imagine? Do you conjure up images of the geography—the rugged Rocky Mountains, quaint New England towns, the vastness of the Great Plains? Do you think of the diversity of the American people? Of a Thanksgiving meal or Fourth of July fireworks? What does America mean to you?

Douglas Sonders/NPR

Shankar Vendantam

The Huddled Masses and the Myth of America

Shankar Vendantam is the host of *Hidden Brain: A Conversation About Life's Unseen Patterns*, a program created by National Public Radio. In an episode aired on January 15, 2018, Vendantam revisits an earlier interview with Maria Cristina Garcia about attitudes toward immigration, in the context of comments made by the U.S. president in 2018. Garcia is a historian and professor of American Studies at Cornell University.

AS YOU READ: Ask yourself, how have attitudes and assumptions around immigration changed over time? How do the attitudes held by those in power compare or contrast with those of the larger population? How might attitudes toward immigration change in the future?

O ur airwaves are filled with debates about immigrants° and refugees.° Who should be in the United States, who shouldn't, and who should decide?   1

These modern debates often draw upon our ideas about *past* waves of immigration. We sometimes assume that earlier generations of newcomers quickly learned English and integrated into American society. But historian Maria Cristina Garcia says these ideas are often false.   2

"Most immigrants who came to the United States did not immigrate to become American," she says. "In many cases immigrants came to replicate the best of the old country in more favorable circumstances."   3

Garcia says in the nineteenth century, it often took a long time for new immigrants to learn English. "Our founding documents were all published in German to accommodate the German-speaking populations. For most of the nineteenth century, instruction in public schools across the country—from Pennsylvania to Texas to Wisconsin—occurred entirely in languages other than English, or bilingually. And this practice was not abolished until the first decades of the 20th century."   4

Nor did immigrants of that era classify themselves as legal or illegal.   5

"They just didn't think in those terms," she says. "During much of our history people moved across our borders with ease. If your ship docked outside of New York City, chances were you weren't even interviewed. So when someone says to me, 'My ancestors immigrated legally, why can't [immigrants today]?,' my first question is, 'When did your ancestors immigrate?' Because if they immigrated in the nineteenth century or in the early twentieth century, they simply didn't use that vocabulary. They didn't think in those terms."   6

[In the following interview], Shankar revisits [a] 2016 conversation with Maria Cristina Garcia, which explored the underlying frames and assumptions at play in our discussions about immigrants and their place in American society.   7

---

immigrant: A person who emigrates from one country to another country to take up permanent residence.   **refugee:** A displaced person; someone who has been forced to leave their country to escape persecution, violence, or disaster.

This is *Hidden Brain*. I'm Shankar Vedantam. We were almost done working on this week's show when news broke Thursday evening, news that required an on-air warning before our colleagues could even discuss it.   8

(SOUNDBITE OF ARCHIVED BROADCAST)

RACHEL MARTIN, BYLINE: An Oval Office conversation turns vulgar.   9

DAVID GREENE, BYLINE: And I want to acknowledge what I'm about to   10
say could offend some people. He asked why the United States would admit people from African nations, which he called shithole countries. Trump then told lawmakers he would rather see more immigrants from Norway. The vulgar comment. . . .

(SOUNDBITE OF ARCHIVED RECORDING)

PRESIDENT DONALD TRUMP: No, I'm not a racist. I am the least racist   11
person you have ever interviewed.

VEDANTAM: In light of President Trump's comments as well as ongoing   12
debate over the program known as Deferred Action for Childhood Arrivals, or DACA,° we thought we'd switch gears and bring you this conversation from October 2016. As a journalist, I think this conversation is timely. As an immigrant myself, I think it's essential.

(SOUNDBITE OF MUSIC)

VEDANTAM: Our airwaves are filled with debates about migrants, refugees   13
and undocumented immigrants—who should be in the United States? Who shouldn't? And, who should decide? It's an issue that seems to get to the core of who we are, who we want to be and where we're headed as a nation. Today we're going to take a fresh look at the issue by exploring what history can teach us about the patterns and paradoxes° of immigration in a nation of immigrants.

(SOUNDBITE OF MUSIC)

VEDANTAM: My guest today is Maria Cristina Garcia. She's a historian and   14
professor of American Studies at Cornell University. Maria Cristina, welcome to *Hidden Brain*.

MARIA CRISTINA GARCIA: Thank you.   15

VEDANTAM: So we call ourselves a nation of immigrants. And, you know,   16
that's more than a saying. It's more than even a fact. It's a foundational story of the United States. And I want to start with this idea. Many of us take genuine pride in being a country whose most famous symbol is the Statue of Liberty.

Deferred Action for Childhood Arrivals (DACA): A U.S. policy meant to protect young undocumented immigrants by preventing their deportation and providing a work permit; this protection expires after two years but can be renewed.   **paradox:** A statement or idea that seems contradictory or absurd but in reality is possibly true; a person or thing that has a contradictory nature.

GARCIA: That's correct. Immigrants and refugees are central to the Amer-   17
ican national mythology, to the stories that we tell about ourselves as a
people. We honor this history with museums and historical markers. We
commercialize it with celebrations like St. Patrick's Day and now Cinco de
Mayo.° But despite the centrality° of immigrants and immigration to the
American story, many of us have been wary of immigrants. And we see this
all throughout history. We have a tension there. We have a contradiction. It's
always been there.

One has only to read Benjamin Franklin, for example, to get a sense of   18
these contradictions. In the 1750s, for example, Franklin called the German
residents of Pennsylvania stupid. He complained about their inability to learn
English and he warned his readers that they would soon overrun, that Ger-
mans would soon overrun the American continent. And yet it's also important
to note that Benjamin Franklin published one of the first German language
newspapers in the colonies. So there was that contradiction there, right?

So fast-forward also to the early national period. Immigration was wel-   19
come because it was important to nation building. We needed immigrants.
The new nation needed immigrants to work in the mills and the factories, to
work in the mines, to harvest the crops, to build the infrastructure of American towns and cities. In many communities you didn't even need to be a citizen in order to vote. And yet, you know, a couple of decades later, by the 1840s
and 1850s, we see the emergence of the Know-Nothing Party, immensely hostile to German and Irish Catholic immigrants, demanding federal restrictions
on immigration and trying to prevent immigrants from voting and holding
public office.

There are so many other examples I could give you. You mentioned the   20
Statue of Liberty during the 1870s and 1880s. As the Statue of Liberty is
going up in New York Harbor to celebrate the end of slavery, Americans are
demanding at this time that the Chinese be barred from immigrating to the
United States, and Congress complies° in 1882 with the Chinese Exclusion
Act. So we see these tensions and these contradictions all throughout American history.

VEDANTAM: I understand that you yourself came to the United States as a   21
refugee, and your own family, your own history of first arriving in the United
States and being seen by others and then your own family's history in terms
of how you see other people coming in or how your family sees other people
coming in reflects this broader pattern, this tension or this paradox in how
we think about immigration.

GARCIA: Yes. You're right. My family immigrated in the 1960s. I was just a   22
toddler. We immigrated from Cuba. We were privileged compared to other
immigrants. We were privileged because we were refugees arriving during the
Cold War from a communist country, and so the proverbial red carpet was

---

Cinco de Mayo: A celebration held on the fifth of May, mainly by Mexican-Americans,
commemorating victory against the French in the 1862 Battle of Puebla.   **centrality:** The
state of being at the center, of being essential.   **comply:** To abide by, act in accordance with.

rolled out for us. But just two decades later, we see another migration from Cuba during the 1980 Mariel Boatlift.° And by the 1980s, those Cubans who had arrived earlier and were more established and had managed to move up the economic ladder and were feeling much more secure in their position began to feel very nervous about the new arrivals who were coming in from Cuba in 1980. They wondered if these new Cubans who had grown up in a communist regime could truly understand democratic institutions, rather, they could understand capitalism. And so these older Cubans, more established Cubans, wondered if the new arrivals would undermine everything that they had accomplished in South Florida and in other communities where they had settled. We see this with every immigrant group when you look at American history. Again, history can teach us a lot.

You know, for example, in the nineteenth century, some of the most 23 vitriolic° voices of the anti-Chinese movement were Irish immigrants and their children, who themselves had been much maligned, and now in turn they were directing a lot of that hostility towards newer arrivals, this time from China. German Jews who had arrived in the early nineteenth century were also highly suspicious and worried about the Eastern European Jews who migrated at the end of the nineteenth century because they too feared that their status in society would be undermined by the newer arrivals. So I guess it's a very human response for those who are more established to worry about what the newer arrivals might do to undermine their hard work.

VEDANTAM: So this is such a fascinating idea that people come to the 24 United States and within a couple of decades their point of view shifts from the point of view of people who say, we really want to make it in the United States, to being really worried about whether the people coming after them are going to be able to make it in the United States. And we sort of see this pattern writ large in all manner of ways.

You know, in the current debates that we have about immigration, I've 25 heard people say, you know — people whose families have been here for many generations — they say that, you know, when their ancestors came to America, they wanted to become Americans, to leave old ways behind. And some of these people worry that more recent immigrants are less interested in assimilation. But from what I'm hearing you say, that might not actually be grounded in historical reality in terms of how immigration patterns have unfolded over the years.

GARCIA: You're so right. Many Americans today believe that the new immi- 26 grants are too culturally different, that they're coming here to take American jobs or mooch° off of welfare, that they have the wrong politics, that they don't want to learn English, that they don't want to assimilate,° that they're national security threats. But these attitudes, they're not new. Americans have been saying this about every immigrant group throughout American history.

Mariel Boatlift: A massive emigration of Cubans to the United States in 1980.   **vitriolic:** bitterly critical; malicious.   **mooch:** To ask for or acquire something without paying for it.   **assimilate:** To become part of a group, country, or society; to adapt, adjust, fit in.

According to American immigration mythology, those who came, say, in the nineteenth century or in the early twentieth century were the ideal immigrants. They learned English quickly. They wanted to be Americans. But the study of history doesn't bear that up. When you study history, it challenges those assumptions that we have about the older immigrants versus the new immigrants.

So for example, let me give you a couple of examples. From the study of history, we now know that not everyone who came to the United States stayed. The two groups that had the lowest return rates were the nineteenth-century Irish and Eastern European or Russian Jews. Every other immigrant group had return rates ranging between 20 and 80 percent. We also know from the study of history that most of most immigrants who came to the United States did not immigrate to become American. In many cases, in most cases, immigrants came to replicate the best of the old country in more favorable circumstances in the new. As I said earlier, in many communities you didn't even need to be a citizen in order to vote.   27

We also know from the study of history that in the nineteenth-century immigrants didn't learn English quickly. From the very beginning, this was a multilingual society. And it oftentimes took several generations for English to become the dominant language on Main Street. Our founding documents were all published in German to accommodate the German-speaking populations. For most of the nineteenth century, instruction in public schools across the country, from Pennsylvania to Texas to Wisconsin, occurred entirely in languages other than English, or bilingually. And this practice was not abolished until the first decades of the twentieth century. So our preoccupation today in the early twenty-first century with requiring linguistic and cultural conformity, that's really a recent phenomena.°   28

From the study of history, we also know that immigrants didn't think of themselves as legal or illegal. They just didn't think in those terms. During much of our history, people moved across our borders with ease. If your ship docked outside of New York City, chances were you weren't even interviewed. Congress passed the first immigration laws to control the movement of people beginning in the 1870s, but the mechanisms to enforce those laws were pretty few until the twentieth century. Indeed, the first Border Patrol consisted of only a couple dozen men on horseback.   29

So when someone says to me, my ancestors immigrated legally, why can't they, my first question is, when did your ancestors immigrate? Because if they immigrated in the nineteenth century or in the early twentieth century, they simply didn't use that vocabulary. They didn't think in those terms. . . .   30

VEDANTAM: You recently wrote an essay about the current debates over immigration in which you said generations from now, students in U.S. history classes — many of them the children of immigrants arriving today — will read what our political candidates, editorialists, bloggers, and talking heads had to say about their ancestors and shudder. What did you mean by that?   31

---

phenomena: (plural of phenomenon) An occurrence or situation that exists but cannot be easily explained; a remarkable person, thing, or event.

GARCIA: When I teach courses in immigration history and we read the edi-   32
torials and the newspaper articles and the broadsides that were published in
the nineteenth and in the early twentieth century, my students often shake
their heads and wonder how Americans could have ever had those feelings or
those thoughts or perspectives. They laugh nervously. But then when we compare those editorials and newspaper articles and broadsides to some of the
editorials and blogs and newspaper articles today, they see the continuities.

And so I suspect that 20 years from now, 30 years from now, I suspect that   33
my students reading the thoughts, the articles of today will also find them
ridiculous, will also shudder, will also wonder why Americans felt the way
they did. But I hope not. There's this part of me that hopes that we will do
better, that we will be better.

(SOUNDBITE OF MUSIC)

VEDANTAM: That was historian Maria Cristina Garcia. She's a professor of   34
American Studies at Cornell University.

Questions to Start You Thinking

1. **Considering Meaning:** According to Maria Cristina Garcia, what are
   some myths held by many in the United States about past waves of immigrants (paragraphs 2–3, 6)?

2. **Identifying Writing Strategies:** Shankar Vedantam mentions that he is
   an immigrant and that his guest, Garcia, arrived in the U.S. as a refugee
   (paragraphs 12; 21–22). Why does Vedantam choose to include this information?

3. **Reading Critically:** Among the myths about past immigration that
   Garcia refutes is the idea that most immigrants came to the U.S. to
   become "Americans." Were you surprised to learn that most immigrants
   did not have this in mind and that many even returned to their home
   countries (paragraphs 25–27)? Why or why not?

4. **Expanding Vocabulary:** In paragraph 29, Garcia says, that "immigrants
   didn't think of themselves as *legal* or *illegal*." What does she mean, and
   how does that observation relate to her larger argument about attitudes
   toward immigration, past and present?

5. **Making Connections:** The words used to discuss immigration change
   over time. Garcia says: "From the study of history, we . . . know that immigrants didn't think of themselves as legal or illegal. They just didn't think
   in those terms" (paragraph 29). How do her observations about language
   align with those made in Yesenia Padilla's essay, "What Does 'Latinx'
   Mean?" (pp. 366–69)?

Suggestions for Writing

1. According to Garcia, history shows that when a new group of immigrants arrives in the United States, there can be friction between the newcomers and the more established immigrants. What is the basis of that friction? Have you or members of your family or community experienced this, whether as newcomers or as established immigrants? If so, how did you or they address or overcome that friction?

2. Looking back at some extremely low moments in U.S. history — such as the internment of Japanese immigrants and citizens or the turning away of the *SS St. Louis*, a ship carrying hundreds of passengers, many of whom later died in Nazi death camps — how can we reconcile the past with the present? What can we do today, to fight against the fear and racist assumptions that allow for such devastating things to happen?

Judith Ortiz Cofer

More Room

Tanya Cofer

Born in Puerto Rico and raised in Paterson, New Jersey, Judith Ortiz Cofer (1952–2016) was the Regents' and Franklin Professor of English and Creative Writing, Emerita, at the University of Georgia, and won numerous awards and honors for her work, which includes published works of poetry, fiction, essays, and memoir. In the following essay, Ortiz Cofer explores the significance of her grandmother getting her own room in the home she shared with her husband and many children. This piece appeared in *Silent Dancing*, a collection of essays and poetry.

AS YOU READ: What details does Ortiz Cofer provide to show the significance of her grandmother and of her grandmother's room?

My grandmother's house is like a chambered nautilus;° it has many rooms, yet it is not a mansion. Its proportions are small and its design simple. It is a house that has grown organically, according to the needs of its inhabitants. To all of us in the family it is known as *la casa de Mamá*. It is the place of our origin; the stage for our memories and dreams of Island° life.   1

I remember how in my childhood it sat on stilts; this was before it had a downstairs. It rested on its perch like a great blue bird, not a flying sort of bird, more like a nesting hen, but with spread wings. Grandfather had built it soon after their marriage. He was a painter and housebuilder by trade, a poet and meditative° man by nature. As each of their eight children were born, new rooms were added. After a few years, the paint did not exactly match, nor the materials, so that there was a chronology° to it, like the rings of a tree, and Mamá could tell you the history of each room in her *casa,* and thus the genealogy° of the family along with it.   2

chambered nautilus: A spiral-shaped seashell that has many separate internal compartments. **Island:** A reference to Puerto Rico. **meditative:** Thoughtful. **chronology:** Time-based order. **genealogy:** History; ancestry.

Her room is the heart of the house. Though I have seen it recently, and 3 both woman and room have diminished in size, changed by the new perspective of my eyes, now capable of looking over countertops and tall beds, it is not this picture I carry in my memory of Mamá's *casa*. Instead, I see her room as a queen's chamber where a small woman loomed° large, a throne-room with a massive four-poster bed in its center which stood taller than a child's head. It was on this bed where her own children had been born that the smallest grandchildren were allowed to take naps in the afternoons; here too was where Mamá secluded herself to dispense private advice to her daughters, sitting on the edge of the bed, looking down at whoever sat on the rocker where generations of babies had been sung to sleep. To me she looked like a wise empress right out of the fairy tales I was addicted to reading.

Though the room was dominated by the mahogany four-poster, it also 4 contained all of Mamá's symbols of power. On her dresser instead of cosmetics there were jars filled with herbs: *yerba buena, yerba mala,*° the making of purgatives° and teas to which we were all subjected during childhood crises. She had a steaming cup for anyone who could not, or would not, get up to face life on any given day. If the acrid° aftertaste of her cures for malingering° did not get you out of bed, then it was time to call *el doctor.*

And there was the monstrous chifforobe° she kept locked with a little 5 golden key she did not hide. This was a test of her dominion° over us; though my cousins and I wanted a look inside that massive wardrobe more than anything, we never reached for that little key lying on top of her Bible on the dresser. This was also where she placed her earrings and rosary at night. God's word was her security system. This chifforobe was the place where I imagined she kept jewels, satin slippers, and elegant sequined, silk gowns of heartbreaking fineness. I lusted after those imaginary costumes. I had heard that Mamá had been a great beauty in her youth, and the belle of many balls. My cousins had other ideas as to what she kept in that wooden vault: its secret could be money (Mamá did not hand cash to strangers, banks were out of the question, so there were stories that her mattress was stuffed with dollar bills, and that she buried coins in jars in her garden under rosebushes, or kept them in her inviolate° chifforobe); there might be that legendary gun salvaged from the Spanish-American conflict over the Island. We went wild over suspected treasures that we made up simply because children have to fill locked trunks with something wonderful.

On the wall above the bed hung a heavy silver crucifix. Christ's agonized 6 head hung directly over Mamá's pillow. I avoided looking at this weapon suspended over where her head would lay; and on the rare occasions when I was allowed to sleep on that bed, I scooted down to the safe middle of the mattress, where her body's impression took me in like a mother's lap. Having taken care of the obligatory religious decoration with a crucifix, Mamá covered the

---

loomed: Towered.   *yerba buena, yerba mala:* Spanish for "good herb" and "bad herb," respectively.   **purgatives:** Agents, often laxatives, that rid the body of perceived toxins.   **acrid:** Sharp or bitter.   **malingering:** A pretend illness.   **chifforobe:** A piece of furniture that has both drawers and space for hanging clothes.   **dominion:** Power or control.   **inviolate:** Undisturbed.

other walls with objects sent to her over the years by her children in the States. *Los Nueva Yores°* were represented by, among other things, a postcard of Niagara Falls from her son Hernán, postmarked, Buffalo, N.Y. In a conspicuous gold frame hung a large color photograph of her daughter Nena, her husband and their five children at the entrance to Disneyland in California. From us she had gotten a black lace fan. Father had brought it to her from a tour of duty with the Navy in Europe (on Sundays she would remove it from its hook on the wall to fan herself at mass). Each year more items were added as the family grew and dispersed, and every object in the room had a story attached to it, a *cuento* which Mamá would bestow on anyone who received the privilege of a day alone with her. It was almost worth pretending to be sick, though the bitter herb purgatives of the body were a big price to pay for the spirit revivals of her story-telling.

Mama slept alone on her large bed, except for the times when a sick grand-   7
child warranted the privilege, or when a heartbroken daughter came home in need of more than herbal teas. In the family there is a story about how this came to be.

When one of the daughters, my mother or one of her sisters, tells the   8
cuento of how Mamá came to own her nights, it is usually preceded by the qualifications that Papá's exile from his wife's room was not a result of animosity between the couple, but that the act had been Mamá's famous blood-less coup° for her personal freedom. Papá was the benevolent° dictator of her body and her life who had had to be banished° from her bed so that Mamá could better serve her family. Before the telling, we had to agree that the old man was not to blame. We all recognized that in the family Papá was as an *alma de Dios,°* a saintly, soft-spoken presence whose main pleasures in life, such as writing poetry and reading the Spanish large-type editions of *Reader's Digest,* always took place outside the vortex° of Mamá's crowded realm. It was not his fault, after all, that every year or so he planted a baby-seed in Mamá's fertile body, keeping her from leading the active life she needed and desired. He loved her and the babies. Papá composed odes° and lyrics to celebrate births and anniversaries and hired musicians to accompany him in singing them to his family and friends at extravagant pig-roasts he threw yearly. Mamá and the oldest girls worked for days preparing the food. Papá sat for hours in his painter's shed, also his study and library, composing the songs. At these celebrations he was also known to give long speeches in praise of God, his fecund wife, and his beloved island. As a middle child, my mother remembers these occasions as a time when the women sat in the kitchen and lamented° their burdens, while the men feasted out in the patio, their rum-thickened voices rising in song and praise for each other, *compañeros°* all.

Los Nueva Yores: The way that Puerto Ricans sometimes refer to the United States. **coup:** Overthrow of an existing order. **benevolent:** Kind. **banished:** Sent away. *alma de Dios:* Spanish for "a good person." **vortex:** A powerful force that draws things into it. **odes:** Poems. **lamented:** Felt sorry about; regretted. *compañeros:* Spanish for "companions."

It was after the birth of her eighth child, after she had lost three at birth or   9
in infancy, that Mamá made her decision. They say that Mamá had had a special way of letting her husband know that they were expecting, one that had
begun when, at the beginning of their marriage, he had built her a house too
confining for her taste. So, when she discovered her first pregnancy, she supposedly drew plans for another room, which he dutifully executed. Every time
a child was due, she would demand, *more space, more space.* Papá acceded° to
her wishes, child after child, since he had learned early that Mamá's renowned
temper was a thing that grew like a monster along with a new belly. In this
way Mamá got the house that she wanted, but with each child she lost in
heart and energy. She had knowledge of her body and perceived that if she
had any more children, her dreams and her plans would have to be permanently forgotten, because she would be a chronically ill woman, like Flora
with her twelve children: asthma, no teeth, in bed more than on her feet.

And so, after my youngest uncle was born, she asked Papa to build a large   10
room at the back of the house. He did so in joyful anticipation. Mamá had
asked him special things this time: shelves on the walls, a private entrance.
He thought that she meant this room to be a nursery where several children
could sleep. He thought it was a wonderful idea. He painted it his favorite
color, sky blue, and made large windows looking out over a green hill and
the church spires beyond. But nothing happened. Mamá's belly did not grow,
yet she seemed in a frenzy of activity over the house. Finally, an anxious Papá
approached his wife to tell her that the new room was finished and ready to
be occupied. And Mamá, they say, replied: "Good, it's for *you*."

And so it was that Mamá discovered the only means of birth control avail-   11
able to a Catholic woman of her time: sacrifice. She gave up the comfort of
Papá's sexual love for something she deemed° greater: the right to own and
control her own body, so that she might live to meet her grandchildren — me
among them — so that she could give more of herself to the ones already there,
so that she could be more than a channel for other lives, so that even now that
time has robbed her of the elasticity of her body and of her amazing reservoir
of energy, she still emanates° the kind of joy that can only be achieved by living according to the dictates° of one's own heart.

acceded: Agreed. **deemed:** Believed to be. **emanates:** Beams with. **dictates:** Guiding
principles.

Questions to Start You Thinking

1. **Considering Meaning:** Why did Cofer's grandmother want to have her
   own room? Why did Cofer's grandfather think she had asked for this
   room?

2. **Identifying Writing Strategies:** Cofer offers vivid, detailed descriptions
   throughout her essay. What main impression do these descriptions create
   of the grandmother and of her room? (For more on how a main impression is conveyed by descriptions, see Chapter 4.)

3. **Reading Critically:** Cofer includes just a brief bit of dialogue in the final paragraph of her essay. Where else might she have added dialogue? What might be the benefit of these additions?

4. **Expanding Vocabulary:** One definition of *secluded* is "withdrawn from or involving little human social activity." How does Cofer's use of the word *secluded* in paragraph 3 broaden and enrich this definition?

5. **Making Connections:** Cofer describes her grandfather as "a benevolent dictator of [her grandmother's] body. . . a saintly, soft-spoken presence" (paragraph 9). How do you think he conforms or fails to conform to "dominant conceptions of masculinity" as described in "The High Cost of Manliness" (pp. 22–24). What effect does this have on the relationship between Papa and his family?

Suggestions for Writing

1. Cofer suggests that by getting her own room, her grandmother dramatically improved her life: she achieved "the kind of joy that can only be achieved by living according to the dictates of one's own heart" (paragraph 11). Write about something (such as a fulfilled request, an event, a new relationship, or a stroke of luck) that dramatically changed your life for the better. How, specifically, did your life change? Why has this change been so important or meaningful to you?

2. Compare and contrast the attitudes of Cofer's grandmother and grandfather about the benefits versus the burdens of having more children. Do the grandfather's attitudes seem dated to you, or do you think they persist in any way among today's fathers? Support your conclusions with examples.

Cristin Young

Sophie Egan

The American Food Psyche

Sophie Egan writes about food and culture. Her work has appeared many publications, including the *New York Times* food blog, the *Washington Post*, *Time*, the *Wall Street Journal*, *Bon Appétit*, *WIRED*, and *Eating Well*. She is a program director at the Culinary Institute of America. The following essay is from Egan's first book, *Devoured: How What We Eat Defines Who We Are*.

AS YOU READ: Ask yourself, how are your food choices like—or different from—those of your parents or grandparents?

American *food culture* is the set of customs, values, and behaviors related to eating and drinking. These form the scaffolding° of daily life.   1

scaffolding: Structure.

Here are some examples of American food culture: 2

- Fast food. This is arguably the best-known feature of our food culture, and the one we've exported most widely around the globe. Not just the food but the way it's consumed, at drive-thrus or taking it to go.
- When we watch movies, we eat popcorn.
- At state fairs, food is fried. Foods you didn't even know could be fried are fried.
- In the summer, we invite friends over for barbecues.
- Unlike in Britain, Canada, or Ireland, in the United States, bacon is supposed to be crispy.
- Don't eat anything when riding the subway.
- Eat pizza. All kinds. Any time.
  - When eating pizza, adhere to some very important rules regarding the delivery of the slice into your mouth: New York style = fold it. Chicago deep dish = fork and knife. Otherwise, no utensils involved. Unless, of course, you want to look like an Italian, in which case: Pinkies up. . . .

Michael Pollan, author of *The Omnivore's° Dilemma: A Natural History of*   3
Four Meals and many other books about food, has said that, given Americans' multiethnic makeup and our relatively new status as a nation, we have never had a stable food culture — as in passing on customs of eating from one generation to the next. This leaves us vulnerable to marketing and the latest nutrition study, "willing to throw it all out every few years," as he once said in an interview.

In other words, without an enduring set of social norms° around eating,   4
we are constantly reinventing them. The support for this idea is in strong supply, but there is an untapped layer that deserves inspecting: how this unstable food culture is shaped by our core values as a country. . . . They help explain why we eat the things we eat and the ways we eat them — and they equip us to understand how we might eat in the future. . . .

A melting pot is defined as "a place where a variety of races, cultures, or   5
individuals assimilate° into a cohesive° whole." Americans take immense pride in this notion. How this concept influences our eating relates to the term's second definition: "a process of blending that often results in invigoration° or novelty."° This means that the hope for the future of food in America sits on the positive side of the coin of reinvention. It's why we are willing to embrace new norms around dining, like wine for the masses, food trucks, Tex-Mex, and Italian food that is really a distinct Italian *American* genre,° without which there would be no "American" food to speak of. . . .

omnivore: A person who eats both animal- and plant-based foods.   **social norms:** An accepted pattern of behavior of a particular group that individuals are expected to conform to. **assimilate:** To become part of a group, country, or society; to adapt, adjust, fit in.   **cohesive:** Tightly unified.   **invigoration:** Animation, stimulation.   **novelty:** Something that is new, original, different.   **genre:** A category of composition that has a specific style, format, or type of content.

When Americans order takeout and delivery, Chinese, Mexican, and Italian top the list; when we eat at a restaurant, the most popular types of international cuisines are sushi, Thai, Vietnamese, Brazilian/Argentinian, Greek, and Southeast Asian. That's according to a 2015 study conducted on behalf of the National Restaurant Association, entitled "Global Palates:° Ethnic Cuisines and Flavors in America." 6

But historians and food studies experts point to Italian food as the original symbol of a broader phenomenon:° the gradual incorporation of foreign cuisines° into traditionally bland American palates. Two-thirds of Americans now eat a greater variety of cuisines from around the world than they did just five years ago. The vast majority of us enjoy eating these types of food both at restaurants that serve only that type of food — what you might consider the more authentic experiences — *and* as part of "mainstream menus," as the study called them, at other types of restaurants. 7

Spaghetti and meatballs is a great case study of our ever-more-daring tastes, and the quests for culinary° adventure, that *today* define American appetites. The dish reveals the making of a true fusion° cuisine in American culture. 8

In the culinary community, "fusion" gets a bad rap. It tends to be taken as meaning the food has no identity. But this is misguided. I'm referring to our cuisine at large. 9

And when I ask the question, What does our food show about who we are?, the story of spaghetti and meatballs suddenly isn't just about Italian American food. It's the story of the melting pot, and the novel, distinctly American cuisine that bubbles up out of it. Spaghetti and meatballs is merely one of countless dishes and ways of eating that never existed anywhere else. And collectively, these comprise° a national food culture. One you might call Immigrant American. 10

Chinese immigrants also found certain dishes that could appeal to American tastes — General Tso's chicken not least among them. This adaptation, the mixing and compromising to create entirely new foods, was much the same. One difference between Italian food and other immigrant cuisines in America, though, is the way Italian Americans responded to its Americanization. Chinese Americans, as Harvey Levenstein writes in *Food in the USA*, "generally found the concoctions served in 'chop suey'° houses and made-in-Minnesota canned 'chow mein'° to be abominations,"° while "Italian-Americans generally shared the native-born WASP's° enthusiasm for 11

---

palate: A person's appreciation for taste and flavor. **phenomenon:** An occurrence or situation that exists but cannot be easily explained; a remarkable person, thing, or event. **cuisine:** A style of cooking, especially one attributed to a specific place or culture. **culinary:** Related to cooking, especially cooking developed as a skill or art form. **fusion:** Joining two or more things to create something new; blending elements of two or more culinary traditions to create a new style of cooking. **comprise:** To consist of; to include or contain. **chop suey, chow mein:** Two popular dishes of American Chinese cuisine made of stir-fried meat and vegetables, mixed in a cornstarch-based sauce and served over rice or noodles. **abomination:** Something that is extremely disliked, disgusting, or vile. **WASP:** White Anglo-Saxon Protestant; refers the elements of American culture associated with the dominant ethnic group, composed of European Americans, often used in a derogatory way.

the Americanized version of their cuisine." They were proud that non-Italian Americans gave their food recognition.

Not long ago, Harvey Levenstein points out, many Americans "equated   12
tacos and frijoles refritos° with stomach cramps and diarrhea." Consider, for a moment, that by 1991 salsa outsold ketchup in retail stores. By $40 million. Now, Chipotle is the envy of every restaurateur in the land.

"In 2009, the dollar share of 'ethnic' frozen meals (Asian, Mexican, etc.)   13
surpassed the dollar share of traditional American recipes (e.g., beef Stroga-noff,° Salisbury steak,° mac and cheese, etc.)," reads a presentation slide by the Hartman Group. . . . Hartman also notes that a little fewer than one in eight adult meals eaten at home involves an "emerging global food," while at a restaurant it's more than one of every five meals.

What's driving the *accelerated*° integration° of global cuisines into main-   14
stream culture, then, is the increased number of meals we eat outside the home. The greater percentage of the total bites we eat in a given day or week that are made by someone else. Why *not* give lamb adobo° a try on your Munchery app? Chicken tikka masala° from the Trader Joe's prepared food section looks whirl-worthy. What these and other new food-service mod-els have done from an innovation standpoint, from an industry disruption standpoint, is make foreign dishes more accessible to the masses.

It's the silver lining, if you will, that comes from our not cooking as much   15
anymore.

Two novel business models have dramatically heightened the pace at   16
which — and the fervor° with which — American consumers embrace the exotic: food trucks and the Chipotle format of fast-casual dining. Some people are happy committing a whole Saturday night to trying a family-run Himalayan restaurant, or driving to a retail district where they don't recog-nize the letters on the signs. But some people are not. It's far easier to shift, say, one turkey sandwich you'd normally have for lunch on Tuesday to a kati roll° if the food truck is parked right outside your office. The same thinking goes for everything from Indian "nanini"° and Filipino pork sisig° rice bowls to Vietnamese banh mi° and Austrian schnitzel.° The speed and price point of food truck food — you'll be on your way for under ten dollars in under ten minutes — further reduces barriers to consumption.

---

frijoles refritos: A dish associated with Mexican and Tex-Mex cuisine made of cooked and mashed pinto beans.   **beef Stroganoff:** A Russian dish made of beef and mushrooms with a sour-cream sauce served over egg noodles.   **Salisbury steak:** An American dish popular in the 1960s.   **accelerated:** Something that has been brought about quickly, or more quickly than expected.   **integration:** The act of uniting or bending; the incorporation of parts into a larger whole.   **adobo:** A Spanish marinade, seasoning, or sauce   **chicken tikka masala:** A South-Asian-inspired dish made of chicken marinated in a spicy yogurt sauce.   **fervor:** Intensity of feeling.   **kati roll:** An Indian street food made of a kebab wrapped in a flat-bread.   **nanini:** A combination of the words *naan*, an Indian flatbread, and *panini*, grilled Italian sandwiches.   **sisig:** A dish of Filipino origin made of pig's head and liver, seasoned with local citrus fruit and peppers.   **banh mi:** A sandwich of Vietnamese origin with French influences, made of a baguette filled with pork, pickled vegetables, and pate.   **schnitzel:** Originally from Austria, coated and fried veal.

Fast-casual restaurants with the create-your-own format — also offering   17
that ten-dollar, ten-minute mark — have a similar effect: You start with a base,
pick a protein, and add sauces and toppings as you like. Importantly, that
cheffing° includes tailoring the spiciness and complexity of flavors to your
comfort level.

As the author John Hooper notes, there is a crucial distinction between   18
diversity and disunity. We are a country of political, cultural, and ideological
diversity, spread across many far-reaching geographic subsections. But there
are features that reveal themselves in the foods we eat that characterize us
broadly as a people.

Various arguments try to explain why Americans like "foreign" food, such   19
as increased international travel, shifts in immigration policies that have
altered our country's demographics,° and so on. But it comes down to one
uniquely American value: As a people, we are curious, open to the new — the
unknown or lesser known. We care about discovery.

All within certain limits of course, because don't forget, all this "mutant°   20
mash-up food," as Anthony Bourdain has called it, is happening *alongside*
an only deepened popularity of our old standbys: the Five Guys and Shake
Shacks selling burgers and milkshakes, except better (apparently), or the craft
beer boom with brewpubs selling Reubens and grilled cheese and fries, except
with, you know, truffle° seasoning. All at a time when the average American
still eats three hamburgers a week.

American fare is far from a thing of the past. It's just a matter of how   21
American fare is defined. So it's not as if we've hopped on another bandwagon
entirely — we've welcomed a whole caravan of new wagons into our fleet.

In 2014, *Bon Appetit*'s Andrew Knowlton featured a restaurant in San   22
Antonio, Texas, called Hot Joy, an Asian fusion joint he called "rule-breaking"
and "trendsetting." Knowlton writes: "Chef Quealy Watson has never been to
Asia. Everything he knows about Chinese, Japanese, Indian, or the rest of that
vast region's cuisine he picked up from cookbooks and the Internet. But who
cares anymore? Authenticity° and rigid adherence° to tradition are overrated.
Deliciousness is king."

So it turns out that one of our biggest problems as eaters, our unstable   23
food culture, is also one of our greatest strengths: The idea that anything
goes — that in throwing it all into the mix something wonderful emerges — is
why we have culinary gems you can't find anywhere else.

Korean tacos and naan pizza and California rolls. Some might consider   24
these horrors. Sullied° versions of the *true* cultural entities. But not us. In
America, collisions are commendable.°

---

cheffing: Working as a chef   demographic: Statistical characteristic of a human population;
a market segment.   mutant: A deviation; can mean something that is monstrous.   truffle:
A highly-valued fungus that grows underground   authenticity: Real-ness; not false.
adherence: The act of holding fast, sticking by.   sullied: Stained, damaged, polluted,
spoiled.   commendable: Praiseworthy.

Questions to Start You Thinking

1. **Considering Meaning:** According to Egan, when it comes to food, why are Americans so willing to try new things, and even reinvent food?

2. **Identifying Writing Strategies:** Egan writes that certain dishes and ways of eating "comprise a national food culture. One you might call Immigrant American" (paragraph 10). What examples and details does Egan draw on to support this statement?

3. **Reading Critically:** For what audience does Egan write this essay? How can you tell?

4. **Expanding Vocabulary:** In her final sentence (paragraph 24), Egan writes, "In America, collisions are commendable." What does she refer to and what does she mean?

5. **Making Connections:** Think about Egan's essay in relation to Shankar Vendantam's "The Huddled Masses and the Myth of America" (pp. 332–37). What "myths" about American eating are suggested in Egan's essay?

Suggestions for Writing

1. Write about a food that you enjoy. To what extent does this food define you? What does it say (or not say) about who you are?

2. Egan mentions an American Asian fusion restaurant created by a chef who has never been to Asia, but who learned about Asian foods through cookbooks and the Internet. She writes of authenticity in cuisine (paragraph 22): "[W]ho cares anymore? Authenticity and rigid adherence to tradition are overrated. Deliciousness is king." Do you agree with her view? Why or why not?

Stephen Kinzer

Joining the Military Doesn't Make You a Hero

Watson Institute

Stephen Kinzer is a prize-winning foreign-correspondent and author. He wrote for more than twenty years for the *New York Times*, with work appearing in the *Guardian* and the *Boston Globe*, where the following article was first published. Kinzer has taught international studies at Brown University and journalism and political science at Northwestern University.

AS YOU READ: Ask yourself, what makes someone a hero? Is it fair to automatically deem someone a hero? What is the effect of doing so?

Who is a hero? In today's America, it is someone who chooses a military career, puts on a uniform, and prepares for war. Placing soldiers and veterans on this kind of pedestal° is a relatively new phenomenon.° 1

pedestal: The base of an upright structure, column or statue; a position of esteem.
phenomenon: An occurrence or situation that exists but cannot be easily explained; a remarkable person, thing, or event.

Past generations of Americans saw soldiers as ordinary human beings. 2
They were like the rest of us: big and small, smart and dumb, capable of good
and bad choices. Now we pretend they are demi-gods.°

One reason Americans have come to view soldiers as our only protectors 3
is that we have accepted the idea that our country is under permanent threat
from fanatics who want to kill us and destroy our way of life. Yet we also felt
this way at the height of the Cold War,° and we did not fetishize° soldiers
then the way we do now. Perhaps that was because few were coming home in
body bags.

Many were killed during the Vietnam War, though, and that did not move 4
us to worship everyone who put on a uniform. We recognized, as all societies
do, that some soldiers are true heroes — but because of their individual acts,
not simply because they chose military careers. We are mature enough to
know that a banker's suit does not always reflect honesty and that a cleric's°
robe may not cloak a pure soul. Yet we readily believe that the olive-green uniform automatically raises its wearer to saintly status.

At sports stadiums, many games now include a ceremony at which a uni- 5
formed "honor guard" marches in formation bearing ceremonial weapons.
Then, during a break in the action, a soldier appears on the field or court, waving to the adoring crowd as an announcer recounts service in Iraq, Afghanistan, or the "war on terror." These rituals feed the fantasy that military service
turns one into a better, more selfless human being.

To admire soldiers who have performed acts of bravery is fully justified. 6
Not all combat heroes, however, are eager to stand before thousands of people and accept the honor they deserve. If we truly want to promote a positive
form of hero-worship, we should not only abandon the idea that uniforms
automatically transform ordinary people into giants. We should also recognize the other giants who protect and defend our society.

Out communities are full of everyday heroes. These are the nurses, school- 7
teachers, addiction counsellors, community organizers, social workers,
coaches, probation officers, and other civilians who struggle to keep Americans
from slipping toward despair, sickness, or violence. They guide people away
from hopelessness and toward productive lives. Society collapses without these
people. Yet we rarely give them the chance to acknowledge the gratitude of
cheering multitudes. That honor is reserved for those whose individual merit
may be limited to their choice — perhaps motivated by a variety of factors — to
put on a uniform.

When soldiers were part of society, people recognized them as ordinary 8
human beings. Now, with the emergence of the all-volunteer army, society has
transferred the burden of war to a small, self-contained caste° cut off from

demi-god: A mythological being with more power than a mortal, but less than a god.
Cold War: The state of political hostility between the United States and its allies against
the Soviet bloc countries, from 1945 to1990.   **fetishize:** To become obsessed with; to fixate
on something as an object of sexual or spiritual worship.   **cleric:** A priest or other religious
leader.   **caste:** A class or other division of society rigidly based on differences in wealth,
inherited rank, occupation, or race.

the American mainstream. This distance allows civilians to develop extravagant fantasies about soldiers that feed the militarist impulse. If we believe our soldiers are superheroes, it makes sense to send them to faraway battlefields to solve our perceived problems in the world. That is why, in this era of seemingly endless war, politicians, the defense industry, and even big-time sports compete with each other to promote hero-worship of soldiers and veterans.

This serves the cynical° interests of those who, for political or business   9
reasons, want to encourage American involvement in foreign wars. Even worse, it distracts attention away from the scandalous way we treat our veterans. Cheering for them in public and saluting them in cliché-ridden° speeches is a way to disguise the fact that our society callously° discards many of them. Shocking rates of unemployment, mental illness, homelessness, addiction, and suicide among our veterans constitute a national disgrace. It is far easier, however, to spend a few seconds applauding a smiling soldier than to contemplate a troubled veteran left behind by an uncaring country.

The soldier acknowledging cheers at a ball game is a fantasy figure we can   10
easily admire. Veterans in need are more disturbing, so we keep them invisible. If we truly considered our uniformed fighters heroic, we would show them real gratitude rather than the phony kind that gives us a shiver of momentary pride but does them little good.

cynical: Distrustful of human nature and motives.   cliché-ridden: Plagued by unoriginal, overused expressions or ideas.   callously: Done without sympathy or emotion.

Questions to Start You Thinking

1. **Considering Meaning:** According to Kinzer, why do Americans treat soldiers the way they do (paragraphs 1–3)?

2. **Identifying Writing Strategies:** Kinzer writes, the hero-worship of soldiers "distracts attention away from the scandalous way we treat our veterans. . . . Shocking rates of unemployment, mental illness, homelessness, addiction, and suicide among our veterans constitutes a national disgrace" (paragraph 9). What is the impact of these statements on Kinzer's overall argument?

3. **Reading Critically:** Do you consider Kinzer's argument to be pro-soldier/veteran? Why or why not?

4. **Expanding Vocabulary:** What does Kinzer mean when he says that Americans "fetishize" soldiers (paragraph 2)? What examples does he provide to support this claim (paragraph 5, for example)?

5. **Making Connections with the Paired Essay:** Based on your reading of this essay, how would Kinzer likely respond to Sidra Montgomery's argument against approaching veterans to say, "Thank You for Your Service" (pp. 350–55)? Support your argument with examples from both texts.

Suggestions for Writing

1. Kinzer writes (paragraph 4): "We are mature enough to know that a banker's suit does not always reflect honesty and that a cleric's robe may not cloak a pure soul." Do you agree? Does Kinzer's generalization about how Americans tend to view business leaders or the clergy align with your experience? How questioning are we when it comes to authority figures in our society—even in our own lives? Write an essay in which you address these questions, supporting your argument with examples. Consider closing your essay by noting the human qualities and actions that earn your trust, respect, and admiration.

2. Kinzer argues (paragraphs 6–7) that we should recognize the "everyday" heroes in our lives. Can you think of an ordinary person in your own life who deserves to be recognized? Write an essay in which you identify that person (or people) and provide reasons why he/she/they deserve to be considered heroic.

Sidra Montgomery

Sidra Montgomery

The Emotion Work of "Thank You for Your Service"

Sidra Montgomery earned her PhD in Sociology from the University of Maryland, College Park. For her dissertation, she researched the concept of the "wounded warrior" and its impact on veterans. Montgomery is a researcher at Insight Policy Research, where she provides data and evaluation on issues affecting vulnerable populations. As a Navy Spouse, she has served on the advisory board for MFAN (Military Family Advisory Network). The following essay was first published by Veteran Scholars (https://veteranscholars.com), a group that is affiliated with the University of Maryland, College Park, Department of Sociology, and the Center for Research on Military Organization.

AS YOU READ: Ask yourself, when you see a veteran, what do you do? Do you approach that person? Thank them for your service? If you are a veteran yourself, has anyone approached you to thank you for your service? If so, how did you feel about that?

In the post-9/11° era, "thank you for your service" (TYFYS) has become the new mantra of public support bestowed upon the veteran community. In the early 2000s, as the wars in Afghanistan° and Iraq° began escalating, "Support Our Troops" car magnets increasingly appeared on the trunks of cars across America. After well over 15 years of war, public gratitude is now most commonly expressed in small interactions between veterans and the public they've served—with strangers saying TYFYS or offering to pay for a coffee or meal. If you ask any recent servicemember or veteran how they feel when someone says TYFYS, you'll probably hear them express a strong opinion

1

post-9/11: Occurring after the terrorist attacks on the United States of September 11, 2001.   **Afghanistan:** A country in south central Asia that the U.S. has been engaged in war with since 2001.   **Iraq:** A country in southwestern Asia that the U.S. was at war with from 2003 to 2011.

about the phrase. While some view it positively and enjoy these interactions, most find it awkward, uncomfortable or irritating. The message of support and gratitude that well-meaning Americans are attempting to express is often lost in translation with veterans.

A collection of op-ed° pieces have addressed why servicemembers find TYFYS to be a point of disconnection rather than connection. James Kelly, an active-duty Marine, says that he hears the phrase so often it has become an "empty platitude,"° something people say only because it is "politically correct."° Matt Richtel, a *New York Times* reporter, highlights how veterans feel the phrase can be self-serving; civilians get to pat themselves on the back because they are doing something for veterans, alleviating any sense of guilt in the era of an all-volunteer service. Another common complaint is that TYFYS doesn't start the conversation between veterans and civilians—it stunts° it—leaving veterans feeling more isolated and less connected to the America they served. Veterans commonly remark that civilians don't even know what they are saying "thank you" for. Elizabeth Samet, a professor at West Point, argues that we've come to the other "unthinking extreme" with TYFYS as an attempt for atonement° after the poor treatment of Vietnam veterans.

While many have tried to explain *why* veterans find TYFYS to be lacking, few have examined *how these interactions affect veterans.* Having interviewed servicemembers and veterans for the past 3 years in my professional life, and being a military spouse for the past 5 years, I have always been intrigued by how veterans handle these moments and interactions. I watch the discomfort when strangers approach my interview subjects or friends and say TYFYS—it becomes an awkward stumble for the veteran to find a way to muster their appreciation for a gesture that doesn't necessarily square with its intent.

Emotion Work

As I analyzed the data I collected for my dissertation,° a total of 39 interviews with wounded, injured, and ill post-9/11 veterans, I realized these interactions require veterans to engage in *emotion work,* a sociological concept defined by Arlie Hochschild. Emotion work is defined by Hochschild as "trying to change, in degree or quality, an emotion or feeling" (1979: 561). It is an active attempt to shape and direct one's feelings to match the appropriate emotions for a given situation. For example, when someone thanks you for something you've done—you're supposed to feel good, right? Gratitude should give you that warm fuzzy feeling inside. This is called "feeling rules"; it's how we know what we should be feeling in any given moment.

For veterans who genuinely appreciate and enjoy hearing TYFYS and other acts of gratitude—there is no "work" necessary because their feelings are

---

op-ed: Short for "opposite the editorial page" or "opinion editorial," an opinion piece that appears in a newspaper, magazine, or other publication.   **platitude:** A trite, dull, or bland remark.   **politically correct:** Conforming to a belief that language or actions that could offend should be eliminated.   **stunt:** To hinder the normal growth or progress of.   **atonement:** amends for an offense or injury.   **dissertation:** An extensive piece of writing focused on a specific subject; a paper submitted for a doctorate degree.

appropriate given the situation. For Alex, a wounded Marine veteran, TYFYS makes him feel as though he is "seen" and that his service is validated:°

> I like it. I really like it when people acknowledge my service. I'm not out there trying to get someone to do it, but when someone takes time out of their day to shake my hand and say, 'Thank you for your service.' It's like, 'Wow. You know this country — it was worth it. You know it's — proud of your service to the country'. . . That's something special.

Alex's emotions are in line with what we expect to feel when someone   6
says thank you and acknowledges something that we have done. He doesn't have to control or wrangle° his emotions because they already align with the socially prescribed° "feeling rules" and expectations.

My dissertation data suggests that 15 to 20% of veterans share Alex's feel-   7
ings; they enjoy and appreciate when people thank them for their service or demonstrate their gratitude through other acts and gestures. Personally and anecdotally,° I've found about the same split: 10–20% find TYFYS gratifying and associate it with positive feelings, and 80–90% of servicemembers and veterans feel uncomfortable or upset about the phrase.

For the majority of wounded veterans I interviewed, who don't have posi-   8
tive associations with TYFYS, these interactions necessitate emotion work. As they go about their day-to-day life, they are thrust into situations where they must acknowledge and negotiate the gratitude of total strangers through their own emotional response: emotions that do not match their true feelings in the situation. Luis, a young Marine Corps veteran with visible injuries, describes how he wrestles with having to do emotion work in these interactions:

> When people say thank you for your service, thank you for what you did . . . it's kind of lost it's shock value or something. I've heard it so much that I'm embarrassed that I can't give them . . . like that first time when some-one said thank you for your service . . . I feel like I don't give them enough sincerity, I feel bad . . . I feel embarrassed for myself because I can't do that, you know? . . . I just hear it sooooo much.

Luis wants to give others a genuine emotional reaction each time they   9
thank him for his service, but he feels he can't because of the overwhelming number of times this happens to him. From this quote it's clear he is blaming himself for even having to perform emotion work in the first place. Connor, an Army veteran with invisible injuries, discusses how he handles TYFYS:

> I give the standard, thanks, appreciate it or happy to do it. Or I don't get into it. Even if I know it's totally fake I'm like, yeah, appreciate it. And I'll give just a fake answer. As fake as I got [from them], that's how much I'll give back . . . It'll be like . . . 'oh, thanks' with the plastic smile. You know what I mean?

---

validated: Made valid; supported or recognized as correct.   **wrangle:** To dispute; to heard, control, and care for livestock.   **prescribed:** Specified or dictated.   **anecdotally:** Done in a way that suggests a story, that is based on unscientific observation.

Connor attempts to mirror the level of sincerity in the interaction,   10
aligning his own response with it. His comment about how he puts on a
"plastic smile" describes how he engages in surface acting: a way to present the necessary emotion to others even though his own feelings haven't
changed.

Another common strategy for veterans, especially wounded veterans who   11
are frequently thanked for their service, is the use of predetermined° responses.
Having a rolodex° of appropriate responses minimizes impromptu° emotion
work. Jackson, a Marine Corps veteran who has visible injuries, says that hearing TYFYS *"just gets old"* because he hears it so much. When I asked him how
he usually responds, he said:

> [I will say] '...no, *thank you.'* Another one is like some people [say] 'thank
> *you guys* for what *you do*...you guys made coming home so much easier and
> so much more worth it.' So make them feel just as adequate in a way.

Jackson reveals the set of responses that he (and others) normally give.   12
These prepackaged responses increase the efficiency of Jackson's emotion
work by creating sentiments that acknowledge and reciprocate the gratitude–
an intentional move on Jackson's part.

Several years after her Marine Corps service, Susan, an invisibly injured   13
veteran, has gained a new perspective on the TYFYS issue. She is now able to
see it from another point of view:

> You get to finally a point — I finally went, you know, these people are very
> sincere, and you've got to let them just say the thing. Because they gener-
> ally want to thank you. And this is so not your experience. You don't have
> to have it with them. And then it became okay going, you know what,
> they're really caring, lovely people most of the time . . .

Susan describes taking away her own investment in these interactions as a   14
way to distance herself from constantly engaging in emotion work whenever
someone says "thank you." She understands the moment to be more about
the other person than herself. She also describes her engagement with deep
acting: working to change the way she truly feels about these interactions; trying to bring her own emotions in line with what's expected.

The Cumulative° Effect for Visibly Injured Veterans

For current servicemembers, veterans, and invisibly injured veterans these   15
moments of invited gratitude from strangers happen occasionally or in concentrated environments where they know they may be thanked or approached.
For visibly injured veterans, these interactions happen every day. Visibly
injured veterans are disproportionately burdened with doing the emotional

---

predetermined: predestined, determined beforehand.   **rolodex:** A list of friends and
business contacts (based on the old "Rolodex" brand of circular file cards).   **impromptu:**
Unplanned, improvised.   **cumulative:** Made up of accumulated parts or additions.

work surrounding public gratitude because their status as wounded veterans can't be hidden or "taken off" like a uniform. And their visible injury only amplifies feelings of gratitude among the public, causing them to experience more of these moments and interactions.

Thomas, an Army veteran with visible injuries, describes: 16

> [Civilians] . . . they just all want to do the right things. And I mean, to that person they have one chance to make a difference to one person. But if it's you, they're the 100th person today to say 'thank you for your service.'

The cumulative effect of these interactions wears on Thomas and other   17
visibly injured veterans:

> And what if everybody did that to me? Like, everywhere I went, what if every single person thought they were doing me a favor and said "thank you for your service." I would spend my whole life giving to other people. I could literally go every five feet and just be doling out good feelings to everybody. And I'm sorry, I'm an emotional bank account, we're all just emotional bank accounts.

Thomas' comments clearly reveal how visibly injured veterans can quickly   18
become exhausted from the emotion work of receiving TYFYS and other gestures of gratitude. What seems like a small interaction in the moment is continually repeated for wounded veterans like Thomas.

The treatment of U.S. veterans has significantly changed over time, from   19
the prosperous return of World War II veterans to the protests and mistreatment of Vietnam veterans to the new era of the all-volunteer force. It is important that as a nation, we engage in a constant reflection process of how we treat our veterans, from the largest of government programs to the smallest interpersonal interactions. The well-meaning intent behind TYFYS isn't always received by post-9/11 veterans in the same way.

Practical Suggestions: What Should We Be Doing to Show Our Gratitude and Appreciation?

Inevitably, after presenting these issues with TYFYS I get asked: *"well, what   20
should we be doing*?" This is both a prudent° and complicated question, and there is no one-size-fits-all answer. We all have our own personal preferences of what is meaningful to us based on our personality, life experiences, and our thoughts. I'm not here to say that I have *the* answer, but I have a couple suggestions based on my work with veterans:

1. **Judge whether the military member or veteran seems open to conversation with a stranger.** You know how you can tell whether the person next to you on a plane wants to talk or wants to be left alone? The

prudent: Marked by wisdom and good judgment.

same should go for your interactions with veterans, servicemembers, and wounded veterans. Do they appear willing to engage with others (i.e., making eye contact or already engaging in a friendly conversation with you), or do they look like they just want to grab their coffee and go about their day? If the latter—let them go about their day and reflect privately on your gratitude for their willingness to lay their life on the line for our freedom.

2. **If you want to show your support for veterans, find a local organization that helps veterans in your community.** Do your research, find out what organizations are doing to serve veterans and improve their lives. Give your financial support or your time (through volunteering).

3. **Go beyond "thank you for your service."** Ask them why they served, ask them when and where they served, ask them what they most enjoyed about their service. Dig deeper; cultivate° gratitude for their service by learning more about it.

cultivate: To foster the growth of.

Questions to Start You Thinking

1. **Considering Meaning:** How do most veterans feel about being thanked for their service? What is "emotion work" (paragraph 4)? To what degree do we require "emotion work" of veterans when we thank them for their service (paragraphs 4–14)?

2. **Identifying Writing Strategies:** To support her discussion of the impact of "emotion work" on veterans, Montgomery includes quotations from several veterans she has interviewed. What is the overall effect of these voices on her argument? How do these voices impact your experience as a reader?

3. **Reading Critically:** Montgomery writes of Jackson, a Marine Corps veteran, "[His] prepackaged responses increase the efficiency of Jackson's emotion work" (paragraphs 11–12). What does she mean?

4. **Expanding Vocabulary:** According to this essay, what is the difference between "surface acting" (paragraph 10) and "deep acting" (paragraphs 13–14)?

5. **Making Connections with the Paired Essay:** Both Montgomery and Stephen Kinzer (see "Joining the Military Doesn't Make You a Hero," on pp. 347–49) discuss the ways that Americans can isolate or create distance between themselves and veterans. Reread each essay, taking note of examples of this distance, and write an essay in which you compare their ideas and argue for a way to better communicate with veterans. Support your ideas with examples from the texts.

Suggestions for Writing

1. In paragraph 20, Montgomery suggests some specific ways of showing appreciation toward veterans that do not include approaching them to thank them for their service. Which of the three options would you be most likely to try, and why? Alternatively, what options not provided in the essay might you explore?

2. Montgomery addresses the differences in day-to-day social experiences between veterans with visible wounds and veterans with invisible wounds. How might their experiences be similar? How might they be different? How would those factors affect how you interact with those veterans?

Krystyna Szulecka/Alamy

Responding to an Image

Jaume Plensa is a sculptor and artist from Spain. His installation *29 Palms*, shown above, is a 164-foot curtain composed of steel-cut letters comprising his favorite poems. The letters are designed to cast fluid shadows across the wall and floor. In the photo, a visitor touches the letters to make them "sing," as Plensa encourages. Reflect on this tactile, three-dimensional, multimedia presentation of letters, which we often encounter in static settings, like books and screens. What does Plensa's installation seem to be saying about the role of words in our world, and its relationship to language?

Jenny Jarvie

Trigger Happy

Jenny Jarvie is a former reporter for the *Los Angeles Times* and a freelance writer whose work has appeared in the *Atlantic*, the *Telegraph*, and *Poetry Magazine*. Jarvie is the recipient of the Catherine Pakenham Award for the most promising young female writer in Britain. In the following article, originally published in the the *New Republic*, Jarvie discusses the negative effects of trigger warnings.

AS YOU READ: What are trigger warnings, and how are they being used on college campuses and in American media?

The "trigger warning" has spread from blogs to college classes. Can it be stopped?

The headline above would, if some readers had their way, include a "trigger warning" — a disclaimer to alert you that this article contains potentially traumatic subject matter. Such warnings, which are most commonly applied to discussions about rape, sexual abuse, and mental illness, have appeared on message boards since the early days of the Web. Some consider them an irksome tic of the blogosphere's most hypersensitive fringes, and yet they've spread from feminist forums and social media to sites as large as the *Huffington Post*. The trigger warning has gained momentum beyond the Internet — at some of the nation's most prestigious universities.

In recent years, student leaders at the University of California, Santa Barbara, passed a resolution urging officials to institute mandatory trigger warnings on class syllabi. Professors who present "content that may trigger the onset of symptoms of Post-Traumatic Stress Disorder"° would be required to issue advance alerts and allow students to skip those classes. According to UCSB newspaper the *Daily Nexus*, Bailey Loverin, the student who sponsored the proposal, decided to push the issue after attending a class in which she "felt forced" to sit through a film that featured an "insinuation"° of sexual assault and a graphic depiction of rape. A victim of sexual abuse, she did not want to remain in the room, but she feared she would only draw attention to herself by walking out.

On college campuses across the country, students have demanded trigger warnings on class content. Many instructors are obliging with alerts in handouts and before presentations, even e-mailing notes of caution ahead of class. At Scripps College, lecturers give warnings before presenting a core curriculum class, the "Histories of the Present: Violence," although some have questioned the value of such alerts when students are still required to attend class. Oberlin College has published an official document on triggers, advising faculty members to "be aware of racism, classism, sexism, heterosexism, cissexism,° ableism,° and other issues of privilege and oppression," to remove triggering material when it doesn't "directly" contribute to learning goals

Post-Traumatic Stress Disorder: A mental health disorder triggered by a traumatic event; can lead to flashbacks and severe anxiety.   **insinuation:** Subtle hinting at something derogatory.   **cissexism:** The privileging and enforcing of gender binaries resulting in prejudice toward those who identify as transgender.   **ableism:** Discrimination favoring able-bodied people.

and "strongly consider" developing a policy to make "triggering material" optional. Chinua Achebe's *Things Fall Apart*, it states, is a novel that may "trigger readers who have experienced racism, colonialism, religious persecution, violence, suicide, and more." Warnings have been proposed even for books long considered suitable material for high-schoolers: a Rutgers University sophomore suggested that an alert for F. Scott Fitzgerald's *The Great Gatsby* say, "TW: suicide, domestic abuse, and graphic violence."

What began as a way of moderating Internet forums for the vulnerable and mentally ill now threatens to define public discussion both online and off. The trigger warning signals not only the growing precautionary approach to words and ideas in the university, but a wider cultural hypersensitivity to harm and a paranoia about giving offense. And yet, for all the debate about the warnings on campuses and on the Internet, few are grappling with the ramifications° for society as a whole.   5

Not everyone seems to agree on what the trigger warning is, let alone how it should be applied. Initially, trigger warnings were used in self-help and feminist forums to help readers who might have post-traumatic stress disorder to avoid graphic content that might cause painful memories, flashbacks, or panic attacks. Some Web sites, like *Bodies Under Siege*, a self-injury support message board, developed systems of adding abbreviated topic tags — from SI (self injury) to ED (eating disorders) — to particularly explicit posts. As the Internet grew, warnings became more popular, and critics began to question their use. Susannah Breslin wrote in the website *True/Slant* that feminists were applying the term "like a Southern cook applies Pam cooking spray to an overused nonstick frying pan" — prompting *Feministing* to call her a "certifiable asshole," and *Jezebel* to lament that the debate has "been totally clouded by ridiculous inflammatory rhetoric."   6

The term only spread with the advent of social media. The *Awl*'s Choire Sicha argued that it had "lost all its meaning." Since then, alerts have been applied to topics as diverse as sex, pregnancy, addiction, bullying, suicide, sizeism, ableism, homophobia, transphobia, slut shaming, victim-blaming, alcohol, blood, insects, small holes, and animals in wigs. Certain people, from rapper Chris Brown to sex columnist Dan Savage, have been dubbed "triggering." Some have called for trigger warnings for television shows such as *Scandal* and *Downton Abbey*. Even the *New Republic* has suggested the satirical news site the *Onion* carry trigger warnings.   7

Slate declared that trigger warnings have become the target of humor. *Jezebel,* which does not issue trigger warnings, raised hackles° by using the term as a headline joke: "It's Time To Talk About Bug Infestations [TRIGGER WARNING]." Such usage, one critic argued, amounted to "trivializing" such alerts and "trolling people who believe in them." And in Britain, Suzanne Moore, a feminist columnist for the *Guardian*, was taken to task when she put a trigger warning on her Twitter bioline, mocking those who followed her feeds only to claim offense. Some critics have ridiculed her in turn: "Trigger   8

---

ramifications: Consequences.   **raised hackles:** Angered, or bred resentment.

warning, @Suzanne_moore is talking again." (Moore's Twitter bio now reads, "Media Whore.")

The backlash° has not stopped the growth of the trigger warning, and now 9 that they've entered university classrooms, it's only a matter of time before warnings are demanded for other grade levels. As students introduce them in college newspapers, promotional material for plays, even poetry slams, it's not inconceivable that they'll appear at the beginning of film screenings and at the entrance to art exhibits. Will newspapers start applying warnings to articles about rape, murder, and war? Could they even become a regular feature of speech? "I was walking down Main Street last night when — trigger warning — I saw an elderly woman get mugged."

The "Geek Feminism Wiki" states that trigger warnings should be used 10 for "graphic descriptions or extensive discussion" of abuse, torture, self-harm, suicide, eating disorders, body shaming, and even "psychologically realistic" depictions of *the mental state* of people suffering from those; it notes that some have gone further, arguing for warnings before the "depiction or discussion of any consensual sexual activity [and] of discriminatory attitudes or actions, such as sexism or racism." The definition on the *Queer Dictionary Tumblr* is similar, but expands warnings even to discussion of *statistics* on hate crimes and self-harming.

As the list of trigger warning–worthy topics continues to grow, there's 11 scant research demonstrating how words "trigger" or how warnings might help. Most psychological research on PTSD suggests that, for those who have experienced trauma, "triggers" can be complex and unpredictable, appearing in many forms, from sounds to smells to weather conditions and times of the year. In this sense, anything can be a trigger — a musky cologne, a ditsy pop song, a footprint in the snow.

As a means of navigating the Internet, or setting the tone for academic 12 discussion, the trigger warning is unhelpful. Once we start imposing alerts on the basis of potential trauma, where do we stop? One of the problems with the concept of triggering — understanding words as devices that activate a mechanism or cause a situation — is it promotes a rigid, overly determin- istic approach to language. There is no rational basis for applying warnings because there is no objective measure of words' potential harm. Of course, words can inspire intense reactions, but they have no intrinsic danger. Two people who have endured similarly painful experiences, from rape to war, can read the same material and respond in wholly different ways.

Issuing caution on the basis of potential harm or insult doesn't help us 13 negotiate our reactions; it makes our dealings with others more fraught. As Breslin pointed out, trigger warnings can have the opposite of their intended effect, luring in sensitive people (and perhaps connoisseurs of graphic content, too). More importantly, they reinforce the fear of words by depicting an ever-expanding number of articles and books as dangerous and requiring of regulation. By framing more public spaces, from the Internet

---

backlash: A strong, negative reaction, especially to a social or political movement.

to the college classroom, as full of infinite yet ill-defined hazards, trigger warnings encourage us to think of ourselves as more weak and fragile than we really are.

What's more, the fear of triggers risks narrowing what we're exposed to. 14 Raechel Tiffe, an assistant professor in Communication Arts and Sciences at Merrimack College, Massachusetts, described a lesson in which she thought everything had gone well, until a student approached her about a clip from the television musical comedy *Glee* in which a student commits suicide. For Tiffe, who uses trigger warnings for sexual assault and rape, the incident was a "teaching moment" — not for the students, but for her to be more aware of the breadth of students' sensitivities.

As academics become more preoccupied with students' feelings of harm, 15 they risk opening the door to a never-ending litany of requests. When students at Wellesley College protested a sculpture of a man in his underwear because, according to the *Change.org* petition, it was a source of "triggering thoughts regarding sexual assault." While the petition acknowledged the sculpture may not disturb everyone on campus, it insisted we share a "responsibility to pay attention to and attempt to answer the needs of all of our community members." Even after the artist explained that the figure was supposed to be sleepwalking, students continued to insist it be moved indoors.

Trigger warnings are presented as a gesture of empathy, but the irony 16 is they lead only to more solipsism, an over-preoccupation with one's own feelings — much to the detriment of society as a whole. Structuring public life around the most fragile personal sensitivities will only restrict all of our horizons. Engaging with ideas involves risk, and slapping warnings on them only undermines the principle of intellectual exploration. We cannot anticipate every potential trigger — the world, like the Internet, is too large and unwieldy.° But even if we could, why would we want to? Bending the world to accommodate our personal frailties does not help us overcome them.

unwieldy: Difficult to manage.

Questions to Start You Thinking

1. **Considering Meaning:** Jarvie states in paragraph 5 that trigger warnings threaten "to define public discussion both online and off." How does she support this argument?

2. **Identifying Writing Strategies:** In paragraph 8, Jarvie notes that trigger warnings have "become the target of humor" in some publications. Why do you think she includes these details? How does this section help support her argument?

3. **Reading Critically:** In paragraph 12, Jarvie writes, "as a means of navigating the Internet, or setting the tone for academic discussion, the trigger warning is unhelpful." What does she mean by "unhelpful"? How does she support this position?

4. **Expanding Vocabulary:** How would you define the word *backlash*, which appears in paragraph 9? What types of backlash has Jarvie identified in her essay?

5. **Making Connections:** In "What Does 'Latinx' Mean?" (pp. 366–68), Yesenia Padilla presents her ideas about language and inclusivity. How do you think she would respond to the idea of trigger warnings? Use quotes from the article to support your position.

Suggestions for Writing

1. Argue in an essay for or against the use of trigger warnings. Make sure you define the term and determine what types of specific trigger warnings you are arguing for or against. Also include where these warnings are or are not appropriate, including on college syllabi, in newspaper articles, on television, and in films.

2. At the end of the essay, Jarvie fears that the use of trigger warnings will lead to restrictions of free speech. Write an argument that either defends or refutes this claim.

Bettmann/Getty Images

James Baldwin

If Black English Isn't a Language, Then Tell Me, What Is?

James Baldwin (1924–87) was a novelist, playwright, and essayist. The grandson of a slave, he was born in Harlem, in New York City, but spent the later part of his life in France. Among his major works are *Nobody Knows My Name: Notes of a Native Son*, *The Fire Next Time*, and *Go Tell It on the Mountain*. The following essay originally appeared in 1979 in the *New York Times*.

AS YOU READ: What is black English? How did it evolve? Why should it be considered as a language unto itself?

The argument concerning the use, or the status, or the reality, of black English is rooted in American history and has absolutely nothing to do with the question the argument supposes itself to be posing. The argument has nothing to do with language itself but with the *role* of language. Language, incontestably, reveals the speaker. Language, also, far more dubiously, is meant to define the other — and, in this case, the other is refusing to be defined by a language that has never been able to recognize him.

People evolve a language in order to describe and thus control their circumstances, or in order not to be submerged by a reality that they cannot articulate. (And, if they cannot articulate it, they *are* submerged.) A Frenchman living in Paris speaks a subtly and crucially different language from that of the man living in Marseilles; neither sounds very much like a man living in

Quebec;° and they would all have great difficulty in apprehending what the man from Guadeloupe, or Martinique,° is saying, to say nothing of the man from Senegal° — although the "common" language of all these areas is French. But each has paid, and is paying, a different price for this "common" language, in which, as it turns out, they are not saying, and cannot be saying, the same things: They each have very different realities to articulate, or control.

What joins all languages, and all men, is the necessity to confront life, in order, not inconceivably, to outwit death: The price for this is the acceptance, and achievement, of one's temporal identity. So that, for example, thought it is not taught in the schools (and this has the potential of becoming a political issue) the south of France still clings to its ancient and musical Provençal, which resists being described as a "dialect."° And much of the tension in the Basque countries,° and in Wales,° is due to the Basque and Welsh determination not to allow their languages to be destroyed. This determination also feeds the flames in Ireland for many indignities the Irish have been forced to undergo at English hands is the English contempt for their language.

It goes without saying, then, that language is also a political instrument, means, and proof of power. It is the most vivid and crucial key to identify: It reveals the private identity, and connects one with, or divorces one from, the larger, public, or communal identity. There have been, and are, times, and places, when to speak a certain language could be dangerous, even fatal. Or, one may speak the same language, but in such a way that one's antecedents are revealed, or (one hopes) hidden. This is true in France, and is absolutely true in England: The range (and reign) of accents on that damp little island make England coherent° for the English and totally incomprehensible for everyone else. To open your mouth in England is (if I may use black English) to "put your business in the street": You have confessed your parents, your youth, your school, your salary, your self-esteem, and, alas, your future.

Now, I do not know what white Americans would sound like if there had never been any black people in the United States, but they would not sound the way they sound. *Jazz*, for example, is a very specific sexual term, as in *jazz me, baby*, but white people purified it into the Jazz Age. *Sock it to me*, which means, roughly, the same thing, has been adopted by Nathaniel Hawthorne's descendants with no qualms or hesitations at all, along with *let it all hang out* and *right on! Beat to his socks* which was once the black's most total and despairing image of poverty, was transformed into a thing called the Beat Generation, which phenomenon was, largely, composed of *uptight*, middle-class white people, imitating poverty, trying to *get down*, to get *with it*, doing their *thing*, doing their despairing best to be *funky*, which we, the blacks, never dreamed of doing — we *were* funky, baby, like *funk* was going out of style.

3

4

5

Quebec: A French-speaking province of Canada.   **Guadeloupe or Martinique:** Two French-Caribbean islands.   **Senegal:** A West African nation, formerly a French colony.   **dialect:** A variety of a language used in a particular region or by a particular group.   **Basque Countries:** An autonomous region on the border of Spain and France, where the Basque language is spoken.   **Wales:** A country in Great Britain where the Welsh language is spoken.   **coherent:** Understandable.

Now, no one can eat his cake, and have it, too, and it is late in the day to attempt to penalize black people for having created a language that permits the nation its only glimpse of reality, a language without which the nation would be even more *whipped* than it is.

6

I say that the present skirmish° is rooted in American history, and it is. Black English is the creation of the black diaspora.° Blacks came to the United States chained to each other, but from different tribes: Neither could speak the other's language. If two black people, at that bitter hour of the world's history, had been able to speak to each other, the institution of chattel slavery° could never have lasted as long as it did. Subsequently, the slave was given, under the eye, and the gun, of his master, Congo Square,° and the Bible — or in other words, and under these conditions, the slave began the formation of the black church, and it is within this unprecedented° tabernacle° that black English began to be formed. This was not, merely, as in the European example, the adoption of a foreign tongue, but an alchemy° that transformed ancient elements into a new language: A language comes into existence by means of brutal necessity, and the rules of the language are dictated by what the language must convey.

7

There was a moment, in time, and in this place, when my brother, or my mother, or my father, or my sister, had to convey to me, for example, the danger in which I was standing from the white man standing just behind me, and to convey this with a speed, and in a language, that the white man could not possibly understand, and that, indeed, he cannot understand, until today. He cannot afford to understand it. This understanding would reveal to him too much about himself, and smash that mirror before which he has been frozen for so long.

8

Now, if this passion, this skill, this (to quote Toni Morrison°) "sheer intelligence," this incredible music, the mighty achievement of having brought a people utterly unknown to, or despised by "history" — to have brought this people to their present, troubled, troubling, and unassailable° and unanswerable place — if this absolutely unprecedented journey does not indicate that black English is a language, I am curious to know what definition of language is to be trusted.

9

A people at the center of the Western world, and in the midst of so hostile a population, has not endured and transcended by means of what is patronizingly called a "dialect." We, the blacks, are in trouble, certainly, but we are not doomed, and we are not inarticulate because we are not compelled to defend a morality that we know to be a lie.

10

---

skirmish: A fight or battle that is usually unplanned.   **diaspora:** A large group of people living away from their original homeland.   **chattel slavery:** A type of slavery in which an enslaved person (and children, and children's children) is treated as property and is bought, sold, and owned forever.   **Congo Square:** An outdoor space in New Orleans where Black slaves met on Sundays to socialize and make music.   **unprecedented:** Never done or never known before.   **tabernacle:** A house or other meeting place used for worship.   **alchemy:** A type of ancient philosophy and medieval chemistry that dealt with trying to change metal into gold.   **Toni Morrison:** An American author, best known for her novel *Beloved*.
unassailable: Untouchable, not liable to doubt or attack.

The brutal truth is that the bulk of white people in American never had   11
any interest in educating black people, except as this could serve white purposes. It is not the black child's language that is in question, it is not his language that is despised: It is his experience. A child cannot be taught by anyone
who despises him, and a child cannot afford to be fooled. A child cannot be
taught by anyone whose demand, essentially, is that the child repudiate° his
experience, and all that gives him sustenance,° and enter a limbo° in which
he will no longer be black, and in which he knows that he can never become
white. Black people have lost too many black children that way.

And, after all, finally, in a country with standards so untrustworthy, a   12
country that makes heroes of so many criminal mediocrities,° a country
unable to face why so many of the nonwhite are in prison, or on the needle,
or standing, futureless, in the streets — it may very well be that both the child,
and his elder, have concluded that they have nothing whatever to learn from
the people of a country that has managed to learn so little.

repudiate: Deny, refuse to accept.   **sustenance:** Nourishment, means of support.
limbo: A place of uncertainty or transition.   **mediocrities:** An ordinary, or middling, person
or entity.

Questions to Start You Thinking

1. **Considering Meaning:** What does Baldwin mean when he writes: "Black
   English is the creation of the black diaspora" (paragraph 4)?

2. **Identifying Writing Strategies:** In paragraph 2, Baldwin gives several
   examples of how black English has become mainstream, including words
   and phrases such as *jazz, sock it to me,* and *funky.* What do these examples
   add to his argument?

3. **Reading Critically:** In what sense is "the black church" (paragraph 4) the
   foundation of black English? According to Baldwin, what is a practical
   reason for the creation of black English (paragraph 5)?

4. **Expanding Vocabulary:** Baldwin describes the creation of black English
   as the result of "an alchemy that transformed ancient elements into a
   new language" (paragraph 4). What is the effect of choosing the word
   "alchemy"? Why might Baldwin have chosen that word?

5. **Making Connections:** Compare the attitudes toward language held by
   James Baldwin and by Yesenia Padilla (see "What Does 'Latinx' Mean?" on
   pp. 366–68). How are their views similar? Draw on each text to support
   your answer.

Suggestions for Writing

1. In paragraph 9 of the essay, Baldwin writes: "[I]f this absolutely unprecedented journey does not indicate that black English is a language, I am
   curious to know what definition of language is to be trusted." Who is
   Baldwin writing to — and why? Write an essay in which you address purpose and audience in relation to Baldwin's essay.

2. Baldwin writes: "A language comes into existence by means of brutal necessity, and the rules of the language are dictated by what the language must convey" (paragraph 7). Write an essay in which you agree or disagree with that statement, drawing on examples from life in America today to support your view.

Yesenia Padilla

Yesenia Padilla

What Does "Latinx" Mean? A Look at the Term That's Challenging Gender Norms

Yesenia Padilla is an essayist, poet, founding editor of *Lumen Magazine*, and community organizer based in Southern California. She identifies Xicanx. The following essay first appeared on *Complex*, a website focusing on the convergence of American subcultures.

AS YOU READ: What is the purpose behind the creation of the term "Latinx"? What do people think of the term? How does it work in practice?

If you've been online at all in the past year, you've probably seen the word "Latinx"and thought: What does it mean? 1

Latinx (pronounced "La-TEEN-ex") is a gender-inclusive way of referring to people of Latin American descent.° Used by activists and some academics, the term is gaining traction° among the general public, after having been featured in publications such as *NPR* to *Latina*. But where did Latinx originate,° and is everybody on board with using it? 2

Ungendering the Spanish Language

Spanish is a gendered language, which means that every noun has a gender (in general, nouns that end in "a" tend to be feminine, and nouns that end in "o" tend to be masculine). While some nouns keep their gender when they become plural, others change based on the gender composition of a given group of people. 3

This approach, however, always defers° to the masculine as the dominant gender. For example, if you had a room full of girlfriends, it'd be full of *amigas*, with the "a" denoting everyone's gender as female. But the entire group's gender changes as soon as one guy enters the room, making it full of *amigos*; the "o" denotes the presence of at least one man—no matter how many women are in the room. Some members of Latin American communities claim this gendered language reinforces patriarchal° and heterosexist° norms, so "Latin@" was later introduced as a way to push back against it. 4

---

descent: Ancestry.   **gaining traction:** Increasing in popularity or acceptance.   **originate:** Begin, arise.   **defers:** Yields to, gives way to.   **patriarchal:** Relating to patriarchy, a social structure in which men dominate women.   **heterosexist:** Displaying prejudice by heterosexuals against those who are not heterosexual.

Using "@" as a suffix° became a way to represent male and female genders.   5
Instead of *amigas* or *amigos*, it was *amig@s*. But the term, which was adopted by
left-leaning activists and even used in academic texts, didn't include gender-
queer° and gender-nonconforming° people. Consequently, Latin@ began to
hit its limit, as those who didn't conform to the male-female gender binary°
gained more visibility.

The Rise of Latinx

According to Google Trends data, Latinx began emerging as early as 2004, but   6
really started popping up in online searches some time in late 2014. During
this period, the term had mostly been used in left-leaning and queer communities as a way to promote inclusivity in language. But thanks to social media
users on sites like Tumblr and Twitter, Latinx gained a foothold by mid-2015,
and its use began spreading beyond LGBTQIA° communities.

"Once the term 'Latinx' was made more visible, it certainly aligned with   7
what I had been learning about gender non-conformity," said Filiberto
Nolasco Gomez, founder of Latin American culture blog *El Huateque*. "It
seemed like the right direction for my website to embrace 'Latinx' as a political statement and a dismantling° of binaries."

By dismantling some of the gendering within Spanish, Latinx helped   8
modernize the idea of a pan-Latin American experience — or *Latinidad* — one
that reflects what it means to be of Latin American descent in today's world.
The term also better reflects Latin America's diversity, which is more in line
with intersectionality, the study of the ways that different forms of oppression (e.g., sexism, racism, classism, and heterosexism) intersect.

"The use of the 'x' is really important to me," according to Chicanx perfor-   9
mance artist Artemisa Clark. "The 'x' shows a development of broader Latinx
movements, one more actively concerned with issues of gender and queerness."

Resistance in Progress

In their takedown of an article that says "Latinx" denotes "a lack of respect for   10
the sovereignty° of Spanish," professors María R. Scharrón-del Río and Alan
A. Aja defend the term, arguing that it should replace "Latino" when referring
to people of Latin American descent.

They say moving towards non-gendered language is a way to escape   11
the ghost of colonialism° that still haunts Latin American culture.
"Latinx" actually represents the people the term is supposed to represent, so

---

suffix: A part of a word that is attached at the end.   **genderqueer:** Relating to a person whose
gender identity cannot be categorized as male or female.   **gender-nonconforming:** The
degree to which a person's appearance, behavior, and self-concept do not fit into conventional
norms of masculinity or femininity.   **binary:** Something having two parts.   **LGBTQIA:**
Acronym for lesbian, gay, bisexual, transgender, queer or questioning, intersex, and asexual
or allied.   **dismantling:** Taking apart; disconnecting the pieces of something.   **sovereignty:**
Supreme power; autonomy.   **colonialism:** The practice by which one country takes control
of and occupies a less powerful country; colonizers take the resources of the colonized to
increase their power and wealth.

it's "a concerted attempt at inclusivity" that "fosters solidarity° with all of our Latinx community," Scharrón-del Río and Aja write.

Still, even with the gender inclusivity of a term like "Latinx," there are still issues that arise when grouping a very diverse population—like that of Latin America—under one umbrella term.   12

"I think there has been a lot of communication and travel between communities and countries within the Americas for centuries, and Latinx kind of gives that some coherence," said Ken Eby-Gomez, a San Francisco-based activist and graduate student. "But . . . it would be a mistake to essentialize° any meaning or characteristics of Latinx."   13

In other words, creating a single Latin American identity can be problematic because it may lead to the erasure of marginalized identities (e.g., indigenous° people), while highlighting lighter-skinned *mestizos* (i.e., people of mixed Spanish and indigenous ancestry).   14

Life after Latinx

Writer Monse Arce argues that the identifier "Latino" erases indigenous history and culture from Latin America. Indeed, using a term like "Latino/@/x" emphasizes the privileges of *mestizos*, reinforcing colorism amongst Latin American people. "Latino/@/x" also implies a uniformity of experience, when in reality, people of Latin American descent have wildly different lives and narratives, she adds.   15

"The root of [Latinx] bothers me in that it's colonial, and my heart rages against [it]," said Eusebio Ricardo Lopez-Aguilar, a Salvadoran activist and census worker based in Winnipeg, Canada. "I haven't used it to describe myself, but I also haven't found a word that works."   16

Many young people of Latin American descent are exploring their complex indigenous roots, and forging new, more personal identities. While some resist using "Latinx," others recognize it as the most inclusive option available, for now. "I guess first-level identification is 'Chicanx' [a political and cultural identifier for Mexican-Americans] and second-level is 'Latinx'," said performance artist Clark.   17

"Latinx" is not the perfect identifying term, so it shouldn't be treated as the answer in the ongoing quest° to develop a cohesive° postcolonial° identity. Given Latin America's turbulent° history and the continued disapora° of its people, the process of figuring out one's identity is both deeply personal and political. Still, using "Latinx" is a positive step towards recognizing all of *nuestro gente* — our people — and will hopefully challenge every Latin American to think about what it truly means to be part of this complex culture.   18

---

solidarity: Unity based on common interests.   **essentialize:** Characterize in terms of stereotypes.   **indigenous:** Native; originating in a particular place.   **quest:** A long search for something.   **cohesive:** Tightly unified.   **postcolonial:** Occurring after colonial rule.   **turbulent:** Rough, stormy.   **diaspora:** A large group of people living away from their original homeland.

Questions to Start You Thinking

1. **Considering Meaning:** Why has the word "Latinx" been created? In Padilla's view, how useful is it?

2. **Identifying Writing Strategies:** In her discussion of the term "Latinx," Padilla brings in the perspectives of many people. Which perspectives are most interesting to you, and why? How effective is this strategy in supporting her overall argument about the word?

3. **Reading Critically:** Padilla writes that the term Latinx "shouldn't be treated as the answer in the ongoing quest to develop a cohesive postcolonial identity" (paragraph 18). What does she mean by that? How does the concept of colonialism figure into the argument she makes about language?

4. **Expanding Vocabulary:** What is "gendered language" (paragraphs 3–4), and why do people consider it to be a problem? What are some ways to "ungender" words?

5. **Making Connections:** Re-read Padilla's essay in the context of Richard Rodriguez's discussion of public and private language (pp. 369–74). How does the term "Latinx" function as public and/or private language?

Suggestions for Writing

1. How do words function as political statements? How do words reflect who does and does not have power? Write an essay in which you explore this question, drawing on the Padilla essay for examples.

2. Padilla writes that Latinx "represents the people the term is supposed to represent," and quotes two professors who say that Latinx is "'a concerted attempt at inclusivity' that 'fosters solidarity with all of our Latinx community'" (paragraph 11). Is it important for language to be inclusive? Why or why not? Support your argument with examples from Padilla, other texts, and/or everyday life in America.

Richard Rodriguez

Public and Private Language

Richard Rodriguez has served as a contributing editor for *Harper's Magazine*, *U.S. News & World Report*, and the Sunday Opinion section of the *Los Angeles Times*. He was a long-time editor for the Pacific News Service and a regular contributor to PBS's *NewsHour*. Among his books, which often draw on autobiography to explore race in America, is his early and well-known memoir, *Hunger of Memory*. The following essay, from that memoir, recounts the origin of his complex views of bilingual education.

Chris Felver/Getty Images

AS YOU READ: How did learning English change Rodriguez's life and his relationship with his family?

Supporters of bilingual education today imply that students like me miss a great deal by not being taught in their family's language. What they seem not to recognize is that, as a socially disadvantaged child, I considered Spanish to be a private language. What I needed to learn in school was that I had the right — and the obligation — to speak the public language of *los gringos.*° The odd truth is that my first-grade classmates could have become bilingual, in the conventional sense of that word, more easily than I. Had they been taught (as upper-middle-class children are often taught early) a second language like Spanish or French, they could have regarded it simply as that: another public language. In my case such bilingualism could not have been so quickly achieved. What I did not believe was that I could speak a single public language.

Without question, it would have pleased me to hear my teachers address me in Spanish when I entered the classroom. I would have felt much less afraid. I would have trusted them and responded with ease. But I would have delayed — for how long postponed? — having to learn the language of public society. I would have evaded — and for how long could I have afforded to delay? — learning the great lesson of school, that I had a public identity.

Fortunately, my teachers were unsentimental about their responsibility. What they understood was that I needed to speak a public language. So their voices would search me out, asking me questions. Each time I'd hear them, I'd look up in surprise to see a nun's face frowning at me. I'd mumble, not really meaning to answer. The nun would persist, "Richard, stand up. Don't look at the floor. Speak up. Speak to the entire class, not just to me!" but I couldn't believe that the English language was mine to use. (In part, I did not want to believe it.) I continued to mumble. I resisted the teacher's demands. (Did I somehow suspect that once I learned public language my pleasing family life would be changed?) Silent, waiting for the bell to sound, I remained dazed, diffident,° afraid.

Because I wrongly imagined that English was intrinsically° a public language and Spanish an intrinsically private one, I easily noticed the difference between classroom language and the language of home. At school, words were directed to a general audience of listeners. ("Boys and girls.") Words were meaningfully ordered. And the point was not self-expression alone but to make oneself understood by many others. The teacher quizzed: "Boys and girls, why do we use that word in this sentence? Could we think of a better word to use there? Would the sentence change its meaning if the words were differently arranged? And wasn't there a better way of saying much the same thing?" (I couldn't say. I wouldn't try to say.)

Three months. Five. Half a year passed. Unsmiling, ever watchful, my teachers noted my silence. They began to connect my behavior with the difficult progress my older sister and brother were making. Until one Saturday morning three nuns arrived at the house to talk to our parents. Stiffly, they

---

los gringos: Spanish for "foreigners," often used as a derogatory term for English-speaking Americans.   **diffident:** Shy.   **intrinsically:** Essentially; inherently.

sat on the blue living room sofa. From the doorway of another room, spying the visitors, I noted the incongruity° — the clash of two worlds, the faces and voices of school intruding upon the familiar setting of home. I overheard one voice gently wondering, "Do your children speak only Spanish at home, Mrs. Rodriguez?" While another voice added, "That Richard especially seems so timid and shy."

That Rich-heard!

6

With great tact the visitors continued, "Is it possible for you and your husband to encourage your children to practice their English when they are home?" Of course, my parents complied. What would they not do for their children's well-being? And how could they have questioned the Church's authority which those women represented? In an instant, they agreed to give up the language (the sounds) that had revealed and accentuated our family's closeness. The moment after the visitors left, the change was observed. "*Ahora,*° speak to us *en inglés,*"° my father and mother united to tell us.

7

At first, it seemed a kind of game. After dinner each night, the family gathered to practice "our" English. (It was still then *inglés,* a language foreign to us, so we felt drawn as strangers to it.) Laughing, we would try to define words we could not pronounce. We played with strange English sounds, often overanglicizing our pronunciations. And we filled the smiling gaps of our sentences with familiar Spanish sounds. But that was cheating, somebody shouted. Everyone laughed. In school, meanwhile, like my brother and sister, I was required to attend a daily tutoring session. I needed a full year of special attention. I also needed my teachers to keep my attention from straying in class by calling out, *Rich-heard* — their English voices slowly prying loose my ties to my other name, its three notes, *Ri-car-do.* Most of all I needed to hear my mother and father speak to me in a moment of seriousness in broken — suddenly heartbreaking — English. The scene was inevitable: one Saturday morning I entered the kitchen where my parents were talking in Spanish. I did not realize that they were talking in Spanish however until, at the moment they saw me, I heard their voices change to speak English. Those *gringo* sounds they uttered startled me. Pushed me away. In that moment of trivial misunderstanding and profound insight, I felt my throat twisted by unsounded grief. I turned quickly and left the room. But I had no place to escape to with Spanish. (The spell was broken.) My brother and sisters were speaking English in another part of the house.

8

Again and again in the days following, increasingly angry, I was obliged to hear my mother and father: "Speak to us *en inglés.*" (*Speak.*) Only then did I determine to learn classroom English. Weeks after, it happened: one day in school I had my hand raised to volunteer an answer. I spoke out in a loud voice. And I did not think it remarkable when the entire class understood. That day, I moved very far from the disadvantaged child I had been only days earlier. The belief, that calming assurance that I belonged in public, had at last taken hold.

9

---

incongruity: Lack of harmony or appropriateness.   *Ahora:* Spanish for "now."   *en inglés:* Spanish for "in English."

Shortly after, I stopped hearing the high and loud sounds of *los gringos*.   10
A more and more confident speaker of English, I didn't trouble to listen to
how strangers sounded, speaking to me. And there simply were too many
English-speaking people in my day for me to hear American accents anymore.
Conversations quickened. Listening to persons whose voices sounded eccen-
trically pitched, I usually noted their sounds for an initial few seconds before
I concentrated on *what* they were saying. Conversations became content-full.
Transparent. Hearing someone's *tone* of voice — angry or questioning or sarcastic or happy or sad — I didn't distinguish it from the words it expressed.
Sound and word were thus tightly wedded. At the end of a day, I was often
bemused, always relieved, to realize how "silent," though crowded with words,
my day in public had been. (This public silence measured and quickened the
change in my life.)

At last, seven years old, I came to believe what had been technically true   11
since my birth: I was an American citizen.

But the special feeling of closeness at home was diminished by then. Gone   12
was the desperate, urgent, intense feeling of being at home; rare was the experience of feeling myself individualized by family intimates. We remained a
loving family, but one greatly changed. No longer so close; no longer bound
tight by the pleasing and troubling knowledge of our public separateness.
Neither my older brother nor sister rushed home after school anymore. Nor
did I. When I arrived home there would often be neighborhood kids in the
house. Or the house would be empty of sounds.

Following the dramatic Americanization of their children, even my par-   13
ents grew more publicly confident. Especially my mother. She learned the
names of all the people on our block. And she decided we needed to have a
telephone installed in the house. My father continued to use the word *gringo*.
But it was no longer charged with the old bitterness or distrust. (Stripped of
any emotional content, the word simply became a name for those Americans
not of Hispanic descent.) Hearing him, sometimes, I wasn't sure if he was pronouncing the Spanish word *gringo* or saying gringo in English.

Matching the silence I started hearing in public was a new quiet at home.   14
The family's quiet was partly due to the fact that, as we children learned
more and more English, we shared fewer and fewer words with our parents.
Sentences needed to be spoken slowly when a child addressed his mother
or father. (Often the parent wouldn't understand.) The child would need to
repeat himself. (Still the parent misunderstood.) The young voice, frustrated,
would end up saying, "Never mind" — the subject was closed. Dinners would
be noisy with the clinking of knives and forks against dishes. My mother
would smile softly between her remarks; my father at the other end of the
table would chew and chew at his food, while he stared over the heads of his
children.

My *mother!* My *father!* After English became my primary language, I no   15
longer knew what words to use in addressing my parents. The old Spanish
words (those tender accents of sound) I had used earlier — *mamá* and *papá* —
I couldn't use anymore. They would have been all-too-painful reminders of
how much had changed in my life. On the other hand, the words I heard

neighborhood kids call *their* parents seemed equally unsatisfactory. *Mother* and *Father*; *Ma, Papa, Pa, Dad, Pop* (how I hated the all-American sound of that last word especially) — all these terms I felt were unsuitable, not really terms of address for *my* parents. As a result, I never used them at home. Whenever I'd speak to my parents, I would try to get their attention with eye contact alone. In public conversations, I'd refer to "my parents" or "my mother and father."

My mother and father, for their part, responded differently, as their children spoke to them less and less. My mother grew restless, seemed troubled and anxious at the scarcity of words exchanged in the house. It was she who would question me about my day when I came home from school. She smiled at the small talk. She pried at the edges of my sentences to get me to say something more. (What?) She'd join conversations she overheard, but her intrusions often stopped her children's talking. By contrast, my father seemed reconciled to the new quiet. Though his English improved somewhat, he retired into silence. At dinner he spoke very little. One night his children and even his wife helplessly giggled at his garbled English pronunciation of the Catholic Grace before Meals. Thereafter he made his wife recite the prayer at the start of each meal, even on formal occasions, when there were guests in the house. Hers became the public voice of the family. On official business, it was she, not my father, one would usually hear on the phone or in stores, talking to strangers. His children grew so accustomed to his silence that, years later, they would speak routinely of his shyness. (My mother would often try to explain: both his parents died when he was eight. He was raised by an uncle who treated him like little more than a menial servant. He was never encouraged to speak. He grew up alone. A man of few words.) But my father was not shy, I realized, when I'd watch him speaking Spanish with relatives. Using Spanish, he was quickly effusive.° Especially when talking with other men, his voice would spark, flicker, flare alive with sounds. In Spanish, he expressed ideas and feelings he rarely revealed in English. With firm Spanish sounds, he conveyed confidence and authority English would never allow him. 16

The silence at home, however, was finally more than a literal silence. Fewer words passed between parent and child, but more profound was the silence that resulted from my inattention to sounds. At about the time I no longer bothered to listen with care to the sounds of English in public, I grew careless about listening to the sounds family members made when they spoke. Most of the time I heard someone speaking at home and didn't distinguish his sounds from the words people uttered in public. I didn't even pay much attention to my parents' accented and ungrammatical speech. At least not at home. Only when I was with them in public would I grow alert to their accents. Though, even then, their sounds caused me less and less concern. For I was increasingly confident of my own public identity. 17

---

effusive: Talkative; unreserved.

Today I hear bilingual educators say that children lose a degree of 18
"individuality" by becoming assimilated into public society. (Bilingual schooling was popularized in the seventies, that decade when middle-class ethnics
began to resist the process of assimilation — the American melting pot.) But
the bilingualists simplistically scorn the value and necessity of assimilation.
They do not seem to realize that there are *two* ways a person is individualized. So they do not realize that while one suffers a diminished sense of *private*
individuality by becoming assimilated into public society, such assimilation
makes possible the achievement of *public* individuality.

Questions to Start You Thinking

1. **Considering Meaning:** What created the new "silence" in the Rodriguez
   household? Explain why.
2. **Identifying Writing Strategies:** How does Rodriguez use comparison
   and contrast to convey his experience learning English?
3. **Reading Critically:** How does Rodriguez use dialogue to make the experience he recalls more vivid for his readers? Is this strategy effective in
   helping him achieve his purpose? Why, or why not?
4. **Expanding Vocabulary:** Rodriguez uses the terms *private* and *public*.
   What do these words mean when used as adjectives to describe "language" and "identity"?
5. **Making Connections with the Paired Essay:** Both Rodriguez and Amy
   Tan ("Mother Tongue," pp. 375–79) grew up in homes in which English
   was spoken as a second language. Compare and contrast how each writer's mastery of English affected his or her parents.

Suggestions for Writing

1. If you speak a second language, write an essay recalling your experience learning it. What were some of your struggles? Can you relate to
   Rodriguez's experience? How do you use that language today? If you
   do not know a second language, write an essay in which you analyze
   possible benefits of learning one. What language would you like to
   learn? Why?
2. According to Rodriguez, "Supporters of bilingual education today imply
   that students like me miss a great deal by not being taught in their family's
   language" (paragraph 1). Rodriguez counters this assumption by showing
   how his immersion in English allowed him to develop a public identity that
   ultimately led to his success. At the same time, however, his English-only
   immersion hurt his family life. Write an essay in which you take a stand
   on the complex topic of bilingual education, using further reading and
   research to support your position about how it does or does not benefit
   students.

Amy Tan

Mother Tongue

Novelist Amy Tan was born in Oakland, California, to parents who had recently immigrated to the U.S. from China. Her first short story became the basis for her first novel, *The Joy Luck Club*, which was a phenomenal bestseller and was made into a movie. The following essay, "Mother Tongue" first appeared in *Threepenny Review*. In it, Tan explores the effect of her mother's "broken" English—the language Tan grew up with—on her life and writing.

AS YOU READ: Identify the difficulties Tan says exist for a child growing up in a family that speaks nonstandard English.

Will Ragozzino/Getty Images

I am not a scholar of English or literature. I cannot give you much more than personal opinions on the English language and its variations in this country or others. 1

I am a writer. And by that definition, I am someone who has always loved language. I am fascinated by language in daily life. I spend a great deal of my time thinking about the power of language — the way it can evoke an emotion, a visual image, a complex idea, or a simple truth. Language is the tool of my trade. And I use them all — all the Englishes I grew up with. 2

Recently, I was made keenly aware of the different Englishes I do use. I was giving a talk to a large group of people, the same talk I had already given to half a dozen other groups. The nature of the talk was about my writing, my life, and my book, *The Joy Luck Club*. The talk was going along well enough, until I remembered one major difference that made the whole talk sound wrong. My mother was in the room. And it was perhaps the first time she had heard me give a lengthy speech, using the kind of English I have never used with her. I was saying things like, "The intersection of memory upon imagination" and "There is an aspect of my fiction that relates to thus-and-thus" — a speech filled with carefully wrought° grammatical phrases, burdened, it suddenly seemed to me, with nominalized° forms, past perfect tenses, conditional phrases, all the forms of Standard English that I had learned in school and through books, the forms of English I did not use at home with my mother. 3

Just last week, I was walking down the street with my mother, and I again found myself conscious of the English I was using, and the English I do use with her. We were talking about the price of new and used furniture and I heard myself saying this: "Not waste money that way." My husband was with us as well, and he didn't notice any switch in my English. And then I realized why. It's because over the twenty years we've been together I've often used that same kind of English with him, and sometimes he even uses it with me. It has become our language of intimacy, a different sort of English that relates to family talk, the language I grew up with. 4

So you'll have some idea of what this family talk I heard sounds like, I'll quote what my mother said during a recent conversation which I videotaped 5

wrought: crafted.   **nominalized:** Made into a noun from a verb.

and then transcribed.° During this conversation, my mother was talking about a political gangster in Shanghai who had the same last name as her family's, Du, and how the gangster in his early years wanted to be adopted by her family, which was rich by comparison. Later, the gangster became more powerful, far richer than my mother's family, and one day showed up at my mother's wedding to pay his respects. Here's what she said in part:

"Du Yusong having business like fruit stand. Like off the street kind. He   6
is like Du Zong—but not Tsung-ming Island people. The local people call putong, the river east side, he belong to that side local people. That man want to ask Du Zong father take him in like become own family. Du Zong father wasn't look down on him, but didn't take seriously, until that man big like become a mafia. Now important person, very hard to inviting him. Chinese way, came only to show respect, don't stay for dinner. Respect for making big celebration, he shows up. Mean gives lots of respect. Chinese custom. Chinese social life that way. If too important won't have to stay too long. He come to my wedding. I didn't see, I heard it. I gone to boy's side, they have YMCA dinner. Chinese age I was nineteen."

You should know that my mother's expressive command of English   7
belies° how much she actually understands. She reads the *Forbes* report, listens to *Wall Street Week,* converses daily with her stockbroker, reads all of Shirley MacLaine's books with ease—all kinds of things I can't begin to understand. Yet some of my friends tell me they understand fifty percent of what my mother says. Some say they understand eighty to ninety percent. Some say they understand none of it, as if she were speaking pure Chinese. But to me, my mother's English is perfectly clear, perfectly natural. It's my mother tongue. Her language, as I hear it, is vivid, direct, full of observation and imagery. That was the language that helped shape the way I saw things, expressed things, made sense of the world.

Lately, I've been giving more thought to the kind of English my mother   8
speaks. Like others, I have described it to people as "broken" or "fractured" English. But I wince when I say that. It has always bothered me that I can think of no way to describe it other than "broken," as if it were damaged and needed to be fixed, as if it lacked a certain wholeness and soundness. I've heard other terms used, "limited English," for example. But they seem just as bad, as if everything is limited, including people's perceptions of the limited English speaker.

I know this for a fact, because when I was growing up, my mother's   9
"limited" English limited *my* perception of her. I was ashamed of her English. I believed that her English reflected the quality of what she had to say. That is, because she expressed them imperfectly her thoughts were imperfect. And I had plenty of empirical evidence to support me: the fact that people in department stores, at banks, and at restaurants did not take her seriously, did not give her good service, pretended not to understand her, or even acted as if they did not hear her.

---

transcribed: Made a written copy of what was said.   **belies:** Contradicts; creates a misleading impression.

My mother has long realized the limitations of her English as well. When I was fifteen, she used to have me call people on the phone to pretend I was she. In this guise, I was forced to ask for information or even to complain and yell at people who had been rude to her. One time it was a call to her stockbroker in New York. She had cashed out her small portfolio and it just so happened we were going to go to New York the next week, our very first trip outside California. I had to get on the phone and say in an adolescent voice that was not very convincing, "This is Mrs. Tan." 10

And my mother was standing in the back whispering loudly, "Why he don't send me check, already two weeks late. So mad he lie to me, losing me money." 11

And then I said in perfect English, "Yes, I'm getting rather concerned. You had agreed to send the check two weeks ago, but it hasn't arrived." 12

Then she began to talk more loudly. "What he want, I come to New York tell him front of his boss, you cheating me?" And I was trying to calm her down, make her be quiet, while telling the stockbroker, "I can't tolerate any more excuses. If I don't receive the check immediately, I am going to have to speak to your manager when I'm in New York next week." And sure enough, the following week there we were in front of this astonished stockbroker, and I was sitting there red-faced and quiet, and my mother, the real Mrs. Tan, was shouting at his boss in her impeccable broken English. 13

We used a similar routine just five days ago, for a situation that was far less humorous. My mother had gone to the hospital for an appointment, to find out about a benign brain tumor a CAT scan had revealed a month ago. She said she had spoken very good English, her best English, no mistakes. Still, she said, the hospital did not apologize when they said they had lost the CAT scan and she had come for nothing. She said they did not seem to have any sympathy when she told them she was anxious to know the exact diagnosis, since her husband and son had both died of brain tumors. She said they would not give her any more information until the next time and she would have to make another appointment for that. So she said she would not leave until the doctor called her daughter. She wouldn't budge. And when the doctor finally called her daughter, me, who spoke in perfect English—lo and behold—we had assurances the CAT scan would be found, promises that a conference call on Monday would be held, and apologies for any suffering my mother had gone through for a most regrettable mistake. 14

I think my mother's English almost had an effect on limiting my possibilities in life as well. Sociologists and linguists probably will tell you that a person's developing language skills are more influenced by peers. But I think that the language spoken in the family, especially in immigrant families which are more insular,° plays a large role in shaping the language of the child. And I believe that it affected my results on achievement tests, IQ tests, and the SAT. While my English skills were never judged as poor, compared to math, English could not be considered my strong suit. In grade school I 15

---

insular: Detached or isolated; keeping to oneself.

did moderately well, getting perhaps B's, sometimes B-pluses, in English and scoring perhaps in the sixtieth or seventieth percentile on achievement tests. But those scores were not good enough to override the opinion that my true abilities lay in math and science, because in those areas I achieved A's and scored in the ninetieth percentile or higher.

This was understandable. Math is precise; there is only one correct answer. Whereas, for me at least, the answers on English tests were always a judgment call, a matter of opinion and personal experience. Those tests were constructed around items like fill-in-the-blank sentence completion, such as, "Even though Tom was _____ , Mary thought he was _____ ." And the correct answer always seemed to be the most bland combinations of thoughts, for example, "Even though Tom was shy, Mary thought he was charming," with the grammatical structure "even though" limiting the correct answer to some sort of semantic° opposites, so you wouldn't get answers like, "Even though Tom was foolish, Mary thought he was ridiculous." Well, according to my mother, there were very few limitations as to what Tom could have been and what Mary might have thought of him. So I never did well on tests like that.

The same was true with word analogies, pairs of words in which you were supposed to find some sort of logical, semantic relationship — for example, "*Sunset* is to *nightfall* as _____ is to _____ ." And here you would be presented with a list of four possible pairs, one of which showed the same kind of relationship: *red* is to *stoplight, bus* is to *arrival, chills* is to *fever, yawn* is to *boring*. Well, I could never think that way. I knew what the tests were asking, but I could not block out of my mind the images already created by the first pair, "*sunset* is to *nightfall*" — and I would see a burst of colors against a darkening sky, the moon rising, the lowering of a curtain of stars. And all the other pairs of words — *red, bus, stoplight, boring* — just threw up a mass of confusing images, making it impossible for me to sort out something as logical as saying: "A sunset precedes nightfall" is the same as "a chill precedes a fever." The only way I would have gotten that answer right would have been to imagine an associative situation, for example, my being disobedient and staying out past sunset, catching a chill at night, which turns into feverish pneumonia as punishment, which indeed did happen to me.

I have been thinking about all this lately, about my mother's English, about achievement tests. Because lately I've been asked, as a writer, why there are not more Asian Americans enrolled in creative writing programs. Why do so many Chinese students go into engineering? Well, these are broad sociological questions I can't begin to answer. But I have noticed in surveys — in fact, just last week   that Asian students, as a whole, always do significantly better on math achievement tests than in English. And this makes me think that there are other Asian American students whose English spoken in the

16

17

18

semantic: Relating to the meaning of language.

home might also be described as "broken" or "limited." And perhaps they also have teachers who are steering them away from writing and into math and science, which is what happened to me.

Fortunately, I happen to be rebellious in nature and enjoy the challenge of disproving assumptions made about me. I became an English major my first year in college, after being enrolled as pre-med. I started writing nonfiction as a freelancer the week after I was told by my former boss that writing was my worst skill and I should hone my talents toward account management.   19

But it wasn't until 1985 that I finally began to write fiction. And at first I wrote using what I thought to be wittily crafted sentences, sentences that would finally prove I had mastery over the English language. Here's an example from the first draft of a story that later made its way into *The Joy Luck Club*, but without this line: "That was my mental quandary in its nascent° state." A terrible line, which I can barely pronounce.   20

Fortunately, for reasons I won't get into today, I later decided I should envision a reader for the stories I would write. And the reader I decided upon was my mother, because these were stories about mothers. So with this reader in mind — and in fact she did read my early drafts — I began to write stories using all the Englishes I grew up with: the English I spoke to my mother, which for lack of a better term might be described as "simple"; the English she used with me, which for lack of a better term might be described as "broken"; my translation of her Chinese, which could certainly be described as "watered down"; and what I imagined to be her translation of her Chinese if she could speak in perfect English, her internal language, and for that I sought to preserve the essence, but neither an English nor a Chinese structure. I wanted to capture what language ability tests can never reveal: her intent, her passion, her imagery, the rhythms of her speech, and the nature of her thoughts.   21

Apart from what any critic had to say about my writing, I knew I had succeeded where it counted when my mother finished reading my book and gave me her verdict: "So easy to read."   22

nascent: Beginning; only partly formed.

Questions to Start You Thinking

1. **Considering Meaning:** What are the Englishes that Tan grew up with? What other Englishes has she used in her life? What does each English have that gives it an advantage over the other Englishes in certain situations?

2. **Identifying Writing Strategies:** What examples does Tan use to analyze the various Englishes she uses? How has Tan been able to synthesize her Englishes successfully into her present style of writing fiction?

3. **Reading Critically:** Although Tan explains that she writes using "all the Englishes" she has known throughout her life (paragraph 21), she doesn't do that in this essay. What are the differences between the English Tan

uses in this essay and the kinds she says she uses in her fiction? How does the language she uses here fit the purpose of her essay?

4. **Expanding Vocabulary:** In paragraph 9, Tan writes that she had "plenty of empirical evidence" that her mother's "limited" English meant that her mother's thoughts were "imperfect" as well. Define *empirical*. What does Tan's use of this word tell us about her present attitude toward the way she judged her mother when she was growing up?

5. **Making Connections with the Paired Essay:** Tan and Richard Rodríguez ("Public and Private Language," pp. 369–74) recount learning English as they grew up in homes where English was a second language. In what way did they face similar experiences and obstacles? How did learning English affect their self-image and influence their relationship with their family?

Suggestions for Writing

1. In a personal essay explain an important event in your family's history, using your family's various Englishes or other languages.

2. Take note of and, if possible, transcribe a conversation you have had with a parent or other family member, with a teacher, and with a close friend. Write an essay comparing and contrasting the "languages" of the three conversations. How do the languages differ? How do you account for these differences? What might happen if someone used "teacher language" to talk to a friend or "friend language" in a class discussion or paper?

Popular Culture

Responding to an Image

How do you think about pop culture — what defines it, and how does it defines us? How does the photo above reflect how we live today? It seems to suggest that we are a society that places value on pop culture and lives much of its life digitally, through smartphones and social media. Who is taking the photo within the picture above, and where is that individual? Is the situation pictured here familiar to you and easy for you to identify? Why or not?

BERTRAND LANGLOIS
/AFP/Getty Images

Stephen King

Why We Crave Horror Movies

Stephen King (born 1947) is a bestselling author of well-known horror novels, including *The Shining, Pet Sematary, Misery, Carrie, Firestarter, The Green Mile,* and others, many of which have been adapted on television and film. He's also written screenplays, teleplays, short fiction, essays, e-books, and a book about writing called *On Writing: A Memoir of the Craft.* The following essay was first published in *Playboy* in 1981.

AS YOU READ: What needs does King says horror movies fulfill for viewers?

I think that we're all mentally ill; those of us outside the asylums only hide it a little better — and maybe not all that much better, after all. We've all known people who talk to themselves, people who sometimes squinch their faces into horrible grimaces when they believe no one is watching, people who have some hysterical fear — of snakes, the dark, the tight place, the long drop . . . and, of course, those final worms and grubs that are waiting so patiently underground. 1

When we pay our four or five bucks and seat ourselves at tenth-row center in a theater showing a horror movie, we are daring the nightmare. 2

Why? Some of the reasons are simple and obvious. To show that we can, that we are not afraid, that we can ride this roller coaster. Which is not to say that a really good horror movie may not surprise a scream out of us at some point, the way we may scream when the roller coaster twists through a complete 360 or plows through a lake at the bottom of the drop. And horror movies, like roller coasters, have always been the special province° of the young; by the time one turns forty or fifty, one's appetite for double twists or 360-degree loops may be considerably depleted. 3

We also go to reestablish our feelings of essential normality; the horror movie is innately conservative, even reactionary.° Freda Jackson as the horrible melting woman in *Die, Monster, Die!* confirms for us that no matter how far we may be removed from the beauty of a Robert Redford or a Diana Ross, we are still light-years from true ugliness. 4

And we go to have fun. 5

Ah, but this is where the ground starts to slope away, isn't it? Because this is a very peculiar sort of fun indeed. The fun comes from seeing others menaced — sometimes killed. One critic suggested that if pro football has become the voyeur's° version of combat, then the horror film has become the modern version of the public lynching. 6

It is true that the mythic, "fairy-tale" horror film intends to take away the shades of gray. . . . It urges us to put away our more civilized and adult 7

---

province: Sphere; area of interest.   **reactionary:** Marked by reaction opposed to progress.
voyeur: One who takes inordinate pleasure in the act of watching.

penchant° for analysis and to become children again, seeing things in pure blacks and whites. It may be that horror movies provide psychic relief on this level because this invitation to lapse into simplicity, irrationality, and even outright madness is extended so rarely. We are told we may allow our emotions a free rein . . . or no rein at all.

If we are all insane, then sanity becomes a matter of degree. If your insan- 8 ity leads you to carve up women like Jack the Ripper or the Cleveland Torso Murderer, we clap you away in the funny farm (but neither of those two amateur-night surgeons was ever caught, heh-heh-heh); if, on the other hand, your insanity leads you only to talk to yourself when you're under stress or to pick your nose on your morning bus, then you are left alone to go about your business . . . though it is doubtful that you will ever be invited to the best parties.

The potential lyncher is in almost all of us (excluding saints, past and 9 present; but then, most saints have been crazy in their own ways), and every now and then, he has to be let loose to scream and roll around in the grass. Our emotions and our fears form their own body, and we recognize that it demands its own exercise to maintain proper muscle tone. Certain of these emotional muscles are accepted — even exalted — in civilized society; they are, of course, the emotions that tend to maintain the status quo° of civilization itself. Love, friendship, loyalty, kindness — these are all the emotions that we applaud, emotions that have been immortalized in the couplets of Hallmark cards and in the verses (I don't dare call it poetry) of Leonard Nimoy.

When we exhibit these emotions, society showers us with positive rein- 10 forcement; we learn this even before we get out of diapers. When, as children, we hug our rotten little puke of a sister and give her a kiss, all the aunts and uncles smile and twit and cry, "Isn't he the sweetest little thing?" Such coveted treats as chocolate-covered graham crackers often follow. But if we deliberately slam the rotten little puke of a sister's fingers in the door, sanctions follow — angry remonstrance° from parents, aunts, and uncles; instead of a chocolate-covered graham cracker, a spanking.

But anticivilization emotions don't go away, and they demand periodic 11 exercise. We have such "sick" jokes as "What's the difference between a truckload of bowling balls and a truckload of dead babies?" (You can't unload the truckload of bowling balls with a pitchfork . . . a joke, by the way, that I heard originally from a ten-year-old.) Such a joke may surprise a laugh or a grin out of us even as we recoil, a possibility that confirms the thesis: if we share a brotherhood of man, then we also share an insanity of man. None of which is intended as a defense of either the sick joke or insanity but merely as an explanation of [how] the best horror films, like the best fairy tales, manage to be reactionary, anarchistic,° and revolutionary all at the same time.

The mythic horror movie, like the sick joke, has a dirty job to do. It delib- 12 erately appeals to all that is worst in us. It is morbidity unchained, our most

---

penchant: Strong inclination.   **status quo:** The existing state of affairs; the way things are.
remonstrance: Objection.   **anarchistic:** Rejecting all forms of control.

base instincts let free, our nastiest fantasies realized . . . and it all happens, fittingly enough, in the dark. For those reasons, good liberals often shy away from horror films. For myself, I like to see the most aggressive of them — *Dawn of the Dead,* for instance — as lifting a trapdoor in the civilized forebrain and throwing a basket of raw meat to the hungry alligators swimming around in that subterranean river beneath.

Why bother? Because it keeps them from getting out, man, it keeps them down there and me up here. It was Lennon and McCartney who said that all you need is love, and I would agree with that.   13

As long as you keep the gators fed.   14

Questions to Start You Thinking

1. **Considering Meaning:** What does King mean when he says that "we're all mentally ill" (paragraph 1)? Is this a serious statement? Why or why not?

2. **Identifying Writing Strategies:** How does King use analysis, breaking a complex topic into parts, to support his argument?

3. **Reading Critically:** Why do you think King uses the inclusive pronoun "we" so frequently throughout his essay? What effect does the use of this pronoun have on your response to his argument?

4. **Expanding Vocabulary:** Define *innately* (paragraph 4). What does King mean when he says horror movies are "innately conservative"? Does he contradict himself when he says they are also "reactionary, anarchistic, and revolutionary" (paragraph 11)? Why, or why not?

5. **Making Connections:** In "Black Men and Public Space" (pp. 429–32), Brent Staples writes about the reflexive fear and anxiety he arouses in people when walking at night. How might King's view of human nature help explain the reactions to Staples?

Suggestions for Writing

1. Do you agree with what King sees as the benefits of horror movies? What about his idea that there's a "potential lyncher" (paragraph 8) in all of us who needs to be "let loose to scream and roll around on the grass" occasionally? Does this outlet for satisfying our more primal, violent instincts seem plausible? Or would you argue the opposite — that we become more violent *because* of such movies? Write an essay that either supports King's points or argues against them.

2. King comes up with a colorful metaphor for the human psyche in paragraph 12. Think about human psychology and the image he presents (of the civilized forebrain, and the feeding of the alligators swimming beneath). When and where have you seen "alligators" coming to the surface, despite that civilized forebrain? What, if anything, else would you add to the picture King gives us here? Write about this metaphor and how it lines up with your experience. Bring in your personal observations as evidence.

Kurt Dean Squire and Matthew Gaydos

No, Fortnite Isn't Rotting Kids' Brains. It May Even Be Good for Them.

Kurt Dean Squire is a professor of informatics at the University of California, Irvine, and the author of *Video Games and Learning* (Teachers College Press, 2011). Matthew Gaydos is a design researcher at the Teaching Systems Lab at Massachusetts Institute of Technology. This article was published in *Education Week*, an online news magazine focused on educational policy for students from pre-K through grade 12.

Kurt Squire

Matthew Gaydos

AS YOU READ: Do you think there are benefits to online gaming, even when those games are violent?

Kids around the country, if not the world, spent the year mimicking Fortnite dances, discussing Ninja's scoperless-sniper rifle shots, and being generally obsessed with the popular video game. Is Fortnite something we should be concerned about? 1

What does research say about this latest kid obsession? 2

As researchers, educators, gamers, and parents whose kids play Fortnite, we see little to be concerned about with the game, but some things that could be encouraging. Playing video-game shooters, we now know, is not a major contributor to youth violence. Granted, kids' enthusiasm for Fortnite can be a little much, but we are old enough to remember Garbage Pail kids and have played Pokemon.° 3

For kids, coming home and playing Fortnite is very similar to playing army men in the woods and building forts. From purely a safety standpoint, playing digital laser tag is probably safer than having crabapple battles with garbage can lids as shields like we did, or shooting each other with BB guns. 4

In fact, as a play experience, there are parts of Fortnite that may even be valuable. Fortnite is, in many respects, a classic "third place" — a place that is neither home nor school, but where kids can socialize and play beyond the watchful eyes of parents or teachers. These are places where kids learn to negotiate conflict, become independent, and explore what kind of person 5

Pokemon: A Japanese media franchise released in 1996 that includes cards, television, and movies.

they want to be. They are important experiences that we too often design out of our kids' lives through structured activities and all of the shuffling back and forth we do in today's busy world.

This isn't to say that we should just let kids go it alone online. Recent 6
news highlights how racism, xenophobia,° and bullying have come out of the shadows and are thriving online. It's more important than ever that we talk with kids about what is appropriate behavior, what's acceptable humor—and what's not.

In our work with Esports in California's Orange County school system, 7
we've seen that one of the best things educators can do is bystander° training. That is, we can teach kids appropriate ways to respond when they see distrustful, harassing, or hateful behavior. Researchers have found that interrupting inappropriate behavior, publicly supporting the harmed person, and calling for help when appropriate are useful ways to combat toxic situations.

Can we really blame kids for being so taken by Fortnite? The game 8
itself—a combination of army guys, building forts, and king-of-the-hill battles—would have taken place with sticks or toy guns in the vacant lots or wooded strands that are increasingly designed out of today's suburban neighborhoods. Further, many children do homework or are engaged in extracurricular activities until long after the pole lights come on, which means that online spaces are the last available place to socialize.°

We are lucky to be writing this from a neighborhood where there are still 9
undeveloped spaces where kids roam on bikes and play these same games offline with Nerf guns. Research shows that, if anything, access to these informal play spaces is good for you. Strong communities, peer relationships (including those forged through gaming), and belonging (including to groups like gaming guilds) can maximize youths' resilience against issues such as substance abuse and depression.

As researchers with decades of experience studying youth and games, 10
we encourage educators to look beyond the immediate content of the game (its characters and themes), and focus more intently on what kids are doing with it. Are kids making new friends? Becoming more confident? Or are they becoming more withdrawn? Are they picking up any toxic° or negative views? Are there signs that game-play might be an indication that something else in their lives is wrong?

Although there are no established links between games and violence, there 11
are some obvious connections between gaming too much and wider problems. More than 25 hours of gaming per week while also in school is not a sustainable schedule, for instance. Wrangling over what extent games are the cause or the symptom somewhat misses the point; unhealthy game play can be a signal. When one of us was teaching middle school, he saw a student online after midnight and used that as an opening to ask if everything was OK at home. It turned out that his parents were getting divorced. The

---

xenophobia: Fear or hatred of foreigners.   **bystander:** An onlooker.   **socialize:** To mingle with others; to make friends.   **toxic:** Poisonous.

occasion was a good chance to talk through how the student was dealing with it, and how he could manage it better.

Similarly, there are some indicators that not playing games can be a problem if kids are being left out of important socializing experiences. Being left out of the nightly hijinks° and inside jokes about new Fortnite dances is not only not fun, but can lead toward broader alienation.° There is some evidence that youths (especially boys) who are not gaming at all can become disconnected and enter down bad paths.

Rather than focusing on what games kids are playing, we should attend more to who they are meeting and gaming with online, what type of talk they are engaged in, and what kinds of groups they are becoming a part of. Online peer groups can lead to strong, lasting friendships, but they can also be toxic and evolve in less healthy directions — just like offline ones. As with most issues around education, we hesitate to give rigid advice, other than this: Get to know and stay connected to your kids, make spaces for them to write or read around their interests, and engage them in conversations around their gaming whenever possible. Many young people are eager to talk about their games and can be brought into conversations about how to manage their gaming productively.

If you're feeling bold, you might see if your school has a gaming club or would be interested in sponsoring one. Gaming together is one of the best ways to build trust outside the classroom that can spill back in and create a positive learning climate.

hijinks: Antics or lively, carefree behavior.   **alienation:** The state of being isolated.

Questions to Start You Thinking

1. **Considering Meaning:** What do the authors think parents and educators should focus on when they see kids playing *Fortnite*? How does their advice differ from the usual warnings and concerns about online gaming?

2. **Identifying Writing Strategies:** There are three rhetorical questions placed for effect in this essay. What purpose do they serve? How do they influence the tone of the essay? What do you notice about their placement?

3. **Reading Critically**: How do Squire and Gaydos make *Fortnite* seem more ordinary and appealing to people who grew up without online gaming? Do you think their comparisons hold weight? Why or why not?

4. **Expanding Vocabulary:** In this article, *Fortnite* is lauded as a game that helps build *resilience* (paragraph 9) in the world, in particular against substance abuse and mental health issues. What does it mean to be *resilient*? Why is it a desirable trait, particularly for teenagers?

5. **Making Connections:** Do you think Stephen King (p. 382) and Squire and Gaydos share any opinions on why we seek out violent movies and games? Where is their thinking similar, and where is it different?

Suggestions for Writing

1. The appeal of online gaming can sometimes be hard for older generations to grasp. If you grew up comfortable with online gaming, think about your parents or grandparents. Did your interests and activities overlap with theirs in any way? In writing, describe the things you did for fun and try to make connections between your fun and the fun had by an older generation.

2. Think about Squire and Gaydos's description of a "third place" where kids socialize and unwind without parent or teacher supervision. What are the benefits of such a place, and what are the dangers? Weigh the pros and cons equally and write an essay that offers an analysis of a virtual third place like *Fortnite* without a desire to portray that space as overwhelmingly positive or negative.

Robbie Quinn

Kate O'Neill

Facebook's "10-Year Challenge" Is Just a Harmless Meme — Right?

Kate O'Neill is the founder and CEO of KO Insights, a strategic advisory firm that explores how data and technology influence humanity. She is the author of *Tech Humanist* and *Pixels and Place: Connecting Human Experience Across Physical and Digital Spaces*.

AS YOU READ: Do you follow and participate in "harmless memes" on Facebook? Do you ever wonder about the implications of your participation?

I f you use social media, you've probably noticed a trend across Facebook, Instagram, and Twitter of people posting their then-and-now profile pictures, mostly from 10 years ago and this year. 1

Instead of joining in, I posted the following semi-sarcastic tweet: 2

Kate O'Neill
✓ @kateo

Me 10 years ago: probably would have played along with the profile picture aging meme going around on Facebook and Instagram
Me now: ponders how all this data could be mined to train facial recognition algorithms° on age progression and age recognition

24.9K

4:25 PM - Jan 12, 2019

Twitter Ads info and privacy

11.7K people are talking about this

algorithm: A series of steps used to solve a mathematical problem.

My flippant° tweet began to pick up traction.° My intent wasn't to claim 3
that the meme° is inherently° dangerous. But I knew the facial recognition
scenario was broadly plausible and indicative of a trend that people should be
aware of. It's worth considering the depth and breadth of the personal data
we share without reservations. Of those who were critical of my thesis, many
argued that the pictures were already available anyway. The most common
rebuttal was: "That data is already available. Facebook's already got all the
profile pictures."

Of course they do. In various versions of the meme, people were instructed 4
to post their first profile picture alongside their current profile picture, or
a picture from 10 years ago alongside their current profile picture. So, yes:
These profile pictures exist, they've got upload time stamps, many people
have a lot of them, and for the most part they're publicly accessible.°

But let's play out this idea. 5

Imagine that you wanted to train a facial recognition algorithm on age-re- 6
lated characteristics and, more specifically, on age progression (e.g., how
people are likely to look as they get older). Ideally, you'd want a broad and
rigorous dataset with lots of people's pictures. It would help if you knew they
were taken a fixed number of years apart — say, 10 years.

Sure, you could mine° Facebook for profile pictures and look at posting 7
dates . . . . But that whole set of profile pictures could end up generating a
lot of useless noise. People don't reliably upload pictures in chronological°
order, and it's not uncommon for users to post pictures of something other
than themselves as a profile picture. A quick glance through my Facebook
friends' profile pictures shows a friend's dog who just died, several cartoons,
word images, abstract patterns, and more.

In other words, it would help if you had a clean, simple, helpfully labeled 8
set of then-and-now photos . . . .

Thanks to this meme, there's now a very large dataset of carefully curated 9
photos of people from roughly 10 years ago and now.

Of course, not all the dismissive° comments in my Twitter mentions were 10
about the pictures being already available; some critics noted that there was
too much crap data to be usable. But data researchers and scientists know
how to account for this. As with hashtags that go viral, you can generally place
more trust in the validity of data earlier on in the trend or campaign — before
people begin to participate ironically or attempt to hijack the hashtag for
irrelevant purposes.

As for bogus pictures, image recognition algorithms are plenty sophisti- 11
cated enough to pick out a human face. If you uploaded an image of a cat 10
years ago and now — as one of my friends did, adorably — that particular sample would be easy to throw out.

---

flippant: Glibly disrespectful.　　**traction:** The degree to which an idea becomes accepted.
inherent: An essential characteristic of.　　**meme:** An element of pop culture (often video,
text, or image) transmitted from one person to another over and over.　　**accessible:** Available.
mine: To extract.　　**chronological:** Arranged in order by time.　　**dismissive:** Disdainful.

For its part, Facebook denies having any hand in the #10YearChallenge. "This is a user-generated meme that went viral on its own," a Facebook spokesperson responded. "Facebook did not start this trend, and the meme uses photos that already exist on Facebook. Facebook gains nothing from this meme (besides reminding us of the questionable fashion trends of 2009). As a reminder, Facebook users can choose to turn facial recognition on or off at any time." 12

But even if this particular meme isn't a case of social engineering, the past few years have been rife with examples of social games and memes designed to extract and collect data. Just think of the mass data extraction of more than 70 million US Facebook users performed by Cambridge Analytica. 13

Is it bad that someone could use your Facebook photos to train a facial recognition algorithm? Not necessarily; in a way, it's inevitable. Still, the broader takeaway here is that we need to approach our interactions with technology mindful of the data we generate° and how it can be used at scale. I'll offer three plausible use cases for facial recognition: one respectable, one mundane, and one risky. 14

The benign scenario: Facial recognition technology, specifically age progression capability, could help with finding missing kids. Last year police in New Delhi reported tracking down nearly 3,000 missing kids in just four days using facial recognition technology. If the kids had been missing a while, they would likely look a little different from the last known photo of them, so a reliable age progression algorithm could be genuinely helpful here. 15

Facial recognition's potential is mostly mundane: Age recognition is probably most useful for targeted advertising. Ad displays that incorporate cameras or sensors and can adapt their messaging for age-group demographics (as well as other visually recognizable characteristics and discernible contexts) will likely be commonplace before very long. That application isn't very exciting, but stands to make advertising more relevant. But as that data flows downstream and becomes enmeshed with our location tracking, response and purchase behavior, and other signals, it could bring about some genuinely creepy interactions. 16

Like most emerging technology, there's a chance of fraught consequences. Age progression could someday factor into insurance assessment and health care. For example, if you seem to be aging faster than your cohorts, perhaps you're not a very good insurance risk. You may pay more or be denied coverage. 17

After Amazon introduced real-time facial recognition services in late 2016, they began selling those services to law enforcement and government agencies, such as the police departments in Orlando and Washington County, Oregon. But the technology raises major privacy concerns; the police could use the technology not only to track people who are suspected of having committed crimes, but also people who are not committing crimes, such as protesters and others whom the police deem a nuisance. 18

The American Civil Liberties Union asked Amazon to stop selling this service. So did a portion of Amazon's shareholders and employees, who asked 19

generate: To create.

Amazon to halt the service, citing concerns for the company's valuation and reputation.

It's tough to overstate the fullness of how technology stands to impact 20 humanity. The opportunity exists for us to make it better, but to do that we also must recognize some of the ways in which it can get worse. Once we understand the issues, it's up to all of us to weigh in.

So is this such a big deal? Are bad things going to happen because you 21 posted some already-public profile pictures to your wall? Is it dangerous to train facial recognition algorithms for age progression and age recognition? Not exactly.

Regardless of the origin or intent behind this meme, we must all become 22 savvier about the data we create and share, the access we grant to it, and the implications for its use. If the context was a game that explicitly stated that it was collecting pairs of then-and-now photos for age progression research, you could choose to participate with an awareness of who was supposed to have access to the photos and for what purpose.

The broader message, removed from the specifics of any one meme or even 23 any one social platform, is that humans are the richest data sources for most of the technology emerging in the world. We should know this, and proceed with due diligence and sophistication . . . .

We should demand that businesses treat our data with due respect, by all 24 means. But we also need to treat our own data with respect.

Questions to Start You Thinking

1. **Considering Meaning:** How does the "10-year challenge" meme generate data about Facebook users? In what way does it streamline the information?

2. **Identifying Writing Strategies:** Kate O'Neill inserts one of her own tweets into this article. Why do you think she does this? Is there any irony to the statement that precedes it: "Instead of joining in, I posted the following semi-sarcastic tweet"?

3. **Reading Critically:** Are most people aware of how their information is being collected and used online? What makes you think so? What is O'Neill's claim about such memes and our awareness of them?

4. **Expanding Vocabulary:** In paragraph 2, O'Neill refers to her "semi-sarcastic" tweet about the Facebook 10-year challenge. What does it mean if something is *sarcastic*? Why would O'Neill make the qualification that her tweet is *semi-sarcastic*, and how might she describe the other part of her tweet?

5. **Making Connections:** Both O'Neill in this article and Squire and Gaydos in "No, Fortnite Isn't Rotting Kids' Brains . . ." (p. 385) address electronic worlds (social media and gaming) and how we act/what we reveal when we are in them. Both articles carry warnings, but do either of them suggest we do away with these worlds? In what way are their instructions for online living similar?

Suggestions for Writing

1. Think about your participation in and presence on social media. Do you think you give away information online? What type of information? Do you do it willingly or unthinkingly? What memes have you participated in and what information do you put online? What protections are available to you? In a short essay, describe your online presence and the information trail you leave behind, no matter how little or how much you use social media; if you don't have an online presence, describe your experience of hearing about others' social media use.

2. O'Neill's article examines the implications of facial recognition technology on social media and the ways in which we give away our information online. Do you think you have a complete picture of what this technology is and what it is used for, based on this article? What questions are you left with? Write a list of 1) what you know based on this article, 2) your questions about the technology, based on this article, and 3) your position on the use of facial recognition technology on social media. Support your position by referencing your answers to 1) and 2).

Jason Johnson

How Stan Lee, Creator of Black Panther, Taught a Generation of Black Nerds about Race, Art, and Activism

Jason Johnson is a professor at the School of Global Journalism and Communication at Morgan State University in Baltimore. He's an MSNBC political contributor and the politics editor at TheRoot.com, where this article was published in 2018. In addition to being a political analyst and public speaker, Johnson is the author of *Political Consultants and Campaigns: One Day to Sell*.

AS YOU READ: What can comic books teach us about the world we live in? What in particular did Stan Lee do for comic books and the people who read them?

When I was a kid, I didn't live close enough to a comic book shop to get there on my bike. My parents would have to take me to Fair Oaks Mall in Fairfax, Va., and I'd get my comics off the old spinner racks at Waldenbooks. As the years went on and specialty comic shops opened, my friends and I had a comic book ritual° of sorts. 1

Matt, Jeff and I would borrow one of our parents' cars, drive out to our favorite comic shop, then go to Jeff's room and read comics until we had to go home. Stacks of X-Men, Captain America and Spider-Man comics would be spread out all over the floor. 2

This is how I spent my '90s childhood. 3

And while at the time the Martin Luther King Jr. holiday was still up for debate, Al Sharpton was considered controversial° and Public Enemy wasn't 4

ritual: A ceremony or practice often related to religious customs.   **controversial:** Subject to controversy, or the expression of opposing viewpoints.

played on "mainstream" radio — in a strange way all of that comic reading gave me a racial and political education that my lily-white suburban Virginia life never did. And it's all thanks to Stan Lee, the creative and driving force behind Marvel comics for half a century, who passed away [in 2018] at the tender age of 95. He gave a black kid a place to play in the cosmos° and beyond, and the world is a little less bright after his passing.

After his death we heard how Stan Lee is credited with creating Daredevil, 5 Thor, Iron Man, Ant-Man, Dr. Strange, the Wasp, the Hulk the Avengers, the Fantastic Four, Spider-Man and, of course, Black Panther. What we didn't hear as much is how he was screaming from the rafters about racism and discrimination while providing a curriculum for black kids like myself when public schools and all other forms of pop culture summarily shut us out.

Stan Lee didn't just develop the modern superhero, he brought activist° 6 heroes and storylines to the mainstream when most other white publishers let alone newspapers were still playing footsie with Nazis, terrorists and bigots.°

It is hard to overstate how important Lee is to black kids growing up in 7 the 1980s and '90s back when comic books were considered a "white" thing. I have literally teared up a few times while writing and thinking about how much joy he brought to youngsters like me, and how much his passion and excitement for comic books helped validate° this hobby and the culture that goes with the genre. More than any other golden age comic creator Lee's characters put blackness and the black experience at the forefront.

When Lee created the X-Men in 1963, the battle between Magneto and Pro- 8 fessor X was meant to be a rough allegory° for the integrationist vs. nationalist philosophies of Martin Luther King Jr. and Malcolm X. Yes, the idea of black oppression and philosophy being played out by mostly protestant white guys like Cyclops and Ice-Man is problematic in hindsight (Magneto is Jewish), but it was a radical idea at the time. It also laid the groundwork for a comic that always spoke to racial injustice, even to kids like me who loved comics but seldom saw themselves in the stories and shows of the genre.

By the '90s, the ideas Stan Lee established had evolved, and I was spend- 9 ing my Saturday afternoons reading about Genosha, the apartheid state that forced mutants into labor for regular (read: white) humans. When my class wasn't talking about apartheid, I was learning it from Stan Lee's creations. Lee's creations seamlessly integrated "blackness" into comics in a way that was revolutionary and organic all at the same time.

Peter Parker was a poor, white kid who was mentored by his black edi- 10 tor at the Daily Bugle newspaper, Robbie Robertson. Captain America's best friend was the Falcon (played by Anthony Mackie in the movies) who wore technologically advanced wings built by Black Panther (in the comics). Black Panther was the king of a super technologically advanced, never-conquered, African nation called Wakanda that introduced me to afro-futurism° before I

---

cosmos: The entire universe as an orderly harmonious system.   **activist:** Advocate of a cause.   **bigot:** A person who is intolerant of others.   **validate:** To make valid; to confirm or give approval to.   **allegory:** A symbolic narrative.   **afro-futurism:** An idea that blends aspects of the African diaspora culture with technology.

even knew what afro-futurism was. Stan Lee created all of those black characters, from kings to sidekicks; from father figures to managers.

It wasn't until later in life, when I started studying and teaching about comics instead of just reading them, that I learned that none of this was a fluke.° Stan Lee was an activist artist, a Jewish guy born to Romanian immigrant parents in New York who hated bigotry. He was explicit about it in his *Stan's Soapbox* editorials that ran across all Marvel Comics. He called bigots "Low IQ Yo-Yos," he said that anybody who generalized about blacks, women, Italians or whoever hadn't truly evolved as a person.

He was doing this in *comic pages* when mainstream newspaper editorials were still deciding if black folks should be able to live where they wanted. When Marvel Comics were afraid that the Black Panther character would be associated with the Black Panther political movement, Stan Lee pushed for T'Challa to keep his name (at one point they wanted to call him Coal Tiger). All of this at a time when even having a black person in a comic was still considered controversial. As recently as October 2017, Lee posted a spontaneous° video on the Marvel's YouTube page stating the foundation of Marvel Comics was to fight for equality and battle against bigotry and injustice.

I don't know if it was Charlottesville,° Va., or Donald Trump that inspired the video but the fact remains that Stan Lee was steadfast in his belief that superheroes should look and sound like the world around us; that they needed to reflect the best in people while tackling the worst of human instincts.

I'm not a kid anymore, I'm not waking up to hear Stan Lee's voice narrate Spider-Man and his Amazing Friends on Saturday mornings. I can drive myself to the movies where I see Stan Lee cameos in Marvel and DC films. I don't look up at the ceilings in Washington, D.C.'s Union Station and imagine what it would it would be like to climb on the walls like Spider-Man (well, actually I still do but not as often).

Yet, every week I teach a class at Morgan State University about comic book politics and history, I still go to the comic shop every Wednesday, I have interviewed Ta-Nehisi Coates twice about the Black Panther comic book, I wrote about how the Falcon made the Captain America movies the blackest Marvel film ever. I've waxed poetic about how the X-Men are the single most progressive pop culture icons in Gen-X culture.

All of this is thanks to Stan Lee, who showed this kid that a love of art and politics didn't have to exist in separate universes; that blackness was as heroic as anything else; and that when you have power — even just the power to draw a few characters on a page — you have a responsibility to make those characters count for something.

Lee would end most of his personal appearances and cameos with *"Excelsior"* — the Latin phrase that translates roughly as "higher."

11

12

13

14

15

16

17

---

fluke: An accident.   **spontaneous:** Arising without effort or premeditation.
Charlottesville, VA: The site of a white supremacist rally in 2017, where a neo-Nazi sympathizer deliberately drove his car into the crowd, killing one person and injuring 40 others.

Thanks for all your help, Stan Lee. I hope you're out there somewhere   18
exploring the cosmos, swinging from the ceilings, knowing that you made the
world a better place.

Excelsior, indeed.   19

Questions to Start You Thinking

1. **Considering Meaning:** What does Jason Johnson say he learned from
   Stan Lee? How did Lee teach him those lessons?

2. **Identifying Writing Strategies:** In his essay, Johnson paints a picture of
   his childhood and of a time period (the 1990s). Is it important that this
   article look backward in time? What would be missing without it?

3. **Reading Critically:** Who is Johnson's intended audience? Why do you
   think so? What is the purpose of writing this article? How, specifically,
   does Johnson reveal his audience and purpose?

4. **Expanding Vocabulary:** In paragraph 9, Johnson mentions the *apartheid*
   state. Where else might you have heard this term? Where does the word
   come from and what does it mean?

5. **Making Connections with the Paired Essay:** In paragraph 16, Johnson says Stan Lee taught him that "when you have power — even just the
   power to draw a few characters on a page — you have a responsibility to
   make those characters count for something." How does that responsibility compare with the thought behind marketing superheroes in Jeffrey
   Brown's "'I'm the Goshdarn Batman!'" (p. 396)?

Suggestions for Writing

1. Think about people you admire from your childhood, whether they are
   alive or dead. Choose one and write a short homage that points out the
   way they affected you, what they taught you, and why you admire them.

2. Johnson indicates that Lee believed his characters should "reflect the best
   in people while tackling the worst of human instincts" (paragraph 13).
   Read a Marvel comic or watch a Marvel movie and write short report on
   how Lee's characters embody this belief.

Jeffrey A. Brown

"I'm the Goshdarn Batman!" The Rise of Cute Superheroes

Jeffrey A. Brown is a professor in the Department of Popular Culture at Bowling
Green State University. He is the author of *Batman and the Multiplicity of Identity:
The Contemporary Comic Book Superhero as Cultural Nexus*; *Black Superheroes:
Milestone Comics and Their Fans*; *Dangerous Curves: Action Heroines, Gender,
Fetishism, and Popular Culture*; and *Beyond Bombshells: The New Action Heroine
in Popular Culture*. This selection was excerpted from an article published in the
Journal of Graphic Novels and Comics in 2018.

AS YOU READ: What traits do you associate with comic book characters?

Comic books have always been stigmatized as a simple and childish form   1
of mass media. The conflation° of comic books as a medium within
the dominant genre of superhero adventures contributes to the perception
that comics are immature fantasies. But, rather than children's fare, modern
superhero comic books often grapple with mature issues of morality, violence,
sexuality, and politics. In fact, the persistent (mis)identification of superhero
comics as childish elides° the reality that, since the late 1980s, children represent a much smaller portion of the comic-book-reading audience. The rise
of comic book specialty stores and direct marketing removed comics from the
traditional convenience store outlets where young consumers of generations
past would often first encounter monthly issues. Likewise, the decline of
print as a popular medium in deference° to digital media, and the steady dis-
appearance of brick-and-mortar bookstores, has hindered children's access to
comic books. The industry's increasing reliance on its core adult consumers,
and the natural maturing of the superhero genre, has also meant an emphasis
on more grown-up story content and more nuanced° character depictions.

Despite the unprecedented popularity currently enjoyed by superheroes in   2
Western culture, and around the world, due primarily to blockbuster movies
and hit television programs, the comic book industry is faced with the challenge of attracting young readers. According to a Nielsen Company market
study commissioned by DC Comics, . . . fewer than 2% of readers are estimated
to be under the age of 18. As the industry website Comics Alliance notes: "The
results are troubling, and raise serious questions about DC's ability to expand
their audience base' (Hudson 2012, para. 1). "The dismally low numbers for
young readers," the review continues "should worry anyone who cares about
the future of superhero comics, and its ability to sustain an audience into the
future" (para. 4). . . .

Marvel and DC may be slow to fully embrace comics aimed at young read-   3
ers, but they have begun to cater to younger consumers through several superhero series and a plethora° of cute superhero merchandise designed to attract
even pre-literate fans. Most of the comic book series recast the superheroes
as younger and more gleeful: Superheroing as a fun playful activity rather
than grim and gritty. . . While these strategies have met with varying degrees
of success, what I want to focus on here is the rather peculiar approach of
infantilizing° superhero characters, which has become increasingly popular
and specifically targets very young consumers and, to a lesser extent, female
audiences. Inspired by the global success of Japanese *kawaii* (cute) aesthetics,
American media forms have begun to mimic the simple lines, bright colors,
and innocent aura that pervades popular Japanese characters/products
such as Hello Kitty and Pokemon. As primarily illustrated characters that
already exist across numerous media platforms and through a range of different visual styles, superheroes are easy to depict according to the aesthetic°

---

conflation: Fusion.   **elide:** Suppress, leave out.   **deference:** Respectful submission.
nuanced: Subtly changed.   **plethora:** Excess.   **infantilizing:** Reducing to or treating like
an infant.   **aesthetics:** A particular concept or approach to beauty.

conventions of cuteness. Cherub-like, cutesy versions of all the most recognisable superheroes from both DC and Marvel have become mainstays in the comics and in popular toy and collectable figures lines from merchandising partners such as Funko, Cosbaby, Hallmark, Jada Toys, Mezco Toyz, Lego, Duplo, Hasbro Playskool, and Fisher-Price. The image of cute superheroes transcends the comic book, television or filmic versions of the characters and appears as an alternative conception of superheroes available on everything from T-shirts and mugs to phone cases, keychains and notebooks. The consumers of these infantilized superheroes range from toddlers to seniors by tapping into an aesthetic of cuteness at odds with the traditionally violent action of superhero stories. The juxtaposition° of the cute and the dramatic versions of superheroes exposes the affective means by which the characters are enjoyed by fans for various purposes and across different points of personal development.

Rather than undermining the general seriousness of modem superheroes,   4
the emergence of cute versions of the characters exploits and capitalizes on existing representational variety within comic books. Superheroes have a long history in the comics of being illustrated and written in vastly different, and often conflicting, styles. The addition of cute superheroes to the lexicon° of representation is novel, but not without precedent° in the world of superheroes. Henry Jenkins (2009) argues that contemporary comic book characters exist in a narrative dynamic of multiplicity.° Characters can, and do, appear in the comics (and other media forms) in very different ways simultaneously. In some stories Batman may be in his 60s, in others he is a young adult; Batman may be Superman's best friend, or his worst enemy; he might be a steampunk Batman, or medieval Bat-Knight, or old west gunslinger Batman. As Jenkins (2009, 20–21) observes:

> Readers may consume multiple versions of the same franchise, each with different conceptions of the character, different understandings of the relationships with the secondary figures, different moral perspectives, exploring different moments in their lives, and so forth.

The idea and acceptance of multiplicity has become part and parcel of   5
superhero fictions. This multiplicity can extend beyond character representations to incorporate entirely different narrative worlds. . . . The addition of cute superheroes fits so neatly alongside the dynamic of multiplicity in the comics that DC simply designated "Earth 42" as the home of the impish variety of their characters. The cute version of superheroes does not disrupt the overall image of any particular character as much as it adds a new perspective, one that seeks to attract an under-represented audience.

Likewise, the emergence of cute superheroes . . . reflects the current industrial use of multimedia "worlds" to support audience expansion. Instead of   6

---

juxtaposition: An instance of things placed side by side for comparison.   **lexicon:** A particular vocabulary.   **precedent:** An earlier event or example that guides other situations.
multiplicity: A large number.

diluting the identity of characters, the abundance of cute superhero cartoons, toys, shirts and other collectibles, boosts overall brand recognition. In this era of corporate synergy where Marvel is owned by Disney and DC Comics is owned by Time-Warner, superheroes have been at the forefront of media convergence. . . . Aaron Taylor (2014, 182) argues . . . that each variation of any given superhero character does not dilute or contradict some core identity, but rather promotes and reinforces the overall brand of that character and/or its parent corporation. Cute superhero merchandise simply extends the concept of those characters into a different representational realm and appeals to different market segments. . . .

Cute li'l superheroes

While many artistic styles in contemporary superhero comic books have elements that can be subjectively deemed "cute," I want to focus on the infantilizing styles that are far more objectively and intentionally "cute." The cute superhero look is clearly exemplified by Skottie Young's work on various *Little Marvel* books and as a variant cover artist on almost every Marvel title Art Baltazar's illustration of DC's *Tiny Titans* and *The Superman Family Adventures,* Eric Jones' art for *Supergirl: Cosmic Adventures in the 8th Grade,* and Dustin Nguyen's art for *Batman: Li'l Gotham* and *Study Hall of Justice.* Rather than the standard bulging muscularity of supermen and the eroticised curves of superwomen (see Brown 2016; Cocca 2016), these cute versions look more like toddlers or babies with oversized heads, rounded torsos, stubby limbs and huge eyes. This type of cute superhero depiction is reproduced and reinforced far beyond the comic books themselves, in popular cartoons such as *Teen Titans Go!* (2013-current), *DC Super Hero Girls* (2015-current) and *Marvel's Superhero Squad* (2009–2011), and through the successful merchandising of products such as Funko's Pop Style Bobbleheads, Li'l Bombshells and Dorbz rounded mini-figures, Quantum Mechanix Q-Pop figures, Disney's line of MXYZ and Tsum Tsum merchandise, Fisher Price's line of Little People and Imaginext superhero toys, and Cosbaby's collectible figures. 7

The trend of infantile superhero depictions is part of a larger cute aesthetic that pervades modem consumer culture. "Cute" is a defining feature of everything from humorous costumes for pets, to cartoon-inspired purses and high-top sneakers, to Victoria's Secret's Pink line of exercise clothes. As Anthony P. McIntyre (2015, 422–423) argues: 8

> Cuteness is a powerful affective° register° whose social proliferation since the turn of the millennium has been striking. Whether in the form of YouTube videos of kittens, the increasing prevalence of cupcakes, or the emoticons that terminate many text messages, the rise of the cute has left few areas of life untouched by its ebullient° reverberations°. . . .

affective: Related to emotions.   **register:** The style of language used in a particular situation.
ebullient: Full of enthusiasm.   **reverberations:** A constantly echoing sound.

The current widespread proliferation of a cute aesthetic in American culture is generally credited to the spread of Japanese *kawaii* (cute) media and consumer products on the international market. Post Second World War Japanese youth, especially but not exclusive females, embraced kawaii aesthetics in various subcultural styles as well as in merchandising and media forms. Lolita-inspired schoolgirl uniforms, Harajuku girls, Sailor Moon, Pokemon, Hello Kitty, and countless anima and manga are emblematic° of the dominant kawaii aesthetic that has been adopted by Western cultures. In fact, exported forms of kawaii popular culture are often regarded as Japan's most valuable international commodity. "Cuteness gives Japan 'cultural power' and is something Japanese are 'polishing' overseas," observes Allison (2003, 383) in her analysis of Pokémon in a global economic context . . . . As Granot et al. (2014, 69, italics in original) observe: "Within the last 30 years *cute* has evolved from a Japanese cultural phenomenon into the ubiquitous chant of almost every (female) teenager: 'that's cute.'". . . 9

The qualities associated with cuteness (small, soft, rounded) imply not just an abstract artistic or aesthetic style, but specifically a sense of the object's infantile vulnerability. Cuteness signifies weakness, dependency and helplessness. . . . Daniel Harris (2000, 4) outlines the relationship between being cute and being needy: "Something becomes cute not necessarily because of a quality it has but because of a quality it lacks, a certain neediness and inability to stand alone." Likewise, Ngai observes how "the formal properties associated with cuteness—smallness, compactness, softness, simplicity and pliancy—call forth specific affects: helplessness, pitifulness, and even despondency"° (Ngai 2005, 816). It is this association between the appearance of cuteness and perception of helplessness that creates an affective and emotional response in consumers. . . . 10

Certainly a key to the novelty of the cute superheroes is their radical departure from the traditional depiction and characterization of superheroes as big, powerful, self-reliant, and sexual. The cute superhero inverts many of the core attributes of the standard superhero persona, literally revisioning superheroes as child-like and child-friendly characters. The cute versions of superheroes clearly places the characters in the domain° children's entertainment, a relatively innocent world where heroic adventures are pure play rather than dangerous adventures. . . . 11

The stark contrast between traditional comic book superheroes and cute superheroes is explicitly addressed in *Superman/Batman* issues 51 and 52 (2008), written by Michael Green and Mike Johnson and illustrated by Rafael Albuquerque. The "Li'l Leaguers" story features a team-up adventure between the conventional Superman and Batman and their cute counterparts from a parallel dimension. . . . Li'l Superman saves the President, catching Air Force One before it crashes, but witnesses are dumbfounded to see a tiny Superman. Likewise. Li'l Batman stops a mugging in Gotham but the criminals are 12

---

emblematic: Symbolic.   **despondency:** Dejection.   **domain:** A particular territory.

shocked to see a diminutive dark knight, the miniature Batman punching them with little fists and scowling at them with oversized anime eyes. When the adult Superman and Batman meet their tiny doppelgangers° Li'l Superman is a caricature of Superman's optimistic persona, gleefully exclaiming: "That's awesome! I'm Superman too! It's *so cool!* We can team up and fight crime together! This is going to be so *great!*" Conversely, the Batmen scowl at each other, and Li'l Batman's expression of toughness is framed as ridiculous: "I'm *Batman!*" the knee-high caped crusader growls. When the adult Batman disagrees, his little counterpart screams: *"I'm the goshdarn Batman!"* The humorous use of "goshdarn" stresses the childish nature of cute Batman as a direct reference to the excessively macho "I'm the god damned Batman!" catchphrase introduced by Frank Miller in *All-Star Batman & Robin* (2005) that has been used repeatedly in the adult oriented comics, and turned into a popular online meme. . . .

The strength and competence of the Li'l superheroes is also depicted as childish. While the cute heroes ostensibly have the same powers as the adult ones, they are noticeably weaker and more vulnerable. The tiny Superman and Batman are confounded by their experience in this strange, big world: when they try to stop a supervillain from robbing a bank Li'l Batman screams "Oww! What is happening to my arm?" because he has never felt pain before, and when Li'l Superman is thrown against a wall he exclaims: *"I felt that!* Usually we just bounce off everything!" Rather than the bloody and violent world depicted in most superhero narratives, the milieu° of the cute heroes is one devoid of any real danger — a cuter, softer, friendlier kid-safe fantasy world populated by cuddly costumed heroes (and villains). Bullets are replaced with suction cups, arrows are replaced with plungers, bombs are replaced with whoopee cushions, and lasers are replaced with silly string. Most of the cute superhero books marketed to children forego traditional adventures all together in favor of unthreatening juvenile humor. For example, in the comic book series *Tiny Titans,* the Li'l heroes have tea parties, play with their pets, and try to find a perfect home for their tree house. . . .

Overall, the cute superheroes suggest a complete erasure of the darker elements fundamental to caped avengers in order to make the genre appropriate for the extremely young target audiences. The "Li'L Leaguers" story reveals how different the cute superheroes are by reworking the basic beginnings of the heroes. The cute superheroes origins are repositioned as a sanitized version of one of the most important conventions in the genre: personal tragedy. Li'l Superman cheerfully reveals that in his reality he is not the lone survivor of the doomed planet Krypton. Li'l Krypton is fine, cute Superman sees his birth parents all the time . . . they just sent him to Earth to keep him dry when it got rainy on Krypton. Likewise, Li'l Batman's origin humorously rewrites one of the most famous and tragic scenes in popular culture. Rather than witnessing his parents being murdered in an alley, Li'l Batman dramatically explains that his parents were simply "pushed to the ground. Two shoves, and nothing was ever the same again. I swore that night that *no one* would ever

13

14

---

doppelganger: A double or look-alike.   **milieu:** Surroundings.

be bullied in Gotham City." The adult Batman is incredulous,° and decides to preserve Li'l Batman's innocence by not revealing the gruesome death of his own parents. As figures that are not shaped by the type of tragedies that provide the motivation for almost every mature version of the superhero, the cute superheroes remain firmly ensconced° in the realm of childhood. Having never lost their innocence through tragedy, the cute superheroes are an effective means to rewrite the characters for preschool-aged audiences. These are versions of popular characters that little kids can identify with, without the frightening spectre of parents being killed. . . .

In their landmark essay "I'm Not Fooled By That Cheap Disguise" Uricchio and Pearson (1991) argue that the death of Bruce Wayne's parents is the most important and consistent element of the Batman mythos. . . . In other words, the death of Bruce Wayne's parents is the unalterable foundation upon which everything Batman is built. This tragic event defines the character's motivations and actions no matter how much the depiction of Batman may be altered by individual creators, different eras and different mediums. . . . Audiences know he is always Batman, a grim avenger, dedicating his life to fighting crime because he witnessed the murder of his parents. "The merest reference to the origin events," Uricchio and Pearson (1991, 196) point out, "activates an intertextual° frame which insists upon the Batman's motivation and key traits/attributes while permitting for variant elaboration." Above all else, Batman *is* Batman because of the murder of his parents.

In reducing the tragic murder of the Waynes to the humorous "shoving" of the Waynes, the Li'l Leaguers storyline emphasises how fundamentally different the implications of cute superheroes are. The cute superhero aesthetic leverages° the familiar attributes of recognizable superheroes (costumes, powers, gadgets, etc.) but repositions them as signifiers of innocence and helplessness. Cute superheroes represent harmless superhero play for young consumers. The Li'l superheroes are still an imaginative path to empowerment, but without the risk of exposing children to ideas of real violence. Defeating "bad guys" is just a simple game. Part of the appeal of cute and cuddly superheroes for preschool-aged children is relatively obvious: they are a safe and simple way to introduce children to a world of imaginative play where they learn the basic principles of right and wrong, good guys and bad guys, without any age-inappropriate content. The helpless and infantile qualities of the cute superheroes allows children to not just identify with the characters, but to also feel a sense of possession or mastery over them. Children can revel in the harmless stories and the funny aspects of the hero's powers, and feel a sense of superiority as well as inclusion.

---

incredulous: Skeptical.   **ensconced:** Settled securely.   **intertextual:** Having to do with the relationship between texts.   **leverages:** Uses to an advantage.

References

Allison, A. 2003. "Portable Monsters and Commodity Cuteness Pokemon as Japan's New Global Power." *Postcolonial Studies* 6 (3): 381–398. doi:10.1080/136887903 2000162220.

Brown, J. A. 2016. *Superhero Movies: Popular Genre and American Values.* New York: Routledge Press.

Cocca, C. 2016. *Superwomen: Gender, Power, and Representation.* New York: Bloomsbury Academic.

Granot, E., Alejandro, T. B., & Russell, L. T. 2014. "A Socio-Marketing Analysis of the Concept of Cute and Its Consumer Culture Implications." *Journal of Consumer Culture,* 14 (1): 66–87. https://doi.org/10.1177/1469540513485274.

Harris, D. 2000. *Cute, Quaint, Hungry and Romantic: The Aesthetics of Consumerisrn.* New York: Basic Books.

Hudson, L. 2012. "DC Comics Survey Reports 'New 52' Readership 93% Male, Only 5% New Readers." *ComicsAlliance.com,* February 10.

Jenkins, H. 2009. "'Just Men in Tights': Rewriting Silver Age Comics in an Era of Multiplicity." In *The Contemporary Comic Book Superhero,* edited by A. Ndalianis. New York: Routledge.

McIntyre, A. P. 2015. "Isn't She Adorkable! Cuteness as Political Neutralization in the Star Text of Zoey Deshanel." *Television & New Media* 16 (5): 422–438. doi:10.1177/1527476414524284.

Ngai. S. 2005. "The Cuteness of the Avant-Garde." *Critical Inquiry* 31 (2): 811–847.

Taylor, A. 2014. "Avengers Dissemble! Transmedia Superhero Franchises and Cultic Management." *Journal of Adaptation in Film & Performance* 7 (2): 181–194. doi:10.1386/jafp.7.2.181_1.

Uricchio, W., and R. Pearson, eds. 1991. *The Many Lives of the Batman: Critical Approaches to a Superhero and His Media.* New York: BFL.

Questions to Start You Thinking

1. **Considering Meaning:** In what way does the introduction of "cute" superheroes complement, rather than detract from, the superheroes as portrayed by DC and Marvel comics?

2. **Identifying Writing Strategies:** Consider the quotations integrated into this article. Identify where they are used. How are they introduced? What effect do they have on Brown's text? How does their placement support the article's points?

3. **Reading Critically:** Brown states, "The cute superhero inverts many of the core attributes of the standard superhero persona, literally revisioning superheroes as child-like and child-friendly characters" (paragraph 11). What evidence supports this idea? What are the original attributes of the superheroes?

4. **Expanding Vocabulary:** Brown ends paragraph 9 with a quote that makes reference to the phrase "that's cute" as *ubiquitous*. How might you define *ubiquitous* given the context? How did you come to that definition?

5. **Making Connections with the Paired Essay:** Both Jason Johnson's "How Stan Lee . . . Taught a Generation" (p. 392) and "'I'm the Goshdarn Batman!'" touch on the deeper and darker themes found in comic books. How might Johnson respond to Brown's analysis of the way superheroes have been given cute, childlike personas?

Suggestions for Writing

1. Have you read many comic books? How many movies made from comic books have you seen? What superhero merchandise have you encountered in your lifetime? Based on what you know, write an essay that compares the audience for comic books with the consumer of the spinoffs and merchandise surrounding them. Does your comparison reflect Brown's argument or not?

2. According to this article, many DC and Marvel superheroes have been infantilized in various ways to market them to a younger audience, including those so young they are not even reading yet. Choose a favorite superhero and do some research: write an essay that examines how one specific comic book character has been made "cute" and what that designation adds to their character.

24 Inequality

Alex Wong/Getty Images

Responding to an Image

This picture shows US Representative Alexandria Ocasio-Cortez (D-NY) speaking during a news conference to introduce the Paycheck Fairness Act. This 2019 bill aimed to close the wage gap between men and women, with women earning only about 80 cents for every dollar that men earn. What can you tell about this moment based on the people pictured here — their gender, race, facial expressions, or other details? Although the event was focused on wage equality, how does the image reflect a shift in other types of equality in the United States? How might a similar picture of elected officials in the United States (and their concerns) look in a photo taken fifty years before this one, or one to two hundred years earlier? How does this image reflect inequality through US history and the government's attempt to combat it?

Vanessa De Luca

Serena Williams Was Blamed for Defending Herself. That's Nothing New for Black Women.

Vanessa De Luca is a media consultant, award-winning journalist, and former editor-in-chief of *Essence* Magazine.

Vanessa K. De Luca

AS YOU READ: Have you ever noticed different standards held for professional athletes due to race, or gender, or both?

Imagine being blamed for defending your integrity.° Then understand that being attacked for speaking up is part of daily life for black women. See April Ryan, Maxine Waters, Kamala D. Harris, Susan E. Rice and Michelle Obama for a few examples of how black women have been admonished° for their public statements. Somehow it seems to happen when we challenge male authority.

It has happened before to Serena Williams, in collisions with tennis's ruling organizations, but never as dramatically as in the women's final of the U.S. Open on Saturday

I had a bad feeling from the moment that Williams walked over to chair umpire Carlos Ramos during the second set of her match against Naomi Osaka, defending herself against his accusation° that she was being guided by coach Patrick Mouratoglou from a courtside box. This would be a turning point in the match, I sensed, and not a good one for Williams.

Ramos did not openly state that Williams was cheating, but the implication° of the umpire's decision left little room for doubt that he believed she was trying to gain an unfair advantage. Williams insisted, "I'm telling you I don't cheat to win, I'd rather lose, and I'm just letting you know." The crowd's effusive° applause after the exchange made clear that the spectators thought she was in the right.

Yet, instead of warning Mouratoglou, Ramos had penalized Williams—a professional athlete with 23 Grand Slam singles titles, and therefore well versed in tennis rules and regulations—for her male coach's faux pas. Mouratoglou later admitted that he had been gesturing to Williams and was mystified that a common practice among coaches at tennis tournaments was suddenly being punished. Not only did Williams have to bear the brunt° of the umpire's decision, but she also had to accept that it was a violation not of her doing.

And it was a turning point. Distressed and frustrated, Williams clearly lost her concentration. She broke her racket after badly misplaying a shot—and was penalized for it, the only justified ruling against her in what turned out to be a fateful trio. With two violations, she was assessed a one-point penalty, in a match where every point was vital.

During a break, Williams was still waiting for Ramos to acknowledge that she had not cheated: "You're attacking my character. Yes you are. You owe me

1

2

3

4

5

6

7

---

integrity: Moral character.   **admonished:** Scolded.   **accusation:** A charge of wrongdoing.
implication: Suggestion.   **effusive:** Unrestrained.   **brunt:** Main thrust or force.

an apology." She did not want her integrity to be tainted° by a man's false characterization. Ramos could have defused the situation simply by saying that he understood her point — and then warning her that if she continued to speak, he would penalize her for a third time.

Instead, he let Williams go on, until she made the apparently unforgivable point that Ramos was a "thief" for stealing a point from her. No one listening would seriously believe that Williams was literally accusing him of theft, yet at that instant Ramos — defending *his* integrity — assessed a third violation. That automatically meant a one-game penalty against Williams, a disaster in a match where she was trying to come back from dropping the first set. Losing the second set meant losing the match, and she did.   8

Some of the media descriptions of Williams's actions on the court as a "furious rant," "an outburst," a "shocking tirade°" and a "meltdown" only support the stereotyping and unconscious bias that permeate° our culture, eager to characterize black women as angry and women in general as incapable of controlling our emotions.   9

"I'm here fighting for women's rights and for women's equality and for all kinds of stuff," Williams told reporters after the match, noting of Ramos that "he's never taken a game from a man because they said 'thief.' For me, it blows my mind. But I'm going to continue to fight for women."   10

She showed this with her warm embrace of winner Osaka during the awards ceremony. Osaka, the 20-year-old daughter of a Haitian father and Japanese mother, was in tears after what must have been an overwhelming experience in winning her first Grand Slam title.   11

The victory was a hollow one, alas, forever tainted by the same old sexist, misogynistic° tropes that women, and black women in particular, have been dealing with for centuries. Osaka says she grew up idolizing° Williams. And well she should have, not just for the way Williams has played the game but also for what she has represented throughout her career. Thanks to Williams, the path that Osaka follows in tennis and in life maybe a little less difficult, but there is plenty of work left to be done.   12

tainted: Marked or affected negatively.   **tirade:** A long, angry speech.   **permeate:** To spread throughout.   **misogynistic:** Having to do with the hatred of women.   **idolizing:** Worshipping.

Questions to Start You Thinking

1. **Considering Meaning:** What was the implication of the umpire Ramos's calls on Serena Williams in her US Open match against Naomi Osaka?
2. **Identifying Writing Strategies:** Does the essay leave you thinking more about Serena Williams or more about black women in general? Does De Luca achieve any balance between the two?
3. **Reading Critically:** How is the example of what happened to Serena Williams an example of "daily life for black women" (paragraph 1)? Why is Williams singled out as the example?

4. **Exploring Vocabulary:** Where does the phrase *faux pas* (paragraph 5) originate from? From what language is it borrowed? What does it mean?

5. **Making Connections:** Think about De Luca's account of the assumptions that were made about Serena Williams in the tennis match against Osaka. Now consider how, in his essay "Black Men and Public Space" (p. 429), people respond to Brent Staples. What assumptions are made about Staples in that essay? Are there any connections between these two essays? Explain your thinking.

Suggestions for Writing

1. Can you think of an example in which a professional athlete (or political figure or celebrity) received deferential or disrespectful treatment because of race or gender (or age or disability)? Write a few paragraphs on when and how the situation took place. Who was involved? Who was watching? Can you remember any dialogue? How did things end up?

2. In her opening paragraph, De Luca mentions several other black women who have "been admonished for their public statements." In a short essay, compare the experience of one of those women to Serena Williams's experience described here. You may have to do some research to gather information on what De Luca is referring to.

Shanna Kattari

The Health Care Discrimination Transgender and Non-Binary People Face Every Day

Shanna Kattari teaches at the University of Michigan School of Social Work. She is a researcher in the fields of sexuality and social justice. She is also a certified sexologist.

AS YOU READ: Have you ever faced discrimination in a health care setting? Why?

Shanna Katz Kattari

Many people may experience anxiety when seeking medical treatment. They might worry about wait times, insurance coverage or how far they must travel to access care.   1

Transgender and non-binary° individuals have an added fear: gender-related discrimination.° This can involve being outed due to a name or gender mismatch on an insurance card, being completely denied care or even being left to die.   2

Most recently, the White House has begun to seriously weigh removing transgender and intersex° individuals from definitions of gender completely.   3

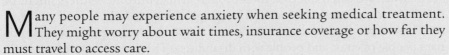

non-binary: Not identifying with or conforming to either male or female gender.
discrimination: Differential treatment, usually having a negative connotation.   **intersex:** Describing an individual with both male and female sex organs.

If enacted, such a change would almost certainly lead to problems for transgender and non-binary people as they seek a variety of health services. Growing scientific evidence shows that this population faces significant hurdles in many domains,° including when seeking medical and mental health care.

Rates of discrimination

Transgender and non-binary individuals are those whose gender does not   4
align with the social expectations connected to the sex they were assigned at birth. Sex, usually assigned male or female at birth, is based on genitalia, while gender is a complete sense of who one knows themselves to be.

It's difficult to estimate what percent of the population is transgender   5
or non-binary. Gender identity is not included in the U.S. census or on most national or statewide data collection efforts. However, research shows that approximately 0.6 percent of U.S. adults identify with a gender expansive identity, such as transgender, non-binary, genderqueer or agender.

Younger people are more likely to have one of these identities compared   6
to adults. Somewhere between 0.7 and 3.8 percent of high school-aged youth report that they identify as transgender, non-binary or another identity besides the sex they were assigned at birth.

This population has many challenging experiences when compared to   7
individuals who are not transgender. Some problems include employment and housing discrimination, as well as higher rates of partner violence. Many of these experiences are connected to transphobia, or discrimination against transgender and non-binary individuals.

Health researchers such as myself have been working to better understand   8
the discrimination that this group faces in medical settings. For example, approximately one-fifth of transgender and non-binary individuals have been denied equal treatment when trying to access doctors or hospitals.

Discrimination can come in many different forms. Medical providers   9
might assume that all health issues are correlated with one's gender identity – for example, assuming that pneumonia is somehow connected to hormone use, or that all anxiety must be due to being transgender. These and other such issues are often referred to as broken arm syndrome. Others might be refused care, or experience harmful language or harassment.

These experiences of discrimination are elevated for transgender and non-bi-   10
nary people of color and people with disabilities. This is true not only in medical settings, but in places like mental health centers, domestic violence centers, drug treatment programs and rape crisis centers. In fact, those with multiple types of disabilities—whether physical, socioemotional or learning-related—are over three times more likely to experience discrimination in all four settings as compared to non-disabled people.

domains: Realms or regions.

Making health care more inclusive

Societal stigma° and bias can leave transgender and non-binary people feeling   11
marginalized. But there are steps that medical providers can take to promote
resiliency° and well-being among this population.

Transgender and non-binary individuals have higher rates of depression   12
and thoughts about suicide. They are also significantly more likely to attempt
suicide. These increased rates are not due to being transgender, but from dealing with stigma, lack of acceptance and abuse.

One study showed that, when transgender and non-binary individuals   13
had a primary care provider that they considered to be inclusive, they had
lower rates of depression and suicidal thoughts. About 54 percent of those
without an inclusive provider reported current depression, compared to only
38 percent of those with such a provider.

I believe that medical and nursing schools, social work, counseling and   14
psychology training programs, and community organizations should make
a tangible effort to better train all health providers and social service professionals. Staff should have more comfort treating members of this community,
especially those who hold multiple marginalized identities, like transgender
people of color.

This training could include information on different language used by   15
this community; guidance on how to correctly use a variety of pronouns; or
best health care practices for working with members of this community. It
could even simply start by providing a basic understanding of the difference
between gender and sex.

Training could help reduce these alarming rates of discrimination faced   16
by this community – as well as bolster° their overall health and well-being.

---

stigma: A mark of shame.   **resiliency:** An ability to bounce back from a negative situation.   **bolster:** To support.

Questions to Start You Thinking

1. **Considering Meaning:** What are some of the failures by medical professionals noted by Kattari in terms of care of transgender and non-binary
   people?

2. **Identifying Writing Strategies:** Look at the title of this article. Based on
   the title, what do you expect the article to focus on? Does it? How does
   Kattari's ending take the article in a different direction?

3. **Reading Critically:** What sort of training do medical professionals need
   in order to end the discrimination felt by members of the transgender
   and non-binary community?

4. **Expanding Vocabulary:** How do you define *transphobia* (paragraph 7)?
   How might you guess at its meaning before looking it up? What about
   broken arm syndrome (paragraph 9)? What does the term mean, and are
   there any clues to the meaning before you search for it?

5. **Making Connections:** How would Kattari respond to Sally Hines's "The False Opposition Between Trans and Feminist Rights" (p. 441) argument about how feminists treat transgender and non-binary people? Does the treatment of transgender/non-binary people by feminists share any similarity with the discrimination they experience by the medical community? Explain the connection.

Suggestions for Writing

1. Research other articles on the experiences of transgender and non-binary people in terms of their health care. You can start by simply googling "non-binary gender and health care" as search terms. Note the credentials of the writer or website before you assume the article is valid for research purposes. How do any other arguments you find compare with Kattari's assessment? Do they support, disagree with, or add to Kattari's perspective? Write a short comparison essay that presents your findings, and be sure to cite your sources using MLA format.

2. Consider Kattari's description of how the transgender/non-binary community is failed or inadequately cared for by medical practitioners and medical insurance. Are there other areas of life many of us take for granted that might also be failing those communities? Which ones? Try to come up with one area and describe, in writing, the difficulties those particular communities might face.

Victoria Rosenboom and Kristin Blagg

Disconnected from Higher Education

Victoria Rosenboom is a research analyst for the Center on Education Data and Policy at the Urban Institute. Prior to that, she was a research assistant at the Center for Research on Children in the US at Georgetown University. Kristin Blagg is a research associate for the Center on Education Data and Policy at the Urban Institute. She focuses on K-12 and post-secondary education.

AS YOU READ: What are some of the roadblocks to higher education faced in certain communities? Does everyone stand an equal chance of attaining higher education?

Approximately 3 million American adults lack access to higher education based on where they live. These people live more than 25 miles from a broad-access public university and do not have access to the high-speed internet connection needed for online education.

Previous work on education deserts has identified areas where access to physical universities is limited (Hillman and Weichman 2016). Our study is the first to examine access to online education. Although online education is not a perfect substitute for learning in a physical classroom, increasing access to online coursework is a common response to the issue of education deserts. Previous studies of online education have found that the least-prepared students perform worse in online courses than in face-to-face courses (Alpert, Couch, and Harmon 2016; Bettinger and Loeb 2017). For the most part, students in hybrid° courses that include both face-to-face and online coursework perform about the same as students in face-to-face courses (Alpert, Couch, and Harmon 2016; Bowen et al. 2014). One study found that students taking the same course in a hybrid format instead of the traditional face-to-face format had a small negative impact on student performance (Joyce et al. 2014). Additionally, a recent study on Georgia Tech's online master of science degree in computer science found that online education expands access to higher education rather than only acting as a substitute for face-to-face courses (Goodman, Melkers, and Pallais 2016).

Our work examines how many students (who are physically isolated from higher education) have the opportunity to access online education and how many are still isolated. Using data from the Integrated Postsecondary Education Data System (IPEDS) and the Federal Communications Commission (FCC), we identify three types of education deserts: physical education desert only, online education desert only, and both a physical and online education desert.   3

After looking at where these deserts are physically located, we used data from the American Community Survey and the US Census to determine who lives in these deserts. Although some students move to enroll in college, the further prospective° students live from a college or university, the less likely they are to enroll (Goodman, Hurwitz, and Smith 2015; Kennedy and Long 2015). Additionally, prospective students who have work and family commitments may be less likely to move to attend college. People living in an education desert are among those with the least access to higher education.   4

Defining Education Deserts

In line with an existing definition of physical education deserts, we define physical deserts as either having no colleges or universities within 25 miles or having access to a single community college as the only broad-access public institution within 25 miles (Hillman and Weichman 2016). The second half of this definition is an important distinction because community colleges and other broad-access public institutions serve their local communities, more so than private institutions or selective public universities. Using the FCC's benchmark for measuring broadband internet access, we define online education deserts as areas where internet speeds are below 25 megabits per second (Mbps) for downloads and 3 Mbps for uploads (FCC 2016a).   5

---

hybrid: A composite.   **prospective:** Potential.

Who Is More Likely to Live in a Complete Education Desert?

Our estimates of the number of adults living in physical education deserts are 6
similar to estimates in previous work, even though we employ a different analytic strategy. We find that 17.6 percent of adults live in a physical education desert. Although many people who live in these deserts have sufficient broadband service to access online education, 1.3 percent of adults (3.1 million) have access to neither physical nor online education (a complete education desert, table 1).

Table 1 Types of Education Deserts and Share of Adults Living in Each Type

	Online education desert	Not an online education desert
Physical education desert	Complete education desert: 1.3%	Physical education desert: 16.3%
Not a physical education desert	Online education desert: 0.8%	Not an education desert: 81.6%

Source: Urban Institute analysis of American Community Survey, Census Bureau, Integrated Postsecondary Education Data System, and Federal Communications Commission data.

Previous work on physical education deserts found that although people 7
living in physical education deserts are primarily white, a disproportionately large number of Native Americans live in physical education deserts. The same holds true for people living in complete education deserts. Only 1.3 percent of the US population lives in a complete education desert, but 11.8 percent of American Indians and Alaska Natives live in education deserts (figure 1).

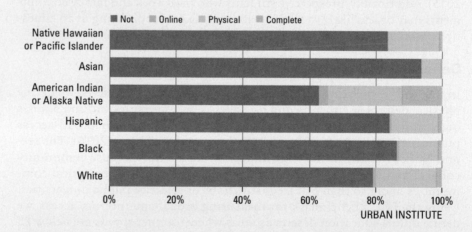

Figure 1 Share of Adults Living in Each Type of Education Desert, by Race or Ethnicity

Source: Urban Institute analysis of American Community Survey, Census Bureau, Integrated Postsecondary Education Data System, and Federal Communications Commission data.
Note: People who identified themselves as non-Hispanic white are included in the "White" category, and all people who identified themselves as Hispanic are included in the "Hispanic" category.

Older Americans are more likely to live in complete education deserts than   8
the average American. Because 82 percent of people living in education deserts are in rural areas, these age demographics may be because of migration°
trends in rural counties. According to the US Department of Agriculture, the
older age of the population in rural counties is likely a function of younger
adults leaving and older retirees moving into the area.[1]

Communities in complete education deserts have lower median family   9
incomes than communities that are not in complete education deserts. The
median family incomes, weighted by population, for families not living in an
education desert and those living in a complete education desert are approximately $56,500 and $41,000, respectively.

Communities without access to higher education have lower levels of   10
educational attainment than those with access to online and physical higher
education. People living in a complete education desert and those not in an
education desert have similar levels of high school or GED completion, but
these two communities are less similar with respect to college enrollment. The
educational attainment gap in high school completion is only 6 percentage
points, the gap in college enrollment is 16 percentage points, and the gap in
college completion is 18 percentage points. About 45 percent of the people in
a complete education desert enrolled in college, compared with 61 percent of
those not living in an education desert.

Conclusion

For most disadvantaged students, the problem is not necessarily enrolling in col-   11
lege, but completing college (Sawhill 2013). But for prospective students who
have work or family commitments and live in education deserts, enrollment
might be the primary problem. Most research focuses on improving college
enrollment to increase access, but our study adds to the growing body of research
that shows that researchers should also focus on the geography of college access
(Hillman and Weichman 2016; Kennedy and Long 2015; López Turley 2009).

Further, we believe our estimate represents a lower bound for the   12
prevalence° of online education deserts. First, although we find that 2.2 percent of adults lack access to 25 Mbps download and 3 Mbps upload service,
a recent FCC report, using data at the census block level instead of the block
group level, found that 10 percent of Americans lack this access (FCC 2016b).
If we assume that the proportion of online deserts that are also physical deserts (two out of three) remains the same, the true share of Americans living in
complete education deserts may be closer to 6 or 7 percent.

Second, the FCC report notes that the maximum advertised speed is not   13
necessarily the speed available to all consumers in a given area and that actual
speeds vary by provider (FCC 2016b). This suggests that the estimate in our
study is a lower bound of the number of Americans who lack broadband
access through an internet provider. Third, research on physical education
deserts suggests that estimates of the number of adults living in a physical
education desert are conservative (Hillman and Weichman 2016). Thus, the

migration: Movement from one place to another.   **prevalence:** Frequency.

number of people living in education deserts may be higher than we have estimated here.

Our findings suggest potential remedies.° To expand physical access in education deserts, some have suggested that selective private or selective public institutions operating in deserts could form partnerships with local community colleges, which are better designed to serve their communities than selective institutions (Hillman and Weichman 2016). Through these partnerships, local community colleges could find ways to expand degree options beyond associate degrees by improving the transfer and articulation process to the nearby selective four-year school. To expand online access in education deserts, the federal government could decrease the cost of broadband deployment.[2] In addition, the FCC recently inquired about benchmarking mobile broadband access and including both mobile and fixed broadband access in their analyses (FCC 2017). Although these two are not substitutes, we need to learn more about the differences between these services when it comes to caps on downloads and costs. Mobile broadband deployment may be more beneficial for minorities and adults, but these benefits might not translate into online education access (Prieger 2015).[3]

Increasing access to broadband is an important part of increasing access to online education, but this solves only part of the access issue. Prospective students still need access to the appropriate hardware and software for their online programs. Currently, institutions are allowed to include the costs of purchasing or renting a personal computer in their aid allowances for books, supplies, transportation, and miscellaneous personal expenses (Federal Student Aid Handbook 2015).

This study demonstrates what many Native Americans, rural Americans, and other Americans living in education deserts already know: the internet has not untethered° all of us from our geographic locations. As long as broadband access depends on geography, place still plays an important role in access to higher education.

remedies: Treatments to cure an illness or solve a problem.   **untethered:** Released from being fastened.

References

Alpert, William T., Kenneth A. Couch, and Oskar R. Harmon. 2016. "A Randomized Assessment of Online Learning." *American Economic Review* 106 (5): 378–82.

Bettinger, Eric, and Susanna Loeb. 2017. "Promises and Pitfalls of Online Education." Washington, DC: Brookings Institution.

Bowen, William G., Matthew M. Chingos, Kelly A. Lack, and Thomas I. Nygren. 2014. "Interactive Learning Online at Public Universities: Evidence from a Six-Campus Randomized Trial." *Journal of Policy Analysis and Management* 33 (1): 94–111.

FCC (Federal Communications Commission). 2016a. *2016 Broadband Progress Report.* Washington, DC: FCC.

———. 2016b. 2016 *Measuring Broadband America: Fixed Broadband Report.*
Washington, DC: FCC.

———. 2017. "Thirteenth Section 706 Report Notice of Inquiry."
Washington, DC: FCC.

Federal Student Aid Handbook. 2015. *Federal Student Aid Handbook.*
Washington, DC: Federal Student Aid.

Goodman, Joshua, Michael Hurwitz, and Jonathan Smith. 2015. *College
Access, Initial College Choice, and Degree Completion.* Working Paper 20996.
Cambridge, MA: National Bureau of Economic Research.

Goodman, Joshua, Julia Melkers, and Amanda Pallais. 2016. *Can Online
Delivery Increase Access to Education?* Working Paper 22754. Cambridge,
MA: National Bureau of Economic Research.

Hillman, Nicholas, and Taylor Weichman. 2016. *Education Deserts: The
Continued Significance of "Place" in the Twenty-First Century.* Washington,
DC: American Council on Education.

Joyce, Theodore J., Sean Crockett, David A. Jaeger, Onur Altindag, and
Stephen D. O'Connell. 2014. *Does Classroom Time Matter? A Randomized Field
Experiment of Hybrid and Traditional Lecture Formats in Economics.* Working
Paper 20006. Cambridge, MA: National Bureau of Economic Research.

Kennedy, Alec, and Mark Long. 2015. *Optimal Spatial Distribution of Colleges.*
Paper presented at the Association for Public Policy Analysis and
Management fall conference, Miami, FL, November 12–14.

López Turley, Ruth N. 2009. "College Proximity: Mapping Access to
Opportunity." *Sociology of Education* 82 (2): 126–46.

Prieger, James E. 2015. "The Broadband Digital Divide and the Benefits of
Mobile Broadband for Minorities." *Journal of Economic Inequality* 13 (3):
373–400.

Sawhill, Isabel. 2013. "Higher Education and the Opportunity Gap."
Washington, DC: Brookings Institution.

Questions to Start You Thinking

1. **Considering Meaning:** What do Rosenboom and Blagg mean by "education deserts" (paragraph 2)? Can you describe what "education deserts" look like? How do they affect people?

2. **Identifying Writing Strategies:** Describe the tone and structure of this article. What effect does the tone and structure have on the reader? Who is the intended audience? How can you tell?

3. **Reading Critically:** In the conclusion, Rosenboom and Blagg state that their study "demonstrates what many Native Americans, rural Americans, and other Americans living in education deserts already know: the internet has not untethered all of us from our geographic locations" (paragraph 16). What does their study reflect about the Internet and geography? Why are Native Americans and rural Americans named here?

4. **Expanding Vocabulary:** How do you define a *broad-access* institution, based on what you read in this article? What is not considered *broad access,*

and why? When Rosenboom and Blagg talk about improving the *transfer and articulation* process (paragraph 14) used between schools, what do you think they mean?

5. **Making Connections:** Can any connections be made between the argument by Rosenboom and Blagg about discrimination felt by those living in education deserts and the argument by Shanna Kattari (p. 407) about discrimination felt by transgender and non-binary people in terms of their access to healthcare? Are there healthcare deserts as well as education deserts? Where are Rosenboom and Blagg's arguments similar to those made by Kattari, and where are they different?

Suggestions for Writing

1. Did you experience any difficulty achieving your goals to get into college? If so, what problems did you face? If not, what advantages did you have as you set out? Write a personal essay about your experience preparing for college, applying to college, paying for college, and taking part in any online aspects of the process (either applying or taking online classes). How does your experience validate any of the data presented by Rosenboom and Blagg? In your conclusion, please address their argument as you wrap up your essay.

2. Do some research on different aspects of online education. Does your college offer online courses? How many credits are offered for them, and what are the expectations of the class? Who are the courses geared toward? Are there colleges that exist entirely online? What courses and degrees are offered? Do you think online education makes education more accessible? Write an essay in conversation with the argument Rosenboom and Blagg make about online education and accessibility to higher education.

Elizabeth Kolbert

Elizabeth Kolbert

The Psychology of Inequality

Elizabeth Kolbert is a staff writer for the *New Yorker*. Her books include *The Prophet of Love: And Other Tales of Power and Deceit*, *Field Notes from a Catastrophe*, and *The Sixth Extinction*, which won the 2015 Pulitzer Prize for general nonfiction. She is the editor of *The Best American Science and Nature Writing 2009*.

AS YOU READ: How does inequality, in terms of income, affect our perceptions of ourselves?

In 2016, the highest-paid employee of the State of California was Jim Mora, the head coach of U.C.L.A.'s football team. (He has since been fired.) That year, Mora pulled in $3.58 million. Coming in second, with a salary of $2.93 million, was Cuonzo Martin, at the time the head coach of the men's basketball team at the University of California, Berkeley. Victor Khalil, the chief dentist at the Department of State Hospitals, made six hundred and eighty-six thousand dollars; Anne Neville, the director of the California Research Bureau, earned a hundred and thirty-five thousand dollars; and John Smith, a seasonal clerk at the Franchise Tax Board, earned twelve thousand nine hundred dollars.

I learned all this from a database maintained by the Sacramento *Bee*. The 2 database, which is open to the public, is searchable by name and by department, and contains precise salary information for the more than three hundred thousand people who work for California. Today, most state employees probably know about the database. But that wasn't the case when it was first created, in 2008. This made possible an experiment.

The experiment, conducted by four economists, was designed to test rival 3 theories of inequity. According to one theory, the so-called rational-updating model, people assess° their salaries in terms of opportunities. If they discover that they are being paid less than their co-workers, they will "update" their projections about future earnings and conclude that their prospects of a raise are good. Conversely,° people who learn that they earn more than their co-workers will be discouraged by that news. They'll update their expectations in the opposite direction.

According to a rival theory, people respond to inequity not rationally but 4 emotionally. If they discover that they're being paid less than their colleagues, they won't see this as a signal to expect a raise but as evidence that they are underappreciated. (The researchers refer to this as the "relative income" model.) By this theory, people who learn that their salaries are at the low end will be pissed. Those who discover that they're at the high end will be gratified.

The economists conducting the study sent an email to thousands of 5 employees at three University of California schools—Santa Cruz, San Diego, and Los Angeles—alerting them to the existence of the *Bee's* database. This nudge produced a spike in visits to the Web site as workers, in effect, peeked at one another's paychecks.

A few days later, the researchers sent a follow-up email, this one with ques- 6 tions. "How satisfied are you with your job?" it asked. "How satisfied are you with your wage/salary on this job?" They also sent the survey to workers who hadn't been nudged toward the database. Then they compared the results. What they found didn't conform to either theory, exactly.

As the relative-income model predicted, those who'd learned that they 7 were earning less than their peers were ticked off. Compared with the control group, they reported being less satisfied with their jobs and more interested in finding new ones. But the relative-income model broke down when it came to those at the top. Workers who discovered that they were doing better than their colleagues evinced° no pleasure. They were merely indifferent. As the economists put it in a paper that they eventually wrote about the study, access to the database had a "negative effect on workers paid below the median for their unit and occupation" but "no effect on workers paid above median."

The message the economists took from their research was that employ- 8 ers "have a strong incentive" to keep salaries secret. Assuming that California

---

assess: Estimate the value of.   **conversely:** In an opposite way.   **evinced:** Proved.

workers are representative of the broader population, the experiment also suggests a larger, more disturbing conclusion. In a society where economic gains are concentrated at the top—a society, in other words, like our own—there are no real winners and a multitude of losers.

Keith Payne, a psychologist, remembers the exact moment when he learned he was poor. He was in fourth grade, standing in line in the cafeteria of his elementary school, in western Kentucky. Payne didn't pay for meals—his family's income was low enough that he qualified for free school lunch—and normally the cashier just waved him through. But on this particular day there was someone new at the register, and she asked Payne for a dollar twenty-five, which he didn't have. He was mortified.° Suddenly, he realized that he was different from the other kids, who were walking around with cash in their pockets.

"That moment changed everything for me," Payne writes, in "The Broken Ladder: How Inequality Affects the Way We Think, Live, and Die." Although in strictly economic terms nothing had happened—Payne's family had just as much (or as little) money as it had the day before—that afternoon in the cafeteria he became aware of which rung on the ladder he occupied. He grew embarrassed about his clothes, his way of talking, even his hair, which was cut at home with a bowl. "Always a shy kid, I became almost completely silent at school," he recalls.

Payne is now a professor at the University of North Carolina, Chapel Hill. He has come to believe that what's really damaging about being poor, at least in a country like the United States—where, as he notes, even most people living below the poverty line possess TVs, microwaves, and cell phones—is the subjective experience of *feeling* poor. This feeling is not limited to those in the bottom quintile; in a world where people measure themselves against their neighbors, it's possible to earn good money and still feel deprived. "Unlike the rigid columns of numbers that make up a bank ledger, status is always a moving target, because it is defined by ongoing comparisons to others," Payne writes.

Feeling poor, meanwhile, has consequences that go well beyond feeling. People who see themselves as poor make different decisions, and, generally, worse ones. Consider gambling. Spending two bucks on a Powerball ticket, which has roughly a one-in-three-hundred-million chance of paying out, is never a good bet. It's especially ill-advised for those struggling to make ends meet. Yet low-income Americans buy a disproportionate share of lottery tickets, so much so that the whole enterprise is sometimes referred to as a "tax on the poor."

One explanation for this is that poor people engage in riskier behavior, which is why they are poor in the first place. By Payne's account, this way of thinking gets things backward. He cites a study on gambling performed by Canadian psychologists. After asking participants a series of probing questions about their finances, the researchers asked them to rank themselves along something called the Normative Discretionary Income Index. In fact,

9

10

11

12

13

mortified: Humiliated.

the scale was fictitious and the scores were manipulated. It didn't matter what their finances actually looked like: some of the participants were led to believe that they had more discretionary income than their peers and some were led to believe the opposite. Finally, participants were given twenty dollars and the choice to either pocket it or gamble it on a computer card game. Those who believed they ranked low on the scale were much more likely to risk the money on the card game. Or, as Payne puts it, "feeling poor made people more willing to roll the dice."

In another study, this one conducted by Payne and some colleagues, participants were divided into two groups and asked to make a series of bets. For each bet, they were offered a low-risk / low-reward option (say, a hundred-percent chance of winning fifteen cents) and a high-risk / high-reward option (a ten-percent chance of winning a dollar-fifty). Before the exercise began, the two groups were told different stories (once again, fictitious) about how previous participants had fared. The first group was informed that the spread in winnings between the most and the least successful players was only a few cents, the second that the gap was a lot wider. Those in the second group went on to place much chancier bets than those in the first. The experiment, Payne contends, "provided the first evidence that inequality *itself* can cause risky behavior." 14

People's attitude toward race, too, he argues, is linked to the experience of deprivation.° Here Payne cites work done by psychologists at N.Y.U., who offered subjects ten dollars with which to play an online game. Some of the subjects were told that, had they been more fortunate, they would have received a hundred dollars. The subjects, all white, were then shown pairs of faces and asked which looked "most black." All the images were composites that had been manipulated in various ways. Subjects in the "unfortunate" group, on average, chose images that were darker than those the control group picked. "Feeling disadvantaged magnified their perception of racial differences," Payne writes. 15

"The Broken Ladder" is full of studies like this. Some are more convincing than others, and, not infrequently, Payne's inferences seem to run ahead of the data. But the wealth of evidence that he amasses is compelling. People who are made to feel deprived see themselves as less competent. They are more susceptible to conspiracy° theories. And they are more likely to have medical problems. A study of British civil servants showed that where people ranked themselves in terms of status was a better predictor of their health than their education level or their actual income was. 16

All of which leads Payne to worry about where we're headed. In terms of per-capita income, the U.S. ranks near the top among nations. But, thanks to the growing gap between the one per cent and everyone else, the subjective effect is of widespread impoverishment. "Inequality so mimics poverty in our minds that the United States of America . . . has a lot of features that better resemble a developing nation than a superpower," he writes. 17

---

deprivation: Lack or loss.   **conspiracy:** A secret plot to do something wrong.

Questions to Start You Thinking

1. **Considering Meaning:** How do you explain the statement "In a society where economic gains are concentrated at the top—a society, in other words, like our own—there are no real winners and a multitude of losers" (paragraph 8)? How does Kolbert's research support this statement?

2. **Identifying Writing Strategies:** How is Kolbert's introduction different from the rest of the essay? Why do you think Kolbert begins the essay this way?

3. **Reading Critically:** Why do poor people engage in risky behaviors such as gambling? Why might you expect the opposite to be true?

4. **Expanding Vocabulary:** Define *inequity* (paragraph 3); *incentive* (paragraph 8); *disproportionate* (paragraph 12); *inferences* (paragraph 16); *subjective* (paragraph 17); and *quintile* (paragraph 11). What do these words reflect about the subject matter or indicate about the writer of this article?

5. **Making Connections with the Paired Essay:** Explain how an experiment or argument made by Keith Payne that's mentioned in Kolbert's essay is similar to the one in the excerpt from "The Broken Ladder" (below). What are the commonalities that characterize all of Payne's work as you see it here?

Suggestions for Writing

1. Consider the quote by Keith Payne that Elizabeth Kolbert uses in her conclusion: "Inequality so mimics poverty in our minds that the United States of America has a lot of features that better resemble a developing nation than a superpower" (paragraph 17). Write a persuasive essay arguing whether that statement is true or false, and why. Use both the Kolbert essay and outside research to back up your position.

2. Go to the salary database Kolbert mentions in paragraph 2 and explore it. Look up some salaries: https://www.sacbee.com/site-services/databases/state-pay/article2642161.html. Do you think this database is a good idea? Is it ethical? Is it a violation of privacy, or should everyone know everyone else's salary? What problems does it create, beyond the ones mentioned by Kolbert? Whether you think it's a good or bad idea to have a public database like this one, defend your opinion persuasively.

Keith Payne

Keith Payne

from *The Broken Ladder*

Dr. Keith Payne is a professor of Psychology and Neuroscience at the University of North Carolina, Chapel Hill. This essay is excerpted from his book, *The Broken Ladder: How Inequality Affects the Way We Think, Live, and Die.*

AS YOU READ: Do we make assumptions about people based on socio-economic status? What assumptions do we make about economic policies designed to help the poorer people in our society?

Decades of studies have found a strong correlation° between dislike of black people and opposition to social welfare° policies aimed at helping the poor. For example, political scientist Martin Gilens found that most Americans believe inequality is too high, and seven in ten think that government spending to help the poor should be increased. And yet, by the same margin, Americans think welfare spending should be cut. "Welfare" simply refers to the suite of race-neutral government programs aimed at helping the poor, so these results don't make much sense on their surface. 1

But it turn out that when Americans talk about "the poor," they mean something veq different from when they talk about "welfare recipients." The best predictor of wanting to slash funding for welfare recipients is racial prejudice. People who believe that black Americans are lazy and undeserving are the most likely to oppose welfare spending. 2

Racial bias is not the only reason that people could be against welfare spending, of course. Economists have pointed out that middle- and upper-class citizens have a rational° interest in opposing welfare spending. From their perspective, cutting taxes on the affluent° and cutting benefits to the poor is simply the self-interested thing to do. People might similarly oppose welfare spending on principled ideological grounds. They might value hard work and self-reliance, and as such regard welfare as a dependency trap, a position often taken by politicians and political elites. But Gilens's studies find no evidence that these are major motivations for ordinary citizens. Statistically speaking, if you want to predict who is predisposed° against welfare, you can mostly ignore their economic principles. What you really need to know is their prejudices. 3

While it may not be surprising that the average person views welfare in racially tinged terms, the truth is that welfare recipients are about evenly divided among white, black, and Hispanic recipients. But when Gilens analyzed depictions of welfare recipients in television and newsmagazines since the 1960s, he found a clear racial bias: When welfare recipients were depicted as the "deserving poor," they were mostly white, but when they were portrayed as lazy and dishonest, they were overwhelmingly black. 4

This cultural messaging linking welfare to lazy people in general and lazy black people in particular makes it difficult to discuss welfare without racial overtones. This association fuels debates about "dog-whistle politics," in which many people hear coded messages about race in what are ostensibly° straightforward policy statements. Ronald Reagan's famous comments about "welfare queens" driving Cadillacs outraged Democrats, though Reagan denied his remark had anything to do with race. His case was not helped when his adviser Lee Atwater described coded racial messages as a central component of the Republican "Southern strategy" in a 1981 interview: "By 1968 you can't say 'ni**er'—that hurts you. Backfires. So you say stuff like 5

---

correlation: Relationship between two things. **welfare:** A set of government programs providing financial support to those in need. **rational:** Based on reason. **affluent:** Wealthy. **predisposed:** Inclined to something. **ostensibly:** Apparently.

forced busing, states' rights and all that stuff. You're getting so abstract now you're talking about cutting taxes, and all these things you're talking about are totally economic things and a byproduct of them is blacks get hurt worse than whites. And subconsciously maybe that's part of it."

More recently, House Speaker Paul Ryan was accused of dog-whistling 6 when he explained poverty as a "tailspin of culture, in our inner cities in particular, of men not working and just generations of men not even thinking about working ...." He, too, later claimed that his comment had nothing to do with race.

We can't know for certain what the intent of these leaders was. Did they 7 mean to stir up racial divisions in the minds of white voters while maintaining plausible deniability? Or did they genuinely seek to be racially neutral while members of the opposing party interpreted their comments cynically? The fact is, if you support Reagan and Ryan, you will be inclined to give them the benefit of the doubt. But if you distrust them, you are more likely to view them as making none-too-subtle racially tinged comments.

The interesting observation from a psychological point of view is that 8 the intention of the speaker ultimately doesn't matter. What does matter is how the audience interprets his words. The notion of racially coded messaging—intentional or not—assumes a psychological leap on the part of listeners. It assumes that when politicians talk about policies, voters naturally connect them to race. My collaborators Jazmin Brown-Iannuzzi, Erin Cooley, Ron Dotsch, and I recently tested whether people really make this psychological leap. We wanted to determine whether, when citizens are asked about welfare recipients, their mind's eye viewed them as black people.

To find that out, we needed a way to visualize our subjects' mental representations. We began by creating a composite photo consisting of selected 9 facial features from a black man, a black woman, a white man, and a white woman. To this androgynous biracial face, we added random visual noise, like static on a TV screen. We repeated this exercise hundreds of times until we had a large set of faces where each looked slightly different and slightly blurry. We then showed research participants pairs from this group of photos and asked them to select which one looked more like a welfare recipient. By morphing together all of the images that had been judged to be the "welfare recipient" and then morphing those that had been chosen as the "non-welfare recipient," we then created two new composite photos.

The images that emerged captured subjects' images of what a welfare 10 recipient looked like. When we showed pairs of unlabeled images to a new set of participants, they described the welfare recipient image as a black man and the image of the non-recipient as a white man. They judged the welfare recipient as looking lazy, irresponsible, hostile, and unintelligent. Chillingly, they also regarded the welfare recipient as being less human. You can see clearly defined eyes in the image of the non-recipient, but the eyes of the welfare recipient are hollow.°

hollow: Empty.

Next, we tested whether these mental images actually cause differences 11 in support for welfare benefits. We showed the images of the typical welfare recipient and the non-recipient, without identifying them, to another group of subjects and asked whether they would be in favor of providing food stamps and cash assistance to each. When they imagined giving benefits to the non-recipient, they were generally supportive. But when they pictured giving benefits to the welfare recipient, they were opposed. The very qualities that people envision° about welfare recipients are the qualities that lead them to oppose giving them benefits.

Economic inequality creates a status-based us-and-them mentality 12 that heightens race bias. And the close connections between race, poverty, and deservingness in the minds of citizens are a major obstacle to reducing economic inequality. Many people simply don't feel very motivated to support fighting poverty when they imagine that minorities will be the beneficiaries.

Acknowledging the existence of racial bias makes many citizens feel 13 hopeless, because it seems so hard to change. Implicit bias seems especially difficult, because it resides not just in the minds of individuals but in the nebulous° current of people and ideas that make up the culture around us. Recent research, however, raises some grounds for optimism. Millions of people have taken an implicit bias test at projectimplicit.com, a website where you can test yourself for biases related to race, gender, age, and other social groups. Psychologist Dominic Packer investigated which American states showed the highest and lowest levels of race bias, and what elements distinguished them.

One of the most important factors was income inequality. States with lower 14 inequality had less implicit bias, even after accounting for average income and regional differences between the North and South. Low-inequality states like Oregon, Washington, and Vermont had much less bias than high-inequality Louisiana, New Jersey, or Pennsylvania. Although it may be difficult to change people's hearts and minds, economic policies can certainly reduce income inequality.

envision: Visualize.   **nebulous:** Unclear.

Questions to Start You Thinking

1. **Considering Meaning:** In Payne's research, how did most subjects envision a welfare recipient? What characteristics did they attribute to a welfare recipient? What about to a non-welfare recipient?

2. **Identifying Writing Strategies:** Where in the essay does Payne discuss cultural messaging? How does the passage on cultural messaging influence the section about his research experiment?

3. **Reading Critically:** How do we tackle implicit bias in social policy and other areas? What starting point does Payne suggest, and what other ways can you think of to lessen or remove such biases?

4. **Expanding Vocabulary:** What do you think Payne means by *plausible deniability* (paragraph 7)? How do you define the two words that make up that phrase?

5. **Making Connections with the Paired Essay:** Both Payne and Elizabeth Kolbert (p. 416) are writing about psychological responses to socioeconomic realities. How does their research overlap? Compare and contrast the research and argument in Payne's essay with the research and argument in Kolbert's essay.

Suggestions for Writing

1. Do a freewriting exercise. On one piece of paper write "welfare recipient" and on another write "deserving poor." For each one, write without stopping and with as little censoring as possible until the page is filled. You do not need to write in complete sentences or form paragraphs. Once you have both pages filled, circle any words that show the sort of bias that Payne is talking about. Underline any words that surprise you. Talk about your findings in class discussion.

2. In a short paper, analyze Payne's argument. Do you think his data is conclusive? Is anything missing from his argument? Is there any information you wish he'd spent more time explaining? How do his anecdotes about politicians Paul Ryan and Ronald Reagan fit into the argument? Answer these and ask and answer other questions in your essay.

Gender

Carol Yepes/Getty Images

Responding to an Image

From gendered clothing to gendered toys to gender reveal parties, our culture often categorizes people and objects as "boy" or "girl." What do the divided halves in this image indicate about cultural depictions of gender? Do you make automatic assumptions based on the colors and featured items? Which ones? Think about where those messages come from in our societies and our families, and why we assume that one side reflects girls and the other side boys. What if the items were mixed up, or the colors different? Does the photo above support gender as a spectrum? If you feel resistant to this interpretation of gender, how would you arrange the picture? Might you even change the question in the text box?

Hannelore Foerster/Getty
Images

Chimamanda Ngozi Adichie

Happy Feminist

Chimamanda Ngozi Adichie was born in Nigeria in 1977. She is an award-winning novelist and short story writer and recipient of a MacArthur Foundation Fellowship and the Orange Broadband Prize for Fiction. Her works include the novels *Purple Hibiscus, Half of a Yellow Sun*, and *Americanah*, as well as a short story collection, *The Thing around Your Neck*. Adichie's latest book, *Dear Ijeawele, or, a Feminist Manifesto in Fifteen Suggestions*, is a bestseller that argues for gender equality. The following reading is excerpted from her book-length essay, *We Should All Be Feminists* (2014), which was adapted from a TEDx talk that she gave in London (2012). Adichie resides in Nigeria and in the United States.

AS YOU READ: Ask yourself, do you consider yourself to be a feminist? Why or why not?

1 In 2003, I wrote a novel called *Purple Hibiscus*, about a man who, among other things, beats his wife, and whose story doesn't end too well. While I was promoting the novel in Nigeria, a journalist, a nice, well-meaning man, told me he wanted to advise me. (Nigerians, as you might know, are very quick to give unsolicited° advice.) He told me that people were saying my novel was feminist,° and his advice to me — he was shaking his head sadly as he spoke — was that I should never call myself a feminist, since feminists are women who are unhappy because they cannot find husbands.

2 So I decided to call myself a Happy Feminist.

3 Then an academic,° a Nigerian woman, told me that feminism was not our culture, that feminism was un-African and I was only calling myself a feminist because I had been influenced by western books. (Which amused me, because much of my early reading was decidedly unfeminist: I must have read every single Mills & Boon° romance published before I was 16. And each time I try to read those books called "classic feminist texts," I get bored, and I struggle to finish them.)

4 Anyway, since feminism was un-African, I decided I would now call myself a Happy African Feminist. Then a dear friend told me that calling myself a feminist meant that I hated men. So I decided I would now be a Happy African Feminist Who Does Not Hate Men. At some point I was a Happy African Feminist Who Does Not Hate Men And Who Likes To Wear Lip Gloss And High Heels For Herself And Not For Men.

5 Gender° matters everywhere in the world. But it is time we should begin to dream about and plan for a different world. A fairer world. A world of happier men and happier women who are truer to themselves.

---

unsolicited: Not asked for. **feminist:** A person who advocates for the rights of women and girls and for equality with men and boys. **academic:** A teacher or scholar who works at a college or university. **Mills & Boon:** A publisher of popular, mass-market romances. **gender:** The cultural, behavioral, and psychological traits typically associated with one's sex.

Gender is not an easy conversation to have. It makes people uncomfort- 6
able, sometimes even irritable. Both men and women are resistant to talk
about gender, or are quick to dismiss the problems of gender. Because thinking of changing the status quo° is always uncomfortable.

Some people ask, "Why the word *feminist*? Why not just say you are a 7
believer in human rights, or something like that?" Because that would be dishonest. Feminism is, of course, part of *human rights* in general — but to choose
to use the vague expression human rights is to deny the specific and particular problem of gender. It would be a way of pretending that it was not women
who have, for centuries, been excluded. It would be a way of denying that the
problem of gender targets women. That the problem was not about being
human, but specifically about being a female human. For centuries, the world
divided human beings into two groups and then proceeded to exclude and
oppress° one group. It is only fair that the solution to the problem should
acknowledge that.

Some men feel threatened by the idea of feminism. This comes, I think, 8
from the insecurity triggered by how boys are brought up, how their sense of
self-worth is diminished° if they are not "naturally" in charge as men.

Other men might respond by saying, "Okay, this is interesting, but I don't 9
think like that. I don't even think about gender."

Maybe not. 10

And that is part of the problem. That many men do not actively think 11
about gender or notice gender. That many men say that things might have
been bad in the past but everything is fine now. And that many men do nothing to change it. If you are a man and you walk into a restaurant and the
waiter greets just you, does it occur to you to ask the waiter, "Why have you
not greeted her?" Men need to speak out in all of these ostensibly° small
situations.

Because gender can be uncomfortable, there are easy ways to close this 12
conversation. Some people will bring up evolutionary biology° and apes, how
female apes bow to male apes — that sort of thing. But the point is this: we are
not apes. Apes also live in trees and eat earthworms. We do not. Some people
will say, "Well, poor men also have a hard time." And they do.

But that is not what this conversation is about. Gender and class are dif- 13
ferent. Poor men still have the privileges of being men, even if they do not have
the privileges of being wealthy. I learned a lot about systems of oppression°
and how they can be blind to one another by talking to black men. I was once
talking about gender and a man said to me, "Why does it have to be you as
a woman? Why not you as a human being?" This type of question is a way
of silencing a person's specific experiences. Of course I am a human being,
but there are particular things that happen to me in the world because I am

---

status quo: Latin, meaning the current state of things.   **oppress:** To mistreat, to unjustly exercise authority to keep someone subservient.   **diminished:** Made less of; belittled.   **ostensibly:**
Seemingly, supposedly.   **evolutionary biology:** The scientific discipline that studies how
diverse life forms on Earth, including human beings, developed over time from common ancestors.   **oppression:** Tyranny; the suffering caused by the abuse of power.

a woman. This same man, by the way, would often talk about his experience as a black man. (To which I should probably have responded, "Why not your experiences as a man or as a human being? Why a black man?")

So, no, this conversation is about gender. Some people will say, "Oh, but women have the real power: bottom power." (This is a Nigerian expression for a woman who uses her sexuality to get things from men.) But bottom power is not power at all, because the woman with bottom power is actually not powerful; she just has a good route to tap another person's power. And then what happens if the man is in a bad mood or sick or temporarily impotent°?   14

Some people will say a woman is subordinate to men because it's our culture. But culture is constantly changing. I have beautiful twin nieces who are 15. If they had been born a hundred years ago, they would have been taken away and killed. Because a hundred years ago, Igbo° culture considered the birth of twins to be an evil omen.° Today that practice is unimaginable to all Igbo people.   15

What is the point of culture? Culture functions ultimately to ensure the preservation and continuity of a people. In my family, I am the child who is most interested in the story of who we are, in ancestral lands, in our tradition. My brothers are not as interested as I am. But I cannot participate, because Igbo culture privileges men, and only the male members of the extended family can attend the meetings where major family decisions are taken. So although I am the one who is most interested in these things, I cannot attend the meeting. I cannot have a formal say. Because I am female.   16

Culture does not make people. People make culture. If it is true that the full humanity of women is not our culture, then we can and must make it our culture.   17

My great-grandmother, from stories I've heard, was a feminist. She ran away from the house of the man she did not want to marry and married the man of her choice. She refused, protested, spoke up whenever she felt she was being deprived of land and access because she was female. She did not know that word feminist. But it doesn't mean she wasn't one. More of us should reclaim that word. My own definition of a feminist is a man or a woman who says, "Yes, there's a problem with gender as it is today and we must fix it, we must do better."   18

All of us, women and men, must do better.   19

---

impotent: Powerless; for males, unable to maintain a state of sexual arousal.   **Igbo:** An ethnic group native to south-central and southeastern Nigeria.   **omen:** Something believed to signal a future event.

Questions to Start You Thinking

1. **Considering Meaning:** For Adichie, why is it important to stand up for herself as a woman, and not, as others have suggested, simply "as a human being" (paragraph 13)?

2. **Identifying Writing Strategies:** What "unsolicited advice" (paragraph 1) and specific anecdotes does Adichie share, and how do they relate to her overall argument?

3. **Reading Critically:** How does culture function, and what needs to happen to culture, according to Adichie (paragraphs 16 and 17)?

4. **Expanding Vocabulary:** When Adichie writes that "more of us should reclaim" the word *feminist* (paragraph 18), what does she mean?

5. **Making Connections:** Based on what you've learned of Adichie's views through this essay, how would she likely respond to Sally Hines's argument ("The False Opposition between Trans and Feminist Rights," pp. 441–42) about trans and feminist rights?

Suggestions for Writing

1. Adichie writes that "some men feel threatened by the idea of feminism" (paragraph 8). What is the reason for this, according to the author? Are there other reasons besides those named by Adichie? Write an essay in which you make an argument about why the term *feminist* is threatening to men and to some women. Draw on additional sources, including other readings in this book, if needed.

2. In paragraph 14, Adichie writes that some people claim that, "women have the real power: bottom power," referring to women who use their sexuality to get things from men. She responds that such women are not actually powerful, that they "just ha[ve] a good route to tap another person's power." What does she mean? What are some other scenarios in which someone appears to have power, but really does not? What is the cultural impact of that situation?

Brent Staples

Black Men and Public Space

Brent Staples is an author and journalist who has had a long career with the *New York Times.* He wrote a memoir called *Parallel Time: Growing Up in Black and White,* which won the Anisfield-Wolf Book Award in 1995 and was also a finalist for the *Los Angeles Times* Book Prize.

AS YOU READ: Why do other pedestrians respond to Staples with anxiety?

Fred R. Conrad/The New York Times/Redux

My first victim was a woman — white, well dressed, probably in her late twenties. I came upon her late one evening on a deserted street in Hyde Park, a relatively affluent neighborhood in an otherwise mean, impoverished section of Chicago. As I swung onto the avenue behind her, there seemed to be a discreet, uninflammatory distance between us. Not so. She cast back a worried glance. To her, the youngish black man — a broad six feet two inches with a beard and billowing hair, both hands shoved into the pockets of a bulky military jacket — seemed menacingly close. After a few more quick glimpses, she picked up her pace and was soon running in earnest. Within seconds, she disappeared into a cross street.

That was more than a decade ago. I was twenty-one years old, a graduate student newly arrived at the University of Chicago. It was in the echo of that terrified woman's footfalls that I first began to know the unwieldy inheritance I'd come into—the ability to alter public space in ugly ways. It was clear that she thought herself the quarry of a mugger, a rapist, or worse. Suffering a bout of insomnia, however, I was stalking sleep, not defenseless wayfarers. As a softy who is scarcely able to take a knife to a raw chicken—let alone hold one to a person's throat—I was surprised, embarrassed, and dismayed all at once. Her flight made me feel like an accomplice in tyranny.° It also made it clear that I was indistinguishable from the muggers who occasionally seeped into the area from the surrounding ghetto. The first encounter, and those that followed, signified that a vast, unnerving gulf lay between nighttime pedestrians—particularly women—and me. And I soon gathered that being perceived as dangerous is a hazard in itself. I only needed to turn a corner into a dicey situation, or crowd some frightened, armed person in a foyer somewhere, or make an errant move after being pulled over by a policeman. Where fear and weapons meet—and they often do in urban America—there is always the possibility of death.

In that first year, my first away from my hometown, I was to become thoroughly familiar with the language of fear. At dark, shadowy intersections, I could cross in front of a car stopped at a traffic light and elicit the *thunk, thunk, thunk, thunk* of the driver—black, white, male, or female—hammering down the door locks. On less traveled streets after dark, I grew accustomed to but never comfortable with people crossing to the other side of the street rather than pass me. Then there were the standard unpleasantries with policemen, doormen, bouncers, cabdrivers, and others whose business it is to screen out troublesome individuals *before* there is any nastiness.

I moved to New York nearly two years ago and I have remained an avid night walker. In central Manhattan, the near-constant crowd cover minimizes tense one-on-one street encounters. Elsewhere—in SoHo, for example, where sidewalks are narrow and tightly spaced buildings shut out the sky—things can get very taut indeed.

After dark, on the warrenlike° streets of Brooklyn where I live, I often see women who fear the worst from me. They seem to have set their faces on neutral, and with their purse straps strung across their chests bandolier-style, they forge ahead as though bracing themselves against being tackled. I understand, of course, that the danger they perceive is not a hallucination. Women are particularly vulnerable to street violence, and young black males are drastically overrepresented among the perpetrators of that violence. Yet these truths are no solace against the kind of alienation that comes of being ever the suspect, a fearsome entity with whom pedestrians avoid making eye contact.

2

3

4

5

---

tyranny: Injustice or abuse.   **warrenlike:** Like a maze.

It is not altogether clear to me how I reached the ripe old age of twenty-two without being conscious of the lethality nighttime pedestrians attributed to me. Perhaps it was because in Chester, Pennsylvania, the small, angry industrial town where I came of age in the 1960s, I was scarcely noticeable against a backdrop of gang warfare, street knifings, and murders. I grew up one of the good boys, had perhaps a half-dozen fistfights. In retrospect, my shyness of combat has clear sources.

As a boy, I saw countless tough guys locked away; I have since buried several, too. They were babies, really — a teenage cousin, a brother of twenty-two, a childhood friend in his mid-twenties — all gone down in episodes of bravado played out in the streets. I came to doubt the virtues of intimidation early on. I chose, perhaps unconsciously, to remain a shadow — timid, but a survivor.

The fearsomeness mistakenly attributed to me in public places often has a perilous flavor. The most frightening of these confusions occurred in the late 1970s and early 1980s, when I worked as a journalist in Chicago. One day, rushing into the office of a magazine I was writing for with a deadline story in hand, I was mistaken for a burglar. The office manager called security and, with an ad hoc° posse, pursued me through the labyrinthine halls, nearly to my editor's door. I had no way of proving who I was. I could only move briskly toward the company of someone who knew me.

Another time I was on assignment for a local paper and killing time before an interview. I entered a jewelry store on the city's affluent Near North Side. The proprietor excused herself and returned with an enormous red Doberman pinscher straining at the end of a leash. She stood, the dog extended toward me, silent to my questions, her eyes bulging nearly out of her head. I took a cursory look around, nodded, and bade her good night.

Relatively speaking, however, I never fared as badly as another black male journalist. He went to nearby Waukegan, Illinois, a couple of summers ago to work on a story about a murderer who was born there. Mistaking the reporter for the killer, police officers hauled him from his car at gunpoint and but for his press credentials would probably have tried to book him. Such episodes are not uncommon. Black men trade tales like this all the time.

Over the years, I learned to smother the rage I felt at so often being taken for a criminal. Not to do so would surely have led to madness. I now take precautions to make myself less threatening. I move about with care, particularly late in the evening. I give a wide berth° to nervous people on subway platforms during the wee hours, particularly when I have exchanged business clothes for jeans. If I happen to be entering a building behind some people who appear skittish, I may walk by, letting them clear the lobby before I return, so as not to seem to be following them. I have been calm and extremely congenial° on those rare occasions when I've been pulled over by the police.

And on late-evening constitutionals° I employ what has proved to be an excellent tension-reducing measure: I whistle melodies from Beethoven and

---

ad hoc: Spur of the moment.   **berth:** Space.   **congenial:** Sociable.   **constitutionals:** Walks taken for the purpose of pleasure or health.

Vivaldi and the more popular classical composers. Even steely New Yorkers hunching toward nighttime destinations seem to relax, and occasionally they even join in the tune. Virtually everybody seems to sense that a mugger wouldn't be warbling bright, sunny selections from Vivaldi's *Four Seasons*. It is my equivalent of the cowbell that hikers wear when they know they are in bear country.

Questions to Start You Thinking

1. **Considering Meaning:** What misconceptions do people have about Staples because he is a young black man? What does he feel causes such misconceptions?

2. **Identifying Writing Strategies:** At the end of the essay, how does Staples use comparison to explain his behavior?

3. **Reading Critically:** What kinds of appeals — emotional, logical, ethical — does Staples use? Are his appeals appropriate for the purpose of his essay? Why, or why not? (For an explanation of kinds of appeals, see p. 142)

4. **Expanding Vocabulary:** Define *affluent, uninflammatory* (paragraph 1), *unwieldy, quarry, errant* (paragraph 2), *bandolier, solace* (paragraph 5), *lethality* (paragraph 6), *bravado* (paragraph 7), and *labyrinthine* (paragraph 8). Why do you think Staples uses such formal language in this essay?

5. **Making Connections:** Although Brent Staples focuses on space and James Baldwin focuses on language, both "Black Men in Public Spaces" and "If Black English Isn't a Language, Tell Me, What Is?" (pp. 362–65) address the threat of physical harm when black men are in close proximity to white people. How do you think Baldwin would respond to Staples's argument?

Suggestions for Writing

1. Staples describes his feelings about being the object of racial fear. Have you or someone you know ever been the object of that fear or other misconceptions based on prejudice or stereotyping? Write a short personal essay discussing the causes and effects of the experience. What preconceptions were involved? How did you or your acquaintance respond?

2. What do you think causes the stereotype of African American men that Staples is addressing? Write an essay that analyzes this stereotype, drawing on several outside sources to support your analysis.

Peggy Orenstein

"Dress to Respect Yourself": Enforcing Female Modesty in Schools

Peggy Orenstein is the author of several best-selling nonfiction works, including *Cinderella Ate My Daughter: Dispatches from the Front Lines of the New Girlie-Girl Culture*; *Waiting for Daisy*, a memoir; *Don't Call Me Princess: Essays on Girls, Women, Sex, and Life*; and *Girls and Sex: Navigating the Complicated New Landscape*, from which this excerpt is taken. She is a contributing writer to the *New York Times Magazine*.

Allen J. Schaben/Los Angeles Times/Getty Images

AS YOU READ: Should girls be told what to wear to school (or women be told what to wear to work)? Is insisting that females dress modestly perpetuating a rape culture in which the victim is to blame?

Camila Ortiz and Izzy Lang had heard it all before. They were seniors at a large California high school—with a campus of over 3,300 students—so this was their fourth September, their fourth "welcome back" assembly. They sat toward the rear of the auditorium, alternately daydreaming and chatting with friends as administrators droned on about the importance of attendance ("especially for you seniors"); the behaviors that could get you suspended; the warnings about cigarettes, alcohol, and weed. Then the dean of students addressed the girls in the crowd. "He was like, 'Ladies, when you go out you need to dress to respect yourself and respect your family,' " recalled Izzy. Blond and blue-eyed, she had a dimple° in one cheek that deepened as she spoke. "'This isn't the place for your short shorts or your tank tops or your crop tops. You need to ask yourself: if your grandmother looks at you, will she be happy with what you're wearing?'"

Camila, whose left nostril was pierced with a subtle crystal stud, jumped in, her index finger wagging. "'You need to cover that up because you need to have respect for yourself.' *You need to respect yourself. You need to respect your family.* That idea was just . . . repeated and repeated. And then he went from that immediately into the slides defining sexual harassment. Like there was a connection. Like maybe if you don't 'respect yourself' by the way you dress you're going to get harassed, and that's your own fault because you wore the tank top."

Growing up in this very school system, Camila had learned the importance of challenging injustice, of being an "upstander." So she began to shout the dean's name. "Mr. Williams! Mr. Williams!" she yelled. He invited her to the front of the auditorium and handed her the mic. "Hi, I'm Camila," she said. "I'm a twelfth-grader and I think what you just said is not okay and is extremely sexist and promoting 'rape culture.' If I want to wear a tank top and shorts because it's hot, I should be able to do that and that has no correlation° to how much 'respect' I hold for myself. What you're saying is just continuing this cycle of blaming the victim." The students in the auditorium cheered, and Camila handed back the mic.

dimple: A hollow or crease usually found in the cheek or chin. **correlation:** A mutual relation between things.

"Thank you, Camila. I totally agree," Mr. Williams said as she walked back   4
to her seat. Then he added, "But there's a time and a place for that type of
clothing."

This was not the first earful I'd gotten about girls' provocative dress: from   5
parents, from teachers, from administrators, from girls themselves. Parents
went to battle over the skimpiness of shorts, the clingy V-necks, the tush-
cupping yoga pants that showed "everything." *Why do girls have to dress like that?*
moms asked, even as some wore similar outfits themselves. Principals tried
to impose decorum,° but ended up inciting rebellion. In suburban Chicago,
eighth-graders picketed a proposed policy against leggings. High-schoolers in
Utah took to the Internet when they discovered digitally raised necklines and
sleeves added to female classmates' shirts in their yearbook photos.

Boys run afoul of dress codes when they flout authority: "hippies" defying   6
the establishment, "thugs" in saggy pants. For girls, the issue is sex. Enforcing
modesty is considered a way both to protect and to contain young women's
sexuality; and they, by association, are charged with controlling young men's.
After the assembly, the dean of attendance, who was female, stopped Camila
in the hallway. "I totally get that you're trying to empower° yourself," she told
the girl, "but it's a bit distracting. You have male teachers, and there are male
students."

"Maybe you shouldn't be hiring male teachers that are focused on staring   7
at my boobs!" Camila shot back. The dean said they could continue the conversation later. "Later" never came.

That was three months ago, and Camila was still furious. "The truth   8
is, it doesn't matter what I wear," she said. "Four out of five days going to
school I will be catcalled, I will be stared at, I will be looked up and down, I
will be touched. You just accept it as part of going to school. I can't help my
body type, and it's super distracting to *me* to know that every time I get up to
sharpen my pencil there's going to be a comment about my butt. That doesn't
happen to guys. No guy has ever had to walk down the hall and had girls
going, 'Hey, boy, your calves are looking great! Your calves are *hot*.'"

Camila is right. Addressing boys directly is the only way to challenge the   9
assumption by some that girls' bodies exist for them to judge — and even
touch — however and whenever they wish. The previous year at the girls' high
school, a group of boys created an Instagram account to "expose" the campus THOTs, an acronym for That Ho Over There. (Every generation seems to
invent a new *Scarlet Letter*° word — *strumpet, hussy, tramp, slut, skank, ho* — with
which to demonize° girls' sexuality.) They down-loaded pictures from girls'
Instagram or Twitter accounts (or snapped one in the hallways), captioning
each with the girl's purported sexual history. All the girls singled out were
black or Latina. Camila was one of them. "It was such a violation," she said.
"Part of the caption was 'I dare you to go f--- her for a good time.' I had to

---

decorum: Propriety.   **empower:** To give authority or strength to.   ***Scarlet Letter:*** A novel by
Nathaniel Hawthorne in which the main character is forced to wear a red *A* on her chest as
punishment for her sin of adultery. **demonize:** To turn into something evil.

go to school with that out there." When she lodged a formal complaint, she was placed in a room with four male school security guards who, she said, asked whether she had actually performed the acts attributed to her on the site. Humiliated, she let the matter drop. The Instagram account eventually petered out; perpetrators were never caught.

Whether online or IRL ("in real life"), Camila's was hardly an isolated case. 10 Another girl, a high school junior in nearby Marin County, California, who played varsity volleyball, told me how boys from the soccer team gathered in the bleachers to harass° her teammates during practice, yelling things like "Nice gooch!" (urban dictionary slang for perineum°) when the girls lunged to make a shot. (There are, incidentally, hundreds of close-up, rear-view photos of underage girls in volleyball shorts on the Internet.) A senior in San Francisco described how, within days of arriving at an elite° summer journalism program she attended in Chicago, the boys created a "slut draft" (akin to a fantasy football league), ranking their female peers in order of "who they wanted to [have sex with]."

"The girls were pissed off," she told me, "but we couldn't complain because 11 of all the implications, right? If you complain and you're on the list, you're a prude. If you complain and you're not on it, you're ugly. If you complain about it being sexist, then you're a humorless feminist bitch and a lesbian."

I heard about a boy who, claiming to have "magic arms," would hug 12 random girls in his New York City public school hallway and then announce his assessment of their bra size; about a high school boy who sauntered up to a stranger at a party in Saint Paul, Minnesota, and asked, "Can I touch your boobs?"; about boys at dances everywhere who, especially after a few (or more) drinks, felt free to "grind" against girls from behind, unbidden. Most girls had learned to gracefully disengage from such situations if uninterested. Boys rarely pursued. Several young women, though, said a dance partner had gone further, pushing aside their skirts and sliding a quick finger into their underwear. By college, girls attending a frat party may not make it to the dance floor at all unless they passed what one called the "pretty test" at the front door, where a designated brother "decides whether you are accepted or rejected, beautiful or ugly. He's the reason you better wear a crop top in subzero weather or you'll end up home alone eating microwave popcorn and calling your mom."

I'm going to say this once here, and then—because it is obvious—I will 13 not repeat it in the course of this book: not all boys engage in such behavior, not by a long shot, and many young men are girls' staunchest allies. However, every girl I spoke with, *every single girl*—regardless of her class, ethnicity, or sexual orientation; regardless of what she wore, regardless of her appearance—had been harassed in middle school, high school, college, or, often, all three. Who, then, is truly at risk of being "distracted" at school?

---

harass: To pester or attack.   **perineum:** The area between external sex organs and the anus.
elite: The best of something.

Questions to Start You Thinking

1. **Considering Meaning:** Why does Camila stand up and challenge her principal? What does she hear him saying, and what does she say back?

2. **Identifying Writing Strategies:** Describe how this essay is constructed. Is there a central speaker? Who is it? When do they appear, and how do you make sense of who they are?

3. **Reading Critically:** Answer Orenstein's ending question: "Who, then, is truly at risk of being 'distracted' at school?" Girls or boys? What does that "distraction" look like? What should the policy be at schools and elsewhere, if not a dress code aimed at girls?

4. **Expanding Vocabulary:** What is a *culture*? What are some of the different *cultures* you experience in life? What is meant by *rape culture*?

5. **Making Connections**: Assumptions are made about Brent Staples because of his race and the way he dresses in "Black Men and Public Space" (pp. 429–32). Assumptions are also made about the girls described in *Girls and Sex*. How would Camila answer the question about who needs to change and why, and would Staples's answer be similar or different? Explain.

Suggestions for Writing

1. Choose a topic that is meaningful to you, or begin an essay about a topic like this one—how women dress and the implications of how people react. As you write, start with an anecdote, or set a scene with characters—real people—as Orenstein does here. When in the essay could you switch points of view and begin to write from your own perspective? Craft an introductory paragraph to an essay—one paragraph only—that finishes with a thesis statement that stands independently from the anecdote or characters you started with.

2. What is rape culture? Define the term and then give examples of how it manifests. How does it affect people's thinking? How does it affect popular culture? How does it shape the ways we think about sex, gender, and rape itself? Write about this phenomenon and explain how Orenstein's article addresses it.

Alina Bradford

What Is Transgender?

Alina Bradford is a contributing writer to *CNET*'s "Smart Home" section, *MTV News*'s tech section, and *Live Science*'s reference section.

AS YOU READ: What does it mean to be transgender?

"Transgender" is an umbrella term that describes people whose gender identity or expression does not match the sex they were assigned at   1

Alina Bradford

birth. For example, a transgender person may identify as a woman despite having been born with male genitalia.°

Nearly 700,000 adults in the United States identify as transgender, according to 2011 research by the Williams Institute at the University of California, Los Angeles. However, being transgender means different things to different people, according to the National Center for Transgender Equality (NCTE).

"There's no one way to be transgender, and no one way for transgender people to look or feel about themselves," the organization says on its website.

A person's internal sense of being male, female or something else is their gender identity. For cisgender,° or non-transgender people, their gender identity matches their sex at birth. For transgender people, the two do not match.

Sometimes, a person's gender identity doesn't fit neatly into two choices. People who see themselves as being both male and female, neither male nor female or as falling completely outside these categories may identify as genderqueer, according to the Human Rights Campaign, an LGBTQ advocacy organization. (LGBTQ refers to the community of lesbian, gay, bisexual, transgender and queer or questioning individuals.)

How a person communicates their gender identity — through dress, behavior, voice or body characteristics — is their gender expression. A person's gender expression may or may not line up with society's expectations of masculinity or femininity, according to the HRC. The term "gender non-conforming" refers to people whose gender expression is different from conventional expectations of masculinity or femininity. However, not all gender-non-conforming people identify as transgender, and not all transgender people identify as gender non-conforming.

The public's understanding of gender identity and expression is evolving as more transgender people share their stories, according to the HRC.

Sex versus gender

Sex and gender are two different concepts. A person's sex refers to his or her biological status as either male or female. The determination of a person's sex depends primarily on various physical characteristics, including chromosomes,° reproductive anatomy and sex hormones, according to the American Psychological Association (APA).

Gender, on the other hand, is a societal construct that deals with the expected behaviors, roles and activities typically associated with the different sexes, the APA said. Gender roles, which vary across cultures, influence how people act and feel about themselves.

Sexual orientation is different from gender identity. Sexual orientation is a person's physical, emotional or romantic attraction to another person, while gender identity is about one's own sense of self, according to GLAAD,

---

genitalia: External reproductive organs.   **cisgender:** A person whose identity corresponds to biological sex from birth.   **chromosomes:** Threads that carry genes in a particular order.

an anti-discrimination organization. Transgender people may be straight, lesbian, gay or bisexual. For example, a person born with male genitalia may transition to being female but may be attracted to females. In this case, the person may identify as lesbian even though she was born with male genitalia.

Making the transition

Trying to change a person's gender identity is no more successful than trying to change a person's sexual orientation, GLAAD said. In other words, it can't be changed. Some people may take steps to better align their sex with their gender using hormones and surgery. HRC points out, however, that many transgender people cannot afford medical treatment or have no desire to pursue surgeries.   11

"So-called 'gender reassignment surgery' (more commonly called 'gender-affirmation surgery' by both medical professionals and transgender individuals) usually references transgender genital surgery," said Dr. Joshua Safer, medical director of the Center for Transgender Medicine and Surgery at Boston Medical Center (BMC), who is also in the BMC Department of Endocrinology. "There are also chest-reconstruction surgeries and facial feminization surgeries, among other options."   12

Genital surgery is typically reserved for transgender individuals over the age of 18 who have been treated with hormones, if that is what is medically indicated, and who have lived for at least a year in the gender roles that match their gender identities, Safer said. Candidates for surgery are reviewed by a medical team that considers mental health and physical health in determining the best treatment strategy, potentially including surgery, for each person.   13

Altering the voice so that it better matches gender identity can also be important to those transitioning. "Here, we envision a world where a transgender person feels no need to change their voice or speech — that is, they would live in a world where people accept and respect them as whatever gender they claim, regardless of how their voice sounds," said Dr. Leah Helou, a speech pathologist who leads the University of Pittsburgh Voice Center's transgender voice and communication services.   14

"However, in the absence of such radical and global acceptance, many trans individuals feel that their communication style is a top priority for making their external self congruent° with their inner self," Helou said. "Our goal is to serve and support those people, while advocating° for broader acceptance of the transgender population."   15

Names and pronouns

After transitioning, transgender people often change their names — either to one that matches their gender or to something neutral. A critical step in transitioning is changing legal documents, including driver's licenses, Social   16

---

congruent: In agreement.   **advocating:** Supporting.

Security cards, passports and credit cards. They often have to go to court to order the changes to be made — an expensive, time-consuming task, according to the NCTE.

It is considered rude to call people who have transitioned by their former   17 name (called "dead-naming"), and it is appropriate to respectfully ask them their name and which pronouns they prefer, according to the HRC.

Most transgender people prefer to be identified with the pronoun that   18 corresponds to the gender with which they identify, according to the HRC. A transgender woman should be called "she" or "her," if that's what she prefers. Some transgender people don't believe in binary gender appellations° and prefer "they" or a non-gendered pronoun.

Discrimination

Being transgender is not a mental disorder. It cannot be "cured" with treat-   19 ment. Transgender people do experience a persistent° disconnect between their assigned sex and their internal sense of who they are, according to the HRC. Medical professionals refer to this disconnect as gender dysphoria because it can cause pain and distress in the lives of transgender people.

The American Psychiatric Association in 2012 announced that a new ver-   20 sion of the Diagnostic and Statistical Manual of Mental Disorders (DSM-5) would replace the term "gender identity disorder" with the more neutral term "gender dysphoria."

Research has shown that transgender people are at high risk of experienc-   21 ing prejudice and mental-health problems. The 2014 National Transgender Discrimination Survey found that 60 percent of health care providers refuse treatment to transgender people. Additionally, the research found that 64 to 65 percent of the transgender people surveyed suffered physical or sexual violence at work, and 63 to 78 percent suffered physical or sexual violence at school. Transgender people often face discrimination even when using the bathroom. In a 2016 poll of Americans by CBS and *the New York Times*, 46 percent of respondents said those who are transgender should use the bathrooms assigned to their birth genders, while 41 percent said such individuals should be able use the bathroom that matches their identities. In May 2016, the U.S. Education and Justice departments stepped in to advise school districts to permit transgender students to use bathrooms and locker rooms that matched the students' gender identities. In response, several states joined in a lawsuit, stating that the federal government had overreached its authority.

Because of discrimination and other factors, the suicide rate among trans-   22 gender people is high. The Suicide Prevention Resource Center reports that more than 83 percent of transgender people had thought about suicide and 54 percent had attempted it. (The National Suicide Prevention Lifeline is 1-800-273-8255.)

---

appellations: Names.   **persistent:** Lasting.

Help for parents

Parents who think their children may be transgender should seek the assistance of experts. "Determining if children are transgender can be a challenge and should be done with careful evaluation from a knowledgeable multidisciplinary team," Safer said. 23

It is important to note that many children question their gender identities without being transgender. Safer advised parents to be respectful of the child's feelings and recognize that there will be no actual medical intervention until the child begins puberty. Even then, initial medical treatments are reversible, he said. 24

Questions to Start You Thinking

1. **Considering Meaning:** What is the difference between sex and gender? What are some of the ways in which we understand and identify gender?

2. **Identifying Writing Strategies:** Who is the intended audience for this article? How can you tell from how it is structured?

3. **Reading Critically:** What difficulties do transgendered individuals run up against as they transition? What are some of the courses of action they take to deal with those difficulties?

4. **Expanding Vocabulary:** What is a *transition*? Can you guess at the meaning based on its shared root with *transgender*? What does it mean, in the context of this article, to *transition* genders?

5. **Making Connections with the Paired Essay:** Both Bradford and Sally Hines (p. 441) are challenging traditional ideas of what it means to be a woman. How would Bradford defend Hines's position against anti-trans feminists? Using either article, explain how the anti-trans feminists (described by Hines) and those who discriminate against transgendered people (described by Bradford) view gender.

Suggestions for Writing

1. Bradford makes a point of talking about the various ways we understand gender, and then drawing a distinction between sex and gender. Try to summarize Bradford's main points about gender and the differences between sex and gender in a paragraph or two.

2. The article ends with a section on discrimination experienced by transgendered people and help for parents of transgendered children. Think about why people might discriminate against transgendered people. Why would transgendered children in particular need protection and/or counseling? Write a report about specific vulnerabilities of transgendered people mentioned or alluded to in this article and try to elaborate on them. You can add extra research for evidence but be sure to cite your research using MLA format.

Sally Hines

The False Opposition between Trans and Feminist Rights

Sally Hines is a professor of sociology and gender identities in the school of sociology at the University of Leeds, in West Yorkshire, England. She has written several books, including *Gender Diversity, Recognition and Citizenship: Towards a Politics of Difference* and *Is Gender Fluid? A Primer for the 21st Century*. This essay was published in a blog on the website of the London-based weekly magazine, the *Economist*.

Sally Hines

AS YOU READ: How do you define feminism?

What is a woman? Who can be a feminist? These questions have been central to feminist theory and activism since the 1970s, proving to be particularly controversial° in the relationship between feminist and transgender activism. In recent years, these questions have returned to haunt feminism. 1

For some feminist theorists the category of "woman" is developed out of the biological characteristics of being female. However, a universal understanding of "woman" (as distinct from "man") fractured during the 1970s as feminists of colour, working class and disabled feminists challenged the capabilities of a largely white, middle-class, able-bodied movement to articulate and organise around their interests. 2

This led to the development of more complex models of feminist analysis. By the 1990s multi-faceted° gender identities and experiences were embraced by feminist scholars who wrote against a biologically-determined feminist theory that excluded trans women. Similarly, the development of several queer movements positively acknowledged difference and argued against the understanding of identity categories as fixed. 3

I am deeply saddened that in recent years there has been renewed antagonism° from a section of feminism towards trans people, and especially towards trans women. The small number of feminists loudly opposing changes to the Gender Recognition Act (which would merely make the administrative process of gender recognition less bureaucratic°) are using a simplistic reading of biology that negates the natural diversities of physical sex characteristics and disregards the realities of trans people's lives. While anti-trans viewpoints are a minority position within feminism, they are championed by several high-profile writers, many of whom reinforce the extremely offensive trope of the trans woman as a man in drag who is a danger to women. 4

The refusal to acknowledge trans women as women is fuelling rhetoric of paranoia and hyperbole° as trans women's long-existing access to public toilets, changing rooms, refuges and hospital wards is disputed. 5

As a feminist I am profoundly concerned by anti-trans feminist rhetoric. I find the current volatile° temperament of feminist political discourse 6

---

controversial: Likely to cause disagreement.   **multi-faceted:** Faving many sides.
antagonism: Hostility, opposition.   **bureaucratic:** Having to do with the running of an organization.   **hyperbole:** Exaggeration.   **volatile:** Unpredictable.

hugely worrying. Despite strong historic and contemporary links between many sections of feminist and trans communities, the anti-transgender sentiments expressed by some leading journalists and amplified through the use of social media are extremely problematic. While anti-transgender feminists are a minority, they have a high level of social, cultural and economic capital.

Within these narratives, trans and feminist rights are being falsely cast in opposition.° Feminist principles of bodily autonomy are abandoned as some anti-trans campaigners query other women's genitals. Reductive° models of biology and restrictive understandings of the distinction between sex and gender are used in defence of this position.   7

For politely disagreeing with their views, I have been harassed by anti-trans campaigners who threw aside feminist principles to bizarrely accuse me of supporting rape by being trans-inclusive, of having an ugly man's face, and of not really being a woman because I am a professor. As women publicly debated my appearance and my genitals on Twitter, I experienced a small degree of the dehumanisation trans people are daily subjected to.   8

These exclusionary practices have a very significant impact. The trans body becomes the body of fear. The separation of bodies in public space is the cornerstone of segregation policy and has long been practised to regulate bodies in relation to race, but also gender, age, class, disability and sexuality. These practices have been vehemently challenged by social-justice movements, including many strands of feminism. Moreover, public scrutiny of the bodies of black women, women athletes and of intersex people through degrading "sex-verification" practices has a long history, which feminist writers and activists have challenged.   9

Bodily autonomy and self-determination of gender are basic civil rights. As a feminist scholar and activist I oppose the current wave of embodied° segregation and sex verification that is in operation as some feminists seek to police the bodies of others. Trans and feminist activists and writers, and their allies, have been countering anti-transgender feminism through public debate, scholarship and policy recommendations for decades. Nevertheless, those currently airing trans-exclusionary discourse repeatedly profess that there has been no debate.   10

Anti-transgender feminism needs to be explicitly recognised as being in breach of the goals of equality and dignity. Indeed, anti-trans feminism must be held up as a doctrine that runs counter to the ability to fulfill a liveable life or, often, a life at all.   11

opposition: Dissent, disagreement.   **reductive:** Simplified.   **embodied:** Represented, in tangible form.

Questions to Start You Thinking

1. **Considering Meaning:** Why do some feminists insist transgender women can't call themselves feminists? What does Hines say is wrong with that position?

2. **Identifying Writing Strategies:** Think about how Hines opens her essay. What is the effect of her opening remarks on the introduction? On the essay as a whole? Can you think of another writer (either in this book or that you've read elsewhere) who started an essay, speech, or story in a similar way?

3. **Reading Critically:** What do you think Hines means when she refers to the "realities of trans people's lives"? Another way of asking the question is: what does Hines see as the "false opposition" of trans and feminist rights?

4. **Expanding Vocabulary:** What is meant by *discourse*? What do you think Hines is referring to when she talks about the "trans-exclusionary discourse" happening around her?

5. **Making Connections with the Paired Essay:** In paragraph 8, Hines writes, "As women publicly debated my appearance and my genitals on Twitter, I experienced a small degree of the dehumanisation trans people are daily subjected to." With that statement in mind, reflect on Bradford's article about what being transgender means, and the relevance of her sections on discrimination and help for parents.

Suggestions for Writing

1. Feminism has taken many shapes over the years and represented many different people. Hines charts some of the history of feminism in her essay. In a short research paper, identify the beginnings of the modern feminist movement in the United States and write about some of the ways that movement has changed, or fractured, to use Hines's term. You are welcome to investigate the thread of feminism that has grown to include trans women. Be sure to cite all sources and include a Works Cited page at the end.

2. Think about the insults Hines says she's received for standing up for trans women's rights. Why do you think people have reacted to her in that way? What is the purpose of such remarks? Have you ever experienced that kind of treatment when you stood up for something you believed in or wrote something that others didn't agree with? When? What happened? In a reflective essay, write about Hines's experience and what's behind it, and if you have a personal story to share that is parallel to hers, connect what happened to you to Hines's story.

A WRITER'S RESEARCH MANUAL

Contents

Introduction: The Nature of Research

How is climate change affecting weather patterns?

Should law enforcement officers be required to wear body cameras?

Should professional athletes draw legal consequences for hard on-field hits?

Is it true that over a million children in the United States are homeless?

Why is cyberbullying so widespread?

When you ask questions like these, discuss them with friends, or read about them, you're conducting informal research to satisfy your curiosity. In your day-to-day life, you may want to buy a tablet, consider an innovative medical treatment, or plan a vacation. To become better informed, you may talk with friends, search the Internet, request product information, compare prices, read articles, and check advertising. You gather and weigh as much information as you can, preparing yourself to make a well-informed decision based on the available evidence. At work you may do the same — gather information, pull it together, and use it to make decisions about feasibility, marketing, or best practices.

In college, too, you'll conduct research. Joining the academic exchange often requires information literacy — the capacity to handle information effectively — as well as critical reading and thinking. Rather than merely pasting together information and opinions from others, you'll need to engage actively: inquiring, searching, accessing, evaluating, integrating, and synthesizing information from sources. The goal of college research is to draw original conclusions and arrive at your own fresh view.

Defining Your Research Project **26**

The research process is complex and made up of many stages. Once you have a topic that intrigues you, you'll move from gathering and organizing preliminary information to synthesizing that information. Then you'll draft, revise, and edit the material about your topic.

Understanding your assignment will help you determine which parts of the research process you will need to focus on. For example, smaller projects like proposals or annotated bibliographies will probably not require as much planning and drafting as a full research paper. Whatever stages of the research process your project involves, keep in mind that research is a recursive process, meaning that you'll likely need to move back and forth through at least some of the stages as you progress.

Learning by Doing 🖝 Reflecting on Research

Have you ever written a research paper? Do you feel confident that you can handle a college research assignment? Or does even the word *research* make you feel anxious? Sum up your past experience. Then list the skills you've already developed in this class that might help you begin your current research project.

Research Assignments: Working from Sources

Research assignments for college courses can take many different forms, but all research assignments will require you to work with outside sources. Sometimes assignments call for just one stage of a research project, such as an annotated bibliography. This chapter will help you define and manage your project to help you prepare for the most basic to the most formidable research tasks. The first step is to find a topic that appeals to you, and to develop a focused research question about it.

The Research Process

ENGAGE Explore a topic that intrigues you, following your assignment (see pp. 450–52).

INQUIRE Narrow your topic to a workable research question and working thesis (see pp. 452-53).

SEARCH Seek and evaluate reliable sources that might help you answer your question (see Chs. 27 and 28).

ORGANIZE Start your working bibliography and annotate possible sources when useful (see pp. 482–85).

INVESTIGATE Work with your sources to obtain details; quote, paraphrase, summarize, and cite information from sources (see pp. 485–92).

SYNTHESIZE Integrate reliable evidence to support your answer to your research question (see pp. 492–93).

PLAN AND DRAFT Starting with a thesis statement that answers your research question, **draft a paper** that uses evidence from sources (see pp. 495–97).

REVISE AND EDIT Allow time to **revise and edit** your paper, making sure you have integrated and **documented** sources correctly (see pp. 498–99).

| WEEK 1 | WEEK 2 | WEEK 3 | WEEK 4 | WEEK 5 | WEEK 6 | WEEK 7 | WEEK 8 |

The Research Proposal

Find a topic that intrigues you, and develop a focused research question about it. Conduct some preliminary research, and adjust your focus if necessary. Once you have a rough picture of how you expect to answer your question, draft a proposal that explains your idea.

Your proposal should include the following:

- background information explaining your interest in the project and how you arrived at your question

- a summary of your preliminary findings and a likely answer to your research question

- an explanation of possible obstacles you may face in conducting your research

- a list of two to three sources you find promising, with complete bibliographic information (for MLA style, see pp. 506–07; for APA style, see pp. 535–36)

For a sample research proposal assignment, see pp. 453–56.

The Source Evaluation

Once you have a research question, conduct some preliminary research, and choose two sources — one print and one online — that are relevant to your topic. For each source, evaluate the following:

- the author's credibility — is the writer a well-known journalist or a novice? Does he or she have a bias?

- the source's (publisher's or sponsor's) reliability

- the author's authority on the topic

- the publication date — is the source current?

For a sample source evaluation assignment, see pp. 480–81.

The Annotated Bibliography

Broader than a single source evaluation, an annotated bibliography is a closer look at five to eight sources that are the most relevant and worthwhile for your purposes. It not only considers what the source says but how you will use that information in your essay. For each source, provide the following:

- complete bibliographic information (for MLA style, see pp. 506–07; for APA style, see pp. 535–36)

- a summary of the source's main thesis and supporting evidence

- a description of how the source relates to your research question

- an explanation of how the source relates to other sources you are researching. (Is it generally in agreement with, or in opposition to, other sources?)

For a sample annotated bibliography assignment, see pp. 483–84.

The Outline

After conducting whatever research is necessary, synthesize the information you assemble to develop your own reasonable answer to the research question.

Then create an outline of how you would present your evidence in a paper. Your outline should include the following main entries:

For details on preparing an outline, see pp. 273–80.

- thesis statement
- supporting evidence (three or more sections)
- responses to opposing viewpoints
- concluding point

The Research Paper

Write a research paper, following the steps outlined in Chapters 26–30: once you have developed a focused research question about your topic, conduct research, evaluating your sources and keeping the information you assemble organized and manageable. Develop your own reasonable answer to your research question and use evidence from sources to support your claim. Then draft, revise, and edit your paper, persuasively using a variety of source material to convey your conclusions. The paper should include the following key features:

For a sample research paper in MLA style, see pp. 521–28; for a sample research paper in APA style, see pp. 549–56.

- introduction with thesis statement
- supporting evidence for thesis
- clear body paragraphs with transitions
- responses to opposing viewpoints
- conclusion that summarizes the main point
- appropriate documentation of five to eight sources

Creating a Schedule

If your instructor doesn't assign a series of small assignments or deadlines for your research project, create your own. Small assignments may take only a week or two, but a full research paper may take several weeks or an entire semester to complete. A schedule can keep you motivated and organized, with time to find, evaluate, and synthesize your sources. Be sure you've allowed enough time to draft and redraft your argument and document your sources appropriately.

Research groups, in class or at work, require cooperative effort but can often accomplish more than one individual could achieve. If your project is collaborative, your team might share the research but produce separate papers or presentations. With your instructor's approval, divide the tasks so that all members are responsible for their own portions. Then agree on your due dates and when to assemble for group meetings.

Choosing a Topic

Many research assignments require you to begin by choosing a topic that interests you. Like explorers in new territory, research writers first take a broad look at promising viewpoints, changes, and trends. Then they zero in on a small area to examine.

Narrowing Your Topic

Narrow a topic by focusing on a particular aspect of it or by considering issues from a local (rather than national or global) perspective.

Broad Topic	Narrower Topic
Military life	Helping veterans reintegrate into civilian life
U.S. education	Measuring learning with standardized tests
World hunger	Aiding hungry children in your community

If you need ideas, listen to the academic exchanges around you. For example, perhaps the reading, writing, or discussion in your geography course alerts you to global environmental threats. Or maybe you hear a podcast about the harms of deforestation. Once you find your area of interest, you can target your research, maybe narrowing "global threats to forests" to "farming practices that threaten rain forests." Consider what you have observed, read, or heard recently that interests you, what life experiences have raised questions for you, or what problem you would like to solve.

For more about brainstorming writing ideas, see Chs. 1 and 15.

Go Online. Online searches can turn up many sources but little focus, so your task will be to narrow the search results to a more workable collection. Always consider the validity of your sources; not everything found on the web is equally reliable!

For more on electronic searches, see Ch. 31.

Browse the Library. For more academic sources, visit your campus library or its Web site, or speak to your reference librarian. The library probably subscribes to many general databases (such as Academic Search Premier, Academic OneFile, and Gale Virtual Reference Library), as well as field-specific resources.

Talk with Experts. Meet with a professor who specializes in the area you're considering. Seek out events or virtual groups relevant to your topic and chat with knowledgeable individuals.

For more on interviewing, see Ch. 5 and p. 469.

Revisit Your Purpose and Audience. Refine your purpose and your audience as you search. Consider what goal you'd like your research project to accomplish — whether it's in your personal life, for a college class, or on the job.

For more on purpose and audience, see pp. 8–14 and p. 265.

Satisfy curiosity	Analyze a situation
Take a new perspective	Substantiate a conclusion
Make a decision	Support a position
Solve a problem	Advocate for change

Turning a Topic into a Question

Once you settle on a topic, formulate questions you think would be worth investigating. By asking more precise questions, your task will emerge into focus.

BROAD OVERVIEW	Family structures
TOPIC	Blended families
SPECIFIC QUESTION	How do blended families today differ from those a century ago?
BROAD OVERVIEW	Contemporary architecture
TOPIC	Landscape architecture
SPECIFIC QUESTION	In what ways have the principles of landscape architecture shaped the city's green design?

If your question is too broad, you'll be swamped with information. If it has been overdone, you'll struggle to sound fresh. You need to find a question that's debatable and that allows you to formulate your own opinion.

Moving from Research Question to Working Thesis

For more on stating and using a thesis, see pp. 266–71.

Some writers find a project easier to tackle if they have in mind not only a question but also a possible answer, maybe even a working thesis. Be flexible, however, ready to change either your possible answer or your question as your research progresses. Until you start your research, you can't know how fruitful your initial question will be. If it doesn't lead you to definite facts or reliable opinions, or if it doesn't encourage you to think critically about those facts or opinions, revise it or throw it out and ask a new question.

RESEARCH QUESTION	How does a nutritious lunch benefit students?
WORKING THESIS	Nutritious school lunches can improve students' classroom performance.

Make a list of terms you can use in your research or points to develop in an outline. You probably will revise or replace your working thesis before you finish, but this early exploration will help you pursue the sources and information you need.

Plan Your Research

For Internet and library search strategies, see Ch. 27.

Conduct a quick search of your library's catalog to test your question. You'll need enough ideas, opinions, facts, statistics, and expert testimony to create a substantial essay. If you turn up a skimpy list, change search terms. If your search results in hundreds of sources, refine your question. Aim for a question that yields twelve to twenty available sources. If you need help, talk to a reference librarian.

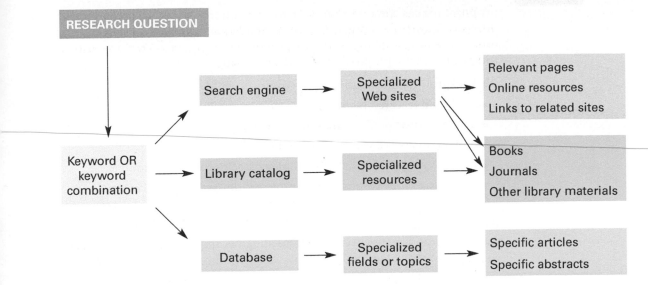

Using your research question to guide your search

Also decide which types of sources to target. Some questions require a wide range, while others a narrower range restricted by date or discipline. The list below describes a number of source types you can investigate.

For advice on creating a working bibliography, see pp. 483–85.

- **Opinions on controversies.** Turn to newspaper editorials, opinion columns, blog posts, issue-oriented sites, and partisan groups for diverse views.
- **News and analysis.** Look for stories from newsmagazines, newspapers, news services, and TV or radio broadcasting.
- **Statistics and facts.** Try census or other government data, library databases, annual fact books, and almanacs.
- **Professional or workforce information.** Look for reports and surveys with academic, government, and corporate sponsors to reduce bias.
- **Research-based analysis.** Try scholarly or well-researched nonfiction, government reports, specialized references, and academic databases.
- **Original records or images.** Check archives, online historical records, and materials held by institutions such as the Library of Congress.

Sample Assignment: Creating a Research Proposal

A research proposal may be an early part of a larger project or it may be a self-contained assignment. In either case, the basic steps in creating a proposal are the same, so follow your instructor's guidelines. A good research proposal makes the case that your topic is interesting, that your research question is worth investigating, and that adequate sources are available. In order to demonstrate the merit of a proposed research project, many instructors require that a proposal include the following:

- background information on the topic
- a focused research question
- a summary of preliminary research findings
- a likely answer to your research question
- a search plan, with a list of possible obstacles to finding sources
- a working bibliography with complete bibliographic information in a specific style, such as MLA or APA

For his assignment, student Marshall Rivera chose the topic of Head Start, an early childhood intervention program aimed at improving educational outcomes for low-income children. He created the following brief proposal.

Marshall Rivera

English 102: Writing and Research

Professor Willard

24 October 2019

Research Proposal: The Cost-Effectiveness of Head Start

Background: Head Start is a federal program created in 1965 as part of President Lyndon B. Johnson's larger initiative of ending poverty in the United States. Operated by the Department of Health and Human Services, Head Start's focus is on preparing young children from low-income families to be ready for school.

Argument made by a source — Head Start claims that children who benefit from early intervention programs are more likely to perform better in school and are therefore more likely to become productive members of society. *Counterargument made by other sources* — But critics claim that Head Start is costly and has no lasting effect on the lives of poor children.

Research question addresses a debatable issue — **Research Question:** Is Head Start an effective enough program to be worth the federal tax dollars required to run it?

Summary of Preliminary Findings: My early research shows mixed reviews of Head Start. Some sources, such as Lindsey Burke at FoxNews.com, strongly criticize the program as a corrupt waste of taxpayer money. Others, such as Amanda Moreno of the *Huffington Post*, insist that Head Start has many worthwhile benefits, even if long-term educational outcomes cannot be clearly demonstrated.

Likely Answer to Research Question: My initial thinking is that Head Start is worth the money, although there is probably room for improvement. For example, maybe Head Start should be held accountable for the performance of the children it helps, similar to the way schools are held accountable for student performance as part of the No Child Left Behind Act. On the other hand, critics of Head Start need to understand the many factors that are out of the agency's control, such as child abuse, substance abuse, school violence, and learning disabilities. In some situations, education alone cannot solve all the problems faced by a child. I suspect that Head Start could be part of a successful series of programs that are aimed at improving all aspects of a child's life, from education to nutrition to safety.

Question allows room for Marshall's opinion, which is then elaborated upon

Search Plan: I plan to uncover sources from both sides of the research question: those in favor of funding Head Start and those opposed to it. My goal is to understand how and why these sources have such different interpretations of the same evidence, which is primarily a large 2010 government study on the effectiveness of Head Start. I also plan to look carefully at the neutral sources that suggest that Head Start is flawed but could be made more effective with some changes. One obstacle I may face in my research is finding unbiased sources. Government sources, which are typically considered reliable, may demonstrate bias in favor of this government-funded program. Many nonprofit and educational sites may also demonstrate this same bias. Likewise, conservative groups that oppose taxes for many federal social programs will probably be automatically biased against Head Start.

Marshall is aware of the need to note bias in his sources.

The bibliography is formatted according to MLA style.

The bibliography has an even mix of opinion and research-based analysis.

Working Bibliography

Burke, Lindsey M. "Head Start's Sad and Costly Secret—What Washington Doesn't Want You to Know." *FoxNews.com*, 14 Jan. 2013, www.foxnews.com/us/2013/01/14/head-starts-sad-and-costly-secret-what-washington-doesnt-want-you-to-know.html.

Colleluori, Salvatore. "Media Cherry-Pick Facts to Falsely Label Head Start Program a Failure." *Media Matters for America*, 16 Jan. 2013, mediamatters.org/research/2013/01/16/media-cherry-pick-facts-to-falsely-label-head-s/192284.

Moreno, Amanda. "Why the Head Start Headlines Are Wrong." *The Huffington Post*, 24 Jan. 2013, www.huffingtonpost.com/amanda-moreno-phd/head-start-early-education_b_2533443.html

Schanzenbach, Diane Whitmore, and Lauren Bauer. "The Long-Term Impact of the Head Start Program." *Brookings Institute*, 19 Aug. 2016, www.brookings.edu/research/the-long-term-impact-of-the-head-start-program/.

United States Department of Health and Human Services, Administration for Children and Families. *Office of Head Start*, www.acf.hhs.gov/programs/ohs. Accessed 16 Oct. 2019.

Finding Sources

27

Although research begins with an intriguing question or issue, it quickly becomes a fast-paced hunt, moving among electronic, print, and human resources. Efficient search strategies will help you find substantial, relevant sources.

Many instructors advocate beginning your research via the campus library, through whose resources you can identify and access reliable information, especially "peer-reviewed" articles — those whose scholarship and research methods have been assessed by experts in the field before publication. Such high-quality sources allow you to draw solid, well-grounded conclusions for your academic audience.

For news-oriented topics or opinions on trending social issues, you also can find up-to-the-minute (though not necessarily reliable) information on the Internet. Where you begin your research may depend on your experience and the nature of your topic. Even if you start looking for a topic on the web, turn to your campus library for focus and depth.

Searching the Internet

The Internet contains resources that vary greatly in quality and purpose. A quick search may turn up intriguing topic ideas, but it may also turn up thousands — maybe millions — of pages of uncertain relevance and timeliness. Some of these pages are motivated by the desire to sell something or by apparent — or hidden — bias. Search returns also will not necessarily be designed to meet any academic standards. And a web search will not include the thousands of private, corporate, or government sites that require passwords, limit access, or simply aren't indexed. The sheer bulk of online information makes searching for relevant research materials both too easy and too difficult, but a few basic principles can help.

Smart Online Searching

When you look for Internet sources, you'll want to keep your search as focused as possible to save time and retrieve the most appropriate sources.

For more on campus library resources, see pp. 460–68.

Find Recommended Internet Resources. Go first to online resources recommended by your instructor. Their recommendations save search time, help you avoid outdated sites, and take you directly to respected resources prepared by experts (scholars or librarians) for academic researchers (like you). Your college library, on campus or online, will offer many more resources and can direct you specifically to research websites maintained by academic institutions, to government sites that allow specialized searches of their collections, and to digitized texts now out of copyright.

Make the Most of Search Engines. Each online search engine has its own system of locating material, categorizing it, and establishing the sequence for reporting results. One search site, patterned on a library index, might be selective. Another might separate advertising from search results, while a third lists "sponsors" who pay advertising fees first, even though sites listed later might be better matches.

Learning by Doing 📷 Comparing Web Searches

Working with some classmates, agree on the topic and terms for a test search. (Or agree to test terms each of you selects.) Have everyone conduct the same search using different search engines, and then compare results. If possible, sit together, using your laptops or campus computers so that you can easily see, compare, and evaluate the search engine results. Ask yourselves these questions:

- What does the search engine's home page suggest its typical users want — academic information, business news, sports, shopping, music?
- What does the search engine gather or index — information from and about a web page (Bing), academic sources (Google Scholar), or a collection of other search engines (Dogpile)?
- What can you learn from a search engine's About, Search Tips, or Help?
- How well does the search engine target your query — the words that define your specific search?
- Does the search engine take questions (Ask), categorize by source type (text, images, news), or group by topic (About)?

Report your conclusions to the class.

Focus the Search Terms. If the keywords you enter into a search engine are too general, you may be overwhelmed with information. For example, a search for sources on *minimum wage* on Bing that produced 26.8 million entries. For more relevant results, consider which aspects of the topic are most necessary to your research and limit your search accordingly. In the example below, focusing the search on a particular aspect (*minimum wage + fast food workers*) produced fewer sources.

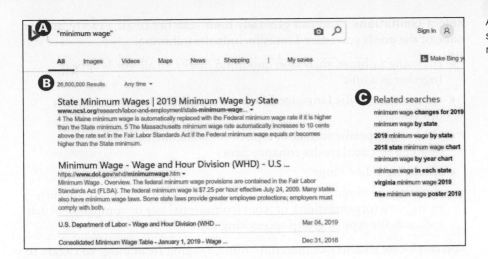

A general keyword search yields 26.8 million results.

A Search term
B Total number of entries located
C Suggested related searches

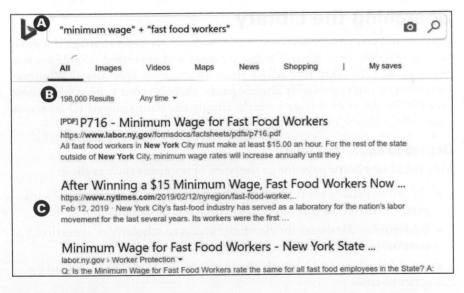

An advanced search with additional terms yields 198,000 results.

A Focusing the search with specific search terms
B Total number of entries located
C Search results

Select Limitations. You can generally limit searches to all, exactly, any, or none of the words you enter. Limits include the following:

- enclosing a phrase, such as in quotation marks, so all words appear together as a unit

- choosing a specific language (human or computer), such as English or Python

- choosing a specific format or type of software, such as a PDF file or audio or visual media enhancements

- specifying a date range

- choosing a domain such as .edu (educational institution), .gov (government), .org (organization), or .com (commercial site or company), which indicates the type of group sponsoring the site

For more on evaluating sources, see Ch. 28.

You can locate a variety of material online, ranging from blogs to tweets to video. For the most up-to-date news stories, use a search engine or go to the website for an established news outlet (e.g., the *Guardian*, CNN, NBC, the *New York Times*, NPR, Reuters, or the *Wall Street Journal*). Be careful to distinguish expertise from opinion and speculation. Pay attention to author credentials and watch for bias. Evaluate and use blogs, personal sites, and social media cautiously.

Searching the Library

What would you pay for access to a 24/7 website designed to make the most of your research time? What if it also screened and organized reliable sources for you — and tossed in free advice from information specialists? Whatever your budget, you've probably already paid — through your tuition — for these services. To get your money's worth, simply use your student ID to access your college library, online or on campus.

Getting to Know the Library

Visit the library home page for an overview of resources such as these:

- the online catalog for finding the library's own books, journals, newspapers, and materials you can read or check out on campus

- subscription databases for electronic access to scholarly or specialized citations, abstracts, articles, and other resources

- interlibrary loan (ILL), which allows you access to materials owned by other libraries

- links for finding specialized campus archives or collections

- pages, tutorials, and tours for advice on using the library productively

To introduce you to the campus library, your instructor may arrange a class orientation. If not, visit the library website and campus facility yourself.

ACCESSING LIBRARY RESOURCES

☐ How do you gain online access to the library from your own computer? What should you do if you have trouble logging in?

☐ How can you get live help from library staff: by drop-in visit, appointment, phone, email, text message, chat, or other technology?

☐ What resources — such as the library catalog and databases — can you search in the library, on campus, or off campus?

☐ How can you identify databases useful for your project? What tutorials from the library or database provider show how to use them efficiently?

☐ How are print books, journals, magazines, or newspapers organized?

☐ How do you find specialized resources such as government documents, maps, legal records, statistics, videos, images, recordings, or local historical archives? Have you consulted a subject librarian?

Home page of the Fullerton College Library.

Ⓐ Overview of library services and information

Ⓑ Search bar for library catalog, databases, and journals

Ⓒ Library hours

Ⓓ Chat with reference librarians

Ⓔ Contact information for librarians

Target Your Search. Your campus library may surprise you with its sophisticated technology and easy access to an overwhelming array of resources. Alone or with help from your reference librarian, you will be able to compile:

- A mixture of sources, including books, journal articles, reference books, or government sites. Use the catalog or databases, or try WorldCat, if it's offered.

- Current or historical information. Try regularly published newspapers, magazines, and journals, or turn to scholarly books.

- Articles from peer-reviewed or refereed journals. Consult *Ulrich's Periodicals Directory* or other databases.

- Opinions about current issues. Search for newspapers or magazines that carry opinion pieces, editorials, or investigative articles. Consult blogs too, but avoid sites devoted to one side of an issue.

- Facts and statistics, from state or federal agencies or nonprofit groups.

Use the Resources. Your campus library can help you become a more efficient and productive student. It provides a wide variety of resources, advice, and tools: e-books, audio books, podcasts, videos, tutorials, workshops, citation managers, source organizers, and apps for academic tasks (e.g., note takers, time managers, project schedules, group organizers, and file hosting services).

Many libraries also supply Library Guides or lists of well-regarded starting points for research within a field. These valuable shortcuts help you quickly find a cluster of useful resources by discipline. The chart below supplies only a small sampling of the specialized indexes, dictionaries, encyclopedias, handbooks, yearbooks, and other resources available.

Using the Library Catalog

A library's catalog is an index of all materials — books, periodicals, digital collections, historical archives, and so on — that the library houses. The catalog may also provide a listing of external materials that may be retrieved through interlibrary loan. The purpose of the catalog is to allow you to find basic information, such as title, author, and date, on materials that you can access through the library.

Search Creatively. Electronic catalogs may allow many search options. These include keyword, Library of Congress subject, author, title, call number, and publication date searches. Consult a librarian or follow the prompts to find out which searches your catalog allows.

Specialized Resources by Discipline

	Specialized Online Indexes	Print Reference Works	Online Government Resources	Internet Resources
Film and Theater	*Film & Television Literature Index; Films on Demand*	*The Oxford Encyclopedia of Theatre and Performance*	Smithsonian Archives Center: Film, Video, and Audio Collections	Cambridge Companions Online
History	*Historical Abstracts America: History and Life*	*Dictionary of Concepts in History*	The Library of Congress: American Memory	WWW Virtual Library: History Central Catalogue
Literature	*MLA International Bibliography; Essay and General Literature Index; JSTOR*	*Encyclopedia of the Novel*	EDSITEment (NEH)	American Studies Journals; Voice of the Shuttle
Social Sciences	*Social Sciences Citation Index*	*International Encyclopedia of the Social and Behavioral Sciences*	Fedstats	e-Source from the National Institutes of Health
Education	*Education Abstracts*	*International Encyclopedia of Education*	National Center for Education Statistics	ERIC: Education Resources Information Center
Political Science	*Worldwide Political Science Abstracts*	*State Legislative Sourcebook*	FedWorld	Political Resources on the Net; National Security Archive
Women's Studies	*Women's Studies International*	*Women in World History: A Biographical Encyclopedia*	U.S. Department of Labor Women's Bureau	Institute for Women's Policy Research
Science and Technology	*General Science Abstracts; Web of Science*	*McGraw-Hill Encyclopedia of Science and Technology*	National Science Foundation	EurekAlert!
Earth Sciences	*GeoRef*	*Facts on File Dictionary of Earth Science*	USGS (U.S. Geological Survey): Science for a Changing World	Center for International Earth Science Information Network
Environmental Studies	*Environmental Abstracts*	*Encyclopedia of Environmental Science*	EPA: U.S. Environmental Protection	EnviroLink
Life Sciences	*Biological Abstracts*	*Encyclopedia of Human Biology*	National Agricultural Library	CAPHIS Top 100 List

Results from a
keyword search for
U.S. immigration
using a library
catalog.

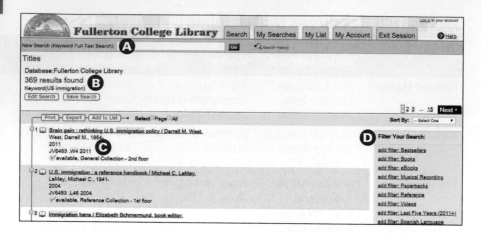

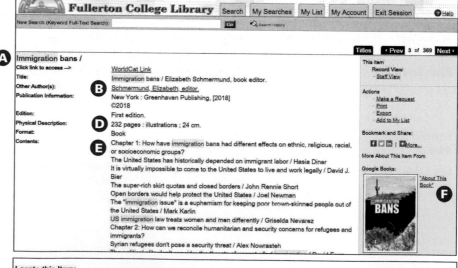

(A) Search box

(B) Number of results found

(C) Numbered results, with call number, location, and availability of each item

(D) Additional filters to narrow your search

When your search produces a list of possible sources, click on the most promising items to learn more about them. Besides the call number or shelf location, the record will identify the author, the title, the place of publication, the date, and often the resource's contents, length, and scope and search terms that may help focus your search. Use these clues to help you select options wisely.

One record from
the keyword search
results.

A Search term is highlighted

B Title and author

C Call number, location, and availability

D Format and number of pages

E Contents

F Preview of the book on another website

Learning by Doing 🖉 Brainstorming for Search Terms

Start with a rough idea for a research question. Working with a classmate or small group, brainstorm a list of keywords that might be useful search terms for each person's topic. Test your terms by searching several places — the library catalog, a subject-area database, a newspaper database, a reliable consumer web page, a relevant government agency, or other library resources. Compare search results in terms of type, quantity, quality, and relevance of sources. Then refine your search terms — add limitations, change keywords, narrow the ideas, and so forth, trying to increase the relevance of what you find.

Browse the Shelves. A call number, like an address, tells where a book or other resource "resides." College libraries generally use the Library of Congress system, with letters and numbers, rather than the numerical Dewey decimal system, but both systems group items by subject. With a call number from an online record, follow the library map and section signs to the shelf with a promising book. Once there, browse through its intriguing neighbors, which often treat the same subject.

Searching Library Databases

Databases gather information. Your library may subscribe to dozens or hundreds to give you easy access to current screened resources, including hard-to-find fee-based web sources. Check the library site for its database descriptions and lists by topic or field. A librarian can help match your research question to the databases most likely to provide what you need.

- **General-interest databases** with citations, abstracts, or full-text articles from many fields as well as news and culture: Academic Search Premier, General OneFile, LexisNexis, OmniFile Full Text; Readers' Guide Full-Text or Retrospective (popular periodicals); Historical New York Times, America's Historical Newspapers, LexisNexis (news)

- **Specialized databases by type of material:** JSTOR, Project MUSE, Sage (scholarly journals); Biological Abstracts (summaries of sources); WorldCat (books); American Periodicals Series Online (digitized magazines from 1741 to 1900)

- **Specialized databases by field:** MedlinePlus, ScienceDirect, GreenFILE (biology, medicine, health); ABI/INFORM (business); AGRICOLA (agriculture)

- **Issue-oriented databases:** PAIS International (public affairs); CQ Researcher (featured issues); Opposing Viewpoints in Context (debatable topics)

- **Reference databases:** Gale Virtual Reference Library, Oxford Reference, Credo Reference

For specific information, select a database that covers the exact field, scholarly level, type of source, or time period that you need. Databases identify sources only in publications they analyze and only for dates they cover. Take tricky research problems to a subject librarian, who may suggest using a different database or older print or CD-ROM indexes for historical research.

Keywords. Start your search with the keywords in your research question:

college costs   voting   forest fires

If your first search produces too many sources, narrow your terms:

college tuition increases

voter suppression

California forest fires

Or add specifics, such as an author, a title, or a date.

Advanced Searches. Fill in the database's advanced search screen to restrict by date or other options. For example, a database might allow wildcard or truncation symbols to find all forms of a term; often * is used for multiple characters.

child*   children, childcare, childhood

A database also might allow Boolean searches that combine or rule out terms:

AND (narrows: all terms must appear in a result)   Colorado and River

OR (expands: any one of the terms must appear)   Colorado or River

NOT (rules out: one term must not appear)   Colorado not River

Boolean searches

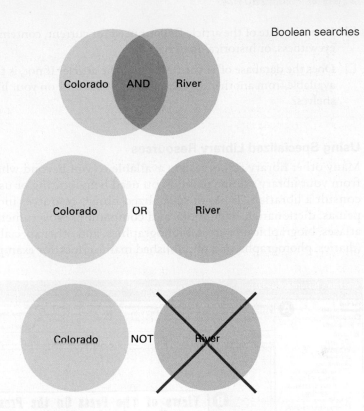

Your search calls up a list of records or entries that include your search terms. Click on one of these for specifics about the item (title, author, publication information, date, other details) and possibly a description or summary (often called an *abstract*) or a link to the full text of the item. If the database supplies only an abstract, read it to decide whether you need to track down the full article elsewhere.

SEARCHING WITH DATABASES

☐ What does the periodical title suggest about its audience, interest area, and popular or scholarly orientation? How likely are its articles to supply what you need?

☐ Have the periodical articles been peer-reviewed by other scholars prior or edited and fact-checked by journalists?

☐ Does the title or description of the article suggest that it will answer your research question?

☐ Does the date of the article fit your need for current, contemporary, eyewitness, or historical material?

☐ Does the database offer the full text of the article? If not, is the periodical available from another database, on its website, or on your library's shelves?

Using Specialized Library Resources

Many other library resources are available to you beyond what's accessible from your library's home page. If you need help locating or using materials, consult a librarian. Types of specialized library resources include encyclopedias, dictionaries, handbooks and companions, government documents, atlases, biographical sources, bibliographies, and other specialized materials (diaries, photographs, and unpublished manuscripts, for example).

Search results from America's Historical Newspapers. Readex, a division of NewsBank Inc.

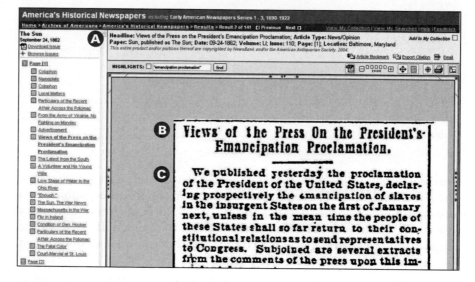

A Publication name, date, volume number, page number
B Article title (and author, if available)
C Text of article

Finding Sources in the Field

The goal of field research is the same as that of library and Internet research — to gather the information you need to answer your research question and to marshal persuasive evidence to support your conclusions. When you interview, observe, or ask questions of people, you generate your own firsthand (or primary) evidence. Before you begin, find out from your instructor whether you need institutional approval for research involving other people ("human subjects approval") from your school's institutional review board (IRB).

Interviewing

Interviews — conversations with a purpose — may be your main source of field material. Whenever possible, interview an expert in the field or, if you are researching a group, someone representative or typical. Prepare carefully.

For more on interviewing, see Ch. 5.

TIPS FOR INTERVIEWING

- Be sure your prospect is willing to be quoted in writing.
- Schedule the interview with enough time — an hour if possible — for a thorough talk.
- Arrive promptly, with carefully thought-out questions to ask.
- Come ready to take notes, including key points, quotations, and descriptive details. If you also want to record, ask permission.
- Listen attentively and be flexible; allow the interview to move in unanticipated directions.
- If a question draws no response, don't persist; go on to the next one.
- At the end of the interview, thank the interviewee, and arrange for an opportunity to clarify comments and confirm direct quotations. Make any additional notes directly following the interview.

If you can't talk in person, try a phone or Skype interview. Federal regulations, by the way, forbid recording a phone interview without notifying the person talking that you are doing so. Always be sure to notify your subject if you are recording them electronically, in addition to taking notes.

Observing

An observation may provide you with essential information about a setting such as a workplace or a school. Some organizations will insist on your displaying valid identification; in advance, ask your instructor for a statement written on college letterhead declaring that you are a student doing field research. Make an appointment with the organization or individual and identify yourself and your purpose. Before you depart, be sure to thank the necessary parties for arranging the observation.

For more on observing, see Ch. 4.

TIPS FOR OBSERVING

- Establish a clear purpose — decide exactly what you want to observe and why.
- Take notes to record important facts, telling details, and sensory impressions. Notice the features of the place, the people there, or whatever relates to the purpose of your observation.
- Consider taking photos or recording video if doing so doesn't distract you from the scene. Photographs can illustrate your paper and help you recall and interpret details while you write. If you are in a private place, get written permission first.

- Pause, look around, fill in missing details, and check the accuracy of your notes before you leave.
- Thank the person who arranged your observation.

Using Questionnaires

Questionnaires, or surveys, are useful for gathering the responses of a large number of people to a fixed set of questions. Online sites such as SurveyMonkey allow you to quickly develop and deploy questionnaires for free. Professional researchers carefully design sets of questions and then randomly select representative people to respond in order to reach reliable answers. Because your survey will not be that extensive, avoid generalizing about your findings. It's one thing to say that "many students" who filled out a questionnaire hadn't read a newspaper in the past month; it's another to claim that this is true of 72 percent of the students at your school—especially when your questionnaires went only to students in a specific major, and only half of them responded to the email invitation.

A more reliable way to treat questionnaires is as group interviews: assume that you collect typical views, use them to build your overall knowledge, and cull responses for compelling details or quotations. Use a questionnaire to concentrate on what a group thinks as a whole or when an interview to cover all your questions is impractical. (See below for a sample questionnaire.)

TIPS FOR USING A QUESTIONNAIRE

- Ask yourself what you want to discover with your questionnaire. Then thoughtfully invent questions to fulfill that purpose.
- State questions clearly, and supply simple directions for easy responses. Test your questionnaire on classmates or friends first.
- Ask questions that so that you can tally responses easily; formats include checking options, marking *yes* or *no*, or circling a number on a five-point scale. Try to ask for one piece of information per question.
- If you wish to consider differences based on age, gender, or other variables, include some demographic questions.
- Write unbiased questions to elicit factual responses. Don't ask *How religious are you?* Instead ask *How often do you attend religious services?* Then you can report actual numbers.
- Try to distribute questionnaires at a set location or event, and collect them as they are completed. If you're conducting the questionnaire online, try to send it out at a time when you know students won't be too busy to respond (such as finals week), and consider sending a reminder as the deadline approaches.

QUESTIONNAIRE

Thank you for completing this questionnaire. All information you supply will be kept strictly confidential.

1. What is your age? _____

2. What is your gender? _____

3. What is your class?

   _____ First-year   _____ Sophomore   _____ Junior   _____ Senior

4. Where do you live?

   _____ On campus   _____ Off campus

5. Do you use the on-campus dining facilities?

   _____ Yes   _____ No

6. If you answered "no," please specify why you do not use the on-campus dining facilities.

   _____ The meal plans are too expensive.

   _____ My schedule and commitments preclude me from being on campus for meals.

   _____ The available food options are not suitable to my dietary needs.

   _____ The available food options are of poor nutritional quality.

   _____ Other (please explain) _____

7. On a scale of 1 to 5, how satisfied are you with the overall quality of food served in on-campus dining facilities?

   (dissatisfied)   1   2   3   4   5   (extremely satisfied)

Questionnaire asking students about dining preferences

Corresponding

Does your interview subject live too far away for you to speak to him or her in person? Search online for an email address, phone number, or social media profile. Introduce yourself and specify your query. Do you need information from a group, such as the American Red Cross, or an elected official? The organization's website should provide contact information.

TIPS FOR CORRESPONDING

- Plan ahead, and allow plenty of time for responses to your requests.
- Make your message short and polite. Identify yourself, and explain your request. List any questions. Thank your correspondent.
- Include your email address in your message. If corresponding by mail, enclose a stamped, self-addressed envelope with the letter.

Attending Public and Online Events

A lecture or conference can be a source of fresh ideas and an excellent introduction to the language of a discipline. Take notes, recording who attended the event and what was said; these details may be useful in your writing later. If you join an online discussion, you can observe, ask a question, or save or print the transcript for your records.

Reconsidering Your Field Sources

Each type of field research can raise particular questions. Consider the credibility and consistency of your field sources. Did your source seem biased or prejudiced? Did your source provide evidence to support or corroborate claims? Have you compared different people's opinions, accounts, or evidence? Is any evidence hearsay — one person telling you the thoughts of another or recounting actions that he or she hasn't witnessed? If so, can you check the information with another source or a different type of evidence? Did your source seem to respond consistently, seriously, and honestly? Remember that a random sampling of people might not be truly representative, and that people aware of being observed sometimes change their behavior.

Evaluating Sources

28

After you locate and collect information, you need to think critically and evaluate — in other words, judge — your sources.

For more on critical reading and thinking, see Chs. 2 and 3.

- Which of your sources are reliable? How do you know?
- What types of sources are you working with?
- What evidence from these sources is most useful for your paper?

This chapter will help you answer these types of questions and evaluate the sources you have found.

Assessing Reliability

Not every source you locate will be equally reliable. You should watch for an author's or a publisher's point of view, which may shape the content of the source. To determine which evidence is best, do what experienced researchers do — ask key questions about the author, the publisher, and the source itself.

Who Is Responsible for the Source?

Learn the credentials, affiliation, and reputation of each author and publisher you plan to use. Any source you use to shape or support your ideas should be reliable and trustworthy.

Credentials. Check for the author's background in the preface, introduction, or concluding note in an article or a book. Discover who — or what organization — is behind a web source and if a publisher has ties to particular advertisers or sponsors. Look for links leading to other articles by the author. If necessary, conduct a web search to learn more about an author's background and expertise.

Reputation. Think about the reputation of the publisher of the source you are using. What other types of books or websites do they publish? A good measure of someone's credibility is the regard of other experts. Does your instructor or a campus expert recognize or recommend the author or publisher? Does a search for the author on Google Scholar produce other sources that cite the author? Is the publisher well established and known for producing quality materials?

Material with No Author Identified. If no author is given, try to identify the sponsor, publisher, or editor. On a website, check the home page or search for a disclaimer, contact information, or an About page. Does the material push a particular point of view? Avoid any source with no identifiable author or publisher.

What Type of Source Is It?

Sources can generally be categorized as either primary or secondary, and both types of sources should be carefully examined for authorship and bias. Most research projects benefit from a combination of primary and secondary sources.

Primary Sources. A *primary source* is a firsthand account written by an eyewitness or a participant. It contains raw data and immediate impressions. Examples include diaries, letters, news articles written by eyewitnesses to an event, and official data such as census or labor statistics.

Secondary Sources. A *secondary source* is an analysis or interpretation of information contained in primary sources. Secondary sources include articles and books analyzing primary sources. A biography of Cleopatra by a modern historian would be a secondary source because it relies on the historian's interpretation of events described in primary sources. An autobiography, on the other hand, is a firsthand source because it is written by the person who experienced the events it covers.

Is the Source Scholarly or Popular?

Most secondary sources can be considered either scholarly or popular, depending on the publisher or author affiliation.

Scholarly Sources. Scholarly sources generally include articles in academic journals and websites as well as books published by university presses. The material is written by scholars or researchers in the field, and it is usually reviewed by other experts before publication. Scholarly sources generally include extensive in-text citations and bibliographies to document their research. Examples of scholarly sources include the *Journal of the American Medical Association* and the *Social Psychology Quarterly*. These sources are written for an expert audience, so some materials may be too specialized for your use.

Popular Sources. Unlike scholarly sources, popular sources are usually written by journalists or non-scholarly writers and are published for a broader audience. Although they are not typically reviewed by experts in the field, reputable popular sources are edited for clarity and accuracy. Examples include the *New York Times, Scientific American,* BBC.com, and *Smithsonian*; these sources can provide important evidence for your research project.

Be wary of articles found circulating on social media. Social media is known for generating "buzz" around news that may be exaggerated, somewhat inaccurate, or completely untrue. If you want to use a source you found on social media, be sure to verify the information it contains by checking other reputable sources. Beware also of advertisements that look like articles with outrageous or shocking titles; these are often paid content sponsored by advertisers.

What Is the Source's Purpose?

Whether primary or secondary, popular or scholarly, reputable or not, authors and publishers often have a purpose in mind when they publish a text. Your job as a researcher is to critically question whether the author or publisher is motivated by a political, a religious, a corporate, or another agenda. To understand the purpose or intention of a source, ask yourself what its purpose is. Does it aim to explain or inform? To report new research? To persuade? To add a viewpoint? To sell a product? Is its purpose transparent, acknowledged in its preface, mission statement, or About Us or FAQ (Frequently Asked Questions) page?

When Was the Source Published?

A source that is up-to-date or at least still timely will be able to address current information and trends in a field. News may appear first in web postings, media broadcasts, and newspapers and eventually in magazines, although such sources may not have allowed time for experts to consider the information thoughtfully. Later, as material is more fully examined, it may appear in scholarly articles and books. For this reason, while it is important to look for the *most* recent evidence related to your research, older materials can supply a valuable historical, theoretical, or analytical focus.

Assessing Bias

Because most authors and publishers have opinions on their topics, there's little point in asking whether they are biased. Instead, ask how their viewpoint affects the presentation of information and opinion. What are the author's or sponsor's allegiances? Does the source treat one side of an issue more favorably than another? Is that bias hidden or stated? Is any important information — especially evidence that might refute this source's argument — notably missing? If you spot such bias early, proceed cautiously, and be sure to look for other viewpoints to avoid lopsided analyses.

Recognizing Biases across the Political Spectrum

Some sources for news and analysis are grounded in conservative or liberal political ideology. For instance, Fox News features conservative hosts and experts, and its following is predominantly conservative viewers. On the other end of the spectrum, the *Washington Post* takes liberal stances on most issues, and its readership is primarily liberal. Both news organizations can be valid sources of information, but recognizing each one's bias will help you judge whether you are getting the full story.

Assessing Relevance

Even a highly reliable source needs to be relevant to your research question and your ideas about how to answer that question. An interesting fact or opinion could be just that — interesting. Instead, you need facts, expert opinions, information, and quotations that relate directly to your purpose and audience.

Considering Your Purpose

For a review of selecting sources, see B in the Quick Research Guide, pp. Q-24–Q-25.

For more on testing evidence, see pp. 138–40.

As you collect sources, consider what makes one source better than another. Think about whether the information it includes is useful for your purposes. Would its strong quotations or hard facts be effective? Does it tackle the topic in a relevant way? For one paper, you might appropriately rely on a popular magazine; for another, you might need the scholarly findings on which the magazine relied. Look for the best sources for your purpose, asking not only *Will this do?* but also *Would something else be better?*

Evaluating Online Sources with Healthy Skepticism

Doing research online can be convenient and fast, but it demands careful attention and a good dose of skepticism to distinguish between authentic sources and unreliable ones.

Understanding a Site's Purpose

Like all sources, online postings, blogs, and websites reflect the biases, interests, or information gaps of their writers or sponsors. Even sites with useful material will provide only what supports their goals — selling their products, serving their clients, enlisting new members, or persuading others to accept their activities or views. The image on p. 477 identifies several features of a website that provides both informative and persuasive materials.

Keep in mind that many online sources do not go through the traditional editorial or review processes that generally make printed sources more reliable. Unlike academic journals or books, they have not been reviewed by experts in the field. Because anyone can create a website, it's especially important to learn as much as you can about the author and publisher of a site. As the "About Us" tab explains, this site focuses on animal welfare. It features photographs of cute dogs and cats in need, images that are meant to appeal to the readers' emotions and encourage them to donate money, time, or both to save animals' lives.

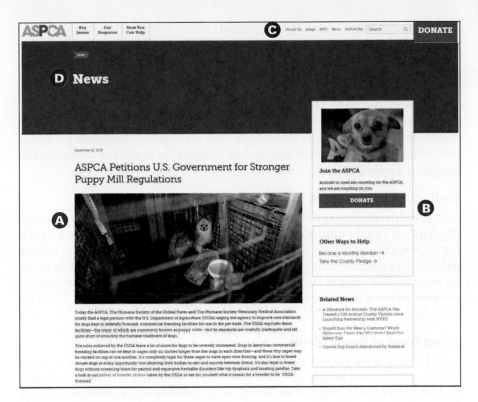

Evaluating a document on a website that identifies as an organization (.org).

A Uses engaging animal images

B Appeals for support

C About Us tab links to page explaining purpose of group

D News section provides searchable collection of articles

Fighting "Fake News"

Anyone who has been paying attention to national events in recent years will recognize the phrase "fake news." The term has been thrown about in tweets, news analyses, political cartoons, and late-night talk shows. "Fake news" can be anything from flat-out false stories, to advertisements formatted to look like news, to real news stories distorted by being taken out of context. Some sources try to maintain the illusion of credibility by providing both real news and the fake stuff, hoping to confuse readers and weaken their belief in the facts. There are also satirical sites mocking events and people in the news (think of *The Onion*); it's easy to be fooled by one of these stories, even though such sites don't intend to be taken seriously.

Although most websites that provide news, information, and analysis are authentic, the ones that spread "fake news" may reach more readers more quickly, thanks to the power of social media.

Recognizing "Clickbait"

Some companies deliberately publish false stories, doctored photographs, and misleading headlines as "news." The motive is often money; if a headline is outrageous enough, more readers will click on it, generating more profit for the company. If a headline or description of an article seems too far-fetched to be true, it probably isn't true after all.

Distinguishing between News and Advertisements

Some websites incorporate advertisements — often called "sponsored content" or "paid content" — into their home pages. Pay attention to such labels, which mean that a sponsoring company or organization paid the website to promote this content. Be aware that paid content often lacks an author. Although it may be published alongside news stories or feature articles written by reporters, learn to distinguish paid content from its neighbors.

Being Wary of Social Media

Social media is the perfect vehicle for false stories. Research shows that social media is how most adults get their news, through links, articles, headlines, and images passed along online. Social media enables fake news to travel with extraordinary speed, and once a story seems to be everywhere, it is harder to refute it.

Remember too that the content you see on social media is not random. Using data analytics, companies can track users' reading habits and identify potential customers for their products. If you have ever searched for something online — say, snow boots — and then were surprised to see an ad showing the very boots you were considering, you have experienced just how targeted such advertising can be. Groups that spread misinformation use similar strategies to reach readers who might be sympathetic or vulnerable to their point of view.

Authenticating Information

Given all these cautions, how can you know what to trust online? If you are suspicious of an article you find, or if you simply aren't sure of a source for whatever reason, try to authenticate the information in the source. Look for two or three other sources that contain the same information, statistics, or evidence or that cite the same research. If you can corroborate the information across several distinct sources, it's more likely to be trustworthy.

Use Fact-Checking Sites. Consult sites like Snopes.com to research stories that seem unbelievable, or check Politifact.com and FactCheck.org to verify whether politicians' claims are accurate or not.

Look for the Evidence. If a source includes evidence supporting a claim, follow the trail and verify the quotations, statistics, or facts. Be suspicious of a source that makes a claim without any evidence to back it up.

Consider Photographs Carefully. We have all heard the expression "A picture is worth a thousand words." But not every picture is equally trustworthy. Photographs can be easily manipulated using graphic design software, so don't assume that anything appearing in a photo is absolute truth. See if the photo has an attribution or a source, and if so, follow it.

Consult Your Research Librarian. When in doubt, go to the experts in researching effectively—your campus librarian. Librarians can help you find reliable sources and authenticate the data inside them.

Diversifying Your News Sources

Recent studies have shown that most Americans get their news from the same few sources, according to where they stand on the political spectrum. In order to obtain a broad range of political points of view, aim for diversity in the news sources you regularly consult. If you tend to consume liberal content such as the *Huffington Post* or *NPR*, check out a conservative source such as the the *Wall Street Journal* or *National Review*. The same is true in reverse. Regardless of your political leanings, push yourself to hear opposing points of view.

Use the checklist that follows to take extra precautions when researching online.

EVALUATING ONLINE SOURCES

☐ Check the URL's domain name (.com, .edu, .gov, etc.) to determine what type of organization is sponsoring the site.

   .com: business or commercial site

   .edu: educational site

   .gov or .us: government site

   .mil: military site

   .org: nonprofit organization site

☐ Carefully check the URL to confirm you've reached the site you wanted, not a site with a similar-sounding name.

☐ Review the site's About page for information on the organization's purpose and affiliations. If no About page is available, you should be skeptical.

☐ Check the publication date or most recent update. Sites that haven't been updated in more than two years should be treated with caution.

☐ Beware of websites with excessive ads or links to commercial sites. Many unreliable sites exist purely as "clickbait," designed solely to earn advertising revenue.

Reviewing Your Sources

Once you've gathered and evaluated a reasonable collection of sources, it's time to step back and consider them as a group. Think about whether the information they include is useful for your purposes. Ask yourself the following questions about your sources and the information they convey:

- Have you found enough relevant and credible sources to satisfy the requirements of your assignment? Have you found enough to suggest sound answers to your research question?

- Are your sources thought provoking? Can you tell what is generally accepted, controversial, or possibly unreliable? Have your sources enlightened you while substantiating, refining, or changing your ideas?

- Are your sources varied? Have they helped you achieve a reasonably complete view of your topic, including other perspectives, approaches, alternatives, or interpretations? Have they deepened your understanding and helped you reach well-reasoned, balanced conclusions?

- Are your sources appropriate? Do they answer your question with evidence your readers will find persuasive? Do they have the range and depth necessary to achieve your purpose and satisfy your readers?

Use these questions to check in with yourself. Make sure that you have a clear direction for your research—whether it's the same direction you started with or a completely new one.

Sample Assignment: Preparing a Source Evaluation

A source evaluation may be a small part of a larger project or it may be a self-contained assignment. Use the source evaluation to demonstrate your understanding of how to judge the reliability of a source as well as its relevance to your paper.

For her assignment, student Ella Jackson chose to evaluate an online source related to the health benefits of eating organic foods. She used MLA citation style.

Ella Jackson

English 101: Composition

Professor Cosby

14 October 2019

Source Evaluation: Blog Post on the Health
Benefits of Eating Organic Foods

Watson, Stephanie. "Organic Food No More Nutritious than
Conventionally Grown Food." *Harvard Health Blog*, Harvard
Medical School, 5 Sept. 2012, www.health.harvard.edu/
blog/organic-food-no-more-nutritious-than-conventionally
-grown-food-201209055264.

This source is directly related to my research question, "Is ———— relevance
organic food healthier than nonorganic food?" It cites a report by
Stanford University researchers, who found "very little difference
in nutritional content" between organic and conventionally
grown food. On the other hand, the same study showed that
conventional produce had about one-third more pesticides than
organic produce. According to this report, it is unknown whether
the pesticide level in conventional foods, which meets current
safety standards, may be more damaging to long-term health than
the lower amount of pesticides found in organic foods. Perhaps
another source can provide some insight into this question.

This source is highly reliable because it was published on ———— reliability
a site sponsored by a well-known and highly regarded medical
school (Harvard), and it includes evidence from another highly
regarded school (Stanford). The author is not a medical expert,
but she is an experienced medical journalist who has written ———— author credibility
and edited more than two dozen books and who served as the
executive editor of *Harvard Women's Health Watch* for two years.

The language in the source seems balanced and unbiased.
It does not take a strong stand on whether organics are worth
the extra cost to consumers, instead stating that whether or not
to buy organic food is a personal choice.

One potential problem with the source is its date. I will ———— timeliness
need to find out if more recent studies have disproven the
results of the 2012 Stanford report.

29 Working with Sources

Working effectively with research sources includes being able to navigate, manage, and take notes on sources as well as marshalling evidence from sources in the form of quotations, paraphrases, and summaries. It also means introducing those sources clearly and citing them correctly.

Managing Your Sources

It is never too early in a research project to begin keeping track of the sources you find. Rather than relying on memory, develop efficient techniques that work best for your research purpose.

Taking Advantage of Digital Tools

When you're researching sources online, become familiar with the tools at your disposal. As a precaution, regularly back up all electronic files you create.

- Download or email search results from library databases to your own computer or storage device, making it easier to find and access these materials again.
- Bookmark useful websites or use a curating site such as Scoop.it to manage your most promising online sources.
- Create a folder to save links, emails, online posts, transcripts of chats, and database records. Give each file a descriptive name so that you can retrieve the information quickly later on.
- If a database or Internet search is productive, note where you searched and what keywords you used so you can easily repeat the search if necessary.

Organizing on Paper

- Summarize sources on sticky notes or index cards so that you can quickly rearrange them.
- Use a poster board to sketch a "storyboard" for the main "events" that you want to cover in your paper.
- Copy or scan book passages and articles, print out electronic sources (noting the site or database and date of access), and keep documents

from field research. Be sure the author (or title) and page number appear on each page so you can accurately credit your source.

Keeping a Working Bibliography

Your working bibliography is a detailed and evolving list of articles, books, websites, and other resources that may contribute to your research. It guides your research by recording the sources you plan to consult and adding notes about those you do examine. A working bibliography also offers two other benefits. First, carefully keeping track of sources will help you sort out source material from your own words, an important part of avoiding plagiarism. Second, your bibliography will provide you with essential information when you are ready to complete your assignment.

Record as much of the publication information as you can for each source:

- Complete name of the author(s); names of editor, compiler, translator, or contributor, if any
- Title and subtitle of the book, magazine, journal, or website where the source was published; title of any special issue or book series, if any
- Volume and issue of the magazine or journal or edition number of the newspaper, if any
- Publication date
- Page numbers of the source; section number or letter of the newspaper, if any
- DOI (digital object identifier) of the source if any; URL of the source, if any

Saving this information now will put you in good shape when it's time to compile your final Works Cited list (MLA) or References list (APA).

You can record this information several ways. Choose what works efficiently for you: note cards (one source per card); a small notebook, writing on one side of the page; a Google doc or digital file; citation management software.

Sample Assignment: Developing an Annotated Bibliography

An annotated bibliography is a list of sources with a short summary or annotation for each entry. This common assignment quickly informs a reader about the direction of your research. It also shows your mastery of two major research skills: identifying a source and writing a summary.

For a sample source evaluation, see pp. 480–81.

For more on MLA and APA formats, see Chs. 31 and 32.

To develop an annotated bibliography, find out which format you're expected to use to identify sources and what your annotations should do—summarize only, evaluate, or meet a special requirement (such as to interpret).

Martina Schwartz prepared an annotated bibliography for her research question, *How can education be improved in Native American communities?* She identified each source as primary (a firsthand or an eyewitness account) or secondary (a secondhand analysis based on primary material), summarized it, and described how she expected it to support her position. The following is a portion of her annotated bibliography.

Brayboy, Bryan McKinley Jones. "Culture, Place, and Power: Engaging the Histories and Possibilities of American Indian Education." *History of Education Quarterly*, vol. 54, no. 3, 2014, pp. 395-402. *Wiley Online Library*, doi: 10.1111/hoeq.12075.

Secondary source. Brayboy, an anthropologist, writes that learning happens not only in the classroom but also in every aspect of life. I plan to use Brayboy's claim to support my argument that education must be reformed to be more cultural and holistic in order to have improved outcomes in Native American communities.

Center for Native Youth. *2018 State of Native Youth Report. The Apsen Institute.* Nov. 2018, www.cnay.org/docs/CNAY_AR2018_FINAL_Web_110618.pdf.

Secondary source. This report interprets numerous statistics and facts as well as powerful quotations by Native American youth. It includes extensive information about a wide range of issues that are important to Native Americans, from how Native youth are disproportionately affected by school discipline and the child welfare system to how climate change is endangering certain sacred sites. The chapter on education and jobs argues for "re-indigenizing" the classroom by inviting the participation of Native American elders and incorporating traditional forms of learning. I will use this report to demonstrate that education needs to be targeted to the needs of the Native American community.

"I will stop 1,800 kids from becoming dropouts." American Indian College Fund, 2012, creativity-online.com/work/american-indian-college-fund-help-a-student-help-a-tribe-3/26344

Primary source. One of a series of print ads that encourages donations to this fund that assists Native Americans in attending college. According to the text below the photograph, the subject ("Allen") is a student studying early childhood education at a college in Washington. Allen is quoted as saying that children who grow up on reservations don't have positive role models from their own culture, which makes it difficult from them to be successful. I will use this ad as an example of how educational charities aim to help Native American communities.

Learning by Doing 🖊 Writing an Annotation

Select one of your sources (or a reading from this book) and write a few sentences summarizing the source and describing why it is relevant to your project. If your instructor has specified a particular approach, tailor your annotation to follow those directions. Exchange annotation drafts with a classmate or small group, and discuss ways to clarify contents or relevance.

Taking Notes

Taking accurate notes — in the form of quotations, paraphrases, and summaries — is essential for any research project. Your goal in capturing source information is to record enough notes and citations that, once they're written, you are independent of the source. Start by reading each source critically and actively; then decide what — and how much — to record so you dig out the useful nuggets without distorting the meaning.

For more examples of capturing information from sources, see pp. 193–97 and D in the Quick Research Guide, pp. Q-27–Q-31.

Reading Actively

Read the entire article or section of a book before beginning to take notes. On your second reading, take notes by annotating, highlighting, quoting, paraphrasing, and summarizing. Such methods help you absorb, evaluate, and select information from a source. They also help you identify potentially useful materials and, later, integrate them smoothly into your paper.

Decide What You Need. Weighing each source carefully and considering how you might use it — even as you are reading — is part of the dynamic process of research. Distinguish what material is significant for answering your research question and what's only slightly related. If you wish, add your own ratings (*, +, !!, or – , ??) at the top or in the margin.

Identify What Comes from Where. Clearly identify the author of the source, a brief title if needed, and the page number or URL where a reader could find the information. These details connect each source note to your corresponding bibliography entry. Adding a keyword at the top of each note will help you cluster related material in your paper.

For more on critical reading and annotating texts, see Ch. 2. For more on evaluating research sources, see Ch. 28.

Decide How to Record Information. When it comes time to draft your paper, you'll incorporate your source material in three basic ways: quoting, paraphrasing, and summarizing.

- **Quoting** is transcribing the author's exact words directly from the source. As you read, you can identify a lively or concrete quotation with a highlighter or by highlighting text in a digital document.
- **Paraphrasing** is fully rewording the author's ideas in your own words. You can paraphrase an important passage in the margin of a printout or on a note card, or in a computer file.

■ **Summarizing** is reducing the author's main point down to the essentials. To remind you of what your sources say, you can attach a summary to the first page of a printout or insert it at the top of a computer file.

Quoting

To quote from a source directly, copy the quotation carefully by hand or paste it electronically. Reproduce the words, spelling, order, and punctuation exactly, even if they're unusual. Put quotation marks around the material so you'll remember that it's a direct quotation, and record the page number(s) where the quotation appears in the source. If you take out one or more irrelevant words, indicate the omission with an ellipsis mark (. . .). If you need to add wording, especially so that a selection makes sense, enclose your addition in brackets [like this].

Quote sparingly, selecting only strong passages that might add support and authority to your assertions. A quotation might contain especially convincing evidence, or it might be a passage where the author has captured a point eloquently.

Paraphrasing

For more on quotations and ellipsis marks, see D3 in the Quick Editing Guide, beginning on p. Q-61, or handbook sections 33 and 35.

Paraphrasing is fully rewording the author's ideas in your own words. It is a useful way to walk your readers through the points made in the original source. When paraphrasing, express an author's ideas, fairly and accurately, in your own words and sentences. Avoid judging, interpreting, or merely echoing the original. A good paraphrase may retain the organization, emphasis, and details of the original, so it's generally similar in length to the original.

ORIGINAL SOURCE	"In staging an ancient Greek tragedy today, most directors do not mask the actors."
PARAPHRASE THAT'S TOO CLOSE TO THE ORIGINAL	Most directors, in staging an ancient Greek play today, do not mask the actors.
GOOD PARAPHRASE	Few contemporary directors of Greek tragedy insist that their actors wear masks.

To write a good paraphrase, read the entire passage through several times. Divide the passage into its most important ideas or points, either in your mind or by highlighting or annotating the passage. Without looking at the original, restate each idea or point in your own words. Aim to convey the ideas from the source faithfully, without repeating its words or sentence structure. Revise your paraphrase if necessary.

Summarizing

Sometimes you simply want to capture the main ideas of a source "in a nutshell." A summary can save space, distilling detailed text into one or two succinct sentences in your own words. Be careful as you reduce a long passage not to distort the original meaning or emphasis. To remind yourself of what your sources say, you can attach a summary to the first page of a printout or insert it at the top of a computer file.

TAKING NOTES WITH QUOTATIONS, PARAPHRASES, AND SUMMARIES

☐ For each source note, have you identified the source (by the author's last name or a keyword from the title) and the exact page(s) or section where the material appears?

☐ Have you added a companion entry to your working bibliography for each new source?

☐ Have you remained true to the meaning of the original source?

☐ Have you quoted sparingly — selecting striking, short passages?

☐ Have you quoted exactly? Do you use quotation marks around significant words, phrases, and passages from the original sources? Do you use ellipsis marks to show where any words have been omitted and brackets to show where words have been added?

☐ Are most notes in your own words — created by paraphrasing or summarizing?

☐ Have you avoided too closely paraphrasing the source?

Learning by Doing 🎯 Capturing Information from Sources

Identify a substantial paragraph or passage from a source you might use for your research paper or from a reading in this book (selected by you, your small group, or your instructor). Study the passage until you understand it thoroughly. Then use it as you respond to the following activities.

1. Quoting

   Identify one notable quotation from the passage you selected. Write a brief paragraph justifying your selection, explaining why you find it notable and why you might use it in a paper. Share your paragraph with classmates. In what ways were your reasons for selection similar to or different from those of your classmates?

2. Paraphrasing

   Write a paraphrase of your passage. Use your own language to restate what it says without parroting its words or sentence patterns. Share your paraphrase with classmates. What are its strengths and weaknesses? Where might you freshen the language?

3. **Summarizing**

In one or two sentences, summarize the passage you selected. Capture its essence in your own words. Share your summary with classmates. What are its strengths and weaknesses? Where might you simplify or clarify it?

Citing Sources

Once you have good notes full of powerful quotations, useful paraphrases, and concise summaries, you can use this material to support your thesis and main points. Add this support responsibly, identifying both the sources and the ideas or exact words captured from them.

Identifying the Source

Clearly identify when you are using material that comes from a source — whether a quotation, summary, or paraphrase. One effective way to do so is to use a signal phrase, a brief statement that gives credit to the author of the source and announces to your readers that the material that follows comes from a source. Whenever possible, help readers see why you have selected particular sources, why you find their evidence pertinent, or how they support your conclusions. Select the verb that conveys to readers each source's contribution. Here is a list of common signalling verbs:

agrees	denies	expresses	reports
argues	describes	interprets	says
asserts	discusses	notes	states
challenges	emphasizes	observes	suggests
claims	explains	points out	writes

Note that APA style generally uses the past tense: *In his 2019 study of drought-resistant farming practices, Tomassino concluded that . . .*). See Ch. 32 for more on APA style.

Signal phrases show that not only have you read your sources but that you have also absorbed and applied what those sources say about your research question. Try the following strategies to strengthen your introduction of source material.

- Name the author in the sentence that introduces the source:

    As Wood explains, the goal of American education continues to fluctuate between gaining knowledge and applying it (58).

- Add the author's name in the middle of the source material:

    In *Romeo and Juliet*, "That which we call a rose," Shakespeare claims, "By any other name would smell as sweet" (2.2.43–44).

- Note the professional title, affiliation, or relevant experience of a source to add authority and increase the credibility of your source:

> According to Jan Lewis, a tax attorney at Sands and Gonzales, . . .
>
> Recalling her tour of duty in Iraq, Sergeant Nelson noted . . .

- Identify information you collected through field research:

  > When interviewed about the campus disaster plan, Natalie Chan, director of Campus Services, confirmed . . .

- Name the author only in the source citation in parentheses if you want to keep your focus on the topic:

  > A second march on Washington followed the first (Whitlock 83).

- Explain for the reader why you have selected and included the material:

  > As Serrano's three-year investigation of tragic border incidents shows, the current policies carry high financial and human costs.

- Interpret what you see as the point or relevance of the material:

  > Stein focuses on stem-cell research, but his discussion of potential ethical implications (18) also applies to other medical research.

- Relate the source clearly to the thesis or point it supports:

  > Although Robinson analyzes workplace interactions, her conclusions (289–92) suggest the need to look at the issues in schools as well.

- Compare or contrast the point of view or evidence of two sources:

  > While Desmond emphasizes the European economic disputes, Lewis turns to the social stresses that also set the stage for World War II.

Citing the Location of the Source Material

Naming each source in the text of your essay both credits it and helps locate it at the end of your paper in the list of sources, called "Works Cited" (MLA) or "References" (APA). There you provide full publication information so that readers can find your original sources if they wish. To make this connection clear, identify the author and the specific location of the source material you used by tucking it into parentheses after the cited material. (In APA style, also add the date.) If you have already identified the author in a signal phrase, you do not need to repeat it in parentheses.

SOURCE AND LOCATION IDENTIFIED IN PARENTHESES

Teenage girls are especially vulnerable to the focus on body size that permeates popular culture (Saunders 41).

SIGNAL PHRASE IDENTIFIES THE SOURCE

As Saunders notes, teenage girls are especially vulnerable to the focus on body size that permeates popular culture (41).

Learning by Doing Identifying and Citing Your Sources

Work on a section of your draft that mentions several sources. In your file or on a printout, highlight each time you use material from a source. First, check each highlighted passage to be sure that you have named the author or source in a signal phrase and stated the page number for a quotation or paraphrase. (Also add the date in APA style; if no page numbers are listed, give the paragraph number or section heading of the cited material.) Next, check each passage to be sure that you have clearly conveyed to a reader the value or contribution of each source — what it adds to your understanding, how it supports your conclusion, or why you have included it. Exchange drafts with a classmate to benefit from a second opinion.

Integrating Material from Sources

Successfully integrating ideas from sources requires more than just a signal phrase at the beginning of a sentence and a parentheses at the end. To illustrate the art of integrating source material, let's look at a passage from historian Barbara W. Tuchman. In *A Distant Mirror: The Calamitous Fourteenth Century* (Knopf, 1978), Tuchman describes the effects of the famous plague known as the Black Death. In her foreword, she admits that any historian dealing with the Middle Ages faces difficulties. For one, large gaps exist in the records. Here is Tuchman's original wording:

ORIGINAL

A greater hazard, built into the very nature of recorded history, is overload of the negative: the disproportionate survival of the bad side — of evil, misery, contention, and harm. In history this is exactly the same as in the daily newspaper. The normal does not make news. History is made by the documents that survive, and these lean heavily on crisis and calamity, crime and misbehavior, because such things are the subject matter of the documentary process — of lawsuits, treaties, moralists' denunciations, literary satire, papal Bulls [official decree]. No Pope ever issued a Bull to approve of something. Negative overload can be seen at work in the religious reformer Nicolas de Clamanges, who, in denouncing unfit and worldly prelates in 1401, said that in his anxiety for reform he would not discuss the good clerics because "they do not count beside the perverse men."

Disaster is rarely as pervasive as it seems from recorded accounts. The fact of being on the record makes it appear continuous and ubiquitous whereas it is more likely to have been sporadic both in time and place. Besides, persistence of the normal is usually greater than the effect of disturbance, as we know from our own times. After absorbing the news of today, one expects to face a world consisting entirely of strikes, crimes, power failures, broken water mains, stalled trains, school shutdowns, muggers, drug addicts, neo-Nazis, and rapists. The fact is that one can come home in the evening — on a lucky day — without having encountered more than one or two of these phenomena.

Integrating Quotations and Paraphrases

Although you might highlight this passage as you read it, it is too long to include in your paper. Quoting it directly would let your source overshadow your own voice. Instead, you might quote a striking line or so and paraphrase the rest by restating the details in your own words. Here, a writer puts Tuchman's ideas into other words but retains the source author's major points and credits Tuchman.

PARAPHRASE WITH QUOTATION

Tuchman points out that historians find some distortion of the truth hard to avoid for more documentation exists for crimes, suffering, and calamities than for the events of ordinary life. As a result, history may overemphasize the negative. The author reminds us that we are familiar with this process in our news coverage, which treats bad news as more interesting than good news. If we believed that news stories told all the truth, we would feel threatened at all times by technical failures, crime, and violence — but we are threatened only some of the time, and normal life goes on. The good, dull, ordinary parts of our lives do not make the front page, and the praiseworthy tend to be ignored. "No Pope," says Tuchman, "ever issued a Bull to approve of something." But in truth, social upheaval did not prevail as widely as we might think from the surviving documents of medieval life (xviii).

Signal phrase identifying Tuchman as the source

Paraphrase of Tuchman's ideas

Quotation integrated into writer's own statement

Page number of the quotation provided in parentheses

Note that this paraphrase is about half as long as the original, although it conveys most of Tuchman's points. The student doesn't interpret or evaluate Tuchman's ideas — she only passes them on. Paraphrasing helps her emphasize ideas important to her research, letting readers know how these ideas support her thesis than a quoted passage would.

Integrating Summaries

A good summary does not preserve everything from the original but instead captures the gist of the main idea faithfully. Extract the gist of a passage by paring away examples, details, modifiers, and nonessentials. Here is how one student marked up a copy of the excerpt from Tuchman, crossing out elements she decided to omit from her summary.

~~A greater hazard,~~ built into the ~~very~~ nature of recorded history, is ~~overload of the negative:~~ the disproportionate survival of the bad side — ~~of evil, misery, contention, and harm. In history~~ this is exactly the same as in the daily newspaper. ~~The normal does not make news. History is made by the~~ documents that survive, ~~and these~~ lean heavily on crisis and calamity, crime and misbehavior, because such things are the subject matter of the documentary process ~~— of lawsuits, treaties, moralists' denunciations, literary satire, papal Bulls. No Pope ever issued a Bull to approve of something. Negative overload can be seen at work in the religious reformer Nicolas de Clamanges, who, in denouncing unfit and worldly prelates in 1401, said that in his anxiety for reform he would no discuss the good clerics because "they do not count beside the perverse men."~~

Disaster is rarely as pervasive as it seems from recorded accounts. ~~The fact of being on the record makes it appear continuous and ubiquitous whereas~~ it is more likely to have been sporadic both in time and place. Besides, persistence of the normal is usually greater than the effect of disturbance, as we know from our own times. ~~After absorbing the news of today, one expects to face a world consisting entirely of strikes, crimes, power failures, broken water mains, stalled trains, school shutdowns, muggers, drug addicts, neo Nazis, and rapists. The fact is that one can come home in the evening — on a lucky day — without having encountered more than one or two of these phenomena.~~

Rewording what was left, she wrote the following condensed version:

SUMMARY

History, like a morning newspaper, reports more bad than good. Why? Because the documents that have come down to us tend to deal with upheavals and disturbances, which are seldom as extensive and long-lasting as history books might lead us to believe (Tuchman xviii).

For more on avoiding plagiarism and using accepted methods of adding source material, see Ch. 11 and D1 in the Quick Research Guide, p. Q-28.

This summary works because the student did not simply omit the phrases she had crossed out, which would have been choppy and still long. She also didn't use Tuchman's exact words: that would be plagiarism. To make a compact, honest summary that would fit smoothly into her paper, the student had to condense the passage into her own words and express the idea in her own voice.

Synthesizing Ideas and Sources

Regardless of whether you are using quotations, paraphrases, or summaries, you need to figure out how to integrate and synthesize them effectively. Inserting transitional phrases (*in addition, in contrast, more recently, despite*) can guide readers and clarify the relationships among your sources. However, transitions alone are not enough. When you synthesize sources, you are combining the voices of multiple sources into a coherent voice of your own. Although this voice relies on outside sources, it should present an original point of view. After synthesizing sources, you will integrate — combine and mix — the explanations, evidence, and details from your sources with your own thoughts and conclusions. Together these components form a unified whole that conveys your perspective and the evidence that logically supports it.

For more on stating a thesis, see pp. 266–70.

To make sure that your voice isn't drowned out by those of your sources, keep your research question and working thesis — which may still be evolving — in front of you as you integrate information.

Integrating source notes into your own writing generally requires positioning materials in a sequence, fitting them in place, and then reworking and interpreting them to convert them into effective evidence that advances your case. Synthesizing sources and evidence weaves them into a unified whole.

Build your synthesis on critical reading and thinking: pulling together what you read and think, relating ideas and information, and drawing conclusions that go beyond those of your separate sources. If you have a sure sense of your paper's direction, you may find this synthesis fairly easy. On the other hand, if your research question or working thesis has changed or you have unearthed persuasive information at odds with your original direction, consider these questions:

- Taken as a whole, what does all this research indicate?
- What does it actually tell you about the answer to your research question?
- What's the most important thing you've learned?
- What's the most important thing you can tell your readers?

Using Sources Ethically

The complex, lively process of research is enriched by the exchange of ideas. However, discussions of research ethics sometimes reduce that topic to one issue: plagiarism. Plagiarists present someone else's work as their own — whether they dishonestly submit as their own a paper purchased from the Web, pretend that passages copied from an article are their own writing, present the ideas of others without identifying sources, or use someone else's graphics without acknowledgment or permission. Plagiarism is viewed especially seriously in college because it shows a deep disrespect on the part of the offender for the work of the academic world — investigating, evaluating, analyzing, interpreting, and synthesizing ideas. And it may have serious consequences — a failing grade on a paper, a failing grade for a course, or dismissal from the institution.

Although individuals often plagiarize on purpose, it's possible to unintentionally plagiarize others' work, too. Most campus policies penalize both intentional and unintentional plagiarism. Working carefully with sources and treating ideas and expressions of others respectfully can build the skills necessary to avoid attribution mistakes. Educating yourself about the standards of your campus, instructor, and profession also can protect you from ethical errors with heavy consequences.

Avoiding Plagiarism

Keep careful records on what information came from which sources, and check your text citations against your concluding list of sources to be sure that the two correspond. Never use another writer's words or ideas without giving that writer due credit and transforming them into words of your own. If you do use words or ideas without giving credit, you are plagiarizing. When using the first-person pronoun *I* in your essay, be sure that what follows is in fact your own idea, not something you learned from a source. Muddling your own idea with that of your source is just as dishonest as quoting without using quotation marks.

AVOIDING PLAGIARISM

See Ch. 31 for more on citing in MLA style and Ch. 32 for more on citing in APA style.

☐ Have you identified the author of material you quote, paraphrase, or summarize? Have you credited the originator of the facts and ideas you use?

☐ Have you cited the location where the material was published?

☐ Have you clearly shown where another writer's ideas stop and yours begin?

☐ Have you checked each paraphrase or summary against the original for accuracy? Do you use your own words? Do you avoid echoing the words and sentence structures of the original? Do you avoid distorting the original meaning?

☐ Have you checked each quotation against the original for accuracy? Have you used quotation marks for both passages and significant words taken directly from your source? Have you noted the page in the original?

☐ Have you used an ellipsis mark (. . .) to show your omissions from the original? Have you used brackets ([ ]) to indicate your changes or additions to a quotation? Have you avoided distorting the original meaning?

☐ Have you checked that each citation in the text of your essay corresponds to an entry in the Works Cited or References list at the end of your essay?

Writing a Research Paper

Moving from nuggets of information to a smooth, persuasive analysis or argument can be the most challenging part of the research process. Remember that the steps in writing a research paper are similar to the stages in most other writing processes, but in the case of research, you're using outside sources to support your ideas.

Planning with a Thesis Statement

You began gathering material from the library, Internet, and field sources with a question in mind. By now, if your research has been thorough and fruitful, you know your answer and have refined into a clear and direct thesis statement. Working with that thesis in mind, you can organize your ideas and evidence into an outline.

For advice on stating a thesis, see pp. 266–69.

Refine Your Thesis. Your thesis clearly, precisely states the point you want to make. It helps you decide what to say and how to say it. When it is clear to your readers, it prepares them for your scope and general message.

If you've used a working thesis to guide your research, sharpen and refine it before drafting, even if you change it later. Explicitly stating it in your opening is only one option. Sometimes you can craft your opening so that readers know exactly what your thesis is even though you only imply it. (Check this option with your instructor if you're unsure about it.) Make your thesis precise and concrete; don't claim more than you can show. If your paper is argumentative—you take a stand, propose a solution, or evaluate something—make your stand, solution, or appraisal clear.

TOPIC	high cost of child care
RESEARCH QUESTION	What are the consequences of the high costs of child care in America?
THESIS	Working parents, children, and caregivers all lose when child care is so expensive.
REFINED THESIS	The federal government should fund a high-quality child care system, which would benefit families, employers, and caregivers alike.

495

For more on organizing,
drafting, and
developing ideas,
see Chs. 16–18.

Organize Your Ideas. It isn't enough for your paper to describe your research steps or to string data together. Instead, you need to report the significance of what you found, explaining what it means and why it matters. If you began with a clear research question, select and organize your evidence to answer it. But don't be afraid to reorganize around a new question.

If your material resists taking shape, arrange your source notes in an order that makes sense. This new order then becomes a plan to follow as you write. You can write out an informal or a formal outline, perhaps using your software's outline tool. Outlining can help you identify any holes in your research; if you lack source notes for a certain section, reconsider your plan or seek other sources to fill the gap.

Interpret Your Sources. On their own, your source notes are only pieces of information. They need your interpretation to transform them into effective evidence. What does each mean in the context of your thesis? Is it strong enough to bear the weight of your claim? Do you need more evidence to shore up an interesting but ambiguous fact? Keep your sources in their supporting role and your voice in the lead. Alternate statements and support to sustain this balance.

Leave Out Unnecessary Information. Include only material that answers your research question and supports your thesis. When material does fit, consider how to incorporate it effectively and ethically.

Drafting

For more on outlining,
see pp. 273–80.

An outline is only a skeleton until you flesh it out with details. Use yours as a working plan, but change the sections or sequence if you discover a better way as you draft. Even if everything isn't in perfect order, get something down on paper. Start at the beginning or wherever you feel most comfortable.

Citing Your Sources as You Draft

For more on citing
source material,
see pp. 199–200 and
488–90.

Citing sources as you draft saves time when you put your paper into final form. And it prevents unintentional plagiarism. Introduce every idea, fact, quotation, paraphrase, or summary captured from your reading or field research, and immediately provide your readers with the exact source of your material. In MLA style, name the author and give the page of the source. (In APA style, add the date, and give a paragraph number, section heading, or other locator.) If you quote a field source, name the speaker, if possible.

When you use a quotation in your draft, copy and paste the passage from your notes, setting it off with quotation marks. Then include a phrase to integrate the source and show why you've quoted it or what authority it lends to your paper.

If no transition occurs to you as you place a quotation or borrowed idea in your draft, don't sit around waiting for one. A series of slapped-in summaries and quotations makes rough reading, but you can add connective tissue later. Highlight these spots so it's easy to return to them.

Beginning and Ending

Perhaps you will think of a good beginning and conclusion only after you have written the body of your paper. The head and tail of your paper might simply showcase your answer to your initial question. But that is not the only way to begin and end a research paper.

Build to Your Finish. You might start out slowly with a clear account of an event to draw your readers into the paper. You could then build up to a strong finish, saving your strongest argument for the end — after you have presented the evidence to support your thesis. Suppose your paper argues that American children are harmed by the national obsession with sports:

- Begin with a real event so you and your reader are on the same footing.
- Explore that event's implications to prepare your reader for your view.
- State your thesis: "The national obsession with sports must end."
- Present each assertion, and support it with evidence captured from well-chosen sources, moving to your strongest argument.
- End with a rousing call to action to stop sports mania.

For more strategies for opening and concluding, see pp. 286–90.

Sum Up the Findings of Others. Another way to begin a research paper is to summarize the work of other scholars. One research biologist, Edgar F. Warner, has reduced this time-tested opening to a formula.

For more on transitions, see pp. 290–92.

> First, in one or two paragraphs, you review everything that has been said about your topic, naming the most prominent earlier commentators. Next you declare why all of them are wrong. Then you set forth your own claim, and you spend the rest of your paper supporting it.

That pattern may seem cut-and-dried, but it is useful because it places your research and ideas into a historical and conceptual framework. If you browse in specialized journals, you may be surprised to see how many articles begin this way. Of course, one or two other writers may be enough to argue with. For example, a student writing on the American poet Charles Olson starts her research paper by disputing two views of him.

> To Cid Corman, Charles Olson of Gloucester, Massachusetts, is "the one dynamic and original epic poet twentieth-century America has produced" (116). To Allen Tate, Olson is "a loquacious charlatan" (McFinnery 92). The truth lies between these two extremes, nearer to Corman's view.

Whether or not you fully stated your view at the beginning, you will certainly need to make it clear in your closing paragraph. A suggestion: before writing the last lines of your paper, read over what you have written. Then, without referring to your paper, try to put your view into writing.

Learning by Doing 🖋 Focusing with a Reverse Outline

We often think of an outline as something writers make before writing a paper. However, a reverse outline can be created using a piece that has already been written. Using the rough draft of your research paper, create a reverse outline. Strip away most of the writing to reveal the structure of the essay itself: central points, main ideas, topic sentences, and important pieces of evidence or support. What do you notice about the overall outline form? Do the paragraphs seem balanced? Do you see any gaps in logic or supporting evidence? Can you identify areas that might benefit from a different organization? Would your argument be improved if information was organized from least important to most important or vice versa?

For advice on integrating sources and avoiding plagiarism, see Ch. 29.

For more revising and editing strategies, see Ch. 19.

Revising and Editing

Looking over your draft, you may find your essay changing. Don't be afraid to develop a whole new interpretation, shift the organization, strengthen your evidence, drop a section, or add a new one.

For more on using your own voice, see pp. 200–02.

REVISING YOUR DRAFT

☐ Have you said something original, not just heaped up statements by others? Does your voice interpret and unify so that your ideas, not those of your sources, dominate?

For a sample student essay in MLA style, see pp. 521–28; for a sample APA essay, see pp. 549–56.

☐ Is your thesis (or main idea) clear? Do all your points support your main idea? Does all your evidence support your points?

☐ Does each new idea follow from the one before it? Can you see any stronger arrangement? Have you used transitions to connect the parts?

☐ Do you need more — or better — evidence to back up any point? If so, where might you find it?

☐ Are the words that you quote truly memorable? Are your paraphrases and summaries accurate and clear? Have you introduced your sources clearly?

☐ Is the source of every quotation, fact, or idea unmistakably clear?

After you have revised your research paper, edit and proofread it. Pay attention to the details. Carefully check the grammar, word choice, punctuation, and mechanics — and then correct any problems. Check your documentation, too — how you identify sources and how you list the works you cite.

Peer Response ⚙Writing Your Research Paper

For general questions for a peer editor, see p. 309.

Have a classmate or friend read your draft and suggest how you might make your paper more informative, tightly reasoned, and interesting. Ask your peer editor to answer questions such as these about writing from sources:

- What is the research question? Does the writer answer that question?

- How effective is the opening? Does it draw you into the paper?

- How effective is the conclusion? Does it merely restate the introduction? Is it too abrupt or too hurried?

- Is the organization logical and easy to follow? Are there any places where the essay is hard to follow?

- Can you identify which ideas are the writer's and which are from sources?

- Do you have any questions about the writer's evidence or the conclusions drawn from the evidence? Point out any areas where the writer has not fully backed up his or her conclusions.

- If this paper were yours, what is the one thing you would be sure to work on before handing it in?

EDITING FOR CLARITY

For quick reviews of other issues, find the relevant checklist sections in the Quick Editing Guide, on p. Q-37. Turn also to the Quick Format Guide, beginning on p. Q-1. For more detailed help with grammatical issues, see Chs. 33–38.

☐ Have you used commas correctly, especially in complicated sentences that quote or refer to sources? — Quick Editing Guide, D1

☐ Have you punctuated quotations correctly? — Quick Editing Guide, D3

☐ Have you used capital letters correctly, especially in titles of sources? — Quick Editing Guide, D1

☐ Have you used correct manuscript form? — Quick Format Guide, A

☐ Have you used correct documentation style? — Chs. 31 and 32

Documenting Sources

A research paper calls on you to follow special rules for documenting your sources—citing them as you write and listing them at the end of your paper. In humanities courses and the social sciences, most writers follow the style of the Modern Language Association (MLA) or the American Psychological Association (APA). Your instructor will probably suggest which style to follow; if you are not told, use MLA. The first time you prepare a research paper in either style, you'll need extra time to look up exactly what to do in each situation. (See Ch. 31 or 32.)

For more on documentation, see Ch. 31 (MLA), Ch. 32 (APA), or the Quick Research Guide, beginning on p. Q-20.

31 MLA Style for Documenting Sources

For a brief overview of MLA style, see E1–E2 in the Quick Research Guide, pp. Q-31–Q-36. Turn also to the Quick Format Guide beginning on p. Q-1.

For advice about using APA style, see Ch. 32.

For detailed visuals on citing sources in MLA style, see the Source Navigators on pp. 510, 511, 513, and 516.

The *MLA Handbook,* Eighth Edition (MLA, 2016), supplies guidance on crediting sources. MLA style is often used in the humanities, including composition, literature, and foreign languages. Although other disciplines follow other style guides, MLA style can help you get used to scholarly practice. MLA style uses a two-part system to credit sources.

- **In-text citations.** Briefly cite or identify the source in your text, usually by noting the author's last name in your discussion or in parentheses right after the information from the source. In most cases, complete the in-text citation with the page number in the source. To cite sources properly in your text, follow the guidelines in the Citing Sources in MLA Style section on page 502.

- **The Works Cited list.** Provide a full description of the source in a concluding alphabetical list, called "Works Cited." The particular information you list will depend on the type of source you are using — a book, a journal article, a document from a website, a film, a review, a podcast, and so on. To list sources properly in your Works Cited list, look up the model for each type of source in the Listing Sources in MLA Style section beginning on page 506. Follow the model's formatting, punctuation, and spacing.

Credit your source every time you quote, paraphrase, or sum up someone else's ideas. The only general exception is "common knowledge," uncontested information that readers in a field know and accept. Examples might include dates, facts about events, and popular expressions such as proverbs. Identify your source any time your readers would — or might — wonder about it, especially if you are unsure what they consider controversial. At the end, make sure that every source cited in the text of your final draft also appears in your list of works cited.

Citing and Listing Sources in MLA Style

Skim the following directory to find models to guide you as you cite and list your sources. The models are organized according to questions you might ask about the source. See pages 520–28 for a sample paper that illustrates MLA style.

(continued)

Citing and Listing Sources in MLA Style *(continued)*

Citing Sources in MLA Style

The core of an MLA citation is the author of the source. Giving that person's last name in your text points your readers to the corresponding entry in your list of works cited. In addition to this name, provide a specific location, usually a page number, identifying where the material appears in the original source, such as (Valero 231). This basic form applies whatever the type of source — article, book, or web page.

As you check your MLA style, keep in mind these three questions:

- Who is the author?
- What type of source is it?
- How are you capturing the source material?

Who Is the Author?

Individual Author Not Named in the Sentence

Place the author's last name in parentheses, right after the source information, to keep readers focused on the sequence and content of your sentences.

One approach to the complex politics of Puerto Rican statehood is to return to the island's colonial history (Negrón-Muntaner 3).

Author with page

Individual Author Named in the Sentence

Name the author in your sentence, perhaps with credentials or experience noted, to capitalize on the persuasive value of the author's "expert" status.

The analysis of filmmaker and scholar Frances Negrón-Muntaner connects Puerto Rican history and politics with cultural influences (xvii).

Author
Page

Two Authors

Include each author's last name either in your sentence or in parentheses.

Ferriter and Toibin note Irish historical objectivity about the famine (5).

Irish historians tend to report the famine dispassionately (Ferriter and Toibin 5).

Three or More Authors

Name the first author in parentheses and follow it with "et al." (the Latin abbreviation for "and others"). Identify the source the same way in your list of works cited.

Between 1870 and 1900, cities grew at an astonishing rate (Roark et al. 671).

Organization as Author

If a source is sponsored by a corporation, a professional society, or another group, name the organization as the author if no one else is specified. Don't give page numbers for web sources unless they are specifically listed on the site.

Each year, the Kids Count program alerts children's advocates about the status of children in their state (Annie E. Casey Foundation).

Author of a Work in a Collection

Cite the author of the specific work, not the editor of the collection, in the text of your essay. Later, in the Works Cited list, you'll list that editor as well.

Amy Tan explains the "Englishes" of her childhood and family (32).

Unidentified Author

For a source with an unknown author, supply the complete title in your sentence or the first main word or two of the title in parentheses.

Due to download codes and vinyl's beauty, album sales are up ("Back to Black" 1).

Same Author with Multiple Works

If you are citing several works by the same author, the author's name alone won't identify which work you mean. Add the full title, or identify it with a few key words. For example, you would cite two books by Bill McKibben, *Deep Economy* and *Eaarth: Making a Life on a Tough New Planet,* as follows.

McKibben cites advocates of consistent economic expansion (*Deep Economy* 10) yet calls growth "the one big habit we finally must break" (*Eaarth* 48).

Different Authors of Separate Works Cited Together

Occasionally you may want to cite more than one source for the same information. List these sources in parentheses and separate them with a semicolon.

Ray Charles and Quincy Jones worked together for many years and maintained a strong friendship throughout Charles's life (Jones 58-59; Lydon 386).

What Type of Source Is It?

Because naming the author is the core of a citation, the basic form applies to any type of source. Even so, a few types of sources may require additional information.

> Use quotation marks in MLA style for titles of articles. Use italics for titles of books, periodicals, and websites. For more style conventions, see pp. 506–07.

Multivolume Work

Add both volume and page numbers, with a colon between.

Malthus has long been credited with this conservative shift in population theory (Durant and Durant 11: 400-03).

Volume number ⎯⎯⎯⎯⎯

Indirect Source

If possible, find the original source. If you can't access it, add "qtd. in" to show that the material was "quoted in" the source you cite.

Author of original source ⎯⎯⎯⎯ Zill says that, psychologically, children in stepfamilies, even those living in a two-parent
Author of source you used ⎯⎯⎯⎯ household, most resemble children in single-parent families (qtd. in Derber 119).

Visual Material

For advice about permission to use visuals, see B1 in the Quick Format Guide, p. Q-8.

When you include a visual, help your reader connect it to your text. In your discussion, identify the artist or the artwork, and refer to its figure number.

Johnson's 1870 painting *Life in the South* is a sentimental depiction of African Americans after the Civil War (see fig. 1).

Below the visual, supply a figure number and title, including the source.

Fig. 1. Eastman Johnson, *Life in the South*, High Museum of Art, Atlanta.

Source without Page Numbers

Web sources rarely supply page numbers. Only list a section, paragraph, or screen number if one is given.

The new arts initiative will bring community-based art therapies to military patients and veterans around the country (National Endowment for the Arts).

Iyengar notes that proximity to public transportation can be a significant factor in the success of a new restaurant (par. 12).

How Are You Capturing the Source Material?

For more on capturing and integrating source material, see Ch. 29.

How you capture source material—summarizing it, paraphrasing it in your own words, or quoting it in a short or long quotation—affects how you credit it. Always set off the source's words using quotation marks or the indented form for a long "block" quotation.

If material, quoted or not, comes from a specific place in a source, add a page number or other location, such as the section number listed in an electronic source or the chapter or line in a literary work. No page number is needed for general material (an overall theme or concept) or a source without page numbers (a website, film, recording, performance).

Summary of an Entire Work

Terrill's *Malcolm X: Inventing Radical Judgment* takes a fresh look at the rhetorical power and strategies of Malcolm X's speeches.

Specific Summary or Paraphrase

One analysis of Malcolm X's 1964 speech "The Ballot or the Bullet" concludes that it exhorts listeners to the radical action of changing vantage point (Terrill 129-31).

If you paraphrase or summarize a one-page article, no page number is needed because it will appear in your Works Cited list.

Vacuum-tube audio equipment is making a comeback, with aficionados praising the warmth and glow from the tubes, as well as the sound (Patton).

Blended Paraphrase and Quotation

When integrate part of a quotation into your own sentence, clearly distinguish the two. Use quotation marks to set apart the words of your source.

To avoid generalizing about "people-with-dementia" (Pearce xxii), the author simply uses names.

Brief Quotation Introduced Formally

Vecsey states his claim for baseball: "No other sport has this endurance" (6).

Brief Quotation Integrated in the Sentence

"No other sport" (6), according to Vecsey's *Baseball: A History of America's Favorite Game*, requires players to tolerate double- or tripleheaders.

Double- and tripleheaders require more stamina than any "other sport" (Vecsey 6).

Only baseball, according to Vecsey, "has this endurance" (6).

Long Quotation

When a quotation is longer than four typed lines, double-space and indent the entire quotation one-half inch instead of using quotation marks. If it is one paragraph or less, begin its first line without extra paragraph indentation. Use ellipsis marks (. . .) to show any omission from the middle. Move the parentheses with the location after the final period of the quoted material.

Cynthia Griffin Wolff comments on Emily Dickinson's incisive use of language:

> Language, of course, was a far subtler weapon than a hammer. Dickinson's verbal maneuvers would increasingly reveal immense skill in avoiding a frontal attack; she preferred the silent knife of irony to the strident battering of loud complaint. . . . Scarcely submissive, she had acquired the cool calculation of an assassin. (170-71)

Colon follows complete sentence

No quotation marks

Indent ½"

Page numbers listed after final period

Quotation from a Sacred Text

Instead of the page, note the version, book, chapter, and/or verse numbers.

Once again, the author alludes to the same passage: "What He has seen and heard, of that He testifies" (*New American Bible*, John 3.32).

Literary Quotation

For a quotation from a novel or short story, first give the page number in your own copy. If possible, add the section or chapter so that the passage could be found in any edition.

In *A Tale of Two Cities*, Dickens describes Stryver as "shouldering himself (morally and physically) into companies and conversations" (110; bk. 2, ch. 4).

For a quotation from a play, list the act, scene, and line numbers, separated by periods.

In Shakespeare's *Othello*, Iago says that love "is merely a lust of the blood and a permission of the will" (1.3.326).

For a quotation from a poem, add a slash to show where a new line begins. Use "line" or "lines" in the first reference but only numbers in subsequent references, as in these examples from William Wordsworth's "The World Is Too Much with Us." The first reference:

Slash between lines —— "The world is too much with us; late and soon, / Getting and spending, we lay waste our powers" (lines 1-2).

The next reference:

Line number —— "Or hear old Triton blow his wreathed horn" (14).

Separate part and line numbers by a period.

In "Ode: Intimations of Immortality," Wordsworth ponders the truths of human existence, "Which we are toiling all our lives to find, / In darkness lost, the darkness of the grave" (8.116-17).

CITING IN-TEXT SOURCES IN MLA STYLE

☐ Have you acknowledged all material from a source?

☐ Have you placed your citation right after your quotation, paraphrase, summary, or other reference to the source?

☐ Have you identified the author of each source in your text or in parentheses?

☐ Have you noted a page number or other location, if available, in parentheses after the source material?

☐ Have you listed volume or poetry line numbers when needed?

☐ Have you checked your final draft to be sure that every source cited in your text also appears in your list of works cited?

Listing Sources in MLA Style

For a sample Works Cited page, see pp. 527–28 and p. Q-3 in the Quick Format Guide.

At the end of your paper, list the sources from which you have actually cited material. Center the title "Works Cited" at the top of a new, double-spaced page. Alphabetize entries by authors' last names or, for works with no author, by title. When an entry exceeds one line, indent the following lines one-half inch. (In Microsoft Word, use your software menu — Format-Paragraph-Indentation — to set this special "hanging" indentation.)

In your Works Cited entry, list the author and title, following each one with a period. Next, you'll need to list information for what MLA calls "containers" — the larger work where you found the source. If you are citing a specific story in an anthology, that story title is the title of your source, and the anthology is its container. If an encyclopedia entry is your source, the encyclopedia is its container. Some sources may have more than one container. If a container is itself part of a larger container (a scholarly journal that you found in an academic database, for example), list the larger container (the database) after the smaller one (the journal). Some sources are self-contained; for example, if you're citing an entire book, the book title is the title of your source, and there is no separate container.

The elements of a container — including, when applicable, its title; the names of contributors such as editors or translators; the version or edition; the volume and issue numbers; the publisher; the date of publication; and a location such as the page number, DOI, permalink, or URL — are separated by commas. The end of a container is marked by a period. By listing these containers, you are ensuring that other researchers can find the same sources you found. For detailed visuals on citing sources in MLA style, see the Source Navigators on pages 510, 511, 513, and 516.

Here are a few general formatting guidelines for your citations:

- Italicize the titles of longer works, such as books, magazines, and websites.
- Place the titles of shorter works, such as articles or poems, in quotation marks.
- Look on the title page for the publisher's name; if no name is listed there, look on the copyright page (usually on the back of the title page). Use publishers' complete names, except for terms such as *Inc.* and *Co.*; retain terms such as *Books* and *Press*. Use *U* and *P* for *University* and *Press*.
- MLA no longer requires you to list location information for book publishers.
- List the latest publication date as listed on the copyright and title pages. For a website, use the copyright date or the date of the most recent update. Check the bottom of a web page or the "About" page to find the date.
- If the title of a website and the publisher are the same or similar, list only the title of the site.
- Abbreviate all months except May, June, and July.
- If the source has no date, give your date of access at the end: Accessed 24 Nov. 2019.
- Give a permalink or a DOI (digital object identifier) if a source has one. If it doesn't, include a URL (omitting the protocol, such as http://).

Who Is the Author?

Individual Author

Shapiro, Dani. *Inheritance: A Memoir of Genealogy, Paternity, and Love.* Knopf, 2019.

Two Authors

Name the authors in the order in which they are listed on the title page.

Last name first to alphabetize ⟶
Regular name order ⟶

Vincent, Lynn, and Sarah Vladic. *Indianapolis: The True Story of the Worst Sea Disaster in U. S. Naval History*. Simon & Schuster, 2018.

Three or More Authors

Name all the authors, or follow the name of the first author with the abbreviation "et al." (Latin for "and others"). Identify the source in the same way you cite it in the text.

Hunt, Lynn, et al. *The Making of the West*. 6th ed., Bedford/St. Martin's, 2019.

Same Author with Multiple Works

Arrange the author's works alphabetically by title. Use the author's name for the first entry only; for the rest, replace the name with three hyphens.

Coates, Ta-Nehisi. *Between the World and Me*. Spiegel & Grau, 2015.

---. *We Were Eight Years in Power: An American Tragedy*. One World, 2017.

Organization as Author

When the author is a corporation, a government agency, or some other organization, begin with the name of the organization.

Author ⟶

National Environmental Health Association. *Professional Food Manager*. 5th ed., Wiley, 2017.

Author and Editor

If your paper focuses on the work or its author, cite the author first.

Joyce, James. *A Portrait of the Artist as a Young Man: Centennial Edition*. 1916. Edited by Seamus Deane, Penguin Books, 2016.

If your paper focuses on the editor or the edition used, cite the editor first.

Deane, Seamus, editor. *A Portrait of the Artist as a Young Man: Centennial Edition*. By James Joyce, 1916. Penguin Books, 2016.

Author and Translator

If your paper focuses on the translation, cite the translator first.

Dostoyevsky, Fyodor. *Crime and Punishment*. Translated by Oliver Ready, Penguin Books, 2015.

Ready, Oliver, translator. *Crime and Punishment*. By Fyodor Dostoyevsky, Penguin Books, 2015.

Unidentified Author

"2012 Cars: Safety." *Consumer Reports*, Apr. 2012, pp. 72–76.

What Type of Source Is It?

Once you find the author format that fits, think about the type of source you are using. Did you consult a printed version of the source, or did you view it electronically? Look for the model that best matches how you found your source, or adapt a model if needed. Review the Source Navigators on pages 510, 511, 513, and 516 for a closer look.

Periodical Articles

Article from a Print Journal

Provide the volume number, issue number, season or month and year, and page numbers for all journal articles.

Pollmann-Schult, Matthias. "Parenthood and Life Satisfaction: Why Don't Children Make People Happy?" *Journal of Marriage and Family,* vol. 76, no. 2, Apr. 2014, pp. 319-36.

> Issue — Volume — Pages

Article from an Online Journal

Supply the information that you would for a print article, and include the URL of the article. If the article is paginated, include page numbers.

Giorgio-Pirkey, Lucy. "Journeys Inward: Coming to Academic Voice." *English Journal,* vol. 108, no. 3, 2019, ncte.org/library/NCTEFiles/Resources/Journals/EJ/1083-jan2019/EJ1083Jan19Journeys.pdf.

Article Accessed from an Electronic Database

If you find a source through a library database or a subscription service, include the name of the service and a permalink or DOI. If the database does not provide a permalink or a DOI, list only the basic URL for the database home page.

Gross, Magdalena H, and Luke Terra. "What Makes Difficult History Difficult?" *Phi Delta Kappan,* vol. 99, no. 8, May 2018, pp. 51-56. *ERIC,* doi:0.1177/0031721718775680.

Article from a Print Magazine

Give the month and year of the issue or its specific date. If the article's pages are not consecutive, add a + after its initial page.

Hayasaki, Erika. "End Pain Forever." *Wired,* May 2017, pp. 84–91.

Marano, Hara Estroff. "Queen of Consciousness." *Psychology Today,* Feb. 2015, pp. 29+.

Article from an Online Magazine

Christakis, Nicholas A. "How AI Will Rewire Us." *The Atlantic,* Apr. 2019, www.theatlantic.com/magazine/archive/2019/04/robots-human-relationships/583204/.

Article Accessed from an Electronic Database

1 The complete name(s) of the author(s)

2 The title and subtitle of the article

3 The title and subtitle of the journal

4 The volume and issue number, if given

5 The month or season and year of publication

6 The complete page numbers of the article

7 The name of the database

8 The DOI of the article, or, if none, the URL

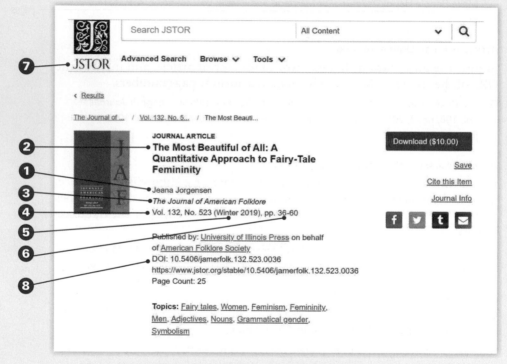

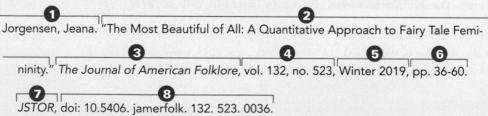

Jorgensen, Jeana. "The Most Beautiful of All: A Quantitative Approach to Fairy Tale Femininity." *The Journal of American Folklore*, vol. 132, no. 523, Winter 2019, pp. 36-60. *JSTOR*, doi: 10.5406. jamerfolk. 132. 523. 0036.

Article from a Print Magazine

① The complete name(s) of the author(s)

② The title and subtitle (if any) of the article

③ The title of the magazine

④ The date of publication

⑤ The complete page numbers for the article

PORTFOLIO

② BEATS GENERATION

The Nigerian musicians who are changing the sound of global pop.

PHOTOGRAPHS BY NAMSA LEUBA

Nearly two decades ago, in 2000, a CD called "Body & Soul: The Beginning" showed up in the markets of Lagos, Nigeria—an album that quickly became a regional hit, and, more gradually, helped spark a musical movement that has changed the sound of global pop. It was the work of Plantashun Boiz, a young trio that might accurately have been described as a boy band. The members—known as Tuface, BlackFace, and Faze—sometimes performed in matching outfits and often sang in matching voices, delivering plaintive, briskly syncopated love songs that bore traces of R. Kelly and Destiny's Child. Careful listeners heard something else, too: a declaration of local pride. "Ememma," one of the most popular tracks, captured the emergence of a hybrid new form of R. & B., propelled by a loping kick-drum beat and slippery verses delivered in Idoma, Tuface's native language.

Tuface was born Innocent Idibia, and his musical education was influenced by his father's record collection, which included albums by such Nigerian heroes as Fela Kuti, the funk-obsessed firebrand, and Bongos Ikwue, a singer-songwriter who specialized in an easeful sort of dance music. Like many pioneers, Idibia is less a virtuoso than a brilliant synthesist, with a knack for drawing together far-flung influences to create songs that seem plainspoken and homegrown. In 2004, recording under the name 2Face Idibia, he released a single called "Nfana Ibaga," which pointed toward the future of Nigerian pop. Idibia's song was talky but tuneful, drawing from hip-hop and dancehall reggae, and it built to an infectious, polyglot chorus:

Nfana ibaga
Never give another man yawa o
So the reason why I say "*nfana ibaga*"
Is that I got my conscience on my side.

The titular phrase is an expression from the Efik language that means, essentially, "no problem." *Yawa* is a Nigerian Pidgin term for "problem." The song became not just a local hit but a global export; Beenie Man, the Jamaican star, appeared on the remix, trying and failing to upstage his host.

In the years since Idibia's solo début, the Lagos music scene has produced a riot of new stars and new sounds. The music, which tends to be frenetic but playful, is sometimes called Afrobeats. (The term is often pluralized, to distinguish it from Afrobeat, Fela Kuti's brand of funk.) It lives not just in Lagos but also in London, a secondary hub, and in other cities worldwide. One of its biggest boosters has been the Canadian rapper Drake, who made a series of recordings with the Afrobeats star WizKid; their collaboration "One Dance," from 2016, is among the most popular songs of this decade in any genre.

This summer, the photographer Namsa Leuba went to Lagos to photograph performers from the city's astonishingly fertile music scene. Idibia was there; he is now known as 2Baba and treated as a kind of Afrobeats godfather. (In 2015, he threw himself a fortieth-birthday party that was simultaneously a national celebration and an all-star concert.) Also on hand were a number of younger performers, all of whom have inherited Idibia's conviction that the sound of Lagos can—in fact, should—echo across the globe.

—Kelefa Sanneh **①**

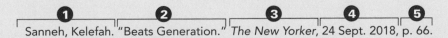

Sanneh, Kelefah. "Beats Generation." *The New Yorker*, 24 Sept. 2018, p. 66.

① **②** **③** **④** **⑤**

Article from a Print Newspaper

If the newspaper has different editions, indicate after the date the one where the article can be found. For example, for the national edition you would include "natl. ed." If the pages for the article are not consecutive, add a + after its initial page.

Santora, Marc, and John Surico. "Angry about Fare Cuts, Uber Drivers in New York Warn of Reprisals." *The New York Times*, 2 Feb. 2016, New York ed., p. A23.

Article from an Online Newspaper

Pope, Denise. "The Right Way to Choose a College." *The Wall Street Journal*, 22 Mar. 2019, www.wsj.com/articles/the-right-way-to-choose-a-college-11553266896.

Editorial

Rampell, Catherine. "Americans' Loyalty to Employers and Insurance Plans Is Costing Them Billions." *The Washington Post*, 10 Nov. 2015, www.washingtonpost.com/opinions/americans-loyalty-to-employers-and-insurance-plans-is-costing-them-billions/2015/11/09/8e04a9de-8726-11e5-be39-0034bb576eee_story.html. Editorial.

Letter to the Editor

If the letter has no title, place "Letter" at the end of the entry.

Berlinger, Nancy. *The New Yorker*, 24 Aug. 2015, www.newyorker.com/magazine/2015/08/24/the-mail-from-the-august-24-2015-issue. Letter.

Review

Include the words "Review of" before the title of the work reviewed.

Boyagoda, Randy. "The Great Calvinist American Novel." Review of *Lila,* by Marilynne Robinson. *The National Review*, 31 Dec. 2014, pp. 47-49.

Books

Print Book

Page, Scott E. *The Model Thinker: What You Need to Know to Make Data Work for You.* Basic Books, 2018.

Online Book

After the print publication information, include the title of the site in italics and the DOI, if available, or URL for the work.

Bricker, Darrell, and John Ibbitson. *Empty Planet: The Shock of Global Population Decline.* McClelland & Stewart, 2019. *Google Books*, books.google.com/books?id=D3ZCDwAAQBAJ&source=gbs_navlinks_s.

Print Book

1 The complete author's name

2 The title and subtitle of the book

3 The publisher

4 The date of publication

FREDERICK

DOUGLASS

PROPHET *of* FREEDOM

2

DAVID W. BLIGHT

1

3

Simon & Schuster

NEW YORK   LONDON   TORONTO   SYDNEY   NEW DELHI

Copyright © 2018 by David W. Blight

4

All rights reserved, including the right to reproduce this book or portions thereof
in any form whatsoever. For information, address Simon & Schuster Subsidiary
Rights Department, 1230 Avenue of the Americas, New York, NY 10020.

1　　　　2　　　　　　　3　　　4

Blight, David W. *Frederick Douglass: Prophet of Freedom.* Simon & Schuster, 2018.

E-book

Turkle, Sherry. *Reclaiming Conversation: The Power of Talk in a Digital Age*. Kindle
ed., Penguin Press, 2015.

Multivolume Work

To cite the full work, add the number of volumes ("vols.") after the date or
dates of publication.

Bindman, David, and Henry Louis Gates, Jr. *The Image of the Black in Western Art*.
Belknap Press of Harvard UP, 2010-14. 5 vols.

To cite only one volume, give its number before the publisher. If you wish,
you then can add the total number of volumes after the date or dates.

Bindman, David, and Henry Louis Gates, Jr. *The Image of the Black in Western Art*. Vol. 3,
Belknap Press of Harvard UP, 2010-14. 5 vols.

Revised Edition

Comins, Neil F. *Discovering the Essential Universe*, 6th ed., W. H. Freeman, 2015.

Book Published in a Series

After the publication information, add the series name as it appears on the
title page, followed by any series number.

Whatmore, Richard. *What Is Intellectual History?* Polity Press, 2015. What Is History?

Parts of a Book

Give the author of the part first. Add the editor of the book after its title. For
print books or PDF files with fixed page numbers, include the selection page
numbers after the publication information.

Selection from a Book

Katz, Jonathan Ned. "The Invention of Heterosexuality." *Race, Class, and Gender in
the United States*, edited by Paula S. Rothenberg, 10th ed., Worth Publishers,
2016, pp. 47-58.

Two or More Works from the Same Edited Collection

If you list more than one selection from an anthology, prepare and refer to an
entry for the collection (instead of repeating it for each selection).

Beauchamp, Tom L. "Justifying Physician-Assisted Deaths." LaFollette, pp. 85-91.

LaFollette, Hugh. *Ethics in Practice: An Anthology*. 4th ed., Wiley-Blackwell, 2014.

Velleman, J. David. "Against the Right to Die." LaFollette, pp. 92-100.

Preface, Introduction, Foreword, or Afterword

Davis, Angela. Foreword. *When They Call You a Terrorist: A Black Lives Matter
Memoir*, by Patrice Khan-Cullors and Asha Bandele, St. Martin's P, 2018, pp. v-xiv.

Article from a Reference Work

For online reference works or well-known references such as *Webster's, World Book Encyclopedia,* or *Encyclopaedia Britannica,* you do not need to include an editor, publisher, or place of publication. For works that are organized alphabetically, you do not need to list the volume or page numbers. If an article's author is identified by initials, check the list of contributors, which should supply the full name.

Durante, Amy M. "Finn Mac Cumhail." *Encyclopedia Mythica,* 17 Apr. 2011,
    www.pantheon.org/articles/f/finn_mac_cumhail.html.

Other Printed or Electronic Documents

Government Document

Generally, the "author" will be the government, the name of the department, and the agency, if there is one, separated by commas. If the document identifies an author or editor, give that name after the title.

United States, Department of Health and Human Services. *Using Evidence*
    to Drive Decision-Making in Government. Office of the Assistant Secre-
    tary for Planning and Evaluation, 6 Mar. 2019, aspe.hhs.gov/pdf-report/
    using-evidence-drive-decision-making-government.

Pamphlet

U.S. Food and Drug Administration Office of Women's Health. *Your Glucose Meter.*
    FDA Office of Women's Health, 2014.

Doctoral Dissertation

If the study is unpublished, place the title in quotation marks; if published, italicize the title. For a dissertation, follow the title with "Dissertation."

Cameron, Kelsey. "The Matter of Identity: Digital Media, Television, and Embodied
    Difference." Dissertation, U of Pittsburgh, 2019.

Online Sources

Entire Website

If a website does not have an update date or publication date, include your date of access at the end. If the site has no author (neither individual nor organizational), begin with the title. If the site has no title, include an identification such as "Home page."

Glazier, Loss Pequeño, director. *Electronic Poetry Center.* U of Pennsylvania, 2019, writing.
    upenn.edu/epc/.

Short Work from a Website

1 The complete name of the author(s), if any

2 The title and subtitle of the work

3 The title of the website

4 The publication date of the work or the date the site was last updated

5 The URL

6 (If no date for #4) The date you accessed the site

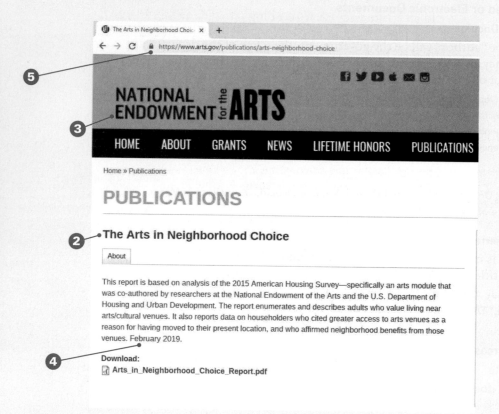

2 "The Arts in Neighborhood Choice." **3** *National Endowment for the Arts,* **4** Feb. 2019,

5 www.arts.gov/publications/arts-neighborhood-choice.

Short Work from a Website

Place the short work in quotation marks before the name of the site. If no author is given, begin with the title.

Waldman, Annie. "How Hospitals Are Failing Black Mothers." *ProPublica*, 27 Dec. 2017,
    www.propublica.org/article/how-hospitals-are-failing-black-mothers.

Home Page for a Campus Department or Course

Department of Sociology. *Syracuse University, Maxwell School of Citizenship and Public
    Affairs*, www.maxwell.syr.edu/soc/.

See the directory on pp. 501-02 for entries for other electronic sources, including books and articles.

Blog or Blog Post

Cite a blog as you would an entire website. Cite a blog post as you would a short work from a website.

Eye Level. Smithsonian American Art Museum, 2019, americanart.si.edu/blog/.

Ho, Melissa. "American Art and the Vietnam War." *Eye Level*, Smithsonian American Art
    Museum, 14 Mar. 2019, americanart.si.edu/blog/american-art-and-vietnam-war.

Social Media Post

Insert the entire post in quotation marks and position it as the title.

Bedford English. "Bedford New Scholar Skye Roberson shares details on Scaffold-
    ing Multimodal Projects through Collaborative Learning: http://ow.ly/Wbtf-
    50n7OAg." *Facebook*, 16 Mar. 2019, www.facebook.com/BedfordEnglish/
    posts/10156251571174607.

The Nobel Prize. "The human body contains about 60% water—without it humans
    wouldn't survive. Read about how some Nobel Laureates have been inspired to inves-
    tigate this liquid further." *Twitter*, 22 Mar. 2019, 8:09 a.m., twitter.com/NobelPrize/
    status/1109109734752337921.

Visual or Audio Sources

Advertisement

Oceania Cruises. *Travel + Leisure*, Apr. 2019, p. 16. Advertisement.

Comic or Cartoon

Start with the cartoonist's name, and end with a label identifying the work as a comic strip or cartoon.

Flake, Emily. *The New Yorker*, 14 Sept. 2015, p. 54. Cartoon.

Photograph or Work of Art

Supply the place (museum or gallery and city) where the photograph is housed. If you are citing it from a published source, provide that source's publication information at the end. For a family or personal photograph, identify who took it and when.

Stieglitz, Alfred. *Self Portrait.* J. Paul Getty Museum, Los Angeles. *Stieglitz: A Beginning Light*, by Katherine Hoffman, Yale UP, 2004, p. 251.

Mann, Sally. *Jessie #25.* 2004, National Gallery of Art, Washington, D.C. Photograph.

Botticelli, Sandro. *The Birth of Venus.* 1482-86, Uffizi Gallery, Florence.

Online Visual

For graphs, charts, or other visuals accessed online, include the name of the website and the URL.

"Religious Affiliation in the US: 2003-17." *ABC News*, 10 May. 2019, abcnews.go.com/ Politics/protestants-decline-religion-sharply-shifting-religious-landscape-poll/ story?id=54995663.

Sound Recording

Begin with the name of the artist, composer, speaker, writer, or other contributor, based on your interest in the recording. For an audio clip accessed on the Web, end with the URL.

Bach, Johann Sebastian. *Bach: Violin Concertos.* Performances by Itzhak Perlman and Pinchas Zukerman, English Chamber Orchestra, EMI, 2002.

Podcast

Begin with the name of the performer or host, based on your interest in the podcast. After the recording date, list the URL.

Graber, Cynthia, and Nicola Twilley. "Can Diet Stop Alzheimer's?" *Gastropod*, season 12, 11 Mar. 2019, gastropod.com/can-diet-stop-alzheimers/.

Television or Radio Program

If you are citing a specific episode, place it in quotation marks. Place the name of the program in italics. Include the network. If you viewed the program online, include a URL.

"The Pension Gamble." *Frontline*, PBS, WGBH, Boston, 23 Oct. 2018.

"At Last, a Fitting Farewell for Richard III." *Weekend Edition*, National Public Radio, KCFR, Denver, 28 Mar. 2015.

Film or Video

If you are citing the work of a particular person, start with that individual's name.

Coogler, Ryan, director. *Black Panther.* Walt Disney Studios Motion Pictures, 2018.

For videos found on the Web, give the URL after the publication information.

"Tornadoes 101." *National Geographic*, accessed 3 June 2019, video.nationalgeographic. com/video/news/101-videos/00000144-0a31-d3cb-a96c-7b3d903d0000.

Live Performance

A Doll's House, Part 2. By Lucas Hnath, directed by Les Waters. Huntington Theatre Company, Boston, 5 Jan. 2019.

Field Sources

Personal Interview

Sokol, Allegra. Personal interview, 5 Aug. 2019.

Broadcast Interview

Begin with the name of the person who was interviewed, followed by "Interview by" and the interviewer's name, if relevant.

Johnson, Mat. "Mat Johnson on 'Loving Day' and Life as a 'Black Boy' Who Looks White." Interview by Terry Gross. *Fresh Air*, National Public Radio, KCFR, Denver, 29 May 2015.

Published Interview

Musk, Elon. "Interviewing Elon Musk." Interview by David Gelles. *The New York Times*, 19 Aug. 2018, p. A2.

Speech or Lecture

Carr, Nicholas. "The World Is Not the Screen: How Computers Shape Our Sense of Place." Radcliffe Institute for Advanced Study, Harvard University, Cambridge, 3 Mar. 2015.

Personal Letter

Rosenthal, Mark. Letter to the author, 1 Oct. 2019.

Email

After the author, list the subject line in quotation marks, followed by the recipient and the date.

Olayo, Sonja. "Upcoming Lecture." Received by Dan Levine, 23 May 2019.

Posting to an Electronic Mailing List

Yen, Jessica. "Quotations within Parentheses (Study Measures)." Copyediting-L, 18 Mar. 2016, list.indiana.edu/sympa/arc/copyediting-l/2016-03/msg00492.html.

Daniel-Gittens, Kathy-Ann. "Debate: Is There a Role for Badges in Higher Education?" *Humanities and Social Sciences Online*, 9 Oct. 2015, tlcwebinars.wordpress.com/2015/10/08/debate-is-there-a-role-for-badges-in-higher-educatio/.

FORMATTING THE WORKS CITED LIST

☐ Have you begun each entry with the right pattern for the author's name?

☐ Have you used quotation marks and italics correctly for titles?

☐ Have you followed the exact punctuation — periods, commas, colons, parentheses — in your entry?

☐ Have you accurately recorded the name of the author, title, and publisher?

☐ Have you checked any entry from a citation management system as carefully as your own entries?

☐ Have you arranged your entries in alphabetical order?

☐ Have you checked your final list against your text citations so that every source appears in both places?

☐ Have you double-spaced your list and set one-inch margin on all sides?

☐ Have you begun the first line of each entry at the left margin, indenting each additional line one-half inch?

A Sample MLA Research Paper

For more on MLA paper format, see the Quick Format Guide, p. Q-20.

In her paper "Meet Me in the Middle: The Student, the State, and the School," Candace Rardon investigates the rising costs of a college education and how schools have responded to the problem. Besides incorporating many features of effective research papers, this paper also illustrates the conventions for citing and listing sources in MLA style. The marginal annotations explain MLA formatting and citation guidelines and point out effective research writing practices. No cover page is needed for an MLA paper. Because an outline was required by this student's instructor, it precedes the paper shown here. Although this sample paper is presented for easy reading in a textbook, your paper should use the type style and size that MLA suggests: Times New Roman font, 12-point size. Set one-inch margins on all sides, double-space all lines, and turn off automatic hyphenation. Use your software's Help feature or visit the campus computer lab for assistance setting up this format for your file.

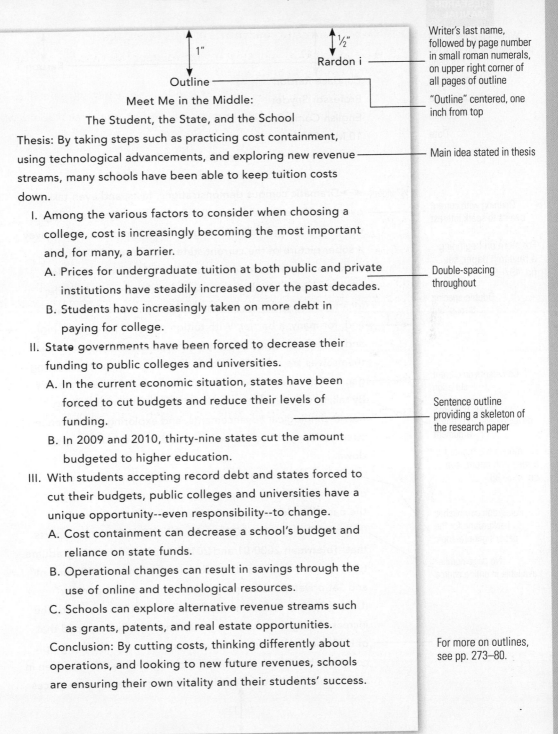

1"

½"

Rardon i

Outline

Meet Me in the Middle:

The Student, the State, and the School

Thesis: By taking steps such as practicing cost containment, using technological advancements, and exploring new revenue streams, many schools have been able to keep tuition costs down.

I. Among the various factors to consider when choosing a college, cost is increasingly becoming the most important and, for many, a barrier.

A. Prices for undergraduate tuition at both public and private institutions have steadily increased over the past decades.

B. Students have increasingly taken on more debt in paying for college.

II. State governments have been forced to decrease their funding to public colleges and universities.

A. In the current economic situation, states have been forced to cut budgets and reduce their levels of funding.

B. In 2009 and 2010, thirty-nine states cut the amount budgeted to higher education.

III. With students accepting record debt and states forced to cut their budgets, public colleges and universities have a unique opportunity--even responsibility--to change.

A. Cost containment can decrease a school's budget and reliance on state funds.

B. Operational changes can result in savings through the use of online and technological resources.

C. Schools can explore alternative revenue streams such as grants, patents, and real estate opportunities.

Conclusion: By cutting costs, thinking differently about operations, and looking to new future revenues, schools are ensuring their own vitality and their students' success.

For more on outlines, see pp. 273–80.

Writer's last name and page number ½" from top of page

1"

½"

Rardon 1

Writer's name
Instructor's name
Course
Date

Candace Rardon

Professor Snyder

English Composition I

10 May 2019

Title, centered

Meet Me in the Middle:

The Student, the State, and the School

½" indent ←→ Dramatic campus demonstrations, fasts, and even take-

Opening with current events to spark interest

For more on beginning a research paper, see pp. 497–98.

overs continue, especially in California (Altavena), as college

costs keep rising (Walker). Images of student protesters convey

a sober picture of the current state of college tuition costs

in the country. For students, among the factors to consider

when choosing a college--academics, athletics, student life,

location, and so on--cost is increasingly the most important

Double-spacing throughout

1"

and, for many, a barrier. With tuition prices at an all-time high

1"

and state funding reduced by economic recession, universities

themselves are now in a unique position to bridge the funding

Comments on current situation

gap and to meet students and states in the middle of the crisis.

Thesis previews development and central argument

By taking steps such as practicing cost containment, using

new technological advancements, and exploring new revenue

For more on a thesis for a research paper, see pp. 495–96.

streams, many schools have been able to keep tuition costs

down.

Prices for undergraduate tuition at both public and

private institutions have progressively increased over

Paragraph establishes background for the paper's general topic

the past decades and now "exceed inflation every year"

(Hayden). The National Center for Education Statistics reports

No page number available in online source

that "[b]etween 2000-01 and 2010-11, prices for undergraduate

tuition, room, and board at public institutions rose 42 percent"

and "at private, not-for-profit institutions rose 31 percent"

(United States). In fact, as CreditUnions.com has reported, the

increase in higher education prices has steadily outpaced that

Figure cited in text

of both medical costs and house prices (see fig. 1). This graph

compares how much the cost of a college education has risen in

recent years with how much health care costs and house prices

1"

Rardon 2

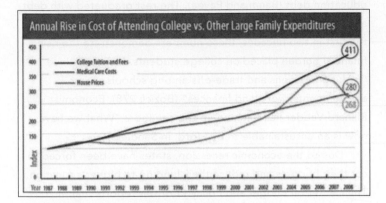

Fig. 1. Annual Rise in Cost of Attending College.

Source: Bureau of Labor Statistics, Consumer Price Index, and
All Urban Consumers, Standard & Poor/Case-Shiller Home Price
Composite-10 Index (Hoffman).

Figure labeled in caption;
source information
provided

Source presents and
credits findings of
another study

have gone up over the same period. While the cost of all
three has gone up, the expense of college has increased the
most.

As the graph shows, the prices of tuition, medical care, and
houses are plotted against both time and the consumer price
index. Computed by the Department of Labor's Bureau of Labor
Statistics, the consumer price index is a calculation generally
used to measure inflation over a period of time, based on how
the prices of common goods and services change. From 1989 to
2008, the price of higher education has consistently risen more
than the prices of medical care and houses, a burden that often
falls on the student.

Key term is defined

Trends in student borrowing point to a crisis in the amount
of debt that students and families have to shoulder to afford an
education. *Trends in Student Aid 2012,* a College Board report,
states that in 2010-11, only 43% of students who graduated with a
bachelor's degree from a public four-year institution did so without

For an explanation of
statistics as evidence,
see p. 137.

Rardon 3

education debt (Baum and Payea). The rest graduated with debt averaging $23,800. Despite a recent 4% drop in borrowing, the first in two decades, these numbers demonstrate the rising financial burden placed on college students. Many continue "making decisions and trade-offs among schools, living arrangements, work, and finances" (Bozick 278). Economist Richard Vedder has summed up the situation: "What we have now is an unsustainable trend" (qtd. in Sandler 199).

Due to the economic recession, states have been forced to cut their budgets and reduce their funding to higher education. The Center on Budget and Policy Priorities reports that in 2009 and 2010, thirty-nine states decreased their budgets for higher education, leading to "reductions in faculty and staff in addition to tuition increases" (Johnson et al. 6). Like California, the state of Florida was forced to raise tuition by 15% in 2009-10. The tuition increases that result from a lack of state funds have become a nationwide threat.

With students accepting record debt and states forced to cut their budgets, public colleges and universities have a unique opportunity--even responsibility--to change. Instead of raising tuition to make up for lost state funds, many schools have begun to cut costs. Through cost containment, schools can decrease their operating budgets and their reliance on state funds. In an article for *Time*, Sophia Yan outlines reductions on more than twenty campuses. For instance, Harvard University saved $900,000 by cutting hot breakfasts during the week in the dining halls. Western Washington University saved $485,000 by cutting its football team, and Whittier College saved $50,000 by cutting first-year orientation by a day. On the theory that "every little bit helps," schools are finding ways to save money.

Margin annotations:

Only one citation needed for material in sequence in a paragraph and clearly from the same source

Facts and statistics support main point

Page numbers provided for quotations

Original quote from another source

Paper continues to lay out background of argument

Transition from background to central argument

First way to avoid raising tuition is explained

Specific examples provide evidence for point

For more on integrating sources, see Ch. 29.

Rardon 4

Going beyond cutbacks in services, schools have also considered operational changes that will result in even more savings. The Delta Project on Postsecondary Education Costs, Productivity, and Accountability, a nonprofit group that analyzes college costs and spending trends, recommends ways to increase productivity:

> Make investments in course redesign and other curricula changes that will make for a more cost-effective curriculum. . . . This includes redesigning large undergraduate courses, creating cost-effective developmental education modules that can be delivered statewide; and redesigning the general education curriculum to enhance community college transfer. (4)

Other suggestions include making buildings more energy efficient and creating work opportunities for jobless students as interns or research assistants (4). Such changes can lead to substantial savings and help schools across the country.

Another alternative to raising tuition is for schools to embrace technological advances. As Kamenetz observes, "Whether hybrid classes, social networks, tutoring programs, games, or open content, technology provides speed skates for students and teachers, not crutches." Specific models have come from the National Center for Academic Transformation, a nonprofit organization that uses information technology to raise student performance and lower costs. Its six course redesign models vary in the amount of in-class instruction replaced by technology (Natl. Center, "Six Models" 1). When the University of Alabama adopted the emporium model for Intermediate Algebra and replaced lectures with an online learning resource center (3), the redesign increased student success, met individual needs, and saved 30% of costs (Natl. Center, "Program"). Of course, such course

---

Point from last paragraph used for transition to new point

Signal phrase refers to organization as author

Direct quotation longer than four lines set off from text without quotation marks, followed by page number in parentheses

Transition leads to second way to avoid raising tuition

Quotation source clearly identified but pages are not numbered in source

Short title added to distinguish two sources by the same author

Basic models are explained before giving a specific example

Statistics support claims

Rardon 5

redesign cannot always be applied across the curriculum, but schools giving serious thought to current technology can transform the classroom, saving money and helping students.

Finally, schools can supplement income from student tuition by considering additional sources of revenue. *BusinessWeek* writer Francesca Di Meglio reports that many schools already look to grants, patents, real estate, and popular graduate courses to "protect [their] bottom line from fiscal and demographic trends that are making the college business more challenging." As early as the 1950s, three Indiana University researchers patented Crest toothpaste, and its returns went on to fund an on-campus dental research institute. Similarly, in 2004 Emmanuel College in Boston allowed Merck, a large pharmaceuticals company, to build a research facility on an acre of land with a 75-year lease for $50 million. Di Meglio's examples show how schools can tap into these alternative income streams and reduce some of the pressure on tuition.

Rising tuition costs, growing student borrowing, and shrinking government funding have endangered widespread access to a college education. As former President Obama himself said in the 2010 State of the Union address, "in the United States of America, no one should go broke because they chose to go to college. . . . It's time for colleges and universities to get serious about cutting their own costs--because they, too, have a responsibility to help solve this problem." In an era of economic strain, schools can embrace this chance to think creatively about the way they operate. By cutting costs where they spent money in the past, thinking differently about how they operate in the present, and looking to new ways of bringing in revenue in the future, schools can ensure their own vitality and their students' success. When public colleges and universities take such steps to ensure that a college education is available to everyone, meeting students and **states** in the middle with innovative ideas, students can stop protesting and start welcoming in an era of increased college access.

Margin annotations:

Third way to avoid raising tuition is introduced

Signal phrase names publication and author

Brackets identify words added to original text

Paraphrase of original source

Final sentence in paragraph connects examples from source with overall argument

For more on concluding a research paper, see pp. 296–90.

Ellipses show where words are omitted

Conclusion emphasizes critical points in argument

Conclusion returns to events in opening

1″   ½″

Rardon 6

Works Cited

Altavena, Lily. "California State Students Protest by Fasting."
The New York Times, 7 May 2012, nyti.ms/23uNvzJ.

Baum, Sandy, and Kathleen Payea. Trends in Student Aid 2012.
College Board, 2012, trends.collegeboard.org/sites/default/
files/student-aid-2012-full-report.pdf.

Bozick, Robert. "Making It through the First Year of College:
The Role of Students' Economic Resources, Employment,
½″ and Living Arrangements." Sociology of Education, vol.
80, no. 3, 2007, pp. 216-84. JSTOR, www.jstor.org/sta-
ble/20452709.

The Delta Project on Postsecondary Education Costs,
Productivity, and Accountability. "Postsecondary Education
Spending Priorities for the American Recovery and
Reinvestment Act of 2009." The National Center for Higher
Education Management, Feb. 2009, nchems.org/news/
documents/ARRAStatementFebruary.2009.pdf.

Di Meglio, Francesca. "Colleges Explore Alternative Revenue
Streams." BusinessWeek.com, Bloomberg, 7 Aug. 2008,
www.bloomberg.com/news/articles/2008-08-08/colleges-
explore-alternative-revenue-streamsbusinessweek-business-
news-stock-market-and-financial-advice.

Hayden, Tom. "Rising Cost of College? We Can't Afford to Be
Quiet." The Chronicle of Higher Education, 28 Mar. 2010.
Academic OneFile, go.galegroup.com.proxy.emerson.edu/ps.

Hoffman, Teri. "Graph of the Week: Annual Rise in Cost of
Attending College vs. Other Large Family Expenditures."
CreditUnions.com. Callahan & Associates, 27 July
2009,www.creditunions.com/articles/graph-of-the-week-
annual-rise-in-cost-of-attending-college-vs-other-large-
family-expenditures/.

List of works cited on a separate page

List alphabetized by names of authors or by titles (when no author is named); names match source citations in text

First line of entry at left margin, additional lines indented ½″

All lines double-spaced, within and between entries

Rardon 7

Johnson, Nicholas, et al. "An Update on State Budget Cuts."
Center on Budget and Policy Priorities. Center on Budget
and Policy Priorities, 19 Apr. 2010, www.cbpp.org/research/
an-update-on-state-budget-cuts.

Kamenetz, Anya. "The Virtual University." *The American
Prospect,* vol. 21, no. 4, 2010, pp. 22+. *LexisNexis
Academic,* www.lexisnexis.com.proxy.emerson.edu.

The National Center for Academic Transformation. "Program in
Course Redesign: The University of Alabama." *The National
Center for Academic Transformation,* 2005, www.thencat.
org/PCR/R2/UA/UA_Overview.htm.

---. "Six Models for Course Redesign." *The National Center
for Academic Transformation,* 2008, www.thencat.org/
R2R/R2R%20PDFs/Six%20Models%20for%20Course%20
Redesign.pdf.

Obama, Barack. "Remarks by the President in State of the
Union Address." United States Capitol, Washington, D.C.,
27 Jan. 2010.

Sandler, Corey. *Cut College Costs Now! Surefire Ways to Save
Thousands of Dollars.* Adams Media, 2006.

United States, Department of Education, National Center for
Education Statistics. "Fast Facts: Tuition Costs of Colleges
and Universities." *Digest of Education Statistics,* 2011, nces.
ed.gov/fastfacts/display.asp?id=76.

Walker, Brianne. "UC, CSU Tuition Increases: The Causes and
Consequences." *Neon Tommy: Annenberg Digital News,* USC
Annenberg School of Journalism and Communication, 13
Dec. 2011, www.neontommy.com/news/2011/12/california-
public-colleges-lead-nation-highest-tuition-and-fees.

Yan, Sophia. "Colleges Find Creative Ways to Cut Back." *Time,*
21 Sept. 2009, p. 81.

Three hyphens replace repeating exact name from previous entry

APA Style for Documenting Sources

The American Psychological Association (APA) details the style most commonly used in the social sciences in its *Publication Manual,* Seventh Edition (APA, 2020). For advice and updates, visit apastyle.org, purchase the manual, or use a library copy.

For a brief overview of APA style, see E2 in the Quick Research Guide, pp. Q-35–Q-36.

APA style uses a two-part system to credit sources.

- **In-text citations.** Briefly cite or identify the author and date of the source in your text, either by mentioning them in your sentence or by noting them in parentheses right after the source material. In many cases, you also supply the page number, paragraph number, or other location in the original source. To cite sources properly in your text, follow the guidelines in the Citing Sources in APA Style section below.

- **The References list.** Provide full publication information for the source in your concluding list, arranged alphabetically by author. This list is called "References." To list sources properly in your References list, look up the model for each type of source in the Listing Sources in APA Style section on page 535. Follow the model's formatting, punctuation, and spacing.

Citing Sources in APA Style

The author and date of a source form the core of an APA citation. That author's last name links your use of the source in your paper with its full information in your list of references. The date tells readers its current or classic status. Include both each time you cite a source in parentheses.

For detailed visuals on citing sources in APA style, see the Source Navigators on pp. 539, 540, 542, and 545.

Citing and Listing Sources in APA Style

Skim the following directory to find sample entries to guide you as you cite and list your sources. Notice that the examples are organized according to questions you might ask and that comparable print and electronic sources are grouped together. See pages 549–56 for a sample paper that illustrates APA style.

(continued)

Citing and Listing Sources in APA Style *(continued)*

A common addition is a specific location, such as a page number (using "p." for "page" or "pp." for "pages"), that tells where the material appears in the original source. If a source lacks page numbers, give a paragraph number, section heading, figure number, or time-stamp. This information is required for quotations and recommended for paraphrases and key concepts. When you supply these elements in parentheses, separate them with commas: (Westin, 2013, p. 48). This basic form applies whatever the type of source—article, book, or web page.

As you check your APA style, keep in mind these three questions:

- Who wrote it?
- What type of source is it?
- How are you capturing the source material?

Who Is the Author?

Individual Author Not Named in the Sentence

Climate change is being taught as a fact rather than as a scientific theory (Tice, 2015, p. 315).

Author, date, and page cited at end of sentence

Individual Author Named in the Sentence

Tice (2015) voiced his concern that climate change is being taught as a fact rather than as a scientific theory (p. 315).

Author and date named in the sentence

Page reference cited at end of sentence

Two Authors

List the last names of coauthors in the order in which they appear in the source. If you mention them in your sentence, join the names with "and"; if you mention them in the parenthetical citation, use an ampersand (&).

Seifried and de Wilde (2014) have demonstrated the importance of sports marketing in the creation of indoor arenas in the 1920s (p. 453).

Sports marketing played an important role in the creation of indoor arenas in the 1920s (Seifried & de Wilde, 2014, p. 453).

Ampersand ⎯⎯⎯

Three or More Authors

For three or more authors, list only the first author with "et al." (for "and others").

Compulsive buying behavior has traditionally been described as a type of addiction or pathological disorder (Spinella et al., 2014, p. 670).

New research by Spinella et al. (2014), however, suggests that such behavior may be more closely linked to general attitudes about money (p. 671).

Learning disabilities occur with each other, with emotional or attention disorders, or with social deficits (Fletcher et al., 2006, p. 9).

Fletcher et al. (2006) characterized this likelihood as "co-morbidity" (p. 9).

Organization as Author

Section heading for an online source ⎯⎯⎯

The United States has recognized more than five hundred Native American tribal governments as sovereign and self-governing (Smithsonian, 2019, Background section).

Author of a Work in a Collection

Cite the author of the individual work; later you will list the collection editor in your references.

The body's melatonin production is inhibited by light (Boyle, 2014, p. 49).

Unidentified Author

Identify the source with its title in your sentence or in the first few words in parentheses, so it is easy to locate in your alphabetical list of references.

It is essential that parents monitor their child's online activities ("Social Networking," 2019).

Same Author with Multiple Works

The publication year distinguishes multiple works by the same author.

Three significant trends in parent-school relations evolved (Grimley, 2007) after the original multistate study (Grimley, 1987).

Different Authors of Separate Works Cited Together

Within a single citation, list the authors of multiple works in alphabetical order (as in your reference list). Separate the works with semicolons.

Several studies have demonstrated a link between celebrity worship and cosmetic surgery among adolescents (Abraham & Zuckerman, 2011; Huh, 2012; Maltby & Day, 2011; Swami et al., 2013).

What Type of Source Is It?

Naming the author is the core of a citation, regardless of the type of source used. Even so, a few types may present complications.

Online Source

Provide an in-text citation for an online source the same way you would for any other source, noting the author and date. List paragraph numbers, figure or table numbers, or a section heading if the source does not have page numbers.

The first artifact in the collection that eventually grew into the National Museum of the American Indian was acquired in 1897 ("Significance of the Collections," 2019).

To cite an entire website, include the URL in the text, but not in your reference list.

The Common Sense Media website (http://www.commonsensemedia.org) provides parents with age-appropriate ratings for movies, books, and television shows.

Indirect Source

If possible, locate and cite the original source. Otherwise, begin your citation with "as cited in" and name your source.

According to Keri Johnson, men are in our culture are allowed to express anger, but women "are expected to express their displeasure with sadness" (as cited in Chemaly, 2018, p. 4).

Government or Organization Document

If no specific author is identified, treat the sponsor as the author. Give its full name in your first citation. If the name is complicated or commonly shortened, you may add an abbreviation in parentheses. In later citations, use just the abbreviation and the date: (APA, 2010).

In *The Impact of Food Advertising on Childhood Obesity* (2010), the American Psychological Association (APA) reported a direct link between number of hours of television watched by and rates of obesity among children.

Source without a Date

When the date is unknown, use "n.d." ("no date").

Interval training encourages rotation between high-intensity spurts and "active recovery, which is typically a less-intense form of the original activity" (*Interval Training*, n.d., para. 2).

Sacred or Classical Text

If the original date is unknown, use "n.d." ("no date"); otherwise, include it before the date of your edition's date: (Burton, 1621/1977). For ancient texts, use the year of the translation: (Homer, trans. 1990). For a quotation, identify lines, sections, or other standard divisions to help readers locate a passage in any edition. For biblical references, specify the version in your initial citation. For all classic works — ancient or religious — specify the version in your internal citation.

Many cultures affirm the importance of religious covenant in accounts as varied as the biblical "Behold, I make a covenant" in Exodus 34:10 (King James Version) and *The Iliad* (Homer, trans. 1990), which opens with the cause of the Trojan War, "all because Agamemnon spurned Apollo's priest" (Book 1, line 12).

Specific Section of a Source

List a specific section (dedication, preface, foreword, afterword, etc.) in your text. In your references list, include an entry for the entire work.

In his foreword to Anthony Ray Hinton's moving book (2018), Bryan Stevenson wrote . . . (p. iv).

Visual Material

To refer to your own figure or table, mention its number in your sentence: "As Figure 2 shows, . . ." Clearly cite a visual from a source.

Use of pro-social media among teenagers is likely to result in more empathetic behavior in real life (Prot et al., 2014, Table 2).

To include or adapt a source's table or visual, you may need to request permission from the author or copyright holder. Many sources — from scholarly journals to websites — state their permissions policy in the issue or on the site. (Ask your instructor's advice if you are unsure how to proceed.) Credit the material in a "From" or "Adapted from" note below it.

Personal Communication

The APA considers face-to-face, online, or phone interviews, letters, memos, text messages, and email to be personal communications. Omit these from your reference list because your readers won't be able to find and use such sources. Simply name your source and the date of the communication in your paper.

Nathan Emmanuel (personal communication, October 10, 2019) has made specific suggestions for stimulating the local economy.

For more on capturing and integrating source material, see Ch. 29.

How Are You Capturing the Source Material?

The way you capture source material — in your own words or in a quotation — affects how you will present and credit it. Always identify words taken directly from a source by using quotation marks or the indented form for a long "block" quotation. Specify the location of quoted words. If you paraphrase material from a source in your own words, APA also recommends that you add a locator. For general information, such as your summary of an overall finding, no location is needed in your citation.

Identify the location of cited material by supplying the page number. For an unpaginated source, especially online, give the paragraph number or the section name (or a shortened version), and identify the paragraph within the section (Methods section, para. 2). If appropriate, identify other parts: Chapter 5, Figure 2, Table 3.

Overall Summary or Important Idea

In *Down, Girl: The Logic of Misogyny*, Manne (2018) examined harassment, domestic violence, and sexual assault as ways of punishing women who challenge patriarchal power.

Blended Paraphrase and Quotation

According to McKibben (2019), the pernicious air pollution over much of India and China is "the biggest public health crisis on the planet" (p. 19).

Brief Quotation Integrated in the Sentence

Ho (2019) observed that the late 1960s saw "a small but influential wave of artists choosing to engage — with the present moment, with politics, and with the public sphere" (para. 11).

Paragraph number provided for an online source.

Long Quotation

If you quote forty words or more, indent the quotation one-half inch and double-space it instead of using quotation marks. After it, add your citation with no additional period, including whatever information you have not already mentioned in your signal phrase.

Emma Willard and Catharine Beecher fought for female educational opportunities, such as a more inclusive curriculum and higher educational opportunities. In 1848, Elizabeth Cady Stanton published the "Declaration of Sentiments" at the Seneca Falls Convention to address and rectify the wrongs done to women, including this resolution:

> That the speedy success of our cause depends upon the zealous and untiring efforts of both men and women, for the overthrow of the monopoly of the pulpit, and for securing to woman an equal participation with men in the various trades, professions, and commerce. (p. 73)

CITING IN-TEXT SOURCES IN APA STYLE

☐ Have you acknowledged all material from a source?

☐ Have you inserted your in-text citation right after a quotation or specific reference to a source?

☐ Have you identified the author and date of each source in your sentence or in parentheses?

☐ Have you added a page number or other location whenever needed?

☐ Have you checked your final draft to be sure that every source cited in your text also appears in your list of references?

Listing Sources in APA Style

List your sources at the end of your paper on a new page with the title "References" centered in boldface at the top. Include only sources that you actually cite in your paper unless your instructor requests otherwise. Format each entry with a "hanging indent" so that subsequent lines are indented one-half inch (about five to seven spaces), just as a paragraph is.

For a sample reference page, see p. 556 or p. Q-6 in the Quick Format Guide.

Double-space your list, and organize it alphabetically by authors' last names; use the title for works without an identified author. To cite several works by the same author, arrange them by date, moving from earliest to most recent. If an author has two works published in the same year, arrange these alphabetically, and add a letter after each date (2019a, 2019b). Use this same date and letter in your in-text citation, too.

APA style uses the following guidelines:

- Supply only initials (with a space between them) for an author's first and middle names (Barr, T. W.)

- Use an ampersand (&, as in a citation in parentheses), not "and" (as you would write in your paper), before the name of the last of more than one author.

- Capitalize only the first word, proper names, and the first word after a colon in the title of a book, article, or website. Capitalize all main words in the title of a journal or other periodical.

- Do not use quotation marks or italics for an article title in your reference list (but use quotation marks if you mention it in your text).

- Spell out names of months, but abbreviate terms common in academic writing (such as "p.m.," "Vol." for "Volume," or "No." for "Number").

- Italicize the title of a website, book, or periodical title (and its volume number).

- Shorten the name of a publisher, but include "Press" and "Books."

- If the author and publisher are the same, list the organization in the author position and omit the publisher.

- For an article, give volume, issue, and any digital object identifier (DOI), a unique number that identifies it with a permanent web address. If no DOI is available for an online article, supply the URL if readers will be able to access the work.

- Include an access date only for online sources that are likely to change.

- Omit a final period after the DOI or URL.

Keep in mind these two key questions, which are used to organize the sample entries that follow:

- Who wrote it?
- What type of source is it?

As you prepare your entries, begin with the author. The various author formats apply whatever your source — article, book, web page, or other material. Then, from the following examples, select the format for the rest of the entry, depending on the type of source you have used. Follow its pattern in your entry, supplying the same information in the same order with the same punctuation and other features.

Who Wrote It?

Individual Author

Kotlowitz, A. (2018). *An American summer: Love and death in Chicago.* Nan A. Talese.

Two Authors

Diamandis, P. H., & Kotler, S. (2014). *Abundance: The future is better than you think.* Free Press.

Three or More Authors

Provide names for up to twenty authors; for more than twenty, list the first nineteen names, and insert an ellipsis before the final author's name.

Schiller, B., Hill, C., & Wall, S. (2016). *The economy today* (14th ed.). McGraw-Hill.

Same Author with Multiple Works

Arrange the titles by date, the earliest first. If some share the same date, arrange them alphabetically, and insert a letter after the date.

Mukherjee, S. (2010). *The emperor of all maladies: A biography of cancer.* Scribner.

Mukherjee, S. (2015a). Blood feuds. *Blood, 126,* 1264-1265. https://doi.org/10.1182/blood-2015-07-659540

Mukherjee, S. (2015b). *The laws of medicine: Field notes from an uncertain science.* TED Books.

Organization as Author

American Lung Association. (2015). *New ozone standards will save lives, protect health.*

Publisher is omitted since it is the same as the author

Editor of a Work or Collection

Wilson, J., & Fuller, A. (Eds.). (2019). *The best American travel writing 2019.* Houghton Mifflin Harcourt.

Author and Translator

Piketty, T. (2014). *Capital in the twenty-first century* (A. Goldhammer, Trans.). Belknap Press. (Original work published 2013)

Unidentified Author

Vets shine in arts, sciences, public service. (2015, December). *Vietnam, 28*(4), 16.

What Type of Source Is It?

Once you have found the author format that fits, look for the type of source that matches. Mix and match the patterns illustrated as needed. For example, the revised edition of an edited collection of articles might send you to several examples until you have identified all elements.

Article in a Print or Online Periodical

Article from a Journal

Italicize the volume number as well as the journal title. If there is an issue number, insert it in parentheses, without italics, immediately after the volume number. End with the DOI, if provided.

Schwartz, A. (2017). What Van Halen can teach us about the care of older patients. *JAMA Internal Medicine, 177*(3), 309-310.

To see how to create the listing for an online journal article, see p. 539.

No period added after
the DOI

Dreby, J. (2015). U.S. immigration policy and family separation: The consequences for children's well-being. *Social Science & Medicine, 132,* 245-251. https://doi.org/10.1016/j.socscimed.2014.08.041

Ampersand before the
final author

Molano, A., Torrente, C., & Jones, S. (2015). Relative risk in context: Exposure to family and neighborhood violence within schools. *Journal of Latino-Latin American Studies, 7*(1), 9-32.

If you want to list a special issue about a topic, rather than singling out an article, begin with the issue editor or, if none, with the issue title.

Internet memes [Themed issue]. (2015). *Journal of Visual Culture, 13*(3).

To see how to create
the listing for an
online journal article,
see p. 539.

Article Accessed through a Subscription Database

Supply the DOI, if one is given. Omit the database unless it is the *only* way to access the work (for example, a dissertation in a dissertation archive)

Powell, A. (2015). Youth "at risk"? Young people, sexual health and consent. *Youth Studies Australia, 26*(4), 21-28.

Abstract for an Article

If you use only the abstract, cite it, not the full article. Add "Abstract" in brackets after the title.

Bordun, T. (2015). Onscreen and off-screen flesh and blood: Performance, affect and ethics in Catherine Breillat's films [Abstract]. *Studies in European Cinema, 12*(2), 132-143. https://doi.org/10.1080/17411548.2015.1037572

To see how to create
the listing for a
magazine article, turn
to p. 540.

Article from a Print Magazine

Donnelly, K. (2019, June). Shaman or showman? *Travel and Leisure,* 64-67.

Article from an Online Magazine

Freund, C. (2019, May 28). Climate change is almost too big a problem to study. The solution? Volcanoes. *Salon.com.* https://www.salon.com/2019/05/28/climate-change-is-almost-too-big-a-problem-to-study-the-solution-volcanoes_partner/

Online Article

1 The last name and initials of the author(s)

2 The date of publication (year for a journal, complete date for a magazine and newspaper)

3 The title and subtitle of the article

4 The name of the periodical

5 Volume number

6 Page numbers

7 DOI, if available, or URL that readers can use to access the work

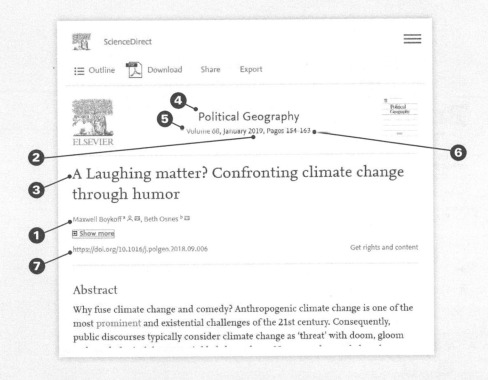

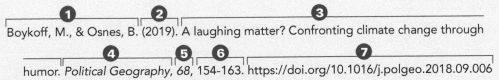

Boykoff, M., & Osnes, B. (2019). A laughing matter? Confronting climate change through humor. *Political Geography, 68,* 154-163. https://doi.org/10.1016/j.polgeo.2018.09.006

Article from a Print Magazine

① The last name and initials of the author(s)

② The date of publication

③ The title and subtitle of the article

④ The name of the periodical

⑤ Volume and issue number, if given

⑥ Page numbers

⑦ DOI, if available, or direct-link URL

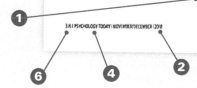

③

Bypassing the Blood-Brain Barrier

The body has developed powerful protections to keep foreign substances out of the brain. Scientists must creatively evade those safeguards in order to treat brain disorders. **BY ABIGAIL FAGAN**

①

HE BRAIN IS our most treasured possession. It coordinates our movements, our words, our relationships, and the ability to pass on our genes. Our body therefore protects the organ fiercely: The central nervous system polices particles traveling through the bloodstream and invites only the safest into our cognitive chamber. This selective process occurs due to a protective boundary known as the blood-brain barrier. The barrier serves a vital role, but it also poses a tremendous challenge for scientists developing drugs to treat brain-based disorders such as Alzheimer's disease, stroke, and brain cancer.

A key component of the barrier's biology involves the endothelial cells that line blood vessels, which are packed

38 | PSYCHOLOGY TODAY | NOVEMBER/DECEMBER | 2018

⑥　④　②

① ② ③ ④
Fagan, A. (2018, November/December). Bypassing the blood-brain barrier. *Psychology*

⑤ ⑥
Today, 51(6), 38-39.

Article from a Newsletter

Grose, J. (2015, October23). How to negotiate your maternity leave at a small company. *Lenny.* http://www.lennyletter.com/culture/news/a107/ how-to-negotiate-your-maternity-leave-at-a-small-company/

Article from a Print Newspaper

Weisman, R. (2015, November 12). For Biogen's growth, a new prescription. *The Boston Globe,* C1.

Article from an Online Newspaper

Bowley, G. (2019, May 28). Leader of Smithsonian's African American museum to direct entire institution. *The New York Times.* https://www.nytimes.com /2019/05/28/arts/design/lonnie-bunch-smithsonian.html

Editorial

Eradicating disease [Editorial]. (2015, October 10). *The Economist, 417*(8959), 13.

Gavin Newsom wants to stop rent gouging. Will lawmakers finally stand up for tenants? [Editorial]. (2019, September 4). *Los Angeles Times.* https://lat.ms/2lBlRm1

Letter to the Editor

Sims, D. (2014, December 31). A kinder, gentler intelligence [Letter to the editor]. *National Review, 66*(24), 2.

Doran, K. (2019, October 11). When the homeless look like grandma or grandpa [Letter to the editor]. *The New York Times.* https://nyti.ms/33foD0K

Review

Greenberg, G. (2019, April). Psychology's incurable hubris [Review of the book *Mind fixers,* by A. Harrington]. *The Atlantic.* https://www.theatlantic.com/magazine/ archive/2019/04/mind-fixers-anne-harrington/583228/

Douthat, R. (2019, October 14). A hustle gone wrong [Review of the film *Hustlers,* by L. Scafaria, Dir.]. *National Review, 71*(18), 47.

Books

Print Book

To see how to create a listing for a book, turn to p. 542.

Damour, L. (2019). *Under pressure: Confronting the epidemic of stress and anxiety in girls.* Random House.

Online Book

Einstein, A. (1920). *Relativity: The special and general theory.* http://www.gutenberg. org/ebooks/30155

Kilby, P. (2019). *The green revolution: Narratives of politics, technology and gender.* Routledge. https://doi.org/10.4324/9780429200823

Print Book

1 The last name and initials of the author(s)   **3** The title and subtitle of the book
2 The date of publication   **4** The publisher

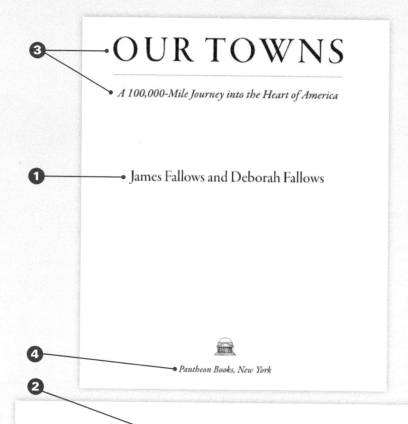

3 OUR TOWNS

A 100,000-Mile Journey into the Heart of America

1 James Fallows and Deborah Fallows

4 *Pantheon Books, New York*

2 Copyright © 2018 by James Fallows and Deborah Fallows

All rights reserved. Published in the United States by Pantheon
Books, a division of Penguin Random House LLC, New York, and
distributed in Canada by Random House of Canada, a division of
Penguin Random House Canada Limited, Toronto.

1 **2** **3**

Fallows, J., & Fallows, D. (2018). *Our towns: A 100,000-mile journey into the heart*

4

of America. Pantheon.

Multivolume Work

McInness, M., Everad, M., Finlayson, C. M., & Davidson, N. (Eds.). (2016). *Encyclopedia of wetlands* (Vol. 2). Springer.

Revised Edition

Pierce, B. (2016). *Genetics essentials: Concepts and connections* (11th ed.). Worth.

Book without a Date

Reade, T. (n.d.). *American Originals.* Midtown Press.

Sacred or Classical Text

New International Version Bible. (2011). Biblica. https://www.biblica.com/bible/ (Original work published 1978)

Homer. (2018). *The odyssey* (E. Wilson, Trans.). W. W. Norton & Company. (Original work published ca. 675–725 B.C.E.)

Parts of a Book

Chapter from an Edited Book

Willis, D. (2018). In search of beauty: Charles White's exposures. In S. K. Oehler & E. Adler (Eds.), *Charles White: A retrospective* (pp. 85-93). Art Institute of Chicago.

Article from a Reference Work

Norman, C. E. (2003). Religion and food. In *Encyclopedia of food and culture* (Vol. 3, pp. 171-176). Scribner.

Brue, A. W., & Wilmshurst, L. (2018). Adaptive behavior assessments. In B. B. Frey (Ed.), *The SAGE encyclopedia of educational research, measurement, and evaluation* (pp. 40–44). SAGE Publications. https://doi.org/10.4135/9781506326139.n21

Other Print or Electronic Documents

Many research reports and similar documents are collaborative products, prepared under the auspices of government, academic, or other organizational sponsors. Start with the specific department name if no author is identified. In parentheses, add any report number assigned by the agency right after the title. Add the publisher (any larger agency) before the URL (if there is one).

Government Document

National Center for Education Statistics. (2018). *The condition of education 2018.* U.S. Department of Education. https://nces.ed.gov/pubs2018/2018144.pdf

Research Report

National Institute on Drug Abuse. (2014). *Principles of adolescent substance use disorder treatment: A research-based guide* (NIH Publication No. 14-7953). https://d14rmgtrwzf5a.cloudfront.net/sites/default/files/podata_1_17_14.pdf

Report from an Academic Institution

Tavoni, M., & van Vuuren, D. P. (2015). *Regional carbon budgets: Do they matter for climate policy?* Harvard Kennedy School, Belfer Center for Science and International Affairs.

Pamphlet

Label the source in brackets as a brochure.

Author is also publisher — U.S. Department of Veterans Affairs. (2012). *Federal benefits for veterans, dependents, and survivors* [Brochure].

Doctoral Dissertation

If the dissertation was informally published by a dissertation indexing service, include the indexing service in the source position. List the DOI if one has been assigned.

Bacaksizlar, N. G. (2019). *Understanding social movements through simulations of anger contagion in social media* (Publication No. 13805848) [Doctoral dissertation, University of North Carolina at Charlotte]. ProQuest Dissertations & Theses.

Online Sources

To help a reader find the same material you used, identify a specific document and give its direct-link URL.

See the directory on pp. 530-31 for entries for other online sources, including books and articles.

Document from a Website

If the publisher of the website is not the author, include its name before the URL.

Rist, R. C., Martin, F. P., & Fernandez, A. M. (2015). *Poverty, inequality, and evaluation: Changing perspectives.* World Bank Group. http://documents.worldbank.org /curated/en/2015/10/25161477/poverty-inequality-evaluation-changing-perspectives

Publisher ——

BBC News. (2019, October 31). *Goats help save Ronald Reagan Presidential Library.* https://bbc.com/news/world-us-canada-50248549

For updates to online formats, visit the APA website at apastyle .org.

Section from an Online Document

World Health Organization. (2018). Global trends in adolescent nutrition. In *Implementing effective actions for improving adolescent nutrition.* https://www.who.int/nutrition/ publications/guidelines/effective-actions-Improving-adolescent/en/

Publisher is same as author —

Document from a Website

1 The last name and initials of the author(s)
2 The date of publication
3 The title and subtitle of the document
4 The name of the publisher
5 The direct-link URL

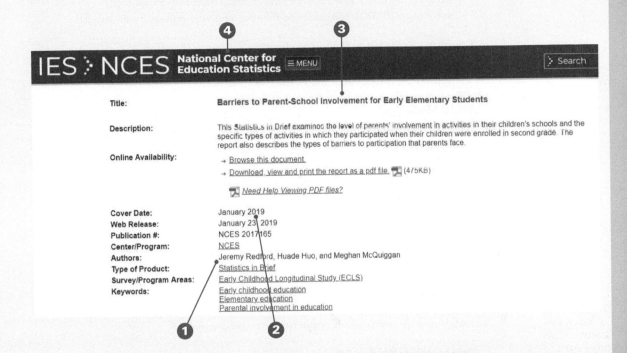

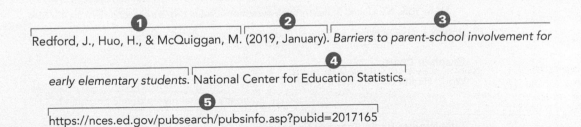

Redford, J., Huo, H., & McQuiggan, M. (2019, January). *Barriers to parent-school involvement for early elementary students.* National Center for Education Statistics. https://nces.ed.gov/pubsearch/pubsinfo.asp?pubid=2017165

Document from a Campus Website

Identify the university and sponsoring program or department (if applicable) before giving the URL for the specific page or document.

Shulsinger, T. (2017). *Six time management tips for online students*. Graduate Programs, Northeastern University. https://www.northeastern.edu/graduate/blog/time-management-tips-online-students/

Blog Post

Maier, J. M. (2019, March 15). Gender, confidence, and who gets to be an expert [Blog post]. *The Society Pages*. https://thesocietypages.org/socimages/2019/03/15/gender-confidence-and-who-gets-to-be-an-expert/

Computer Software or Mobile Application Software (App)

Google LLC. (2019). *Google earth* (Version 9.3.3) [Mobile app]. App Store. https://apps.apple.com/us/app/google-earth/id293622097

Social Media Post

Include the entire post or caption (up to the first 20 words—each emoji, hashtag, or link counts as a word), or use a description of the post in square brackets. List images or recordings in brackets following the title. Include an access date if the content is likely to change.

Georgia Aquarium. (n.d.). *Home* [Facebook page]. Facebook. Retrieved October 15, 2019, from https://www.facebook.com/GeorgiaAquarium/

Georgia Aquarium. (2019, October 10). *Meet the bigfin reef squid* [Video]. Facebook. https://www.facebook.com/GeorgiaAquarium/videos/2471961729567512/

Visual or Audio Sources

Advertisement

Jeep [Advertisement]. (2018, May). *National Geographic*, 19.

Photograph or Work of Art

O'Keeffe, G. (1930). *Black hollyhock blue larkspur* [Painting]. Metropolitan Museum of Art, New York, NY, United States. https://www.metmuseum.org/art/collection/search/487764

Botero, F. (1992). *Horse* [Sculpture]. Plaza Botero, Medellin, Colombia.

Graph or Chart

World Health Organization. (2108). *Summary of the global HIV epidemic 2017* [Chart]. https://www.who.int/hiv/data/2017_summary-global-hiv-epidemic.png?ua=1

Television or Radio Series or Episode

Waller-Bridge, P., Williams, H., & Williams, J. (Executive Producers). (2016–2019). *Fleabag* [TV series]. Two Brothers Pictures; BBC.

Waller-Bridge, P. (Writer), & Bradbeer, H. (Director). (2019, March 18). The provocative request (Season 2, Episode 3) [TV series episode]. In P. Waller-Bridge, H. Williams, & J. Williams (Executive Producers), *Fleabag*. Two Brothers Pictures; BBC.

Film or Video

Petzold, C. (Director). (2019). *Transit* [Motion picture]. France: Neon Productions.

If you accessed the film or video online, list the website as the publisher.

Wray, B. (2019, May). *How climate change affects your mental health* [Video].
TED Conferences. https://www.ted.com/talks/britt_wray_how_climate_
change_affects_your_mental_health

If you access the video via YouTube, list that as the publisher and the account that uploaded the video as the author.

TED. (2019, September 20). *Britt Wray: How climate change affects your mental health*
[Video]. YouTube. https://www.youtube.com/watch?v=-llDkCEvsYw

Sound Recording

Carlile, B. (2018). The mother [Song]. On *By the way, I forgive you*. Low Country
Sound; Elektra.

Podcast

Kaczmarek, J. (Host). (2019, February 21). Against all odds [Audio podcast episode].
In *Selected shorts*. New York Public Radio, WNYC Studios. https://www.wnyc.org/
story/0b77e52d8b93477befcb5a44/

Lecture, Speech, or Recorded Interview

Warren, E. (2019, September 16). *Senator Elizabeth Warren speech in Washington
Square Park* [Speech video recording]. C-SPAN. https://www.c-span.org/
video/?464314-1/senator-elizabeth-warren-campaigns-york-city

Online Forum Post

ScienceModerator. (2018, November 16). *Science discussion: We are researchers
working with some of the largest and most innovative companies using DNA
to help people* [Online forum post]. Reddit. https://www.reddit.com/r/science/
comments/9xlnm2/science_discussion_we_are_researchers_working/

Field Sources

Personal Interview

Omit a personal interview from your reference list because it's not accessible to readers. Instead, mention it in your paper as a personal communication.

Email or Electronic Posting

Cite inaccessible, nonpublic messages as personal communications.

LISTING SOURCES IN APA REFERENCES LIST

- ☐ Have you started each entry with the appropriate pattern for the author's name? Have you left spaces between the initials for each name?
- ☐ Have you used "&" (not "and") before the last coauthor's name, up to twenty authors?

☐ Have you included the date in each entry?

☐ Have you followed the sample pattern for the type of source used?

☐ Have you used capitals and italics correctly for the titles in your entries?

☐ Have you included the conventional punctuation — periods, commas, colons, parentheses — in your entry?

☐ Have you correctly typed or pasted in the DOI or URL of an electronic source? Have you ended without adding a final period after a DOI or URL?

☐ Have you arranged your entries in alphabetical order?

☐ Have you checked your final list of references against your text citations so that every source appears in both places?

☐ Have you double-spaced your reference list and formatted it with an inch margin on all sides?

☐ Have you begun the first line of each entry at the left margin and indented each additional line one-half inch (or five to seven spaces)?

☐ Have you checked any entry from a citation management system as carefully as your own entries?

A Sample APA Research Paper

For more on APA format, see the Quick Format Guide, p. Q-1.

In "Sex Offender Lists: A Never-Ending Punishment," Jenny Lidington explores the goal of the sex offender registry and its many functional problems. Her scholarly approach is designed to help readers grasp the complexities of a difficult societal issue that often generates strong feelings. Notice how thoughtfully she tackles the topic: defining terms, making distinctions, reviewing history, tracing consequences, distinguishing differences, and establishing the basis for her questions. Her paper illustrates APA paper format, including an abstract and keywords, as well as the APA conventions for citing and listing sources. The marginal annotations explain APA formatting and citation guidelines, as well as point out effective research writing practices. Although this sample paper is presented for easy reading in a textbook, your paper should use the type style and size that APA suggests: Times New Roman font, 12-point size. Set one-inch margins on all four sides, double-space all the lines, and turn off automatic hyphenation. Use your software's Help feature or visit the campus computer lab for assistance setting up this format for your file.

1"

1 Page number

Sex Offender Lists: A Never-Ending Punishment — Title

Jenny Lidington ——— Author
Department of Sociology, Tufts University ——— School
SOC 112, Urban Sociology
Dr. Sasha Wayne
November 26, 2019

2

Title centered —————————— **Sex Offender Lists: A Never-Ending Punishment**

½" indent (or 5 to ◄─►Whether someone is 18 years old having consensual
7 spaces)
sex with his 17-year-old high school sweetheart or 40 years

old preying on young children, both are considered sexual

Double-spaced ———————— predators in the eyes of the law. In both cases, jail time and
throughout
registration as a sex offender are the penalties for those caught

and convicted. No real distinction is made over the severity

of the crime when one is labeled a sex offender, even though

the extent of the sexual misconduct can vary tremendously.

All those deemed sex offenders are required to register their

addresses with local police or be rearrested; the police then

release this information to the general public. Although the

sex offender lists were created with the honorable intention of

raising awareness of dangerous citizens in communities, they

ultimately inflict unwarranted punishment on offenders in the

interest of protecting potential victims. Not only are these

lists unconstitutional, but the public's misunderstanding and

1" misuse of the provided information can lead to unintended and 1"

◄─► sometimes heinous consequences. ◄─►

First-level heading, bold
and centered (second- —————————— **History of Sex Offender Registration**
level heading is bold, at
left margin) The earliest form of sex offender registration was

Background presented in ——— implemented over 50 years ago in California and slowly spread
chronological order
to a handful of states. The early registries were primarily used

to create a database, accessible only to local authorities for

reference when sex crimes occurred, of the whereabouts of

potentially dangerous citizens. However, with these registries

came a "sex crime panic," strongly enhanced by media

Specific pages noted ———————— coverage of more extreme sex crimes (Thomas, 2011, p. 37).

During this panic, the public began to push heavily for more

stringent legislation.

The tipping point came with the case of a young

Minnesota boy named Jacob Wetterling. On October 22,

1"

3

1989, Jacob was bicycling with his brother and a friend when a masked gunman intercepted them and kidnapped Jacob. It was believed at the time that he had been sexually assaulted and murdered, and in 2016, police were led to Jacob's remains by his attacker, and this longstanding belief was confirmed. In light of this tragedy, the Jacob Wetterling Act was established in 1994, requiring states to create and maintain sex offender registries. Notably, the information on the registries was accessible only to appropriate authorities. While this policy had monumental implications, it did not satisfy the public as communities wanted access to records of sex offenders' residences (Thomas, 2011, p. 42).

On July 29, 1994, another horrific and highly publicized incident occurred that substantiated the argument for public notification and would significantly impact sex offenders' quality of life. Megan Kanka, a 7-year-old girl from New Jersey, was raped and murdered by her neighbor, Jesse Timmenequas. Jesse, unbeknownst to the community, was a repeat sex offender. This event spurred legislators to create the registry reforms the public desired by passing Megan's Law. This legislation amended the Jacob Wetterling Act by requiring community notification of nearby sex offenders' residences. Along with publishing the registration information, other methods of notification were encouraged. Louisiana, for example, required sex offenders "to post signs at their homes declaring their status as sex offenders" (Thomas, 2011, p. 45).

Constitutional Questions about Sex Offender Registries

Overlooking the rights of perpetrators of abominable crimes can be easy; however, the constitutionality of sex offender registration is entirely questionable. Whatever the crime, the rights of the convicted should be upheld. Because the registration process occurs after an offender is released from incarceration, these lists fail to comply

Figures (not words) used for pages, dates, ages, and numbers with more than one digit

4

with the ex post facto clause, which prohibits the creation of laws that add punishments after a crime has been committed. These lists have been taken to court on grounds of retrospection, though rulings have not favored the offenders (Pattis, 2011, para. 6), and also on grounds of due process, as offenders have no opportunity to argue against community notification.

A third constitutional issue is whether the residential restrictions imposed by the lists constitute banishment, an illegal form of punishment under the constitution. In many states, sex offenders are not allowed within a few blocks of schools, daycare centers, or playgrounds. Particularly in communities with many facilities, acceptable livable areas for registered offenders may be limited or nonexistent. "I never realized how many schools and parks there were until I had to stay away from them," a registered sex offender conceded in Levenson and Cotter's 2005 survey (as cited in Thomas, 2011, p. 129). Essentially, these restrictions, intended to make given areas safer, create potentially dangerous sex-offender communities. This was the case in Broward County, Florida, where 95 registered sex offenders lived within a five-block tract (Thomas, 2011, p. 129). Those who cannot find housing or afford available housing are left homeless though commonly banished from homeless shelters and hostels, too (Thomas, 2011, p. 129).

Public Misconceptions

Those who argue that sex offender registries are constitutional often maintain that the lists are not punitive and provide the public with vital information that can prevent future sex crimes. Even those who admit that the lists may infringe upon offenders' rights argue that any minor violations are outweighed by the contribution to public safety. This argument might be the case if the critically flawed information in sex offender

---

Multiple authors joined by *and* in text

Additional source cited in source where it was mentioned

5

lists was not subject to public misinterpretation. One shortcoming is a lack of specificity: A person who urinated in public is on the same list as one who repeatedly raped young children. In California, one of each 375 adults is registered as a sex offender, a testament to this loose definition of sex crimes (Leon, 2011, p. 119). Although offenders are ranked on a scale of one to three (the worst) in terms of likelihood of reoffending, people tend to ignore these distinctions. As a police officer stated for the *Seattle Times*, "People look at them in a bucket. They say 'Any kind of sex offender is a sex offender, and always will be a sex offender'" (Farley, 2011, para. 13).

Another flaw lies in the accuracy of the rankings. Most crimes require a post-incarceration evaluation to determine whether the criminal is still a threat to society, but sex offenders have no follow-up. When they are released from prison, their names go into a sex offender registry, no matter how much time has passed since the crime. The "threat level" classification represents the level at the time of the crime, not the offender's current risk level. Therapy sessions both during and after prison could result in the offender no longer posing a threat to the community. Studies show that within three years of being released from prison, only 5% of sex offenders are rearrested for another sex crime (Office of Sex Offender Monitoring, 2017; Alper & DuRose, 2019, p. 8), though longer-term studies suggest higher rates of recidivism.

In addition, due to the potentially inaccurate classifications, offenders may be assigned inappropriate punishments for their given crime. For example, many sex offenders whose crimes were not against children (or who may be children themselves) are given the same living restrictions as child rapists. The man imprisoned for having sex with his girlfriend days before she was legally old enough to give consent does not pose enough risk to

Paragraph number supplied for online article without numbered pages

6

restrict him from living near playgrounds and schools. Although some states such as New Jersey and Washington are working to assess risks more accurately, they are the exceptions (Leon, 2011, pp. 141-142).

Consequences of a Lack of Privacy

These major flaws in the sex offender registry system can have counterproductive and tragic effects. When sex offenders must register, their personal information is not given on a need-to-know basis; it is blazoned across the community where they live. Their names, photographs, license plate numbers, and home and work addresses are posted online for the world to view. They may struggle to find housing, to avoid public disapproval or embarrassing exposure of their pasts, and to pass background checks necessary to find work. Because these offenders are often shunned by the adult world, they may seek companionship with children, which potentially tempts some to offend again. With their faces plastered on local bulletin boards or email alerts, offenders can grow increasingly aggravated, which also may lead them to new crimes (Chen, 2009).

This lack of privacy also makes offenders vulnerable to public vigilantes who can inflict harsh punishments. According to a Los Angeles County study by Gallo et al.,

> A number of judges felt that although the avowed purpose of the registration statute is to facilitate the process of law enforcement by providing a list of suspects... the information obtained under section 290 is subject to some abuse — either through police harassment or by indiscriminate revelation to unauthorized persons. (as cited in Leon, 2011, pp. 68-69)

Tragically, public harassment can lead to suicides and murders of registered sex offenders, as was the case for 24-year-old William Elliot. At age 20, Elliot was sentenced

Long quotation (40 words or longer) indented ½" without quotation marks

7

to four months in jail for having sex with his girlfriend who was two weeks away from turning 16 (the legal age of consent in Maine). Four years later, a young man named Stephen Marshall found Elliot's residential information on an online sex-offender database. Marshall used this information to stalk Elliot and shoot him to death in his own home (Ahuja, 2006). This incident is a horrific example of the unintended effects of public misinterpretation of sex offender lists, but it also calls into question whether these lists can be considered nonpunitive.

Violations of Rights of Citizens

Perceived as monsters, fiends, and psychopaths, sex offenders are not easily seen as victims; however, as American citizens, they have the same right to life, liberty, and the pursuit of happiness as anyone else. Although the sex registry laws were created with the best of intentions, they violate these constitutional rights and can have gruesome unintended consequences. Most importantly, they are not especially effective.

Many people believe that the typical sex crime is child rape when in reality most sex crimes are much more benign. The dramatic cases encourage regulation that far exceeds what is necessary for most offenders, placing those who have urinated publicly in the same category as pedophiles (Bonnar-Kidd, 2010, p. 416). However, the sex-crime taboos make it difficult for the public to override emotionally charged ideas of the misconduct that the lists represent and then to see the critical flaws in the current registry system. If these lists are to continue to exist, they should no longer serve as dehumanizing blacklists for the public to use at its own discretion.

Page numbering continues

8

Heading centered

First line of entry at left margin, additional lines indented ½"

List alphabetized by last names of authors, or by titles (when no author is named); names match source citations in text

Supply only initials for authors' first and middle names; leave space between first and middle initials

No period after URL

First word in title and after colon and all proper nouns capitalized

References

Ahuja, G. (2006, April 18). Sex offender registries: Putting lives at risk? ABC News. https://abcnews.go.com/amp/US/story?id=1855771

Alper, M., & DuRose, M. R. (2019, May). *Recidivism of sex offenders released from state prison (2005–2014)* (NCJ 251773). https://www.bjs.gov/content/pub/pdf/rsorsp9yfu0514.pdf

Bonnar-Kidd, K. K. (2010). Sexual offender laws and prevention of sexual violence or recidivism. *American Journal of Public Health, 100,* 412-419. https://doi.org/10.2105/AJPH.2008.153254

Chen, S. (2009, February 19). After prison, few places for sex offenders to live. *The Wall Street Journal.* https://www.wsj.com/articles/SB123500941182818821

Farley, J. (2011, January 1). Sex-offender rankings: Is there room for gray areas? *The Seattle Times.* https://www.seattletimes.com/seattle-news/sex-offender-rankings-is-there-room-for-gray-areas/

Leon, C. S. (2011). *Sex fiends, perverts, and pedophiles: Understanding sex crime policy in America.* New York University Press.

Office of Sex Offender Sentencing, Monitoring, Apprehending, Registering, and Tracking. (2017, May). *Adult sex offender recidivism.* U.S. Department of Justice. https://www.smart.gov/pdfs/AdultSexOffenderRecidivism.pdf

Pattis, N. (2011, February 7). Time to revisit ex post facto clause for sex offenders [Blog post]. *Pattis Blog.* https://www.pattisblog.com/index.php?article=Time_To_Revisit_Ex_Post_Facto_Clause_For_Sex_Offenders_2983

Thomas, T. (2011). *The registration and monitoring of sex offenders: A comparative study.* Routledge.

A WRITER'S HANDBOOK

Contents

Introduction:
Grammar, or The Way Words Work

Hundreds of times a day, with wonderful efficiency, we perform tasks of understanding and constructing complex sentences. Isn't it possible to write well without contemplating grammar at all? Yes. If your innate sense of grammar is reliable, you can write clearly and logically and forcefully without knowing a subjective complement from a handsaw. Most successful writers, though, have gained this sense through many years of practice. When you doubt a word or a construction, a handbook can clear up your confusion and restore your confidence—just as a dictionary can help your spelling.

This handbook explains the most common grammatical conventions—accepted ways in which skilled writers put words together to convey meaning clearly. The college writer can learn by following these examples, just as an athlete, an artist, or a mechanic can learn by watching professionals.

Learning by Doing 🖉 Creating an Error Log

Keeping track of errors will dramatically improve your writing skills. To make the most of feedback, keep a running list of errors your instructor or writing tutors have noted on your drafts. Keep track of the date, the name of the error and its symbol or abbreviation ("pronoun agreement" might be "pn agr," for example), a sample sentence or word group, and a note about how to fix the mistake. You may also wish to note the type of error: matters of **grammar** are addressed in Chapter 34, **style** is covered in Chapter 35, **word choice** is in Chapter 36, **punctuation** is in Chapter 37, and **mechanics** are in Chapter 38. If you are unsure of the meaning of a grammatical term, check Chapter 33 for a **review of common elements** such as parts of speech or look in the index for specific page numbers.

Basic Grammar

The English language has rules about how to put words together to create clear sentences. These rules are called "grammar," and they are the subject of all the chapters in this handbook. This first chapter, Basic Grammar, gives an overview of the building blocks of language and grammar. Rather than focusing on grammatical correctness, this chapter explains the pieces — parts of speech, parts of sentences, and types of sentences — you'll need to understand to grasp the rules in later chapters.

1 | Parts of Speech

English has eight basic parts of speech: nouns, pronouns, verbs, adjectives, adverbs, prepositions, conjunctions, and interjections. Each part of speech performs a specific function in a sentence.

1a Nouns

Nouns are words that name people, places, objects, or ideas, and they can be either common or proper. Most nouns are **common** — they refer to people, places, and things in general, and they are usually not capitalized. **Proper nouns** are specific, unique names, and they are usually capitalized.

TYPES OF NOUNS at a glance

	Common *(general)*	Proper *(specific)*
person	woman	Serena Williams
place	country	Mexico
thing	book	*The Bedford Guide for College Writers*

Nouns can perform several different roles in a sentence, primarily as subject (see 2) and object (see 1f and 3a).

 ## Guidelines for Multilingual Writers
What Are Count and Noncount Nouns and Articles?

Count Nouns and Articles

Nouns referring to items that can be counted are called **count** (or **countable**) nouns. Count nouns can be made plural.

> *table, chair, egg*   two *tables,* several *chairs,* a dozen *eggs*

Singular count nouns must be preceded by a **determiner.** The class of words called determiners includes **articles** (*a, an, the*), **possessives** (*John's, your, his, my,* and so on), **demonstratives** (*this, that, these, those*), **numbers** (*three, the third,* and so on), and **indefinite quantity words** (*no, some, many,* and so on).

> *a* dog, *the* football, *one* reason, *the first* page, *no* chance

Noncount Nouns and Articles

Nouns referring to items that cannot be counted are called **noncount** (or **uncountable**) nouns. Noncount nouns cannot be made plural.

> I need to learn more grammars.

- Common categories of noncount nouns include types of **food** (*cheese, meat, bread*), **solids** (*dirt, salt, chalk*), **liquids** (*milk, juice, gasoline*), **gases** (*methane, hydrogen, air*), and **abstract ideas,** including emotions (*democracy, gravity, love*).

- Another category of noncount nouns is **mass** nouns, which usually represent a large group of countable nouns (*furniture, mail, clothing*).

- The only way to count noncountable nouns is to use a countable noun with them, usually to indicate a quantity or a container.

> one *piece* of furniture, two *quarts* of water, an *example* of jealousy

- Noncount nouns, such as *advice*, are never preceded by an indefinite article; they are often preceded by *some*.

    > She gave us ~~a~~ good advice.
    >
    > *(some inserted above "a")*

- When noncount nouns are *general* in meaning, no article is required, but when the context makes them specific (usually in a phrase or a clause after the noun), the definite article is used.

    GENERAL   Good continues to fight *evil*.

    SPECIFIC   The *evil* that humans do lives after them.

Guidelines for Multilingual Writers
What Are Definite and Indefinite Articles?

The Definite Article (*the*)

- Use *the* with a specific count or noncount noun already mentioned in a piece of writing or familiar to both the writer and the reader.

    > She got a huge box in the mail. *The* box contained oranges from Florida. [*The* is used the second time the noun (*box*) is mentioned.]
    >
    > Did you feed *the* baby? [Both reader and writer know which baby.]

- Use *the* before specific count or noncount nouns when the reader has enough information to identify what is being referred to.

    > *The* furniture in my apartment is old and faded. [Specific furniture]

- Use *the* before a singular count noun to state a generality.

    > *The* dog has been a companion for centuries. [*The dog* refers to all dogs in general.]

- Use *the* before some geographical names.

    > *Collective Nations:* the United States, the United Kingdom
    >
    > *Groups of Islands:* the Bahamas, the Canary Islands
    >
    > *Large Bodies of Water* (except lakes): the Atlantic Ocean, the Dead Sea, the Monongahela River, the Gulf of Mexico
    >
    > *Mountain Ranges:* the Rockies, the Himalayas

- Use *the* or another determiner when plural count nouns name a definite or specific group; use no article when they name a general group.

    > Hal is feeding *the horses* in the barn, and he has already fed *his cows*.
    >
    > *Horses* don't eat meat, and neither do *cows*.

(continued)

The Indefinite Article (*a, an*)

- Use *a* or *an* with a nonspecific, singular count noun when it is not known to the reader or to the writer.

    Jay has *an* antique car. [The car's identity is unknown to the reader.]

    I saw *a* dog in my backyard this morning. [The dog's identity is unknown to the writer.]

- Use *a* or *an* when the noun is first used; use *the* when it is repeated.

    I saw *a* car that I would love to buy. *The* car was red with tan seats.

- Use *some* or no article with general noncount or plural nouns.

    I am going to buy ~~a~~ furniture for my apartment.
    ^{some}

1b   Pronouns

A **pronoun** is a word that takes the place of a noun. The noun that the pronoun refers to is called the antecedent.

ANTECEDENT (NOUN)   PRONOUN

     Nelson gave the book to Miranda before *he* went to Texas. [*He* takes the place of the antecedent, *Nelson*.]

There are several different types of pronouns, and they perform a variety of different roles in a sentence.

Personal Pronouns

Personal pronouns serve as subjects (see 2), objects (see 3a), or possessives (see 32). The personal pronoun form changes depending on the pronoun's role in the sentence.

PERSONAL PRONOUNS at a glance

	SUBJECTIVE		OBJECTIVE		POSSESSIVE	
	Singular	*Plural*	*Singular*	*Plural*	*Singular*	*Plural*
First Person	I	We	me	us	my/mine	our/ours
Second Person	you	You	you	you	your/yours	your/yours
Third Person	he	They	him	them	his	their/theirs
	she		her		her/hers	
	it		it		its	

SUBJECTIVE
PRONOUN

She will run for president in the next election.

OBJECTIVE
PRONOUN

The catcher tossed the ball to *us*.

POSSESSIVE
PRONOUN

The family on the corner just sold *their* house.

Indefinite Pronouns

Indefinite pronouns do not refer to a specific noun.

INDEFINITE PRONOUNS

all	everyone	no one
any	everything	nothing
anybody	few	one (of)
anyone	many	several
anything	much	some (of)
both	neither (of)	somebody
each (of)	nobody	someone
either (of)	none	something
everybody		

Something must be done about skyrocketing tuition costs.

Relative Pronouns

Relative pronouns relate a group of descriptive words to a noun in a sentence.

RELATIVE PRONOUNS

that	which	whomever
what	who	whose
whatever	whom	

DESCRIPTIVE WORD GROUP

California, *which* is experiencing a drought, has imposed tough water restrictions. [*Which* relates the descriptive word group to the noun *California*.]

Interrogative Pronouns

Interrogative pronouns are used to introduce questions.

INTERROGATIVE PRONOUNS

what	whom
which	whose
who	

What is for dinner tonight?

Demonstrative Pronouns

Demonstrative pronouns specify a particular noun.

> DEMONSTRATIVE PRONOUNS
> that   this
> these   those

> *This* building was constructed before *those* roads were paved.

Reflexive and Intensive Pronouns

Reflexive and intensive pronouns end with the suffix *-self* or *-selves*.

REFLEXIVE AND INTENSIVE PRONOUNS at a glance

	Singular	*Plural*
First Person	myself	ourselves
Second Person	yourself	yourselves
Third Person	himself	
	herself	
	itself	themselves

Reflexive pronouns are used as objects when renaming nouns or pronouns that are subjects.

> Juanita gave *herself* a raise.

Intensive pronouns are used to restate a noun or pronoun for emphasis or clarity.

> The *bride* and *groom* made the wedding cake *themselves*. [*Themselves* clarifies the *bride* and *groom* as the makers of the cake.]

For details on using pronouns correctly, see 10, 11, and 12.

1c Verbs

Verbs are words that usually express action (*swim, eat, sleep*) or being (*is, become, seem, feel*) in a sentence.

Action Verbs

Action verbs are so named because they show action.

> The street performer *sings* a different song each evening.

Linking Verbs

Linking verbs such as *is, become, seem,* and *feel* show a state of being by linking a noun with a word that renames or describes it.

> Although the temperature *is* higher, the air *feels* cooler.

Helping Verbs

Helping or **auxiliary verbs** (*have, must, can*) accompany a main verb to add information about its action.

> I probably *am going* to France this summer. [main verb *going* + helping verb *am*]

For more details on the way verbs are used in sentences, see 3. For more on using verbs correctly, see 8 and 9.

1d Adjectives

An **adjective**'s job is to provide information about the person, place, object, or idea named by the noun or pronoun. Adjectives answer questions such as *Which one? What kind?* and *How many?* They may appear before or after the noun or pronoun they are describing.

> The *small red* car was *expensive*.

For details on using adjectives and adverbs correctly, see 13.

1e Adverbs

An **adverb** describes a verb, an adjective, or another adverb by answering questions such as *How? When? Where? Why?* and *To what degree?* Adverbs often end in *-ly*, and they may appear before or after the word they describe.

> The *very* tall tree stood *majestically* above the rest. [*Very* describes how *tall* the tree is; *majestically* describes how the tree *stood*.]

1f Prepositions

Prepositions are small but important words that connect a noun or pronoun to another part of a sentence.

COMMON PREPOSITIONS

about	before	except	of	to
above	behind	for	off	toward
across	below	from	on	under
after	beneath	in	out	until
against	beside	inside	outside	up
along	between	into	over	upon
among	by	like	past	with
around	down	near	since	within
at	during	next to	through	without

The entire word group that begins with a preposition and ends with a noun is called a **prepositional phrase**. The noun in the prepositional phrase is called the **object** of the preposition.

PREPOSITIONAL PHRASE

> The museum allows visitors to sleep *under* the blue *whale*.

1g Conjunctions

Conjunctions are used to connect related words or word groups in a sentence. The two main types of conjunctions are coordinating and subordinating.

Guidelines for Multilingual Writers
How Do I Use Prepositions of Location and Time
(*in, on, at*)?

Location Expressions

> Elaine lives *in* Manhattan *at* a swanky address *on* Fifth Avenue.

- *In* means "within" or "inside of" a place, including geographical areas, such as cities, states, countries, and continents.

> I packed my books *in* my backpack and left to visit my cousins *in* Canada.

- Where *in* emphasizes *location* only, *at* is often used to refer to a place when a specific *activity* is implied: *at the store* (to shop), *at the office* (to work), *at the theater* (to see a play), and so on.

> Angelo left his bicycle *in* the bike rack while he was *at* school.

- *On* means "on the surface of" or "on top of" something and is used with floors of buildings and planets. It is also used to indicate a location *beside* a lake, river, ocean, or other body of water.

> The service department is *on* the fourth floor.

> We have a cabin *on* Lake Michigan.

- *In, on*, and *at* can all be used in addresses. *In* is used to identify a general location, such as a city or neighborhood. *On* is used to identify a specific street. *At* is used to give an exact address.

> We live *in* Boston *on* Medway Street.

> We live *at* 20 Medway Street.

- *In* and *at* can both be used with the verb *arrive*. *In* indicates a large place, such as a city, state, country, or continent. *At* indicates a smaller place, such as a specific building or address. (*To* is never used with *arrive*.)

> Alanya arrived *in* Alaska yesterday; Sanjei will arrive *at* the airport soon.

Time Expressions

- *In* indicates the span of time during which something occurs or a time in the future; it is also used in the expressions *in a minute* (meaning "shortly") and *in time* (meaning "soon enough" or "without a moment to spare"). *In* is also used with seasons, months, and periods of the day.

> He needs to read this book *in* the next three days. [During the next three days]

> I'll meet you *in* the morning *in* two weeks. [Two weeks from now]

- **On** is used with the days of the week, with the word *weekend*, and in the expression *on time* (meaning "punctually").

  Let's have lunch *on* Friday.

- **At** refers to a specific time on the clock as well as a specific time of the day (*at night, at dawn, at twilight*).

  We'll meet again next Monday *at* 2:15 p.m.

 ## Guidelines for Multilingual Writers
What Are Phrasal Verbs?

Many two word verbs end with a **particle,** a word that can be used as a preposition on its own but becomes part of a **phrasal verb.** Once the particle is added, the verb takes on a new idiomatic meaning.

  break up: to separate; to end a romantic relationship; to laugh

  decide on: to select or to judge a person or thing

  turn in: to hand in or submit something

  feel for [a person]: to sympathize with another's unhappiness

  take in [a person]: to house a person; to trick by gaining a person's trust

Coordinating Conjunctions

Coordinating conjunctions join elements with equal or near-equal importance. There are seven coordinating conjunctions (shown below), which can be remembered by using the acronym *FANBOYS.*

  COORDINATING CONJUNCTIONS

  for   and   nor   but   or   yet   so

  The suspect has brown hair *and* blue eyes.

  Several people saw the crime, *but* only one witness spoke to police.

Subordinating Conjunctions

Subordinating conjunctions join elements of unequal importance. A subordinating conjunction can make one clause in a sentence have less emphasis than another.

For more on using coordinating and subordinating conjunctions, see 19.

COMMON SUBORDINATING CONJUNCTIONS

after	before	since	until
although	even though	so	when
as	how	so that	whenever
as if	if	than	where
as soon as	in order that	that	wherever
as though	once	though	while
because	rather than	unless	why

SUBORDINATE CLAUSE   MAIN CLAUSE

Even though tickets wouldn't go on sale until Monday, fans started lining

up on Saturday afternoon. [*Even though* is the subordinating conjunction.]

1h   Interjections

Interjections express emotion or surprise and are usually set off from a sentence with a comma or an exclamation point.

> *Wow!* These pictures of Pluto are astonishing!

EXERCISE 1–1 Identifying Parts of Speech

Identify the part of speech of each underlined word or word group in the following sentences. Answers for the lettered sentences appear at the end of the Handbook. Example:

>   *noun* *verb*   *adjectives*   *preposition*
> Bottled <u>water</u> <u>is</u> one of the most <u>popular</u> drinks sold <u>in</u> the United States.

a. Bottled water has been <u>available</u> <u>around</u> the world <u>for</u> <u>centuries</u>.

b. <u>It</u> <u>became</u> <u>very</u> <u>common</u> <u>during</u> the late twentieth century.

c. <u>Americans</u> <u>drink</u> more bottled water than people in other <u>countries</u> <u>do</u>.

d. <u>Interestingly</u>, some <u>American</u> tap water is <u>cleaner</u> than water in <u>most</u> parts <u>of</u> the world.

e. Bottled water companies <u>usually</u> <u>label</u> <u>their</u> products "spring water," "purified water," <u>or</u> "mineral water."

1. <u>Liza</u> <u>hopes</u> to stop the school <u>from</u> selling bottled water <u>on</u> campus.

2. <u>She</u> <u>argues</u> that bottled water is <u>expensive</u> and bad <u>for</u> the <u>environment</u>.

3. <u>It</u> <u>wastes</u> tons of plastic every year, <u>and</u> students <u>spend</u> thousands of dollars on a product that should be <u>free</u>.

4. <u>But</u> plenty of students <u>enjoy</u> the <u>convenience</u> <u>of</u> bottled water.

5. <u>They</u> don't want to bring <u>their</u> own <u>reusable</u> bottles from <u>home</u>.

2 | Subjects

The **subject** of a sentence or clause identifies the main person, place, object, situation, or idea performing an action or being discussed. Subjects are always nouns or pronouns.

> *Honesty* is the best policy.
>
> *She* walks to work every day.

2a Singular and Plural Subjects

Subjects may be singular, meaning only one, or plural, meaning more than one.

> The tennis *ball* went over the fence.
>
> Three *dogs* chased the ball.
>
>   SUBJECT
>
> *Louis* and *Jen* tried to find the ball.

2b Simple and Complete Subjects

The **simple subject** consists only of the noun(s) or pronoun(s) that is performing the action or being discussed. The **complete subject** consists of the simple subject and all the modifiers that surround it.

>   COMPLETE SUBJECT
>
> College *students* who balance their work, school, and family are more likely to succeed at all three. [*Students* is the simple subject.]

2c Finding the Subject in a Sentence

To find the subject of a sentence, start by locating the first noun or pronoun in the sentence (see 1a and 1b).

> *Meg* began writing her paper.

However, the first noun or pronoun is not always the subject of a sentence. Sometimes nouns performing other functions come before the subject. Be sure the noun or pronoun is not part of a prepositional phrase (see 1f). It can help to find prepositions and strike out prepositional phrases.

> PREP   NOUN (NOT SUBJ)
>
> ~~After the holiday~~, when classes resumed, Meg began writing her paper.

Also make sure the noun is not part of a word group beginning with a subordinating conjunction (see 1g). Look for subordinating conjunctions and strike out the word groups that are connected to them.

<pre>
              SUBORD   NOUN
              CONJ   (NOT SUBJ)   SUBJECT
</pre>
~~After the holiday, *when classes* resumed~~, *Meg* began writing her paper.

In imperative sentences (sentences that make a request or give a command), the understood subject *you* is often left out.

> Do not text and drive. [The subject *you* is understood and is not included in the sentence.]

EXERCISE 2–1 Identifying Subjects

Circle the simple subject and underline the complete subject in each of the following sentences. Answers for the lettered sentences appear at the end of the Handbook. Example:

> The popular children's show (Sesame Street) first aired on public television in 1969.

a. Before that time, television shows were made for adults or entire families.

b. Ernie and Bert became familiar characters for all preschoolers.

c. The show inspired countless future programs for children.

d. Although *Sesame Street* was an educational program, it provided entertainment for kids as well.

e. Over 74 million Americans have watched the show since it began.

1. Mika and I spent this morning reviewing our notes for the test.

2. In the bottom drawer, you can find some extra notebooks.

3. Buildings that meet the new flood requirements will not need additional insurance.

4. Customers who bring their own bags to the store earn reward points.

5. After watching all the Harry Potter movies in one weekend, Sadie vowed to read all the books again.

---

3 | Verbs, Objects, and Complements

More information about using verbs correctly can be found in 8, 9, and 21.

Verbs provide information about the subject's action or state of being. **Action verbs** show action (*swim, eat, sleep*), and **linking verbs** (*is, become, seem, feel*) link the subject of a sentence with a word that renames or describes it. A few verbs accompany a main verb to add information about time or possibility; they are called **helping** or **auxiliary verbs** (*have, must, can*).

3a Action Verbs and Objects

Most action verbs (AV) can be followed by one or more objects. A **direct object** (DO) is the target of the verb's action. It usually answers the question *What?* or *Who?*

> AV   DO
> Kevin *drank* three *sodas* at the movies. [The direct object, *sodas*, answers the question "What did Kevin drink?"]

An **indirect object** (IO) is the recipient of the verb's action. It usually answers the question *For what?* or *For whom?*

> AV IO   DO
> Kevin *bought me* some *popcorn* at the movies. [The direct object, *popcorn*, answers the question "What did Kevin buy?"; the indirect object, *me*, answers the question "For whom did Kevin buy some popcorn?"]

Some verbs, known as **transitive verbs**, require an object to make their meaning clear.

> AV   DO
> Elana *fixed* the flat *tire*. [The direct object, *tire*, answers the question "What did Elana fix?" Without the direct object and its modifiers (*the flat*), the sentence ("Elana fixed.") would not make sense.]

 Guidelines for Multilingual Writers
What Preposition Should I Use with Indirect Objects?

These sentences mean the same thing:

> I sent the president a letter.

> I sent a letter to the president.

In the first sentence, *the president* is the **indirect object**: he or she receives the direct object (*a letter*), which was acted on (*sent*) by the subject of the sentence (*I*). In the second sentence, the same idea is expressed using a **prepositional phrase** beginning with *to*.

■ Some verbs can use either an indirect object or the preposition *to*: *give, send, lend, offer, owe, pay, sell, show, teach, tell.* Some verbs can use an indirect object or the preposition *for*: *bake, build, buy, cook, find, get, make.*

> I paid the travel agent one hundred dollars.

> I paid one hundred dollars to the travel agent.

> Margarita cooked her family some chicken.

> Margarita cooked some chicken for her family.

(continued)

- Some verbs cannot have an indirect object; they must use a preposition. The following verbs must use the preposition *to*: *describe, demonstrate, explain, introduce,* and *suggest*.

  Please explain ~~me~~ indirect objects _^ *to me.*

- The following verbs must use the preposition *for*: *answer* and *prepare*.

  He prepared ~~me~~ the punch _^ *for me.*

- Some verbs cannot use a preposition; instead, they can have an indirect object. The following verbs must have an indirect object: *ask* and *cost*.

  Sasha asked _^ *her* a question ~~to her~~.

3b Linking Verbs and Complements

A **linking verb** (LV) shows what the subject of a sentence *is* or *is like*. The linking verb connects the subject with its **subject complement** (SC) — a noun, a pronoun, or an adjective.

> **COMMON LINKING VERBS** at a glance
>
> Some linking verbs tell what a noun is, was, or will be.
>
> > *be, become, remain*: I *remain* optimistic.
> > *grow*: The sky is *growing* dark.
> > *make*: One plus two *makes* three.
> > *prove*: His warning *proved* accurate.
> > *turn*: The weather *turned* cold.
>
> Some linking verbs tell what a noun might be.
>
> > *appear, seem, look*: The child *looks* cold.
>
> Most verbs of the senses can operate as linking verbs.
>
> > *feel, smell, sound, taste*: The smoothie *tastes* sweet.

            LV   SC
Julia will *make* a good *doctor*. [The subject complement, *doctor*, is a noun renaming the subject, *Julia*.]

            LV   SC
Jorge *is* not the *one*. [The subject complement, *one*, is a pronoun renaming the subject, *Jorge*.]

                    LV   SC
London weather *seems foggy*. [The subject complement, *foggy*, is an adjective describing the subject, *weather*.]

A verb may be a linking verb in some sentences and a transitive verb in others. If you focus on what the verb means, you can usually tell how it is functioning.

>   LV   SC
> I often *grow sleepy* after lunch. [The verb *grow* is a linking verb (meaning "become") because it is followed by a subject complement, *sleepy*.]

>   AV   DO
> I often *grow tomatoes* in my garden. [The verb *grow* is a transitive verb (meaning "raise") because it is followed by a direct object, *tomatoes*.]

Object complements are similar to subject complements in that they rename a noun, in this case the object of a verb or preposition. But no linking verb is required with object complements.

>   DO   OC
> The judges rated *Hugo* the best *skater*. [The object complement, *skater*, renames the direct object, *Hugo*.]

3c Helping Verbs

Verbs such as *have, must,* and *can* that accompany a main verb to add information about its action are called **helping** or **auxiliary verbs**. Adding a helping or auxiliary verb to a main verb allows you to express a wide variety of tenses and moods. (See 8.) The parts of this combination, called a **verb phrase,** need not appear together and may be separated by other words.

> HELPING   HELPING   MAIN
> VERB   VERB   VERB
> You *should* not *have scared* that pigeon. [*Should* and *have* add information about the main verb *scared*.]

> ## HELPING VERBS at a glance
>
> Of the twenty-three helping verbs, fourteen can also act as main verbs that identify the central action.
>
> > be, is, am, are, was, were, being, been
> > do, does, did
> > have, has, had
>
> The other nine act only as helping verbs, never as main verbs. They are called modal verbs, and they show actions that are possible, doubtful, necessary, required, and so on.
>
> > can, could, should, would, may, might, must, shall, will

EXERCISE 3–1 Identifying Verbs, Objects, and Complements

Label the underlined word or word group in the following sentences as action verb (AV), linking verb (LV), helping verb (HV), direct object (DO), indirect object (IO), or subject complement (SC). Answers for the lettered sentences appear at the end of the Handbook. Example:

>   *HV*   *MV*
> Many science and technology inventions <u>are</u> <u>inspired</u> by nature.

a. An entrepreneur named Percy Shaw <u>invented</u> <u>reflectors</u> for road signs after seeing a cat's eyes glowing in his headlights on a foggy night.

b. An inventor named George de Mestral <u>noticed</u> <u>burrs</u> in his dog's fur; he then <u>gave</u> the <u>world</u> <u>Velcro.</u>

c. Many scientists <u>are</u> <u>eager</u> to discover new products.

d. Accidents <u>have</u> also <u>inspired</u> <u>inventions.</u>

e. A machine giving off microwave particles <u>melted</u> a chocolate <u>bar,</u> leading to the invention of the microwave oven.

1. Soda and other sugary beverages <u>are</u> at least partly <u>responsible</u> for increasing obesity rates in children.

2. Some schools <u>sell</u> <u>children</u> soft <u>drinks,</u> which nutritionists say is a bad idea.

3. Milk <u>is</u> more <u>important</u> than sugary drinks for developing bones.

4. Some cities and states <u>have</u> <u>passed</u> <u>laws</u> to tax sodas.

5. Others <u>want</u> extra-large <u>sodas</u> to be completely banned.

Learning by Doing 🔲 Finding Subjects and Verbs

Being able to identify subjects and verbs in your own writing will make it much easier to find and fix common grammatical problems such as subject-verb agreement errors. Working with one of your drafts, underline all the main subjects and double underline all the main verbs. Draw a line connecting the subject-verb pairs. Do some subjects have more than one verb? Do some verbs have more than one subject? Do some sentences have multiple subject-verb pairs? All of these situations are acceptable if the correct grammar and punctuation are used.

4 | Clauses and Phrases

Clauses and phrases are word groups that have a specific function in a sentence. Clauses have both a subject and a verb; phrases do not.

4a Clauses

Clauses can be independent or dependent (subordinate). An **independent clause** contains a subject and a verb, expresses a complete thought, and can stand alone as a complete sentence. Independent clauses are often referred to as the **main clause** in a sentence.

MAIN CLAUSE

Stevie Ray Vaughan was inducted into the Rock and Roll Hall of Fame in 2015. [*Stevie Ray Vaughan* is the subject of the clause; *was inducted* is the verb.]

A **subordinate clause** looks very similar to an independent clause, with a subject, a verb, and a complete thought, but it cannot stand alone as a sentence because it opens with a **subordinating conjunction**.

SUBORDINATE CLAUSE

Although he died in 1995

A subordinate clause may be joined to an independent clause for grammatical correctness.

SUBORDINATE CLAUSE   MAIN CLAUSE

Although he died in 1995, *Stevie Ray Vaughan was inducted* into the Rock

and Roll Hall of Fame in 2015. [Note that each clause in this sentence includes a subject and a verb.]

4b Phrases

Phrases are groups of related words that do not contain a subject and a verb.

Prepositional Phrases

A word group that begins with a preposition and ends with a noun is called a **prepositional phrase.** The noun in the prepositional phrase is the object of the preposition. Prepositional phrases can modify nouns or verbs.

PREPOSITIONAL PHRASE

The fox ran *into the woods.* [The prepositional phrase *into the woods* modifies the verb *ran* by describing where the fox ran to.]

PREPOSITIONAL PHRASE

The plants *on the balcony* need water. [The prepositional phrase *on the balcony* describes which plants need water.]

Verbal Phrases

Verbals look like verbs, but they do not function as verbs in a sentence. Verbals include infinitives (*to* + verb), present participles (verb form ending in *-ing*), and past participles (verb form usually ending in *-ed*). (For more on participles, see 8.)

INFINITIVE	PRESENT PARTICIPLE	PAST PARTICIPLE
to walk	walking	walked
to look	looking	looked
to drive	driving	drove

Verbals can be used on their own or in **verbal phrases,** which consist of the verbal plus any related words. Both verbals and verbal phrases can act as nouns, adjectives, or adverbs.

VERBAL PHRASE AS ADVERB

The team worked nights to avoid the scorching sun. [The verbal phrase *to avoid the scorching sun* modifies the verb *worked*. The verbal is the infinitive *to avoid*.]

VERBAL PHRASE AS NOUN/SUBJECT

Bicycling to work is my favorite way to exercise and help the environment. [The verbal phrase *Bicycling to work* is the subject of the sentence. The verbal is the present participle *bicycling*.]

VERBAL PHRASE AS ADJECTIVE

The letter, signed by Halley's attorney, will be on your desk in the morning. [The verbal phrase *signed by Halley's attorney* modifies the noun *letter*. The verbal is the past participle *signed*.]

Appositive Phrases

An **appositive** adds information to a noun or pronoun by identifying it in a different way. An appositive can be a single word or a group of words, sometimes called an **appositive phrase**.

APPOSITIVE

My dog, Laika, destroyed the library book.

APPOSITIVE PHRASE

My dog, a Portuguese water dog, is a strong swimmer.

Absolute Phrases

An **absolute phrase** is an expression, usually a noun followed by a participle, that modifies an entire clause or sentence and can appear anywhere in the sentence.

ABSOLUTE PHRASE

The stallion pawed the ground, chestnut mane and tail swirling in the wind.

EXERCISE 4–1 Identifying Phrases and Clauses

Label each underlined word group in the following sentences as main clause, subordinate clause, prepositional phrase, verbal phrase, appositive phrase, or absolute phrase. Answers for the lettered sentences appear at the end of the Handbook. Example:

> <u>*subordinate clauses*</u>   <u>*main clause*</u>
> When the winner was announced, everybody cheered.

a. <u>Spending the night in an ice hotel</u> is <u>on my bucket list</u>.

b. I will do well <u>on the test</u> <u>because I studied for three hours</u>.

c. The car, <u>a 1957 Chevy</u>, gleamed like it had just come <u>off the assembly line</u>.

d. <u>After searching all morning</u>, <u>we gave up on finding the lost earring</u>.

e. We exited the house hurriedly, <u>dinner still steaming on the table</u>.

1. <u>The Inca site of Machu Picchu is undergoing restoration</u>.

2. The historic city is situated over 7,000 feet <u>above sea level</u>, <u>its terraced fields reaching as high as the clouds</u>.

3. <u>Built by the Incas around 1450</u>, <u>Machu Picchu existed unknown to outsiders for centuries</u>.

4. American Hiram Bingham, <u>who came upon the site in the early twentieth century</u>, embellished the story of his discovery.

5. The city, <u>a UNESCO World Heritage Site</u>, has been open to tourists since 1911.

5 | Sentence Structures

Sentences contain familiar patterns of syntax, or word order, that allow us to make sense of them.

5a Simple Sentences

All sentences consist of at least one main clause, which includes a subject and a verb.

>   S   V
> Alyssa skates.

A sentence with only one main clause is called a **simple sentence**. It may contain modifiers, objects, complements, and phrases in addition to the subject and verb.

>   S   V   DO
> Even amateur stargazers can locate the Big Dipper in the night sky.

Like clauses, simple sentences may contain more than one subject, which is called a **compound subject**.

COMPOUND SUBJECT

Frankie and Bruno played baseball.

Clauses and simple sentences may also contain more than one verb, called a **compound verb**.

COMPOUND VERB

Sarah and Tomas sing, act, and dance.

5b Compound Sentences

Clauses may be combined to form longer, more elaborate sentences. A **compound sentence** consists of two or more main clauses joined by a coordinating conjunction such as *and* or *but,* by a semicolon, or by a semicolon followed by a transition word such as *however* or *nevertheless.*

MAIN CLAUSE   MAIN CLAUSE

I would like to accompany you, but I can't.

MAIN CLAUSE   MAIN CLAUSE

My car broke down; therefore, I missed the first day of class.

5c Complex Sentences

For help with combining clauses correctly, see 19.

A **complex sentence** has one main clause and one or more subordinate clauses.

MAIN CLAUSE   SUBORDINATE CLAUSE

I will be at the airport when you arrive.

5d Compound-Complex Sentences

A **compound-complex sentence** combines a compound sentence (two or more main clauses) and a complex sentence (at least one subordinate clause).

MAIN CLAUSE   SUBORDINATE CLAUSE   MAIN CLAUSE

Nobody saw the accident, and when the police arrived, the driver had

already left the scene.

EXERCISE 5–1 Identifying Sentence Types

Identify each sentence below as simple, compound, complex, or compound-complex. Answers for the lettered sentences appear at the end of the Handbook. Example:

> **Although Jenna is not superstitious, she will not stay on the thirteenth floor of a hotel.** *complex*

a. Manga is a style of Japanese comic book that caught on in the United States in the 1990s.

b. This trunk contains all our old family photos; if it were destroyed, we would have no way to replace them.

c. Carlo visited Jan's fruit stand at the farmers' market, and he mentioned my name.

d. I walked to the station, rode the train for an hour, and took a bus to the other side of town.

e. Ben and Jerry created a successful ice cream company.

1. After the Soviet Union collapsed in 1989, many eastern European countries gained independence.

2. Russia and the United States have never fought directly against each other in a war.

3. For decades, the two countries have had differing viewpoints and have supported opposing sides in smaller wars.

4. The two countries continue to disagree on many global issues, and they accuse each other of inappropriate actions.

5. Even though they rarely see eye-to-eye, the Russians and the Americans have worked together at important times, and they must strive to find more common ground in the future.

6 | Sentence Fragments

A **sentence** is a word group that includes both a subject and a predicate and can stand alone (see 5a).

A **subject** is the part of a sentence that names something—a person, an object, an idea, a situation—about which the verb makes an assertion (see 2).

A **verb** is a word that shows action or a state of being (see 1c and 3).

Unlike a complete sentence, a **fragment** is partial or incomplete. It may lack a subject, a verb, or both. A fragment fails to express a grammatically complete thought. Unless you add what's missing or reword what's incomplete, a fragment cannot stand alone as a sentence. Even so, we all use fragments in everyday speech, where their context and delivery make them understandable and therefore acceptable.

> That bicycle over there.
>
> Good job.
>
> Not if I can help it.

In writing, fragments like these fail to communicate complete, coherent ideas. Notice how much more effective they are as complete sentences.

> I'd like to buy that bicycle over there.
>
> You did a good job sanding the floor.
>
> Nobody will steal my seat if I can help it.

Some writers use fragments on purpose. Advertisers are fond of short, emphatic fragments that command attention, like quick jabs to the head.

> For seafood lovers. Every Tuesday night. All you can eat.

In texts or tweets, writers compress their language because time and space are limited. They rely on the recipient to fill in the gaps.

> Thru with lab. CU @ 8. Pizza?

In college writing, though, it is good practice to express your ideas in complete sentences.

6a If a fragment is a phrase, link it to a nearby sentence, or make it a complete sentence.

You have two choices for revising a fragment if it is a phrase: (1) link it to an adjoining sentence, using punctuation such as a comma or a colon, or (2) add a missing subject or verb to make it a complete sentence.

> Malcolm has two goals. ~~Wealth~~ *: wealth* and power. [The phrase *Wealth and power* has no verb; inserting a colon links it to *goals.*]

> Al ends his stories the way he mixes his martinis. ~~With~~ *, with* a twist. [The prepositional phrase *With a twist* has no subject or verb; inserting a comma links it to the main clause.]

> To stamp out the union. ~~That~~ was the bosses' plan. [The infinitive phrase *To stamp out the union* has no main verb or subject; the revision transforms it into the subject of the sentence.]

> The students *were* taking the final exam in the auditorium. [The helping verb *were* completes the verb and makes a sentence.]

6b If a fragment is a subordinate clause, link it to a nearby sentence, or drop the subordinating conjunction.

Some fragments are missing neither subject nor verb. Instead, they are subordinate clauses, unable to express complete thoughts unless linked with main clauses. When you find a subordinating conjunction at the start or in the middle of a word group, that word group may be a subordinate clause. You can (1) combine the fragment with a main clause (a complete sentence) nearby, or (2) make the subordinate clause into a complete sentence by dropping the subordinating conjunction.

> The new law will help create jobs. ~~If~~ *, if* it passes.

> Because Jay is an avid skier. ~~He~~ *, he* loves winter in the mountains.

A **phrase** consists of two or more related words that work together but may lack a subject, a verb, or both (see 4b).

A **subordinating conjunction** is a word (such as *because, although, if, when*) used to make one clause dependent on, or subordinate to, another (see 19d–19f.)

6c If a fragment has a participle but no other verb, change the participle to a main verb, or link the fragment to a nearby sentence.

A present participle (the *-ing* form of the verb) can serve as the main verb in a sentence only with a form of *be* ("Sally *is working* harder than usual"). A participle alone, used as a main verb, results in a fragment.

> Jon was used to the pressure of deadlines. *, having* ~~Having~~ worked the night shift at the daily newspaper. [The fragment is combined with an adjoining sentence.]

> Jon was used to the pressure of deadlines. *He had* ~~Having~~ worked the night shift at the daily newspaper. [Another form of the verb is used.]

A **compound verb** consists of two or more verbs linked by a conjunction (see 5a).

6d If a fragment is part of a compound verb, add it to the sentence with the subject and the rest of the predicate.

> In spite of a pulled muscle, Jeremy ran the race. *and* ~~And~~ won.

EXERCISE 6–1 Eliminating Fragments

Eliminate any fragments in the following examples. Some sentences may be correct. Possible revisions for the lettered sentences appear at the end of the Handbook. Example:

> Bryan hates parsnips. *and* ~~And~~ loathes squash.

a. Michael had a beautiful Southern accent. Having lived many years in Georgia.

b. Pat and Chris are determined to marry each other. Even if their families do not approve.

c. Jack seemed well qualified for a career in the air force. Except for his tendency to get airsick.

d. Lisa advocated sleeping no more than four hours a night. Until she started nodding off through her classes.

e. They met. They talked. They fought. They reached agreement.

1. Being the first person in his family ever to attend college. Alex is determined to succeed.

2. Does our society rob children of their childhood? By making them aware too soon of adult ills?

3. Richard III supposedly had the young princes murdered. No one has ever found out what really happened to them.

4. For democracy to function, two elements are crucial. An educated populace and a collective belief in people's ability to chart their own course.

5. You must take his stories as others do. With a grain of salt.

EXERCISE 6–2 Eliminating Fragments

Rewrite the following paragraph, eliminating all fragments. Explain why you made each change. Example:

> Many people exercise to improve their health, ~~But~~ *but* may forget that food and sleep are also important. [The second word group is a fragment because it has no subject. The revised sentence links the fragment to the rest of the sentence.]

Exercise alone won't be beneficial if the body isn't fed and rested. The average adult should consume roughly 2,000 to 2,500 calories per day. Those calories should reflect a balanced diet. Including fiber, protein, and essential vitamins and minerals. Healthy adults should sleep 7 to 9 hours every night. And avoid sleeping during the day. The right amount of exercise is also important. Because pushing the body too hard can result in injury. For most adults, 2 to 5 hours of moderate exercise per week will yield significant health benefits. Whether they are trying to lose weight, gain strength, or simply feel better. People should adopt a balanced regimen.

---

7 | Comma Splices and Fused Sentences

Joining two main clauses with only a comma between them yields a faulty construction called a **comma splice.** Here are two perfectly good main clauses, each separate, each able to stand on its own as a sentence:

> The detective wriggled on his belly toward the campfire. The sleeping smugglers didn't notice him.

Splicing those sentences with a comma makes for difficult reading.

> COMMA SPLICE   The detective wriggled on his belly toward the campfire, the sleeping smugglers didn't notice him.

Even more confusing than a comma splice is a **fused sentence** or **run-on:** two main clauses joined without any punctuation.

> FUSED SENTENCE   The detective wriggled on his belly toward the campfire the sleeping smugglers didn't notice him.

Lacking clues from the writer, a reader cannot tell where to pause. To understand the sentence, he or she must halt and reread.

> A **main clause** is a group of words that has both a subject and a verb and can stand alone as a complete sentence (see 4a).

The next two pages show five easy ways to eliminate both comma splices and fused sentences. Your choice depends on the length and complexity of your main clauses and the effect you want to achieve.

A **sentence** is a word group that includes both a subject and a verb and can stand alone (see 5a).

7a Write separate complete sentences to correct a comma splice or a fused sentence.

Freud has been called an enemy of sexual repression, *the* truth is that he is not a friend of free love.

Coordinating **conjunctions** join elements with equal or near-equal importance (see 1g and 19a–19c).

7b Use a comma and a coordinating conjunction to correct a comma splice or a fused sentence.

If both clauses are of roughly equal weight, you can use a comma to link them — as long as you add a coordinating conjunction after the comma.

Hurricane winds hit ninety miles an hour, *and* they tore the roof from every house on Paradise Drive.

7c Use a semicolon or a colon to correct a comma splice or a fused sentence.

A semicolon can connect two closely related thoughts, emphasizing each one.

Hurricane winds hit ninety miles an hour; they tore the roof from every house on Paradise Drive.

If the second thought illustrates or explains the first, add it with a colon.

The hurricane caused extensive damage: it tore the roof from every house on Paradise Drive.

A **main clause** is a group of words that has both a subject and a verb and can stand alone as a complete sentence (see 4a).

For advice on subordination, see 19d–19f. For a list of subordinating conjunctions, see p. 568.

7d Use subordination to correct a comma splice or a fused sentence.

To show that one main clause has more importance, make the less important one subordinate by adding a subordinating conjunction.

When Hurricane winds hit ninety miles an hour, they tore the roof from every house on Paradise Drive.

Hurricane winds *, which* ~~hit ninety miles an hour they~~ tore the roof from every *, hit ninety miles an hour.* house on Paradise Drive.

7e Use a semicolon, conjunctive adverb, and a comma to correct a comma splice or a fused sentence.

If you want to cram more than one clause into a sentence, you may join two clauses with a **conjunctive adverb.** Conjunctive adverbs show relationships such as addition (*also, besides*), comparison (*likewise, similarly*), contrast (*instead, however*), emphasis (*namely, certainly*), cause and effect (*thus, therefore*), or time (*finally, subsequently*). These transitional words and phrases can be a useful way of linking clauses—but only with the right punctuation. Insert the semicolon after the first main clause. Then give the conjunctive adverb, followed by a comma and the rest of the sentence.

> Freud has been called an enemy of sexual repression, ; however, the truth is that he is not a friend of free love.

A writer might consider a comma plus the conjunctive adverb *however* enough to combine the two main clauses, but that glue won't hold. Stronger binding—the semicolon along with a comma—is required.

For a list of conjunctive adverbs, see p. 633.

EXERCISE 7–1 Revising Comma Splices and Fused Sentences

In the following examples, correct each comma splice or fused sentence in two ways, and decide which way works better. Be creative: don't correct all the same way. Some may be correct as written. Possible revisions for the lettered sentences appear at the end of the Handbook. Example:

> Comic book writer Stan Lee created famous characters such as
> Spider-Man and the ~~Hulk, he~~ *Hulk. He* grew up in New York City.

> Comic book writer Stan ~~Lee~~ *Lee, who grew up in New York City,* created famous characters such as
> Spider-Man and the ~~Hulk, he grew up in New York City.~~ *Hulk.*

a. Lee's comic book superheroes are ordinary people with flaws they also have extraordinary abilities.

b. Iron Man (Tony Stark) has a superpowered suit and the ability to fly, he is a heavy drinker and suffers from anxiety.

c. Teenaged nerd Peter Parker is another example he has spider-like abilities to spin webs and scale buildings.

d. Thor is a godlike superhero who comes to Earth with super strength and the ability to fly, his weakness is his fondness for humans.

e. Bruce Banner was a brilliant scientist who studied gamma radiation, an accident caused him to turn into a giant destructive hulk when he gets angry.

1. Other well-known superheroes include Superman and Batman, they originated in the 1930s.
2. Superman is the last survivor of the planet Krypton he has x-ray vision and super strength he is weakened by kryptonite.
3. Batman has no superhuman abilities, he fights crime using his ingenuity and his physical prowess.
4. Wonder Woman came along in 1941 she is a warrior princess based on the Amazons of Greek mythology.
5. Many superhero characters are making comebacks in high-budget films, they feature famous actors and impressive special effects.

EXERCISE 7–2 Revising Comma Splices and Fused Sentences

Revise the following passage, using subordination, a conjunctive adverb, a semicolon, or a colon to correct each comma splice or fused sentence. You may also write separate complete sentences. Some sentences may be correct. Example:

> *because*
> English can be difficult to learn / it is full of expressions that don't mean what they literally say.

Have you ever wondered why you drive on parkways and park on driveways, that's about as logical as your nose running while your feet smell! When you think about it, these phrases don't make sense yet we tend to accept them without thinking about what they literally mean we simply take their intended meanings for granted. Think, however, how confusing they are for a person who is just learning the language. If, for example, you have just learned the verb *park*, you would logically assume that a parkway is where you should park your car, of course when most people see a parkway or a driveway they realize that braking on a parkway would be hazardous, while speeding through a driveway will not take them very far. However, our language is full of idiomatic expressions that may be difficult for a person from another language background to understand. Fortunately, there are plenty of questions to keep us *all* confused, such as why Americans commonly refer to going to work as "punching the clock."

8 | Verb Form, Tense, and Mood

For information on active versus passive voice in verbs, see 21.

Verb forms can change to show **tense**, which indicates the time that the action took place (last year, next month), and **mood**, which indicates the attitude of the thought being expressed (a command, a wish, a statement).

8a Use the correct form of the verb.

Verbs can take one of five forms and stand alone or with helping verbs to indicate the full range of times when an action or a state of being does, did, might, or will occur.

- The **base** is the simple dictionary form of the verb (*go, sing, laugh*) that is used for the present tense for all but the third-person singular: *I/we/you/ they go, sing, laugh*. For the third-person present tense, add an *-s* or *-es* ending: *He/she/it goes, sings, laughs*. The base form preceded by *to* (*to go, to sing, to laugh*) is called the **infinitive.**
- The **past tense** signals completed action (*went, sang, laughed*). (See 8c.)
- The **past participle** is combined with helping verbs to indicate action at various past or future times (*have gone, had sung, will have laughed*). (See 8e.) With forms of *be*, it makes the passive voice. (See 21.)
- The **present participle,** the *-ing* form of the verb (*going, singing, laughing*), is used to make the progressive tenses. (See 8f and 8g.) It also can modify nouns and pronouns ("the *leaking* bottle") or, as a gerund, function as a noun ("*Sleeping all day* pleases me").

8b Use the simple present tense for actions that take place once, repeatedly, or continuously in the present.

The simple present tense is the infinitive form of a regular verb plus *-s* or *-es* for the third-person singular (used with *a singular noun* or *he, she*, or *it*).

I like, I watch	we like, we watch
you like, you watch	you like, you watch
he/she/it likes, he/she/it watches	they like, they watch

> ### VERB TENSES at a glance
>
> Note that these examples show first person only.
>
> **SIMPLE TENSES**
>
> | *Present* | *Past* | *Future* |
> |---|---|---|
> | I cook | I cooked | I will cook |
> | I see | I saw | I will see |
>
> **PERFECT TENSES**
>
> | *Present perfect* | *Past perfect* | *Future perfect* |
> |---|---|---|
> | I have cooked | I had cooked | I will have cooked |
> | I have seen | I had seen | I will have seen |
>
> **PROGRESSIVE TENSES**
>
> | *Present progressive* | *Past progressive* | *Future progressive* |
> |---|---|---|
> | I am cooking | I was cooking | I will be cooking |
> | I am seeing | I was seeing | I will be seeing |
> | *Present perfect progressive* | *Past perfect progressive* | *Future perfect progressive* |
> | I have been cooking | I had been cooking | I will have been cooking |
> | I have been seeing | I had been seeing | I will have been seeing |

The irregular verbs *be* and *have* are special cases for which you should learn the correct forms.

I am, I have	we are, we have
you are, you have	you are, you have
he/she/it is, he/she/it has	they are, they have

You can use the simple present tense for an action happening right now ("I *welcome* this news"), happening repeatedly in the present ("Judy *goes* to church every Sunday"), or ongoing in the present ("Wesley *likes* ice cream"). In some cases, if you want to ask a question, intensify the action, or form a negative, use the helping verb *do* or *does* before the main verb.

I *do think* you should take the job. I *don't think* it will be difficult.

Does Christos *want* it? *Do* you *want* it? *Doesn't* anyone *want* it?

You can use the simple present for future action: "Football *starts* Wednesday." With *before, after,* or *when,* use it to express a future meaning: "When the team bus *arrives,* the players will board." Use it also for a general or timeless truth, even if the rest of the sentence is in a different tense.

Water *freezes* at 32 degrees.

8c　Use the simple past tense for actions already completed.

Use the past tense for an action at a specific past time, whether stated or implied.

Nicole *walked* to the theater yesterday.

Though speakers may not pronounce the *-d* or *-ed* ending, standard written English requires that you add it to regular past tense verbs.

　　　used
I use to wear weird clothes when I was a child.

Most verbs in English are **regular verbs**: they form the past tense in a standard, predictable way. Regular verbs that end in *-e* add *-d* to the base form; those that do not end in *-e* add *-ed.*

Akira *smiled* all night long.

Jack *enjoyed* the party.

At least two hundred **irregular verbs** form the past tense in some way other than by adding *-d* or *-ed.*

　　　drove
Lauren drived home early.

Because irregular verbs do not follow a standard pattern when they take the past tense, the forms must be memorized.

Most irregular verbs, familiar to native English speakers, pose no problem. For more details on verbs that cause trouble when changing tense, see 8h (*be, have,* and *do*) and 8i (*lie/lay* and *sit/set*).

Guidelines for Multilingual Writers
When Do I Use the Past, Present, and Future Tenses of Verbs?

DURATION OR TIME RELATIONSHIP	PAST TIME: *Yesterday, some time ago, long ago*	PRESENT TIME: *Right now, today, or at this moment*	FUTURE TIME: *Tomorrow, soon, or at some expected or possible moment*
ACTION OR STATE *OCCURS ONCE*	**PAST TENSE:** The team *played* the game last week.	**PRESENT TENSE:** The game *starts* now.	**FUTURE TENSE:** The bus *will arrive* at noon on Friday. **PRESENT TENSE:** The bus *arrives* after lunch.
ACTION OR STATE *OCCURS REPEATEDLY*	**PAST TENSE:** The team *played* every Monday of the summer.	**PRESENT TENSE:** The game *starts* on time.	**FUTURE TENSE:** The bus *will arrive* at noon on Fridays. **PRESENT TENSE:** The bus *arrives* at noon on Fridays.
ACTION OR STATE *OCCURS CONTINUOUSLY*	**PAST TENSE:** The team *played* their best all season.	**PRESENT TENSE:** The game always *ends* before dark.	**PRESENT TENSE:** The bus *will arrive* at noon from now on.
ACTION OR STATE *IS A GENERAL OR TIMELESS FACT*		**PRESENT TENSE:** A good game *needs* action and suspense.	
ACTION OR STATE *IS COMPLETED BEFORE THE TIME OF ANOTHER ACTION*	**PAST PERFECT TENSE:** The team *had practiced* for only two weeks before they played their first game.		**FUTURE PERFECT TENSE:** The bus *will have arrived* at six other fields before it reaches our stop.
ACTION OR STATE *WAS BEGUN IN THE PAST BUT IS STILL GOING ON*		**PRESENT PERFECT TENSE:** The game *has provided* enjoyment every week.	

PAST TENSE OF COMMON IRREGULAR VERBS
at a glance

BASE	PAST TENSE
be, am, is, are	was, were
begin	began
choose	chose
do	did
eat	ate
go	went
have	had
speak	spoke

In the past tense, you can use the helping verb *did* (past tense of *do*) to ask a question or intensify the action. Use *did* (or *didn't*) with the base form of the main verb for both regular and irregular verbs.

I walked.	I did walk.	Why did I walk?
You watched.	You did watch.	What did you watch?
She jogged.	She did jog.	Where did she jog?

 Guidelines for Multilingual Writers
How Do I Form Negatives?

You can make a sentence negative by using **not** or another negative adverb such as *seldom, rarely, never, hardly, hardly ever,* or *almost never.*

- With *not*: subject + helping verb + *not* + main verb

  Gina did *not* go to the concert.

  They will *not* call again.

- For questions: helping verb + *n't* (contraction for *not*) + subject + main verb

  Didn't [for *Did not*] Gina go to the concert?

  Won't [for *Will not*] they call again?

- With a negative adverb: subject + negative adverb + main verb *or* subject + helping verb + negative adverb + main verb

  My son *seldom* watches TV.

  Danh may *never* see them again.

- With a negative adverb at the beginning of a clause: negative adverb + helping verb + subject + verb

  Not only does Emma struggle with tennis, but she also struggles with golf.

  Never before have I been so happy.

NOTE: Don't pile up several negatives for intensity or emphasis in a sentence. Readers may consider double negatives (*not never, not hardly, wouldn't not*) sloppy repetition or assume that two negatives cancel each other out.

The students did not ~~never~~ arrive late.

(ever inserted above)

The students ~~did not~~ never ~~arrive~~ late.

(arrived inserted above)

8d Use the simple future tense for actions that are expected to happen but have not happened yet.

Most actions that have not yet taken place are expressed in the simple future tense, including promises and predictions.

> George *will arrive* in time for dinner.

> *Will* you please *show* him where to park?

To form the simple future tense, add *will* to the base form of the verb.

I will climb	we will climb
you will climb	you will climb
he/she/it will climb	they will climb

You can also use *shall* to inject a tone of determination ("We *shall* overcome!") or in polite questions ("*Shall* we dance?").

It is true that the present tense can indicate future action ("We *go* on vacation next Monday" – see 1b), but this is generally informal in tone.

8e Use the perfect tenses for actions completed at the time of another action.

The perfect tenses consist of the verb *have* plus the past participle.

For regular verbs, the past participle is the same as the past tense. For irregular verbs, the past participle follows no set pattern and must be memorized.

See 8h for details on the very irregular verbs *be*, *have*, and *do*; see 8i for details on the confusing verbs *lie/lay* and *sit/set*.

> ### PAST TENSE AND PAST PARTICIPLE at a glance
>
> **REGULAR VERBS**
>
> | Base | Past Tense | Past Participle |
> |---|---|---|
> | hatch | hatched | hatched |
> | look | looked | looked |
> | smile | smiled | smiled |
>
> **IRREGULAR VERBS**
>
> | Base | Past Tense | Past Participle |
> |---|---|---|
> | be, am, is, are | was, were | been |
> | begin | began | begun |
> | burst | burst | burst |
> | choose | chose | chosen |
> | do | did | done |
> | eat | ate | eaten |
> | go | went | gone |
> | lay | laid | laid |
> | lie | lay | lain |
> | set | set | set |
> | sit | sat | sat |
> | speak | spoke | spoken |

In the perfect tenses, the tense of *have* indicates the tense of the whole verb phrase. The action of a **present perfect** verb was completed before the sentence is uttered. Its helping verb is in the present tense: *have* or *has*.

I *have* never *visited* Spain, but I *have visited* Mexico.

Have you *called* Mr. Grimaldi? Mr. Grimaldi *has called* for help.

You can use the present perfect tense for an action completed before some other action: "I *have washed* my hands of the whole affair, but I am watching from a distance." With *for* or *since*, it shows an action begun in the past and still going on: "Max *has worked* in this office for years."

The action of a **past perfect** verb was completed before some other action in the past. Its helping verb is in the past tense: *had*.

The concert *had ended* by the time we found a parking space.

Had you *wanted* to clean the house before your parents arrived?

In informal writing, the simple past may be used when the relationship between actions is made clear by *when*, *before*, *after*, or *until*.

Observers *watched* the plane catch fire before it landed.

The action of a **future perfect** verb will be completed by some point (specified or implied) in the future. Its helping verb is in the future tense: *will have*.

The builders *will have finished* the house by June.

When you acquire the new dime, *will* you *have collected* every coin you want?

The store *will* not *have closed* by the time we arrive.

8f Use the simple progressive tenses for actions in progress.

The progressive tenses consist of a form of *be* plus the present participle (the *-ing* form). The tense of *be* determines the tense of the whole verb phrase.

The **present progressive** expresses an action that began in the past and is taking place now. Its helping verb is in the present tense: *am*, *is*, or *are*.

I *am thinking* of a country in Africa.

Is Stefan *babysitting* while we *are visiting* her sister?

You can express future action with the present progressive of *go* plus an infinitive phrase.

I am *going to sign up* for the CPR class.

The **past progressive** expresses an action that took place continuously at some time in the past, whether or not that action is still going on. Its helping verb is in the past tense: *was* or *were*.

The old men *were sitting* on the porch when we passed.

Lucy *was planning* to take the weekend off.

The **future progressive** expresses an action that will take place continuously at some time in the future. Its helping verb is in the future tense: *will be*.

They *will be answering* the phones while she is gone.

Will we *be dining* out every night on our vacation?

8g Use the perfect progressive tenses for continuing actions that began earlier.

The **present perfect progressive** indicates an action that started in the past and is continuing in the present. Form it by adding the present perfect of *be* (*has been, have been*) to the present participle (*-ing* form) of the main verb. Often *for* or *since* is used with this tense.

Fred *has been complaining* about his neighbor since the wild parties began.

Have you *been reading* Uma's postcards from England?

The **past perfect progressive** expresses a continuing action that was completed before another past action. Form it by adding the past perfect of *be* (*had been*) to the present participle of the main verb.

By the time Khalid finally arrived, I *had been waiting* for half an hour.

The **future perfect progressive** expresses an action that is expected to continue into the future for a specific time and then end before or continue beyond another future action. Form it by adding *will have been* to the present participle of the main verb.

By fall Joanne *will have been attending* school longer than anyone else I know.

EXERCISE 8–1 Identifying Verb Tenses

Underline each verb or verb phrase in the following sentences and identify its tense. Answers for the lettered sentences appear at the end of the Handbook. Example:

> *present progressive*   *simple present*
> John is <u>living</u> in Hinsdale, but he <u>prefers</u> Joliet.

a. He has been living like a hunted animal ever since he hacked into the university computer lab in order to change all his grades.

b. I have never appeared on a reality television show, and I will never appear on one unless my family gets selected.

c. James had been at the party for only fifteen minutes when his host suddenly pitched the caterer into the swimming pool.

d. As of next month, I will have been studying karate for six years, and I will be taking the test for my orange belt in July.

e. The dachshund was running at its fastest speed, but the squirrel strolled toward the tree without fear.

1. As of May 1, Ira and Sandy will have been going together for a year.
2. She will be working in her study if you need her.
3. Have you been hoping that Carlos will come to your party?
4. I know that he will not yet have returned from Chicago.
5. His parents had been expecting him home any day until they heard that he was still waiting for the bus.

8h Use the correct forms of the very irregular verbs *be, have,* and *do.*

The verbs *be, have,* and *do* take very irregular forms in the present and past tenses. Refer to the following chart to avoid confusion.

FORMS OF *BE, HAVE,* AND *DO* at a glance

be

PRESENT TENSE		PAST TENSE	
I am	we are	I was	we were
you are	you are	you were	you were
he/she/it is	they are	he/she/it was	they were

PAST PARTICIPLE

been   I have *been* in line for two hours.

PRESENT PARTICIPLE

being   Kara is *being* extra cautious around her patients.

have

PRESENT TENSE		PAST TENSE	
I have	we have	I had	we had
you have	you have	you had	you had
he/she/it has	they have	he/she/it had	they had

PAST PARTICIPLE

had   Ivan has *had* the flu every year since he can remember.

PRESENT PARTICIPLE

having   Mia is *having* a party on New Year's Eve.

do

PRESENT TENSE

I do	we do	I did	we did
you do	you do	you did	you did
he/she/it does	they do	he/she/it did	they did

PAST TENSE (heading over right columns)

PAST PARTICIPLE

done   Gina had *done* all her homework before the class ended.

PRESENT PARTICIPLE

doing   What were you *doing* last night?

8i Use the correct forms of *lie* and *lay* and *sit* and *set*.

Try taking two easy steps to eliminate confusion between *lie* and *lay*.

- Learn the principal parts and present participles of both (see below).
- Remember that *lie* never takes a direct object: "The island *lies* in the ocean." *Lay* always requires an object to answer "Lay what?": "*Lay* that pistol down."

The same distinction exists between *sit* and *set*. The verb *sit* rarely takes a direct object: "He *sits* on the stairs." *Set* almost always takes an object: "He *sets* the bottle on the counter." Note a few easily memorized exceptions: The sun *sets*. A hen *sets*. Gelatin *sets*. You *sit* the canter in a horse show.

> A **direct object** is the target of a verb that completes the action performed by the subject or asserted about the subject (see 3a).

FORMS OF *LIE* AND *LAY*, *SIT* AND *SET* at a glance

lie, lay, lain, lying: recline

PRESENT TENSE

I lie	we lie	I lay	we lay
you lie	you lie	you lay	you lay
he/she/it lies	they lie	he/she/it lay	they lay

PAST TENSE (heading over right columns)

PAST PARTICIPLE

lain   We have *lain* in the sun long enough.

PRESENT PARTICIPLE

lying   At ten o'clock he was still *lying* in bed.

lay, laid, laid, laying: put in place, deposit

PRESENT TENSE

I lay	we lay	I laid	we laid
you lay	you lay	you laid	you laid
he/she/it lays	they lay	he/she/it laid	they laid

PAST TENSE (heading over right columns)

(continued)

PAST PARTICIPLE

laid   Having *laid* his clothes on the bed, Mark jumped in the shower.

PRESENT PARTICIPLE

laying   *Laying* her cards on the table, Lola cried, "Gin!"

sit, sat, sat, sitting: be seated

PRESENT TENSE		PAST TENSE	
I sit	we sit	I sat	we sat
you sit	you sit	you sat	you sat
he/she/it sits	they sit	he/she/it sat	they sat

PAST PARTICIPLE

sat   I have *sat* here long enough.

PRESENT PARTICIPLE

sitting   Why are you *sitting* on that rickety bench?

set, set, set, setting: place

PRESENT TENSE		PAST TENSE	
I set	we set	I set	we set
you set	you set	you set	you set
he/she/it sets	they set	he/she/it set	they set

PAST PARTICIPLE

set   Paul has *set* the table for eight.

PRESENT PARTICIPLE

setting   Chanh-Duy has been *setting* traps for the mice.

EXERCISE 8–2 Using Irregular Verb Forms

Correct each incorrect irregular verb in the following sentences. Some sentences may be correct. Answers for the lettered sentences appear at the end of the Handbook. Example:

      spoken
  I have ~~spoke~~ to my professor about my absence last week.

a. Do he need a ride to school tomorrow?

b. I laid down to rest because I felt weak.

c. We will be setting here waiting for you after the show.

d. The class has begun reading Shakespeare this semester.

e. Reese sat the flowers on the table before dinner.

1. As a family rule, the kids all turn off their phones and lie them face down at meal time.

2. Dean has choose to visit London instead of Paris.

3. She have everything: a strong marriage, a stable job, and wonderful kids.

4. We been looking for a new car for a few weeks.

5. We have eaten pasta for dinner every night this week.

8j Use verbs in the appropriate mood.

Another characteristic of every verb is its **mood.** The indicative mood is most common. The imperative and subjunctive moods add valuable versatility.

The **indicative mood** is used to state a fact, to ask a question, or to express an opinion.

FACT	Danika *left* home two months ago.
QUESTION	*Will* she *find* happiness?
OPINION	I *think* not.

The **imperative mood** is used to make a request or to give a command or direction. The understood but usually unstated subject of a verb in the imperative mood is *you.* The verb's form is the base form or infinitive.

REQUEST	Please *be* there before noon. [*You* please be there. . . .]
COMMAND	*Hurry*! [*You* hurry!]
DIRECTION	*Drive* east on State Street. [*You* drive east. . . .]

The **subjunctive mood** is used in a subordinate clause to express a wish, requirement, suggestion, or condition contrary to fact. The subjunctive mood suggests uncertainty: the action expressed by the verb may or may not actually take place as specified. In any clause opening with *that* and expressing a requirement, the verb is in the subjunctive mood and takes the base or infinitive form.

> Professor Vogt requires that every student *complete* the essay promptly.
>
> She asked that we *be* on time for all meetings.

When you use the subjunctive mood to describe a condition that is contrary to fact, use *were* if the verb is *be.* For other verbs, use the simple past tense. Wishes, whether present or past, follow the same rules.

> If I *were* rich, I would be happy.
>
> If I *had* a million dollars, I would be happy.
>
> Elissa wishes that Ted *were* more goal oriented.
>
> Elissa wished that Ted *knew* what he wanted to do.

For a condition contrary to fact in the past, use the past perfect tense.

> If I *had been* awake, I would have seen the meteor showers.
>
> If Jessie *had known* you were coming, she would have cleaned her room.

Guidelines for Multilingual Writers
What Are Conditionals?

Conditional sentences usually contain an *if* clause, which states the condition, and a result clause.

- When the condition is true or possibly true in the present or future, use the present tense in the *if* clause and the present or future tense in the result clause. The future tense is not used in the *if* clause.

    If Jane *prepares* her essay early, she usually *writes* very well.

    If Maria *saves* enough money, she *will buy* a car.

- When the condition is not true in the present, for most verbs use the past tense in the *if* clause; for the verb *be*, use *were*. Use *would*, *could*, or *might* + infinitive form in the result clause.

    If Carlos *had* a computer, he *would need* a monitor, too.

    If Claudia *were* here, she *could do* it herself.

- When the condition was not true in the past, use the past perfect tense in the *if* clause. If the possible result was in the past, use *would have, could have,* or *might have* + past participle (*-ed* or *-en* form) in the result clause. If the possible result is in the present, use *would, could,* or *might* + infinitive form in the result clause.

    If Claudia *had saved* enough money, she *could have bought* a car. [Result in the past]

    If Annie *had finished* law school, she *might be* a successful lawyer now. [Result in the present]

An **infinitive** consists of the base form of a verb plus the word to (see 8a).

Although use of the subjunctive has grown scarcer over the years, it still sounds crude to write "If I *was* you. . . ." If you ever feel that the subjunctive makes a sentence sound stilted, rewrite it with an infinitive phrase.

Professor Vogt requires every student *to complete* the essay promptly.

EXERCISE 8–3 Using the Correct Mood of Verbs

Find and correct any errors in mood in the following sentences. Identify the mood of the incorrect verb as well as its correct replacement. Some sentences may be correct. Answers for the lettered sentences appear at the end of the Handbook. Example:

The law requires that each person files a tax return by April 15. [Incorrect: *files*, indicative; correct: *file*, subjunctive]

a. Dr. Belanger recommended that Juan flosses his teeth every day.

b. If I was you, I would have done the same thing.

c. Tradition demands that Daegun shows respect for his elders.

d. Please attends the training lesson if you plan to skydive later today.

1. If she was slightly older, she could stay home by herself.

2. If they have waited a little longer, they would have seen some amazing things.

3. Emilia's contract stipulates that she works on Saturdays.

4. If James invested in the company ten years ago, he would have made a lot of money.

9 | Subject-Verb Agreement

What does it mean for a subject and a verb to agree? Practically speaking, it means that their forms match: plural subjects take plural verbs, third-person subjects take third-person verbs, and so forth. When your subjects and verbs agree, you prevent a mismatch that could distract readers.

9a A verb agrees with its subject in person and number.

Subject and verb agree in person (first, second, or third):

> *I write* my papers on my laptop. [Subject and verb in first person]

> *Eamon writes* his papers in the lab. [Subject and verb in third person]

Subject and verb agree in number (singular or plural):

> *Grace enjoys* college. [Subject and verb singular]

> *She and Jim are* on their vacation. [Subject and verb plural]

The present tense of most verbs is the infinitive form, with no added ending except in the third-person singular. (See 8b–8h.)

I enjoy	we enjoy
you enjoy	you enjoy
he/she/it enjoys	they enjoy

Forms of the verb *be* vary.

I am	we are
you are	you are
he/she/it is	they are

A **subject** is the part of a sentence that names something — a person, an object, an idea, a situation — about which the predicate makes an assertion (see 2).

A **verb** is a word that shows action or a state of being (see 1c and 3).

9b A verb agrees with its subject, not with any words that intervene.

> My *favorite* of O. Henry's short stories *is* "The Gift of the Magi."

A **prepositional phrase** includes the preposition and its object (a noun or pronoun), plus any modifiers (see 1f).

A singular subject linked to another noun or pronoun by a prepositional phrase beginning with wording such as *along with, as well as,* or *in addition to* remains a singular subject and takes a singular verb.

> My cousin *James* as well as his wife and son *plans* to vote for Levine.

9c Subjects joined by *and* usually take a plural verb.

In most cases, a compound subject takes a plural verb.

A **compound subject** is a subject consisting of two or more nouns or pronouns linked by *and* (see 5a).

> *Sugar, salt, and fat* can adversely *affect* people's health.

However, phrases like *each boy and girl* or *every dog and cat* consider subjects individually, as "each one" or "every one," and use a singular verb.

> *Each man and woman* in the room *has* a different story to tell.

Use a singular verb for two singular subjects that form or are one thing.

> *Lime juice and soda quenches* your thirst.

9d With subjects joined by *or* or *nor*, the verb agrees with the part of the subject nearest to it.

> Either they or *Max is* guilty.

Subjects containing *not . . . but* follow this rule also.

> Not we but *George knows* the whole story.

You can remedy awkward constructions by rephrasing.

> Either they are guilty or Max is.

> We do not know the whole story, but George does.

9e Most collective nouns take singular verbs.

A **collective noun** is a singular noun that represents a group of people or items. When a collective noun refers to a group of people acting as one, use a singular verb.

> The *jury finds* the defendant guilty.

When the members of the group act individually, use a plural verb.

> The *jury agree* on the verdict.

If you feel that using a plural verb results in an awkward sentence, reword the subject so that it refers to members of the group individually.

The *jurors agree* on the verdict.

9f Most indefinite pronouns take a third-person singular verb.

Singular indefinite pronouns take a third-person singular verb.

Someone is here for you.

Even when one of these subjects is followed by a phrase containing a noun or pronoun of a different person or number, use a singular verb.

Each of you *is* here to stay.

One of the elephants *seems* dangerously ill.

▶ INDEFINITE PRONOUNS at a glance

Always Singular

anybody	everything	nothing
anyone	much	one (of)
anything	neither (of)	somebody
each (of)	nobody	someone
everybody	no one	something
everyone		

Always Plural

both	few	many	several

May Be Singular or Plural

all	any	either (of)	none	some (of)

9g The indefinite pronouns *all*, *any*, and *some* use a singular or plural verb, depending on their meaning.

I have no explanation. *Is any* needed?

Any of the changes considered critical *have* been made already.

All is lost.

All the bananas *are* gone.

Some of the blame *is* mine.

Some of us *are* Democrats.

None — like *all*, *any*, and *some* — takes a singular or a plural verb, depending on the sense in which the pronoun is used.

None of you *is* exempt.

None of his cats *were* gray.

9h In a subordinate clause with a relative pronoun as the subject, the verb agrees with the antecedent.

A **relative pronoun** is a pronoun that opens a subordinate clause and modifies a noun or pronoun in another clause (see 1b).

To determine the person and number of the verb in a subordinate clause whose subject is *who*, *which*, or *that*, look back at the word to which the pronoun refers. This word, known as an antecedent, is usually (but not always) the noun closest to the relative pronoun.

I have a roommate *who studies* day and night. [The antecedent of *who* is the third-person singular noun *roommate*. Therefore, the verb in the subordinate clause is third-person singular, *studies*.]

Pandas are mammals *that have* trouble reproducing in captivity. [The antecedent of *that* is *mammals*, so the verb is third-person plural, *have*.]

9i A verb agrees with its subject even when the subject follows the verb.

Introductory expressions such as *there* or *here* change the ordinary order so that the subject follows the verb. Remember that verbs agree with subjects and that *here* and *there* are never subjects.

Here *is* a *riddle* for you.

There *are* forty *people* in my law class.

Under the bridge *were* a broken-down *boat and* a worn *tire.*

9j A linking verb agrees with its subject, not its subject complement.

A **linking verb** is a verb that shows a state of being by linking the sentence subject with a word that renames or describes the subject (see 1c and 3b).

When a form of the verb *be* links two or more nouns, the subject is the noun before the linking verb. Nouns that follow the linking verb are subject complements. Make the verb agree with the subject of the sentence, not the subject complement.

Jim is a gentleman and a scholar.

Amy's *parents are* her most enthusiastic audience.

A **subject complement** is a noun, an adjective, or a group of words that follows a linking verb and renames or describes the subject (see 3b).

9k When the subject is a title, use a singular verb.

In sixth grade, *Harry Potter and the Chamber of Secrets was* my favorite book.

"People" sung by Barbra Streisand *is* my aunt's favorite song.

9I Singular nouns that end in -s take singular verbs.

Some nouns look plural even though they refer to a singular subject: *measles, logistics, mathematics, electronics.* Such nouns take singular verbs.

The *news is* that *economics is* now one of the most popular majors.

EXERCISE 9–1 Making Subjects and Verbs Agree

Find and correct any subject-verb agreement errors in the following sentences. Some sentences may be correct. Answers for the lettered sentences appear at the end of the Handbook. Example:

> are
> Addressing the audience tonight is the nominees for club president.
>   ^

a. For many college graduates, the process of looking for jobs are often long and stressful.

b. Not too long ago, searching the classifieds and inquiring in person was the primary methods of job hunting.

c. Today, however, everyone need to use the Internet to search for openings or to post their résumés.

d. My classmates and my teacher recommends specific sites for posting résumés.

e. All the résumés contains keywords that make them appear in searches.

1. There are many people who thinks that interviewing is the most stressful part of the job search.

2. Sometimes only one person conducts an interview, while other times a whole committee conduct it.

3. Either the interviewer or the committee usually begin by asking simple questions about your background.

4. Making eye contact, dressing professionally, and appearing confident is some of the qualities an interviewer may consider important.

5. After an interview, most people sends a thank-you letter to the person who conducted it.

10 | Pronoun Case

Depending on a pronoun's function in a sentence, we say that it is in the **subjective case,** the **objective case,** or the **possessive case.** Some pronouns change form when they change case, and some do not. The personal pronouns *I, he, she, we,* and *they* and the relative pronoun *who* have different forms in the subjective, objective, and possessive cases. Other pronouns, such as *you* and *it,* have only two forms: the plain case (which serves as both subjective and objective) and the possessive case.

> ## PERSONAL PRONOUNS at a glance
>
> | | SUBJECTIVE | | OBJECTIVE | | POSSESSIVE | |
> |---|---|---|---|---|---|---|
> | | Singular | Plural | Singular | Plural | Singular | Plural |
> | *First Person* | I | we | me | us | my/mine | our/ours |
> | *Second Person* | you | you | you | you | your/yours | your/yours |
> | *Third Person* | he | they | him | them | his | their/theirs |
> | | she | | her | | her/hers | |
> | | it | | it | | its | |

10a Use the subjective case for the subject of a sentence or clause.

A **subject** is the part of a sentence that names something—a person, an object, an idea, a situation—about which the verb in the predicate makes an assertion (see 2).

Jed and *I* ate the granola.

Who cares?

Maya recalled that *she* played baseball.

Election officials are the people *who* count.

A pronoun serving as the subject for a verb is subjective even when the verb is only implied, not explicitly stated:

          I
Jed is hungrier than ~~me~~. [The verb *am* is implied: Jed is hungrier than I *am*.]

 Don't be fooled by a pronoun that appears immediately after a verb, looking as if it were a direct object but functioning as the subject of a clause. The pronoun's case is determined by its role, not by its position.

               whoever
We were happy to interview ~~whomever~~ was running. [The subjective pronoun *whoever* is the subject of the verb *was running*.]

10b Use the subjective case for a subject complement.

A **subject complement** is a noun, an adjective, or a group of words that follows a linking verb and renames or describes the subject (see 3b).

When a pronoun functions as a subject complement, it plays essentially the same role as the subject and its case is subjective.

                   he   *I*
The phantom graffiti artist couldn't have been ~~him~~. It was ~~me~~. [The subject pronouns *he* and *I* are subject complements.]

10c Use the subjective case for an appositive to a subject or subject complement.

An **appositive** is a word or group of words that adds information by identifying a subject or object in a different way (see 4b).

A pronoun in an appositive phrase has the same case as the noun it stands beside.

                she
The class officers—Ravi and ~~her~~—announced a senior breakfast. [The subjective pronoun *she* helps rename the subject, *officers*.]

Objective Case

10d Use the objective case for a direct object, an indirect object, the object of a preposition, or the subject of an infinitive.

The custard pies hit *him* and *me*. [The objective pronouns *him* and *me* are direct objects of the verb *hit*.]

Mona threw *us* towels. [The objective pronoun *us* is an indirect object of the verb *threw*.]

Mona threw towels to *him* and *us*. [The objective pronouns *him* and *us* are direct objects of the preposition *to*.]

We always expect *him* to win. [The objective pronoun *him* is the subject of the infinitive *to win*. This is the only case in which an objective pronoun is used as a subject.]

Mona agreed to keep the secret between s̶h̶e̶ her and I̶. me. [The objective pronouns *her* and *me* are direct objects of the preposition *between*.]

10e Use the objective case for an appositive to a direct or indirect object or the object of a preposition.

Mona helped all of us—Mrs. Van Dumont, h̶e̶, him, and I̶. me. [The objective pronouns *him* and *me* refer back to the object *us*.]

Bob gave his favorite students, Tom and s̶h̶e̶, her, an approving nod. [The objective pronoun *her* refers back to the object *students*.]

Possessive Case

10f Use the possessive case to show ownership.

Possessive pronouns can function as adjectives or as nouns. *My, your, his, her, its, our,* and *their* function as adjectives by modifying nouns or pronouns.

My new bike is having *its* first road test today.

The possessive pronoun *its* does not contain an apostrophe. *It's* with an apostrophe is a contraction for *it is*, as in "*It's* a beautiful day for bike riding."

The possessive pronouns *mine, yours, his, hers, ours,* and *theirs* can discharge the whole range of noun duties, serving as subjects, subject complements, direct objects, indirect objects, or objects of prepositions.

SUBJECT	*Yours* is the last vote we need.
SUBJECT COMPLEMENT	This day is *ours*.
DIRECT OBJECT	Don't take your car; take *mine*.
INDIRECT OBJECT	If we're honoring requests, give *hers* top priority.
OBJECT OF A PREPOSITION	Give Mia's request priority over *theirs*.

A **direct object** is the target of a verb that completes the action performed by the subject or asserted about the subject (see 3a).

An **indirect object** is a person or thing affected by the subject's action, usually the recipient of the direct object, through the action indicated by a verb (see 3a).

The **object of a preposition** is the noun or pronoun that follows the preposition, connecting it to the rest of the sentence (see 4b).

An **infinitive** consists of the base form of a verb plus the word *to* (see 8a).

10g Use the possessive case to modify a gerund.

A **gerund** is a form of a verb, ending in *-ing,* that functions as a noun (see 8a).

A possessive pronoun (or possessive noun) is the appropriate escort for a gerund. As a noun, a gerund requires an adjective for a modifier.

> *his*
> Mary is tired of ~~him~~ griping. [The possessive pronoun *his* modifies the gerund *griping.*]
>
> *their* *his*
> I can stand ~~them~~ being late every day but not ~~him~~ sleeping on the job.
> [The possessive pronoun *their* modifies the gerund *being;* the possessive pronoun *his* modifies the gerund *sleeping.*]

A **present participle** is a form of a verb ending in *-ing* that cannot function alone as a main verb but can act as an adjective (see 8a).

However, editing possessives can be confusing because two different verb forms both end in *-ing:* gerunds that act as nouns and present participles that act as adjectives. If you are not sure whether to use a possessive for a gerund or an objective pronoun with a word ending in *-ing,* look closely at your sentence. Which word — the pronoun or the *-ing* word — is the object of your main verb? That word functions as a noun; the other word modifies it.

> Mr. Phipps remembered *them* smoking in the boys' room. [Mr. Phipps remembers *them,* those students. *Them* is the object of the verb, so *smoking* is a participle modifying *them.*]

> Mr. Phipps remembered *their* smoking in the boys' room. [Mr. Phipps remembers *smoking,* that habit. The gerund *smoking* is the object of the verb, and the possessive pronoun *their* modifies it.]

EXERCISE 10–1 Using Pronoun Case Correctly

Replace any pronouns used incorrectly in the following sentences. Explain why each was incorrect. (Consider all these examples as written — not spoken — English, so apply the rules strictly.) Some sentences may be correct. Answers for the lettered sentences appear at the end of the Handbook. Example:

> *she*
> That is ~~her,~~ the new university president, at the podium. [*She* is a subject complement.]

  a. I didn't appreciate you laughing at her and I.

  b. Lee and me would be delighted to serenade whomever will listen.

  c. The managers and us servers are highly trustworthy.

  d. The neighbors were driven berserk by him singing.

  e. Jerry and myself regard you and she as the very people who we wish to meet.

  1. Have you guessed the identity of the person of who I am speaking?

  2. It was him asking about the clock that started me suspecting him.

  3. They — Jerry and her — are the troublemakers.

  4. Mrs. Van Dumont awarded the prize to Mona and I.

  5. The counterattack was launched by Dusty and myself.

11 | Pronoun Reference

The main use of pronouns is to refer in a brief, convenient form to some **antecedent** that has already been named. A pronoun usually has a noun or another pronoun as its antecedent. Often the antecedent is the subject or object of the same clause in which the pronoun appears.

> Josie hit the *ball* after *its* first bounce.
>
> Smashing into *Greg*, the ball knocked off *his* glasses.

The antecedent also can appear in a different clause or even a different sentence from the pronoun.

> *Josie* hit the *ball* when *it* bounced back to *her*.
>
> The *ball* smashed into *Greg*. *It* knocked off *his* glasses.

A pronoun as well as a noun can be an antecedent.

> My *dog* hid in the closet when *she* had *her* puppies. [*Dog* is the antecedent of *she*; *she* is the antecedent of *her*.]

11a Name the pronoun's antecedent: don't just imply it.

When editing, be sure you have identified clearly the antecedent of each pronoun. A writer who leaves a key idea unsaid is likely to confuse readers.

> Norwegians
> Ted wanted a Norwegian canoe because he'd heard that ~~they~~ produce the lightest canoes afloat.

To clarify what noun or pronoun *they* refers to, the writer must supply an antecedent for *they*.

An **antecedent** is the word to which a pronoun refers (see 1b).

Guidelines for Multilingual Writers
How Do I Use Relative Pronouns Correctly?

Be sure to use relative pronouns (*who, whose, which, that*) correctly in sentences with adjective clauses. Use *who*, not *which*, for a person. Select *that* to introduce necessary information that defines or specifies; reserve *which* for additional, but not defining, information.

- Do not omit the relative pronoun when it is the subject within the adjective clause

  > who
  > The woman gave us directions to the museum told us not to miss the Picasso exhibit. [*Who* is the subject of the adjective clause.]

- In speech and informal writing, you can imply (rather than state) a relative pronoun when it is the object of a verb or preposition within the adjective clause. In formal writing, you should use the relative pronoun.

For more on choosing *that* or *which*, see 28e.

(continued)

> FORMAL   Jamal forgot to return the book *that I gave him*. [*That* is the object of *gave*.]
>
> INFORMAL   Jamal forgot to return the book *I gave him*. [The relative pronoun *that* is implied.]
>
> FORMAL   This is the box *in which we found the jewelry*. [*Which* is the object of the preposition *in*.]
>
> INFORMAL   This is the box *we found the jewelry in*. [The relative pronoun *which* is implied.]
>
> *NOTE:* When the relative pronoun is omitted, the preposition moves to the end of the sentence but must not be left out.
>
> - *Whose* is the only possessive form of a relative pronoun. It is used with persons, animals, and things.
>
>   *whose*
>   I bought a chair ~~that its~~ legs were wobbly.
>
> *NOTE:* When in doubt about a pronoun, you can rephrase the sentence: I bought a chair *with wobbly legs*.

Watch out for possessive nouns. They won't work as antecedents.

his   *William*
On ~~William's~~ canoe, ^he painted a skull and bones.

the   *Hemingway*
In ~~Hemingway's~~ story, ^he describes the powerful sea.

11b Give the pronoun *it, this, that,* or *which* a clear antecedent.

*An **antecedent** is the word to which a pronoun refers (see 1b).*

Vagueness arises, thick as fog, whenever *it, this, that,* or *which* points to something a writer assumes is said but indeed isn't. Often the best way out of the fog is to substitute a specific noun or expression for the pronoun.

my solitary life
I was an only child, and ^~~it~~ was hard.

Because
^Judy could not get along with her younger brother, ~~This is the reason~~ she wanted to get her own apartment.

11c Make the pronoun's antecedent clear.

Confusion strikes if a pronoun points in two or more directions. When more than one antecedent is possible, the reader wonders which the writer means.

CONFUSING   Hanwei shouted to Kenny to take off his burning sweater.

Whose sweater does *his* mean—Kenny's or Hanwei's? Simply changing a pronoun won't clear up the confusion. The writer needs to revise enough to move the two possible antecedents out of each other's way.

CLEAR	"Kenny!" shouted Hanwei. "Your sweater's on fire! Take it off!"
CLEAR	Flames were shooting from Kenny's sweater. Hanwei shouted to Kenny to take it off.
CLEAR	Hanwei realized that his sweater was on fire and shouted to Kenny for help.

11d Place the pronoun close to its antecedent to keep the relationship clear.

Watch out for distractions that slip in between noun and pronoun. If your sentence contains two or more nouns that look like antecedents to a pronoun, your readers may become bewildered.

| CONFUSING | Harper steered his dinghy alongside the cabin cruiser that the drug smugglers had left anchored under an overhanging willow in the tiny harbor and eased it to a stop. |

What did Harper ease to a stop? By the time readers reach the end of the sentence, they are likely to have forgotten. To avoid confusion, keep the pronoun and its antecedent reasonably close together.

| CLEAR | Harper steered his dinghy into the tiny harbor and eased it to a stop alongside the cabin cruiser that the drug smugglers had left anchored under an overhanging willow. |

Never force your readers to stop and think, "What does that pronoun stand for?" You, the writer, have to do this thinking for them.

EXERCISE 11–1 Making Pronoun Reference Clear

Revise each sentence or group of sentences so that any pronoun needing an antecedent clearly points to one. Possible revisions for the lettered sentences appear at the end of the Handbook. Example:

I took the money out of the wallet and threw ~~it~~ *the wallet* in the trash.

a. I could see the moon and the faint shadow of the tree as it began to rise.

b. Katrina spent the summer in Paris and traveled throughout Europe, which broadened her awareness of cultural differences.

c. Most managers want employees to work as many hours as possible. They never consider the work they need to do at home.

d. I worked twelve hours a day and never got enough sleep, but it was worth it.

e. Kevin asked Mike to meet him for lunch but forgot that he had class at that time.

1. Bill's prank frightened Josh and made him wonder why he had done it.
2. Korean students study up to twenty subjects a year, including algebra, calculus, and engineering. Because they are required, they must study them year after year.
3. Pedro Martinez signed a baseball for Chad.
4. When the bottle hit the windshield, it shattered.
5. My friends believe they are more mature than many of their peers because of the discipline enforced at their school. However, it can also lead to problems.

12 | Pronoun-Antecedent Agreement

A pronoun's job is to fill in for a noun, much as an actor's double fills in for the actor. Pronouns are a short, convenient way to avoid repeating the noun.

> The sheriff drew a six-shooter; he fired twice.

In this action-packed sentence, first comes a noun (*sheriff*) and then a pronoun (*he*) that refers back to it. *Sheriff* is the antecedent of *he*. Just as verbs need to agree with their subjects, pronouns need to agree with the nouns they stand for without shifting number, person, or gender in midsentence.

12a Pronouns agree with their antecedents in person and number.

A pronoun matches its antecedent in person (first, second, or third) and in number (singular or plural), even when intervening words separate the pronoun and its antecedent. Here, noun and pronoun disagree in person (third person *campers*; second person *your*):

> *their*
> All campers should bring ~~your~~ knapsacks.

Here, noun and pronoun disagree in number (singular *camper*; plural *their*):

> *his or her*
> Every camper should bring ~~their~~ knapsack.

12b Most antecedents joined by *and* require a plural pronoun.

> *George*, who has been here before, *and Jenn*, who hasn't, need *their* maps.

A **compound subject** is a subject consisting of two or more nouns or pronouns linked by *and* (see 5a).

If the nouns in a compound subject refer to the same person or thing, they make up a singular antecedent. Use a singular pronoun too.

> The *owner and founder* of this company carries *his* laptop everywhere.

12c **A pronoun agrees with the closest part of an antecedent joined by *or* or *nor*.**

If your subject is two or more nouns (or a combination of nouns and pronouns) connected by *or* or *nor*, look closely at the subject's parts. Are they all singular? If so, your pronoun should be singular.

Neither *Joy nor Jean* remembered *her* book last week.

If *Sam, Arthur, or Dieter* shows up, tell *him* I'm upstairs.

If the part of the subject closest to the pronoun is plural, the pronoun should be plural.

Neither *Joy nor her sisters* rode *their* bikes today.

If you see *Sam, Arthur, or their friends*, tell *them* I'm upstairs.

12d **An antecedent that is a singular indefinite pronoun takes a singular pronoun.**

Most indefinite pronouns (such as *everyone* and *anybody*) are singular in meaning, so the pronouns that refer to them are also singular.

For a list of indefinite pronouns, see p. 563.

Either of the boys can do it, as long as *he* tries.

12e **Most collective nouns used as antecedents require singular pronouns.**

When the members of a group (such as a committee, family, jury, or trio) act as a unit, use a singular pronoun to refer to them.

The *cast* for the play will be posted as soon as the director chooses *it*.

When the group members act individually, use a plural pronoun.

The *cast* will go *their* separate ways when summer ends.

12f **A pronoun agrees with its antecedent in gender.**

If your *mother* brings you to camp, invite *her* for lunch.

EXERCISE 12–1 Making Pronouns and Antecedents Agree

If any nouns and pronouns disagree in number, person, or gender in the following sentences, substitute pronouns that agree with the nouns. If you prefer, strengthen any sentence by rewriting it. Some sentences may be correct. Possible revisions for the lettered sentences appear at the end of the Handbook. Example:

> _it_
> A cat expects people to feed ~~them~~ often.   _Or_
>
> _Cats expect_
> ~~A cat expects~~ people to feed them often.

a. Many architects find work their greatest pleasure.

b. Neither Melissa nor James has received their application form yet.

c. He is the kind of man who gets their fun out of just sipping one's beer and watching his Saturday games on TV.

d. Many a mother has mourned the loss of their child.

e. When one enjoys one's work, it's easy to spend all your spare time thinking about it.

1. All students are urged to complete your registration on time.

2. When a dog doesn't respond to their master's call, they may have suffered hearing loss.

3. Each member of the sorority has to make her own bed.

4. If you don't like the songs the choir sings, don't join them.

5. Young people should know how to protect oneself against AIDS.

13 | Adjectives and Adverbs

Adjectives provide information about the person, place, object, or idea named by the noun or pronoun.

> The _thin, lightweight_ laptop fits in my purse.

 ADJECTIVES AND ADVERBS at a glance

ADJECTIVES
1. Typically answer the question Which? or What kind?
2. Modify nouns or pronouns

ADVERBS
3. Answer the question How? When? Where? or sometimes Why?
4. Modify verbs, adjectives, and other adverbs

An adverb describes a verb, an adjective, or another adverb.

> The phones arrived _yesterday;_ we _quickly_ restocked the shelves with the _incredibly_ popular models.

13a Use an adverb to modify a verb, an adjective, or another adverb.

awfully
It's ~~awful~~ hot today.

Awful is an adjective, so it can modify only nouns or pronouns. An adverb is needed to modify the adjective *hot*.

13b Use an adjective as a subject complement or an object complement.

Her old car looked *awful*. [The adjective *awful* is a subject complement: it follows a linking verb and modifies the subject, *car*.]

An **object complement** completes the description of a direct object and can be an adjective or a noun, but never an adverb.

Early to bed and early to rise makes a man *healthy, wealthy*, and *wise*. [The adjectives modify the direct object *man*.]

When you are not sure whether you're dealing with an object complement or an adverb, look closely at the word's role in the sentence. If it modifies a noun, it is an object complement and should be an adjective.

The coach called the referee *stupid* and *blind*. [*Stupid* and *blind* are adjectives modifying the direct object *referee*.]

If it modifies a verb, you want an adverb instead.

In fact, the ref had called the play *correctly*. [*Correctly* is an adverb modifying the verb *had called*.]

An **object complement** is a noun, an adjective, or a group of words that renames or describes a direct object (see 3b).

13c Use *good* as an adjective and *well* as an adverb.

This sandwich tastes *good*. [The adjective *good* is a subject complement following the linking verb *tastes* and modifying the noun *sandwich*.]

Al's skin healed *well* after surgery. [The adverb *well* modifies the verb *healed*.]

Only if the verb is a linking verb can you safely follow it with *good*. Other kinds of verbs need adverbs, not subject complements.

well
After a bad start, the game ended ~~good~~.

A **linking verb** is a verb that shows a state of being by linking the sentence subject with a word that renames or describes the subject (see 1c and 3b).

Complications arise when we write or speak about health. It is perfectly correct to say *I feel good*, using the adjective *good* as a subject complement after the linking verb *feel*. However, generations of confusion have nudged the adverb *well* into the adjective category, too. A nurse may speak of "a well baby"; greeting cards urge patients to "get well" — meaning, "become healthy." Just as *healthy* is an adjective here, so is *well*.

When someone asks, "How do you feel?" you can duck the issue with "Fine!" Otherwise, in speech *good* or *well* is acceptable; in writing, use *good*.

For advice on using commas with adjectives, see 28d.

🌐 Guidelines for Multilingual Writers
What Is the Order for Cumulative Adjectives?

Cumulative adjectives are two or more adjectives used directly before a noun and not separated by commas or the word *and*.

> She is an *attractive older French* woman.

> His *expressive large brown* eyes moved me.

Cumulative adjectives usually follow a specific order of placement before a noun. Use this list as a guide, but keep in mind that the order can vary.

1. Articles or determiners

   a, an, the, some, this, these, his, my, two, several

2. Evaluative adjectives

   beautiful, wonderful, hardworking, distasteful

3. Size or dimension

   big, small, huge, obese, petite, six-foot

4. Length or shape

   long, short, round, square, oblong, oval

5. Age

   old, young, new, fresh, ancient

6. Color

   red, pink, aquamarine, orange

7. Nation or place of origin

   American, Japanese, European, Bostonian, Floridian

8. Religion

   Protestant, Muslim, Hindu, Buddhist, Catholic, Jewish

9. Matter or substance

   wood, gold, cotton, plastic, pine, metal

10. Noun used as an adjective

    car (as in *car mechanic*), *computer* (as in *computer software*)

13d Form comparatives and superlatives of most adjectives and adverbs with *-er* and *-est* or *more* and *most*.

Comparatives and superlatives are forms that describe one thing in relation to another. Put most adjectives into comparative form (for two things) by adding *-er* and into superlative form (for three or more) by adding *-est*.

The budget deficit is *larger* than the trade deficit.

This year's trade deficit is the largest ever.

We usually form the comparative and superlative of potentially cumbersome long adjectives with *more* and *most* rather than with *-er* and *-est*.

        more beautiful
The lake is ~~beautifuller~~ than I'd imagined.

For short adverbs that do not end in *-ly,* usually add *-er* and *-est*. With all others, use *more* and *most*.

The trade deficit grows *fastest* and *most uncontrollably* when exports fall.

Do not use *more* or *most* in addition to adding *-er* or *-est* to the adjective or adverb.

Eric thought Hitchcock's *Rear Window* was ~~more~~ scarier than *Psycho*. [To say *more scarier* is redundant; deleting *more* corrects the sentence.]

No matter how wonderful something is, we can call it the *best* only when we compare it with more than one other thing. Any comparison between two things uses the comparative form, not the superlative.

                                      better
Chocolate and vanilla are both good, but I like chocolate ~~best~~. [Changing the superlative *best* to the comparative *better* corrects the sentence.]

13e Use the correct comparative and superlative forms of irregular adjectives and adverbs.

Use irregular adjectives and adverbs (such as *bad* and *badly*) with care.

        worse
Tom's golf game is no ~~worser~~ than George's.

For negative comparisons, use *less* and *least* for adjectives and adverbs.

Michael's speech was *less dramatic* than Louie's.

Paulette spoke the *least dramatically* of all.

> ## IRREGULAR ADJECTIVES AND ADVERBS at a glance
>
> | ADJECTIVES | COMPARATIVE | SUPERLATIVE |
> |---|---|---|
> | good | better | best |
> | bad | worse | worst |
> | little | less, littler | least, littlest |
> | many, some, much | more | most |
>
> | ADVERBS | COMPARATIVE | SUPERLATIVE |
> |---|---|---|
> | well | better | best |
> | badly | worse | worst |
> | little | less | least |

13f Omit *most* with an adjective or adverb that is already superlative.

Some words, such as *top*, *favorite*, and *unique*, mark whatever they modify as one of a kind. They need no further assistance to make their point.

> Lisa has a ~~most~~ unique background.

EXERCISE 13–1 Using Adjectives and Adverbs Correctly

Find and correct any incorrect use of adjectives and adverbs in the following sentences. Some sentences may be correct. Answers for the lettered sentences appear at the end of the Handbook. Example:

> The merger worked out ~~good~~ *well* for both companies.

a. The field unit carried out their orders exact.

b. Marin felt badly that her mother could not make it to the ceremony.

c. After living in both the city and the suburbs, Aaron decided he liked the city best.

d. The orphaned dogs appear sadly in the animal shelter's cages.

e. Nico enjoys watching all sports, but his most favorite is basketball.

1. Drones are unpiloted air vehicles that are often remotely controlled by someone on the ground.

2. Opal is one of the rarest gemstones.

3. People sometimes behave strange when they are in a new environment and they are concerned for their safety.

4. The library is a more quieter place to study than the coffee shop.

5. That was the worse dinner I have ever had in my entire life.

14 | Shifts

Just as you can change position to view a scene from different vantage points, in your writing you can change the time or perspective. However, shifting tense or point of view unconsciously or unnecessarily within a passage creates ambiguity and confusion for readers.

14a Maintain consistency in verb tense.

In a passage or an essay, use the same verb tense unless the time changes.

> The driver yelled at us to get off the bus, so I ~~ask~~ _asked_ him why, and he ~~tells~~ _told_ me it ~~is~~ _was_ none of my business.

A verb's **tense** refers to the time when the action of a verb did, does, might, or will occur (see 8).

14b If the time changes, change the verb tense.

To write about events in the past, use past tense verbs. To write about events in the present, use present tense verbs. If the time shifts, change tense.

> I _do_ not _like_ the new television programs this year. The comedies _are_ too realistic to be amusing, the adventure shows _don't have_ much action, and the law enforcement dramas _drag_ on and on. Last year the programs _were_ different. The sitcoms _were_ hilarious, the adventure shows _were_ action packed, and the dramas _were_ fast paced. I _prefer_ last year's reruns to this year's shows.

The time and the verb tense change appropriately from present (_do like, are, don't have, drag_) to past (_were, were, were, were_) back to present (_prefer_), contrasting this year's _present_ with last year's _past_ programming.

NOTE: When writing about literature, the accepted practice is to use present tense verbs to summarize what happens in a story, poem, or play. When discussing other aspects of a work, use present tense for present time, past tense for past, and future tense for future.

> Steinbeck _wrote_ "The Chrysanthemums" in 1937. [Past tense for past time]

> In "The Chrysanthemums," Steinbeck _describes_ the Salinas Valley as "a closed pot" cut off from the world by fog. [Present tense for story summary]

14c Maintain consistency in the voice of verbs.

Shifting unnecessarily from active to passive voice may confuse readers.

> My roommates and I _sit_ up late many nights talking about our problems. _We discuss grades_
> ~~Grades~~, teachers, jobs, money, and dates ~~are discussed~~ at length.

For more on using active and passive voice, see 21.

14d Maintain consistency in person.

Person indicates your perspective as a writer. First person (_I, we_) establishes a personal, informal relationship with readers as does second person (_you_), which brings readers into the writing. Third person (_he, she, it, they_) is more

For more on pronoun forms, see 1b and 10.

formal and objective. In a formal scientific report, second person is seldom appropriate, and first, if used, might be reserved for reporting procedures. In a personal essay, using *he, she,* or *one* to refer to yourself would sound stilted. Choose the person appropriate for your purpose and stick to it.

> College students need transportation, but ~~you~~ **they** need a job to pay for the insurance and the gasoline.

> Anyone can go skydiving if ~~you have~~ **he or she has** the guts.

14e   Maintain consistency in the mood of verbs.

For examples of the three moods of verbs, see 8j.

Avoid shifts in mood, usually from indicative to imperative.

> Counselors advised students to register early. ~~Also~~ **They also advised them to** pay **their** tuition on time.
> [Edits make both indicative.]

14f   Maintain consistency in level of language.

To impress readers, writers sometimes inflate their language or slip into slang. The level of language should fit your purpose and audience throughout an essay. For a personal essay, use informal language.

> INCONSISTENT   I felt like a typical tourist. I carried an expensive digital camera with lots of icons I didn't quite know how to decode. But I was in a quandary because there was such a plethora of picturesque tableaus to record for posterity.

Instead of suddenly shifting to formal language, the writer could end simply: *But with so much beautiful scenery all around, I couldn't decide where to start.*
  For an academic essay, use formal language.

> INCONSISTENT   Puccini's *Turandot* is set in a China of legends, riddles, and fantasy. Brimming with beautiful melodies, this opera is music drama at its most spectacular. It rules!

Cutting the last sentence avoids an unnecessary shift in formality.

EXERCISE 14–1 Maintaining Grammatical Consistency

Revise the following sentences to eliminate shifts in verb tense, voice, mood, person, and level of language. Possible revisions for the lettered sentences appear at the end of the Handbook. Example:

> I needed the job at the restaurant, so I tried to tolerate the insults of my boss, but ~~a person can~~ **I could** take only so much.

a. Dr. Jamison is an erudite professor who cracks jokes in class.

b. The audience listened intently to the lecture, but the message was not understood.

c. Scientists can no longer evade the social, political, and ethical consequences of what they did in the laboratory.

d. To have good government, citizens must become informed on the issues. Also, be sure to vote.

e. Good writing is essential to success in many professions, especially in business, where ideas must be communicated in down-to-earth lingo.

1. Our legal system made it extremely difficult to prove a bribe. If the charges are not proven to the satisfaction of a jury or a judge, then we jump to the conclusion that the absence of a conviction demonstrates the innocence of the subject.

2. Before Morris K. Udall, Democrat from Arizona, resigns his seat in the U.S. House of Representatives, he helped preserve hundreds of acres of wilderness.

3. Anyone can learn another language if you have the time and the patience.

4. The immigration officer asked how long we planned to stay, so I show him my letter of acceptance from Tulane.

5. Archaeologists spent many months studying the site of the African city of Zimbabwe, and many artifacts were uncovered.

Learning by Doing 🖉 Considering Your Rough Draft

One method of finding weak spots in an essay is to read it backward, sentence by sentence. When you read an essay from beginning to end, your brain can insert assumed information and gloss over gaps. Reading backward allows you to take each sentence on its own merit. This method also allows you and your reviewers to better identify sentence fragments, run-on sentences, and missing words. Try this method to see what weak spots you find in your own essay. Write a reflection about what you discover.

35 | Effective Sentences

15 | Misplaced and Dangling Modifiers

The purpose of a **modifier**, such as an adjective or adverb, is to give readers more information. The modifier must be linked clearly to whatever it is meant to modify or describe.

15a Keep modifiers close to what they modify.

Misplaced modifiers — phrases and clauses that wander away from what they modify — produce results more likely to amuse readers than to inform them. Place your modifiers as close as possible to whatever they modify.

in colorful packages.
She offered toys to all the children ~~in colorful packages.~~ [The phrase *in colorful packages* modifies *toys*, not *children*.]

from the crates
We removed the dishes ~~from the crates~~ that got chipped. [The clause *that got chipped* modifies *dishes*, not *crates*.]

15b Place each modifier so that it clearly modifies only one thing.

A **squinting modifier** is one that looks two ways, leaving the reader uncertain whether it modifies the word before or after it. To avoid ambiguity, place your modifier close to the word it modifies and away from another that might cause confusion.

SQUINTING	The book that appealed to Amy *tremendously* bored Marcus.
CLEAR	The book that *tremendously* appealed to Amy bored Marcus.
CLEAR	The book that appealed to Amy bored Marcus *tremendously*.

EXERCISE 15–1 Placing Modifiers

Revise the following sentences, which contain modifiers that are misplaced or squinting. Possible revisions for the lettered sentences appear at the end of the Handbook. Example:

> *Using a flashlight in the dark,*
> ^Patti found the cat ~~using a flashlight in the dark~~.

a. The bus got stuck in a ditch full of passengers.

b. He was daydreaming about fishing for trout in the middle of a meeting.

c. The boy threw the paper airplane through an open window with a smirk.

d. I reached for my sunglasses when the glare appeared in the glove compartment.

e. High above them, Sally and Glen watched the kites drift back and forth.

1. In her soup she found a fly at one of the best restaurants in town.

2. Andy learned how to build kites from the pages of an old book.

3. Alex vowed to return to the island sometime soon on the day he left it.

4. The fish was carried in a suitcase wrapped in newspaper.

5. The reporters were informed of the crimes committed by a press release.

15c State something in the sentence for each modifier to modify.

Generally readers assume that a modifying phrase at the start of a sentence refers to the subject of a main clause that follows it. If readers encounter a modifying phrase midway through a sentence, they assume that it modifies something just before or (less often) after it.

> *Feeling tired after the long hike,* Jason went to bed.
>
> Alicia, *while sympathetic,* was not inclined to help.

A **main clause** is a group of words that has both a subject and a verb and can stand alone as a complete sentence (see 4a).

Sometimes a writer slips up, allowing a modifying phrase to dangle. A **dangling modifier** is one that doesn't modify anything in its sentence.

DANGLING	*Noticing a pain behind his eyes,* an aspirin seemed a good idea.
	[The opening doesn't modify *aspirin* or, in fact, anything.]

To correct a dangling modifier, first figure out what noun, pronoun, or noun phrase the modifier is meant to modify. Then make that word or phrase the subject of the main clause.

CLEAR   *Noticing a pain behind his eyes, he* decided to take an aspirin.

Another way to correct a dangling modifier is to turn the dangler into a clause that includes the missing noun or pronoun.

Although she is talented, her
~~Her~~ progress, ~~although talented,~~ has been slowed by poor work habits.

Sometimes rewriting will clarify what the modifier modifies.

Although   *she*   *hampered*
~~Her progress, although talented,~~ has been ~~slowed~~ by poor work habits.

EXERCISE 15–2 Revising Dangling Modifiers

Revise any sentences that contain dangling modifiers. Some sentences may be correct. Possible revisions for the lettered sentences appear at the end of the Handbook. Example:

Joan realized that   *her*
Angry at her poor showing, geology would never be ~~Joan's~~ favorite class.

a. Unpacking the suitcase, a horrible idea occurred to me.

b. After fixing breakfast that morning, the oven might be left on at home.

c. Trying to reach my neighbor, her phone was busy.

d. Desperate to get information, my solution was to ask my mother to drive over to check the oven.

e. With enormous relief, my mother's call confirmed everything was fine.

1. After working six hours, the job was done.

2. Further information can be obtained by calling the specified number.

3. To compete in the Olympics, talent, training, and dedication are needed.

4. Pressing hard on the brakes, the car spun into a hedge.

5. Showing a lack of design experience, the architect advised the student to take her model back to the drawing board.

16 | Incomplete Sentences

A fragment fails to qualify as a sentence because it lacks a subject or a predicate (or both) or it fails to express a complete thought. However, a sentence with the essentials can still miss the mark. If it lacks a crucial word or phrase, the sentence may be *incomplete*. When you make comparisons and use elliptical constructions, be certain that you complete the thought you want to express.

Comparisons

16a Make your comparisons clear by stating fully what you are comparing with what.

> INCOMPLETE   Roscoe loves spending time online more than Diane.

Does Roscoe prefer the company of a keyboard to the company of his friend? Or, of these two people, is Roscoe (and not Diane) the online addict? Adding a word would complete the comparison.

> CLEAR   Roscoe loves spending time online more than Diane *does*.

> CLEAR   Roscoe loves spending time online more than *with* Diane.

16b When you start to draw a comparison, finish it.

The unfinished comparison is a favorite of advertisers — "Our product is better!" — because it dodges the question "Better than what?" A sharp writer knows that any item must be compared *with* something else.

Scottish tweeds are warmer / *than any other fabric.*

16c Be sure the things you compare are of the same kind.

A sentence that compares should reassure readers on two counts: the items are similar enough to compare, and the terms of comparison are clear.

> INCOMPLETE   The engine of a Ford truck is heavier than a Piper Cub airplane.

What is being compared? Truck engine and airplane? Or engine and engine? Because a truck engine is unlikely to outweigh a plane, we can guess the writer meant to compare engines. Readers, however, should not have to guess at the writer's intended meaning.

> CLEAR   The engine of a Ford truck is heavier than *that of* a Piper Cub airplane.

> CLEAR   A Ford truck's engine is heavier than a *Piper Cub's*.

In this last example, parallel structure (*Ford truck's* and *Piper Cub's*) helps make the comparison concise as well as clear.

For more on parallel structure, see 18.

16d To compare an item with others of its kind, use *any other*.

A comparison using *any* shows how something relates to a group without belonging to the group.

Alaska is larger than *any* country in Central America.

A comparison using *any other* shows how one member of a group relates to other members of the same group.

Death Valley is drier than *any other* place in the United States.

EXERCISE 16–1 Completing Comparisons

Revise the following sentences by adding needed words to any comparisons that are incomplete. (There may be more than one way to complete some comparisons.) Some sentences may be correct. Possible revisions for the lettered sentences appear at the end of the Handbook. Example:

I hate hot weather more than you ^do.   *Or*

I hate hot weather more than ^I hate you.

a. The movie version of *The Brady Bunch* was much more ironic.

b. Taking care of a dog is often more demanding than a cat.

c. I received more free calendars in the mail for 2016 than any year.

d. The crime rate in the United States is higher than Canada.

e. Liver contains more iron than any meat.

1. Driving a sports car means more to Jake than his professors.

2. People who go on vacation aren't necessarily happier, but they will always have experiences to talk about.

3. I don't have as much trouble getting along with Michelle as Karen.

4. A hen lays fewer eggs than a turtle.

5. Singing is closer to prayer than a meal of Chicken McNuggets.

Elliptical Constructions

Robert Frost begins his well-known poem "Fire and Ice" with the following lines:

Some say the world will end in fire, / Some say in ice.

When Frost wrote that opening, he avoided needless repetition by implying certain words rather than stating them. The result is more concise and more effective than a complete version of the same sentence would be:

Some say the world will end in fire, some say the world will end in ice.

This common tactic produces an **elliptical construction** — one that leaves out (for conciseness) words that are unnecessary but clearly understood by readers. Elliptical constructions can be confusing, however, if a writer gives readers too little information to fill in those missing words.

16e When you eliminate repetition, keep all the words essential for clarity.

An elliptical construction avoids repeating what a reader already knows, but it should omit only words that are stated elsewhere in the sentence, including prepositions. Otherwise, your reader may fill the gap incorrectly.

> *to*
> The train neither goes ⌃nor returns from Middletown.

16f In a compound predicate, leave out only verb forms that have already been stated.

Compound predicates are prone to incomplete constructions, especially if the verbs are in different tenses. Be sure no necessary part is missing.

> *voted*
> Lee never has ⌃and never will vote to raise taxes.

A **compound predicate** is a predicate consisting of two or more verbs linked by a conjunction (see 5a).

16g If you mix comparisons using *as* and *than*, include both words.

To contrast two things, use the comparative form of an adjective followed by *than*: *better than, more than, fewer than*. To show a similarity between two things, sandwich the simple form of an adjective between *as* and *as*: *as good as, as many as, as few as*. Often you can combine two *than* or two *as* comparisons into an elliptical construction.

For more on comparative forms, see 13d–13f.

> The White House is smaller [than] and newer than Buckingham Palace.
>
> Some elegant homes are as large [as] and as grand as the White House.

However, merging a *than* comparison with an *as* comparison won't work.

> *than*
> The White House is smaller ⌃but just as beautiful as Buckingham Palace.

EXERCISE 16–2 Completing Sentences

Revise the following sentences by adding needed words to any constructions that are incomplete. (There may be more than one way to complete some constructions.) Some sentences may be correct. Possible revisions for the lettered sentences appear at the end of the Handbook. Example:

> *seen*
> The general should have ⌃but didn't see the perils of invasion.

a. Eighteenth-century China was as civilized and in many respects more sophisticated than the Western world.

b. Pembroke was never contacted, much less involved with, the election committee.

c. I haven't yet but soon will finish my research paper.

d. Ron likes his popcorn with butter, Linda with parmesan cheese.

e. George Washington always has been and will be regarded as the father of this country.

1. You have traveled to exotic Tahiti; Maureen to Asbury Park, New Jersey.

2. The mayor refuses to negotiate or even talk to the civic association.

3. Building a new sewage treatment plant would be no more costly and just as effective as modifying the existing one.

4. You'll be able to tell Jon from the rest of the team: Jon wears white Reeboks, the others black high-tops.

5. Erosion has and always will reshape the shoreline.

17 | Mixed Constructions and Faulty Predication

Sometimes a sentence contains all the necessary ingredients but still doesn't make sense.

17a   Link phrases and clauses logically.

A **mixed construction** results when a writer connects phrases or clauses (or both) that don't work together as a sentence.

> MIXED   In her efforts to solve the tax problem only caused the mayor additional difficulties.

The prepositional phrase *In her efforts to solve the tax problem* is a modifier; it can't act as the subject of a sentence. The writer, however, has used this phrase as a noun—the subject of the verb *caused*. To untangle this mixed construction, the writer has two choices: (1) rewrite the phrase so that it works as a noun, or (2) use the phrase as a modifier, not as a subject.

> REVISED   Her efforts to solve the tax problem only caused the mayor additional difficulties. [With *in* gone, *efforts* becomes the subject.]
>
> REVISED   In her efforts to solve the tax problem, the mayor created additional difficulties. [The phrase now modifies the verb *created*.]

To fix a mixed construction, check your links—especially prepositions and conjunctions.

Jack/ ~~although he~~ was picked up by the police, but was not charged.

Although
~~Jack, although~~ he was picked up by the police, ~~but~~ was not charged.   *Jack*

---

*A **phrase** consists of two or more related words that work together but may lack a subject, a verb, or both (see 4b).*

*A **clause** is a group of related words that includes both a subject and a verb (see 4a).*

*A **preposition** is a transitional word (such as in, on, at, of, from) that leads into a phrase (see 1f).*

Guidelines for Multilingual Writers
How Can I Avoid Mixed Constructions, Faulty Predication, and Subject Errors?

Mixed constructions result when phrases or clauses are joined even though they do not logically go together. Combine clauses with either a coordinating conjunction or a subordinating conjunction, never both.

> Although baseball is called "the national pastime" of the United States, ~~but~~ football is probably more popular.

> *Baseball*
> ~~Although baseball~~ is called "the national pastime" of the United States, but football is probably more popular.

Faulty predication results when a verb and its subject, object, or modifier do not match. Do not use a noun as both the subject of the sentence and the object of a preposition.

> *there are*
> In my neighborhood ~~has~~ several good restaurants.

> *My*
> ~~In my~~ neighborhood has several good restaurants.

Subject errors include leaving out and repeating subjects of clauses.

- Do not omit *it* used as a subject. A subject is required in all English sentences except commands (imperatives).
  > *It is*
  > ~~Is~~ interesting to visit museums.

- Do not repeat the subject of a sentence with a pronoun.
  > My brother-in-law, ~~he~~ is a successful investor.

For more on coordination and subordination, see 19.

Coordinating conjunctions join elements with equal or near-equal importance (see 1g and 19a–19c).

A **subordinating conjunction** is a word (such as *because, although, if, when*) used to make one clause dependent on, or subordinate to, another (see 1g and 19d–19f).

17b Relate the parts of a sentence logically.

Faulty predication refers to a skewed relationship between a verb and some other part of a sentence.

> FAULTY   *The temperature of water freezes at 32 degrees Fahrenheit.*

At first glance, that sentence looks all right. It contains both subject and verb. It expresses a complete thought. What is wrong with it? The writer has mismatched the subject and verb. The sentence tells us that *temperature freezes*, when science and common sense tell us *water freezes*. The writer needs to select a subject and verb that fit each other.

> REVISED   *Water freezes at 32 degrees Fahrenheit.*

Faulty predication also results from a mismatched verb and direct object.

> *the number of students who can attend college.*
> Rising costs diminish ~~college for many students.~~

A **subject** is the part of a sentence that names something—a person, an object, an idea, a situation—about which the verb makes an assertion (see 2).

A **verb** is a word that shows action or state of being (see 1c and 3).

A **direct object** is the target of a verb that completes the action performed by the subject or asserted about the subject (see 3a).

A **linking verb** is a verb that shows a state of being by linking the sentence subject with a word that renames or describes the subject (see 1c and 3b.)

Costs don't *diminish college*. To correct this error, the writer changed the sentence so that its direct object follows logically from its verb. Subtler predication errors result when a writer uses a linking verb to forge a false connection between the subject and a subject complement.

> FAULTY   *Industrial waste* has become *an important modern priority*.

Is it *waste* that has become a *priority*? Or is it *solving problems caused by careless disposal of industrial waste*? A writer who says all that, though, risks wordiness. Why not just replace *priority* with a closer match for *waste*?

> REVISED   *Industrial waste* has become *a modern menace*.

Mismatches between a verb and another part of the sentence are easier to avoid when the verb is active rather than passive.

The idea of giving thanks for a good harvest ~~was not done first by~~ the Pilgrims. _{did not originate with}

17c Avoid starting a definition with *is when* or *is where*.

A definition needs to fit grammatically with the rest of the sentence.

Dyslexia is ~~when you have~~ a reading disorder.

To shoot a layup,
~~A layup is where~~ a player dribbles in close to the basket and then makes a one-handed, banked shot.

17d Avoid using *the reason is because* . . .

Anytime you start an explanation with *the reason is*, what follows *is* should be a subject complement: an adjective, a noun, or a noun clause. *Because* is a conjunction; it cannot function as a noun or an adjective.

that
The reason Al hesitates is ~~because~~ no one supported him last year.

~~The reason~~ Al hesitates ~~is~~ because no one supported him last year.

EXERCISE 17–1 Correcting Mixed Constructions and Faulty Predication

Correct any mixed constructions and faulty predication you find in the following sentences. Possible revisions for the lettered sentences appear at the end of the Handbook. Example:

worsened
The storm ~~damaged~~ the beach erosion.   *Or*

beach.
The storm damaged the ~~beach erosion.~~

a. The cost of health insurance protects people from big medical bills.

b. In his determination to prevail helped him finish the race.

c. The AIDS epidemic destroys the body's immune system.

d. The temperatures are too cold for the orange trees.

e. A recession is when economic growth is small or nonexistent and unemployment increases.

1. The opening of the new shopping mall should draw out-of-town shoppers for years to come.

2. The reason the referendum was defeated was because voters are tired of paying so much in taxes.

3. In the glacier's retreat created the valley.

4. A drop in prices could put farmers out of business.

5. The researchers' main goal is cancer.

18 | Parallel Structure

You use **parallel structure,** or parallelism, when you create a series of words, phrases, clauses, or sentences with the same grammatical form. The pattern created by the series — its parallel structure — emphasizes the similarities or differences among the items, whether they are things, qualities, actions, or ideas.

> My favorite foods are roast beef, apple pie, and linguine with clams.
>
> Louise is charming, witty, intelligent, and talented.
>
> Manuel likes to swim, ride, and run.
>
> Dave likes movies that scare him and books that make him laugh.

Each series is a perfect parallel construction, composed of equivalent words: nouns in the first example, then adjectives, verbs, and adjective clauses.

18a In a series linked by a coordinating conjunction, keep all elements in the same grammatical form.

A coordinating conjunction (*and, but, for, or, nor, so, yet*) cues your readers to expect a parallel structure. Whether your series consists of single words, phrases, or clauses, its parts should balance one another.

For more on coordination, see 19a–19c.

>   *clumsy*
> The puppies are tiny, ~~clumsily bumping into each other,~~ and cute.

Two elements in this series are parallel one-word adjectives (*tiny, cute*), but the third, the verb phrase *clumsily bumping,* is inconsistent.

A **gerund** is a form of a verb, ending in *-ing*, that functions as a noun (see 8a).

An **infinitive** consists of the base form of a verb plus the word *to* (see 8a).

Don't mix verb forms, such as gerunds and infinitives, in a series.

Plan a winter vacation if you like skiing and ~~to skate.~~ *skating.*

Plan a winter vacation if you like ~~skiing~~ *to ski* and to skate.

In a series of phrases or clauses, be sure that all elements in the series are similar in form, even if they are not similar in length.

You can take the key, or ~~don't forget to~~ *you can* leave it under the mat. [The declarative clause starting with *You can* is not parallel to the imperative clause starting with *don't forget.*]

18b In a series linked by correlative conjunctions, keep all elements in the same grammatical form.

A **correlative conjunction** is a pair of linking words such as *either/or* or *not only/but also* that appear separately but work together to join elements of a sentence. When you use a correlative conjunction, follow each part with a similarly structured word, phrase, or clause.

I'm looking forward ~~to~~ either *to* attending Saturday's wrestling match or to seeing it on closed-circuit TV. [*To* precedes the first part (*to either*) but -follows the second part (*or to*).]

Take my advice: try neither ~~to be~~ *to be* first nor last in the lunch line. [*To be* follows the first part but not the second part.]

> ## CORRELATIVE CONJUNCTIONS at a glance
>
> | as . . . as | just as . . . so | not only . . . but also |
> |---|---|---|
> | both . . . and | neither . . . nor | whether . . . or |
> | either . . . or | not . . . but | |

18c Make the elements in a comparison parallel in form.

For more on comparisons, see 16a–16d and 16g.

A comparative word such as *than* or *as* cues the reader to expect a parallel structure. This makes logical sense: to be compared, two things must resemble each other, and parallel structure emphasizes this resemblance.

Philip likes ~~fishing~~ *to fish* better than to sail.

Maintaining railway lines is as important to the public transportation system as ~~to buy~~ *buying* new trains.

18d Reinforce parallel structure by repeating rather than mixing lead-in words.

Parallel structures are especially useful when a sentence contains a series of clauses or phrases. For example, try to precede potentially confusing clauses with *that, who, when, where,* or some other connective, repeating the same connective every time to help readers follow them with ease.

No one in this country needs a government *that* aids big business at the

expense of farmers and workers, $\overset{that}{\wedge}$ ravages the environment in the name of

progress, or $\overset{that}{\wedge}$ slashes budgets for health and education.

If the same lead-in word won't work for all elements in a series, try changing the order of the elements to minimize variation.

The new school building is large $\overset{and\ expensive,\ but\ uncomfortable\ and}{\sout{but\ not\ very\ comfortable,\ and\ expensive,}}$ $\sout{but}$ unattractive.

EXERCISE 18–1 Making Sentences Parallel

Revise the following sentences by substituting parallel structures for awkward ones. Possible revisions for the lettered sentences appear at the end of the Handbook. Example:

In the Rio Grande Valley, the interests of conservationists, government

officials, and $\overset{immigrants}{\sout{those\ trying\ to\ immigrate}}$ collide.

a. The border separating Texas and Mexico marks not only the political boundary of two countries, but it also is the last frontier for some endangered wildlife.

b. In the Rio Grande Valley, both local residents and the people who happen to be tourists enjoy visiting the national wildlife refuges.

c. The tall grasses in this valley are the home of many insects, birds, and there are abundant small mammals.

d. Two endangered wildcats, the ocelot and another called the jaguarundi, also make the Rio Grande Valley their home.

e. Many people from Central America are desperate to immigrate to the United States by either legal or by illegal means.

1. Because the land along the Rio Grande has few human inhabitants and the fact that the river is often shallow, many undocumented immigrants attempt to cross the border there.

2. To stop undocumented immigrants more easily, the U.S. government has cut down tall grasses, put up fences, and the number of immigration patrols has been increased.

3. For undocumented immigrants, crossing the border at night makes more sense than to enter the United States in broad daylight, so the U.S. government has recently installed bright lights along the border.

4. The ocelot and the jaguarundi need darkness, hiding places, and to have some solitude if they are to survive.

5. Neither the immigration officials nor have wildlife conservationists been able to find a solution that will protect both the U.S. border and these endangered wildcats.

19 | Coordination and Subordination

Coordination and subordination can use conjunctions to specify relationships between ideas. Coordination connects thoughts of equal importance; subordination shows how one thought affects another.

19a Use coordination to join clauses or sentences that are related in theme and equal in importance.

> The car skidded for a hundred yards. It crashed into a brick wall.

These two clauses make equally significant statements about the same subject, a car accident. Because the writer has not linked the sentences, we can only guess that the crash followed from the skid.

> The car skidded for a hundred yards, and it crashed into a brick wall.

Now the sequence is clear: first the car skidded; then it crashed. That's coordination. There are three main ways to join clauses using coordination.

1. Join two main clauses with a comma and a coordinating conjunction (*for, and, nor, but, or, yet, so*).

   Ari does not want to be placed on your mailing list/ ~~He does not~~ *, nor does he* want a salesperson to call him.

2. Join two main clauses with a semicolon and a conjunctive adverb. Conjunctive adverbs show relationships such as addition, comparison, contrast, emphasis, cause and effect, or time.

   The guerrillas did not observe the truce/ *; furthermore, they* ~~They~~ never intended to.

3. Join two main clauses with a semicolon or a colon.

   The army wants to negotiate/ *; the* ~~The~~ guerrillas prefer to fight.

   The guerrillas have two advantages/ *; they* ~~They~~ know the terrain, and the people support them.

Sidebar notes:

A **conjunction** is a linking word that connects words or groups of words through coordination or subordination (see 1g).

A **clause** is a group of related words that includes both a subject and a verb (see 4a).

Coordinating conjunctions join elements with equal or near-equal importance.

For a list of common conjunctive adverbs, see p. 633.

For more on semicolons and colons, see 30 and 31.

19b Coordinate clauses only if they are clearly and logically related.

Whenever you hitch together two sentences, make sure they get along. Will the relationship between them be evident to your readers?

> FAULTY   The sportscasters were surprised by Easy Goer's failure to win the Kentucky Derby, but it rained on derby day.

Readers need enough information to see why two clauses are connected.

> COORDINATED   The sportscasters were surprised by Easy Goer's failure to win the Kentucky Derby; *however, he runs poorly on a muddy track*, and it rained on derby day.

Choose a coordinating conjunction, conjunctive adverb, or punctuation mark that accurately reflects this relationship.

> *but*
> The sportscasters all expected Easy Goer to win the Kentucky Derby, ~~and~~
> Sunday Silence beat him.

19c Coordinate clauses only if they work together to make a coherent point.

When a writer strings together several clauses in a row, often the result is excessive coordination. Packing too much information into a single sentence can make readers dizzy, unable to pick out which points really matter. Each key idea deserves its own sentence so readers see its importance.

COORDINATING WORDS at a glance

Coordinating Conjunctions

and, but, for, nor, or, so, yet

Common Conjunctive Adverbs

accordingly	finally	likewise	otherwise
also	furthermore	meanwhile	similarly
anyway	hence	moreover	still
as	however	nevertheless	then
besides	incidentally	next	therefore
certainly	indeed	nonetheless	thus
consequently	instead	now	undoubtedly

> EXCESSIVE   Easy Goer was the Kentucky Derby favorite, and all the sportscasters expected him to win, but he runs poorly on a muddy track, and it rained on derby day, so Sunday Silence beat him.

| REVISED | Easy Goer was the Kentucky Derby favorite, and all the sportscasters expected him to win. However, he runs poorly on a muddy track, and it rained on derby day. Therefore, Sunday Silence beat him. |

Excessive coordination may result from repeating the same conjunction.

| EXCESSIVE | Phil was in meetings all day, so he didn't know about the rain, so he went ahead and bet on Easy Goer, so he lost twenty bucks, so now he wants to borrow money from me. |

| REVISED | Phil was in meetings all day, so he didn't know about the rain. He went ahead and bet on Easy Goer and lost twenty bucks. Now he wants to borrow money from me. |

EXERCISE 19–1 Using Coordination

Revise the following sentences, adding coordination where appropriate and removing faulty or excessive coordination. Possible revisions for the lettered sentences appear at the end of the Handbook. Example:

> The wind was rising, ~~and~~ leaves tossed on the trees, and the air seemed to
>
> crackle with electricity. *We* ~~and we~~ knew that a thunderstorm was on the way.

a. Professional poker players try to win money and prizes in high-stakes tournaments. They may lose thousands of dollars.

b. Poker is not an easy way to make a living. Playing professional poker is not a good way to relax.

c. A good "poker face" reveals no emotions. Communicating too much information puts a player at a disadvantage.

d. Hidden feelings may come out in unconscious movements. An expert poker player watches other players carefully.

e. Poker is different from most other casino gambling games, for it requires skill and it forces players to compete against each other, and other casino gambling pits players against the house, so they may win out of sheer luck, but skill has little to do with winning those games.

1. The rebels may take the capital in a week. They may not be able to hold it.

2. If you want to take Spanish this semester, you have only one choice. You must sign up for the 8 a.m. course.

3. Peterson's Market has raised its prices. Last week tuna fish cost $1.29 a can. Now it's up to $1.59.

4. Joe starts the morning with a cup of coffee, which wakes him up, and then at lunch he eats a chocolate bar, so that the sugar and caffeine will bring up his energy level.

5. The *Hindenburg* drifted peacefully over New York City. It exploded just before landing.

19d Subordinate less important ideas.

Subordination is extremely useful because it shows your readers the relative importance of ideas, how one follows from another or affects another. You stress what counts, thereby encouraging your readers to share your viewpoint. You can subordinate one sentence to another in either of the following ways.

For a list of subordinating words, see p. 636.

1. Turn the less important idea into a subordinate clause by introducing it with a subordinating conjunction such as *because*, *if*, or *when*.

   Jason has a keen sense of humor. He has an obnoxious, braying laugh.

From those sentences, readers don't know what to feel about Jason. Is he likable or repellent? The writer needs to show which trait matters more.

> *Although Jason has a keen sense of humor*, he has an obnoxious, braying laugh.

A **main clause** is a group of words that has both a subject and a verb and can stand alone as a complete sentence (see 4a).

This revision makes Jason's sense of humor less important than his annoying hee-haw. The less important idea is stated as a subordinate clause opening with *Although*; the more important idea is stated as the main clause.

The writer could reverse the meaning by combining the other way:

> *Although Jason has an obnoxious, braying laugh*, he has a keen sense of humor.

That version makes Jason sound fun to be with, despite his mannerism.

Which of Jason's traits to emphasize is up to the writer. What matters is that, in both combined versions, the writer takes a clear stand by making one sentence a main clause and the other a subordinate clause.

2. Turn the less important idea into a subordinate clause by introducing it with a relative pronoun such as *who*, *which*, or *that*.

   Jason, *who has an obnoxious, braying laugh*, has a keen sense of humor.

   Jason, *whose sense of humor is keen*, has an obnoxious, braying laugh.

A **relative pronoun** is a pronoun that opens a subordinate clause and modifies a noun or pronoun in another clause (see 1b).

19e Express the more important idea in the main clause.

Sometimes a writer accidentally subordinates a more important idea to a less important one and turns the sentence's meaning upside down.

FAULTY SUBORDINATION   Although the heroism of the Allied troops on D-Day lives on in spirit, many of the World War II soldiers who invaded Normandy are dead now.

SUBORDINATING WORDS at a glance

Common Subordinating Conjunctions

after	before	since	until
although	even though	so	when
as	how	so that	whenever
as if	if	than	where
as soon as	in order that	that	wherever
as though	once	though	while
because	rather than	unless	why

Relative Pronouns

that, which	what	who	whom
whose	whatever	whoever	whomever

Guidelines for Multilingual Writers
What's the Difference between Prepositions and Conjunctions?

Prepositions and conjunctions may seem similar, but they have different functions in a sentence. To make things even more confusing, some words, such as *but*, *for*, *after*, and *until*, can work as either a conjunction or a preposition. Here are some tips to keep in mind:

- **Coordinating conjunctions** join words, phrases, or clauses.

  WORDS: Jacob excels at English, history, *and* French.

  PHRASES: Cats enjoy sleeping in the daytime *but* creeping around at night.

  CLAUSES: Alicia is taking many science classes, *for* she wants to become a doctor.

- **Subordinating conjunctions** come at the beginning of a clause, giving that clause less emphasis than the main clause in the sentence. Remember that all clauses have a subject and a verb.

  After she finished the book, Deanne began writing a summary.

  The bus driver stayed with the student *until* the ambulance arrived.

- **Prepositions** introduce short phrases that consist of the preposition, a noun (the object of the preposition), and any articles or adjectives. Note that prepositional phrases do not contain subjects or verbs.

  After Thanksgiving dinner, Carla always takes a long walk *around* the neighborhood.

  On New Year's Eve, everyone *but* Isadora stayed awake *until* midnight.

  We waited *for* the package, but it never came.

This sentence is accurate, but by putting *are dead now* in the main clause and *lives on* in the subordinate clause, it stresses death over life. Reversing the two creates a more powerful sentence.

REVISED   Although many of the World War II soldiers who invaded Normandy are dead now, the heroism of the Allied troops on D-Day lives on in spirit.

19f Limit the number of subordinate clauses in a sentence.

Excessive subordination strings too many ideas together without helping readers pick out what matters.

Debate over the Strategic Defense Initiative (SDI), ~~a which~~ was originally *has to some extent focused on the wrong question. The plan* proposed as a space-based defensive shield that would protect America from enemy attack, ~~but which critics~~ *Critics* have suggested *, however, that it* amounts to creating a first-strike capability in space, ~~has to some extent focused on the wrong question.~~

> A **subordinate clause** is a group of words that contains a subject and a verb but cannot stand alone because it depends on a main clause to help it make sense (see 4a and 19d).

EXERCISE 19–2 Using Subordination

Revise the following sentences, adding coordination and removing faulty or excessive coordination where appropriate. Possible revisions for the lettered sentences appear at the end of the Handbook. Example:

The tiny house movement is a social ~~movement. It~~ *movement that* involves people downsizing to homes much smaller than traditional houses.

a. The average cost of a single-family home in the United States is over $275,000. It costs less than one-tenth of that to build a tiny house.

b. American homes average about 2,500 square feet. They have three bedrooms, two bathrooms, and a garage for two or more cars.

c. A tiny house is between 100 and 400 square feet. It enables simpler living in a smaller, more efficient space.

d. Tiny houses come in all shapes, sizes, and forms. They are much more customizable than traditional mobile homes.

e. The tiny house movement, which people are joining for many reasons, is popular because people who want to be environmentally conscious can build a tiny house so that they will have fewer financial concerns once they build the house, which will give them more time and freedom.

1. We may not realize it. Dozens of books are banned every year in schools, classrooms, and libraries.

2. Some communities feel that books contain dangerous themes and inappropriate language. They want to prevent children and teens from gaining access to them.

3. Young adult books such as the Twilight and Harry Potter series focus on what some people consider to be satanic or occult themes. These are often targeted by censorship groups.

4. Books could be made available only to the appropriate age group. They would not need to be banned.

5. If people who want to ban classics such as *The Grapes of Wrath* and *To Kill a Mockingbird* had actually read those books, they would realize that, although they may contain strong themes and language, their overall message is positive.

20 | Sentence Variety

For a review of sentence types, see 5.

Most writers rely on some patterns more than others to express ideas directly and efficiently, but sometimes they combine sentence elements in unexpected ways to emphasize ideas and to surprise readers.

20a Normal Sentences

In a **normal sentence,** a writer puts the subject before the verb at the beginning of the main clause. This pattern is the most common in English because it expresses ideas in the most straightforward manner.

Most college *students* today *want* interesting classes.

20b Inverted Sentences

In an **inverted sentence,** a writer inverts or reverses the subject-verb order to emphasize an idea in the predicate.

NORMAL   *My peers are uninterested* in reading.

INVERTED   How *uninterested* in reading *are my peers!*

20c Cumulative Sentences

In a **cumulative sentence,** a writer piles details at the end of a sentence to help readers visualize a scene or understand an idea.

They came walking out in heavily brocaded yellow and black costumes, the familiar "toreador" suit, heavy with gold embroidery, cape, jacket, shirt and collar, knee breeches, pink stockings, and low pumps.

—Ernest Hemingway, "Bullfighting Is Not a Sport—It Is a Tragedy"

20d Periodic Sentences

The positions of emphasis in a sentence are the beginning and the end. In a **periodic sentence,** a writer suspends the main clause for a climactic ending, emphasizing an idea by withholding it until the end.

Leaning back in his chair, shaking his head slowly back and forth, frustrated over his inability to solve the equation, Franklin scowled.

EXERCISE 20–1 Increasing Sentence Variety

Revise the following passage, adding sentence variety to create interest, emphasize important ideas, and strengthen coherence.

We are terrified of death. We do not think of it, and we don't speak of death. We don't mourn in public. We don't know how to console a grieving friend. In fact, we have eliminated or suppressed all the traditional rituals surrounding death.

The Victorians coped with death differently. Their funerals were elaborate. The yards of black crepe around the hearse, hired professional mourners, and solemn procession leading to an ornate tomb are now only a distant memory. They wore mourning jewelry. They had a complicated dress code for the grieving process. It governed what mourners wore, and it governed how long they wore it. Many of these rituals may seem excessive or even morbid to us today. The rituals served a psychological purpose in helping the living deal with loss.

21 | Active and Passive Voice

| ACTIVE | College students read challenging books. |
| PASSIVE | Challenging books are read by college students. |

These two statements convey similar information, but their emphasis is different. The first sentence is active: the subject (*students*) performs the verb's action (*read*). The second sentence is passive: the subject (*books*) receives the verb's action (*are read*). The active sentence states its idea directly; the passive sentence states its idea indirectly.

21a In most cases, use the active voice rather than the passive voice.

Verbs in the **active voice** consist of principal parts and helping verbs. Verbs in the **passive voice** consist of the past participle (*-ed* or *-en* form) preceded by a form of *be* ("you *are given*," "I *was given*," "she *will be given*"). Most writers prefer the active to the passive voice because it is clearer and simpler, requires fewer words, and identifies the actor and the action more explicitly.

ACTIVE VOICE   *Sergeants give* orders. *Privates obey* them.

Normally the subject of a sentence is the focus of readers' attention. If that subject does not perform the verb's action but instead receives the action, readers may wonder: What did the writer mean to emphasize?

PASSIVE VOICE   *Orders are given* by sergeants. *They are obeyed* by privates.

Other writers misuse the passive voice to try to lend pomp to a humble truth (or would-be truth). For example, "Slight technical difficulties are being experienced" may replace "The airplane needs repairs." Some even use the passive voice to deliberately obscure the truth.

21b Use the passive voice in certain cases.

You do not need to drop the passive voice entirely from your writing. Sometimes the performer of a verb's action is irrelevant, as in a lab report, which emphasizes the research, not the researcher. Sometimes the performer is understood:

> Automobiles are built in Detroit.

Other times the performer is unknown and simply omitted:

> Many fortunes were lost in the stock market crash of 1929.

It's a good idea, though, to substitute the active voice for the passive unless you have a good reason for using the passive:

> I babysat five
> ~~Five~~ children ~~were babysat by me~~ last week.

EXERCISE 21–1 Using Active and Passive Voice Verbs

Revise the following passage, changing the passive voice to the active voice in each sentence, unless you can justify keeping the passive. Example:

> *Many species of animals reached the*
> ~~The~~ Galápagos Islands ~~were reached by many species of animals~~ in ancient times.

The unique creatures of the Galápagos Islands have been studied by many scientists. The islands were explored by Charles Darwin in 1835. His observations led to the theory of evolution, which he explained in *On the Origin of Species*. Thirteen species of finches on the islands were discovered by Darwin, all descended from a common stock; even today this variety of species can be seen by visitors to the islands. Each island species has evolved by adapting to local conditions. A twig is used by the woodpecker finch to probe trees for grubs. Algae on the ocean floor are fed on by the marine iguana. Salt water can be drunk by the Galápagos cormorant, thanks to a salt-extracting gland. Because of the tameness of these animals, they can be studied by visitors at close range.

Learning by Doing 🔟 Considering Language

Examine the sentence style of a written artifact (essay, song, meme, etc.). What problems can you find with its modifiers, parallelism, variety, and other issues discussed in this chapter? Do you think the style choices were intentional? How might you improve the writing?

Word Choice

36

22 | Appropriateness

When you talk to people face-to-face, you can gauge their reactions to what you say. Often their responses guide your tone and your choice of words. When you write, you can't see your readers. Instead, you must imagine yourself in their place, focusing on their responses when you revise.

Besides affecting how well you achieve your purpose as a writer, your language can affect how well you're regarded by others. When you accurately assess the tone, formality, and word choice expected in a situation, you use the power of language to enhance your position. When you misjudge, you risk being misunderstood or judged harshly.

22a Choose a tone appropriate for your topic and audience.

Like a speaker, a writer may come across as friendly or aloof, furious or merely annoyed, playful or grimly serious. This attitude is the writer's **tone,** and it strongly influences the audience's response. For instance, readers might reject as inappropriate a humorous approach to terrorist attacks. To convey your tone, use sentence length, level of language, and vocabulary. The key is to be aware of your readers and their expectations.

22b Choose a level of formality appropriate for your tone.

Considering the tone you want to convey helps you choose words that are neither too formal nor too informal. **Formal** language is typically impersonal and serious. Formal language is marked by relatively complex sentences and a large vocabulary. It doesn't use contractions (such as *doesn't*).

In contrast, **informal** language more closely resembles ordinary conversation. It uses relatively short sentences and common words. It may include contractions, slang, and references to everyday objects and activities. The writer may use *I* and address the reader as *you*.

The right language for most college essays lies somewhere between formal and informal. If your topic and tone are serious (for a research project on homelessness, for example), then your language may lean toward formality. If your topic is not weighty and your tone is light (for a humorous personal essay about giving your dog a bath, for example), then your language may be informal.

EXERCISE 22–1 Choosing an Appropriate Tone and Level of Formality

Revise the following passages to ensure that both the tone and the level of formality are appropriate for the topic and audience. Example:

> I'm sending you this letter because I want you to meet with me and give me some info about the job you do.
>
> *I am writing to request an informational interview about your profession.*

1. Dear Senator Crowley:

   I think you've got to vote for the new environmental law, so I'm writing this letter. We're messing up forests and wetlands — maybe for good. Let's do something now for everybody who's born after us.

   Thanks,

   Glenn Turner

2. The United States Holocaust Memorial Museum in Washington, D.C., is a great museum dedicated to a real bad time in history. It's hard not to get bummed out by the stuff on show. Take it from me, it's an experience you won't forget.

3. Dear Elaine,

   I am so pleased that you plan on attending the homecoming dance with me on Friday. It promises to be a gala event, and I am confident that we will enjoy ourselves immensely. I understand a local group by the name of Electric Bunny will provide musical entertainment. Please call me at your earliest convenience to inform me when to pick you up.

   Sincerely,

   Bill

22c Choose common words instead of jargon.

Jargon is the term for the specialized vocabulary used by people in a certain field, such as music, carpentry, law, or sports. Nearly every academic, professional, and recreational field has its own jargon. To a specialist addressing other specialists, jargon is convenient and necessary. Without technical terms, after all, two surgeons could hardly discuss a patient's anatomy. To an outsider, though, such terms may be incomprehensible. To communicate with readers without confusing them, avoid unnecessary jargon.

>   *caught*   *criminal*
> The police ~~apprehended~~ the alleged ~~perpetrator of the crime~~ in the
> *area*
> ~~vicinity~~ of White Hills, and now they will ~~proceed to book~~ him.
>   *arrest*

Jargon often results in unnecessarily wordy language because the writer is attempting to sound intellectual or seeking to avoid speaking directly about an issue.

For more on wordiness, see 25. For more on euphemisms (indirect wording to avoid unpleasant topics), see 22d.

>   *lowered her blood pressure*   *some*
> Grandma ~~alleviated her hypertension~~ by adding ~~a certain~~
>   *exercise*   *daily routine.*
> ~~amount of mobile activity~~ to her ~~quotidian procedure.~~

Many instances of jargon come from business and technical language. Avoid using technological terms such as *interface* and *input* to refer to nontechnical ideas. Also avoid ending words with the suffix *-ize* (as in *privatize*) and in the hyphenated term *-wise* (as in *time-wise*).

>   *sell*   *to private buyers.*
> The government intends to ~~privatize~~ federal land/
>   *electorate to vote and to express its views to elected officials.*
> A democracy needs the ~~electorate's input.~~

EXERCISE 22–2 Avoiding Jargon

Revise the following sentences to eliminate the jargon. If necessary, revise extensively. If you can't tell what a sentence means, decide what it might mean, and rewrite it so that its meaning is clear. Possible revisions for the lettered sentences appear at the end of the Handbook. Example:

>   *cut*
> ~~The proximity of~~ Mr. Fitton's knife ~~to~~ Mr. Schering's arm ~~produced a~~
> ~~violation of the integrity of the skin.~~

a. Everyone at Boondoggle and Gall puts in face time at the holiday gatherings to maximize networking opportunities.

b. This year, in excess of fifty employees were negatively impacted by Boondoggle and Gall's decision to downsize effective September 1.

c. The layoffs made Jensen the sole point of responsibility for telephone interface in the customer-service department.

d. The numerical quotient of Jensen's telephonic exchanges increased by a factor of three post-downsizing, yet Jensen received no additional fiscal remuneration.

e. Jensen was not on the same page with management re her compensation, so she exercised the option to terminate her relationship with Boondoggle and Gall.

1. The driver-education course prepares the student for the skills of handling a vehicle on the highway transportation system.

2. In the heart area, Mr. Pitt is a prime candidate-elect for intervention of a multiple bypass nature.

3. The deer hunter's activity of quietizing a predetermined amount of the deer populace balances the ecological infrastructure.

22d Use euphemisms sparingly.

Euphemisms are plain truths dressed attractively, sometimes hard facts stated gently. To say that someone *passed away* instead of *died* is a common euphemism—humane, perhaps, in breaking terrible news to an anxious family. In such language, an army that *retreats* makes *a strategic withdrawal,* and a shampoo brightens *silver highlights* not *gray hair.*

22e Avoid slang in formal writing.

Slang, when new, can be colorful ("She's not playing with a full deck"), playful ("He's wicked cute!"), and apt (a *stiff* for a corpse). Most slang, however, quickly seems as old and wrinkled as the Jazz Age's *twenty-three skidoo!* Your best bet is to stick to words that are usual but exact.

EXERCISE 22–3 Avoiding Euphemisms and Slang

Revise the following sentences to replace euphemisms with plainer words and slang with Standard English. Possible revisions for the lettered sentences appear at the end of the Handbook. Example:

> *Someone stole*   *now in debt.*
> ~~Some dude ripped off~~ my wallet, so I am ~~currently experiencing a~~
> ~~negative cash flow.~~

a. At three hundred bucks a month, the apartment is a steal.

b. The soldiers were victims of friendly fire during a strategic withdrawal.

c. Churchill was a wicked good politician.

1. Saturday's weather forecast calls for extended periods of shower activity.

2. The caller to the talk-radio program sounded totally wigged out.

3. We anticipate a downturn in economic vitality.

23 | Exact Words

Good writing depends on knowing what words mean and how to use them precisely.

23a Choose words for their connotations as well as their denotations.

The **denotation** of a word is its basic meaning—its dictionary definition. *Excited, agitated,* and *exhilarated* all denote a similar state of physical and emotional arousal. The **connotations** of a word are the shades of meaning that set it apart from its synonyms. You might be *agitated* by the prospect of exams next week, but *exhilarated* by your plans for the vacation afterward. When you choose one of several options, you base your choice on connotation.

> Advertisers have given light beer a macho image by showing football
> players ~~sipping~~ *guzzling* the product with ~~enthusiasm.~~ *gusto.*

23b Avoid clichés.

A **cliché** is a trite expression, once vivid or figurative but now worn out from too much use. Clichés abound when writers and speakers try hard to sound lively but don't invent anything vigorous, colorful, and new. If your writing includes clichés such as the following, delete them or rewrite them in your own words.

COMMON CLICHÉS

a sneaking suspicion	last but not least
above and beyond the call of duty	make a long story short
add insult to injury	through thick and thin
beyond a shadow of a doubt	tip of the iceberg
few and far between	tried and true

23c Use idioms in their correct form.

Idioms, or **idiomatic expressions,** are phrases that, through long use, have become standard even though their construction may defy logic or grammar. Many idioms require you to choose the right preposition or article to use before a noun. When in doubt, use a dictionary.

> In order to comply ~~to~~ *with* the zoning laws, be sure ~~and~~ *to* check with the building department.

> ## COMMON IDIOMATIC EXPRESSIONS at a glance
>
> abide by (not *abide with*)   sure to (not *sure and*)
> according to (not *according with*) think of, about (not *think on*)
> capable of (not *capable to*)   try to (not *try and*)
> comply with (not *comply to*)   type of (not *type of a*)
> plan to (not *plan on*)

EXERCISE 23–1 Selecting Words

Revise the following passage to replace clichés, faulty idioms, and words with inappropriate connotations. Example:

> The Mayan city of Uxmal is a ~~common~~ *popular* tourist attraction. The ruins have stood alone in the jungle since ~~time immemorial~~ *ancient times*.

We spent the first day of our holiday in Mexico arguing around what we wanted to see on our second day. We finally agreed to a day trip out to some Mayan ruins. The next day we arrived on the Mayan city of Uxmal, which is as old as the hills. It really is a sight for sore eyes, smack-dab in a jungle stretching as far as the eye can see, with many buildings still covered in plants and iguanas moving quickly over the decayed buildings. The view from the top of the Soothsayer's Temple was good, although we noticed storm clouds gathering in the distance. The rain held up until we got off of the pyramid, but we drove back to the hotel in a lot of rain. After a day of sightseeing, we were so hungry that we could have eaten a horse, so we had a good meal before we turned in.

---

24 | Bias-Free Language

Thoughtful writers try to avoid harmful bias in their language. They respect their readers and don't want to insult them, anger them, or impede communication. Be on the lookout for words that insult or stereotype individuals or groups by gender, age, race, ethnicity, sexual orientation, religion, or ability.

24a Avoid terms that include or imply *man*.

Substitute a gender-neutral term for *man* or a word starting with *man*.

> *Human beings study people's cruelty to one another.*
> ~~Mankind studies man's inhumanity to man.~~

Similarly, you need not simply replace the ending -*man* with -*person*. Instead, think about meaning and find a truly neutral synonym.

letter carrier?
Did you leave a note for the ~~mailman~~?

flight attendant
Ask your ~~stewardess~~ for a pillow.

24b Use plural instead of singular forms.

Replace the singular with the plural (*they* and *their* for *he* and *his*).

students value their
Today's ~~student values his~~ education.

When a singular indefinite pronoun is an antecedent, its pronoun must also be singular.

his or her
Everyone is set in ~~their~~ ways. [The combined pronoun *his or her* is singular, so it correctly refers to the singular indefinite pronoun *Everyone*.]

Alternatively, you could recast the sentence with a plural antecedent.

People are
~~Everyone is~~ set in their ways. [Now the plural pronoun *their* agrees with the plural antecedent *People*.]

For more on pronoun-antecedent agreement, see 12.

24c Where possible, omit words that denote gender.

You can make your language more bias-free by omitting pronouns and other words that needlessly indicate gender.

There must be rapport between a stockbroker and ~~his~~ client, a teacher and ~~her~~ student, a doctor and ~~his~~ patient.

Also treat men and women equally in terms of description or title.

husband
I now pronounce you ~~man~~ and wife.

Ms.
Please page Mr. Pease, Mr. Mankodi, and ~~Emily~~ Brillantes.

24d Avoid condescending labels.

A responsible writer does not call women *chicks, babes, woman drivers,* or any other names that imply that they are not to be taken seriously. Nor should an employee ever be called a *girl* or *boy.* Avoid terms that put down individuals or groups because of age (*old goat, the grannies*), race or ethnicity (*Indian giver, Chinaman's chance*), or disability (*gimpy, handicapped*).

administrative assistants
The ~~girls in the office~~ got Mr. Birt a birthday cake.

has old-fashioned ideas.
My neighbor ~~is just an old fogy.~~

When describing a group, try to use the label or term that its members prefer.

           Asian
Alice wants to study ~~Oriental~~ culture.

24e   Avoid implied stereotypes.

Sometimes a stereotype is linked to a title. Aside from obvious exceptions, never assume that all the members of a group are of the same gender.

                                           families.
Pilots have little time to spend with their ~~wives and children.~~

Avoid stereotyping individuals or groups, negatively or positively.

Roberto isn't very good at paying his rent on time, ~~which doesn't surprise me because he is from Mexico~~.

24f   Use *Ms.* for a woman with no other known title.

Ms. is the preferred title of polite address for women because, like *Mr.* for men, it does not indicate marital status. Use *Miss* or *Mrs.* only if you know that the woman prefers this form. If a woman holds a doctorate, professional office, or position with a title, use that title rather than *Ms.*

Ms. Jane Doe, Editor	Dear Ms. Doe:
Professor Jane Doe, Department of English	Dear Professor Doe:
Senator Jane Doe, Washington, D.C.	Dear Senator Doe:

EXERCISE 24–1 Avoiding Bias

Revise the following sentences to eliminate bias. Possible revisions for the lettered sentences appear at the end of the Handbook. Example:

    Firefighters need   *their*
~~A fireman needs~~ to check ~~his~~ equipment regularly.

a. Our school's athletic program will be of interest to black applicants.

b. The new physicians include Dr. Scalia, Anna Baniski, and Dr. Morton.

c. The diligent researcher will always find the sources he seeks.

1. Simon drinks like an Irishman.

2. Like most Asian Americans, Soon Li excels at music and mathematics.

3. Dick drives a Porsche because he likes the way she handles on the road, despite the little old ladies who slow down traffic.

25 | Wordiness

Concise language is clearer than wordy language. Simplify phrases by eliminating words that are redundant or unnecessary.

For strategies for
cutting extra words,
see Ch. 19.

SAMPLE WORDY PHRASES	CONCISE
a large number of	many
a period of a week	a week
arrive at an agreement, conclude an agreement	agree
at an earlier point in time	before, earlier
due to the fact that	because
lend assistance to	assist, aid, help
past experience, past history	experience, history
persons of the Methodist faith	Methodists
plan ahead for the future	plan
resemble in appearance	look like
sufficient number (or amount) of	enough
true facts	facts, truth
utilize, make use of	use

EXERCISE 25–1 Eliminating Wordiness

Revise the following passage to eliminate wordiness. Example:

> ~~At this point in time,~~ a debate ~~pertaining to~~ freedom of speech is raging
> across our campuses.

(annotations above the line: A ; *about* ; *currently*)

The media in recent times have become obsessed with the conflict on campuses across the nation between freedom of speech and the attempt to
protect minorities from verbal abuse. Very innocent remarks or remarks of
a humorous nature, sometimes taken out of context, have gotten a large
number of students into trouble for the violation of college speech codes.
Numerous students have become very vocal in attacking these "politically
correct" speech codes and defending the right to free speech. But is the campaign against the politically correct really pertaining to freedom of speech,
or is it itself a way in which to silence debate? Due to the fact that the
phrase "politically correct" has become associated with liberal social causes
and sensitivity to minority feelings, it now carries a very extraordinary
stigma in the eyes of conservatives. To accuse someone of being politically
correct is to refute their ideas before hearing their argument. The attempt to
silence the opposition is a dangerous sign of our times and suggests that we
are indeed in a cultural war.

Learning by Doing Refining Your Wording

After you have read or skimmed through this chapter, consider which types of words you most often wrestle with. Do you have trouble regulating your tone, your attitude, and your degree of formality? Do you lapse into specialized jargon, slang, or clichés? Do you fall into biased or stereotypical wording rather than sticking to fair, neutral language? Or is your writing wordy? Identify the problem you want to tackle, review the section about it, and plan a strategy — highlighting words to reconsider, applying your instructor's past suggestions in a current paper, or searching for passages to rephrase. After you have made improvements, exchange papers with a peer, and help each other spot any other word choice issues.

26 | Commonly Confused Words

The brief list that follows includes words and phrases that are commonly misspelled or confused. For a more comprehensive list, see the Glossary of Troublemakers on pages Q-50 through Q-59 in the Quick Editing Guide.

▶ COMMONLY CONFUSED HOMONYMS at a glance

accept (v., receive willingly); **except** (prep., other than)
　Mimi could *accept* all of Lefty's gifts *except* his ring.

affect (v., influence); **effect** (n., result)
　If the new rules *affect* us, what will be their *effect*?

capital (adj., uppercase; n., seat of government); **capitol** (n., government building)
　The *Capitol* building in our nation's *capital* is spelled with a *capital C*.

cite (v., refer to); **sight** (n., vision or tourist attraction); **site** (n., place)
　Did you *cite* Aunt Peg as your authority on which *sites* feature the most interesting *sights*?

complement (v., complete; n., counterpart); **compliment** (v. or n., praise)
　For Lee to say that Sheila's beauty *complements* her intelligence may or may not be a *compliment*.

desert (v., abandon; n., hot, dry region); **dessert** (n., end-of-meal sweet)
　Don't *desert* us by leaving for the *desert* before *dessert*.

elicit (v., bring out); **illicit** (adj., illegal)
　By going undercover, Sonny should *elicit* some offers of *illicit* drugs.

---

led (v., past tense of *lead*); **lead** (n., a metal)
> Gil's heart was heavy as *lead* when he *led* the mourners to the grave.

principal (n. or adj., chief); **principle** (n., rule or standard)
> The *principal* problem is convincing the media that the high school *principal* is a person of high *principles*.

stationary (adj., motionless); **stationery** (n., writing paper)
> Hubert's *stationery* shop stood *stationary* until a flood swept it away.

their (pron., belonging to them); **there** (adv., in that place); **they're** (contraction of *they are*)
> Sue said *they're* going over *there* to visit *their* aunt.

to (prep., toward); **too** (adv., also or excessively); **two** (n. or adj., numeral: one more than one)
> Let's not take *two* cars *to* town—that's *too* many unless Hal comes *too*.

who's (contraction of *who is*); **whose** (pron., belonging to whom)
> *Who's* going to tell me *whose* dog this is?

your (pron., belonging to you); **you're** (contraction of *you are*)
> *You're* not getting *your* own way this time!

EXERCISE 26–1 Commonly Confused Words

Edit the following passage to correct any misused words. You may need to refer to the list on pages Q-50 through Q-59 or to a dictionary. Example:

> *There*
> ~~Their~~ are many different ways to use a degree in psychology.

The principal job is of course psychologist, but a master's degree is required too practice therapy. For graduates just starting out with a psychology degree, a good idea would be to except a job in human resources, working on cite for a major corporation. This work is somewhat unique because it exposes employees to a wide variety of careers in a short period of time. In regards to other fields for psychology majors, job seekers might consider either real estate, law enforcement, or market research. The starting salary range for jobs in these areas is anywheres from $35,000 to $50,000 per year. Alot of psychology majors pursue graduate degrees in law, social work, criminal justice, and education. In most cases, an employee with a master's degree will earn more money then one with only a bachelor's degree. Psychology majors should try and consider all their options early so they can focus there education on the career path that suits them best.

37 Punctuation

Learning by Doing 🎯 Tackling Punctuation Patterns

Check comments in past drafts or final papers for punctuation errors that suggest a pattern. Have readers questioned your use of commas? Do you guess about where to put colons? Look up the Handbook guidelines for that punctuation problem and write out useful rules in your own words. Share your rules and any remaining questions with a small group of classmates.

27 | End Punctuation

Three marks can signal the end of a sentence: the period, the exclamation point, and the question mark.

27a Use a period to end a declarative sentence, a directive, or an indirect question.

Most sentences are **declarative,** meaning that they make a statement.

Many people on earth are malnourished.

A period, not a question mark, ends an **indirect question,** which states that a question was asked or is being asked.

For examples of direct questions, see 27c.

> The counselor asked Marcia why she rarely gets to class on time~~?~~.
>
> I wonder why Roland didn't show up~~?~~.

27b Use a period after some abbreviations.

A period within a sentence shows that what precedes it has been shortened.

> Dr. Lene V. Hau's speech will be broadcast at 8:00 p.m.

The names of many organizations (YMCA, PTA), countries (USA, UK), and people (JFK, FDR) are abbreviated using all capitals without periods. Other abbreviations, such as those for designations of time, use periods. When an abbreviation ends a sentence, follow it with one period, not two.

For more on abbreviations, see 36.

27c Use a question mark to end a direct question.

> How many angels can dance on the head of a pin?

The question mark comes at the end of the question even if the question is part of a longer declarative sentence.

> "What'll I do now?" Marjorie wailed.

For advice on punctuating indirect quotations and questions, see 33. For examples of indirect questions, see 27a.

27d Use an exclamation point to end an interjection or an urgent command.

Rarely used in college writing, an exclamation point signals strong emotion.

> We've struck an iceberg! We're sinking! I can't believe it!

It may mark an interjection or emphasize an urgent directive.

> Oh, no! Fire! Hurry up! Help me!

An **interjection** is a word or expression that inserts an outburst of feeling (see 1h).

EXERCISE 27–1 Using End Punctuation

If needed, correct end punctuation in the following sentences. Give reasons for any changes you make. Some sentences may be correct. Answers for the lettered sentences appear at the end of the Handbook. Example:

> Tom asked Cindy if she would be willing to coach him in tennis~~?~~. [Not a direct question]

a. The question that still troubles the community after all these years is why federal agents did not act sooner?

b. I wonder what he was thinking at the time?

c. If the suspect is convicted, will lawyers appeal the case?

1. What will Brad and Emilia do if they can't take vacations at the same time.

2. When a tree falls in a forest, but no one hears it, does it make a sound.

3. What will happen next is anyone's guess.

28 | Commas

Like a split-second pause in conversation, a well-placed comma helps your readers to catch your train of thought. It keeps them from stumbling over a solid block of words or drawing an inaccurate conclusion.

> Lyman paints‸fences‸and bowls.

Without the commas, the sentence reads as if Lyman is a painter who works with both a large and a small brush. The commas clarify that Lyman wields a paintbrush, a sword, and a bowling ball.

28a Use a comma with a coordinating conjunction to join two main clauses.

A **main clause** is a group of words that has both a subject and a verb and can stand alone as a complete sentence (see 4a).

When you join main clauses with a coordinating conjunction (*and, but, for, or, nor, so, yet*), add a comma after the first clause, right before the conjunction.

                                                                COORD CONJ

|←——— MAIN CLAUSE ———→| |←——— MAIN CLAUSE ———→|
The pie whooshed through the air, but the agile Hal ducked.

If your clauses are short and parallel in form, you may omit the comma. Or you may keep the comma to throw emphasis on your second clause.

A **phrase** consists of two or more related words that work together but may lack a subject, a verb, or both (see 4b).

Spring passed and summer came.   Spring passed, and summer came.

They urged but I refused.   They urged, but I refused.

CAUTION: Don't use a comma with a coordinating conjunction that links two verbs or phrases.

> The mustangs galloped⁄ and cavorted across the plain.

> The lights flickered momentarily⁄ and then went out completely.

28b Use a comma after an introductory clause, phrase, or word.

A **clause** is a group of related words that includes both a subject and a verb (see 4a).

Weeping, Lydia stumbled down the stairs.

Before that, Arthur saw her reading an old love letter.

If he knew who the writer was, he didn't tell.

Placed after any such opening word, phrase, or subordinate clause, a comma tells your reader, "Enough preliminaries: now the main clause starts."

EXCEPTION: You do not need a comma after a single introductory word or a short phrase or clause if there is no danger of misreading.

Sooner or later Lydia will tell us the whole story.

EXERCISE 28-1 Using Commas

Add any necessary commas to the following sentences, and remove any commas that do not belong. Some sentences may be correct. Answers for the lettered sentences appear at the end of the Handbook. Example:

> During the guided tour of the Mayan ruins, James had no access to phone service or email.

a. He was so upset about his lack of connection to the outside world that he might as well have not even come on the trip.

b. When we returned to the hotel he couldn't wait to check for any messages.

c. James logged on to the hotel wifi immediately but he was surprised to find that he hadn't gotten any emails all morning.

d. His office hadn't called him nor had his friends left him any messages.

e. He pretended to be relieved that nothing urgent had come up at work but I think he was secretly annoyed that everyone was doing fine without him.

1. Some people say that we are overly wired in this age of modern gadgets but others just can't get enough technology.

2. How often do we stop to look around and talk with other people on the train or in a coffee shop?

3. One family instituted a "tech-free Tuesday" in their home so nobody had access to wifi, telephones, or television.

4. They played games together after dinner, and read books before going to sleep.

5. The teenage kids hated it at first but they ended up enjoying their night off from digital connections.

28c Use a comma between items in a series.

When you list three or more items, whether they are nouns, verbs, adjectives, adverbs, or entire phrases or clauses, separate them with commas.

> Country ham, sweet corn, and potatoes weighted Grandma's table.

> Joel prefers music that shakes, rattles, and rolls.

Notice that no comma *follows* the coordinating conjunction.

> We climbed the Matterhorn, voyaged beneath the sea, and/ flew on a rocket through space.

NOTE: Some writers omit the comma *before* the final item in the series. This custom may throw off the rhythm of a sentence and, in some cases, obscure the writer's meaning. Using the comma in such a case is never wrong and is preferred in academic style; omitting it can create confusion.

> I was met at the station by my cousins, brother and sister.

Are these people a brother-and-sister pair who are the writer's cousins? Or are they a group consisting of the writer's cousins, her brother, and her sister? If they are more than two people, a comma would clear up the confusion.

> I was met at the station by my cousins, brother, and sister.

28d Use a comma between coordinate adjectives but not between cumulative adjectives.

Adjectives that function independently of each other, though they modify the same noun, are called **coordinate adjectives.** Set them off with commas.

> Ruth was a clear, vibrant, persuasive speaker.
>
> Life is nasty, brutish, and short.

CAUTION: Don't use a comma after the final adjective before a noun.

> My professor was a brilliant, caring/ teacher.

To check whether adjectives are coordinate, ask two questions. Can you rearrange the adjectives without distorting the meaning? (*Ruth was a persuasive, vibrant, clear speaker.*) Can you insert *and* between them? (*Life is nasty and brutish and short.*) If the answer to both is yes, the adjectives are coordinate. Removing any one of them would not greatly affect the others. Use commas between them to show that they are separate and equal.

NOTE: If you link coordinate adjectives with *and* or another coordinating conjunction, omit the commas except in a series (see 28c).

> New York City is huge/ and dirty/ and beautiful.

Cumulative adjectives work together to create a single unified picture of the noun they modify. No commas separate them.

> Ruth has two small white poodles.
>
> Who's afraid of the big bad wolf?

Coordinating conjunctions join elements of equal or near-equal importance (see 1g and 19a–19c).

For more on cumulative adjectives, see p. 614.

If you remove, rearrange, or insert *and* between cumulative adjectives, the effect is distorted (*two white small poodles; the big and bad wolf*).

EXERCISE 28-2 Using Commas

In these sentences, add any necessary commas, remove any unneeded ones, and change any incorrect punctuation. Some sentences may be correct. Answers for the lettered sentences appear at the end of the Handbook. Example:

> Mel has been a faithful‸hardworking‸consistent band manager.

a. Mrs. Carver looks like a sweet, little, old lady, but she plays a wicked electric guitar.

b. Her bass player, her drummer and her keyboard player all live in the same retirement community.

c. They practice individually in the afternoon, rehearse together at night and play at the community's Saturday night dances.

d. The Rest Home Rebels have to rehearse quietly, and cautiously, to keep from disturbing the other residents.

e. Mrs. Carver has organized the group, scheduled their rehearsals, and acquired backup instruments.

1. When she breaks a string, she doesn't want her elderly crew to have to grab the guitar change the string and hand it back to her, before the song ends.

2. The Rest Home Rebels' favorite bands are U2, Arcade Fire and Lester Lanin and his orchestra.

3. They watch a lot of MTV because it is fast-paced colorful exciting and informative and it has more variety than soap operas.

4. Just once, Mrs. Carver wants to play in a really, huge, sold-out, arena.

5. She hopes to borrow the community's big, white, van to take herself her band and their equipment to a major, professional, recording studio.

28e Use commas to set off a nonrestrictive phrase or clause.

A **nonrestrictive modifier** adds a fact that, while perhaps interesting and valuable, isn't essential. The sentence would make sense without it. Set off the modifier with commas before and after.

> Potts Alley, *which runs north from Chestnut Street*, is too narrow for cars.
>
> At the end of the alley, *where the fair was held last May*, a getaway car waited.

A **restrictive modifier** is essential. Omit it and you significantly change the meaning of the modified word and the sentence. Such a modifier is called *restrictive* because it limits what it modifies: it specifies this place, person, or

A **modifier** is a word, phrase, or clause that provides more information about other parts of a sentence (see 15).

action and no other. Because a restrictive modifier is part of the identity of whatever it modifies, no commas set it off from the rest of the sentence.

> They picked the alley *that runs north from Chestnut Street* because it is close to the highway.

> Anyone *who robs my house* will be disappointed.

Leaving out the modifier in that last sentence changes the meaning from potential robbers to humankind.

NOTE: Use *that* to introduce (or to recognize) a restrictive phrase or clause. Use *which* to introduce (or to recognize) a nonrestrictive phrase or clause.

> The food *that I love best* is chocolate.

> Chocolate, *which I love*, is not on my diet.

28f Use commas to set off nonrestrictive appositives.

An **appositive** is a word or group of words that adds information by identifying a subject or an object in a different way (see 4b).

Like the modifiers discussed in 28e, an **appositive** can be either restrictive or nonrestrictive. If it is nonrestrictive—if the sentence still makes sense when it is omitted or changed—then set it off with commas before and after.

> My third ex-husband, *Hugo*, will be glad to meet you.

> We are bringing dessert, *a blueberry pie*, to follow dinner.

If the appositive is restrictive—if you can't take it out or change it without changing your meaning—then include it without commas.

> Of all the men I've been married to, my ex-husband *Hugo* is the best cook.

EXERCISE 28–3 Using Commas

Add any necessary commas to the following sentences, and remove any commas that do not belong. Draw your own conclusions about what the writer meant to say, as needed. Some sentences may be correct. Possible revisions for the lettered sentences appear at the end of the Handbook. Example:

> Jay and his wife ˄ the former Laura McCready ˄ were college sweethearts.

a. We are bringing a dish vegetable lasagna, to the potluck supper.

b. I like to go to Central Bank, on this side of town, because this branch tends to have short lines.

c. The colony, that the English established at Roanoke disappeared mysteriously.

d. If the base commanders had checked their gun room where powder is stored, they would have found that several hundred pounds of gunpowder were missing.

e. Brazil's tropical rain forests which help produce the air we breathe all over the world, are being cut down at an alarming rate.

1. The aye-aye which is a member of the lemur family is threatened with extinction.
2. The party, a dismal occasion ended earlier than we had expected.
3. The general warned that the concessions, that the military was prepared to make, would be withdrawn if not matched by the rebels.
4. Although both of Don's children are blond, his daughter Sharon has darker hair than his son Jake.
5. Herbal tea which has no caffeine makes a better after-dinner drink than coffee.

28g Use commas to set off conjunctive adverbs.

When you drop a conjunctive adverb into the middle of a clause, set it off with commas before and after.

For a list of common conjunctive adverbs, see p. 633.

> Using lead paint in homes has been illegal, *however*, since 1973.

> Builders, *indeed*, gave it up some twenty years earlier.

28h Use commas to set off parenthetical expressions.

Use a pair of commas around any parenthetical expression or any aside from you to your readers.

> Home inspectors, *for this reason*, sometimes test for lead paint.

> Cosmic Construction never used lead paint, *or so their spokesperson says*, even when it was legal.

28i Use commas to set off a phrase or clause expressing contrast.

> It was Rudolph, *not Dasher*, who had a red nose.

EXCEPTION: Short contrasting phrases beginning with *but* need no commas.

> It was not Dasher/ but Rudolph/ who had a red nose.

28j Use commas to set off an absolute phrase.

The link between an absolute phrase and the rest of the sentence is a comma, or two commas if the phrase falls in midsentence.

An **absolute phrase** is an expression, usually a noun followed by a participle, that modifies an entire clause or sentence and can appear anywhere in the sentence (see 4b).

> *Our worst fears drawing us together*, we huddled over the letter.

> Luke, *his knife being the sharpest*, slit the envelope.

EXERCISE 28–4 Using Commas

Add any necessary commas to the following sentences, and change any punctuation that is incorrect. Answers for the lettered sentences appear at the end of the Handbook. Example:

> The officer, a radar gun in his hand, gauged the speed of the passing cars.

a. The university insisted however that the students were not accepted merely because of their parents' generous contributions.

b. This dispute in any case is an old one.

c. It was the young man's striking good looks not his acting ability that first attracted the Hollywood agents.

d. Gretchen learned moreover not always to accept as true what she had read in celebrity magazines.

e. The hikers most of them wearing ponchos or rain jackets headed out into the steady drizzle.

1. The lawsuit demanded furthermore that construction already under way be halted immediately.

2. It is the Supreme Court not Congress or the president that ultimately determines the legality of a law.

3. The judge complained that the case was being tried not by the court but by the media.

4. The actor kneeling recited the lines with great emotion.

5. Both sides' patience running thin workers and management carried the strike into its sixth week.

28k Use commas to set off a direct quotation from your own words.

For advice on using punctuation marks with quotations, see 33g–33i; for advice on using quotation marks, see 33a–33d.

When you briefly quote someone, distinguish the source's words from yours with commas (and, of course, quotation marks). When you insert an explanation into a quotation (such as *he said*), set that off with commas. The comma always comes *before* the quotation marks.

> Shakespeare wrote, "Some are born great, some achieve greatness, and some have greatness thrust upon them."

> "The best thing that can come with success," commented the actress Liv Ullmann, "is the knowledge that it is nothing to long for."

EXCEPTION: Do not use a comma with a very short quotation or one introduced by *that*.

Don't tell me "yes" if you mean "maybe."

Jules said that "Nothing ventured, nothing gained" is his motto.

Don't use a comma with any quotation run in to your own sentence and read as part of it. Often such quotations are introduced by linking verbs.

Her favorite statement at age three was "I can do it myself."

Shakespeare originated the expression "my salad days, when I was green in judgment."

A **linking verb** is a verb that shows a state of being by linking the sentence subject with a word that renames or describes the subject (see 1c and 3b).

28l Use commas around *yes* and *no*, mild interjections, tag questions, and the name or title of someone directly addressed.

YES AND NO	*Yes*, I'd like a Rolls-Royce, but, *no*, I didn't order one.
INTERJECTION	*Well*, don't blame it on me.
TAG QUESTION	It would be fun to ride in a Silver Cloud, *wouldn't it*?
DIRECT ADDRESS	Drive us home, *James*.

An **interjection** is a word or expression that inserts an outburst of feeling (see 1h).

28m Use commas to set off dates, states, countries, and addresses.

On June 6, 1995, Ned Shaw was born.

East Rutherford, New Jersey, seemed like Paris, France, to him.

His family moved to 11 Maple Street, Middletown, Ohio.

Do not add a comma between state and zip code: *Bedford, MA 01730.*

EXERCISE 28–5 Using Commas

Add any necessary commas to the following sentences, remove any commas that do not belong, and change any punctuation that is incorrect. Some sentences may be correct. Answers for the lettered sentences appear at the end of the Handbook. Example:

> When Alexander Graham Bell said ⌃ "Mr. Watson ⌃ come here, I want you ⌃" the telephone entered history.

a. César Chávez was born on March 31 1927, on a farm in Yuma, Arizona.

b. Chávez, who spent years as a migrant farmworker, told other farm laborers "If you're outraged at conditions, then you can't possibly be free or happy until you devote all your time to changing them."

c. Chávez founded the United Farm Workers union and did indeed, devote all his time to changing conditions for farmworkers.

d. Robert F. Kennedy called Chávez, "one of the heroic figures of our time."

e. Chávez, who died on April 23, 1993, became the second Mexican American to receive the highest civilian honor in the United States, the Presidential Medal of Freedom.

1. Yes I was born on April 14 1988 in Bombay India.

2. Move downstage Gary, for Pete's sake or you'll run into Mrs. Clackett.

3. Vicki my precious, when you say, "great" or "terrific," look as though you mean it.

4. Perhaps you have forgotten darling that sometimes you make mistakes, too.

5. Well Dotty, it only makes sense that when you say, "Sardines!," you should go off to get the sardines.

29 | Misuses of the Comma

Just as important as including the comma where it belongs is omitting the comma in places where it does *not* belong. Be aware of the following common misuses of the comma.

29a Do not use a comma to separate a subject from its verb or a verb from its object.

The athlete driving the purple Jaguar/ was Jim Fuld. [The comma separated subject from verb.]

The governor should not have given his campaign manager/ such a prestigious appointment. [The comma separated verb from direct object.]

For lists of coordinating words, see p. 633.

29b Do not use a comma with compound subjects or verbs joined by correlative or coordinating conjunctions.

Do not divide a compound subject or verb unnecessarily with a comma.

Neither Peter Pan/ nor the fairy Tinkerbell/ saw the pirates sneaking toward their hideout. [Compound subject]

The chickens clucked/ and pecked/ and flapped their wings. [Compound verb]

29c Do not use a comma before the first or after the last item in a series.

We had to see/ my mother's doctor, my father's lawyer, and my dog's veterinarian/ in one afternoon.

29d Do not use a comma to set off a restrictive word, phrase, or clause.

A restrictive modifier is essential to the definition or identification of whatever it modifies; a nonrestrictive modifier is not.

> The fireworks/that I saw on Sunday/ were the best I've ever seen.

For an explanation of restrictive modifiers, see 28e.

29e Do not use commas to set off indirect quotations.

When *that* introduces a quotation, the quotation is indirect and requires neither a comma nor quotation marks.

> He told us that/ we shouldn't have done it.

For more on quoting someone's exact words, see 33a–33c.

EXERCISE 29–1 Misuses of the Comma

Correct any misuses of the comma in the following sentences. Some sentences may be correct. Answers for the lettered sentences appear at the end of the Handbook. Example:

> Farms that use organic fertilizer/ can be just as large and industrialized as nonorganic farms.

a. The proposed bill would give veterans in rural areas, improved access to medical care, health benefits, and job training.

b. Neither the House of Representatives, nor the Senate, seems likely to vote for increasing the federal minimum wage.

c. The report basically states that, increased testing is not improving student outcomes, even though that was the original intention.

d. During migration, hummingbirds, which weigh less than an ounce, travel distances, that average 500 miles per day.

e. After the party, we found, an earring, two sweaters, a hat, a scarf, and a shoe.

1. Upon hearing the doorbell ring, the dog jumped, and barked, and howled, and spun in circles.

2. Eyewitnesses from the period confirm that, there was, incredibly, a molasses flood in Boston in 1919.

3. The all-inclusive package provides guests with, unlimited food, beverages, and watersports rentals; spa treatments and tennis lessons, however, cost extra.

4. Several players from the team, have volunteered to visit young cancer patients at the local hospital.

5. The painting, that was stolen from the museum twenty years ago, was found, in perfect condition, in an abandoned warehouse.

30 | Semicolons

A semicolon is a sort of compromise between a comma and a period: it creates a stop without ending a sentence.

30a Use a semicolon to join two main clauses not joined by a coordinating conjunction.

Coordinating conjunctions join elements with equal or near-equal importance (see 1g and 19a–19c).

Suppose, having written one statement, you want to add another that is closely related in sense. You decide to keep them both in a single sentence.

> Shooting baskets was my brother's favorite sport; he would dunk them for hours at a time.

A semicolon is a good substitute for a period when you don't want to bring your readers to a complete stop.

> By the yard life is hard; by the inch it's a cinch.

NOTE: When you join a subordinate clause to a main one or join two statements with a coordinating conjunction, use a comma. Reserve the semicolon to emphasize a close connection or to avoid confusion when long, complex clauses include internal punctuation.

30b Use a semicolon to join two main clauses that are linked by a conjunctive adverb.

For a list of common conjunctive adverbs, see p. 633.

You can use a conjunctive adverb to show a relationship between clauses such as addition (*besides*), comparison (*likewise, similarly*), contrast (*instead, however*), emphasis (*namely, certainly*), cause and effect (*thus*), or time (*finally*). When a second statement begins with (or includes) a conjunctive adverb, you can join it to the first with a semicolon. No matter where the conjunctive adverb appears, the semicolon is placed between the two clauses.

> Bert is a stand-out player; *indeed*, he's the one hope of our team.
>
> We yearned to attend the concert; tickets, *however*, were hard to come by.

30c Use a semicolon to separate items in a series that contain internal punctuation or that are long and complex.

The semicolon is especially useful for setting off one group of items from another. More powerful than a comma, it divides a series of series.

> The auctioneer sold clocks, watches, and cameras; freezers of steaks and tons of bean sprouts; motorcycles, cars, speedboats, canoes, and cabin cruisers; and rare coins, curious stamps, and precious stones.

EXERCISE 30–1   Using Semicolons

Add any necessary semicolons to the following sentences, and change any that are incorrectly used. Some sentences may be correct. Answers for the lettered sentences appear at the end of the Handbook. Example:

> The wind picked up and the thunder was getting louder; it was no longer safe to be outside.

a. The research paper was due in six weeks, therefore, Ali got started right away by making a schedule.

b. The committee estimated the extent of violent crime among teenagers, especially those between the ages of fourteen and sixteen, acted as a liaison between the city and schools and between churches and volunteer organizations, and drew up a plan to reduce violence, both public and domestic, in the next decade.

c. The skilled pilot landed the plane in an open field, all passengers made it out safely.

d. The mall no longer seems to attract customers, however; downtown businesses are picking up again.

1. Even though the ivory trade is now banned in most countries, elephant populations continue to be endangered.

2. The day after Thanksgiving is usually the busiest shopping day of the year, nonetheless, my sister is insisting that we check out all the deals.

3. It was a shocking site; all that remained of our house was a pile of rubble and splintered wood.

4. The glass on Leah's phone was so cracked it looked like a spider's web; but she could still make calls and use her apps.

31 | Colons

A colon introduces a further thought, one added to throw light on a first. Some writers use a capital letter to start any complete sentence that follows a colon; others prefer a lowercase letter. Whichever you choose, be consistent. A phrase that follows a colon always begins with a lowercase letter.

31a   Use a colon between two main clauses if the second exemplifies, explains, or summarizes the first.

Like a semicolon, a colon can join two sentences into one. The chief difference is this: a semicolon says merely that two main clauses are related; a colon, like

> A **main clause** is a group of words that has both a subject and a verb and can stand alone as a complete sentence (see 4a).

an abbreviation for *that is* or *for example*, says that the second clause gives an example or explanation of the point in the first clause.

> She tried everything: she scoured the Internet, made dozens of phone calls, wrote emails, even consulted a lawyer.

31b Use a colon to introduce a list or a series.

A colon can introduce a word, a phrase, a series, or a second main clause, sometimes strengthened by *as follows* or *the following*.

> The dance steps are as follows: forward, back, turn, and glide.

When a colon introduces a series of words or phrases, it often means *such as* or *for instance*. A list of examples after a colon need not include *and* before the last item unless all possible examples have been stated.

> On a Saturday night many kinds of people crowd our downtown area: drifters, bored senior citizens, college students out for a good time.

31c Use a colon to introduce an appositive.

An **appositive** is a word or group of words that adds information by identifying a subject or an object in a different way (see 4b).

A colon preceded by a main clause can introduce an **appositive**.

> I have discovered the key to the future: robots.

31d Use a colon to introduce a long or comma-filled quotation.

Sometimes you can't conveniently introduce a quoted passage with a comma. Perhaps the quotation is too long or heavily punctuated, or your introduction demands a longer pause. In either case, use a colon.

> God told Adam and Eve: "Be fruitful, and multiply, and replenish the earth, and subdue it."

31e Use a colon when convention calls for it.

AFTER A SALUTATION	Dear Professor James:
BIBLICAL CITATIONS	Job 9:2 [book, chapter, verse], but Job 9.2 [MLA]
TITLES: SUBTITLES	*Connections: Empowering College and Career Success*
TIME OF DAY	2:02 p.m.

A **main clause** is a group of words that has both a subject and a verb and can stand alone as a complete sentence (see 4a).

31f Use a colon only at the end of a main clause.

In a sentence, a colon always follows a complete sentence, never a phrase. Avoid using a colon between a verb and its object, between a preposition and its object, and before a list introduced by *such as*.

My mother and father are/ Bella and Benjamin.

Many great inventors have changed our lives, such as/ Edison, Marconi, and Glutz.

Many great inventors have changed our lives ; ̶s̶u̶c̶h̶ ̶a̶s̶: Edison, Marconi, and Glutz.

EXERCISE 31–1 Using Colons

Add, remove, or replace colons wherever appropriate in the following sentences. Where necessary, revise the sentences further to support your changes in punctuation. Some sentences may be correct. Possible revisions for the lettered sentences appear at the end of the Handbook. Example:

Yum-Yum Burger has franchises in the following cities; New York, Chicago, Miami, San Francisco, and Seattle.

a. The Continuing Education Program offers courses in: building and construction management, engineering, and design.

b. The interview ended with a test of skills, taking messages, operating the computer, typing a sample letter, and proofreading documents.

c. The sample letter began, "Dear Mr. Rasheed, Please accept our apologies for the late shipment."

1. In the case of *Bowers v. Hardwick,* the Supreme Court decided that: citizens had no right to sexual privacy.

2. He ended his speech with a quotation from Homer's *Iliad,* "Whoever obeys the gods, to him they particularly listen."

3. Professor Bligh's book is called *Management, A Networking Approach.*

---

32 | Apostrophes

Use apostrophes for three purposes: to show possession, to indicate an omission, and to add an ending to a number, a letter, or an abbreviation.

32a To make a singular noun possessive, add -'s.

The *plumber's* wrench left grease stains on *Harry's* shirt.

Add -'s even when your singular noun ends with the sound of *s.*

Felix's roommate enjoys reading *Henry James's* novels.

> **POSSESSIVE NOUNS AND PLURAL NOUNS** at a glance
>
> Both plural nouns and possessive nouns often end with -*s.*
> - Plural means more than one (two *dogs*, six *friends*), but possessive means ownership (the *dogs'* biscuits, my *friends'* cars).
> - If you can substitute *of* for the -*s'* (the biscuits *of* the dogs, the cars *of* my friends), use the plural possessive with an apostrophe after the -*s.*
> - If you can't substitute *of*, you need the simple plural with no apostrophe (the *dogs* are well fed, my *friends* have no money for gas).

Some writers find it awkward to add -'*s* to nouns that already end in an -*s,* especially those of two syllables or more. You may, if you wish, form such a possessive by adding only an apostrophe.

> The Egyptian king *Cheops'* death occurred centuries before *Socrates'.*

32b To make a plural noun ending in -*s* possessive, add an apostrophe.

> Renata wrapped up the *managers'* meeting before attending her *friends'* dinner party.

32c To make a plural noun not ending in -*s* possessive, add -'*s.*

Nouns such as *men, mice, geese,* and *alumni* form the possessive case the same way as singular nouns: with -'*s.*

> What effect has the *women's* movement had on *children's* literature?

32d To show joint possession by two people or groups, add an apostrophe or -'*s* to the second noun of the pair.

> I left my *mother and father's* home with *friends and neighbors'* good wishes.

If the two members of a noun pair possess a set of things individually, add an apostrophe or -'*s* to each noun.

> *Men's* and *women's* marathon records are improving steadily.

32e To make a compound noun possessive, add an apostrophe or -'*s* to the last word in the compound.

A compound noun consists of more than one word (*commander in chief, sons-in-law*); it may be either singular or plural.

> The *commander in chief's* duties will end on July 1.

> Esther does not approve of her *sons-in-law's* professions.

32f To make an indefinite pronoun possessive, add -'s.

Indefinite pronouns such as *anyone*, *nobody*, and *another* are usually singular; they form the possessive case with -'s. (See 32a.)

> What caused the accident is *anybody's* guess, but it was *no one's* fault.

Indefinite pronouns do not refer to a specific noun (see 1b).

32g To indicate the possessive of a personal pronoun, use its possessive case.

The personal pronouns are irregular; each has its own possessive form, none with an apostrophe. Resist adding an apostrophe or -'s.

NOTE: *Its* (no apostrophe) is always a possessive pronoun.

> I retreated when the Murphys' German shepherd bared *its* fangs.

It's (with an apostrophe) is always a contraction of *it is*.

> *It's* [It is] not our fault.

Personal pronouns stand for a noun that names a person or thing (see 1b).

32h Use an apostrophe to indicate an omission in a contraction.

> *They're* [They are] too sophisticated for me.
>
> Pat *didn't* [did not] finish her assignment.
>
> Americans grow up admiring the Spirit of *'76* [1776].
>
> *It's* [It is] nearly eight *o'clock* [of the clock].

32i Use an apostrophe to form the plural of a letter or word mentioned as a word.

LETTER	How many *n*'s are there in *Cincinnati*?
WORD	Try replacing all the *should*'s in that list with *could*'s.

No apostrophes are needed for plural numbers and most abbreviations.

DECADE	The *2000s* differed greatly from the 1990s.
NUMBER	Cut out two *3s* to sew on Larry's shirt.
ABBREVIATION	Do we need *IDs* at YMCAs in other towns?

EXERCISE 32–1 Using Apostrophes

Correct any errors in the use of the apostrophe in the following sentences. Some sentences may be correct. Answers for the lettered sentences appear at the end of the Handbook. Example:

> ~~Youd~~ *You'd* better put on ~~you're~~ *your* new shoes.

a. Joe and Chucks' fathers were both in the class of 90.

b. They're going to finish their term papers as soon as the party ends.

c. It was a strange coincidence that all three womens' cars broke down after they had picked up their mother's-in-law.

d. Don't forget to dot you're *is* and cross you're *ts*.

e. Mario and Shelley's son is marrying the editor's in chief's daughter.

1. The Hendersons' never change: their always whining about Mr. Scobee farming land thats rightfully their's.

2. Its hard to join a womens' basketball team because so few of them exist.

3. I had'nt expected to hear Janice' voice again.

4. Don't give the Murphy's dog it's biscuit until it's sitting up.

5. Isnt' it the mother and fathers' job to tell kid's to mind their *ps* and *qs*?

33 | Quotation Marks

For more on quoting, paraphrasing, and summarizing, see Ch. 29 in *A Writer's Research Manual*.

For capitalization with quotation marks, see 37j.

Quotation marks always come in pairs: one at the start and one at the finish of a quoted passage. In the United States, the double quotation mark (") is preferred over the single one (') for most uses. Use quotation marks to set off quoted or highlighted words from the rest of your text.

> "Injustice anywhere is a threat to justice everywhere," wrote Martin Luther King Jr.

33a Use quotation marks around direct quotations from another writer or speaker.

Enclose someone's exact words in quotation marks.

> Malala Yousafzai reflected the importance of women's education when she said, "We cannot succeed when half of us are held back."

Use an indirect quotation to credit and report someone else's idea accurately. Do not use his or her exact words or quotation marks.

> Malala Yousafzai asserted the importance of women's education.

33b Use single quotation marks around a quotation inside another quotation.

Sometimes you may quote a source that quotes someone else or puts words in quotation marks. When that happens, use single quotation marks around the internal quotation (even if your source used double ones); put double quotation marks around the larger passage you are quoting.

> "My favorite advice from Socrates, 'Know thyself and fear all women,'" said Dr. Blatz, "has been getting me into trouble lately."

Guidelines for Multilingual Writers
What Is the Difference between Direct and Indirect
Quotations?

When you quote directly, use the exact words of the original writer or
speaker; set them off with double quotation marks. When you change
a direct quotation into an indirect quotation (someone else's idea
reported without using his or her exact words), be sure to reword the
quotation. Do not repeat the original wording from a source.

■ Be sure to change the punctuation and capitalization. You also may
need to change the verb tense.

DIRECT QUOTATION   Pascal said, "The assignment is on Chinua
                     Achebe, the Nigerian writer."

INDIRECT QUOTATION   Pascal said that the assignment was on Chinua
                     Achebe, the Nigerian writer.

■ If the direct quotation is a question, you must change the word order
in the indirect quotation.

DIRECT QUOTATION   Jean asked, "How far is it to Boston?"

INDIRECT QUOTATION   Jean asked how far it was to Boston.

NOTE: Use a period, not a question mark, with questions in indirect
quotations.

■ You often must change pronouns for an indirect quotation.

DIRECT QUOTATION   Antonio said, "I think you are mistaken."

INDIRECT QUOTATION   Antonio said that he thought I was mistaken.

33c Instead of using quotation marks, indent longer quotations.

Suppose you are writing an essay about the meaning of a college education.
You might include a lengthy quotation, like this:

> In her 2014 commencement address at Brooklyn College, writer
> Edwidge Danticat spoke about the importance of bravery:
>> The great Maya Angelou has said that courage is the most important
>> of all virtues. . . . I wish for you the courage to continue to walk
>> boldly and freely in this world. I wish for you the courage to rule out
>> no dream as too big and no hope as too small. I wish for you the
>> courage to live fiercely though not recklessly both for yourself and
>> others. Be brave and creative as you put all the theories and

knowledge that you have learned to work. Be brave in spirit; be brave in mind. Because only those with imagination and courage are able to reach beyond the ordinary and take us to the next frontier.

For more on the MLA and APA styles, see Chs. 31–32.

Indenting the passage shows it is a direct quotation without adding quotation marks. In MLA style, indent quotations of five lines or more by one-half inch. In APA style, indent quotations of forty words or more by one-half inch. Follow the same practice if you quote four or more lines of a poem. In both, double-space the quoted lines, and cite the source.

For advice on capitalization and quotations, see 37j.

33d In dialogue, use quotation marks around a speaker's words, and mark each change of speaker with a new paragraph.

Randolph gazed at Ellen and sighed. "What extraordinary beauty."

"They are lovely," she replied, staring at the roses, "aren't they?"

33e Use quotation marks around the titles of a speech, an article in a newspaper or magazine, a short story, a poem shorter than book length, a chapter in a book, a song, and an episode of a television or radio program.

For advice on italicizing titles, see 39a and the chart on p. 688.

The article "Alice Munro's Magic" begins with a description of "Home," from Munro's collection *Family Furnishings*.

In Chapter 5, "Expatriates," Schwartz discusses Eliot's famous poem "The Love Song of J. Alfred Prufrock."

33f Avoid using quotation marks to show slang, wit, or irony.

By the time I finished my ⸙chores,⸙ my ⸙day off⸙ was over.

No quotation marks are needed after *so-called* or similar words.

The meet included many so-called ⸙champions.⸙

33g Put commas and periods inside quotation marks.

For more on commas with quotations, see 28k.

A comma or a period is always placed before quotation marks, even if it is not part of the quotation.

We pleaded, "Keep off the grass," in hope of preserving the lawn.

The sign warned pedestrians: "Keep off the grass."

33h Put semicolons and colons outside quotation marks.

We said, "Keep off the grass"; they still tromped onward.

33i **Put other punctuation inside or outside quotation marks depending on its function in the sentence.**

Parentheses that are part of the quotation go inside the quotation marks. Parentheses that are your own, not part of the quotation, go outside.

> We said, "Keep off the grass (unless it's artificial turf)."

> They tromped onward (although we had said, "Keep off the grass").

If a question mark, exclamation point, or dash is part of the quotation, place it inside the quotation marks. Otherwise, place it after them.

> Who hollered "Fire"? She hollered, "Fire!"

Don't close a sentence with two end punctuation marks, one inside and one outside the quotation marks. If the quoted passage ends with a dash, an exclamation point, a question mark, or a period, you need not add any further end punctuation. If the quoted passage falls within a question asked by you, however, the sentence should finish with a question mark, even if that means dropping other end punctuation (*Who hollered "Fire"?*).

EXERCISE 33–1 Using Quotation Marks

Add quotation marks wherever they are needed in the following sentences, and correct any other errors. Answers for the lettered sentences appear at the end of the Handbook. Example:

> Annie asked him, "Do you believe in free will?"

a. What we still need to figure out, the police chief said, is whether the victim was acquainted with his assailant.

b. A skillful orator, Patrick Henry is credited with the comment Give me liberty or give me death.

c. I could hear the crowd chanting my name—Jones! Jones!—and that spurred me on, said Bruce Jones, the winner of the 5,000-meter race.

d. The video for the rock group Guns N' Roses' epic song November Rain is based on a short story by Del James.

e. In response to a possible asteroid strike on Earth, former astronaut Rusty Schweickart says, Every country is at risk.

1. That day at school, the kids were as "high as kites."

2. Notice, the professor told the class, Cassius's choice of imagery when he asks, Upon what meat doth this our Caesar feed, / That he is grown so great?

3. "As I was rounding the bend," Peter explained, "I failed to see the sign that said Caution: Ice.

4. John Cheever's story The Swimmer begins with the line It was one of those midsummer Sundays when everyone sits around saying, I drank too much last night.

5. Who coined the saying Love is blind?

34 | Dashes

A **dash** is a horizontal line used to separate parts of a sentence — a dramatic substitute for a comma, semicolon, or colon. Your software may automatically turn two hyphens without any spaces into a dash.

34a Use a dash to indicate a sudden break in thought or shift in tone.

The dash signals that a surprise is in store: a shift in viewpoint, perhaps, or an unfinished statement.

> Ivan doesn't care which team wins—he bet on both.
>
> I didn't notice my parents' accented speech—at least not at home.

34b Use a dash to introduce an explanation, an illustration, or a series.

An **appositive** is a word or group of words that adds information by identifying a subject or an object in a different way (see 4b).

Use a dash to add an informal preparatory pause or to introduce an appositive that needs drama or contains commas.

> My advice to you is simple—stop complaining.
>
> Longfellow wrote about three young sisters—grave Alice, laughing Allegra, and Edith with golden hair—in "The Children's Hour."

34c Use dashes to set off an emphatic aside or a parenthetical expression from the rest of a sentence.

> It was as hot—and I mean *hot*—as the Fourth of July in Death Valley.

34d Avoid overusing dashes.

To compare dashes with commas, see 28, and with parentheses, see 35a–35b.

The dash becomes meaningless if used too often. Use it only when a comma, colon, or parentheses don't seem strong enough.

> Algy's grandmother—a sweet old lady—asked him to pick up some things at the store—milk, eggs, and cheese.

EXERCISE 34–1 Using Dashes

Add, remove, or replace dashes wherever appropriate in the following sentences. Some sentences may be correct. Possible answers for the lettered sentences appear at the end of the Handbook. Example:

Stanton had all the identifying marks/boating shoes, yellow slicker,

sunblock, and an anchor/of a sailor.

a. I enjoy going hiking with my friend John — whom I've known for fifteen years.

b. Pedro's new boat is spectacular: a regular seagoing Ferrari.

c. The Thompsons devote their weekends to their favorite pastime, eating bags of potato chips and cookies beside the warm glow of the television.

1. The sport of fishing — or at least some people call it a sport — is boring, dirty — and tiring.

2. At that time, three states in the Sunbelt, Florida, California, and Arizona, were the fastest growing in the nation.

3. LuLu was ecstatic when she saw her grades, all A's!

35 | Parentheses, Brackets, and Ellipses

Parentheses (singular, *parenthesis*) work in pairs. So do brackets. Both surround bits of information to make a statement perfectly clear. An ellipsis mark is a trio of periods inserted to show that something has been cut.

Parentheses

35a Use parentheses to set off interruptions that are useful but not essential.

Franklin D. Roosevelt (commonly known as "FDR") won four elections.

He occupied the White House for so many years (1933 to mid-1945) that babies became teens without having known any other president.

The material within parentheses may be helpful, but it isn't essential. Use parentheses to add a qualification, a helpful date, or a brief explanation — words that, in conversation, you might add in a changed tone of voice.

35b Use parentheses around letters or numbers indicating items in a series.

> Archimedes asserted that, given (1) a lever long enough, (2) a fulcrum, and (3) a place to stand, he could move the earth.

No parentheses are needed for numbers or letters in an indented list.

EXERCISE 35–1 Using Parentheses

Add, remove, or replace parentheses wherever appropriate in the following sentences. Some sentences may be correct. Possible answers for the lettered sentences appear at the end of the Handbook. Example:

> The Islamic fundamentalist Ayatollah Khomeini—1900–1989— *(1900-1989)* was a cleric and leader of Iran in the late twentieth century.

a. Our cafeteria serves the four basic food groups: white — milk, bread, and mashed potatoes — brown — mystery meat and gravy — green — overcooked vegetables and underwashed lettuce — and orange — squash, carrots, and tomato sauce.

b. The hijackers will release the hostages only if the government, 1, frees all political prisoners and, 2, allows the hijackers to leave the country.

c. When Phil said he works with whales (as well as other marine mammals) for the Whale Stranding Network, Lisa thought he meant that his group lures whales onto beaches.

1. The new pear-shaped bottles will hold 200 milliliters, 6.8 fluid ounces, of lotion.

2. World War I, or "The Great War," as it was once called, destroyed the old European order forever.

3. The Internet is a mine of fascinating, and sometimes useless, information.

Brackets

Brackets work in pairs like parentheses. Their special purpose is to mark changes in quoted material.

For advice on quoting, paraphrasing, and summarizing, see Ch. 29 in *A Writer's Research Manual.*

35c Use brackets to add information or to make changes within a direct quotation.

A quotation must be quoted exactly. If you add or alter a word or a phrase in a quotation from another writer, place brackets around your changes.

Suppose you are writing about James McGuire's being named chairman of the board of directors of General Motors. In your source, the actual words are these: "A radio bulletin first brought the humble professor of philosophy the astounding news." But in your paper, you want readers to know the professor's identity. So you add that information in brackets.

> "A radio bulletin first brought the humble professor of philosophy [James McGuire] the astounding news."

Never alter a quoted statement any more than you have to. Ask yourself: Do I really need this quotation, or should I paraphrase?

35d Use brackets around *sic* to indicate an error in a direct quotation.

When you faithfully quote a statement that contains an error, follow the error with a bracketed *sic* (Latin for "so" or "so the writer says"). Usually you're better off paraphrasing an error-riddled passage.

> The book *Cake Wrecks* includes a photo of a cake with this message written on top in icing: Happy Thanksgiven [*sic*].

Ellipses

35e Use ellipses to signal that you have omitted part of a quotation.

Occasionally you will want to quote just the parts of a passage that relate to your topic. Acknowledge your cuts with *ellipses*: three periods with a space between each one (. . .). If ellipses conclude a sentence, precede them with a period placed at the end of the sentence. Suppose you want to quote from Marie Winn's book *Children without Childhood* (Penguin, 1984) but omit some of its detail. Use ellipses to show each cut:

> According to Winn, children's innocence can be easily lost: "Today's nine- and ten-year-olds . . . not infrequently find themselves involved in their own parents' complicated sex lives, . . . at least as advisers, friendly commentators, and intermediaries."

35f Avoid using ellipses at the beginning or end of a quotation.

Even though a source continues after a quoted passage, you don't need ellipses at the end of your quotation. Nor do you need to begin a quotation with three dots. Save the ellipses for words you omit *inside* whatever you quote. If you cut more than a section or two, think about paraphrasing.

For more on quoting, paraphrasing, and summarizing, see Ch. 29 in *A Writer's Research Manual*.

EXERCISE 35–2 Using Brackets and Ellipses

The following is a passage from an essay. The sentences that follow use quoted material from the passage. Correct any faulty use of brackets and ellipses, and add brackets and ellipses if necessary. Some sentences may be correct. Answers for the lettered sentences appear at the end of the Handbook.

> Darwin himself was not entirely consistent in the language he used to describe his beliefs. And of course his views changed over the course of his life. Starting in 1876 he began writing a private autobiography for his children and grandchildren. In it he mentioned the change in his religious views. A gradual skepticism towards Christianity and the authenticity of the Bible gradually crept over him during the late 1830s — leaving him not a Christian, but no atheist either; rather a sort of theist. To be a "theist" in Darwin's day was to believe that a supernatural deity had created nature or the universe but did not intervene in the course of history.
>
> —John van Wyhe, "Was Charles Darwin an Atheist?"

a. According to van Wyhe, "Darwin was not consistent in the language he used to describe his beliefs."

b. John van Wyhe notes that "Darwin's views on religion changed over the course of his life."

c. John van Wyhe points out that Darwin wrote privately about his shift in beliefs.

1. According to van Wyhe, "A gradual skepticism towards Christianity gradually crept over Darwin during the late 1830s."

2. John van Wyhe writes that Darwin was "not a Christian, but no atheist either; rather a sort of theist."

3. John van Wyhe explains that theists such as Darwin believed in "a supernatural deity that had created nature or the universe but did not intervene in the course of history."

Mechanics

Learning by Doing 🔘 Understanding Conventions

Working with a group, select a convention for using hyphens, italics, or other mechanics — one that you find difficult. Read through the section about that rule and try to figure out why this convention is expected in academic writing. Come up with an example or two that will help you and others apply it correctly.

36 | Abbreviations

Abbreviations enable a writer to include necessary information in capsule form. Limit abbreviations to those common enough for readers to recognize, or add an explanation so that a reader does not wonder, "What does this mean?" Remember: when in doubt, spell it out.

36a Use abbreviations for some titles with proper names.

Abbreviate the following titles :

Mr. and Mrs. Vernon Collins   Dr. Elinor Ostrom

Ms. Marta Torres   St. Matthew

For advice on punctuating abbreviations, see 27b.

Write out other titles in full.

General Douglas MacArthur   Senator Dianne Feinstein

Spell out most titles that appear without proper names.

Tomás is studying to be a ~~dr.~~ doctor

When an abbreviated title (such as an academic degree) follows a proper name, set it off with commas. Don't add commas otherwise.

Alice Martin, CPA, is the accountant for Charlotte Cordera, PhD.

My brother has a BA in economics.

Avoid repeating forms of the same title before and after a proper name. Use either *Dr. Jane Doe* or *Jane Doe, DDS,* but not *Dr. Jane Doe, DDS.*

36b Use *a.m., p.m., BCE, AD,* and *$* with numbers.

9:05 a.m.   3:45 p.m.   2000 BCE   AD 1066

For exact prices that include cents and for amounts in the millions, use a dollar sign with figures (*$17.95, $10.52, $3.5 billion*). Avoid combining an abbreviation with wording that means the same thing : *$1 million,* not *$1 million dollars; 9:05 a.m.* or *9:05 in the morning,* not *9:05 a.m. in the morning.*

36c Avoid abbreviating names of months, days of the week, units of measurement, or parts of literary works.

NAMES OF MONTHS AND DAYS OF THE WEEK

After their session on September 3, they did not meet until Friday, December 12.

UNITS OF MEASUREMENT

It would take 10,000 pounds of concrete to build a causeway 25 feet by 58 inches.

PARTS OF LITERARY WORKS

Von Bargen's reply appears in volume 2, chapter 12, page 187.

Leona first speaks in act 1, scene 2 [or the second scene of act 1].

36d Use the full English version of most Latin abbreviations.

For the use of *sic* to identify an error, see 35d.

Follow the conventions of your citation style if you use Latin abbreviations in source citations, parentheses, and brackets. However, unless you are writing for an audience of ancient Romans, translate most Latin abbreviations into English in your text.

COMMON LATIN ABBREVIATIONS	ENGLISH
et al. (*et alia*)	and others, and the others (people)
etc. (*et cetera*)	and so forth, and others, and the rest
i.e. (*id est*)	that is
e.g. (*exempli gratia*)	for example, such as

36e Use abbreviations for familiar organizations, corporations, and people.

Most sets of initials that are capitalized and read as letters do not require periods between the letters (CIA, JFK, UCLA). A set of initials that is pronounced as a word is called an **acronym** (NATO, AIDS, UNICEF) and never has periods between letters.

To avoid misunderstanding, write out an organization's full name the first time you mention it, followed by its initials in parentheses. Then, in later references, you can rely on initials alone. (For very familiar initials, such as FBI or CBS, you need not give the full name.)

36f Avoid abbreviations for countries.

When you mention the United States or another country in your text, give its full name unless the repetition would weigh down your paragraph.

                                    United States   *United Kingdom*
The president will return to the US on Tuesday from a trip to the UK.

EXCEPTION: Unlike *US* as a noun, the abbreviation, used consistently with traditional periods or without, is acceptable as an adjective: *US Senate, U.S. foreign policy*. For other countries, find an alternative: *British ambassador*. Follow your citation style when you cite or list government documents.

EXERCISE 36–1 Using Abbreviations

Substitute abbreviations for words and vice versa as appropriate in the following sentences. Correct any incorrectly used abbreviations. Answers for the lettered sentences appear at the end of the Handbook. Example:

                                                      Wednesday, April
Please return this form no later than noon on Wed., Apr. 7.

a. Prof. Garcia has office hours on Mon. and Tues., beginning at 10:00 a.m.

b. Emotional issues, e.g., abortion and capital punishment, cannot be settled easily by compromise.

c. The red peppers are selling for three dollars and twenty-five cents a lb.

1. Hamlet's famous soliloquy comes in act three, sc. one.
2. A.I.D.S. has affected people throughout U.S. society, not just gay men and IV-drug users.
3. The end of the cold war between the U.S. and the Soviet Union complicated the role of the U.N. and drastically altered the purpose of N.A.T.O.

37 | Capital Letters

For capitalization following a colon, see 31.

Use capital letters only with good reason. If you think a word will work in lowercase letters, you're probably right.

37a Capitalize proper names and adjectives made from proper names.

Proper names designate individuals, places, organizations, institutions, brand names, and certain other distinctive things. Any proper noun can have an adjective form, also capitalized.

Miles Standish	University of Iowa	Australian beer
India	a Volkswagen	a Renaissance man
United Nations	a Xerox copier	Shakespearean comedy

37b Capitalize a title or rank before a proper name.

During her second term, Senator Wilimczyk proposed several bills.

In his lecture, Professor Jones analyzed fossil evidence.

Titles that do not come before proper names usually are not capitalized.

Ten senators voted against the research appropriation.

Jones is the department's only full professor.

EXCEPTION: The abbreviation of an academic or professional degree is always capitalized. The informal name of a degree is not capitalized.

Dora E. McLean, MD, also holds a BA in music.

Dora holds a bachelor's degree in music.

37c Capitalize a family relationship only when it is part of a proper name or when it substitutes for a proper name.

Do you know the song about Mother Machree?

I would like you to meet my aunt, Emily Smith.

37d **Capitalize the names of religions, their deities, and their followers.**

Christianity	Muslims	Jehovah	Krishna
Islam	Methodists	Allah	the Holy Spirit

37e **Capitalize proper names of places, regions, and geographic features.**

Los Angeles	the Black Hills	the Atlantic Ocean
Death Valley	Big Sur	the Philippines

Do not capitalize *north, south, east,* or *west* unless it is part of a proper name (*West Virginia, South Orange*) or refers to formal geographic locations.

Drive south to Chicago and then east to Cleveland.

Tanya, who has always lived in the South, likes to read about the Northeast.

A common noun such as *street, avenue, boulevard, park, lake,* or *hill* is capitalized when part of a proper name.

Meinecke Avenue	Hamilton Park	Lake Michigan

37f **Capitalize days of the week, months, and holidays, but not seasons or academic terms.**

During spring term, by the Monday after Passover, I have to choose between the January study plan and junior year abroad.

37g **Capitalize historical events, periods, and documents.**

Black Monday	the Roaring Twenties
the Civil War [*but* a civil war]	Magna Carta
the Holocaust [*but* a holocaust]	Declaration of Independence
the Bronze Age	Atomic Energy Act

37h **Capitalize the names of schools, colleges, departments, and courses.**

West School, Central High School [*but* middle school, high school]

Reed College, Arizona State University [*but* the college, a university]

Department of History [*but* history department, department office]

Feminist Perspectives in British Literature [*but* literature course]

37i **Capitalize the first, last, and main words in titles.**

When you write the title of a paper, book, article, work of art, television show, poem, or performance, capitalize the first and last words and all main words in between. Do not capitalize articles (*a, an, the*), coordinating conjunctions (*and, but, for, or, nor, so, yet*), or prepositions (such as *in, on, at, of, from*) unless they come first or last in the title or follow a colon.

ESSAY	"Ticket to the Fair"
NOVEL	*Native Son*
VOLUME OF POETRY	*American Primitive*
POEM	"A Valediction: Of Weeping"

For advice on using quotation marks and italics for titles, see 33e and 39a.

37j Capitalize the first letter of a quoted sentence.

Oscar Wilde wrote, "The only way to get rid of a temptation is to yield to it."

For advice on punctuating quotations, see 33g–33i.

Only the first word of a quoted sentence is capitalized, even when you break the sentence with words of your own.

"The only way to get rid of a temptation," wrote Oscar Wilde, "is to yield to it."

If you quote more than one sentence, start each one with a capital letter.

For advice on using brackets to show changes in quotations, see 35c.

"Art should never try to be popular," said Wilde. "The public should try to make itself artistic."

EXERCISE 37–1 Using Capitalization

Correct any capitalization errors in the following sentences. Answers for the lettered sentences appear at the end of the Handbook. Example:

Speaking of Cuba, ~~president~~ President Barack Obama said, "~~a~~ A future of greater peace, security, and democratic development is possible if we work together."

a. The great Shakespearean Tragedy *Macbeth*, which was written around 1600, opens in the scottish countryside and includes the famous character lady Macbeth.

b. Colleen's favorite class at Arizona State university is Literature. She also enjoys taking Weekend hiking trips to the grand canyon.

c. Jake's Great-Aunt was the author Kate Chopin, who wrote the famous work of fiction "The story of an hour" two Decades after the civil war.

1. During ramadan, the ninth month of the islamic calendar, all healthy muslims are required to fast from dawn to dusk.

2. After calling us in to dinner for the third time with no response, mom called into the yard, "okay, the dog is getting an extra-large meal tonight!"

3. My Grandfather recalls that the roaring twenties came to a screeching halt when the great depression hit at the end of 1929.

38 | Numbers

Unless you are writing in a scientific field or your essay relies on statistics, you'll generally want to use words (*twenty-seven*). Figures (*27*) are most appropriate in contexts where readers are used to seeing them, such as times and dates (*11:05 p.m. on March 15*).

38a In general, write out a number that consists of one or two words, and use figures for longer numbers.

Short names of numbers are easily read (*ten, six hundred*); longer ones take more thought (*two thousand four hundred eighty-seven*). For numbers of more than a word or two, use figures.

> Two hundred fans paid twenty-five dollars apiece for that shirt.

> A frog's tongue has 970,580 taste buds; a human's has six times as many.

EXCEPTION: For multiples of a million or more, use a figure plus a word.

> The earth is 93 million miles from the sun.

> ▶ **FIGURES** at a glance
>
> | | |
> |---|---|
> | ADDRESSES | 4 East 74th Street; also, One Copley Place, 5 Fifth Avenue |
> | DATES | May 20, 2007; 450 BCE; also, Fourth of July |
> | DECIMALS | 98.6° Fahrenheit; .57 acres |
> | FRACTIONS | $3\frac{1}{2}$ years; $1\frac{3}{4}$ miles; half a loaf, three-fourths of voters |
> | PARTS OF | volume 2, chapter 5, page 37 |
> | LITERARY WORKS | act 1, scene 2 (*or* act I, scene ii) |
> | PERCENTAGES | 25 percent; 99.9 percent; also, 25%, 99.9% |
> | EXACT PRICES | $1.99; $200,000; also, $5 million, ten cents, a dollar |
> | SCORES | a 114–111 victory; a final score of 5 to 3 |
> | STATISTICS | men in the 25–30 age group; odds of 5 to 1 (*or* 5–1 odds); height 5'7"; also, three out of four doctors |
> | TIMES | 2:29 p.m.; 10:15 tomorrow morning; also, half past four, three o'clock (always with a number in words) |

38b Use figures for most addresses, dates, decimals, fractions, parts of literary works, percentages, exact prices, scores, statistics, and times.

Using figures is mainly a matter of convenience. If you think words will be easier for your readers to follow, you can always write out a number.

38c Use words or figures consistently for numbers in the same category throughout a passage.

For more on the plurals of figures (6s, 1960s), see 32i.

Switching between words and figures for numbers can be distracting to readers. Choose whichever form suits similar numbers in your passage, and use that form consistently for all numbers in the same category.

> Of the 276 representatives who voted, 97 supported a 25 percent raise, while 179 supported a 30 percent raise over five years.

38d Write out a number that begins a sentence.

When a number starts a sentence, either write it out, move it deeper into the sentence, or reword the opening.

> Five percent of the frogs in our aquarium ate sixty-two percent of the flies.

> Ten thousand people packed an arena built for 8,550.

EXERCISE 38–1 Using Numbers

Correct any inappropriate uses of numbers in the following sentences. Some sentences may be correct. Answers for the lettered sentences appear at the end of the Handbook. Example:

> As Feinberg notes on page 197, a delay of ~~3~~ *three* minutes cost the researchers ~~5~~ *five* years' worth of work.

a. A program to help save the sea otter transferred more than eighty animals to a new colony over the course of 2 years; however, all but 34 otters swam back home again.

b. 12 percent or so of the estimated fifteen billion plastic water bottles purchased annually in the United States are recycled.

c. In act two, scene nine, of Shakespeare's *The Merchant of Venice*, Portia's 2nd suitor fails to guess which of 3 caskets contains her portrait.

1. *Fourscore* means 4 times 20; a *fortnight* means 2 weeks; and a *brace* is two of anything.

2. 50 years ago, traveling from New York City to San Francisco took approximately 15 hours by plane, 50 hours by train, and almost 100 hours by car.

3. At 7 o'clock this morning the temperature was already ninety-seven degrees Fahrenheit.

39 | Italics

Italic type—as in this line—slants to the right. In handwriting, indicate italics by underlining. Slightly harder to read than perpendicular type, italic is usually saved for emphasis or other special uses.

39a Italicize certain titles, names, and words.

> We read the story "Araby" in James Joyce's book *Dubliners*.
>
> The Broadway musical *My Fair Lady* was based on Shaw's play *Pygmalion*.

Use italics for the types of titles, names, and words shown on page 688.

39b Use italics sparingly for emphasis.

When you absolutely *must* stress a term, use italics. In most cases, the structure of your sentence should give emphasis where emphasis is due.

> He put the package *under* the mailbox, not *into* the mailbox.
>
> People living in affluent countries may not be aware that nearly *sixteen thousand children per day* die of starvation or malnutrition.

EXERCISE 39–1 Using Italics

Add or remove italics as needed as you rewrite the following sentences. (Use underline to show italics, if you are writing by hand.) Some sentences may be correct. Answers for the lettered sentences appear at the end of the Handbook. Example:

> Does *avocado* mean "lawyer" in Spanish?

a. Hiram could not *believe* that his parents had seen *the Beatles'* legendary performance at Shea Stadium.

b. During this year's *First Night* celebrations, we heard Verdi's Requiem and Monteverdi's Orfeo.

c. It was fun watching the passengers on the Europa trying to dance to *Blue Moon* in the midst of a storm.

1. Jan can never remember whether Cincinnati has three n's and one t or two n's and two t's.

2. My favorite comic bit in "The Pirates of Penzance" is Major General Stanley's confusion between "orphan" and "often."

3. In Tom Stoppard's play "The Real Thing," the character Henry accuses Bach of copying a *cantata* from a popular song by *Procol Harum*.

For titles that need to be placed in quotation marks, see 33e.

▶ ITALICS at a glance

Titles

MAGAZINES, NEWSPAPERS, AND SCHOLARLY JOURNALS
Newsweek   the *Oregonian*   *Film & History*

LONG LITERARY WORKS
The Bluest Eye (a novel)   *The Less Deceived* (a collection of poems)

FILMS
Psycho   *Casablanca*   *Mad Max: Fury Road*

PAINTINGS AND OTHER WORKS OF ART
Four Dancers (a painting)   *The Thinker* (a sculpture)

LONG MUSICAL WORKS
Aïda   *Handel's Messiah*

ALBUMS
25   *The Chronic*

TELEVISION AND RADIO PROGRAMS
The Walking Dead   *All Things Considered*

Other Words and Phrases

NAMES OF AIRCRAFT, SPACECRAFT, SHIPS, AND TRAINS
the *Orient Express*   the *Challenger*

FOREIGN-LANGUAGE WORD OR PHRASE NOT IN EVERYDAY USE
Gandhi taught the principles of *satya* and *ahimsa*: truth and nonviolence.

LETTER, NUMBER, WORD, OR PHRASE DEFINED OR REFERRED TO AS A WORD
The neon *5* on the door identified the club's address.

The rhythmic motion of the alimentary canal is called *peristalsis*.

What do you think *fiery* suggests in the second line?

SYNONYM OR TRANSLATION (italicize the word; put its definition in quotation marks.)

The word *orthodoxy* means "conformity."

Trois, drei, and *tres* are all words for "three."

Exceptions: The names of the Bible (King James Version, Revised Standard Version), the books of the Bible (Genesis, Matthew), and other sacred books (the Qur'an, the Rig-Veda) are not italicized.

40 | Hyphens

The hyphen is used to join words and to connect parts of words.

40a Use hyphens in compound words that require them.

Compound words in the English language take three forms :

1. Two or more words combined into one (*crossroads, salesperson*)
2. Two or more separate words that function as one (*gas station, high school*)
3. Two or more words linked by hyphens (*sister-in-law, window-shop*)

Compounds fall into these categories more by custom than by rule. When you're not sure which way to write a compound, refer to a current collegiate dictionary. If the compound isn't listed, write it as two words.

Use a hyphen in a compound word containing one or more elements beginning with a capital letter.

> Bill says that, as a *neo Marxist* living in an *A frame* house, it would be politically incorrect for him to wear a Mickey Mouse T-shirt.

40b Use a hyphen in a compound adjective preceding, but not following, a noun.

> Jerome, a devotee of *twentieth-century* music, has no interest in the classic symphonies of the *eighteenth century*.

> I'd like living in an *out-of-the-way* place better if it weren't so far *out of the way*.

In a series of hyphenated adjectives with the same second word, you can omit that word (but not the hyphen) in all but the last adjective of the series.

> Julia is a lover of eighteenth-, nineteenth-, and twentieth-century music.

The adverb *well*, when coupled with an adjective, follows the same hyphenation rules as if it were an adjective.

> It is *well known* that Tony has a *well-equipped* kitchen, although his is not as *well equipped* as the hotel's.

Do *not* use a hyphen to link an adverb ending in *-ly* with an adjective.

> The sun hung like a newly minted penny in a freshly washed sky.

40c Use a hyphen after the prefixes all-, ex-, and self- and before the suffix -elect.

> Lucille's *ex-husband* is studying *self-hypnosis*.

> This *all-important* debate pits Senator Browning against the *president-elect*.

40d **Use a hyphen in most cases if an added prefix or suffix creates a double vowel, a triple consonant, or an ambiguous pronunciation.**

The contractor's *pre-estimate* did not cover any *pre-existing* flaws.

The recreation department favors the *re-creation* of a summer program.

It is also acceptable to omit the hyphen in the case of a double *e: reeducate.*

40e **Use a hyphen in spelled-out fractions and compound whole numbers from twenty-one to ninety-nine.**

When her sister gave Leslie's age as six and *three-quarters,* Leslie corrected her: "I'm six and *five-sixths*!"

The fifth graders learned that *forty-four* rounds down to forty while *forty-five* rounds up to fifty.

40f **Use `a hyphen to indicate inclusive numbers.**

The section covering the years 1975-1980 is found on pages 20-27.

40g **Use a hyphen to break a word between syllables at the end of a line.**

Academic style guides (such as MLA and APA) prefer that you turn off your word processor's automatic hyphenation. If you're designing a text that requires breaking a word, check your dictionary for its syllable divisions.

EXERCISE 40–1 Using Hyphens

Add necessary hyphens and remove incorrectly used hyphens in the following sentences. Some sentences may be correct. Answers for the lettered sentences appear at the end of the Handbook. Example:

> *ex-husband*
> Her ~~exhusband~~ works part-time as a short-order cook.

a. Jimmy is a lively four year old boy, and his sister is two years old.

b. The badly damaged ship was in no condition to enter the wide-open waters beyond the bay.

c. Tracy's brother in law lives with his family in a six room apartment.

1. Heat-seeking missiles are often employed in modern air-to-air combat.

2. *The Piano* is a beautifully-crafted film with first-rate performances by Holly Hunter and Harvey Keitel.

3. Nearly three fourths of the money in the repair and maintenance account already has been spent.

41 | Spelling

English spelling so often defies the rules that many writers wonder if, indeed, there *are* rules. How, then, are you to cope? You can proofread carefully and use your spell checker. You can refer to lists of commonly misspelled words and of **homonyms,** words that sound the same, or almost the same, but are spelled differently.

For a list of commonly confused homonyms, see pp. 650–51.

You can also use several tactics to teach yourself to be a better speller.

1. *Use mnemonics.* To make spellings stick in your memory, invent associations. Using such mnemonic devices (tricks to aid memory) may help you. *Weird* behaves *weirdly.* Rise ag*ain,* Brit*ain*! *Separate* has *a rate.* Why isn't *math*ematics like *athle*tics? You write a *letter* on stationery. Any silly phrase or sentence will do, as long as it helps.

2. *Keep a list of words you misspell.* Each time you proofread a paper or receive one back from your instructor, add words you've misspelled. Then practice pronouncing, writing, and spelling them out loud until they stick.

3. *Check any questionable spelling by referring to your dictionary.* Check words as you find them and double-check them as you proofread and edit. A good dictionary will distinguish American and British spellings (*color, colour; terrorize, terrorise*).

4. *Learn commonly misspelled words.* If you're likely to confuse words that sound alike, turn to the list of Commonly Confused Homonyms and the Glossary of Troublemakers in the Quick Editing Guide. Spell every troublesome word out loud; write it ten times. Spend a few minutes each day going over them. Do the same with any common problem words that your spell checker routinely catches, such as *nucular* for *nuclear* or *exercize* for *exercise.* Your spelling will improve rapidly.

Answers for Lettered Exercises

EXERCISE 1–1 ▪ Identifying Parts of Speech, p. 568

a. *available*: adjective; *around*: preposition; *for*: preposition; *centuries*: noun
b. *It*: pronoun; *became*: verb; *very*: adverb; *common*: adjective; *during*: preposition
c. *Americans*: noun; *drink*: verb; *countries*: noun; *do*: verb
d. *Interestingly*: adverb; *American*: adjective; *cleaner*: adjective; *most*: adjective; *of*: preposition
e. *usually*: adverb; *label*: verb; *their*: pronoun; *or*: conjunction

EXERCISE 2–1 ▪ Identifying Subjects, p. 570

a. *television shows*: complete subject; *shows*: simple subject
b. *Ernie and Bert*: complete subject; *Ernie and Bert*: simple subject
c. *The show*: complete subject; *show*: simple subject
d. *it*: complete subject; *it*: simple subject
e. *Over 74 million Americans*: complete subject; *Americans*: simple subject

EXERCISE 3–1 ▪ Identifying Verbs, Objects, and Complements, p. 574

a. *invented*: AV; *reflectors*: DO **b.** *noticed*: AV; *burrs*: DO; *gave*: AV; *world*: IO; *Velcro*: DO **c.** *are*: LV; *eager*: SC **d.** *have*: HV; *inspired*: MV; *inventions*: DO **e.** *melted*: AV; *bar*: DO

EXERCISE 4–1 ▪ Identifying Phrases and Clauses, p. 577

a. *Spending the night in an ice hotel*: verbal phrase; *on my bucket list*: prepositional phrase
b. *on the test*: prepositional phrase; *because I studied for three hours*: subordinate clause
c. *a 1957 Chevy*: appositive phrase; *off the assembly line*: prepositional phrase
d. *After searching all morning*: subordinate clause; *we gave up on finding the lost earring*: main clause
e. *dinner still steaming on the table*: absolute phrase

EXERCISE 5–1 ▪ Identifying Sentence Types, p. 579

a. complex **b.** compound/complex **c.** compound
d. simple **e.** simple

EXERCISE 6–1 ▪ Eliminating Fragments, p. 582

Suggested revisions:

a. Michael had a beautiful Southern accent, having lived many years in Georgia.
b. Pat and Chris are determined to marry each other, even if their families do not approve.

c. Jack seemed well qualified for a career in the air force, except for his tendency to get airsick.
d. Lisa advocated sleeping no more than four hours a night until she started nodding off through her classes.
e. Complete sentences

EXERCISE 7–1 ▪ Revising Comma Splices and Fused Sentences, p. 585

Suggested revisions:

a. Lee's comic book superheroes are ordinary people with flaws; they also have extraordinary abilities. *Or*
  Lee's comic book superheroes are ordinary people with flaws, yet they also have extraordinary abilities.
b. Although Iron Man (Tony Stark) has a superpowered suit and the ability to fly, he is a heavy drinker and suffers from anxiety. *Or*
  Iron Man (Tony Stark) has a superpowered suit and the ability to fly; however, he is a heavy drinker and suffers from anxiety.
c. Teenaged nerd Peter Parker is another example: he has spider-like abilities to spin webs and scale buildings. *Or*
  Teenaged nerd Peter Parker, who has spider-like abilities to spin webs and scale buildings, is another example.
d. Thor is a godlike superhero who comes to Earth with super strength and the ability to fly; his weakness is his fondness for humans. *Or*
  Thor is a godlike superhero who comes to Earth with super strength and the ability to fly, but his weakness is his fondness for humans.
e. Bruce Banner was a brilliant scientist who studied gamma radiation. An accident caused him to turn into a giant destructive hulk when he gets angry. *Or*
  Bruce Banner was a brilliant scientist who studied gamma radiation until an accident caused him to turn into a giant destructive hulk when he gets angry.

EXERCISE 8–1 ▪ Identifying Verb Tenses, p. 593

a. *has been living*: present perfect progressive; *hacked*: simple past
b. *have never appeared*: present perfect; *will never appear*: simple future; *gets selected*: simple present
c. *had been*: past perfect; *pitched*: simple past
d. *will have been studying*: future perfect progressive; *will be taking*: future progressive
e. *was running*: past progressive; *strolled*: simple past

EXERCISE 8–2 ▪ Using Irregular Verb Forms, p. 596

a. Change *Do* to *Does* **b.** Change *laid* to *lay* **c.** Change *setting* to *sitting* **d.** Correct **e.** Change *sat* to *set*

EXERCISE 8–3 ▪ Using the Correct Mood of Verbs, p. 598

a. Dr. Belanger recommended that Juan *floss* his teeth every day. (Incorrect *flosses,* indicative; correct *floss,* subjunctive)
b. If I *were* you, I would have done the same thing. (Incorrect *was,* indicative; correct *were,* subjunctive)
c. Tradition demands that Daegun *show* respect for his elders. (Incorrect *shows,* indicative; correct *show,* subjunctive)
d. Please *attend* the training lesson if you plan to skydive later today. (Incorrect *attends,* indicative; correct *attend,* imperative)

EXERCISE 9–1 ▪ Making Subjects and Verbs Agree, p. 603

a. For many college graduates, the process of looking for jobs *is* often long and stressful.
b. Not too long ago, searching the classifieds and inquiring in person *were* the primary methods of job hunting.
c. Today, however, everyone *needs* to use the Internet to search for openings or to e-mail *his or her* résumés.
d. My classmates and my cousin *send* most résumés over the Internet because it costs less than mailing them.
e. All of the résumés *contain* keywords that make them appear in searches.

EXERCISE 10–1 ▪ Using Pronoun Case Correctly, p. 606

a. I didn't appreciate *your* laughing at her and *me.* (*Your* modifies the gerund *laughing; me* is an object of the preposition *at.*)
b. Lee and *I* would be delighted to serenade *whoever* will listen. (*I* is a subject of the verb phrase *would be delighted; whoever* is the subject of the clause *whoever will listen.*)
c. The managers and *we* servers are highly trustworthy. (*We* is a subject complement.)
d. The neighbors were driven berserk by *his* singing. (The gerund *singing* is the object of the verb *driven;* the possessive pronoun *his* modifies *singing.*) *Or*
  Correct as is. (*Him* is the object of the verb *driven; singing* is a participle modifying *him.*)
e. Jerry and *I* regard you and *her* as the very people *whom* we wish to meet. (*I* is a subject of the verb *regard; her* is a direct object of the verb *regard; whom* is the object of the infinitive *to meet.*)

EXERCISE 11–1 ▪ Making Pronoun Reference Clear, p. 609

Suggested revisions:

a. As the moon began to rise, I could see the faint shadow of the tree.

b. While she spent the summer in Paris, Katrina broadened her awareness of cultural differences by traveling throughout Europe.
c. Most managers want employees to work as many hours as possible. They never consider the work their employees need to do at home.
d. My working twelve hours a day and never getting enough sleep was worth it.
e. Kevin asked Mike to meet him for lunch but forgot that Mike had class at that time. *Or*
  Kevin forgot that he had class at the time he asked Mike to meet him for lunch.

EXERCISE 12–1 ▪ Making Pronouns and Antecedents Agree, p. 611

Suggested revisions:

a. Correct
b. Neither Melissa nor James has received an application form yet. *Or*
  Melissa and James have not received their application forms yet.
c. He is the kind of man who gets his fun out of just sipping his beer and watching his Saturday games on TV.
d. Many a mother has mourned the loss of her child. *Or*
  Many mothers have mourned the loss of their children.
e. When you enjoy your work, it's easy to spend all your spare time thinking about it. *Or*
  When one enjoys one's work, it's easy to spend all one's spare time thinking about it.

EXERCISE 13–1 ▪ Using Adjectives and Adverbs Correctly, p. 616

a. Change *exact* to *exactly* **b.** Change *badly* to *bad* **c.** Change *best* to *better* **d.** Change *sadly* to *sad* **e.** Delete *most*

EXERCISE 14–1 ▪ Maintaining Grammatical Consistency, p. 618

Suggested revisions:

a. Dr. Jamison is an erudite professor who tells amusing anecdotes in class. (Formal) *Or*
  Dr. Jamison is a funny teacher who cracks jokes in class. (Informal)
b. The audience listened intently to the lecture but did not understand the message.
c. Scientists can no longer evade the social, political, and ethical consequences of what they do in the laboratory.
d. To have good government, citizens must become informed on the issues. Also, they must vote.
e. Good writing is essential to success in many professions, especially in business, where ideas must be communicated clearly.

EXERCISE 15–1 ▪ Placing Modifiers, p. 621

Suggested revisions:

a. The bus full of passengers got stuck in a ditch.
b. In the middle of a meeting, he was daydreaming about fishing for trout.
c. With a smirk, the boy threw the paper airplane through an open window.
d. When the glare appeared, I reached for my sunglasses in the glove compartment.
e. Sally and Glen watched the kites high above them drift back and forth.

EXERCISE 15–2 ▪ Revising Dangling Modifiers, p. 622

Suggested revisions:

a. As I was unpacking the suitcase, a horrible idea occurred to me.
b. After fixing breakfast that morning, I might have left the oven on at home.
c. Although I tried to reach my neighbor, her phone was busy.
d. Desperate to get information, I asked my mother to drive over to check the oven.
e. I felt enormous relief when my mother's call confirmed everything was fine.

EXERCISE 16–1 ▪ Completing Comparisons, p. 624

Suggested revisions:

a. The movie version of *The Brady Bunch* was much more ironic *than the television show.*
b. Taking care of a dog is often more demanding than *taking care of* a cat.
c. I received more free calendars in the mail for the year 2016 than *I have for* any other year.
d. The crime rate in the United States is higher than *it is in* Canada.
e. Liver contains more iron than any *other* meat.

EXERCISE 16–2 ▪ Completing Sentences, p. 625

Suggested revisions:

a. Eighteenth-century China was as civilized *as* and in many respects more sophisticated than the Western world.
b. Pembroke was never contacted *by,* much less involved with, the election committee.
c. I haven't yet *finished* but soon will finish my research paper.
d. Ron likes his popcorn with butter; Linda *likes hers* with parmesan cheese.
e. Correct

EXERCISE 17–1 ▪ Correcting Mixed Constructions and Faulty Predication, p. 628

Suggested revisions:

a. Health insurance protects people from big medical bills.
b. His determination to prevail helped him finish the race.
c. AIDS destroys the body's immune system.
d. The temperatures are too low for the orange trees.
e. In a recession, economic growth is small or nonexistent and unemployment increases.

EXERCISE 18–1 ▪ Making Sentences Parallel, p. 631

Suggested revisions:

a. The border separating Texas and Mexico marks not only the political boundary of two countries but also the last frontier for some endangered wildlife.
b. In the Rio Grande Valley, both local residents and tourists enjoy visiting the national wildlife refuges.
c. The tall grasses in this valley are the home of many insects, birds, and small mammals.
d. Two endangered wildcats, the ocelot and the jaguarundi, also make the Rio Grande Valley their home.
e. Many people from Central America are desperate to immigrate to the United States by either legal or illegal means.

EXERCISE 19–1 ▪ Using Coordination, p. 634

Suggested revisions:

a. Professional poker players try to win money and prizes in high-stakes tournaments; however, they may lose thousands of dollars.
b. Poker is not an easy way to make a living, and playing professional poker is not a good way to relax.
c. A good "poker face" reveals no emotions, for communicating too much information puts a player at a disadvantage.
d. Hidden feelings may come out in unconscious movements, so an expert poker player watches other players carefully.
e. Poker is different from most other casino gambling games, for it requires skill and it forces players to compete against each other. Other casino gambling pits players against the house, so they may win out of sheer luck, but skill has little to do with winning those games.

EXERCISE 19–2 ▪ Using Subordination, p. 637

Suggested revisions:

a. Whereas the average cost of a single-family home in the United States is over $275,000, it costs less than one-tenth of that to build a tiny house.
b. American homes, which average about 2,500 square feet, have three bedrooms, two bathrooms, and a garage for two or more cars.

c. Although a tiny house is between 100 and 400 square feet, it enables simpler living in a smaller, more efficient space.
d. Tiny houses, which come in all shapes, sizes, and forms, are much more customizable than traditional mobile homes.
e. People who are joining the tiny house movement do so for many reasons. The most popular reasons include environmental concerns, financial concerns, and the desire for more time and freedom.

EXERCISE 22–2 ▪ Avoiding Jargon, p. 643

Suggested revisions:

a. Everyone at Boondoggle and Gall attends holiday gatherings in order to meet and socialize with potential business partners.
b. This year, more than fifty employees lost their jobs after Boondoggle and Gall's decision to reduce the number of employees by September 1.
c. The layoffs left Jensen in charge of all telephone calls in the customer-service department.
d. Jensen was responsible for handling three times as many telephone calls after the layoffs compared with before, yet she did not receive any extra pay.
e. Jensen and her managers could not agree on a fair compensation, so she decided to quit her job at Boondoggle and Gall.

EXERCISE 22–3 ▪ Avoiding Euphemisms and Slang, p. 644

Suggested revisions:

a. At three hundred dollars a month, the apartment is a bargain.
b. The soldiers were accidentally shot by members of their own troops while they were retreating.
c. Churchill was an excellent politician.

EXERCISE 24–1 ▪ Avoiding Bias, p. 648

Suggested revisions:

a. Our school's athletic program will be of interest to *many* applicants.
b. The new physicians include Dr. Scalia, *Dr.* Baniski, and Dr. Morton.
c. *Diligent researchers* will always find the sources *they* seek.

EXERCISE 27–1 ▪ Using End Punctuation, p. 653

a. The question that still troubles the community after all these years is why federal agents did not act sooner. [Not a direct question]
b. I wonder what he was thinking at the time. [Not a direct question]
c. Correct

EXERCISE 28–1 ▪ Using Commas, p. 655

a. Correct
b. When we returned to the hotel, he couldn't wait to check for any messages.
c. James logged on to the hotel wifi immediately, but he was surprised to find that he hadn't gotten any e-mails all morning.
d. His office hadn't called him, nor had his friends left him any messages.
e. He pretended to be relieved that nothing urgent had come up at work, but I think he was secretly annoyed that everyone was doing fine without him.

EXERCISE 28–2 ▪ Using Commas, p. 657

a. Mrs. Carver looks like a sweet little old lady, but she plays a wicked electric guitar.
b. Her bass player, her drummer, and her keyboard player all live in the same retirement community.
c. They practice individually in the afternoon, rehearse together at night, and play at the community's Saturday night dances.
d. The Rest Home Rebels have to rehearse quietly and cautiously to keep from disturbing the other residents.
e. Correct

EXERCISE 28–3 ▪ Using Commas, p. 658

Suggested revisions:

a. We are bringing a dish, vegetable lasagna, to the potluck supper.
b. I like to go to Central Bank on this side of town because this branch tends to have short lines.
c. The colony that the English established at Roanoke disappeared mysteriously.
d. If the base commanders had checked their gun room, where powder is stored, they would have found that several hundred pounds of gunpowder were missing.
e. Brazil's tropical rain forests, which help produce the air we breathe all over the world, are being cut down at an alarming rate.

EXERCISE 28–4 ▪ Using Commas, p. 660

a. The university insisted, however, that the students were not accepted merely because of their parents' generous contributions.
b. This dispute, in any case, is an old one.
c. It was the young man's striking good looks, not his acting ability, that first attracted the Hollywood agents.
d. Gretchen learned, moreover, not always to accept as true what she had read in celebrity magazines.
e. The hikers, most of them wearing ponchos or rain jackets, headed out into the steady drizzle.

EXERCISE 28–5 ▪ Using Commas, p. 661

a. César Chávez was born on March 31, 1927, on a farm in Yuma, Arizona.
b. Chávez, who spent years as a migrant farmworker, told other farm laborers, "If you're outraged at conditions, then you can't possibly be free or happy until you devote all your time to changing them."
c. Chávez founded the United Farm Workers union and did, indeed, devote all his time to changing conditions for farmworkers.
d. Robert F. Kennedy called Chávez "one of the heroic figures of our time."
e. Correct

EXERCISE 29–1 ▪ Misuses of the Comma, p. 663

a. The proposed bill would give veterans in rural areas improved access to medical care, health benefits, and job training.
b. Neither the House of Representatives nor the Senate seems likely to vote for increasing the federal minimum wage.
c. The report basically states that increased testing is not improving student outcomes, even though that was the original intention.
d. During migration, hummingbirds, which weigh less than an ounce, travel distances that average 500 miles per day.
e. After the party, we found an earring, two sweaters, a hat, a scarf, and a shoe.

EXERCISE 30–1 ▪ Using Semicolons, p. 665

a. The research paper was due in six weeks; therefore, Ali got started right away by making a schedule.
b. The committee estimated the extent of violent crime among teenagers, especially those between the ages of fourteen and sixteen; acted as a liaison between the city and schools and between churches and volunteer organizations; and drew up a plan to reduce violence, both public and domestic, in the next decade.
c. The skilled pilot landed the plane in an open field; all passengers made it out safely.
d. The mall no longer seems to attract customers; however, downtown businesses are picking up again.

EXERCISE 31–1 ▪ Using Colons, p. 667

Suggested revisions:

a. The Continuing Education Program offers courses in building and construction management, engineering, and design.
b. The interview ended with a test of skills: taking messages, operating the computer, typing a sample letter, and proofreading documents.
c. The sample letter began, "Dear Mr. Rasheed: Please accept our apologies for the late shipment."

EXERCISE 32–1 ▪ Using Apostrophes, p. 669

a. Joe's and Chuck's fathers were both in the class of '90.
b. Correct
c. It was a strange coincidence that all three women's cars broke down after they had picked up their mothers-in-law.
d. Don't forget to dot your *i*'s and cross your *t*'s.
e. Mario and Shelley's son is marrying the editor in chief's daughter.

EXERCISE 33–1 ▪ Using Quotation Marks, p. 673

a. "What we still need to figure out," the police chief said, "is whether the victim was acquainted with his assailant."
b. A skillful orator, Patrick Henry is credited with the comment "Give me liberty or give me death."
c. "I could hear the crowd chanting my name — 'Jones! Jones!' — and that spurred me on," said Bruce Jones, the winner of the 5,000-meter race.
d. The video for the rock group Guns N' Roses' epic song "November Rain" is based on a short story by Del James.
e. In response to a possible asteroid strike on Earth, former astronaut Rusty Schweickart says, "Every country is at risk."

EXERCISE 34–1 ▪ Using Dashes, p. 675

Suggested revisions:

a. I enjoy going hiking with my friend John, whom I've known for fifteen years.
b. Pedro's new boat is spectacular — a regular seagoing Ferrari.
c. The Thompsons devote their weekends to their favorite pastime — eating bags of potato chips and cookies beside the warm glow of the television.

EXERCISE 35–1 ▪ Using Parentheses, p. 676

Suggested revisions:

a. Our cafeteria serves the four basic food groups: white (milk, bread, and mashed potatoes), brown (mystery meat and gravy), green (overcooked vegetables and underwashed lettuce), and orange (squash, carrots, and tomato sauce).
b. The hijackers will release the hostages only if the government (1) frees all political prisoners and (2) allows the hijackers to leave the country.
c. Correct

EXERCISE 35–2 ▪ Using Brackets and Ellipses, p. 677

a. According to van Wyhe, "Darwin . . . was not . . . consistent in the language he used to describe his beliefs."
b. John van Wyhe notes that "[Darwin's] views [on religion] changed over the course of his life."
c. Correct

EXERCISE 36–1 ▪ Using Abbreviations, p. 681

a. *Professor* James has office hours on Monday and Tuesday, beginning at 10:00 a.m.
b. Emotional issues, *for example,* abortion and capital punishment, cannot be settled easily by compromise.
c. The red peppers are selling for *$3.25 a pound.*

EXERCISE 37–1 ▪ Using Capitalization, p. 684

a. The great Shakespearean tragedy *Macbeth,* which was written around 1600, opens in the Scottish countryside and includes the famous character Lady Macbeth.
b. Colleen's favorite class at Arizona State University is literature. She also enjoys taking weekend hiking trips to the Grand Canyon.
c. Jake's great-aunt was the author Kate Chopin, who wrote the famous work of fiction "The Story of an Hour" two decades after the Civil War.

EXERCISE 38–1 ▪ Using Numbers, p. 686

a. A program to help save the sea otter transferred more than eighty animals to a new colony over the course of *two* years; however, all but *thirty-four* otters swam back home again.

b. *Twelve percent* or so of the estimated *15* billion plastic water bottles purchased annually in the United States are recycled.
c. In act 2, scene 9, of Shakespeare's *The Merchant of Venice,* Portia's *second* suitor fails to guess which of *three* caskets contains her portrait [or act II, scene ix, as directed].

EXERCISE 39–1 ▪ Using Italics, p. 687

a. Hiram could not believe that his parents had seen the Beatles' legendary performance at Shea Stadium.
b. During this year's First Night celebrations, we heard Verdi's *Requiem* and Monteverdi's *Orfeo.*
c. It was fun watching the passengers on the *Europa* trying to dance to "Blue Moon" in the midst of a storm.

EXERCISE 40–1 ▪ Using Hyphens, p. 690

a. Jimmy is a lively four-year-old boy, and his sister is two years old.
b. Correct
c. Tracy's brother-in-law lives with his family in a six-room apartment.

Quick Format Guide

When you think about a newspaper, a specific type of publication comes to mind because the newspaper is a familiar *genre*, or form. Almost all printed newspapers share a set of defined features: a masthead, headlines, pictures with captions, graphics, and articles arranged in columns of text. Popular magazines, academic journals, letters of recommendation, corporate annual reports, and many other types of writing can be identified and distinguished by such features.

Readers also have expectations about how a college paper should look, sometimes including the presentation of visual material such as graphs, tables, photographs, or other illustrations, depending on the field and the assignment. How can you find out what's expected? Check your course materials. Look for directions about format, advice about common problems, requirements for a specific academic style — or all three.

A | Following the Format for an Academic Paper

You can easily spot the appealing features of a magazine, newspaper, or website with bold headlines, colorful images, and creative graphics. These lively materials serve their purpose, attracting your attention and promoting the interests of the publication's owners, contributors, or sponsors. In contrast, academic papers may look plain, even downright dull. However, their aim is not to entertain you but to engage your mind. The conventions — the accepted expectations — for college papers vary by field but typically support core academic values: to present ideas, reduce distractions, and integrate sources. A conventional format reassures readers that you respect the values behind the guidelines.

MLA First Page

Running head with writer's last name and page number on every page

Writer's name
Instructor's name
Course
Date

Title, centered

Double-spaced 12-point Times New Roman font recommended

Right margin uneven with no hyphenation

Thesis previews paper's development

Signal phrase names publication and author

Long quotation (5 prose or 4 poetry lines or more) indented without quotation marks

Ellipses show omissions, and brackets show additions within a quotation

Page number locates information in source

Electronic sources without page numbers cited only by author or by title with organization as author

---

½"

1"   Williams 1

Christopher Williams
Professor Smith
Composition I
12 May 2019

Watercoolers of the Future

½" indent or 5 spaces →The traditional office environment includes many challenges such as commuting in rush-hour traffic, spending long hours in a cubicle, and missing family events due to strict work hours. These challenges are all changing, however, now that technology is altering how and where people work. With more and more freelance and home-based possibilities, a trend known as co-working has led to the

1"   development of shared workspaces. As technology changes the   1"
traditional office work space, new co-working cooperatives are creating the watercoolers of the future, positive gathering spots where working people can meet and share ideas.

New technology is leading the shift away from corporate offices. In *The Future of Work*, Malone explains this move away from the physical office with four walls:

½"   Dispersed physically but connected by technology, workers are now able . . . to make their own decisions using informa-tion gathered from many other people and places. . . . [They] gain the economic benefits of large organizations, like economies of scale and knowledge, without giving up the human benefits of small ones, like freedom, creativity, motivation, and flexibility. (4)

Working at a distance or from home can take a toll on workers, however. Loneliness and lack of social opportunities are some of the largest problems for people who do not work in a traditional office (Miller). This is where co-working comes in. Independent workers such as freelancers, people starting their own businesses, and telecommuters share office space. They often pay a monthly fee in exchange for use of the rented area and whatever it provides, such as desk space, meeting rooms,

1"

MLA Works Cited

½"

1"

Works Cited

Butler, Kiera. "Works Well with Others." *Mother Jones*, Jan./
    Feb. 2008, pp. 66-69.

Cetron, Marvin J., and Owen Davies. "Trends Shaping
    Tomorrow's World: Economic and Social Trends and Their
    Impacts." *The Futurist*, vol. 44, no. 3, May-June 2010,
    pp. 35-51. *Academic OneFile*, go.galegroup.com.

Citizen Space. "Our Philosophy." *Citizen Space*, citizenspace.
    us/about/our-philosophy/. Accessed 8 Mar. 2019.

Donkin, Richard. *The Future of Work*. Palgrave Macmillan, 2009.

Godin, Seth. "The Last Days of Cubicle Life." *Time*, 14 May
    2009, content.time.com/time/specials/packages/
    article/0,28804,1898024_1898023_1898077,00.html.

Goetz, Kaomi. "Co-working Offers Community to Solo
    Workers." *Morning Edition*, National Public Radio,
    6 Jan. 2010, www.npr.org/templates/story/story.
    php?storyId=122252297.

---. "For Freelancers, Landing a Workspace Gets Harder."
    Morning Edition, National Public Radio, 10 Apr. 2012, www.
    npr.org/2012/04/10/150286116/
    for-freelancers-landing-a-workspace-gets-harder.

Malone, Thomas W. *The Future of Work: How the New Order of
    Business Will Shape Your Organization, Your Management
    Style, and Your Life*. Harvard Business Review Press, 2004.

McConville, Christine. "Freelancers Bag Cheap Office Space."
    The Boston Herald, 15 Aug. 2009, www.bostonherald.com/
    business/general/view.bg?articleid=1191126.

Miller, Kerry. "Where the Coffee Shop Meets the Cubicle."
    Bloomberg Businessweek, 26 Feb. 2007, www.bloomberg.
    com/bw/stories/2007-02-26/where-the-coffee-shop
    -meets-the-cubiclebusinessweek-business-news-stock-
    market-and-financial-advice.

1"

Side notes:

List of works cited on a separate page

Running head continues

List alphabetized by last names of authors or by titles (when no author is named)

First line of entry at left margin

Additional lines indented ½"

Double-spaced throughout

Three hyphens show additional work by same author

APA Title Page

1"

1

Double-spaced 12-point
Times New Roman font
recommended

Title, centered in
boldface type, with one
line space after it

Author

Department and school

Course number and
name

Instructor's name

Due date

Limitations of Pet Health Insurance

Jennifer Miller
Business Department, Springfield College
BUS 121, Personal Finance
Dr. Steven Lopez
April 12, 2019

APA First Page of Text

_{½" (or 5–7 spaces)}

Limitations of Pet Health Insurance

The Humane Society of the United States (2012) reports in *U.S. Pet Owner ship Statistics* that over 78 million dogs and 84 million cats are owned as household pets. However, only 3% of household pets are insured. Furthermore, in 2007, "only 850,000 pet insurance policies [were] in effect . . . according to the National Commission on Veterinary Economic Issues" (Weston, 2010, para. 2). Recent studies suggest that, despite the growing availability of insurance plans for pet health care, these policies may not be the cheapest way to care for a household pet. Pet owners need to consider a number of factors before buying a policy, including the pet's age, any preexisting diseases that an insurance carrier might decide not to cover, and a policy's possible hidden fees.

Types of Pet Health Insurance Currently Available

Pet ownership is important to many people, and pets can do a great deal to improve the mental health and quality of life for their owners (McNicholas et al., 2005, p. 1252). However, paying for a pet's own health care can be stressful and expensive. Mathews (2009) reported on the costs in the *Wall Street Journal*:

This year, pet owners are expected to spend around $12.2 billion for veterinary care, up from $11.1 billion last year and $8.2 billion five years ago, according to the American Pet Products Association. Complex procedures widely used for people, including chemotherapy and dialysis, are now available for pets, and the potential cost of treating certain illnesses has spiked as a result. (Introduction section, para. 4)

Many providers currently offer plans to insure household pets. The largest of the providers is the long-standing Veterinary Pet Insurance (VPI), holding over two-thirds of the country's market (Weston, 2010). Other companies include ASPCA Pet Health Insurance, Petshealth Care Plan, and AKC Pet Healthcare Plan. All offer plans for dogs and cats, yet VPI is one of only a

---

Annotations (margin notes):

Title, centered

Introductory statement names organization as author with date added in parentheses

Double-spaced throughout

Brackets show additions, and ellipses show omissions within a quotation

Electronic source without pages cited by author, date, and paragraph number

Thesis previews paper's dovelopment

First-level heading in bold type and centered

Citation identifies authors, date, and location in the source (required for quotation and preferred for paraphrase)

Long quotation (40 words or more) indented without quotation marks

Section name and paragraph number locate quotation in electronic source without page numbers

Right margin uneven with no automatic hyphenation

APA References

12

Heading, centered

List alphabetized by last names of authors or by titles (when no author is named)

First line of entry at left margin

Additional lines indented ½

Double-spaced throughout

No period after URL

As many as twenty authors named in References

No period after DOI (digital object identifier) for article

Long URL divided before period, slash, or other punctuation mark

References

Barlyn, S. (2008, March 13). Is pet health insurance worth the price? *The Wall Street Journal,* D2.

Busby, J. (2005). *How to afford veterinary care without mortgaging the kids.* Busby International.

Calhoun, A. (2008, February 8). What I wouldn't do for my cat. *Salon.* http://www.salon.com /2008/02/08/my_1300_cat/

Darlin, D. (2006, May 13). Vet bills and the priceless pet: What's a practical owner to do? *The New York Times.* http://www .nytimes.com /2006/05/13/business/13money.html

Humane Society of the United States. (2012). U.S. pet ownership statistics. http://www.humanesociety.org/ issues/pet_overpopulation/facts/pet_ownership_ statistics.html

Kenney, D. (2009). *Your guide to understanding pet health insurance.* PhiloSophia.

Mathews, A. W. (2009, December 9). Polly want an insurance policy? *The Wall Street Journal.* http://online.wsj.com /articles/SB126065217023489175

McNicholas, J., Gilbey, A., Rennie, A., Ahmedzai, S., Dono, J., & Ormerod, E. (2005). Pet ownership and human health: A brief review of evidence and issues. *British Medical Journal, 331,* 1252-1254. https://doi.org/10.1136/bmj.331.7527.1252

Price, J. (2010, April 9). Should you buy pet health insurance? *The Christian Science Monitor.* http://www.csmonitor.com /Business/Christian-Personal-Finance/2010/0409/ Should-you-buy-pet-health-insurance

Weston, L. P. (2010, November 4). Should you buy pet insurance? *MSN Money.* http://money.msn.com/insurance /should-you-buy-pet-insurance-weston.aspx

Common Academic Values	Common Paper Expectations and Format
Clear presentation of ideas, information, and research findings	■ Text printed out on one side of a white sheet of paper, double-spaced, one-inch margins ■ Paper uses black, 12-point Times New Roman type and has numbered pages
Investigation of an intriguing issue, unanswered question, unsolved puzzle, or unexplored relationship	■ Title and running head to clarify focus for reader ■ Abstract in social sciences or sciences to sum up ■ Opening paragraph or section to express thesis, research question, or conclusions ■ Closing paragraph or section to reinforce conclusions
Academic exchange of ideas and information, including evidence from reliable authorities and investigations	■ Quotations from sources identified by quotation marks or block format ■ Paraphrase, summary, and synthesis of sources ■ Citation of each source in the text when mentioned ■ Well-organized text with transitions and cues to help readers make connections ■ Possibly headings to identify sections
Identification of evidence to allow a reader to evaluate its contribution and join the academic exchange	■ Full information about each source in a concluding list ■ Specific format used for predictable, consistent arrangement of detail

MLA (Modern Language Association) style, explained in the *MLA Handbook,* Eighth Edition (MLA, 2016), is commonly used in the humanities. APA (American Psychological Association) style, explained in the *Publication Manual of the American Psychological Association,* Seventh Edition (American Psychological Association, 2020), is commonly used in the social and behavioral sciences. Both MLA and APA, like other academic styles, specify how a page should look and how sources should be credited. (See pp. Q-2–Q-6.)

For examples showing how to cite and list sources in MLA and APA styles, see E in the Quick Research Guide, pp. Q-31–Q-36.

B | Integrating and Crediting Visuals

Visuals in your text can engage readers, convey information, and reinforce your words. The MLA and APA style guides divide visuals into two groups:

- **Tables** are grids that clearly report numerical data or other information in columns (running up and down) and rows (running across).
- **Figures** include charts, graphs, diagrams, drawings, maps, photographs, or other images.

Much of the time you can create pie charts, bar graphs, or tables in your text file using your software, spreadsheet, or presentation options. Try a drawing program for making diagrams, maps, or sketches or an image editor for scanning print photographs or adding your own digital shots.

When you add visuals from other sources, you can photocopy or scan printed material, pick up online graphics, or turn to the computer lab for sophisticated advice. For a complex project, get help well ahead of your deadline, and allow plenty of time to learn new techniques.

Select or design visuals that are clear, easy to read, and informative.

- To present statistical information, use graphs, charts, or tables.
- To discuss a conflict in a certain geographical area, supply a map.
- To illustrate a reflective essay, scan an image of yourself or an event.
- To clarify stages, steps, or directions for a process, add a diagram.

B1 Position visuals and credit sources.

Present each visual: provide a context for it, identify its purpose, explain its meaning, and help a reader see how it supports your point. Following your style guide, identify and number it as a table or figure. Place the visual near the related text discussion so readers can easily connect the two.

Solve any layout problems in your final draft as you arrange text and visual on the page. For instance, align an image with the left margin to continue the text's forward movement. Use it to balance and support, not overshadow, text. Let the visual draw a reader's eye with an appropriate — not excessive — share of the page. For a long table or large photograph on its own page, simply add page breaks before and after it. To include tables or figures for reference, such as your survey forms, place them in an appendix or collect them in an electronic supplement, as APA suggests.

Acknowledge visual sources as carefully as textual sources. Credit material from a source, printed or electronic, as you present the visual. Ask permission, if required, to use an image from a copyrighted source, including most printed books, articles, and other resources; credit the owner of the copyright. If you download an image from the Web, follow the site guidelines for the use of images. If you are uncertain about whether you can use an image from a source, ask your teacher's advice.

B2 Prepare tables using MLA or APA format.

If you conduct a small survey, use the insert or table menu to create a simple table to summarize responses. Supply a table number and a title or caption before the table. Double-space, add lines to separate sections, and use letters to identify any notes. (For APA style, set the table number in boldface, italicize the title, and insert *Note.* before the note, flush left.)

TABLE FORMAT FOR PRESENTING YOUR SURVEY FINDINGS

Table 1

Sources of Financial Support Reported by Survey Participants[a]

Type of Support	First-Year Students (n = 20)	Other Undergraduates (n = 30)
Scholarship or Campus Grant	25%	20%
Student Loans	40%	57%
Work Study	20%	7%
Family Support	50%	40%
Part-Time or Full-Time Job	25%	57%
Employer or Military Contribution	10%	17%
Other	5%	7%

a. Percentages based on the total number of respondents (n) were calculated and rounded to the nearest whole number.

If your results came from only a few students at one campus, you might compare them with state or national findings, as in the next sample table. When you include a table or an image from a source, credit it, and identify it as a source (MLA) or as adapted (APA) if you have modified it.

TABLE FORMAT FOR MLA AND APA SOURCE CREDITS

Table 2

Percentages of Undergraduates Receiving Selected Types of Financial Aid, by Type of Institution, Attendance Pattern, Dependency Status, and Income Level: 2011-12

Institutional Characteristics	Any Grants	Any Student Loans	Work-Study	Veteran Benefits
Public				
2-year				
(non-doctorate)	50.5	17.6	1.9	2.9
4-year	55.3	39.4	5.3	3.2
4-year (doctorate)	59.9	55.5	6.2	2.8

Source: Radwin, David, et al. *2011-12 National Postsecondary Student Aid Study (NPSAS:12): Student Financial Aid Estimates for 2011-12.* National Center for Education Statistics, Aug. 2013, nces.ed.gov/pubs2013/2013165.pdf.

(Marginal annotations)

Table number

Title or caption

Letter keyed to note

Column headings

Pair of rules or lines to enclose heading

Rule or line to mark end

Note of explanation if needed

Table number (boldface for APA)

Title or caption (italics for APA)

Column headings

Spanner heading (for all rows) centered

MLA source credit

The credit on page Q-9 follows MLA style; the credit below follows APA. At the end, add the date and name as any copyright holder requests.

APA source credit

Note. Adapted from U.S. Department of Education, Institute of Education Sciences, National Center for Education Statistics. 2013. *2011-12 National Postsecondary Student Aid Study* (NCES Publication No. NPSAS:12), Table 1.

B3 Add diagrams, graphs, charts, and other figures.

Select or design figures purposefully. Consider your readers' needs as you decide which types might convey information effectively. A diagram can help readers see the sequence of steps in a process. A graph can show how different groups of people behave over time. A sketch of an old building can illustrate the style of its era. Add a clear caption or title to identify what you are illustrating as well as labels for readers to note key elements, add numerical or textual detail, and use visual elements—size, shape, direction, color—to emphasize, connect, or contrast.

- A diagram can simplify a complex process and clarify its stages. Figure Q.1 shows the stages in the studying process.
- A comparative line graph can show how trends change over time. Figure Q.2 illustrates how driver distraction contributes to accidents.

Figure Q.1
A Diagram Showing the Study Process

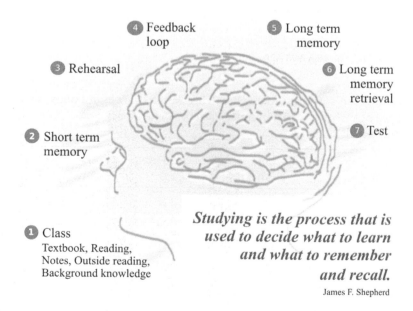

4 Feedback loop

5 Long term memory

3 Rehearsal

6 Long term memory retrieval

2 Short term memory

7 Test

1 Class
Textbook, Reading, Notes, Outside reading, Background knowledge

Studying is the process that is used to decide what to learn and what to remember and recall.

James F. Shepherd

Source: www.howtostudy.org

- A column or bar graph can compare relative values. Figure Q.3 illustrates the same data found in Q.2 in a different format.
- A map can present geographical or spatial data. Figure Q.4 shows the geographical range of the Great Lakes basin, which was the subject of a collaborative FEMA study.

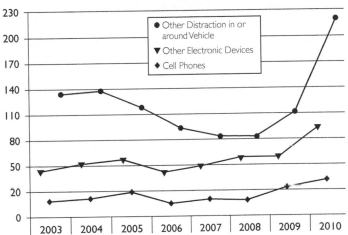

Number of Automobile Accidents Attributed to Driver Distractions in Sedgwick County, 2003-2010

- ● Other Distraction in or around Vehicle
- ▼ Other Electronic Devices
- ◆ Cell Phones

Figure Q.2 Data Represented as a Graph

Sedgwick County Health Department.

Source: Kansas, Sedgwick County, Sedgwick County Health Deptartment. *Sedgwick County Health Department Data Book*. Sedgwick County Health Department, Mar. 2012, p. 14, www.naccho.org/uploads/downloadable-resources/Sedgwick-CHA-Part-1-Data-Book.pdf.

Number of Automobile Accidents Attributed to Driver Distractions in the State of Kansas and Sedgwick County

Figure Q.3 Data Represented as a Table

Sedgwick County Health Department.

Year	Cell Phones		Other Electronic Devices		Other Distraction in or around Vehicle	
	KS	▼ SG	KS	◆ SG	KS	● SG
2003	198	45	81	12	956	133
2004	260	53	111	16	991	138
2005	292	58	104	19	909	119
2006	350	44	104	8	843	96
2007	350	49	111	14	802	84
2008	394	61	102	13	832	84
2009	499	61	201	23	1,020	113
2010	536	95	180	35	1,303	223

Source: Kansas, Sedgwick County, Sedgwick County Health Department. *Sedgwick County Health Department Data Book*. Sedgwick County Health Department, Mar. 2012, p. 14, www.naccho.org/uploads/downloadable-resources/Sedgwick-CHA-Part-1-Data-Book.pdf.

Figure Q.4 Map

FEMA.

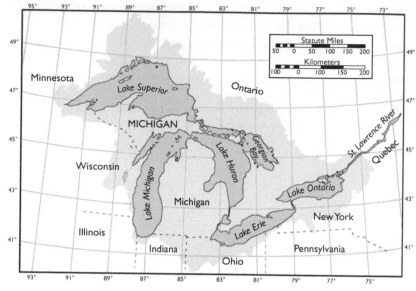

States/Provinces of the Great Lakes Basin.

Source: Department of Homeland Security, Federal Emergency Management Agency. "States/Provinces of the Great Lakes Basin." *Great Lakes Coastal Flood Study Summary Fact Sheet.* Great Lakes Coastal Flood Study, 5 April 2012, p. 1, greatlakescoast.org/pubs/factSheets/GLCFS_FS1_ProgramSummary.pdf.

C | Preparing a Document Template

Unless your teacher encourages creative formatting, avoid experimenting with a college paper. Follow the assigned format and style; check your draft against your instructor's directions and against examples (such as the MLA and APA samples here). Use your software's Help function to learn how to set font, page, format, or template features such as these:

- placement of information on the first page
- margin widths for the top, bottom, and sides of the page (such as 1″)
- name of font (Times New Roman), style (regular roman, italics, or bold), and size of type (12 point)
- running head with automatic page numbering
- double spacing (without extra space between paragraphs)
- text alignment, even on the left but not on the right (left alignment, not centered text, with automatic hyphenation of words turned off)
- width of the paragraph indentation and special "hanging" indentation for your final list of sources
- any other features of the required format

A template simplifies using expected features every time you write a paper with the same specifications. If you have trouble setting features or saving the template, get help from your instructor, a classmate, the writing center, or the computer lab. Follow these steps to create your template:

1. Format your paper the way you want it to look.
2. Create a duplicate copy of your formatted file.
3. Delete all text discussion in the duplicate document.
4. Use the Save As feature to save the file as a document template.
5. Give the template a clear name ("Comp paper" or "MLA form").
6. To open a new file, select this template from your template folder.

D | Solving Common Format Problems

Software programs differ, as do versions of the same software. Watch for default settings or format shifts that do not match an academic format.

- Reset the settings to avoid extra lines between paragraphs or automatic hyphenation.
- Use your software's Help function to look up the feature by naming it (paragraph), identifying the issue (paragraph spacing), or specifying what you want to do (troubleshoot paragraph spacing).

Other problems can arise because academic style guides make their own assumptions about the texts their users are likely to write. For example, MLA style assumes you will write an essay, simply separate items in a list with commas, and probably limit additions to tables and illustrations. On the other hand, APA style assumes you probably need section headings, lists (numbered, bulleted, or lettered within a sentence), and appendices, especially for research materials such as sample questionnaires. In addition, your instructor might require an outline or links for online sources. Follow your instructor's advice if your paper requires formatting that the style you are using (MLA or APA) does not recognize.

Readers appreciate your consideration of their practical problems, too. A clear, neat, readable document is one that readers can readily absorb. For example, your instructor might ask you to reprint a paper if your toner cartridge is nearly empty. Papers in a standard format are easier on the eyes than those with faint print or unusual features. In addition, such papers have margin space for comments so they are easy to grade. If you submit an electronic file, pay attention to online formatting conventions.

E | Designing Other Documents for Your Audience

Four key principles of document design can help you prepare effective documents in and out of the classroom: know your audience, satisfy them with the features and format they expect, consider their circumstances, and remember your purpose.

DESIGNING FOR YOUR AUDIENCE

☐ Who are your readers? What matters to them? How might the format of your document acknowledge their values, goals, and concerns?

☐ What form or genre do readers expect? Which of its features and details do they see as typical? What visual evidence would they find appropriate?

☐ What problems or constraints will your readers face as they read your document? How can your design help reduce these problems?

☐ What is the purpose of your document? How can its format help achieve this purpose? How might it enhance your credibility as a writer?

☐ What is the usual format of your document? Find and analyze a sample.

E1 Select type font, size, and face.

Typography refers to the appearance of letters on a page. In your word-processing program, you can change typeface or font style from roman to bold or italics or change type size for a passage by highlighting it and clicking on the appropriate toolbar icon.

Most college papers and many other documents use Times New Roman in a 12-point size. Signs, posters, and visuals such as slides for presentations might require larger type (with a larger number for the point size). Test such materials for readability by printing samples in various type sizes and standing back from them at the distance of your intended audience. Size also varies with different typefaces because they occupy different amounts of horizontal space on the page. Figure Q.5 shows the space required for the same sentence written in four different 12-point fonts.

Figure Q.5 Space Occupied by Different Typefaces

Times New Roman	An estimated 40 percent of young children have an imaginary friend.
Courier New	An estimated 40 percent of young children have an imaginary friend.
Helvetica	An estimated 40 percent of young children have an imaginary friend.
Calibri	An estimated 40 percent of young children have an imaginary friend.

Fonts also vary in design. Times New Roman and Courier New are called *serif* fonts because they have small tails, or serifs, at the ends of the letters.

Helvetica and the more casual Calibri are *sans serif*—without serifs—and thus have solid, straight lines without tails at the tips of the letters.

Times New Roman (serif)   K k P p
Helvetica (sans serif)   K k P p

Sans serif fonts have a clean look, desirable for headlines, ads, "pull quotes" (in larger type to catch the reader's eye), and text within APA-style figures. More readable serif fonts are used for article (or "body") text. Times New Roman, the common font preferred for MLA and APA styles, was developed for the *Times* newspaper in London. As needed, use light, slanted *italics* (for certain titles) or dark **bold** (for APA headings).

E2 Organize effective lists.

The placement of material on a page—its layout—can make information more accessible for readers. MLA style recognizes common ways of integrating a list within a sentence: introduce the list with a colon or dash (or set it off with two dashes); separate its items with commas, or use semicolons if the items include commas. APA style adds options, preceding each item in a sentence with a letter enclosed by parentheses, such as (a), (b), and (c), or using display lists—set off from text—for visibility and easy reading.

One type of displayed list, the numbered list, can emphasize priorities, conclusions, or processes such as steps in research procedures, how-to advice, or instructions, as in this simple sequence for making clothes:

NUMBERED LIST

1. Lay out the pattern and fabric you have selected.
2. Pin the pattern to the fabric, noting the arrows and grain lines.
3. Cut out the fabric pieces, following the outline of the pattern.
4. Sew the garment together using the pattern's step-by-step instructions.

Another type of displayed list sets off a bit of information with a bullet, most commonly a small round mark (•) but sometimes a square (■), from the toolbar. Bulleted lists are common in résumés and business documents but not necessarily in academic papers, though APA style now recognizes them. Use them to identify items when you do not wish to suggest any order of priority, as in this list of tips for saving energy.

BULLETED LIST

- Let your hair dry without running a hair dryer.
- Commute by public transportation.
- Turn down the thermostat by a few degrees.
- Unplug your phone charger and TV during the day.

E3 Consider adding headings.

In a complex research report, business proposal, or Web document, headings show readers how the document is structured, which sections are most important, and how parts are related. Headings also name sections so readers know where they are and where they're going. Headings at different levels should differ from each other and from the main text in placement and style, making the text easy to scan for key points.

For academic papers, MLA encourages writers to organize by outlining their essays but doesn't recommend or discuss text headings. In contrast, APA illustrates five levels of headings beginning with these two:

First-Level Heading Centered in Bold

Second-Level Heading on the Left in Bold

Besides looking the same, headings at the same level in your document should be brief, clear, and informative. They also should use consistent parallel phrasing. If you write a level-one heading as an *-ing* phrase, do the same for all the level-one headings that follow. Here are some examples of four common patterns for phrasing headings.

For more on parallel structure, see section B2 in the Quick Editing Guide, p. Q-47.

-*ING* PHRASES

Using the College Catalog

Choosing Courses

Declaring a Major

NOUN PHRASES

E-Commerce Benefits

E-Commerce Challenges

Online Shopper Profiles

QUESTIONS

What Is Hepatitis C?

Who Is at Risk?

How Is Hepatitis C Treated?

IMPERATIVE SENTENCES

Initiate Your IRA Rollover

Balance Your Account

Select New Investments

Web pages—especially home pages and site guides—are designed to help readers find information quickly, within a small viewing frame that may change shape and size across devices. For this reason, they generally have more headings than other documents. If you design a Web page or post your course portfolio, consider what different readers might want to find. Then design your headings and content to meet their needs.

F | Organizing a Résumé and an Application Letter

When your reader is a prospective employer, present a solid, professional job application, preferably a one-page résumé and application letter (see pp. Q-18–Q-19). Both should be clearly organized to show why you are a strong candidate for the position. The purpose of your résumé is to organize the details of your education and experience (usually by category and by reverse chronology) so they are easy to review. Wording matters, so use action verbs and parallel structure to convey your experience and enthusiasm. The purpose of your application letter is to highlight your qualifications and motivate the reader to interview and eventually hire you. A follow-up letter might thank your interviewer, confirm your interest, and supply anything requested. Write clearly, and use a standard format; a sloppy letter might suggest that you lack the communication skills employers value.

Your campus career center may provide sample application letters and résumés so you can compare layout variations, evaluate their impact, and effectively design your own. To apply for a professional program, internship, or other opportunity, simply adapt your letter and résumé. For an electronic job application form, select relevant information from your résumé and embed as many key words as possible that might be used to sort or rank applications.

Splits heading with contact information

Catherine Michaels

65 Oakwood Ave. Apt. #105
Somerville, MA 02144
Mobile 617-555-5555
crmichaels@comnet.com

Places current information first

Experience

Research Analyst *June 2018–Present*
Industrial Economist, Incorporated — Cambridge, MA

Develop profit estimation model, adopted as practice area standard, for petroleum bulk stations
Create and implement valuation methodology for a major privately held forestry company

Intern, Global Treasury — **Investment Management Team** *June 2017–August 2017*
State Street Corporation — Boston, MA

Specifies activities

Research and analyze corporate bonds, including economics and industry analyses

Education

Bachelor of Arts — Bates College, Lewiston, ME *September 2014–May 2018*

Major: Economics Related Courses: Calculus; Advanced Statistics and Economics
Minor: Japanese

Skills & Competencies

Uses bold type to highlight categories

Statistical Packages: SAS, STATA, R
Programming Languages & Related: VBA, Python, SQL, LINUX/UNIX, Scripting (KHS/BASH), DOS
Microsoft Office: Advanced Excel, PowerPoint
Other: Cloud Computing (PaaS, AWS, shell interaction, batch processing), Hadoop Ecosystem
Languages and Music: Conversational Japanese, Guitar, Saxophone, Banjo

Labels sections and uses dividers

Leadership & Involvement

Analytic Pro Bono Work (present)
Leverage data mining skills to assist nonprofit organizations
Consult on data collection and management
Improve donation volume and donor retention

Boston Data Science Community
Participate actively in industry groups, Boston Predictive Analytics, Boston R Users

Alpine Climbing (2015–present)
Organize route finding and equipment logistics
Lead trips throughout California, Canadian Rockies, and New England

65 Oakwood Ave. Apt. #105
Somerville, MA 02144
15 May 2019

Ross Landon
Denver Stategists
8866 Larimer Street, Suite 404
Denver, CO 80217

Dear Mr. Landon:

Josh Greenway, formerly a data analyst with Denver Strategists, recommended that I contact you about the upcoming expansion of your Marketing Analysis Group. I am looking for an opportunity to combine my college major in economics with my long-standing interest in statistics. Because your expansion promises an excellent opportunity to do so, I wish to apply for one of your openings for a data analyst.

As my résumé indicates, my college internship with the Investment Management Team at Global Treasury introduced me to the many processes involved in industry analyses. Since graduation, I have worked as a research analyst at Industrial Economics, estimating valuation and profits for clients in diverse industries. In addition, as a pro bono consultant with Boston nonprofit organizations, I have expanded my expertise with statistics packages. For these groups, I have directed my skills to improving data mining and data management in order to help them cultivate and retain contributors more effectively.

I am now looking forward to designing and conducting more complex data mining and data analysis projects. Joining your expansion team would offer me a welcome opportunity to develop my analytic skills, expand my experience with various statistical methods, and gain sophistication working with team colleagues as well as a variety of clients. For me, data analysis is a challenging and rewarding way to combine my skills in math, statistics, and technology with the creativity data science requires. Both my education and my experience have prepared me to address a company's problems or change a client's perspective through data-based analysis.

I would be happy to meet with you to learn more about your plans for the Marketing Analysis Group. Please call me at 617-555-5555, e-mail me at crmichaels@comnet.com, or write to me at the address above. I appreciate your consideration and look forward to hearing from you.

Sincerely,
Catherine Michaels
Catherine Michaels

Enclosure: Résumé

Follows standard letter format

Addresses specific person

Identifies job sought and describes interests

Explains qualifications

Confirms interest

Supplies contact information

Includes resume with letter

Quick Research Guide

When you begin college, you may feel uncertain about what to say and how to speak up. As you gain experience, you will join the academic exchange around you by reading, thinking, and writing with sources. You will turn to articles, books, and websites for evidence to support your thesis and develop your ideas, advancing knowledge through exchange.

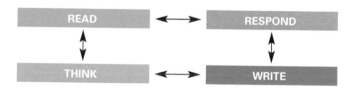

Conducting research requires time to explore, to think, and to respond. However, efficient and purposeful research can produce greater success in less time than optimistic browsing. Maybe you need more confidence or good advice fast: you've procrastinated, you're overwhelmed, or you're uncertain about how to proceed. To help you, this Quick Research Guide concentrates on five key steps.

TURNING TO SOURCES FOR SUPPORTING EVIDENCE

A | Defining Your Quest

Especially when your research goals are specific and limited, you're more likely to succeed if you try to define the hunt in advance.

PURPOSE CHECKLIST

☐ What is the thesis you want to support, point you want to show, question you want to answer, or problem you want to solve?

For more about stating and using a thesis, see pp. 266–71.

☐ Does the assignment require or suggest certain types of supporting evidence, sources, or presentations of material?

☐ Which ideas do you want to support with good evidence?

☐ Which ideas might you want to check, clarify, or change?

☐ Which ideas or opinions of others do you want to verify or counter?

☐ Do you want to analyze material yourself (for example, comparing different articles or websites) or to find someone else's analysis?

For more about types of evidence, see pp 136–38.

☐ What kinds of evidence do you want to use — facts, statistics, or expert testimony? Do you also want to add your own firsthand observation?

TWO VIEWS OF SUPPORTING EVIDENCE

COLLEGE WRITER	COLLEGE READER
• Does it answer my question and support my thesis?	• Is it relevant to the purpose and assignment?
• Does it seem accurate?	• Is it reliable, given academic standards?
• Is it recent enough?	• Is it current, given the standards of the field?
• Does it add enough detail and depth?	• Is it of sufficient quantity, variety, and strength?
• Is it balanced enough?	• Is it typical and fair?
• Will it persuade my audience?	• Does the writer make a credible case?

For evidence checklists, see pp. 138–39 and p. Q-24.

A1 Decide what supporting evidence you need.

When you want to add muscle to college papers, you need reliable resources to supply facts, statistics, and expert testimony to back up your claims. You may not need comprehensive information, but you will want to hunt—quickly and efficiently—for exactly what you do need. That evidence should satisfy you as a writer and meet the criteria of your college readers—instructors and possibly classmates. Suppose you want to propose solutions to your community's employment problem.

WORKING THESIS

Many residents of Aurora need more—and more innovative—higher education to improve their job skills and career alternatives.

Because you already have ideas based on your firsthand observations and the experiences of people you know, your research goals are limited. First, you want to add accurate facts and figures that will show why you believe a compelling problem exists. Next, you want to visit the websites of local educational institutions and possibly locate someone to interview about existing career development programs.

A2 Decide where you need supporting evidence.

As you plan or draft, you may tuck in notes to yourself—figure that out, find this, look it up, get the numbers here. Other times, you may not know exactly what or where to add. One way to determine where you need supporting evidence is to examine your draft, sentence by sentence.

- What does each sentence claim or promise to a reader?

- Where do you provide supporting evidence to demonstrate the claim or fulfill the promise?

The answers to these questions—your statements and your supporting evidence—often fall into a common alternating pattern:

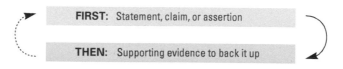

FIRST: Statement, claim, or assertion

THEN: Supporting evidence to back it up

For more about arguments based on claims of substantiation, evaluation, or policy, see pp. 135–36.

For more on inductive and deductive reasoning, see pp. 298–99.

When you spot a string of assertions without much support, you've found a place where you might need more evidence. Select reliable evidence so that it substantiates the exact statement, claim, or assertion that precedes it. Likewise, if you spot a string of examples, details, facts, quotations, or other evidence, introduce or conclude it with an interpretive statement that explains the point the evidence supports. Make sure your general statement connects and pulls together all the particular evidence.

When Carrie Williamson introduced her cause-and-effect paper, "Rain Forest Destruction," she made a general statement and then supported it by quoting facts from a source. Then she repeated this statement-support pattern, backing up her next statement in turn. By using this pattern from the very beginning, Carrie reassured her readers that she was a trustworthy writer who would try to supply convincing evidence throughout her paper.

The tropical rain forests are among the most biologically diverse communities in the world. According to the Rainforest Alliance, "The forests of the Neotropics are the habitat for tens of thousands of plant and wildlife species," as in "a single square mile of tropical forest in Rondonia, Brazil," which is home to "1,200 species of butterflies—twice the total number found in the United States and Canada" ("Conservation"). These amazing communities depend on each part being intact in order to function properly but are being destroyed at an alarming rate. Over several decades, even in protected areas, only 2% increased while 85% "suffered declines in surrounding forest cover" (Laurance et al. 291). Many rain forest conservationists debate the leading cause of deforestation. Regardless of which is the major cause, logging, slash-and-burn farming, and resource exploitation are destroying more of the rain forests each year.

> Statement
>
> Supporting evidence: Information and statistics about species
>
> Statement
>
> Supporting evidence: Facts about destruction
>
> Statement identifying cause-and-effect debate
>
> Statement previewing points to come

The table below shows some of the many ways this common statement-support pattern can be used to clarify and substantiate your ideas.

First: Statement, Claim, or Assertion	Then: Supporting Evidence
Introduces a topic	Facts or statistics to justify the importance or significance of the topic
Describes a situation	Factual examples or illustrations to convey reality or urgency
Introduces an event	Accurate firsthand observations to describe an event that you have witnessed
Presents a problem	Expert testimony or firsthand observation to establish the necessity or urgency of a solution
Explains an issue	Facts and details to clarify or justify the significance of the issue
States your point	Facts, statistics, or examples to support your viewpoint or position
Prepares for evidence that follows	Facts, examples, observations, or research findings to develop your case
Concludes with your recommendation or evaluation	Facts, examples, or expert testimony to persuade readers to accept your conclusion

Use the following checklist to help you decide whether—and where—you might need supporting evidence from sources.

EVIDENCE CHECKLIST

☐ What does your thesis promise that you'll deliver? What additional evidence would ensure that you effectively demonstrate your thesis?

☐ Are your statements, claims, and assertions backed up with supporting evidence? If not, what evidence might you add?

☐ What evidence would most effectively persuade your readers?

☐ What criteria for useful evidence matter most for your assignment or your readers? What evidence would best meet these criteria?

☐ Which parts of your paper sound weak or incomplete to you?

☐ What facts or statistics would clarify your topic?

☐ What examples or illustrations would make the background or the current circumstances clearer and more compelling for readers?

☐ What does a reliable expert say about the situation your topic involves?

☐ What firsthand observation would add authenticity?

☐ Where have peers or your instructor suggested more or stronger evidence?

B | Searching for Recommended Sources

When you need to search efficiently, begin with reliable sources, already screened by professionals. Your college library buys books, subscribes to scholarly journals, and acquires print and electronic resources; these are expected to follow accepted editorial practices. Well-regarded publishers and professional groups turn to peer reviewers—experts in the field—to assess articles or books before they are selected for publication. These quality controls bring readers material that meets academic or professional standards.

B1 Seek advice about reliable sources.

Your challenge is not simply to find any sources but to find solid sources with reliable evidence. The following questions can help you find solid sources fast—ideally already screened, selected, and organized for you.

RESOURCE CHECKLIST

☐ Have you talked with your instructor after class, during office hours, or by e-mail to ask for advice about resources for your topic? Have you checked the assignment, syllabus, handouts, or class website?

☐ Have your classmates recommended useful academic databases, disciplinary websites, or similar resources?

☐ Does the department offering the course have a website with lists of library resources or links to sites well regarded in that field?

☐ Which search strategies and library databases does the librarian at the reference desk recommend for your course and topic?

☐ Which databases or links on your library's website lead to government (federal, state, or local) resources or articles in journals and newspapers?

☐ Which resources are available through the online library catalog or in any periodicals or reference area of your campus library?

B2 Select reliable sources that meet readers' criteria.

For some assignments, you might be expected to use varied sources: reports from journalists, advice from practitioners in the field, accounts of historical eyewitnesses, or opposing opinions on civic policy. For other assignments, you might be expected to turn only to scholarly sources — also identified as peer-reviewed or refereed sources — with characteristics such as these:

- in-depth investigation or interpretation of an academic topic or problem
- discussion of previous studies, which are cited in the text and listed at the end for easy reference by readers
- use of research methods accepted in a discipline or several fields
- publication by a reputable company or sponsoring organization
- acceptance for publication based on the author's credentials and reviews by experts (peer reviewers) who assess the quality of the study
- preparation for publication supervised by academic or expert editors or by authors and professional staff

Your instructors are likely to favor these quality controls. Your campus librarian can help you limit your searches to peer-reviewed journals or check the scholarly reputation of sources that you find.

C | Evaluating Possible Sources

Like the perfect wave or the perfect day, the perfect source is hard to come by. Instead of looking for perfect sources, evaluate sources on the basis of practicality, standards, and evidence.

C1 Evaluate sources as a practical researcher.

Your situation as a writer may determine how long or how widely you can search or how deeply you can delve into the sources you find. If you are worried about finishing on time or about juggling several assignments, you will need to search efficiently, using your own practical criteria.

```
                    ┌─────────────┐
                    │  Accessible │
                    │   sources   │
                    └─────────────┘
  ┌──────────┐                              ┌──────────────┐
  │ Readable │                              │  Up-to-date  │
  │ sources  │                              │ sources with │
  └──────────┘                              │    timely    │
                                            │ information  │
              ┌────────────────────┐        └──────────────┘
              │    A student       │
              │ researcher's       │
              │ criteria for       │
              │ efficient research │
  ┌──────────┐└────────────────────┘        ┌──────────────┐
  │Pertinent │                              │    Sound     │
  │sources   │                              │ sources with │
  │with      │                              │ clear facts  │
  │useful    │       ┌──────────┐           │ and          │
  │details   │       │ Reliable │           │ statistics   │
  │and       │       │sources   │           └──────────────┘
  │examples  │       │with      │
  └──────────┘       │expert    │
                     │testimony │
                     └──────────┘
```

C2 Evaluate sources as your readers would.

If you are uncertain about college requirements, start with recommended sources that are easily accessible, readable, and up-to-date. Look for sources that are chock-full of reliable facts, statistics, research findings, case studies, observations, examples, and expert testimony to persuade your readers.

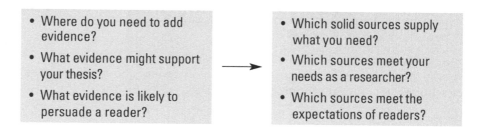

- Where do you need to add evidence?
- What evidence might support your thesis?
- What evidence is likely to persuade a reader?

→

- Which solid sources supply what you need?
- Which sources meet your needs as a researcher?
- Which sources meet the expectations of readers?

C3 Evaluate sources for reliable and appropriate evidence.

When you use evidence from sources to support your points, both you and your readers are likely to hold two simple expectations:

- that your sources are reliable so you can trust their information
- that the information you select from them is appropriate for your paper

After all, how could an unreliable source successfully support your ideas? And what could unsuitable or mismatched information contribute? The difficulty, of course, is learning how to judge what is reliable and appropriate. The following checklist suggests how you can use the time-tested journalist's questions to evaluate print or electronic sources.

SOURCE EVALUATION CHECKLIST

Who?

☐ Who is the author? What are the author's credentials and experience?

☐ Who is the intended audience? Is it general or academic?

☐ Who publishes or sponsors the source? Is this publisher well regarded?

☐ Who has reviewed the source before publication? Only the author?
Expert peer reviewers or referees? An editorial staff?

What?

☐ What is the purpose of the publication or website? Is it trying to sell,
inform, report, or shape opinion?

☐ What bias or point of view might affect the reliability of the source?

☐ What evidence does the source present? Does the source seem trustworthy
and logical? Does it identify its sources or supply active links?

When?

☐ When was the source published or created? When was it revised?

☐ When has it been cited by others in the field?

Where?

☐ Where did you find the source?

☐ Where is the source recommended? Has your library supplied it?

Why?

☐ Why would you use this source rather than others?

☐ Why is its information relevant to your research question?

How?

☐ How would it support your thesis and provide persuasive evidence?

☐ How does the source reflect its author, publisher or sponsor, and audience?
How might you need to qualify its use in your paper?

D | Capturing, Introducing, and Citing Evidence Added from Sources

Sometimes researchers concentrate so hard on hunting for reliable sources that they forget what comes next. The value of every source remains potential until you successfully capture its facts, statistics, expert testimony, examples, or other information in a form that you can incorporate into your paper. Then you need to introduce the information in order to identify its

For examples in both MLA and APA style, see E1–E2.

source or its contribution to your paper. Finally, you must accurately cite or credit, both in the text of your paper and in a final list of sources, each source whose words or ideas you use.

D1 Avoid plagiarism.

Allow enough time to add information from sources skillfully and correctly. Find out exactly how your instructor expects you to credit sources. Even if you do not intend to plagiarize—to use another writer's words or ideas without appropriately crediting them—a paper full of sloppy or careless shortcuts can look just like a paper deliberately copied from unacknowledged sources. Instead, borrow carefully and honestly.

Identify the source of information, any idea, summary, paraphrase, or quotation, right away, as soon as you add it to your notes. Carry that acknowledgment into your first draft and all the drafts that follow. You generally do not need to identify a source if you use what is called "common knowledge"—quotations, expressions, or information widely known and widely accepted. If you are uncertain about the need for a citation, ask your instructor, or simply provide the citation.

D2 Read your source critically.

For more on critical reading, see Ch. 2. For more on evaluating evidence, see pp. 138–39. For more on logical fallacies, see pp. 145–46.

Before you pop outside material into your paper, read critically to evaluate its reliability and suitability. If you cannot understand a source that requires specialized background, don't use it. If its ideas, facts, claims, or viewpoint seem unusual, incorporate only what you can substantiate in unrelated sources. If its evidence seems accurate, logical, and relevant, decide exactly how you might want to add it to your paper. Carefully distinguish it from your own ideas, whether you quote, paraphrase, or summarize.

D3 Quote accurately.

For more on punctuating quotations and using ellipsis marks, see D3 in the Quick Editing Guide, pp. Q-61–Q-62.

As you take notes, record as many quotations as you want if that process helps you master the material. When you add quotations to your paper, be selective. A quotation in itself is not necessarily effective evidence, and too many quotations will suggest that your writing is padded or lacks original thought. Quote exactly, and credit your source using the format expected.

QUOTATION CHECKLIST

☐ Have you quoted only a notable passage that adds support and authority?

☐ Have you checked your quotation word by word, for accuracy?

☐ Have you marked the beginning and the ending with quotation marks?

☐ Have you used ellipses (. . .) to mark any spot where you have left out words in the original?

☐ Have you identified the source of the quotation in a signal phrase (see D6) or in parentheses?

☐ Have you recorded in parentheses the page number or paragraph number where the quotation appears in the source?

D4 Paraphrase carefully.

A paraphrase presents a passage from a source in your own words and sentences. It may include the same level of detail as the original, but it should not slip into the original wording (unless you identify those snippets with quotation marks). Credit the original source as you do when you quote.

For more about how to quote, paraphrase, and summarize, see pp. 193–97.

PARAPHRASE CHECKLIST

☐ Have you read the passage critically to be sure you understand it?

☐ Have you paraphrased accurately, reflecting both the main points and the supporting details in the original?

☐ Does your paraphrase use your own words without repeating or echoing the words or the sentence structure of the original?

☐ Does your paraphrase stick to the ideas of the original?

☐ Have you revised your paraphrase so it reads smoothly and clearly?

☐ Have you identified the source of the paraphrase in a signal phrase (see D6) or in parentheses?

☐ Have you recorded in parentheses the page number or paragraph number where the passage appears in the source?

D5 Summarize fairly.

A summary clearly identifies the source and reduces its ideas to their essence. Using your own words, your summary may boil a book, a chapter, an article, or a section down to a few sentences that accurately and clearly sum up the sense of the original.

SUMMARY CHECKLIST

☐ Have you read critically to be sure you understand the source?

☐ Have you fairly stated the author's main point in your own words?

☐ Have you briefly stated any supporting ideas that you wish to sum up?

☐ Have you stuck to the overall point without bogging down in details?

☐ Is your summary respectful of others, even if you disagree with them?

☐ Have you revised your summary so it reads smoothly and clearly?

☐ Have you identified the source of the summary in a signal phrase (see D6) or in parentheses?

☐ Have you recorded in parentheses the page number or paragraph number where any specific passage appears in the source?

D6 Introduce and cite each quotation, paraphrase, summary, and synthesis.

Weave ideas from sources into your paper so that they effectively support the point you want to make. As you integrate each idea, take three steps.

1. Capture. Begin with the evidence you have captured from your source. Refine this material so that it will fit smoothly into your paper. Reduce your quotation to its most memorable words, freshen the wording of your paraphrase, or tighten your summary. Synthesize by pulling together your own ideas and those of your sources to reach new insights. Position the evidence where it is needed to support your statements.

2. Introduce. Avoid tossing stand-alone quotations into your paper or stacking up a series of paraphrases and summaries. Instead, use your signal phrase to lead smoothly into your source information. Try to draw on the authority of the source, mention the author's credentials, or connect the material to other sources or to your points. Let readers know why you have selected this evidence and what you think it adds to your paper.

For more on signal phrases, see pp. 199–200.

Dalton, long an advocate of "green" construction, recommends . . . (18).

As a specialist in elder law, attorney Tamara Diaz suggests . . . (57).

For more on punctuating quotations, see D3 in the Quick Editing Guide, pp. Q-61–Q-62.

Like Westin, regional director Neil urges that ". . ." (308). Brown, however, takes an innovative approach to local conservation practices and recommends . . . (108).

Another policy analyst, arguing from principles expressed in the Bill of Rights, maintains . . . (Frank 96).

While Congress pits secure borders against individual liberties, immigration analyst Smith proposes a third option that . . . (42).

For examples showing how to cite and list sources in your paper, see section E.

3. Cite. Identify each source briefly yet accurately. Follow MLA, APA, or another academic format.

- Name the author in parentheses (unless named in a signal phrase).
- In APA style, add the date of the source.
- Add an exact page number (or, for APA, a paragraph number, or section heading) to locate the original passage.

- If a source does not name its author, begin the citation with the first words of the title.
- Add a full entry for each source to a list at the end of your paper.

E | Citing and Listing Sources in MLA or APA Style

MLA style is the format for crediting sources that is recommended by the Modern Language Association and often required in English classes. APA style, the format recommended by the American Psychological Association, is often used in social sciences, business, and some composition classes. These two styles are widely used in college papers, but your specialized courses may require other academic styles, depending on the field. Because instructors expect you to credit sources carefully, follow any directions or examples supplied, or refer to the style manual required. Although academic styles all credit sources, their details differ. Stick to the one expected.

In both the MLA and APA styles, your sources need to be identified twice in your paper: first, briefly, at the very moment you draw upon the source material and later, in full, at the end of your paper. The short reference includes the name of the author of the source (or a short form of the title if the source does not name an author), so it's easy for a reader to connect that short entry in your text with the related full entry in the final alphabetical list.

E1 Cite and list sources in MLA style.

Cite in the text. At the moment you add a quotation, paraphrase, or summary, identify the source. Citations generally follow a simple pattern: name the author, and note the page in the original where the material is located.

> (Last Name of Author ##) (Talia 35) (Smitt and Gilbert 152-53)

Place this citation immediately after a direct quotation or paraphrase.

> When "The Lottery" begins, the reader thinks of the "great pile of stones" (Jackson 260) as children's entertainment.

If you name the author in a signal phrase, the citation is even simpler.

> As Hunt notes, the city faced "a decade of deficits and drought" (54).

For quotations from poems, plays, or novels, supply line, act and scene, or chapter numbers rather than page numbers.

> The speaker in Robinson's poem describes Richard Cory as "richer than a king" (line 9), an attractive man who "fluttered pulses when he said, / 'Good-morning' " (7-8).

To find formats for other types of sources, consult the current *MLA Handbook,* often available in the library, or check your research manual or research guide for more information.

If you use only one source, identify it as your essay begins. Then just give page or line numbers in parentheses after each quote or paraphrase.

CITATION CHECKLIST

☐ Have you placed your citation right after your quotation, paraphrase, or summary?

☐ Have you enclosed your citation in parentheses?

☐ Have you provided the last name of the author either in your signal phrase or in your citation?

☐ Have you used a short title for a work without an identified author?

☐ Have you added any available page or other location number (such as a Web paragraph, poetry line, novel chapter, or play act and scene), as numbered in the source, to identify where the material appears?

List at the end. For each source mentioned in the text, supply a corresponding full entry in a list called "Works Cited" at the end of your paper.

WORKS CITED CHECKLIST

☐ Have you followed the sample pattern for the correct source type as exactly as possible?

☐ Have you used quotation marks and italics correctly for titles?

☐ Have you used correct punctuation — periods, commas, colons, parentheses?

☐ Have you checked the accuracy of numbers: pages, volumes, dates?

☐ Have you accurately recorded names: authors, titles, publishers?

☐ Have you correctly typed or copied in the address of an electronic source that a reader could not otherwise find or that your instructor requires?

☐ Have you correctly arranged your entries in alphabetical order?

☐ Have you checked your final list against your text citations so that every source appears in both places?

☐ Have you double-spaced your list just like your paper, without any extra space between entries?

☐ Have you begun the first line of each entry at the left margin and indented each additional line (the same space you would indent a paragraph)?

For format examples, see the Quick Format Guide, pp. Q-1–Q-19.

Follow MLA patterns. Use the following examples as patterns for your entries. For each type of source, supply the same information in the same order, using the same punctuation or other features.

Book
TEXT CITATION

(Blyth 37)

WORKS CITED ENTRY

Author's name   Period   Title of book, in italics   Period   Year of publication

Shapiro, Dani. *Inheritance: A Memoir of Genealogy, Paternity, and Love.* Knopf, 2019.

Publisher   Period

Essay, Story, or Poem from a Book
TEXT CITATION

(Brady 506)

WORKS CITED ENTRY

Author of selection   Title of selection, in quotation marks   Title of book or anthology, in italics

Adichie, Chimamanda Ngozi. "Happy Feminist." *The Bedford Guide for College Writers with Reader*, edited by X. J. Kennedy, Dorothy M. Kennedy, and Marcia F. Muth, 12th ed., Bedford/St. Martin's, 2020, pp. 426-28.

Authors or editors of book   Publisher of book   Year of publication   Page numbers of selection

See the title page of this book and the reading on pp. 426–28 to find the details needed for this entry.

Popular Magazine Article
The author's name and the title generally appear at the beginning of an article. If the author is not identified, simply begin your entry with the title. Typically, the magazine name, the date, and page numbers appear at the bottom of pages. Arrange the date in this order: 4 Oct. 2019.

TEXT CITATION

(Freedman 10)

WORKS CITED ENTRY

Author's name   Title of article, in quotation marks   Title of magazine, in italics

Freedman, David H. "The Happiness App." *Discover*, Jan.-Feb. 2013, pp. 10-11.

Date of publication   Page numbers of article

Scholarly Journal Article
TEXT CITATION

(Calomiris and Khan 78)

WORKS CITED ENTRY

Authors' names   Title of article, in quotation marks

Calomiris, Charles W., and Urooj Khan. "An Assessment of TARP Assistance to
  Financial Institutions." *The Journal of Economic Perspectives*, vol. 29, no. 2,
  Spring 2015, pp. 53-80.

Season   Page numbers   Title of journal,   Volume and issue
and year   of article   in italics   number

For an online article, end with the URL.

Author's name   Title of article, in   Title of journal, in
  quotation marks   italics

Giorgio-Pirkey, Lucy. "Journeys Inward: Coming to Academic Voice." *English
  Journal*, vol. 108, no. 3, 2019, ncte.org/library/NCTEFiles/Resources/
  Journals/EJ/1083-jan2019/EJ1083Jan19Journeys.pdf.

Volume and issue   Year   URL
number

Article from a Library Database

In databases, the original publication details often appear at the top of the
entry. List the details of the original publication first in your works cited
entry, separating each detail with a comma and ending with a period, as
shown below. Then provide information about the database, again separating each detail with a comma and ending with a period. Give a DOI (digital
object identifier) if available; if none is provided, give the URL.

TEXT CITATION

Omit the page number when it is not available online.

(Gross and Terra 54)

WORKS CITED ENTRY

Title of article, in   Name of database,
Authors' names   quotation marks   in italics

Title of magazine or
journal, in italics

Gross, Magdalena H., and Luke Terra. "What Makes Difficult History

Volume and issue
numbers, followed by
month or season of
publication

Difficult?" *Phi Delta Kappan*, vol. 99, no. 8, May 2018, pp. 51-56. *ERIC*,
  dx.doi.org/10.1177/0031721718775680.

DOI   Page numbers, followed
by period

Page from a Website

The page title and site title often appear at the top of a given page. The date
when a site was posted or last updated often appears at the bottom, as does
the name of the sponsor (which also may appear as a link). If the sponsor
name is the same as the site name, omit the sponsor name, as illustrated in
the example below.

TEXT CITATION

A site is identified by title if it does not name an author.

According to the Rainforest Alliance, . . .

WORKS CITED ENTRY

No author identified / Title of page, in quotation marks / Title of site, in italics

"Our Work in Sustainable Forestry." *Rainforest-alliance.org*, 2016, www.rainforest-alliance.org/work/forestry.

Date posted or updated / URL

E2 Cite and list sources in APA style.

Cite in the text. After the author's last name, add the date. Use "p." (for "page") or "pp." (for "pages") or "para." or "paras." (for "paragraphs"), or list the section heading to indicate the location of the cited material.

(Last Name of Author, Date, p. ##) (Harper, 2019, para. 3)

(Wulf, 2015, pp. 396-410)

(Lopez, 2019, Symptoms section)

List at the end. Call your list of sources "References." Include all the sources cited in your text except for personal communications and classics.

Follow APA patterns. Use the following examples as patterns for your entries. For each type of source, supply the same information in the same order using the same punctuation or other features.

To find formats for other types of sources, consult the current *Publication Manual of the American Psychological Association*, often available in the library, or check your research manual or research guide for more information.

Book
TEXT CITATION

(Shapiro, 2019, p. 37)

REFERENCES ENTRY

Shapiro, D. (2019). *Inheritance: A memoir of genealogy, paternity, and love.* Knopf.

Work or Section in a Book
TEXT CITATION

(Adichie, 2020, p. 426)

REFERENCES ENTRY

Adichie, C. N. (2020). Happy feminist. In X. J. Kennedy, D. M. Kennedy, & M. F. Muth (Eds.), *The Bedford guide for college writers* (12th ed., pp. 426-428). Bedford/St. Martin's. (Original work published 2014)

Turn to the title page of this book and the reading selection on pp. 426–28 to find the details needed for this entry.

Popular Magazine Article
TEXT CITATION

(Freedman, 2013, p. 11)

REFERENCES ENTRY

Freedman, D. H. (2013, January-February). The happiness app. *Discover, 34*(1), 10-11.

Scholarly Journal Article

For a magazine or journal article, add any volume number in italics and any issue number in parentheses, without a space or italics.

TEXT CITATION

(Calomiris & Khan, 2015, p. 73)

REFERENCES ENTRY

Calomiris, C. W., & Khan, U. (2015). An assessment of TARP assistance to financial institutions. *The Journal of Economic Perspectives, 29*(2), 53-80.

For an online article, end with the DOI or URL.

Giorgio-Pirkey, L. (2019). Journeys inward: Coming to academic voice. *English Journal, 108*(3), ncte.org/library/NCTEFiles/Resources/Journals/EJ/1083-jan2019/ EJ1083Jan19Journeys.pdf

Article from a Library Database

IN-TEXT CITATION

If an exact page number is not available for an online article, list a paragraph number or section heading.

(Gross & Terra, 2018, p. 53)

(Myers, 2019, para. 6)

REFERENCES ENTRY

End with the DOI. Omit the database unless the work is only available through that database.

Gross, M. H., & Terra, L. (2018). What makes difficult history difficult? *Phi Delta Kappan, 99*(8), 51-56. https://doi.org/10.1177/0031721718775680

Page from a Website

TEXT CITATION

Because the website does not name an author, the signal phrase identifies the site's sponsor.

According to the Rainforest Alliance (2016) . . .

REFERENCES ENTRY

Your access date is not needed unless the material is likely to change.

Rainforest Alliance. (2016). Our work in sustainable forestry. http://www .rainforest-alliance.org/work/forestry

For APA format examples, see the Quick Format Guide, pp. Q-1–Q-19.

Quick Editing Guide

A | Editing for Common Grammar Problems Q-38

B | Editing to Ensure Effective Sentences Q-46

C | Editing for Word Choice Q-48

D | Editing for Common Punctuation Problems Q-59

E | Editing for Common Mechanics Problems Q-62

This Quick Editing Guide provides an overview of grammar, style, word choice, punctuation, and mechanics problems typical of college writing.

EDITING CHECKLIST

Common and Serious Problems in College Writing

Grammar Problems

☐ Have you avoided writing sentence fragments?   A1

☐ Have you avoided writing comma splices or fused sentences?   A2

☐ Have you used the correct form for all verbs in the past tense?   A3

☐ Do all verbs agree with their subjects?   A4

☐ Have you used the correct case for all pronouns?   A5

☐ Do all pronouns agree with their antecedents?   A6

☐ Have you used adjectives and adverbs correctly?   A7

Sentence Problems

☐ Does each modifier clearly modify the appropriate sentence element?   B1

☐ Have you used parallel structure where needed?   B2

Word Choice Problems

☐ Have you used appropriate language?   C1

☐ Is your writing clean and concise?   C2

☐ Have you correctly used commonly confused words?   C3

frag
A

Appendix Quick Editing Guide

Punctuation Problems

☐ Have you used commas correctly? — D1

☐ Have you used apostrophes correctly? — D2

☐ Have you punctuated quotations correctly? — D3

Mechanics Problems

☐ Have you used capital letters correctly? — E1

☐ Have you spelled all words correctly? — E2

For editing and proofreading strategies, see pp. 316–18.

Editing and proofreading are needed at the end of the writing process because writers — *all* writers — find it difficult to write error-free sentences the first time they try. Once you are satisfied that you have expressed your ideas, you should make sure that each sentence and word is concise, clear, and correct. Certain common errors in Standard Written English are like red flags to careful readers: they signal that the writer is either ignorant or careless. Use the editing checklist above to check your paper for these problems; then use the editing checklists in each section to help you correct specific errors. Concentrate on any problems likely to reappear in your writing.

Your grammar checker or software can help you catch some errors, but not others. Always consider the grammar checker's suggestions carefully before accepting them and continue to edit on your own.

- A grammar checker can't always identify the subject or verb in a sentence; it may question whether a sentence is complete or whether its subject and verb agree, even when the sentence is correct.

- Grammar checkers are likely to miss misplaced modifiers, faulty parallelism, possessives without apostrophes, or incorrect commas.

- Most grammar checkers do a good job of spotting problems with adjectives and adverbs, such as confusing *good* and *well*.

- Keep track of your mistakes to develop an "error hit list." Use your software's Find capacity to check for searchable problems such as instances of *each* (always singular) or *few* (always plural) to see if all the verbs agree.

A | Editing for Common Grammar Problems

A **subject** names something — a person, an object, an idea, a situation — about which the verb makes an assertion.

A **verb** is a word that shows action or a state of being.

A1 Check for sentence fragments.

A complete sentence has a subject, has a verb, and can stand on its own. A **sentence fragment** cannot stand on its own as a sentence because it lacks a subject, a verb, or both, or for some other reason fails to convey a complete thought. Though common in ads and fiction, fragments are not usually effective in college writing because they do not express coherent thoughts.

> ### At a glance **GUIDE**
>

To edit for fragments, check that each sentence has a subject and a verb and expresses a complete thought. To correct a fragment, complete it by adding a missing part, dropping an unnecessary subordinating conjunction, or joining it to a nearby sentence, if that would make more sense.

Roberto has two sisters , Maya and Leeza.

were
The children going to the zoo.

were caught in a traffic jam.
The children going to the zoo ,

Last night ~~when~~ we saw Viola Davis's most recent movie.

EDITING CHECKLIST

Fragments

☐ Does the sentence have both a subject and a verb?

☐ If the sentence contains a subordinate clause, does it contain a clause that is a complete sentence too?

☐ If you find a fragment, can you link it to an adjoining sentence, eliminate its subordinating conjunction, or add any missing element?

A2 Check for comma splices or fused sentences.

A complete sentence has a subject and a verb and can stand on its own. When two sentences are combined as one sentence, each sentence within the larger one is called a *main clause*. However, writers need to follow the rules for joining main clauses to avoid serious sentence errors. A **comma splice** is two main clauses joined with only a comma. A **fused sentence** (or **run-on**) is two main clauses joined with no punctuation at all.

A **main clause** is a group of words that has both a subject and a verb and can stand alone as a complete sentence.

COMMA SPLICE	I went to the shop, I bought a new coat.
FUSED SENTENCE	I went to the shop I bought a new coat.

To find these errors, examine the main clauses in each sentence to make sure they are joined correctly. Correct a comma splice or fused sentence in one of these four ways, depending on which makes the best sense:

ADD A PERIOD	I went to the shop. I bought a new coat.
ADD A COMMA AND A COORDINATING CONJUNCTION	I went to the shop, and I bought a new coat.
ADD A SEMICOLON	I went to the shop; I bought a new coat.
ADD A SUBORDINATING CONJUNCTION	I went to the shop, where I bought a new coat.

Coordinating conjunctions (*and, but, for, or, nor, so, yet*) join elements with equal or near-equal importance.

A **subordinating conjunction** is a word (such as *because, although, if, when*) used to make one clause dependent on, or subordinate to, another.

EDITING CHECKLIST

Comma Splices and Fused Sentences

☐ Can you make each main clause a separate sentence?

☐ Can you link the two main clauses with a comma and a coordinating conjunction?

☐ Can you link the two main clauses with a semicolon or, if appropriate, a colon?

☐ Can you subordinate one clause to the other?

A3 Check for correct past tense verb forms.

The **form** of a verb, the way it is spelled and pronounced, can change to show its **tense** — the time when its action did, does, or will occur (in the past, present, or future). A verb about something in the present will often have a different form than a verb about something in the past.

PRESENT	Right now, I *watch* only a few minutes of television each day.
PAST	Last month, I *watched* television shows every evening.

Regular verbs are verbs whose forms follow standard rules; they form the past tense by adding *-ed* or *-d* to the present tense form:

  watch/watched   look/looked   hope/hoped

Check all regular verbs in the past tense for one of these endings.

    asked
I ~~ask~~ my brother for a loan yesterday.
  ^

      raced
Nicole ~~race~~ in the track meet last week.
     ^

TIP: If you say the final *-d* sound when you talk, you may find it easier to add the final *-d* or *-ed* when you write past tense regular verbs.

Because **irregular verbs** do not have standard forms, their unpredictable past tense forms must be memorized. In addition, the past tense may differ from the past participle. Check a dictionary for these forms.

> *lay*
> My cat ~~laid~~ on the tile floor to take her nap.
> ^

> *swum*
> I have ~~swam~~ twenty laps every day this month.
> ^

A **participle** is a verb that cannot function alone as a main verb, including present participles ending in *-ing* and past participles often ending in *-ed* or *-d*.

TIP: In college papers, follow convention by using the present tense, not the past, to describe the work of an author or the events in a literary work.

> *reveals*
> In "The Lottery," Jackson ~~revealed~~ the power of tradition. As the story
> ^

> *opens*   *gather*
> ~~opened~~, the villagers ~~gathered~~ in the square.
> ^   ^

IRREGULAR VERBS at a glance

INFINITIVE (BASE)	PAST TENSE	PAST PARTICIPLE
begin	began	begun
burst	burst	burst
choose	chose	chosen
do	did	done
eat	ate	eaten
go	went	gone
lay	laid	laid
lie	lay	lain
speak	spoke	spoken

EDITING CHECKLIST

Past Tense Verb Forms

☐ Have you identified the main verb in the sentence?

☐ Is the sentence about past, present, or future? Does the verb show this time?

☐ Is the verb regular or irregular? Have you used its correct form?

A4 Check for correct subject-verb agreement.

The **form** of a verb, the way it is spelled and pronounced, can change to show **number**—whether the subject is singular (one) or plural (more than one). It can also show **person**—whether the subject is *you* or *she,* for example.

A **verb** is a word that shows action or a state of being.

A **subject** names something—a person, an object, an idea, a situation—about which the verb makes an assertion.

SINGULAR	Our instructor *grades* every paper carefully.
PLURAL	Most instructors *grade* tests using a standard scale.
SECOND PERSON	You *write* well-documented research papers.
THIRD PERSON	She *writes* good research papers, too.

A verb must match (or *agree with*) its subject in terms of number and person. Regular verbs (whose forms follow a standard rule) are problems only in the present tense. There they have two forms: one that ends in -s or -es and one that does not. Only singular nouns and the subjects *he, she,* and *it* use the verb form that ends in -s or -es.

I *like*	we *like*
you *like*	you *like*
he/she/it/Dan/the child *likes*	they *like*

The verbs *be* and *have* are irregular, so their present tense forms must be memorized. The verb *be* is also irregular in the past tense.

FORMS OF *BE* AND *HAVE* at a glance

PRESENT		PAST	
I am	we are	I was	we were
you are	you are	you were	you were
he/she/it is	they are	he/she/it was	they were

PRESENT		PAST	
I have	we have	I had	we had
you have	you have	you had	you had
he/she/it has	they have	he/she/it had	they had

An **indefinite pronoun** stands for an unspecified person or thing, including singular forms (*each, everyone, no one*) and plural forms (*both, few*).

Problems in agreement often occur when the subject is hard to find, is an indefinite pronoun, or is confusing. Make sure that you include any -s or -es endings and use the correct form for irregular verbs.

writes
Jim ~~write~~ at least fifty e-mails a day.

have
The students ~~has~~ difficulty with the assignment.

was
Every one of the cakes ~~were~~ sold at the fundraiser.

EDITING CHECKLIST

Subject-Verb Agreement

☐ Have you correctly identified the subject and the verb in the sentence?

☐ Is the subject singular or plural? Does the verb match?

☐ Have you used the correct form of the verb?

A5 Check for correct pronoun case.

Depending on the role a pronoun plays in a sentence, it is said to be in the **subjective case, objective case,** or **possessive case.** Use the subjective case if the pronoun is the subject of a sentence, the subject of a subordinate clause, or a subject complement (after a linking verb). Use the objective case if the pronoun is a direct or indirect object of a verb or the object of a preposition. Use the possessive case to show possession.

SUBJECTIVE	*I* will argue that our campus needs more parking.
OBJECTIVE	This issue is important to *me*.
POSSESSIVE	*My* argument will be quite persuasive.

Writers often use the subjective case when they should use the objective case—sometimes trying to sound formal and correct. Instead, choose the correct form based on a pronoun's function in the sentence. If the sentence pairs a noun and a pronoun, try the sentence with the pronoun alone.

FAULTY	My company gave my husband and *I* a trip to Hawaii.
PRONOUN ONLY	My company gave *I* a trip?
CORRECT	My company gave my husband and *me* a trip to Hawaii.

FAULTY	My uncle and *me* had different expectations.
PRONOUN ONLY	*Me* had different expectations?
CORRECT	My uncle and *I* had different expectations.

A **pronoun** is a word that stands in place of a noun.

A **subject** names something—a person, an object, an idea, a situation—about which the verb makes an assertion.

An **object** is the target or recipient of the verb's action.

A **subject complement** is a noun, an adjective, or a group of words that follows a linking verb and renames or describes the subject.

▶ PERSONAL PRONOUN CASES at a glance

SUBJECTIVE	OBJECTIVE	POSSESSIVE
I	me	my, mine
you	you	your, yours
he	him	his
she	her	hers
it	it	its
we	us	our, ours
they	them	their, theirs
who	whom	whose

FAULTY	Jack ran faster than my brother and *me*.
PRONOUN ONLY	Jack ran faster than *me* ran?
CORRECT	Jack ran faster than my brother and *I*.

A second common error with pronoun case involves gerunds. Whenever you need a pronoun to modify a gerund, use the possessive case.

Our supervisor disapproves of ~~us~~ *our* talking in the hallway.

A **gerund** is a form of a verb, ending in *-ing,* that functions as a noun.

EDITING CHECKLIST

Pronoun Case

☐ Have you identified all the pronouns in the sentence?

☐ Does each one function as a subject, an object, or a possessive?

☐ Given the function of each, have you used the correct form?

A6   Check for correct pronoun-antecedent agreement.

The **form** of a pronoun, the way it is spelled and pronounced, can change to show **number** — whether the subject is singular (one) or plural (more than one). It also can change to show **gender** — masculine or feminine, for example — or **person**: first (*I, we*), second (*you*), or third (*he, she, it, they*).

A **pronoun** stands in place of a noun.

SINGULAR	My brother took *his* coat and left.
PLURAL	My brothers took *their* coats and left.
MASCULINE	I talked to Steven before *he* had a chance to leave.
FEMININE	I talked to Stephanie before *she* had a chance to leave.

A pronoun refers to its **antecedent**, usually a specific noun or pronoun nearby. The connection between the two must be clear so that readers know what the pronoun means in the sentence. The two need to match (or *agree*) in number and gender.

A common error is using a plural pronoun to refer to a singular antecedent. This error often crops up when the antecedent is difficult to find, is an indefinite pronoun, or is confusing for another reason. First, find the antecedent, and decide whether it is singular or plural. Then make the pronoun match its antecedent.

Neither Luz nor Pam received approval of ~~their~~ *her* financial aid.

[*Neither Luz nor Pam* is a compound subject joined by *nor*. Any pronoun referring to it must agree with only the nearer part of the compound: *her* agrees with *Pam*, which is singular.]

Indefinite pronouns are troublesome antecedents when they are grammatically singular but create a plural image in the writer's mind. Fortunately, most indefinite pronouns are always singular or always plural.

his
Each of the boys in the club has ~~their~~ own custom laptop.

[The word *each*, not *boys*, is the antecedent. *Each* is an indefinite pronoun and is always singular. Any pronoun referring to it must be singular as well.]

his or her
Everyone in the meeting had ~~their~~ own assistant.

[*Everyone* is an indefinite pronoun that is always singular. Any pronoun referring to it must be singular as well.]

Use the plural to avoid gendered terms and be inclusive to transgender and nonbinary individuals.

All the people in the meeting had their own assistant.

> An **indefinite pronoun** stands for an unspecified person or thing, including singular forms (*each, everyone, no one*) and plural forms (*both, few*).

INDEFINITE PRONOUNS at a glance

ALWAYS SINGULAR			ALWAYS PLURAL
anybody	everyone	nothing	both
anyone	everything	one (of)	few
anything	much	somebody	many
each (of)	neither (of)	someone	several
either (of)	nobody	something	
everybody	no one		

EDITING CHECKLIST

Pronoun-Antecedent Agreement

☐ Have you identified the antecedent for each pronoun?

☐ Is the antecedent singular or plural? Does the pronoun match?

☐ Is the antecedent masculine, feminine, or neuter? Does the pronoun match?

☐ Is the antecedent first, second, or third person? Does the pronoun match?

A7 Check for correct adjectives and adverbs.

Adjectives and **adverbs** describe or give information about (*modify*) other words. Many adverbs are formed by adding *-ly* to adjectives: *simple, simply; quiet, quietly*. Because adjectives and adverbs resemble one another, writers sometimes mistakenly use one instead of the other. To edit, find the word that the adjective or adverb modifies. If that word is a noun or pronoun, use an adjective (to describe which or what kind). If that word is a verb, an adjective, or another adverb, use an adverb (to describe how, when, where, or why).

> **Modifiers** are words, phrases, or clauses that provide more information about other parts of a sentence.

quickly.
Kelly ran into the house ~~quick.~~

terrible
Gabriela looked ~~terribly~~ after her bout with the flu.

Adjectives and adverbs with similar comparative and superlative forms can also cause trouble. Always ask whether you need an adjective or an adverb in the sentence, and then use the correct word.

well
His scar healed so ~~good~~ that it was barely visible.

Good is an adjective; it describes a noun or pronoun. *Well* is an adverb; it modifies or adds to a verb (*heal*, in this case) or an adjective.

> **IRREGULAR ADJECTIVES AND ADVERBS** *at a glance*
>
> | POSITIVE ADJECTIVES | COMPARATIVE ADJECTIVES | SUPERLATIVE ADJECTIVES |
> | --- | --- | --- |
> | good | better | best |
> | bad | worse | worst |
> | little | less, littler | least, littlest |
> | many, some, much | more | most |
> | POSITIVE ADVERBS | COMPARATIVE ADVERBS | SUPERLATIVE ADVERBS |
> | well | better | best |
> | badly | worse | worst |
> | little | less | least |

EDITING CHECKLIST

Adjectives and Adverbs

☐ Have you identified which word the adjective or adverb modifies?

☐ If the word modified is a noun or pronoun, have you used an adjective?

☐ If the word modified is a verb, an adjective, or an adverb, have you used an adverb?

☐ Have you used the correct comparative or superlative form?

B | Editing to Ensure Effective Sentences

B1   Check for misplaced or dangling modifiers.

Modifiers are words, phrases, or clauses that provide more information about other parts of a sentence.

For a sentence to be clear, the connection between a modifier and the thing it modifies must be obvious. Usually a modifier should be placed just before or just after what it modifies. If the modifier is too close to some other sentence element, it is a **misplaced modifier.** If the modifier cannot logically modify anything in the sentence, it is a **dangling modifier.** Both errors can confuse readers—and sometimes create unintentionally humorous images. As you edit, place a modifier directly before or after the word modified and clearly connect the two.

in the refrigerator
Dan found the leftovers when he visited ~~in the refrigerator.~~

[In the faulty sentence, *in the refrigerator* seems to modify Dan's visit. Obviously the leftovers, not Dan, are in the refrigerator.]

I saw that
Looking out the window, the clouds were beautiful.

[In the faulty sentence, *Looking out the window* should modify *I,* but *I* is not in the sentence. The modifier dangles without anything logical to modify until *I* is in the sentence.]

EDITING CHECKLIST

Misplaced and Dangling Modifiers

☐ What is each modifier meant to modify? Is the modifier as close as possible to that sentence element? Is any misreading possible?

☐ If a modifier is misplaced, can you move it to clarify the meaning?

☐ What noun or pronoun is a dangling modifier meant to modify? Can you make that word or phrase the subject of the main clause? Or can you turn the dangling modifier into a clause that includes the missing noun or pronoun?

B2 Check for parallel structure.

A series of words, phrases, clauses, or sentences with the same grammatical form is said to be **parallel.** Using parallel form for elements that are parallel in meaning or function helps readers grasp the meaning of a sentence more easily. A lack of parallelism can distract, annoy, or even confuse readers.

To use parallelism, put nouns with nouns, verbs with verbs, and phrases with phrases. Parallelism is particularly important in a series, with correlative conjunctions, and in comparisons using *than* or *as.*

to ski, to ice skate,
I like to go to Estes Park ~~for skiing, ice skating,~~ and to meet interesting people.

The proposal is neither practical/nor ~~is it~~ innovative.

Teens need a few firm rules rather than ~~having~~ many flimsy ones.

Edit to reinforce parallel structures by repeating articles, conjunctions, prepositions, or lead-in words as needed.

that
His dream was that he would never have to give up his routine but he would still find time to explore new frontiers.

Correlative conjunctions are pairs of linking words (such as *either/or, not only/but also*) that appear separately but work together to join elements of a sentence.

EDITING CHECKLIST

Parallel Structure

☐ Are all the elements in a series in the same grammatical form?

☐ Are the elements in a comparison parallel in form?

☐ Are the articles, conjunctions, prepositions, or lead-in words for elements repeated as needed rather than mixed or omitted?

C | Editing for Word Choice

C1 Use appropriate language.

Your topic, audience, and purpose will help you determine the appropriate tone and level of formality for your writing. For most college and work assignments, your tone will be serious and your language formal.

INFORMAL   Crotchety old banks are getting schooled by newbie outfits like e-wallets and e-tailers.

FORMAL   Traditional banks are facing increasing competition from online payment systems and Internet retailers.

In formal writing, it is best to avoid jargon, euphemisms, slang, and clichés.

TYPE OF LANGUAGE	DEFINITION	EXAMPLES
jargon	Specialized vocabulary used by people in a certain field, especially business and computing	<ul><li>*bandwidth* (for *capacity*)</li><li>*human capital* (for *employees*)</li></ul>
euphemisms	Indirect wording used to avoid unpleasant topics	<ul><li>*pass away* (for *die*)</li><li>*enhanced interrogation* (for *torture*)</li></ul>
slang	Very informal, playful language that goes in and out of style	<ul><li>*delish* (for *delicious*)</li><li>*do time* (for *serve a jail or prison term*)</li></ul>
clichés	A trite expression worn out from overuse	<ul><li>*few and far between*</li><li>*tip of the iceberg*</li></ul>

No matter what level of formality you use in your writing, avoid offending your readers by remaining unbiased, using gender-neutral language, and omitting stereotypes about age, race, ethnicity, culture, education, and so on.

> *Good doctors are*   *their*
> A good doctor is communicative with ~~his~~ patients.

EDITING CHECKLIST

Appropriate Language

☐ Have you used a tone appropriate for your topic and audience?

☐ Have you avoided jargon, euphemisms, slang, and clichés?

☐ Have you remained unbiased, used gender-neutral language, and avoided stereotypes?

C2   Write clearly and concisely.

Strive for short, simple expressions whenever possible.

WORDY	CONCISE
at an earlier point in time	before
due to the fact that	because
make use of, utilize	use
true facts	facts

Choosing exact words with the correct **connotation** (shade of meaning beyond the basic definition or **denotation**) will help your writing remain clear and concise.

>   *skeletal*   *gaunt*
> The political prisoner emerged with a ~~slender~~ body and a ~~chiseled~~
>   *triumphant.*
> face, but his expression was clearly ~~dominant.~~

EDITING CHECKLIST

Appropriate Language

☐ Is your writing concise?

☐ Have you used exact words?

C3 Watch out for commonly confused words.

Usage refers to the way in which writers customarily use certain words and phrases, including matters of accepted practice or convention. The following glossary lists words and phrases whose usage may trouble writers. Not every possible problem is listed — only some that frequently puzzle students.

Glossary of Troublemakers

a, an   Use *an* only before a word beginning with a vowel sound. "*An* asp can eat *an* egg *an* hour." (Some words, such as *hour* and *honest*, open with a vowel sound even though spelled with an *h*.)

above   Using *above* or *below* to refer back or forward in an essay is awkward and may not be accurate. Instead, try "the *preceding* argument," "in the *following* discussion," "on the *next* page."

accept, except   *Accept* is a verb meaning "to receive willingly"; *except* is usually a preposition meaning "not including." "This childcare center *accepts* all children *except* those under two." Sometimes *except* is a verb, meaning "to exempt." "The entry fee *excepts* children under twelve."

advice, advise   *Advice* is a noun, *advise* a verb. When someone *advises* you, you receive *advice*.

affect, effect   Most of the time, the verb *affect* means "to act on" or "to influence." "Too much beer can *affect* your speech." *Affect* can also mean "to put on airs." "He *affected* a British accent." *Effect*, a noun, means "a result": "Too much beer has a numbing *effect*." But *effect* is also a verb, meaning "to bring about." "Pride *effected* his downfall."

agree to, agree with, agree on   *Agree to* means "to consent to"; *agree with*, "to be in accord." "I *agreed to* attend the lecture, but I didn't *agree with* the speaker's views." *Agree on* means "to come to or have an understanding about." "Chuck and I finally *agreed on* a compromise: the children would go to camp but not overnight."

ain't   Don't use *ain't* in writing; it is nonstandard English for *am not, is not (isn't)*, and *are not (aren't)*.

a lot   Many people mistakenly write the colloquial expression *a lot* as one word: *alot*. Use *a lot* if you must, but in writing *much* or *a large amount* is preferable. See also *lots, lots of, a lot of*.

already, all ready   *Already* means "by now"; *all ready* means "set to go." "At last our picnic was *all ready*, but *already* it was night."

altogether, all together   *Altogether* means "entirely." "He is *altogether* mistaken." *All together* means "in unison" or "assembled." "Now *all together* — heave!" "Inspector Trent gathered the suspects *all together* in the drawing room."

among, between   *Between* refers to two persons or things; *among*, to more than two. "Some disagreement *between* the two countries was inevitable. Still, there was general harmony *among* the five nations represented at the conference."

amount, number   Use *amount* to refer to quantities that can't be counted or to bulk; use *number* to refer to countable, separate items. "The *number* of people you want to serve determines the *amount* of ice cream you'll need."

an, a   See *a, an*.

and/or Usually use either *and* or *or* alone. "Tim *and* Elaine will come to the party." "Tim *or* Elaine will come to the party." For three options, write, "Tim *or* Elaine, *or both*, will come to the party, depending on whether they can find a babysitter."

ante-, anti- The prefix *ante-* means "preceding." *Antebellum* means "before the Civil War." *Anti-* most often means "opposing": *antidepressant*. It needs a hyphen in front of *I* (*anti-inflationary*) or in front of a capital letter (*anti-Marxist*).

anybody, any body When *anybody* is used as an indefinite pronoun, write it as one word: "*Anybody* in his or her right mind abhors murder." Because *anybody* is singular, do not write "Anybody in *their* right mind." *Any body,* written as two words, is the adjective *any* modifying the noun *body.* "Name *any body* of water in Australia."

anyone, any one *Anyone* is an indefinite pronoun written as one word. "Does *anyone* want dessert?" The phrase *any one* consists of the pronoun *one* modified by the adjective *any* and is used to single out something in a group: "Pick *any one* of the pies they're all good."

anyplace *Anyplace* is colloquial for *anywhere* and should not be used in formal writing.

anyways, anywheres These nonstandard forms of *anyway* and *anywhere* should not be used in writing.

as Sometimes using the subordinating conjunction *as* can make a sentence ambiguous. "*As* we were climbing the mountain, we put on heavy sweaters." Does *as* here mean "because" or "while"? Whenever using *as* would be confusing, use a more specific term instead, such as *because* or *while.*

as, like Use *as, as if,* or *as though* rather than *like* to introduce clauses of comparison. "Dan's compositions are tuneful, *as* [not *like*] music ought to be." "Jeffrey behaves *as if* [not *like*] he were ill." *Like,* because it is a preposition, can introduce a phrase but not a clause. "My brother looks *like* me." "He runs *like* a duck."

as to Usually this expression sounds stilted. Use *about* instead. "He complained *about* [not *as to*] the cockroaches."

at See *where at, where to.*

bad, badly *Bad* is an adjective; *badly* is an adverb. Following linking verbs (*be, appear, become, grow, seem, prove*) and verbs of the senses (*feel, look, smell, sound, taste*), use the adjective form. "I feel *bad* that we missed the plane." "The egg smells *bad.*" The adverb form is used to modify a verb or an adjective. "The Tartans played so *badly* they lost to the last-place team, whose *badly* needed victory saved them from elimination."

being as, being that Instead of "*Being as* I was ignorant of the facts, I kept still," write "*Because* I was ignorant" or "*Not knowing* the facts."

beside, besides *Beside* is a preposition meaning "next to." "Sheldon enjoyed sitting *beside* the guest of honor." *Besides* is an adverb meaning "in addition." "*Besides*, he has a sense of humor." *Besides* is also a preposition meaning "other than." "Something *besides* shyness caused his embarrassment."

between, among See *among, between.*

between you and I The preposition *between* always takes the objective case. "Between *you* and *me* [not *I*], Joe's story sounds suspicious." "Between *us* [not *we*], what's going on between Bob and *her* [not *she*] is unfathomable."

but that, but what "I don't know *but what* [or *but that*] you're right" is a wordy, imprecise way of saying "Maybe you're right" or "I believe you're right."

can, may Use *can* to show ability. "Jake *can* bench-press 650 pounds." *May* involves permission. "*May* I bench-press today?" "You *may,* if you *can.*"

capital, capitol A *capital* is a city that is the center of government for a state or country. *Capital* can also mean "wealth." A *capitol* is a building in which legislators meet. "Who knows what the *capital* of Tanzania is?" "The renovated *capitol* is a popular attraction."

center around Say "Class discussion *centered on* [or *revolved around*] her paper." In this sense, the verb *center* means "to have one main concern"—the way a circle has a central point. (To say a discussion centers *around* anything is a murky metaphor.)

cite, sight, site *Cite,* a verb, means "to quote from or refer to." *Sight* as a verb means "to see or glimpse"; as a noun it means "a view, a spectacle." "When the police officer *sighted* my terrier running across the playground, she *cited* the leash laws." *Site,* a noun, means "location." "Standing and weeping at the *site* of his childhood home, he was a pitiful *sight.*"

climatic, climactic *Climatic,* from *climate,* refers to meteorological conditions. Saying "climatic conditions," however, is wordy—you can usually substitute "the climate": "*Climatic* conditions are [or "The *climate* is"] changing because of pollution in the atmosphere." *Climactic,* from *climax,* refers to the culmination of a progression of events. "In the *climactic* scene, the hero drives his car off the pier."

compare, contrast *Compare* has two main meanings. The first, "to liken or represent as similar," is followed by *to.* "She *compared* her room *to* a jail cell." The second, "to analyze for similarities and differences," is generally followed by *with.* "The speaker *compared* the American educational system *with* the Japanese system."

 Contrast also has two main meanings. As a transitive verb, taking an object, it means "to analyze to emphasize differences" and is generally followed by *with.* "The speaker *contrasted* the social emphasis of the Japanese primary grades *with* the academic emphasis of ours." As an intransitive verb, *contrast* means "to exhibit differences when compared." "The sour taste of the milk *contrasted* sharply *with* its usual fresh flavor."

complement, compliment *Compliment* is a verb meaning "to praise" or a noun meaning "praise." "The professor *complimented* Sarah on her perceptiveness." *Complement* is a verb meaning "to complete or reinforce." "Jenn's experiences as an intern *complemented* what she learned in class."

could care less This is nonstandard English for *couldn't care less* and shouldn't be used in writing. "The cat *couldn't* [not *could*] *care less* about which brand of cat food you buy."

could of *Could of* is colloquial for *could have* and shouldn't be used in writing.

couple of Write "a *couple of* drinks" when you mean two. For more than two, say "a *few* [or *several*] drinks."

criteria, criterion *Criteria* is the plural of *criterion,* which means "a standard or requirement on which a judgment or decision is based." "The main *criteria* for this job are attention to detail and good computer skills."

data *Data* is a plural noun. Write "The data *are*" and "*these* data." The singular form of *data* is *datum*—which is rarely used. Instead, use *fact, figure,* or *statistic.*

different from, different than   *Different from* is usually the correct form to use. "How is good poetry *different from* prose?" Use *different than* when a whole clause follows. "Violin lessons with Mr. James were *different than* I had imagined."

don't, doesn't   *Don't* is the contraction of *do not*, and *doesn't* is the contraction of *does not*. "They *don't* want to get dressed up for the ceremony." "The cat *doesn't* [not *don't*] like to be combed."

due to   *Due* is an adjective and must modify a noun or pronoun; it can't modify a verb or an adjective. Begin a sentence with *due to* and you invite trouble: "*Due to* rain, the game was postponed." Write instead, "*Because of* rain." *Due to* works after the verb *be*. "His fall was *due to* a banana peel." There, *due* modifies the noun *fall*.

due to the fact that   A windy expression for *because*.

effect, affect   See *affect, effect*.

either   Use *either* when referring to one of two things. "Both internships sound great; I'd be happy with *either*." When referring to one of three or more things, use *any one* or *any*. "*Any one* of our four counselors will be able to help you."

et cetera, etc.   Sharpen your writing by replacing *et cetera* (or its abbreviation, *etc.*) with exact words. Even translating the Latin expression into English ("and other things") is an improvement, as in "high-jumping, shot-putting, and other field events."

everybody, every body   When used as an indefinite pronoun, *everybody* is one word. "Why is *everybody* on the boys' team waving his arms?" Because *everybody* is singular, it is a mistake to write, "Why is *everybody* waving *their* arms?" *Every body* written as two words refers to separate, individual bodies. "After the overture, *every body* was in *its* [not *their*] correct place onstage."

everyone, every one   Used as an indefinite pronoun, *everyone* is one word. "*Everyone* has *his or her* own ideas." Because *everyone* is singular, it is incorrect to write, "*Everyone* has *their* own ideas." *Every one* written as two words refers to individual, distinct items. "I studied *every one* of the chapters."

except, accept   See *accept, except*.

expect   In writing, avoid the informal use of *expect* to mean "suppose, assume, or think." "I *suppose* [not *expect*] you're going on the geology field trip."

fact that   This is a wordy expression that, nearly always, you can do without. Instead of "*The fact that* he was puny went unnoticed," write, "That he was puny went unnoticed." "Because [not *Because of the fact that*] it snowed, the game was canceled."

farther, further   In your writing, use *farther* to refer to literal distance. "Chicago is *farther* from Nome than from New York." When you mean additional degree, time, or quantity, use *further*: "Sally's idea requires *further* discussion."

fewer, less   *Less* refers to general quantity or bulk; *fewer* refers to separate, countable items. "Eat *less* pizza." "Salad has *fewer* calories."

field of   In a statement such as "He took courses in *the field of* economics," omit *the field of* to save words.

firstly   The recommended usage is *first* (and *second*, not *secondly*; *third*, not *thirdly*; and so on).

former, latter   *Former* means "first of two"; *latter*, "second of two." An acceptable but heavy-handed pair, they often oblige your reader to backtrack. Your writing will be clearer if you simply name again the persons or things you mean. Instead of "The *former* great artist is the master of the flowing line, while the *latter* is the master of color," write, "Picasso is the master of the flowing line, while Matisse is the master of color."

further, farther   See *farther, further*.

get, got   *Get* has many meanings, especially in slang and colloquial use. Some are not appropriate in formal writing, such as "Let's start [not *get*] painting," or "His frequent interruptions finally started annoying [not *getting to*] me," or "She's going to take revenge on [not *get*] him." Or better, be even more specific: "She's going to spread rumors about him to ruin his reputation."

good, well   To modify a verb, use the adverb *well*, not the adjective *good*. "Jan dives *well* [not *good*]." Linking verbs (*be, appear, become, grow, seem, prove*) and verbs of the senses (such as *feel, look, smell, sound, taste*) call for the adjective *good*. "The paint job looks *good*." *Well* is an adjective used only to refer to health. "She looks *well*" means that she seems to be in good health. "She looks *good*" means her appearance is attractive.

hanged, hung   Both words are the past tense of the verb *hang*. *Hanged* refers to an execution. "The murderer was *hanged* at dawn." For all other situations, use *hung*. "Jim *hung* his wash on the line to dry."

have got to   In formal writing, avoid using the phrase *have got to* to mean "have to" or "must." "I *must* [not *have got to*] phone them right away."

he, she, he or she   Using *he* to refer to an indefinite person is considered sexist; so is using *she* with traditionally female occupations or pastimes. However, the phrase *he or she* can seem wordy and awkward.

herself   See *-self, -selves*.

himself   See *-self, -selves*.

hopefully   *Hopefully* means "with hope." "The children turned *hopefully* toward the door, expecting Santa Claus." In writing, avoid *hopefully* when you mean "it is to be hoped" or "let us hope." "*I hope* [not *Hopefully*] the posse will arrive soon."

if, whether   Use *whether*, not *if*, in indirect questions and to introduce alternatives. "Father asked me *whether* [not *if*] I was planning to sleep all morning." "I'm so confused I don't know *whether* [not *if*] it's day or night."

imply, infer   *Imply* means "to suggest"; *infer* means "to draw a conclusion." "Maria *implied* that she was too busy to see Tom, but Tom *inferred* that Maria had lost interest in him."

in, into   *In* refers to a location or condition; *into* refers to the direction of movement or change. "She burst *into* the room and found her sweetheart *in* another's arms."

infer, imply   See *imply, infer*.

in regards to   Write *in regard to, regarding,* or *about*.

inside of, outside of   As prepositions, *inside* and *outside* do not require *of*. "The students were more interested in events *outside* [not *outside of*] the building than those *inside* [not *inside of*] the classroom." In formal writing, do not use *inside of* to refer to time or *outside of* to mean "except." "I'll finish the assignment *within* [not *inside of*] two hours." "He told no one *except* [not *outside of*] a few friends."

irregardless   *Irregardless* is a double negative. Use *regardless*.

is because See *reason is because, reason . . . is.*

is when, is where Using these expressions results in errors in predication. "Obesity *is when* a person is greatly overweight." "Biology *is where* students dissect frogs." *When* refers to a point in time, but *obesity* is not a point in time; *where* refers to a place, but *biology* is not a place. Write instead, "Obesity is the condition of extreme overweight." "Biology is a laboratory course in which students dissect frogs."

its, it's *Its* is a possessive pronoun, never in need of an apostrophe. *It's* is a contraction of *it is.* "Every new experience has *its* bad moments. Still, *it's* exciting to explore the unknown."

it's me, it is I Although *it's me* is widely used in speech, don't use it in formal writing. Write "It is *I*," which is grammatically correct. The same applies to other personal pronouns. "It was *he* [not *him*] who started the mutiny."

kind of, sort of, type of When you use *kind, sort,* or *type* — singular words — make sure that the sentence construction is singular. "That *type* of show *offends* me." "Those *types* of shows *offend* me." In speech, *kind of* and *sort of* are used as qualifiers. "He is *sort of* intelligent." Avoid them in writing. "He is *rather* [or *somewhat* or *slightly*] intelligent."

latter, former See *former, latter.*

lay, lie The verb *lay,* meaning "to put or place," takes an object. "*Lay* that pistol down." *Lie,* meaning "to rest or recline," does not. "*Lie* on the bed until your headache goes away." Their principal parts are *lay, laid, laid* and *lie, lay, lain.*

less, fewer See *fewer, less.*

liable, likely Use *likely* to mean "plausible" or "having the potential." "Ben is *likely* [not *liable*] to win." Save *liable* for "legally obligated" or "susceptible." "A stunt man is *liable* to injury."

lie, lay See *lay, lie.*

like, as See *as, like.*

likely, liable See *liable, likely.*

literally Don't sling *literally* around for emphasis. Because it means "strictly according to the meaning of a word (or words)," it will wreck your credibility if you're speaking figuratively. "Professor Gray *literally* flew down the hall" means that Gray traveled on wings. Save *literally* to mean that you're reporting a fact. "Chemical wastes travel on the winds, and the skies *literally* rain poison."

loose, lose *Loose,* an adjective, most commonly means "not fastened" or "poorly fastened." *Lose,* a verb, means "to misplace" or "to not win." "I have to be careful not to *lose* this button — it's so *loose.*"

lots, lots of, a lot of Use these expressions only in informal speech. In formal writing, use *many* or *much.* See also *a lot.*

mankind This term is considered sexist by many people. Use *humanity, humankind, the human race,* or *people* instead.

may, can See *can, may.*

media, medium *Media* is the plural of *medium* and most commonly refers to the various forms of public communication. "Some argue that, of all the *media,* television is the worst for children."

might of *Might of* is colloquial for *might have* and should not be used in writing.

most   Do not use *most* when you mean "almost" or "nearly." "*Almost* [not *Most*] all the students felt that Professor Crey should receive tenure."

must of   *Must of* is colloquial for *must have* and should not be used in writing.

myself   See *-self, -selves*.

not all that   *Not all that* is colloquial for *not very*; do not use it in formal writing. "The movie was *not very* [not *not all that*] exciting."

number, amount   See *amount, number*.

of   See *could of, might of, must of, should of*.

O.K., o.k., okay   In formal writing, do not use any of these expressions. *All right* and *I agree* are possible substitutes.

one   Like a balloon, *one*, meaning "a person," tends to inflate. One *one* can lead to another. "When *one* is in college, *one* learns to make up *one's* mind for *oneself*." Avoid this pompous usage. When possible, substitute *people* or a more specific plural noun. "When *students* are in college, *they* learn to make up their minds for *themselves*."

ourselves   See *-self, -selves*.

outside of, inside of   See *inside of, outside of*.

percent, per cent, percentage   When you specify a number, write *percent* (also written *per cent*). "Nearly 40 *percent* of the listeners responded to the offer." Only use *percentage*, meaning "part," with an adjective, when you mention no number. "A high *percentage* [or *a large percentage*] of listeners responded." *A large number* or *a large proportion* sounds better yet.

phenomenon, phenomena   *Phenomena* is the plural of *phenomenon*, which means "an observable fact or occurrence." "Of the many mysterious supernatural *phenomena*, clairvoyance is the strangest *phenomenon* of all."

precede, proceed   *Precede* means "to go before or ahead of "; *proceed* means "to go forward." "The fire drill *proceeded* smoothly; the children *preceded* the teachers onto the playground."

principal, principle   *Principal* means "chief," whether used as an adjective or as a noun. "According to the *principal*, the school's *principal* goal will be teaching reading." Referring to money, *principal* means "capital." "Investors in high-risk companies may lose their *principal*." *Principle*, a noun, means *rule* or *standard*. "Let's apply the *principle* of equality in hiring."

proved, proven   Although both forms can be used as past participles, *proved* is recommended. Use *proven* as an adjective. "They had *proved* their skill in match after match." "Try this *proven* cough remedy."

quote, quotation   *Quote* is a verb meaning "to cite, to use the words of." *Quotation* is a noun meaning "something that is quoted." "The *quotation* [not *quote*] next to her photograph fits her perfectly."

raise, rise   *Raise*, meaning "to cause to move upward," is a transitive verb and takes an object. *Rise*, meaning "to move up (on its own)," is intransitive and does not take an object: "I *rose* from my seat and *raised* my arm."

rarely ever   *Rarely* by itself is strong enough. "George *rarely* [not *rarely ever*] eats dinner with his family."

real, really   *Real* is an adjective, *really* an adverb. Do not use *real* to modify a verb or another adjective, and avoid overusing either word. "Sula is a *really* [not *real*] fine novel." Even better: "Sula is a fine novel."

reason is because, reason . . . is *Reason . . . is* requires a clause beginning with *that.* Using *because* is nonstandard. "The *reason* I can't come *is that* [not *is because*] I have the flu." It is simpler and more direct to write, "I can't come because I have the flu."

rise See *raise, rise.*

-self, -selves Don't use a pronoun ending in *-self* or *-selves* in place of *her, him, me, them, us,* or *you.* "Nobody volunteered but Jim and *me* [not *myself*]." Use the *-self* pronouns to refer back to a noun or another pronoun and to lend emphasis. "*We* did it *ourselves.*" "Svetlana *herself* is a noted musician."

set, sit *Set,* meaning "to put or place," is a transitive verb and takes an object. *Sit,* meaning "to be seated," is intransitive and does not take an object. "We were asked to *set* our jewelry and metal objects on the counter and *sit* down."

shall, will; should, would The helping verb *shall* formerly was used with first-person pronouns. It is still used to express determination ("We *shall* overcome") or to ask consent ("*Shall* we march?"). Otherwise, *will* is commonly used with all three persons. "I *will* enter medical school in the fall." *Should* is a helping verb that expresses obligation; *would,* a helping verb that expresses a hypothetical condition. "I *should* wash the dishes before I watch TV." "He *would* learn to speak English if you *would* give him a chance."

she, he or she See *he, she, he or she.*

should of *Should of* is colloquial for *should have* and should not be used in writing.

sight See *cite, sight, site.*

since Sometimes using *since* can make a sentence ambiguous. "*Since* the babysitter left, the children have been watching television." Does *since* here mean "because" or "from the time that"? If using *since* might be confusing, use an unambiguous term (*because, ever since*).

sit See *set, sit.*

site See *cite, sight, site.*

sort of See *kind of, sort of, type of.*

stationary, stationery *Stationary,* an adjective, means "fixed, unmoving." "The fireplace remained *stationary* though the wind blew down the house." *Stationery* is paper for letter writing. To spell it right, remember that *letter* also contains *-er.*

suppose to Write *supposed to.* "He was *supposed to* read a novel."

sure *Sure* is an adjective, *surely* an adverb. Do not use *sure* to modify a verb or another adjective. If you mean "certainly," write *certainly* or *surely* instead. "He *surely* [not *sure*] makes the Civil War come alive."

than, then *Than* is a conjunction used in comparisons; *then* is an adverb indicating time. "Marlene is brainier *than* her sister." "First crack six eggs; *then* beat them."

that, where See *where, that.*

that, which Which pronoun should open a clause — *that* or *which*? If the clause adds to its sentence an idea that, however interesting, could be left out, then the clause is nonrestrictive. It should begin with *which* and be separated from the rest of the sentence with commas. "The vampire, *which* hovered nearby, leaped for Sophia's throat."

If the clause is essential to your meaning, it is restrictive. It should begin with *that* and should not have commas around it. "The vampire *that* Mel brought from Transylvania leaped for Sophia's throat." The clause indicates not just any old vampire but one in particular.

Don't use *which* to refer vaguely to an entire clause. Instead of "Jack was an expert drummer in high school, *which* won him a scholarship," write "Jack's skill as a drummer won him . . ."

that, who, which, whose See *who, which, that, whose.*

themselves See *-self, -selves.*

then, than See *than, then.*

there, their, they're *There* is an adverb indicating place. *Their* is a possessive pronoun. *They're* is a contraction of *they are.* "After playing tennis *there* for three hours, Lamont and Laura went to change *their* clothes because *they're* going out to dinner."

to, too, two *To* is a preposition. *Too* is an adverb meaning "also" or "in excess." *Two* is a number. "Janet wanted to go *too*, but she was *too* sick *to* travel for *two* days. Instead, she went *to* bed."

toward, towards *Toward* is preferred in the United States, *towards* in Britain.

try and Use *try to.* "I'll *try to* [not *try and*] attend the opening performance of your play."

type of See *kind of, sort of, type of.*

unique Nothing can be *more, less,* or *very unique. Unique* means "one of a kind."

use to Write *used to.* "Robert *used to* have a beard, but now he is clean-shaven."

wait for, wait on *Wait for* means "await"; *wait on* means "to serve." "While *waiting for* his friends, George decided to *wait on* one more customer."

well, good See *good, well.*

where, that Although speakers sometimes use *where* instead of *that*, you should not do so in writing. "I heard on the news *that* [not *where*] it got hot enough to fry eggs on car hoods."

where . . . at, where . . . to The colloquial use of *at* or *to* after *where* is redundant. Write "*Where* were you?" not "*Where* were you *at*?" "I know *where* she was rushing [not *rushing to*]."

whether See *if, whether.*

which, that See *that, which.*

who, which, that, whose *Who* refers to people, *which* to things and ideas. "Was it Pogo *who* said, 'We have met the enemy and he is us'?" "The blouse, *which* was green, accented her dark skin." *That* refers to things but can also be used for a class of people. "The team *that* increases sales the most will get a bonus." Because *of which* can be cumbersome, use *whose* even with things. "The mountain, *whose* snowy peaks were famous the world over, was covered by fog." See also *that, which.*

who, whom *Who* is used as a subject, *whom* as an object. In "*Whom* do I see?" *Whom* is the object of *see.* In "*Who* goes there?" *Who* is the subject of "goes."

who's, whose *Who's* is a contraction of *who is* or *who has.* "*Who's* going with Phil?" *Whose* is a possessive pronoun. "Bill is a conservative politician *whose* ideas are unlikely to change."

whose, who, which, that See *who, which, that, whose.*

will, shall See *shall, will; should, would.*

would, should See *shall, will; should, would.*

would of *Would of* is colloquial for *would have* and should not be used in writing.

you *You,* meaning "a person," occurs often in conversation. "When *you* go to college, *you* have to work hard." In writing, use *one* or a specific, preferably plural noun. "When *students* go to college, *they* have to work hard." See *one.*

your, you're *Your* is a possessive pronoun; *you're* is the contraction of *you are.* "*You're* lying! It was *your* handwriting on the envelope."

yourself, yourselves See *-self, -selves.*

D | Editing for Common Punctuation Problems

D1 Check for correct use of commas.

The **comma** is a punctuation mark indicating a pause. By setting some words apart from others, commas help clarify relationships. They prevent the words on a page and the ideas they represent from becoming a jumble.

1. Use a comma before a coordinating conjunction (*and, but, for, or, so, yet, nor*) joining two main clauses in a compound sentence.

   The discussion was brief, *so* the meeting was adjourned early.

2. Use a comma after an introductory word or word group unless it is short and can't be misread.

   After the war, the North's economy developed rapidly.

3. Use commas to separate the items in a series of three or more items.

   The chief advantages will be *speed, durability,* and *longevity.*

4. Use commas to set off a modifying clause or phrase if it is nonrestrictive — if it can be taken out of the sentence without significantly changing the essential meaning of the sentence.

   Good childcare, *which is hard to find,* should be available at work.

   Good childcare *that is reliable and inexpensive* is every employee's hope.

5. Use commas to set off a nonrestrictive appositive, an expression that comes directly after a noun or pronoun and renames it.

   Sheri, *my sister,* has a new job as an events coordinator.

6. Use commas to set off parenthetical expressions, conjunctive adverbs, and other interrupters.

The proposal from the mayor's commission, *however,* is not feasible.

An **appositive** is a word or group of words that adds information about a subject or object by identifying it in a different way.

A **parenthetical expression** is an aside to readers or a transitional expression such as *for example* or *in contrast*.

Conjunctive adverbs are linking words that can connect independent clauses and show a relationship between two ideas.

EDITING CHECKLIST

Commas

☐ Have you added a comma between two main clauses joined by a coordinating conjunction?

☐ Have you added commas needed after introductory words or word groups?

☐ Have you separated items in a series with commas?

☐ Have you avoided commas before the first item in a series or after the last?

☐ Have you used commas before and after each nonrestrictive (nonessential) word, phrase, or clause?

☐ Have you avoided using commas around a restrictive word, phrase, or clause that is essential to the meaning of the sentence?

☐ Have you used commas to set off appositives, parenthetical expressions, conjunctive adverbs, and other interrupters?

D2 Check for correct use of apostrophes.

An **apostrophe** is a punctuation mark that either shows possession (*Sylvia's*) or indicates that one or more letters have intentionally been left out to form a contraction (*didn't*). An apostrophe is never used to create the possessive form of a pronoun; use the possessive pronoun form instead.

Mike's
~~Mikes~~ car was totaled in the accident.

Women's   *men's.*
~~Womens~~' pay is often less than ~~mens'~~.

                    didn't
Che ~~did'nt~~ want to stay at home and study.

                         its
The dog wagged ~~it's~~ tail happily.   [It's = it is? No.]

It's
~~Its~~ raining.   [It's = it is.]

POSSESSIVE PERSONAL PRONOUNS *at a glance*

PERSONAL PRONOUN	POSSESSIVE CASE
I	my, mine
you	your, yours (*not* your's)
he	his
she	her, hers (*not* her's)
it	its (*not* it's)
we	our, ours (*not* our's)
they	their, theirs (*not* their's)
who	whose (*not* who's)

EDITING CHECKLIST

Apostrophes

☐ Have you used an apostrophe when letters are left out in a contraction?

☐ Have you used an apostrophe to create the possessive form of a noun?

☐ Have you used the possessive case — not an apostrophe — to show that a pronoun is possessive?

☐ Have you used *it's* correctly (to mean *it is*)?

D3 Check for correct punctuation of quotations.

For more about quotations from sources, see D3 in the Quick Research Guide, p. Q-28.

When you quote the exact words of a person you've interviewed or a source you've read, enclose those words in quotation marks. Notice how student Betsy Buffo presents the words of her subject in this passage from her essay "Interview with an Artist":

> Derek is straightforward when asked about how his work is received in the local community: "My work is outside the mainstream. Because it's controversial, it's not easy for me to get exposure."

She might have expressed and punctuated this passage in other ways:

> Derek says that "it's not easy" for him to find an audience.
> Derek struggles for recognition because his art falls "outside the mainstream."

If your source quotes someone else (a quotation within a quotation), put your subject's words in quotation marks and the words he or she is quoting in single quotation marks. Always put commas and periods inside the quotation marks; put semicolons and colons outside. Include all necessary marks in the correct place or sequence.

> As Betsy Buffo explains, "Derek struggles for recognition because his art falls 'outside the mainstream.'"

Substitute an ellipsis mark (. . .) — three spaced dots — for any words you have omitted from the middle of a direct quotation. If you're following MLA style, place the ellipses inside brackets ([. . .]) when necessary to avoid confusing your ellipsis marks with those of the original writer. If the ellipses come at the end of a sentence, add another period to conclude the sentence. You don't need an ellipsis mark to show the beginning or ending of a quotation that is clearly incomplete.

> In his essay "Four Weeks Vacation," Robinson writes, "The health implications of sleep-deprived motorists weaving their way to the office . . . are self-evident" (481).

EDITING CHECKLIST

Punctuation with Quotations

☐ Are the exact words quoted from your source enclosed in quotation marks?

☐ Are commas and periods placed inside closing quotation marks?

☐ Are colons and semicolons placed outside closing quotation marks?

☐ Do ellipses show where you omit words from the middle of a quote?

E | Editing for Common Mechanics Problems

E1 Check for correct use of capital letters.

Capital letters begin a new sentence; names of specific people, nationalities, places, dates, and things (proper nouns); and main words in titles.

During my ~~Sophomore~~ *sophomore* year in ~~College,~~ *college,* I took ~~World Literature, Biology,~~ *world literature, biology,*

American ~~History, Psychology,~~ *history, psychology,* and French—courses required for a ~~Humanities Major.~~ *humanities major.*

EDITING CHECKLIST

Capitalization

☐ Have you used a capital letter at the beginning of each complete sentence, including sentences that are quoted?

☐ Have you used capital letters for proper nouns and pronouns?

☐ Have you avoided using capital letters for emphasis?

☐ Have you used a capital letter for the first, last, and main words in a title? (Main words exclude prepositions, coordinating conjunctions, and articles.)

CAPITALIZATION *at a glance*

THE FIRST LETTER OF A SENTENCE, INCLUDING A QUOTED SENTENCE
She called out, "Come in! The water's warm."

PROPER NAMES AND ADJECTIVES MADE FROM THEM
Smithsonian Institution   a Mayan city   Marie Curie

RANK OR TITLE BEFORE A PROPER NAME
Ms. Olson   Professor Santocolon   Dr. Frost

FAMILY RELATIONSHIP ONLY WHEN IT SUBSTITUTES FOR OR IS PART OF A PROPER NAME
Grandma Jones   Father Time

RELIGIONS, THEIR FOLLOWERS, AND DEITIES
Islam   Orthodox Jew   Krishna

PLACES, REGIONS, GEOGRAPHIC FEATURES, AND NATIONALITIES
Palo Alto   the Berkshire Mountains   Egyptians

DAYS OF THE WEEK, MONTHS, AND HOLIDAYS
Wednesday   July   Labor Day

HISTORICAL EVENTS, PERIODS, AND DOCUMENTS
the Boston Tea Party   the Middle Ages   the Constitution

SCHOOLS, COLLEGES, UNIVERSITIES, AND SPECIFIC COURSES
Temple University   Introduction to Clinical Psychology

FIRST, LAST, AND MAIN WORDS IN TITLES OF PAPERS, BOOKS, ARTICLES, WORKS OF ART, TELEVISION SHOWS, POEMS, AND PERFORMANCES
The Decline and Fall of the Roman Empire   "The Lottery"

E2 Check spelling.

A **preposition** is a transitional word (such as *in, on, at, of, from*) that leads into a phrase.

Coordinating conjunctions are one-syllable linking words (*and, but, for, or, nor, so, yet*) that join elements with equal or near-equal importance.

An **article** is the word *a, an,* or *the*.

For a list of commonly confused words, see C3.

Misspelled words are difficult to spot in your own writing, as you usually see what you think you wrote. Spell checkers are handy, but you need to know their limitations: a spell checker highlights words that do not appear in its dictionary, including most proper nouns. Spell checkers will not highlight words misspelled as different words, such as *except* for *accept, to* for *too,* or *own* for *won.*

EDITING CHECKLIST

Spelling

☐ Have you checked for the words you habitually misspell?

☐ Have you checked for commonly confused or misspelled words? (See C3.)

☐ Have you checked a dictionary for any words you are unsure about?

☐ Have you run your spell checker? Have you read your paper carefully for errors that the spell checker would miss such as a stray letter?

Acknowledgements

Adichie, Chimamanda Ngozi, "Happy Feminist" from *We Should All Be Feminists* by Chimamanda Ngozi Adichie, copyright © 2014 by Chimamanda Ngozi Adichie. Used by permission of Alfred A. Knopf, an imprint of the Knopf Doubleday Publishing Group, a division of Penguin Random House LLC. All rights reserved.

Baldwin, James, "If Black English Isn't a Language, Then Tell Me, What Is?" Originally published in *The New York Times*. Copyright © 1979 by James Baldwin. Copyright renewed. Collected in *James Baldwin: Collected Essays*, published by Library of America. Used by arrangement with the James Baldwin Estate.

Bennett, James, "If You're Mad about 'DAMN.,' You Probably Need to Listen to More Hip Hop," NewSounds.org, April 17, 2018. New Sounds, from WQXR and New York Public Radio. Reprinted by permission.

Blow, Charles M., "Black Dads Are Doing Best of All." From *The New York Times*, June 30, 2015. Copyright © 2015 The New York Times. All rights reserved. Used under license.

Bradford, Alina, "What Is Transgender?" *Live Science* June 17, 2018. Reprinted by permission of EnVeritas Group

Brown, Jeffrey A. " 'I'm the Goshdarn Batman!' Affect and the Aesthetics of Cute Superheroes," *Journal of Graphic Novels and Comics*, Volume 9, Issue 2, 2018. Reprinted by permission of the publisher, Taylor & Francis Ltd., http://www.tandfonline.com.

Cofer, Judith Ortiz, "More Room," from *Silent Dancing: A Partial Remembrance of a Puerto Rican Childhood* by Judith Ortiz Cofer is reprinted with permission from the publisher (©1990 Arte Publico Press–University of Houston).

De Luca, Vanessa K., "Serena Williams Was Blamed For Defending Herself," *The Washington Post*, September 9, 2018. Reprinted by permission of the author.

Divakaruni, Chitra Banerjee, "Clothes" from *Arranged Marriage* by Chitra Banerjee Divakaruni, copyright © 1995 by Chitra Divakaruni. Used by permission of Doubleday, an imprint of the Knopf Doubleday Publishing Group, a division of Penguin Random House LLC. All rights reserved.

Egan, Sophie, "The American Food Psyche" pp. 14-16, 19-20, 305-9 from *Devoured* by Sophie Egan. Copyright © 2016 by Sophie Egan. Reprinted by permission of HarperCollins Publishers.

Gottschalk, Simon, "In Praise of Doing Nothing," *The Conversation* May 31, 2018. Reprinted by permission of the author.

Harjo, Suzan Shown, "Last Rites for Indian Dead: Treating Remains Like Artifacts Is Intolerable" *Los Angeles Times*, September 16, 1989. Copyright © 1989 Suzan Shown Harjo. Reprinted by permission of the author.

Hines, Sally, "Trans and Feminist Rights Have Been Falsely Cast in Opposition" Republished with permission of The Economist Group Ltd. from *The Economist*, July 13, 2018; permission conveyed through Copyright Clearance Center, Inc.

Jarvie, Jenny, "Trigger Happy: The 'Trigger Warning' Has Spread from Blogs to College Classrooms," *New Republic*, March 3, 2014. Reprinted by permission of the author.

Jensen, Robert, excerpt from "The High Cost of Manliness" www.AlterNet.org, September 8, 2006. Reprinted by permission of the author.

Johnson, Jason, "How Stan Lee Taught a Generation of Black Nerds About Race, Art, and Activism," *The Root*, November 18, 2018. Copyright © 2018 Gizmodo Media Group, LLC. Reprinted by permission.

Kattari, Shanna, "Transgender and Non-Binary People Face Health Care Discrimination Every Day," *The Conversation*, October 23, 2018 Reprinted by permission of the author.

King, Stephen, "Why We Crave Horror Movies," Copyright © 1982 by Stephen King. Originally appeared in *Playboy*, 1982. Reprinted with permission. All rights reserved.

Kinzer, Stephen, "Joining the Military Doesn't Make You a Hero," *The Boston Globe*, December 7, 2014. Reprinted by permission of the author.

Kolbert, Elizabeth, "The Psychology of Inequality," *The New Yorker*, January 15, 2018. Reprinted by permission of the author.

Montgomery, Sidra, "The Emotion Work of 'Thank You for Your Service,'" *Veteran Scholars*, March, 2017. Reprinted by permission of the author.

National Public Radio, Inc. © 2018 News report titled "The Huddled Masses and The Myth Of America" was originally published at npr.org on January 15, 2018, and is used with the permission of NPR. Any unauthorized duplication is strictly prohibited.

O'Neill, Kate, "Facebook's '10 Year Challenge' Is Just Harmless Meme," *Wired*, January 15, 2019. Reprinted by permission of the author.

Orenstein, Peggy, pp 7-11 from *Girls and Sex*. Copyright © 2016 by Peggy Orenstein. Reprinted by permission of HarperCollins.

Padilla, Yesenia, "What does 'Latinx' mean? A look at the term that's challenging gender norms," *Complex*, April 18, 2016. Reprinted by permission of the author.

Payne, Keith, excerpts from *The Broken Ladder: How Inequality Affects the Way We Think, Live, and Die*, copyright © 2017 by Keith Payne. Used by permission of Penguin Books, an imprint of Penguin Publishing Group, a division of Penguin Random House LLC. All rights reserved.

Rhee, Margaret, "Returning to My Father's Koreatown," On She Goes, August 18, 2017. Reprinted by permission of the author.

Rideau, Wilbert, "Why Prisons Don't Work" from *Time* (March 21, 1994). Copyright ©1994 by Wilbert Rideau. Reprinted with the permission of the author c/o The Permissions Company, Inc., www.permissionscompany.com.

Rodriguez, Richard, "Public and Private Language," from *Aria: A Memoir of a Bilingual Childhood*. Copyright (c) 1980 by Richard Rodriguez. Originally appeared in *The American Scholar*. Reprinted by permission of Georges Borchardt, Inc., on behalf of the author.

Ronson, Jon, "How One Stupid Tweet Blew Up Justine Sacco's Life" (NYTmagazine article 2/15/15) from *So You've Been Publicly Shamed* by Jon Ronson, copyright © 2015 by Jon Ronson Ltd. Used by permission of Riverhead, an imprint of Penguin Publishing Group, a division of Penguin Random House LLC. All rights reserved.

Rosenboom, Victoria and Kristin Blagg, "Disconnected from Higher Education." Republished by permission of the Urban Institute, February 3, 2018; permission conveyed through Copyright Clearance Center, Inc.

Sapolsky, Robert, excerpt from "The Origin of Celebrity: Why Julia Roberts Rules the World" (*Nautilus*, Issue 5). Reprinted by permission of the author.

Sinclair, Isaac, "E-Cigarettes Pose a Hidden Danger," *The Iowa State Daily*, January 19, 2017. Reprinted by permission of the author.

Squire, Kurt Dean and Gaydos, Matthew, "No, Fortnite Isn't Rotting Kids' Brains. It May Even Be Good for Them" by *Education Week* (Commentary Section) Vol. 38, Issue 01, August 8, 2018. Reprinted by permission of the authors.

Staples, Brent, "Black Men and Public Space," *Harper's*, December 1986. Repritned by permission of the author.

Tan, Amy, "Mother Tongue." Copyright © 1989 by Amy Tan. First appeared in *The Threepenny Review*. Reprinted by permission of the author and the Sandra Dijkstra Literary Agency.

Toohey, Peter. Excerpted from "Sibling Rivalry, a History" (*The Atlantic*, November 20, 2014) adapted from *Jealousy*. Copyright © 2014 by Yale University Press. Reprinted by permission.

Tyson, Neil deGrasse, from "The Cosmic Perspective," *Natural History*, April 2007. Reprinted by permission of Natural History Magazine, Inc.

INDEX

CORRECTION SYMBOLS

Many instructors use these abbreviations and symbols to mark errors in student papers. Refer to this chart to find out what they mean.

Abbreviation or Symbol	Meaning	See the Handbook	See the Quick Editing Guide
abbr	abbreviation	36 (p. 853)	
adj	misuse of adjective	13 (p. 784)	A7 (p. Q-45)
adv	misuse of adverb	13 (p. 784)	A7 (p. Q-45)
agr	faulty agreement	8 (p. 758), 12 (p. 782)	A4 (p. Q-41), A6 (p. Q-44)
appr	appropriate	22 (p. 814)	C1 (p. Q-48)
awk	awkward		
bias	use bias-free language	24 (p. 819)	
cap	use capital letter	37 (p. 856)	
case	error in case	10 (p. 775)	A5 (p. Q-43)
cl	clause error	4 (p. 746)	
compl	complement error	3 (p. 741)	
coord	faulty coordination	19a–c (p. 804)	
cs	comma splice	7 (p. 755)	A2 (p. Q-39)
dm	dangling modifier	15c (p. 793)	B1 (p. Q-46)
exact	exact words	23 (p. 818)	
frag	fragment	6 (p. 752)	A1 (p. Q-38)
fs	fused sentence	7 (p. 755)	A2 (p. Q-39)
gl or *gloss*	see Glossary of Troublemakers		C3 (p. Q-50)
hyph	error in use of hyphen	40 (p. 863)	
inc	incomplete sentence	16 (p. 794)	
irreg	error in irregular verb		A3 (p. Q-40)
ital	italics	39 (p. 861)	
lc	use lowercase letter	37 (p. 856)	E1 (p. Q-62)
mixed	mixed construction	17 (p. 798)	
mm	misplaced modifier	15a-b (p. 792)	B1 (p. Q-46)
mood	error in mood	8 (p. 758)	
num	error in the use of numbers	38 (p. 859)	
obj	object error	3 (p. 741)	

Abbreviation or Symbol	Meaning	See the Handbook	See the Quick Editing Guide
pass	ineffective passive voice	21b (p. 812)	
phr	phrase error	4 (p. 746)	
pos	part of speech error	1 (p. 730)	
pron agr	pronoun-antecedent error	12 (p. 782)	A6 (p. Q-44)
punct	error in punctuation	27–35 (p. 826)	D (p. Q-59)
ref	error in pronoun reference	11 (p. 779)	A6 (p. Q-44)
rep	too much repetition	25 (p. 822)	
rev	revise	(See Ch. 23.)	
run-on	comma splice or fused sentence	7 (p. 755)	A2 (p. Q-39)
sent	sentence structure error	5 (p. 748)	
shift	shift error	14 (p. 789)	
sp	misspelled word	41 (p. 865)	E2 (p. Q-64)
sub	faulty subordination	19d–f (p. 807)	
subj	subject error	2 (p. 740)	
t or *tense*	error in verb tense	8 (p. 758)	A3 (p. Q-40)
v	voice	14c (p. 789)	
var	sentence variety needed	20 (p. 810)	
vb	error in verb form	8 (p. 758)	A3 (p. Q-40)
vb agr	subject-verb agreement error	9 (p. 771)	A4 (p. Q-41)
wc	word choice	22–26 (p. 814)	C (p. Q-48)
w	wordy	25 (p. 822)	C2 (p. Q-49)
ww	commonly confused word	26 (p. 823)	C3 (p. Q-50)
//	faulty parallelism	18 (p. 801)	B2 (p. Q-47)
x	obvious error		

PROOFREADING SYMBOLS

Use these standard proofreading marks when making minor corrections in your final draft. If extensive revision is necessary, type or print out a clean copy. Add your instructor's own abbreviations and symbols on the right.

Symbol	Meaning
∿	Transpose (reverse order)
≡	Capitalize
/	Lowercase
#	Add space
⌒	Close up space
℘	Delete
⎯	Stet (undo deletion)
∧	Insert
⊙	Insert period
⌄	Insert comma
;/	Insert semicolon
:/	Insert colon
∨	Insert apostrophe
⟨⟨ ⟩⟩	Insert quotation marks
|=|	Insert hyphen
¶	New paragraph
no ¶	No new paragraph

A GUIDE TO THE HANDBOOK